# QU STUDIES

**HARRINGTON PARK PRESS**

NEW YORK, NY • USA

# QUEER STUDIES

## STUDIES

## BEYOND

## BINARIES

**BRUCE
HENDERSON**

Harrington Park Press
Box 331
9 East 8th Street
New York, NY 10003

http://harringtonparkpress.com

Library of Congress Cataloging-in-Publication Data

Names: Henderson, Bruce, 1957– author.
Title: Queer studies : beyond binaries / Bruce Henderson.
Description: New York, NY : Harrington Park Press, [2019] | Includes
bibliographical references and index. Identifiers: LCCN 2019012119
(print) | LCCN 2019013651 (ebook) | ISBN 9781939594341 (ebook) |
ISBN 9781939594334 (hardcover : alk. paper) | ISBN 9781939594327
(pbk. : alk. paper)
Subjects: LCSH: Gay and lesbian studies. | Sexual minorities—Study and
teaching. | Queer theory.
Classification: LCC HQ75.15 (ebook) | LCC HQ75.15 .H46 2019 (print) |
DDC 306.76—dc23
LC record available at https://lccn.loc.gov/2019012119

for Daryl J. Bem, husband,

and in loving memory of
Leland H. Roloff (1927–2015), teacher,
and
Gary J. Zanke (1956–1993), best friend,

all three, forever in my heart

CONTENTS

# PREFACE

*Queer Studies: Beyond Binaries* is designed for undergraduate survey courses in the growing field of queer studies, sometimes referred to as LGBT studies or GLBT studies or some other variation of the acronyms associated with sexual identity and orientation. It grew out of my own experiences in teaching such a class, designed for students at any level of undergraduate study and from any major or minor, with no prerequisite. Thus, it makes no assumptions about its target audience's prior knowledge in sexuality studies, and it takes care to spend time defining and explaining the myriad terms and concepts on which the study of the lives of queer people and of the acts of "queering" are built.

While it uses concepts from both queer theory and queer history throughout, especially as foundations for the more specific and detailed ideas, figures, movements, and case studies in each chapter, the book is not designed for classes strictly in either theory or history. There are a number of accessible and excellent books designed to introduce students to queer theory or history, but this book is designed to give its readers an overview of both various disciplinary and interdisciplinary perspectives on the material, ranging from linguistics through biology through psychology through politics, and ending with aesthetics.

## UNIQUE FEATURES

### Interdisciplinary Approach

I came to the teaching of the course as someone who had taught undergraduate college students for many decades, often using queer texts and concepts in my classes, but never focusing exclusively on queer studies. As a teacher of a general course in queer studies, you may come from specific disciplinary training and teaching but may be eager to expand the reach of your own interest in queer studies to a broader perspective and set of approaches. As a teacher, I myself span both positions, having done my earlier undergraduate and graduate training in communication and performance studies and then later pursuing graduate work in a field that, like queer studies, is by definition and philosophy interdisciplinary, disability studies. My own experience is that the diversity of life experiences and scholarly perspectives my own students bring to this class is itself instructive and has helped form the organization and content of the course. It is also the case that the academy has shifted from strict disciplinary divisions, such as they were, and has been moving increasingly toward approaches that build on dialogues between different disciplines and their similarly

Henderson, Bruce, *Queer Studies: Beyond Binaries*
dx.doi.org/10.17312/harringtonparkpress/2019.09.qsbb.00a
© 2019 by Harrington Park Press

different assumptions, methods, and paradigms. Often, the best of such work involves scholars working in teams, in dialogues between, for example, literary studies and cognitive science, and history and statistics. The book, then, helps model such approaches to the production and understanding of knowledge and offers students an opportunity to begin to enter into the kinds of scholarly and intellectual work they will encounter as they move through their studies.

## Active Voice

This book is written with an active voice that invites students to build on their own experiences and knowledge and apply ideas to their daily lives. By doing this, students take ownership of their forming an understanding of queerness as a concept and of queer lives they either inhabit themselves or encounter among peers, family, and the social worlds with which they interact.

## Exploration of Various Kinds of Binaries

As the subtitle suggests, one of the most significant features of this book is its consistent questioning of various kinds of binaries, those "either-or" pairings that have increasingly come under analysis and criticism. It is one of the principal reasons the term queer studies is used throughout, rather than LGBT(Q). In my experience students of this generation are much more likely to name and identify their sexual identity (and gender expression) in ways that the acronyms tend to restrict. In the book, as in my classroom, I make as few assumptions about the identities and experiences of students as possible, with the hope that the book will be of use as much to heterosexually identified students as to queer students who seek a place to situate their own sense of self in larger contexts.

## Investigative Approach

Each chapter includes at least two "Issues for Investigation," discussion topics that apply the concepts to real-world contexts or activities that can be carried out independently, in small groups, or as a class. The "Issues for Investigation" allow students to move beyond rote memorization of the terms and concepts. Because they are discussion- and activity-driven, they allow students whose learning styles may be more grounded in practical and applied methods of acquiring knowledge to better understand the material. Teachers will find additional questions and suggestions in the Instructor's Resources (details about which are provided below).

## Intersectional Perspectives

While most existing queer studies textbook focus on queerness itself, it is becoming more and more clear that identity is never as simple as inhabiting a single category or characteristic. There is growing interest in what critical race and legal scholars call intersectionality, which recognizes that identity is not a matter of belonging to a single social category. Thus, this textbook takes the increasingly prevalent approach of intersectionality as one of its central tenets: that identity is never singular, but always the product of multiple characteristics, such as sexuality, race, gender, class, and ability or disability. An intersectional approach also allows students who may not identify as queer to understand and engage with the ways in which their own multiple identities are relevant to the study of queerness.

## Flexibility in Content Coverage

The chapters in Part III are designed to be teachable as stand-alone chapters. This allows teachers greater flexibility in designing the organization of classes. For example, some instructors may want to delve into issues of queerness and spirituality, while others may be more interested in issues of wellness or in power.

## Features to Enhance Student Learning

Each chapter contains one or more "Spotlight" sections, in which an individual, a social movement or event, or a text is described and discussed in detail — ranging from the poetry of the queer Latinx writer Richard Blanco to the vocabulary of the queer dialect Polari to an excerpt from the fiction of the novelist Jane Hamilton, an LGBTQ+ ally. The "Spotlight" sections provide case studies, often historical or artistic, to which students can apply larger, more abstract theories. They also introduce students to lived experiences and expressive products of queer people in particular places and in particular moments in time. This, in turn, helps students situate their own lives, experiences, and perceptions in a longer historical tradition and to see beyond their own individual observations.

Each chapter also includes a list of further readings and viewings that a teacher might assign or students might choose for exploring a particular topic in more detail. The Instructor's Resources provide other suggestions, as well.

Key terms are bold-faced when first introduced and are defined in the glossary. A book of this scope includes terms that may be unfamiliar to many students (or their particular usage in queer studies may be new to them), and the glossary can help readers reinforce and review meanings and usages of such terms. Teachers may also find the glossary a useful study guide for their students to review for quizzes and exams, as well as opportunities for classes to debate usage — which is always changing and evolving.

## INTENDED AUDIENCE

While instructors should feel free to supplement the textbook with their own additional readings (such as memoirs, articles, fiction, poetry, visual texts), this book is designed to be used as the sole or primary text in introductory courses on queer or LGBT studies. The book can also be used as a supplementary text in courses on sexuality studies in general (including women's and gender studies), queer/LGBT identity, and disciplinary courses that address issues of identity and society (which may be found in departments of political science, sociology, and psychology, to name a few). The sample syllabi in the Instructor's Resources provide tips on how to use the book in a variety of these courses.

## INSTRUCTOR'S RESOURCES

The Instructor's Resources provides additional materials helpful to both teachers and students. First, instructors will find a number of sample syllabi for introductory courses in queer studies, for both one-semester and one-quarter courses. There are also sample syllabi to demonstrate how to use the text in a more supplementary way for a variety of courses such as Sexuality Studies and Queer Identity. Finally, there are sample syllabi that demonstrate how to emphasize different aspects of the book in various courses. For example, some teachers may want to focus very closely on foundational issues dealing with language and the spectrum of identities and experiences that fall under the heading queer. For them, Parts I and II may be where they spend most of the course.

In addition, the Instructor's Resources features twenty-five to thirty Power-Point slides for each chapter, along with teaching tips and discussion questions tied to the book's "Spotlight" and "Issues for Investigation" sections to help review and highlight central concepts and terms. Tips for making the most of the suggested readings and viewings are also provided for each chapter. Additionally, instructors will find a test bank for those who wish to use content and application exams to measure student learning outcomes. Questions are provided in a variety of formats, including true-false, multiple choice, definitions, and short answer. Essay questions that may be of most use for teachers who wish to give unit or midterm and final exams are also provided. The book's bold-faced key terms along with hotlinks to their definitions, detailed chapter outlines and summaries, and learning objectives are provided for students to use when studying for tests. The resources are available to confirmed adopters. To request the resources, contact coursematerials @columbiauniversitypress.com or bcohen@harringtonparkpress.com.

## ORGANIZATION OF THE BOOK

The book begins with a brief introduction, setting both the binary-critical philosophy of the text and the concept of queering as an active verb that students will be asked to engage in throughout the course (and which defines each of the succeeding parts of the textbook proper). Part I focuses on issues of language, ranging from the basic terms used to classify or name nonheteronormative people and experience, to larger units of speech and writing, drawing on work on dialects and slang as well as on speech act theory. Part II is devoted to issues of identity, in terms both of identity formation and of identity intersections (and the condition of intersectionality, which is critical to much of contemporary identity studies in general). This part begins with a consideration of the meaning of the nature of "desire" as a way of grounding what has been central to much of the field of queer studies, that is, variations of same-sex attraction. From there, the chapters in Part II look at various traditional categories of queerness in sexuality studies, including trans and intersex identities. The design of Part II is intended to continually remind and challenge the students to recognize that no single category of identity is extricable from other nodes of identity, and that within any nameable category, there is a wide range of experiences and variations.

Part III examines queerness in contexts ranging from the most formative in students' lives (school) to those that are more global (such as spirituality and citizenship). There is a logic in the arrangement of chapters, as they move from earliest forms of social context to those that students may enter as they become adults.

Part IV, "Queering Imagination," deals in the most sustained way with issues of representation and creativity, considering such issues as camp, activist art, and mainstream media works, as well as moving students to "imagining" queer utopias, an issue that has been of concern in recent years to scholars and artists alike. This is followed by a brief conclusion, which serves more as a challenge and call to action for students — an encouragement to continue their study of queer life and experiences at the end of the class.

## ACKNOWLEDGMENTS

I wish to thank the people at Harrington Park Press for encouraging this project and providing helpful support throughout the process. In particular, I wish to thank Bill Cohen, publisher, Steven Rigolosi, developmental editor, Patrick Ciano, design director, and Ann Twombly, production coordinator, for their contributions to the process. Debra Riegert was of great assistance in my preparation of the Instructor's Resources.

To the readers of the manuscript, whose insights, support, and always constructive criticism and suggestions have unquestionably improved the book, I owe a large debt. Scott Dillard of Georgia College and State University and Dustin Bradley Goltz of DePaul University read the manuscript in its earliest drafts and made invaluable suggestions about how to tighten the sprawling pages and shape them into what I hope is a useful book for readers. Tony E. Adams of Bradley University and Bernadette Marie Calafell of Gonzaga University offered thoughtful and very helpful insights into such critical areas as the closet, coming out, race, ethnicity, class, and privilege. Paisley Currah of Brooklyn College, CUNY, carefully and thoroughly read the manuscript and offered many invaluable and generous suggestions about issues of trans inclusivity. I am grateful to all who took the time to offer their wisdom and insights.

I am grateful to the various writers who granted permission for use of their texts in this book, thus allowing me to provide undergraduates with primary sources to supplement my own observations. In particular, I owe special debts of gratitude to Richard Blanco, Scott Dillard, Loraine Edwalds, Jim Elledge, John S. Gentile, Jane Hamilton, John Russell Heineman, and Kevin Jennings, all of whom made the process feasible. I am so happy to have your writings in my book, thus enlarging the dialogic process, and I am proud to count many of you also as dear friends. I must single out the brilliantly talented and generous artist Peter Lane, whose elegant and powerful image provides an anchor for the cover of the book.

I offer most sincere thanks to my sister, Mary Danner, and her family for always welcoming me, never judging me, and always making me feel the value of my family of origin. I greatly appreciate those people who, along this pathway of life, befriended me, included me, and helped me feel I always had a "family of choice" (whether they knew it or not): John Dennis Anderson, Gary Balfantz, Amy Darnell, the late Carlos Clarke Drazen, Nancy Greco, Timothy Gura, Katharine Kittredge, Monica Miller, the late Patricia S. Pace, George Piggford, Joshua L. Potter-Dineen, Kay Quinlan, Mary-Kirk Arends Reyff, Gary Schaaf, Julie-Ann Scott, Sue Palmer Stoughton, David C. Sweeney, Sarah Trenholm, and John White. A special collective nod goes to the "DG" (Drama Group) of Oak Park–River Forest High School, from 1971 to 1975, who created a safe, if sometimes highly theatrical (and why not?), place to begin the process of self-discovery.

Thanks to teachers who both challenged me and nurtured me as I grew into myself: at Oak Park–River Forest High School, Helen Barclay, James Eitrheim, Harold Lee Radford, Norma Schultz, Beatrice Soroka, and, always, Leslie A. Wiberg; at Northwestern University, Wallace A. Bacon, Robert S. Breen, Kathleen Galvin, Leland M. Griffin, and Lilla A. Heston; at the University of Illinois at Chicago, Lennard C. Davis, Carol J. Gill, Joy

Hammel, and Timothy Murphy. The late Kevin G. Barnhurst offered a seminar on queer media studies at the University of Illinois at Chicago that I now see was the first planting of the seed that led to this book: while I know he would find much to critique and question in this book, I wish he were still among us to see it, and I would love to have the opportunity to discuss many issues in it.

Carol Simpson Stern, at Northwestern University, must always merit a separate and special paragraph of her own in any work I do. She has, for more than forty years, been my teacher, mentor, coauthor, and friend. Without her confidence and encouragement, I would not be where I am. And I also wish to thank her husband, J. Allyson Stern, who has been generous enough to "share" her with me and always to be there to provide me with goodwill and courage when I was not sure I could summon them for myself.

Thanks also to Ithaca College, which provided me some time off from teaching for the writing of this book through its flexible workload and sabbatical programs, and to Villanova University, which provided me with an exciting chance to teach its fine students and work with wonderful colleagues, as the Harron Family Endowed Professor of Communication in fall 2016. I am especially grateful to colleagues at Villanova who have become friends: Jared Bishop, Sherry Bowen, Shauna MacDonald, Heidi Rose, as well as Maurice Hall, currently at the College of New Jersey.

At Ithaca College I have so many colleagues to thank for helping enlighten me on topics ranging from classical Greece to contemporary culture, gently correcting misconceptions and generously leading me to sources (though any and all errors are, of course, my own responsibility). I must single out Rebecca Plante, of the Sociology Department, who first suggested me to Harrington Park Press as a possible author for this project. In my home department, Communication Studies, Christopher House and Robert Sullivan were always willing and enthusiastic resources, Christopher especially on issues concerning the black church's responses to HIV/AIDS and queer affirmation in general, and Bob in all matters classical, and also for his gift of time and patience, particularly generous, given that he was simultaneously working to complete his own book; he was nonetheless never stinting in making time to answer some of my always a-bit-too-detailed (and garrulous) questions on Greek concepts of love and sexuality. In the Department of History, I owe much to the following individuals: Karin Breuer, Jason Freitag, Matthew Klemm, and Zenon Wasyliw. Jason, in particular, fielded almost daily questions on Islam and sexuality, and the book is all the better for his knowledge and insights. In the Department of Modern Languages and Literatures, Gladys Varona-Lacey was not only a valuable source of information, but one of the best friends one could have; Annette Levine and Michael Richardson were also invaluable in helping me understand queer issues in non-Anglophone cultures. Rebecca Lesses in the Jewish Studies Department helped me think and talk through the complexities of Judaism and queer identity. Carla Golden, both as a brilliant scholar of lesbian psychology and as coordinator of the Women's and Gender Studies Program, gave me the opportunity to teach the college's Queer Studies course, which was the genesis of this book. Luca Maurer, director of the LGBT Center for Education, Outreach, and Services, has provided me with a model of how to work with students across various spectrums of sexuality and other axes of identity.

The students at Ithaca College have constantly provided me with new insights and with lessons their generations still have to teach those of us who came of age earlier. It has been my privilege to work and learn with them for the past thirty years.

Finally, I dedicate this book to the three men whose love and lives I have most cherished — three men who taught me and continue to teach me how to live a proud, thoughtful, and caring life as a gay man.

# QUEER STUDIES

# INTRODUCTION

## Queering "Queering": A Way of Seeing/ Experiencing/Knowing

*Queer Studies: Beyond Binaries* is designed as an introductory textbook for undergraduate courses in this rapidly growing field; it is also a product of my own experiences as a teacher of a semester-long course in this subject over a series of years. Such courses are often developed as part of a call for a broader spectrum of classes that address **identity** issues or diversity education, and students are enrolled for any number of reasons. Some identify as queer (or use a parallel term, such as *gay* or *LGBTQ+*) and are looking for opportunities to study in a systematic way how their own experiences are connected to broader histories and issues of "queerness" in general. Other students wish to expand their toolkit of diversity knowledge, adding to the kinds of education they have often received in courses on race and gender (and, less frequently, class). Still others, when asked why they have enrolled in such a class, may mention that a friend or family member has recently come out, and the students wish to develop ways of understanding experiences of people who are important to them and, in some cases, to work with them as advocates, whether within the domestic sphere of the family (particularly for siblings) or in larger social and political contexts.

My hope is that this book will be of value to each and all of these students. So, readers, whatever your reasons for picking up this book (no doubt most often as a class requirement), I trust that it will speak to you and provide you both with information and perspectives that will enrich and enlarge your ways of thinking about and understanding queerness, both as a way of being and as a way of experiencing and knowing. My goal is to make the material accessible enough so that those who have not studied sexuality in any academic or scholarly way will be able to navigate the myriad perspectives and concepts, while those of you who, either because you have done previous coursework in gender studies or because you "live the life," will find much that is new and illuminating here as well.

Henderson, Bruce, *Queer Studies: Beyond Binaries*
dx.doi.org/10.17312/harringtonparkpress/2019.09.qsbb.00b
© 2019 by Harrington Park Press

Chapter 1 focuses exclusively and in-depth on the language scholars and others use to talk about queerness, but it is useful, in framing the book, to break down some of the central terms of the title, to clarify the basic assumptions of the book and its organization.

## BINARIES

The phrase in the subtitle, "beyond binaries," invokes the term **binary**, which readers may have encountered previously, though perhaps in other disciplines or contexts. In our digital world, most are familiar with the use of the binary pairing of 0 and 1 in computer coding; the electronic transmission of information and language would be very different without this technology. Similarly, if you have studied languages or speech science, you may have learned about "cognate pairs," sounds that share many of the same characteristics but which are distinguished by a single feature. The discovery and study of such binaries has been of great use for those working with people on their spoken language.

The expansion of the search for binaries beyond such microscopic levels led, in the mid-twentieth century, to an intellectual movement called structuralism, in which such writers as the anthropologist Claude Levi-Strauss and the linguist Ferdinand de Saussure identified binary pairs that helped organize analysis of social and cultural phenomena: one of Levi-Strauss's most famous binaries was "the raw and the cooked," which he used to examine food and purity codes and rituals within different cultures. Critics of structuralism, who were often known as poststructuralists or deconstructionists, argued that too rigid an imposition of binary ways of thinking tended to reduce the complexity of the world, in everything from social structures to individual experiences of identities. They looked to "deconstruct" such binaries, remove their "givenness," to get at the ways in which "either-or" categories limit understanding.

This challenge to binaries has more than academic implications, and the relationship between academic perspectives and real-world experiences and structures is at the heart of the use of this alternative to binaries in this book. It was quite common, during much of the twentieth century, to divide human sexual identity and experience into a neat binary: heterosexual-homosexual; in the case of gender there have been and continue to be binaries clustered around such oppositional terms as "male-female" or "masculine-feminine," pairs that trans people and their allies contest and interrogate. Aside from the fact that such a binary omits even the possibility of bisexuality as a genuine axis of identity, it flattens the complex, rich experiences of people who don't find their experiences of attraction, activity, social identity, or embodiment so easily wrapped up in a single word. To put it less academically, binaries can run the risk of forcing people to "pick a side," or, in the case of trans people, to be what the writer Michel Foucault called "docile bodies," to "stay on the side" assigned them either at birth or throughout childhood and adolescent development by medical professionals, family members, or society at large. Human experience is just not that easily categorized.

Indeed, in developing the book, the people at Harrington Park Press and I have had valuable conversations about the title of the book — whether it would be better to use the word **queer** or the term **LGBT**. Ultimately, we have gone with the former, as being more inclusive. While *LGBT* may seem more neutral and, depending on where and when you experience the terms, less negative in its history and connotations than *queer*, the presence of four categories (LGBT) nevertheless continues the spirit of binaries — of asking people to contain their experience of self and others into boxes. And, in fact, as we will discuss at more length, even *LGBT* has become somewhat outmoded, as various, more specific ways of describing sexual identity have come into existence.

One of the most searching and thoughtful discussions of the tensions and possibilities for productive dialogue between LGBT and queer perspectives is that of the late scholar R. Tony Slagle. In his essay "Ferment in LGBT Studies and Queer Theory: Personal Ruminations on Contested Terrain," listed in the Works Cited section of this book, Slagle writes about his own career in the field of communication studies, which he began when the discipline's scholarly and professional association, the National Communication Association (previously the Speech Communication Association), had established, a few years back, a caucus (similar to an interest group, originally designed to raise awareness and do professional activism in the association) for "Gay and Lesbian Concerns": the word "queer" had not yet really or fully entered the lexicon as anything but a slur.

Slagle was one of a new generation of scholars who were reading queer theory and introducing it into their teaching, scholarship, and everyday lives. In the essay, Slagle notes the opposition he faced, sometimes in the form of ad hominem (personal) attacks, for his attraction to queer theory (and for his use of the word *queer* in and of itself, which to the previous generation was both unwelcome and, to their minds, unscholarly), and the essay charts both the personal costs, psychological and professional, that his commitment to *queer* enacted on him, and more recent developments: as of this writing, the association now has a Caucus on Gay, Lesbian, Bisexual, Transgender, and Queer Concerns, as well as a Gay, Lesbian, Bisexual, Transgender, and Queer Communication Studies Group, which focus on scholarship on those identity groups. Slagle's "personal ruminations" articulate with eloquence and honesty the challenges of navigating the waters even (perhaps especially) in scholarly and intellectual contexts. They point not simply to generational differences, but to political commitments, in which those opposed to Slagle's use of *queer* either reject the term as mired in historical offense or view the primary work of their group as dealing with sexual orientation, not gender identity and expression. So, understanding of different people's use of (and preference for) such terms as *LGBT* and *queer* will probably lead to better communication and more productive discussion.

## QUEER STUDIES AND QUEER THEORY

In setting out to develop this textbook, both the publishers and I have agreed from the outset about how we hoped this book might add to the relatively small number of books designed specifically for bright undergraduate students interested both in gaining ways of thinking about queerness (theory) and in applying such thinking to the experiences of people who either identify as queer or have meaningful interactions with queer people (in other words, everyone!). *Queer theory* as a scholarly concept has a history that is typically traced back to the coining of the phrase by the film and literary theorist Teresa de Lauretis and to a central set of scholars, such as Judith Butler, Eve Kosofsky Sedgwick, Alexander Doty, and Michael Warner, who drew on various philosophers and other thinkers to develop a distinctive methodology and set of assumptions in carrying out their work. There are a number of accessible, relatively brief surveys of queer theory already in print (a few are listed at the end of this introduction) and this book does not seek to duplicate or compete with such books.

Queer theory, though it varies in scope and approach, is predicated on the concept of *nonnormativity* as a legitimate, nonpathologized variation in human existence and in its centrality to viewing and acting in the world. It argues, as others have said of critical race theory and feminist theory (with which it shares many points of contact), that the "margins may define the center" as much as the other way around; in simpler terms, the assumed centrality of the "norm" is as much a social construct as the "othering" of those who, by social construction and history of such features as race (usually marked by skin color and assumed geographical point of origin), gender, or sexual orientation, as well as disability and class, have been viewed and treated as "nonnormative." Queer theory, as its name suggests, tends to focus most on sexual orientation and gender identity. It also differs from LGB (or LGBTQ+) studies in that it typically views sexual or gender issues not as static (though an individual's sexual orientation or gender identity may be experienced as continuous and consistent), but as open to change and variation over the course of a lifetime or in different social and cultural contexts. Queer theory also argues for the epistemological (i.e., knowledge-producing) value of, in Alexander Doty's phrase, "seeing things queerly," that is, as opening different and valuable perspectives from the dynamism that *queerness* as a concept encourages.

This book uses the overarching concept of *queering,* drawn from queer theory, as a way of looking at the lives of queer people across a range of concepts and in light of different academic and scholarly disciplines. At its simplest level, we might say that what queer theory brings to the book is a conviction that thinking beyond **normativity** (assumptions that there is a "natural" or "normal" state of being or way of experiencing) yields useful and equally valid knowledge about the world. In a sense, what *queering* (as a gerund or verb) does is to challenge what might be considered the figure-ground proportions usually unchecked or uncritiqued. In this sense, *to queer* is to ask all of us to consider or reconsider what gets emphasized and how seeing from what are often marked as the "margins" may make it possible to produce better, more inclusive knowledge.

As a textbook in queer studies, its scope is somewhat ambitious. *Queer Studies: Beyond Binaries* provides a survey of what cannot be completely inclusive, but nonetheless is a broad span of scholarly disciplines and human experiences, from the foundational study of language with which the book begins to social institutions, psychological experiences, and pedagogical approaches with which we all have experiences — if not as scholars, then as people who make our way in the world, from earliest education to the rituals of marriage, facing the end of life, and advocating for justice. Queer theory informs this book, but the emphasis is on asking readers to engage with all manner of experiences in the world at large.

## ORGANIZATION OF THE BOOK AND SUGGESTIONS FOR ITS USE

The book is divided into twelve chapters (in addition to this introduction and a brief conclusion) and four parts. Each chapter, as the Contents indicates, takes a different topic or area of inquiry and engages in ways of queering the traditional ways of approaching the knowledge associated with the topic. Part I focuses exclusively on issues of language, and it stands alone. To achieve common ground among class members, it is recommended that all classes study and discuss this chapter. Part II consists of five chapters, each examining either a category or categories of queer identity or a facet of queer experience, ranging from such local social units as the family and school to global considerations, such as health and citizenship. While each chapter is relatively self-contained, the recommendation is to have students read and discuss all these chapters, as they are intended to be inclusive of the range of categories of queerness (with the understanding that some of the categories overlap).

Part III, comprising five chapters, takes queerness and brings it into contact with larger contexts — again, with the understanding that many aspects of identity cannot be separated from and indeed emerge from such contexts. These contexts and their associated scholarly disciplines range from education to psychology to health studies to religion and theology to political science and government. While all the chapters can be covered in a standard semester (quarter courses may find themselves rushed if all chapters are required), this is where individual instructors may wish to make their own judgments, based on the goals of their particular class, their own areas of expertise and knowledge, and their institutional characteristics. If an instructor chooses to be more selective about inclusion of various chapters in Part III, this may allow each instructor to spend more than a week's time on the topics and perhaps add supplemental readings, drawn either from the Suggestions for Further Reading and Viewing at the end of each chapter or from their own knowledge base. Part IV, like Part I, stands alone, as it considers how queer artists (thought of broadly) have imagined the worlds in which they live and continue to imagine futures. It serves as a kind of epilogue, a "leading out" beyond the confines of the book and the span of the course.

Each chapter also contains one or more "Spotlights," sections that focus on specific individuals or moments in queer history, which provide opportunities to get a closer look at the people who were and are part of broader movements or moments in queer life. Similarly, each chapter offers a number of "Issues for Investigation," either a series of questions for discussion or suggestions for individual or group activities, to help instructors and students make application of the material in the chapter's body. No doubt teachers will develop their own sets of questions and activities as well. Whether a class addresses these issues, the instructor may find them useful as a way to review the material contained in each chapter.

## QUEERNESS AS A WAY OF INCLUSION, NOT AS A BARRIER

A book of this nature often deals, by necessity, with statements about large groups of people and a certain degree of generalization; needless to say, the experiences of individuals vary considerably, depending not only on when and where they live, but on the complex intersectionalities of the other facets of their lives. As you will see, the term *queer*, which will be the overarching term of the book, is not one all people discussed here would necessarily use to describe themselves or embrace for historical or political reasons. When feasible and when logical, I have endeavored to use the language that individuals would have used, though *queer* remains the default term as a rule when there is no reason to use another. So, it is a delicate balance, and one to remain aware of as you navigate through the book. Similarly, assumptions about the lives and identities of scholars, writers, artists, and other individuals should be suppressed, unless there is historical or autobiographical material to lead to a conclusion. The author Jane Hamilton, for example, whose gay-centered (perhaps even queer) novel, *The Short History of a Prince*, is included, identifies as **heterosexual**, though she has had deep friendships and important relationships with queer folk. The same is true for work on trans issues: the musician David Bowie, who identified as cisgender and, for most of his life, either heterosexual or bisexual, popularized a style of appearance and rock music that built on a complicated resistance to gender binaries. In some cases, individual artists' (or other workers') life narratives have shifted over time. The British comedian-actor Eddie Izzard, who frequently performs in what is marked as traditionally feminine clothing and makeup, has moved, over the course of decades, from describing himself as a heterosexual "drag artist" (they also have appeared and acted in male roles onstage and in film, as well as in stand-up comedy) to now preferring nonbinary pronouns and identity. Izzard may be seen as having always done queer work, especially in terms of trans issues, and their own journey suggests the kind of fluidity *queer* can signify.

At the same time, the question may be complicated in different ways in other contexts or for other individuals. In corresponding with the contemporary New York–based sculptor Peter Lane, who identifies as a gay man (perhaps he would use the word *queer*), I posed the question whether his art is queer (you can find examples of his magnificent — "monumental," to use his own descriptive term — pieces online). He responded to my question with the following statement:

> I don't think there is any connection between my sexual nature and my work, but at the same time, my sexual nature is an important part of who I am. . . . But I digress. Sexual expression is separated from sexual nature by culture and situation. Straight guys *become* gay in prison . . . and flaming queens go ultra-butch under repressive regimes. And I'm lucky enough to remember when, in the immortal words of Jonathan Winters, "the Gideon Bible only gets you so far, and then you gotta go downstairs." Well, we've reached a time when, for better and for worse, you don't have to go downstairs. (personal correspondence)

Lane's statement is an honest description of his own complex sense of how his sexual identity and his art are inextricably entwined, but not necessarily overtly, programmatically, or intentionally "driven" by a desire to make something that could be identified as queer. Is his art queer? Viewers and critics might say yes; he might say the question is not an important one to him.

Take a few minutes and look at this book's cover; its principal image is drawn from Lane's sculptural work. Lane's work is not figurative, as a rule, depicting representations of things; he has used the word *monumental* to describe his style and motivations. While he, as he suggested, does not see himself as overtly or intentionally queer in his aesthetics or in the political implications of his work, consider how the image might be seen as pushing boundaries of the kinds of normativity we might associate with "fine art." In what way, whether overtly or not, does the image lend itself to a queer reading or understanding?

All this is to say that *queer*, as a descriptor, as an experience, as an academic method, requires that we adopt a fluidity of approach and an openness to difference and variation that do not constrain us, any more than we would want to be constrained by a too rigid, formulaic, or prescriptive imposition of a binary such as queer–non-queer. Queer should be a place that allows for exploration, disagreement, and discovery, for honoring of individuals' experience and naming of their own lives and experiences, and for ongoing conversations about possibilities.

## SUGGESTIONS FOR FURTHER READING

Jagose, Annamarie. *Queer Theory: An Introduction.* New York: New York University Press, 1997.

Stryker, Susan, *Transgender History: The Roots of Today's Revolution.* 2nd ed. New York: Seal Press, 2017.

Sullivan, Nikki. *A Critical Introduction to Queer Theory.* New York: New York University Press, 2003.

Wilchins, Riki. *Queer Theory, Gender Theory.* Bronx, NY: Riverdale Avenue Books, 2014.

PART I

# QUEERING LANGUAGE

# QUEERING LANGUAGE
## Words and Worlds

The philosopher and writer Kenneth Burke once wrote, "A choice of words is a choice of worlds," suggesting that not only is it through language that we make decisions about how to make sense of the worlds in which we live, but that we also actually use language to create the worlds themselves. He went on to describe human beings as "wordlings," creatures whose beings and lives are dominated by the power and effects of language—and he extended this notion to include all kinds of symbol making, not just the verbal realm of words and sentences.

**Linguists**, scholars and professionals who study the structure, relationships, meanings, and uses of language, cast their nets wider than the intentional use of language to cause change or to conserve the status quo. Linguists are as interested in the aspects of language that occur in unconscious or even seemingly automatic ways, and how and why they work that way. Linguists are typically considered to be social scientists, using observational and experimental methods to produce knowledge and test hypotheses. In addition, linguists often divide their study between what they refer to as **diachronic** and **synchronic** perspectives. Diachronic linguistics looks at changes in language over the course of time, using historical methods of study; synchronic linguistics studies the use of language at a particular time. These two perspectives, we will find, are complementary rather than oppositional: both are helpful, but they focus on different aspects of the study of language. What is at stake in "queering language," in terms of the words and worlds that are often chosen for or imposed on us? To answer that question requires that we begin with a word that itself has an interesting history (diachronic), as well as a complexity of meaning at any given moment (synchronic): queer.

## QUEER: WHAT'S IN A WORD?

One place to begin is with the language of the description and course title for which you are reading this book. Is it, perhaps, "LGBT Studies," or,

Henderson, Bruce, *Queer Studies: Beyond Binaries*
dx.doi.org/10.17312/harringtonparkpress/2019.09.qsbb.001
© 2019 by Harrington Park Press

alternatively, "GLBT Studies"? Maybe a longer set of letters — "LGBTQ" or "LGBTQA" or "LGBTQIA" — or something even longer? Is it yet another title, such as "Sexuality Studies" or "Sexual Minorities"? Which department or program offers the course? If it is Queer Studies, what expectations does the word *queer* create in you?

The word *queer* has an interesting history. Beginning with the history of the word (and its derivation, which is often referred to as its etymology) can help us situate, in a more in-depth way, the multiple meanings the word has and ways in which it is used in our own time. So, let us look at the earliest recorded uses of the words in the English language and then its changing meanings across time. The linguist Robin Brontsema has studied the word *queer* in some depth. She turns to the *Oxford English Dictionary*, which traces the word back to the Middle High German word *twer*, which carries associations such as "cross" or "oblique," suggesting qualities of "differentness" or "strangeness" (Brontsema, 2). Brontsema goes on to explain that "*queer*'s original significations did not denote nonnormative sexualities, but rather a nonnormativity from sexuality" (ibid.). It simply meant odd or strange.

Brontsema notes that the use of *queer* to mark non**heteronormative** sexuality (as well as nonmonogamous heterosexual arrangements), began to develop in the early part of the twentieth century in the United States and the United Kingdom, though not in an exclusive way. She draws on the work of such historians as George Chauncey to map out the various terms that coexisted with *queer* and notes that, at different times, the word carried different denotative and connotative meanings. At some times, *queer* was a kind of umbrella term for those individuals and groups of people who practiced same-sex behaviors (even if they practiced opposite-sex behaviors as well), often pointing primarily to male homosexuals, in large part because women's sexuality, of any kind, has been given less attention socially and historically.

Chauncey argues that historical evidence indicates that *queer* even marked a different set of characteristics within same-sex-centered communities of men. It was counterposed to the term *fairy*, which described not only a man who desired and practiced sex with other men, but also a way of expressing how that man acted in expressing his gender: *fairy* was frequently a term used to stigmatize men who acted in gender-nonconforming ways, who were considered "effeminate" or "womanly" (terms that today are contested or questionable). Among such men, *fairy* was saved for men who presented themselves in ways the society of the times considered "nonmasculine."

The term **homosexual** has a similarly complex history. Historians of sexuality such as Michel Foucault argue that "the homosexual" as a stable, defined class of identity did not exist before the late nineteenth century, when sexology emerged as an academic and scholarly field of study. Though there were equivalent words, such as **sodomite**, they were typically used to describe people who performed particular acts that were viewed by the society of the time as unnatural, and it was the behavior that was being described, not something that was part of the individual's essential character. But in the Victorian period and beyond (i.e., the middle of the nineteenth century through the first half of the twentieth), the mutation from adjective to noun indicates a significant conceptual shift, a shift that marks an agreement among those who share a language that the concept has become a more defined state of being.

By the middle of the twentieth century, the word *queer* carried sexual connotations, though still in a fairly binary way: people either were or were not queer — that is, most people worked from the general assumption that one was attracted either to one's own sex or to the "opposite" one. (Bisexuality remained undertheorized, often consigned to such categories as "undecided" or "opportunistic," rather than as an authentic category of sexual identity.) While *homosexual* might be seen as the most "objective" term, social attitudes made the act of describing or calling someone a homosexual to be viewed as a negative, stigmatizing act. The word *homosexual* need not inherently be a negative descriptor, but, depending on how, when, where, and why it is used, it can have the effect of making a negative judgment about a person.

Moving back to our central term, *queer*, we can now consider how the word continues its historical evolution to the present day and how it functions in our own time. *Queer* remained a word used primarily in a negative way to describe people who participated in or who were assumed to practice homosexual behaviors and who were defined by them. Indeed, *queer*, like *homosexual*, became used as a noun, often in informal or casual contexts — as a kind of slang. One might suggest that it carried even more force than *homosexual*, both for people who used it as a slur or a derogation against other people and for people who identified as homosexual and who used it among other people with whom they shared this identity. For the former, *queer* was strictly negative, intended as a kind of verbal threat or wound; for the latter, the power of the word was more complex (as it is today).

Brontsema, as do other scholars, identifies yet another important shift in the use of *queer* as occurring around 1990, after the two decades following the Stonewall Riots, which happened in 1969 and are commonly considered to be a major moment in the emergence of what was then called the gay liberation movement, and about one decade into the AIDS epidemic. As a response to what many grassroots radicals viewed as repressive politics under President Ronald Reagan and the accompanying lack of action, including research, financial support, and public discourse, dealing with the growing effects of HIV/AIDS (the virus was not discovered until 1983), a group calling itself Queer Nation formed in 1990. The formation and self-naming of this group are viewed as the first time a coalition of individuals who would have been labeled by society as "queer" (in the sexual sense) decided to take back the word from those individuals and groups who had more political, social, economic, and cultural power, and to use it as an act of self-determination and pride. This use of *queer* coincided with its introduction into scholarly and academic discourse, which is usually marked by Teresa de Lauretis's coining of the phrase *queer theory* in an issue of the feminist journal *Differences*. *Queer* began to include those who practiced gender nonconformity and who inhabited trans identities. It is worth noting that this was accompanied by political tensions over the word, such as a resistance by some members of the organization Queer Nation to including trans identities as "citizens" of such a nation; a Transgender Nation caucus was formed within Queer Nation (Stryker 2008, 146).

Think about how even the very simple, economical phrase *Queer Nation* performs powerful work: we typically associate the word *nation* very strongly with legitimate citizenship, with belonging to a recognized group, occupying a cultural and, typically, geographic "space." Yet, as the political scientist Benedict Anderson has suggested, in addition to these geographic territories (which have historically themselves been open to considerable contest and conflict, as we witness in the Middle East and elsewhere today), all nations are essentially and finally "imagined communities," so that there is no reason that there cannot be a "queer nation," populated by people who claim the word *queer* as central to who they are.

Just as we noted that the shift of *homosexual* from adjective to noun was an important linguistic movement, so is the expansion of *queer,* both in terms of its meaning and in its grammatical range as a signal of significant shifting of attitudes and views, consequential. With the advent of a more positive, empowering set of associations, and particularly with the development of queer theory and queer studies in the academy, the verb *to queer* has become one that has positive potential: it is often used to mean a process by which some phenomenon (a social event, an artistic text, a set of attitudes) is reevaluated and reread in ways that break down assumptions of what is "normal." *To queer* something in a scholarly way means to look at the object of study through lenses that do not simply accept the givens we may have been taught or simply internalized.

*Queering* something in a scholarly way, then, may involve the sexual and gendered aspects of a phenomenon. Some critics have queered the television series *The Big Bang Theory* by shifting the focus from the heterosexual relationships at the center of the show to the nonheteronormative elements that can be seen in it, such as the character Amy's crush on her friend Penny, the "bromance" between Raj and Howard, and the possible asexuality (in early seasons) of Sheldon. Sheldon's resistance to any sexuality made some viewers label him as asexual, itself a queer position. The introduction of Amy as a girlfriend and then fiancée and wife can be seen as a "normatizing" move (though their sex life is anything but "normative"). Queering gender has similarly occurred in stage traditions. Shakespeare's plays (especially his comedies, such as *Twelfth Night* and *The Merchant of Venice*) are doubly queered, as the female roles were played by adolescent male actors because women were not permitted on the stage. More recently, male actors, particularly those of a certain age, have enjoyed playing Oscar Wilde's "dragon-like" prudish female character, Lady Bracknell, in *The Importance of Being Earnest*, which suggests the "female masculinity" of this aggressive Victorian matriarch. J.M. Barrie specified that the title character in his classic *Peter Pan* was to be played by a female actor; interestingly, perhaps the most famous actor to play Peter Pan was the musical comedy star Mary Martin, who won a Tony and performed the role three times on live television, and who always stated that it was her favorite role. Martin's stage personae varied, from the hyperfeminine Venus in *One Touch of Venus* to the ultimately normative, though initially tomboyish, Maria von Trapp in *The Sound of Music*, both on Broadway. Biographers have long speculated that Martin herself was either lesbian or bisexual; it may be that her pleasure in playing Peter was the freedom it allowed her to explore her own sense of gender nonconformity, which, in the mid-twentieth century, could be revealed only as part of stage performances.

But queering need not necessarily be overtly or even unconsciously sexual in its content. To choose another example from popular culture, there have been many scholarly attempts to queer the Harry Potter books (and films), long before their author, J.K. Rowling, declared that the beloved headmaster Dumbledore was gay. Some cultural commentators suggested that this series' phenomenal popularity had to do with the ways in which it queered both the traditional school story and the experience of adolescence itself. Though there is no homosexuality overtly present in the stories, they depict an alternative world, different from the one the rest of us "Muggles" exist in, a world in which there is power in being different or, to use the language of queer theory, "nonnormative." Which "houses" at Hogwarts seemed more queer than others to you, and why?

Recall that Brontsema began her own etymological analysis by noting that the root word *twer* did not have sexual connotations, and that *queer* came to carry widespread sexual associations only in the last century and a half. It would seem that we are now in a place and time where the sexual is once again not a necessary aspect of the word's connotations or use. Some might argue that, even in those instances in which sexual nonnormativity is not explicitly intended, we cannot ever return to a "prehistorical" use of the word, that its identification with a minoritized experience or identity, and one that is associated with the erotic or romantic, will always be somewhere underneath — that the word will always have a "sexiness" about it.

The last aspect we might consider about the word *queer* is what might be considered both political and ethical and falls into the arena of what Brontsema calls "linguistic reclamation." Brontsema argues that the "reclamation of *queer* has been largely fragmented, limitedly accepted, and highly contested" (5). She proceeds to suggest a set of perspectives through which to view the debate over whether it is politically efficacious and ethically warranted to reclaim *queer* and make the decision in a conscious and mindful way to give it an accepted place in public discourse. She starts with the seemingly simple binary opposition of positions on this question: "reclamation opposed" versus "reclamation supported" — the former standing for a belief that the word should not be used, the latter that it should be. Note that the word *reclamation* is central to this pairing — as is the case with any parallel speech acts, much may depend on who is performing the action.

Brontsema argues that the simple binary of "opposed-supported" is insufficient to allow us to have useful and intelligent conversations about what is at stake in such "linguistic reclamations." So she expands the terms of the issue by adding a second set of variables to the binary: "pejoration inseparable" and "pejoration separable." By *pejoration* she means the use of the term in a negative or disparaging way. She proceeds to identify and describe different permutations produced by juxtaposing the "opposed-supported" binary and the "separable-inseparable" binary regarding the word *queer*.

Perhaps the most interesting possibilities are in the less intuitive prospect: that the pejoration is inseparable from the word and that, nonetheless or even because this is the case, there can be good reasons to support reclaiming it. Brontsema summarizes the logic behind this position in terms that get at a particular kind of political stance, both about language and about historical awareness: such a perspective in a sense embraces a history of resistance and ongoing struggle against oppression and wears this condition as a badge of pride. Calling oneself queer, talking about an affinity group as queers, calling on citizens to queer marriage or the military (or any other traditionally normative activity or group) become acts that simultaneously assert a newly acquired and ongoing movement for power, while honoring and acknowledging both the past and present views and acts that would devalue and disempower queers.

An example of how *queer* may both include *trans* and enable it for some individuals comes from the transgender historian Susan Stryker, who writes: "I named myself queer in 1990. . . . The term allowed me to align myself with other antiheteronormative identities and sociopolitical formations without erasing the specificity of my sense of self or the practices I engage to perform myself for others. By becoming queer first, I found I could then become transsexual in a way I had not previously considered" (Stryker 1998, 151). This is an example of how *queer* became a kind of ideological "gateway" to *trans* for Stryker — and then may be seen as also acknowledging a possible place in *queer* for *trans*, or at least an overlap between the two.

Brontsema concludes by acknowledging that we need to keep in mind some thus-far neglected parts of the issue. First, there are (and perhaps always will be, though we cannot say for sure, of course) what she calls "non-queer gays and lesbians," by which she means homosexual people (we will address the sometimes-thorny issues in these terms in the next section of this chapter) who choose not to use *queer* for myriad reasons and whom self-described queers may also not wish to include under the term *queer* (which they may reserve, as Brontsema suggests, for a specific set of political attitudes and actions). She also cautions us to consider the ways in which the word *queer* has been used (and continues to be) as a form of **hate speech**, in which the speaking or writing of the word is intended to cause harm or to threaten. Though she notes this possibility, she finally asserts that hate speech succeeds only if the intended objects allow themselves to be victims of it. If one chooses not to use *queer*, she suggests, it should not be as a result of fear that others will once again usurp its power. Do you think she is right about this?

## LGBTQIA+: ALPHABET SOUP OR LITTLE BOXES?

Certainly, the use of the word *queer* to refer to all people who stand outside normative conceptions of sexual and gender identity, desire, and behavior has distinct advantages in its inclusiveness. That inclusiveness may at the same time be criticized by some as its very weakness. A way to understand the possible pitfalls of *queer* as an inclusive term may be understood through the idea of the **ladder of abstraction**, a concept advanced by the scholar S. I. Hayakawa, who theorized that people move, linguistically and cognitively, up and down levels (like rungs on a ladder) of words that are either more or less abstract and, therefore, represent a concept in more mental or more concrete terms:

**Level Four:** Abstractions

**Level Three:** Noun classes: broad groups

**Level Two:** Noun categories: more definite groups

**Level One:** Specific, identifiable nouns

One could argue that the word *queer* has moved, at different times and in different contexts, from Level Four (simply understood to mean "strange" or "different") to the other levels. If *queer* is used to refer to all people whose sexual lives and identities are nonnormative, perhaps we are using the word in a Level Three sense. If we narrow the meaning of *queer* to refer only to sexuality centered on same-sex interactions or desires, we are probably even farther down, on Level Two. Level One might be a very specific individual's way of understanding their sexuality or gender, or, as suggested in the previous section, might require that the same-sex association or gender nonconformity be tied to a radical, left-wing politics.

This section, then, focuses on language — specifically, words and phrases that name groups, that move in ways more typically specific in their meaning than *queer*, keeping in mind the varied uses of *queer* discussed above (some more abstract, some perhaps more specific than some of the words discussed below). We start by unraveling the code of each letter of our "queer alphabet."

## Gay: All-Purpose Word or Gender Specific?

The word **gay** has a long and often unclear history in the language of sexuality and sexual identity. Like the word *queer*, it has had and continues to have meanings that are entirely unassociated with sexual identity. If you consult dictionaries (including online ones), you will discover that virtually all of them now include *homosexual* as one of the accepted definitions, sometimes with the qualification that it is often used specifically to refer to male homosexuals. In some dictionaries, it is the first definition, which often suggests what the lexicographer considers to be the most common or frequent meaning in use at the time of the publication of the dictionary. It is not the case that the positioning of a definition in a list in a dictionary carries any prescriptive dimensions: that is, the first definition given is not intended to be the "correct" one or even the "preferred" one

The *Oxford English Dictionary* once again helps us trace the historical lineage of the word. The first three definitions focus on nonsexual meanings of the word. Only in definition no. 4 is a sexual quality introduced. The first definition under this subheading is "wanton, lewd, lascivious," followed by the abbreviation *Obs.,* meaning obsolete, or no longer used (the first examples of this usage date to the fifteenth century). Definition number 4c, which immediately precedes the definition of *gay* as homosexual is "of a woman: living by prostitution. Of a place: serving as a brothel" (www.oed.com).

Indeed, if you read writing from the eighteenth century up to some decades in the twentieth, you will find this usage, without any implication of homosexuality. To be a "gay girl" was to be a prostitute. The British word for a man (usually a young man) who either performed homosexual behaviors or did "women's work" was *molly*, and molly houses were houses of prostitution where men could hire such young men, who sometimes (but not always) dressed in female clothing, for sexual purposes. This word was always considered a form of slang, the informal and everyday language of social life. When used in this sense today, it almost always is in reference to the past or to a historical setting: one finds it in novels meant to evoke the eighteenth and nineteenth centuries.

The word *gay* as a specifically homosexual term is first noted by the *OED* as having been in print in a short story by Gertrude Stein. In a sketch called "Miss Furr and Miss Skeene," published in 1922, Stein writes a thinly veiled story about two women she knew. The editors of the *OED* qualify this first instance of the use of the word *gay* to mean homosexual, saying, "It is likely that, although there may be innuendo in some cases, these have been interpreted anachronistically in the light either of the context, . . . or of knowledge about an author's sexuality" (www.oed.com). Nonetheless, read the following brief excerpt from the piece (the story is now in the public domain and can be found in multiple places online), and consider how the repetition of the word starts to become a signifier (a word or symbol) of an ongoing relationship between the title characters: "They stayed there and were gay there, not very gay there, just gay there. They were both gay there, they were regularly working there both of them cultivating their voices there, they were both gay there. Georgine Skeene was gay there and she was regular, regular in being gay, regular in not being gay, regular in being a gay one who was one not being gay longer than was needed to be one being quite a gay one. They were both gay then there and both working there then" (www.gutenberg.org/files/33403/33403-h/33403-h.htm).

The word *gay* as an accepted, commonly understood synonym for homosexual truly emerged for the larger public in the period after the Stonewall Riots, in part because of the emergence of political organizations such as the Gay Liberation Front and the use by those affiliated with such groups claiming the word *gay* as their identity term of choice. It quickly replaced *homosexual* in the language of people identifying as having same-sex desire as a more positive term and one less clinical (i.e., scientific, medically pathologizing) than *homosexual*. There certainly was resistance in various corners to the word *gay*. Some nonhomosexual people asserted that a minority group had somehow appropriated a word that the dissenters viewed as more "innocent" and nonsexual. Conversely, a small but vocal minority of homosexual people suggested that the adoption of *gay* as a synonym for *homosexual* trivialized the significance of sexual orientation and the historical and political oppression of people who struggled for rights and acceptance. One could say that they, too, might have been too close in time to see that the word would become less strongly associated with the frivolous and take on a primary meaning of *homosexual*, thus demonstrating the power of a group of people to use and change language.

One complication many scholars and cultural commentators have noted is that in recent decades there has been a kind of "restigmatizing" use of the word, particularly among adolescent males, as in the cliché "Dude, that's so gay!" in which the word *gay* means stupid, corny, uncool. We suspect many speakers who use the word in this way may be unconscious of the ways in which this redefinition may well once again, however unintentionally, reinforce negative attitudes toward gay people.

One of the ways in which we continue to observe the ever-changing nature of language is in the spreading of uses of the word *gay*. Some people use the word as a noun: the contemporary stand-up comic Kathy Griffin often refers in her performances to "her gays," explaining that she views gay people (men, in particular) with great love, admiration, and support. Her actions generally support this self-characterization: she has been an outspoken heterosexually identified advocate for marriage equality and for admission to the military of LGBTQ+ people. But, some would suggest, the turning of an adjective into a noun (parallels might be "the blacks," or "the disabled") tends to reduce people to a single characteristic.

It is interesting to note that, in twentieth- and twenty-first-century English, there is no single, commonly used noun to identify homosexual men. Since *gay* did have an earlier association with criminalized sexual behaviors (prostitution), some think its association with homosexuality derives from the connection, perceived or real, between female prostitutes and young homosexual men (mollies) both of whom were paid for providing sexual services outside the law. It has also been suggested that *gay* as a term for homosexual men derived from the hobo culture of late nineteenth-century America, in which "gay-cats" were young vagrant men who traveled the country picking up short-term work and often begging for food, shelter, or money, and often attaching themselves to older men "on the bum," as it was colloquially known, and who often either offered sexual services in return for protection or were abused sexually and physically by older men (www.etymonline.com).

Those who oppose the use of the word *gay* as a universal term for all homosexual people argue that it is no less sexist than the universal "he," which, up until the last half century, was considered the appropriate word to use as the singular form for all people. Therefore, many people prefer to use *gay* primarily as a marker of male homosexuality, though there are women who prefer *gay woman* to *lesbian*. When talking about all people who identify as homosexual, the phrase *gay men and lesbians* or *lesbians and gay men* (the question of order will be addressed below) seems preferable for those people who are not comfortable, for whatever reason, with the word *queer*.

## Lesbian: Going Back to Ancient Greece to Coin a Modern Word

The word **lesbian** is clearly at Level Two on Hayakawa's ladder of abstraction — it is always more specific, restricted to women who identify as homosexual or who identify with homosexual women (the term that emerged from what is called second-wave feminism, that of the 1960s into the 1980s, up to the advent of queer theory, perhaps, is often "women-identified women"). Men have no claim on this word, though issues regarding transgender language and experience have called even that restriction into question (as well as what we mean by *men*). Some radical feminists assert that transgender women are actually men, on the basis of both biological and social histories, and they argue against the inclusion of such people in lesbian separatist spaces, such as the Michigan Womyn's Music Festival, and women-only communities.

The word *lesbian* has an ancient history, harkening back to the Greek island of Lesbos, where the first female lyric poet whose work survives, a woman named Sappho, lived and wrote. We have primarily only fragments of Sappho's personal poetry, but scholars have noted in them and in what has been able to be pieced together about Sappho's life that her erotic attractions were directed to both women and men. In modern terms, she might be described as bisexual, but because the word *lesbian* was coined in the late 1800s by English writers to describe erotic and romantic relationships between women, the term is now used principally to provide a category for women whose primary, often exclusive sexual identity is homosexual. Interestingly, ancient Greek had a word, *lesbiazein*, a word used to describe behavior that involved "'sexual initiative and shamelessness' among women" (www.etymonline.com), but it was not used exclusively to denote same-sex relationships.

More recent feminist and lesbian writers have called for a more complex consideration of the term *lesbian*, with interesting and thought-provoking implications, not only for queering language, but for many aspects of the lives of women, homosexual or otherwise. In 1980 the poet and essayist Adrienne Rich wrote an essay she called "Compulsory Heterosexuality and Lesbian Existence," in which she argued for lesbianism as an extension of feminism. Rich, who had been married to a man before coming out and living the rest of her life as a lesbian, suggested that the privileging of heterosexuality as not only the norm but also as a more desirable identity needed to be challenged and that, therefore, it would be politically and personally useful for all women to remove themselves from men and to form some kind of lesbian relationship or have a lesbian experience, even if they identified primarily as heterosexual and even if they returned to a heterosexual coupled arrangement. This was a reaction to what she described as *compulsory heterosexuality*, which she claimed consisted of assumptions and ways of policing thought and behavior that made all people (men and women) value and feel coerced into aspiring to heterosexuality as "better" than other kinds of sexuality.

She suggested that the word *lesbian* as a noun be done away with, arguing that its clinical connotations limited its liberatory value. In its place, she preferred such terms as **lesbian existence** and **lesbian continuum**, the latter of which was meant to map out a space where all women, regardless of their desires or typical sexual practices, might place themselves in women-identified worlds — thus, to hark back to Burke, the words would allow women to choose their worlds. A motto attributed to the lesbian-feminist thinker Ti-Grace Atkinson sums up the thesis nicely: "Feminism is the theory; lesbianism is the practice."

Rich later clarified that she intended her earlier essay not as a broadside arguing either for doing away with heterosexuality or for suggesting that it was in any essential way less valid a sexual identity or experience than lesbian existence; rather, she wished her readers to consider doing what is sometimes called reversing figure and ground. Society, particularly at that time, took heterosexuality so much for granted as the given, and she wanted to encourage her readers to reconsider and imagine a world in which the figure might be viewed in a different, less commanding position. Rich's idea of a lesbian continuum became a very helpful and powerful *heuristic*, a method by which individuals and communities might discover unexpected or unconscious assumptions and possibilities for themselves.

Some feminists of the period described themselves as "political lesbians," typically meaning that though their erotic and romantic attractions were, either exclusively or primarily, for members of the opposite sex, they felt themselves intellectually, politically, and morally in alignment with the goals and practices of lesbian activism. As is true of any complex term, *political lesbian* had and has its detractors, seen by some as co-opting a term of identity by otherwise heterosexual (and, hence, typically more privileged in general) women.

### Bisexual: Both/And — Reinforcing Binaries or Expanding beyond Them?

In the nineteenth century, as the science of biology became more sophisticated, expanded, and standardized, the word **bisexual** entered the lexicon of English usage. Initially, it referred to organisms (typically plants and nonhuman animals) that possessed biological characteristics of male and female members of the species, and such "bisexuality" was a typical occurrence, rather than an anomaly in such species.

It was only in the twentieth century that the word came to have a consistent, commonly accepted meaning in language about human beings and their sexual identities, desires, and behaviors. It was used and continues to be used to categorize humans who describe themselves as having erotic or romantic (or both) attraction to members of their own sex as well as to those they view as belonging to the opposite sex. The very construction of the word has led to confusion, sometimes quite inaccurate assumptions, and often stigmatizing attitudes toward people who either claim the word as their identity or who are described as such by others.

It is *bi-* that may cause some confusion or resistance. In its broadest sense, *bi-* simply means "two." *Bisexual,* then, in the language of sexual identity, has the literal meaning of describing an individual who is attracted to "both" sexes. Myriad questions can arise for people who identify outside bisexual experience, some of which have rightly been viewed as contributing to *biphobism,* a suspicion of, misunderstanding of, or antagonism toward people who identify as bisexual. Is a bisexual person someone who must be *equally* attracted to men and women? Can such people ever have a truly and satisfying monogamous relationship — are they always in a state of desiring experiences with people from multiple sexual categories? Is bisexuality simply a form of deception, whether of the self or the other, perhaps because of stigmas against homosexuality? Can someone who describes their sexual desire as "bi" nonetheless feel more romantic about one gender over the other? Note that the implicit binary of *bi-* is what may cause some people difficulties in understanding and lead them to stigmatizing or to what is often called "bi erasure," either ignoring or questioning the authenticity of the existence and value of people who identify as such.

There is a growing use of *pansexual* by people who wish to identify as not being exclusively attracted to one sex or the other. One advantage to *pansexual* is that it also opens up a space for the inclusion of trans desires — desires either of people who identify as trans and whose attractions may not map as easily on preexisting categories, or of people who are attracted to trans people as a category of possible sexual or romantic partners.

### T: From Transvestite/Transsexual to T+/T*

The prefix *trans-* is from the Latin for "across." It is used in almost every area of life, nature, and technology and does not carry any inherent sexual sense. It is interesting, then, that it has become one of the most hotly debated and highly contested terms in current discourse about sexuality and gender identity. The first use of a word associated with it is **transvestite**, which has typically been defined as a person who dresses in the clothes traditionally associated with the opposite sex. The next word to emerge using *trans-* in a sense associated with sex and sexual identity was **transsexual**: both terms were coined by the German sexologst Magnus Hirschfeld, who worked in the early twentieth century. While individuals who have described the experience of feeling themselves born into a wrongly sexed body have clearly been in the world throughout history, and we have documentation of at least one surgery performed for the purpose of sexual reassignment as early as 1930, the term seems to have come into more common usage in the 1950s. With the development and expansion of sex-reassignment surgeries, the word *transsexualism* came to refer to the psychological state of feeling one has an inappropriate match between body and sexual identity and *transsexual* to individuals who had undergone some form of sex-reassignment surgery (also referred to as gender-affirming surgery today).

As social theorists and social scientists began to draw significant distinctions between the concept of sex as a biological category and gender as a sociocultural one, both of these *trans-* terms began to be subjected to greater scrutiny. Indeed, biologists such as Anne Fausto-Sterling, author of *Myths of Gender*, and psychologists such as Cordelia Fine, author of *Delusions of Gender*, challenge such neat distinctions. The more widely used term today is **transgender**, which attempts to cast a wide net in the way that the words *queer* and, in some cases, *gay* do. It was popularized by the writer and activist Leslie Feinberg to avoid and replace language that came out of a medical and psychopathologizing model of identity and experience. In a sense, *transgender* as a construction aims to underscore the wide variety of individual differences and experiences that may profitably be viewed in a kind of multivoiced dialogue with each other.

Two very recent attempts to link the multiplicity of experiences captured by some of the terms above are **trans\*** and **trans+**. The rhetoric of these terms is one of inclusiveness and diversity. The asterisk (\*) comes from computer/digital culture, in which the \* serves to tell a search engine to look for all occurrences of what has preceded the symbol: thus, "trans\*" symbolically calls on a range of possible positions on a spectrum of sexual diversity for inclusion, respect, and authenticity. The + sign is also used sometimes, and it, too, seems to be mathematical in its symbolic significance, suggesting an ongoing, perhaps infinite set of possibilities.

An important point to keep in mind is that, while to those who live outside the transgender experience, there is sometimes an assumption that all transgender people wish to undergo surgery or surgeries or other forms of medical treatment to align their physical bodies more closely to traditional assumptions about maleness or femaleness (what many people mean when they use *man* or *woman* in anatomical terms), this equation of "trans" with "transsexual" is no longer as dominant as it once was. For some people who identify as transgender, what is at issue is not a desire to change their bodies, either surgically or hormonally, but to be permitted to live openly and with full rights in the gender they claim as their authentic one. So, just as there are many ways to experience oneself as gay, straight, bisexual, and so forth, so there is a wide variety of experiencing the self in personally positive ways as either transgender or cisgender (a term to be defined in the next paragraph). Just as people with disabilities often avoid a discourse of "wrongness" or "defect," but focus on social barriers to personal and collective agency and self-worth, the same can be true for transgender people: it is not the body that is "wrong," but society's views, treatment, and, often, regulation of the body (and the wholeness of the person who inhabits the body).

Another terminological development of comparatively recent coinage is **cisgender** (sometimes abbreviated in common speech as *cis*). It is derived from the Latin root *cis-*, which may be translated as "on this side" or, more helpfully for our purposes, "same as" or "aligned with." The term (or some variation of it, such as *cissexual*) has been in limited use since the late 1990s, but it began to gain more widespread currency during the first decade of the twenty-first century (though it is still less familiar to most people than the term *transgender*). It is used to distinguish between people who identify as transgender and those who experience the gender they were assigned at birth as an accurate and appropriate representation of who they feel themselves to be. It has probably taken longer for the term to be recognized because it names the "unmarked" category: that is, it is fair to say that considerably more people identify as cisgender than as transgender. *Cisgender* still generates some degree of controversy among some people, who oppose it because they see it as a term imposed on them by those outside the group (presumably trans people). Of course, there are many terms that have been developed to label or name people by those outside the group, so this opposition seems more likely to be the product of either transphobia or a perceived loss of linguistic power. And, just as Freud famously said that heterosexuality needed as much explanation as homosexuality, it is useful and important to have a word that specifies the experience of those who identify with the gender assigned at birth as much as it is to have one for those who do not. Otherwise, the unmarked category remains, whether people intend it to or not, the dominant, assumed status of normativity.

## Q: Questioning and/or Queer

LGBT has, for some time, been the alphabetic string most often found in writings about nonnormative sexuality that address relationships between sexual identities beyond a single category. Some add the letter Q to the list. The Q can have two meanings, depending on the intention of the speaker or writer and the implicit or explicit understanding of the audience. When first introduced to the alphabetic string, it was used most often to stand for **questioning**, people who were questioning their sexual identity, particularly their sexual orientation. The term was used and the symbol included in order to provide a space, both conceptually and associationally, for such individuals, perhaps even to provide them with a safeness, to invite them in to explore their status of "not-yet-knowing" without making them feel that they somehow had to choose or declare themselves.

The other and more recent use of *Q* is for *queer*. In some respects, this use may initially seem to be redundant, since *queer* is frequently, perhaps even primarily, used these days to be as broad a term as possible. Nonetheless, those who would include the Q to mean queer offer the reasonable counterargument that *queer* need not necessarily involve same-sex behaviors or orientations, and that it therefore has a place in addition to, rather than as a replacement for, the other letters of identity. Sometimes *Q* is repeated in such an abbreviation, as in *LGBTQQ*. In those cases, it is probably safe to assume that whoever is using the abbreviation wants to include both *questioning* and *queer* as part of the grouping.

## I: Intersex — From Hermaphrodite to DSD

There is a growing inclusion of the letter *I* in the alphabetic string of symbols. It almost universally refers to people who identify as **intersex**, a person who either has genitals associated with both men and women or ambiguous ones (or other related medical conditions that make identification of a single biological sex difficult or arbitrary, or genetic variations from xx-xy binary). In general, people who identify as intersex are conscious of their anomalies (to use the formal medical language) or become aware later in life that they were born with or developed such anomalies. Some of these individuals were (and still are) subjected to surgical interventions, often when still in infancy, to "correct" such anomalies. The term that preceded intersex was **hermaphrodite**, drawn from Greek mythology, after the character Hermaphroditus, the son of the gods Aphrodite and Hermes, who was born a boy but was united with the water nymph (spirit) Salmacis, into a two-sexed being. Because the word *hermaphrodite* has a history of associations with freak shows and monstrosity, the use of word to describe modern-day individuals is much less common than it once was.

It is important to keep in mind that intersex people are as varied and diverse in their physical, psychological, and social experiences as other populations. It is not simply the case that intersex people have all the genitalia of both men and women; some might not present as being that different from people with the "normal" genitalia of one sex or another. We will have more to say about the complexities of intersex people and their lives in chapter 4.

The use of the *I* in the acronym is an interesting one, in that some of the most significant leaders in activism in terms of this identity, such as Cheryl Chase, who founded the Intersex Society of North America (ISNA) in 1993, have moved away from the term *intersex* and have instead suggested the phrase *Differences of Sexual Development* or *Disorders of Sex Developments*, more clinical-sounding terms, abbreviated as *DSD*. There remains considerable controversy over this newer name, as critics suggest that it once again symbolically and, perhaps quite materially, gives power not to the individuals but to parents and especially to medical personnel.

## A: Allies and A-'s

Up until the last few years, if *A* was included, it was understood to stand for allies, those individuals and groups of people who, while not identifying as other than heterosexual themselves, viewed themselves as supporters and advocates, friends and often families of people whose sexuality was labeled as nonheteronormative. The inclusion of the *A* in this sense was to acknowledge and honor the coalitions between queer folk and non-queer folk (or to suggest a kind of "political queerness," analogous to "political lesbianism") and to demonstrate the value of and role of such people in social and political battles. One might conjecture that such inclusion serves a number of possible functions and may derive from some historical events and processes. First, by including this *A*, people working in identity politics and social movements can broaden the potential membership — a far journey from the closeted gatherings that of necessity marked earlier periods in history: this became especially critical in political and care-providing aspects of the AIDS epidemic, when non-queer people stepped up alongside queer people.

In more recent times, the *A* has had an alternative meaning, and it may well be that it is becoming more prominent than the "allies" one. It might be useful to think of an *A* spectrum (not to be confused with a parallel "autism spectrum"): a cluster of ways of participating in and naming an experience of one's sexual or romantic identity: **asexual**, **aromantic**, and **agender**. In the case of these words, the *a-* prefix refers, as it does in other areas, to an absence of the characteristic or experience (or some relative self-reported position on a continuum). Thus, people on this spectrum may identify as having no sexual attraction to any other person of any gender; such individuals *may* report romantic (nonerotic) feelings toward other people, either of their own sex or of another. Aromantic people report never having feelings of romantic love for others; they may report having sexual feelings, and they may describe other kinds of love (such as familial, friendship that qualifies as love, and so forth). Agender people describe themselves as not having a sense of themselves as either male or female (or masculine or feminine); they may be different from people who would describe themselves as **androgynous**, people who report a sense of self as both male and female, or masculine and feminine. (The sets of terms, once kept separate to distinguish between sex and gender, now often are used interchangeably, and not always consistently.) Some of these people prefer the term **nonbinary** (or a variant of it), to describe their sense of gender — that theirs is not an absence of gender, but a sense of gender that does not fit into any either-or description.

## Sequence May Matter

Depending on when material you are reading or viewing was produced, you may find the string *GLBT*, *LGBT*, or some other variation (including omission of one or more letters). Similarly, phrases such as *gay and lesbian* and *lesbian and gay* are often used synonymously to refer to the same populations. Historically, *gay and lesbian* and *GL* were first most widely used, some would argue because of alphabetic order, others because they viewed *gay* as the umbrella term. With the emergence and spread of feminism (especially lesbian feminism), activists and theorists began to question the political and communicative meaning of "ordering" the terms. As an attempt to address historical inequities between men and women, many individuals and groups began to reverse the order, opting for *lesbian and gay* and *LG* (as well as *LGB* and *LGBT* and so forth). By doing so, such groups are making a statement of the importance of always keeping women's issues and experiences and identities present in the cultural and activist work of people affiliated by same-sex desires. A group not choosing to begin with *lesbian* or *L* should not be perceived as diminishing women's lives, however; such a choice is rarely meant to imply a hierarchy of negative valuation.

## QUEER LANGUAGE AND THE SPEAKING OF THE WORLD: SOME PRAGMATIC ISSUES

### "Gayvoice" and "Gaydar": Do They Exist and What Might They Be?

The term **gayvoice** (or *gay voice*) is used to describe certain qualities of speech performed by gay men, often in either a humorous or a scornful way, depending on who is doing the describing and what the context is. Many gay men, in particular, insist that there is a particular way of speaking, unique to gay men, and that the presence of such a voice is "proof positive" that the speaker can be identified as gay. This, in turn, also may lead some people to insist that they possess something they call a **gaydar** — an ability to spot gay persons at first contact: sometimes this gaydar is attributed to voice; other times, it is read nonverbally, through movements, gestures, even clothing. (Recently, scientists at Stanford University claimed they could program a computer to recognize gay male faces, a study that is controversial and critiqued.) Though there has been some research on the voices of lesbians, there are far less data and less agreement on what might constitute a "lesbian voice."

Consider popular culture and media representations of gay men. Think about such situation comedies as *Will and Grace, Modern Family*, and *Looking*. Are some characters depicted as having more gayvoice than others? Is it ever a topic characters discuss — either the gay men or those around them? How do characters talk about the voices of gay men? Is voice sometimes a way a character suspected of being gay is identified? For example, *Will and Grace*, which was first broadcast on NBC from 1998 to 2006 (and which returned to follow its characters in 2017), featured as ongoing characters two gay men, Will Truman and his sidekick, Jack McFarland. Initially, the premise of the series was that Will was the more serious and responsible gay man: a high-achieving lawyer and, probably not coincidentally, a man who could, if and when necessary, pass for straight (heterosexual). Jack, on the other hand, in the tradition of supporting sidekicks, was more cartoonlike, the zany next-door neighbor, somewhat childlike and irresponsible, never seeming to have a way of supporting himself. Watch an episode or two. Do their voices reflect these different social, psychological, and economic positions?

There has been comparatively little empirical scientific study of the phenomenon of gayvoice, and what there is tends to be based on small samples, drawn from limited, often fairly homogeneous subject groups. The design of the studies that have been done (Gaudio; Moonwoman-Baird) dates back to the 1990s. Because language acquisition and development combine biological and sociocultural dimensions, if there were a gayvoice identifiable from the research in the 1990s, we might expect it to have some consistency across time, but also to have the ability, like all features of language, to change over time for communities of speakers.

Earlier linguists of gender wondered if gayvoice (our term, not theirs) might be gendered in the sense of gay men imitating or unconsciously internalizing speech patterns associated with women (McConnell-Ginet). Subsequent research does not seem to bear this out, based on those patterns of intonation, pitch, range, and rate socially associated with female voices. Perhaps it works the other way around: because there has often been an assumption that gay men are like women, their speech patterns and vocalizations have been interpreted as "feminine."

So what are some of the characteristics often associated by nonlinguists with gayvoice? On the basis of the studies done and anecdotal reports by self-identified gay men, they might include some of the following:

1. wider range of intonation than typical in men in general

2. sometimes higher habitual pitch range (*habitual* here refers to the range that feels most comfortable for the speaker)

3. elongation (stretching) of vowels and diphthongs (sometimes to the point of making vowels into two different vowel sounds)

4. hypernasality of vowels (i.e., speaking them through the nose more than is usual for most speakers, particularly male speakers)

5. dentalization (placing the tongue against the teeth to make certain sounds, which are usually made by placing the tongue against the front part of the hard palate or roof of the mouth, often done by what is called "tongue thrusting," pushing the tongue farther forward than most speakers place it — sounds like t and d, sh and zh)

These are perhaps the most audible and recognizable sounds that are often considered part of gayvoice. Of course, even if we were able to generalize, the question might remain: How do gay men "acquire" this way of speaking? Is it innate, or a product of early socialization — exposure to gayvoice, either in everyday life or from the media?

It is difficult to make a good argument for the innateness of gayvoice, without larger databases of voices and without consideration of what gayvoice might sound like in different languages. Similarly, specialists in child acquisition of language do not believe that mere exposure to certain linguistic behaviors necessarily makes a child imitate the behavior. If a male child learns gayvoice through exposure, it is probably not because he is gay and the example has pulled the "true" speech out of him; it seems more likely that he finds the person he is seeing and hearing interesting and that that person provides a positive example of what interests him.

The director David Thorpe has made a documentary film about the very subject, called *Do I Sound Gay?* (2015). Thorpe, building on his own discomfort with "sounding gay," interviewed many gay men about their voices; he talked to speech therapists who indicated that they have clients come to them, wanting help in getting rid of gayvoice, and to cultural commentators such as Dan Savage, who spoke about the politics and social significance of what is at stake in this issue. For gay men and for those who either support or denigrate them, gayvoice may be as serious an issue as a regional dialect in terms of identification with a group or assumptions made about those groups by outsiders.

Throughout a long part of the twentieth century and continuing in some professions and regions today, students interested in entering media broadcasting as a profession were counseled to take courses or lessons in "accent reduction" and to acquire what was called "standard American speech." This is less common today, though strong accents are still "marked" in the media as nonnormative. As there are more and more visible (and audible) queer-identified broadcasters (they may use the terms *gay* and *lesbian*), such as Anderson Cooper, Don Lemon, Rachel Maddow, Philip Rucker, and Robin Roberts, who all identify at some point on the LGBTQ+ spectrum and embody diversity of race, gender, ethnicity, and social class, stereotypes may begin to weaken and elements of gayvoice of any particular media figure may simply not matter as much. There has not been any sustained scholarly or popular discussion about gayvoice in other languages or in the media performances of broadcasters in other languages, though there certainly are some openly queer broadcasters in other cultures and languages.

## Code-Switching and Slang: Speaking with Your "People"

Slang is the language of everyday life. Traditionally, the term has been used to mark linguistic practices that occur outside formal contexts, such as school, the business world, and public places where more standardized language use is either expected or in some cases required. Slang can be a socially and politically controversial topic as well. In particular, people disagree about when and where slang is appropriate, who is entitled to use specific forms of slang associated with or referring to different groups, and what the implications of the use of slang are for social justice and progress — the last might be called the political ethics of slang. Two groups concerned about the use of slang, particularly terms historically used to denigrate minority members or people with less social and political power, are African Americans and women of all races. The use of in-group terms continues to be hotly debated. Like members of these two groups, queer people have both used slang and been the subject of use of slang by others, slang that is specific to the lives, characters, experiences, and valuing or devaluing of queer people.

Are such terms ever acceptable — even when used with intended "affection" by one group member for another? Some gay men find the use of *fag* or *queen* acceptable in a closed-group situation, understanding the term as a kind of insider form of parody or knowledge; other gay men find such terms oppressive and detrimental to the use of language that acknowledges both the historical oppression of gay men and offers more positive possibilities for queer experience. The same is true for lesbians, who may use a term like *dyke* as a way of signaling toughness and strength in the face of oppression, both by heteronormative and patriarchal elements of society; others may find the term offensive. This is also true within groups of transgender people: some may find the use of the word *tranny* (sometimes spelled *trannie*) offensive, both in its casualness and its use of the diminutive; others see it as an insider term, reclaimed as a sign of defiance and strength.

Queer people have also come up with coded phrases and language to communicate with each other that do not, at least on the surface, seem to carry stigma with them. Linguists have a term, **code-switching**, that is used to describe the practice of moving back and forth between the formal, more widely shared language used in settings such as business and school and the language (which may be thought of as a dialect) used at home or with other members of a cultural community, usually one that does not have the same social power as the dominant language. Queer people often engage in code-switching as well, sometimes at the level of word substitutions, but often in terms of other language features. A queer person may use the dominant (sometimes also called *unmarked*) language in an office meeting, and then go back to his office and call another queer person, such as a friend or partner or even another queer coworker, and the prosodic elements (the sense of intonation, pitch, and "melody") of their speech, as well as some of their words and phrases may change dramatically. For many queer people, code-switching not only is a pleasurable language practice on its own terms (private language often has a sense of play and of secret knowledge that is enjoyable for its own sake), but has been and continues to be a form of survival, both in professional worlds, and in everyday lives, where certain terms and interactions can be made safer and more successful by such linguistic strategies.

Queer folk have found ways of integrating normative phrases into "code-switching" contexts for purposes of inclusion and identification. When two queer people are trying to communicate about a third person, who may not be present, one may say, "He (or she) is *family*," a safer way of passing along the message that the third party is queer: this may be the case if the third person is not *out of the closet* (or not universally so, if one ever can claim to be universally "out") or if the situation in which the statement is made is one where it is unclear whether more directly queer identification is safe, either for the third person or for the speakers exchanging the information. In gender-specific contexts, gay men during the 1960s through 1980s sometimes would refer to another gay man as a "friend of Dorothy," a euphemism for saying the man was gay — the origins of this phrase are still discussed, but some argue that *Dorothy* is meant to evoke the 1939 film *The Wizard of Oz*, and Dorothy's friends were the three outcasts who became heroes (the Scarecrow, the Tin Man, and the Cowardly Lion); others associate Dorothy with the actress-singer Judy Garland, who played the role and who was (and remains) for many gay men a cultural icon. "Sings in the choir" is similarly used, more for gay men, but at times for lesbians. This phrase may originate in the stereotype that queer people are "artistic"; it may also have connections with the presence of queer people in church choirs in black churches. Such terms rarely have a single point of origin. How they came to mean what they mean and that they change over time are what is important.

Though discussions of code-switching tend to focus on verbal language, it is important to remember that nonverbal communication accounts for the vast majority of interaction between people and the perceptions they make. This affects all queer people, but especially trans people, and particularly those who describe themselves or are described by others as *non-passing* (not able or not choosing to be perceived in their new or affirmed gender) or those who identify as nonbinary. Such individuals may have to engage in complex physical, kinesthetic, or other performative forms of code-switching in order to gain access to such areas as airport checkpoints or restrooms or other spaces or occasions when there is heightened scrutiny of identity, especially categorical identity such as gender, race, or age.

## SPOTLIGHT ON HISTORY: TALKING POLARI WITH JULIAN "AND MY FRIEND, SANDY"

The phenomenon of **Polari** is a fascinating case study in how communities of queer people developed a variety of language, one that had currency among gay men in Britain during a certain historical period when open discussion of queer lives was not always safe. Paul Baker, its premiere scholar, defines it as "a secret language mainly used by gay men and lesbians, in London and other UK cities with an established gay subculture, in the first 70 or so years of the twentieth century" (1). An interesting term he uses to describe Polari is as an "anti-language" (13), suggesting that one of the functions of it as a speech code was to maintain some degree of secrecy from those outside the subculture of its primary speakers. He traces it back even further to traditions of Cant, "secret code language used by criminals in the sixteenth to eighteenth century" (16).

The word *Polari* is believed to have been derived from the earlier word *Parlyaree*, itself connected to the Italian verb *parlare*, to speak. Baker traces its origins to traveling actors, who often felt the need to speak in codes as a form of self-protection, in some cases because actors and all theater people were viewed in various historical periods as disreputable and not to be trusted. Early on, it drew its lexicon (vocabulary) from various Romance languages (such as Italian, French, and Spanish), as well as from the language of the Romani people (often referred to, disparagingly and inaccurately, as gypsies), from Cockney (the dialect and slang used by people raised in or living in the East End of London, traditionally a low-income area), which often involved rhyming phrases that stood in place for a more obvious or transparent word, and from language used by sailors (perhaps because sailors, like actors, traveled quite a bit, frequented pubs and brothels, and were sometimes viewed as sexually flexible in terms of choice of partners). Baker notes that later in the twentieth century, Polari also introduced words drawn from Jewish cultures, particularly Yiddish, the everyday language of many Jewish people and one that was commonly found in music halls and vaudeville, and in the 1960s from the emerging drug culture. While Baker suggests that, by the time he was doing his primary research in the 1990s, Polari had generally died out as an ongoing language, he notes that in the late 1990s he was aware of a form of speech called Klub Polari, spoken among people who frequented dance clubs, which were heavily populated by queer people. Baker has written that he saw Klub Polari less as a development of the older Polari per se, and more as a kind of rebirth of interest in the traditions and history of Polari.

If you want to hear and see Polari in practice, there are nonetheless still some rich places to experience it. The musician Morrissey, usually identified as queer (he has declared himself as attracted neither to men nor to women, but to humans), recorded an album that he titled *Bona Drag*, which, in Polari, translates as "nice outfit" (*bona* meaning nice or good and *drag*, probably familiar to you as clothing, but often used specifically to refer to a costume or gender-nonconforming outfit); on that album, he performs a song called "Piccadilly Palare" in this language. (It is available on YouTube and other online sources.) The 1998 film *Velvet Goldmine*, set in the glam-rock British club scene of the 1970s, features a scene performed in Polari, and a British novel, *Sucking Sherbet Lemons* by Michael Carson, published in 1988 but set in the 1960s, tells the story of the coming out of a gay, Catholic boy and features Polari.

Polari became popular among people outside queer circles in the 1960s by way of a popular radio show produced and broadcast by the British Broadcasting Company (BBC), *Round the Horne*, a weekly series. It was a comedy-variety show, named after the popular comedian Kenneth Horne. One of the sketches was a visit from a pair of characters named Julian and Sandy. Horne would play "straight man" to Julian and Sandy, who were, in the context of the sketch, inseparable friends, though never described as lovers — in fact, in the last episode of the show, they were revealed to be married to women, a turnabout of expectations calculated to produce a laugh.

Julian would speak first, saying, "I'm Julian and this is my friend Sandy." The sketch, whose setting would vary from week to week, would usually involve Horne walking into some kind of business establishment (a bookstore, a travel agency) run by Julian and Sandy, who would use the occasion to speak to Horne in Polari, and occasionally, in order to make a pun, Horne would use a word from Polari, or a word that would have a different meaning in Polari. Julian and Sandy spoke rapidly, as any native speakers of a language might, but, because they were played by actors, they knew how to use timing, emphasis, and pauses to make the jokes understandable for the presumably non-Polari-fluent listeners.

The code-switching we identified as part of queer speech during this period was evident in virtually all of the Julian and Sandy sketches. To a non-insider listener, Julian and Sandy would seem like two silly, friendly, and harmless men, perhaps "poofs," to use the British slang of the time. Such listeners might enjoy the sketches for their wit and often low humor — the writers and actors were smart enough to realize that the broad audience of the BBC Radio would not want anything that graphically described queer sexual acts (or any overt sexual acts of any kind, given the times), but they found ways to distinguish the proper (though not always too proper) Mr. Horne from the pair.

Baker suggests that, in a twist of irony, it may be that it was the very popularity of the Julian and Sandy broadcasts that began to erode the actual everyday use of Polari by queer folk. Polari functioned for its non-theatrical speakers as a language of shared, often closeted identities. As a broader audience began to understand some of the most frequently used words and conventions of Polari, its usefulness as an underground language began to wane. It showed up at a funeral service for the queer film-maker and activist Derek Jarman, who was one of the leaders in what was called the New Queer Cinema, which pushed boundaries of what and how queer life, bodies, and experiences could be depicted on film; his was one of the most publicly acknowledged, openly identified deaths from AIDS. At the memorial service for Jarman, a radical guerilla (street) theater performance group, which called itself the Sisters of Perpetual Indulgence — they were queer-identified men dressed as nuns, though they often sported facial hair, thus making no effort to disguise their male bodily characteristics or to pass as female — substituted Polari for the traditional Latin sections of the Mass (Jarman was an atheist). This performance was referred to as the Canonization of St. Derek, as it appropriated the rituals and terms of Catholicism for queer purposes. To the people for whom Jarman served as a "holy figure," Polari was a symbol of the underground, transgressive culture to which he belonged (Lucas).

Baker has written a book on Polari, *Polari — The Lost Language of Gay Men*, which you might find interesting to read if you are intrigued by the more elaborate vocabulary and linguistic conventions of Polari. Ian Lucas, who wrote an insightful analysis of the Jarman Mass for an anthology of scholarly writings in queer linguistics, includes what he calls "A Simple Polari Glossary" (92 – 93). Here are a few selections from that glossary.

| | |
|---|---|
| *beancove* | young queen |
| *bingey* | penis |
| *bona* | good |

| | |
|---|---|
| *bona nochey* | good night |
| *cackle* | gossip |
| *cant* | talk |
| *charver* | to have sex |
| *cottage* | public toilet |
| *cove* | friend, "mate" |
| *dolly* | dear |
| *eek* | face |
| *lally* | leg |
| *mince* | walk effeminately |
| *moey* | money |
| *multi* | many |
| *mungaree* | food |
| *naff* | uninteresting (also, "straight") |
| *nanty* | not, none, negative |
| *omie* | man |
| *omiepalone* | homosexual |
| *palone* | woman |
| *parlary* | to talk in Polari |
| *peroney* | for each one |
| *riah* | hair |
| *stampers* | shoes |
| *thews* | arms |
| *trade* | sexual partner |
| *troll* | to walk, look for trade |
| *varda* | to look |
| *yews* | eyes |

Some are exaggerations drawn from physical acts (cackle for gossip); some are built through a process called *backslanging*, in which a new word is made by a reversal of the traditional spelling or pronunciation of a word (*riah* for "hair"); some are derived from other languages (*bona nochey* for "good night," derived from Spanish's *buenas noches*), some share an initial letter (*lallies* for "legs"), and so forth. And a few remain current in queer language today: *trade* still means a sexual partner, though, for most people who use the word, it refers to a non-gay-identified man who is willing (often for money) to engage in sexual acts with another man. *Troll* as a verb can still serve as the equivalent of "cruising," or looking for sex (once upon a time, *trolling* was often associated with strolling or driving through public places, trying to spot possible sexual partners; today, it may be the case that more trolling is done online). *Troll* has become a noun, which, in queer language, usually refers to an older man, often trying to find a younger man for sexual acts; it has expanded in digital culture to refer to people who post on various blogs or other chat sites with the intent to cause trouble or fool people.

## CONCLUSION

Needless to say, we have only scratched the surface of the possibilities of queering language. Language is one of the defining characteristics of what it means to be human and is constantly evolving, as speakers change and needs and contexts for communication alter and develop over time and space. It is, in the terms of philosopher Paul Grice, based on an implicit "cooperative principle," by which speakers learn what information to include, how much to include, when to stop speaking, and so forth. As Mary Bucholtz and Kira Hall suggest, the performative nature of language means that words and larger speech acts "do not merely describe the world, but change it" (491). Language is not only how we know or describe ourselves, others, and the worlds around them, but it is how we *make* ourselves, each other, and our worlds. How we make ourselves — or are made into ourselves by those people and forces that surround us — is the subject of Part II of this book: those sets of ideas, theories, concepts, and acts that we place under the larger area of *identity*.

## ISSUES FOR INVESTIGATION

### 1. Hierarchies of Terms

Make a list of as many different terms you can think of that are used to label people as queer (or LGBTQ+, if those divisions are more manageable for you at this point). Once you have this basic list, divide it into different categories of people — perhaps on the basis of gender (are there some words that are specific to gay men, some to gay women, some to transgender women, some to transgender men?), assumed sexual practices (oral, anal, other), gender expression (not simply whether your assumption about a person is that they are male or female, but *how* they present themselves in gendered ways to the world), tastes, hobbies, professions, activities (such as "opera queen" for a gay man who loves opera, "diesel dyke," sometimes associated with women who work in traditionally male jobs, though now expanded to a more general category of gender expression). Share these lists with your fellow students. Discuss when and where people in your group have heard these words used (or used them themselves). Who has used them and for what reason? What was the effect of the communication act — was the use commented on or challenged? Was it an insider or outsider use of slang?

Then try your hand at ranking the slang terms and phrases. Though this is highly subjective and often quite context-specific, it may be useful to try to order the terms on a continuum from *totally acceptable* to *totally unacceptable*, realizing that context may play a role in where on such a continuum you might place a term. Or you might use the categories from *extremely offensive* to *not offensive at all* as your continuum. Discuss where you place each word or phrase and why. Do not be surprised if there is considerable disagreement among group members — there is no single right or wrong answer to these questions. The point is to try to excavate what is underneath these uses of slang.

Below are some common (and not-so-common) terms and phrases associated with queer people, either emerging from the way queer people talk about and among themselves or emerging from language used by non-queer people about queer people. We have divided them into a number of categories. Compare them to your own:

## General (men, women, and trans people)

| queer | homo | gay | perv |
|-------|------|-----|------|

## Men only

| faggot (also fag) | fairy fruit | cocksucker | |
|-------------------|-------------|------------|---|
| bugger | queen | pansy | poof |
| nance | butt boy | bear | twink |
| mary | swish | chicken | otter |
| chickenhawk | shirt lifter | fudge packer | girl (sometimes "gurl") |
| sister (sissy) | sod (from sodomy) | molly | nance (Nancy) |

## Women only

| | | | |
|---|---|---|---|
| dyke (bulldyke) | bulldagger | lesbo (lezbo/lezzie) | butch |
| muff diver | rug muncher (carpet muncher) | tom | |

LUG
(lesbian until graduation — women only)

## Bisexual men and women

| | | |
|---|---|---|
| switch hitter | AC/DC | heteroflexible (usually for men) |

## Trans

| | | | |
|---|---|---|---|
| tranny | trans man | trans woman | genderqueer |
| nonbinary | boi | Two-Spirit | FTM |
| M2F | MTF | F2M | MTN |
| MTX | FTN | FTX | |

We have intentionally included some that are no longer in current use and some that are more specific to particular English-speaking countries or regions. Are there any that are new to you? (You can find their meaning and history on the Internet and in other resources.) Do you have any to add to the list?

## 2. Speaking and Learning Polari

Working from the selected glossary provided above, see if you can come up with a sentence (or, if you are brave, a conversation) using Polari. While the list provided means your performance would of necessity be a mix of Polari and standard English, see what levels of connotation and nuance the introduction of such coded language achieves. Search the Internet for examples of spoken Polari — there is a short film available that shows two (presumably) gay men in a public park using Polari to communicate; it is called *Putting on the Dish* and can be found on a number of sites. There is a widely available clip that shows queer men in the club scene in the film *Velvet Goldmine*. YouTube and other sites have selections from the recordings made of the "Julian and Sandy" routines, and an anthology of them is available on CD. If you are especially ambitious, you may wish to read Baker's book to attain higher proficiency in Polari.

## SUGGESTIONS FOR FURTHER READING AND VIEWING

*Do I Sound Gay?* Directed by David Thorpe. Sundance, 2015.

Leap, William L. *Beyond the Lavender Lexicon.* Newark, NJ: Gordon & Breach, 1995.

———. *Word's Out: Gay Men's English.* Minneapolis: University of Minnesota Press, 1996.

Livia, Anna, 'd Kira Hall. *Queerly Phrased: Language, Gender, and Sexuality.* New York: Oxford University Press, 1997.

Zimman, Lal, Jenny Davis, and Joshua Raclaw, eds. *Queer Excursions: Retheorizing Binaries in Language, Gender, and Sexuality.* New York: Oxford University Press, 2014.

**PART II**

# QUEERING IDENTITY

# CHAPTER 2

# QUEERING DESIRE
## Knowing "Feeling"

**Desire** is one of the most difficult concepts to define, certainly to the satisfaction of those who would use the word, and often seems to defy the powers of language to produce meaning. We often use it as synonym for other
words — *love, attraction, longing, wanting* — and certainly each of these
words helps us get closer to an understanding of what individuals may
mean by the word, though no single one of them stands satisfactorily in the
place of *desire*. Complicating the problem are the ways in which various of
the human sciences and arts go about defining, describing, and, in some
cases, measuring *desire*, and, indeed, there are those who might scoff at the
idea of being able to quantify desire itself. Similarly, another difficulty is
that the word is more often than not tied to a particular domain of experience: we might ask, is "sexual desire" the same as "desire for peace," or
"desire for chocolate"? Obviously, in each case in the previous sentence, the
object of desire is different (sex, peace, chocolate), but is the nature of what
it means to desire them the same or different? Nonetheless, since much of
what moves people to identify as queer (or to be identified as such by others, including non-queers) originates in desire, it is necessary to explore it,
even if it feels always slightly out of reach — as, indeed, such psychoanalytic theorists as Sigmund Freud, Jacques Lacan, and others suggest is the
nature of desire: that which, if satisfied, no longer exists as desire.

## DESIRE: "THE SPIRIT'S WINGS" OR "THAT FIERY SADNESS"?

The first phrase used to describe desire in the heading above comes from
the German Romantic poet and dramatist Johann Wolfgang von Goethe,
who described desire as that which lifts the spirit (or soul) up and enables
it to take flight and to transcend the everyday things that would interfere
with achievement and happiness. The modern poet, composer, and musical
performer Patti Smith coined the phrase "that fiery sadness" as a metaphor

Henderson, Bruce, *Queer Studies: Beyond Binaries*
dx.doi.org/10.17312/harringtonparkpress/2019.09.qsbb.002
© 2019 by Harrington Park Press

for desire, placing the two primary words "fiery" and "sadness" in close proximity to each other, suggesting a simultaneity of an emotion ("sadness") and an intensity ("fiery"). There are scholars and thinkers who would argue that the identities we claim or that are imposed on us may lead us to engage in certain acts or behaviors: these might be called social or political theories of desire, in that they assume that institutions and ideologies external to us play key roles in creating desire within us. The Marxist philosopher Louis Althusser used the term **interpellation** to describe this process, suggesting that social institutions and structures "hail" us as certain kinds of people, telling us how to be "citizens" in ways considered proper in any given place and time in history. This view of the self as constructed by external forces is often called *materialism,* and it sees any kind of desire as "non-natural" (not "unnatural"), that is, not having any basis in an unmediated experiencing of the world. Thus, for someone who follows this line of reasoning, even sexual desire is a product of a hegemonic (or dominant), power-wielding set of beliefs and practices, and that is as true for heterosexual desire as for any other form.

Before we move to the specifics of sexual desire and what the lesbian psychologist Lisa Diamond calls "romantic attraction," it will be useful to frame the discussion within what might be called an "ethics of desire." This may at first seem a curious phrase, as it raises the question: Isn't desire (distinct from sexual conduct) a neutral term, perhaps even more so if people generally seem to agree that it is something that originates in some way or process outside the conscious choice of individuals? In general, it seems that most people would agree that desire itself may not violate moral principles — it is in the acting on desires that questions of good and bad, right and wrong, which are central to ethics, come into play.

Plato viewed desire as having problematic ethical components built into it. In one of his dialogues, the *Phaedrus,* he has his spokesman, Socrates, on a walk with a handsome younger man named Phaedrus, whom Socrates, it is implied, wishes to seduce, talk about the ethics of sexual pleasure, arguing, initially, in his characteristically ironic, figure-ground-shaking way, that it is actually *more* ethical (i.e., good in a moral sense) for a young man like Phaedrus to bestow his sexual favors on someone who does *not* love him, certainly a reversal of what we might have expected him to say.

In his second major speech of the dialogue, Socrates uses what has come to be called the figure of the noble rider and the two horses to explain how desire, which has the potential to be a form of madness and spiritual degradation, can indeed be integrated into a love of true Beauty (which is a manifestation of what Plato viewed as immortal, ideal forms, not ever fully accessible to human beings, but only to divinities). Socrates builds his argument along these lines: the human being is always the charioteer, trying to keep the two horses, which represent different impulses, one might even say desires, in harmony — the desire for the good (which is associated with the holy, the spiritual, the intellectual) and the desire for the bad or base (which is simple sexual or carnal pleasure, without respect for the welfare of the beloved or, for that matter, of the self). But what Socrates, like many, recognizes, is that even within the realm of desire as an abstract concept, there is space for the good and the bad — and part of our task as citizens and as ethically aspirational, if human, creatures, is to keep the horses working together. He is not arguing against desire per se, but for the control (both of self and of the horses) of what could be mutually divisive attractions.

It is often said that we live in a world today dominated by immediate or instant gratification, that, to use Plato's terms, it is easier for the darker, ignoble horse to win the battle, simply because there are so many ways for that to happen: think of one-click shopping, social media dating sites, and so forth. In whatever sphere of desire (sexual, shopping, food, others), is there still pleasure to be had by having to earn or wait for the fulfillment of desire?

## (HOMO)SEXUAL DESIRE: A SPECIFIC CATEGORY OR A QUEER VARIATION ON DESIRE IN GENERAL?

Sigmund Freud, the first great modern theorist of sexuality and the father of psychoanalytic theory, did not in any a priori way regard homosexuality (which he called *inversion*, though not in a way to stigmatize it, simply as a way of dividing it from normative sexual orientation or development) as more problematic than heterosexuality and famously said that the latter required as much explanation as homosexuality; indeed, he believed all humans are born bisexual (a theory to which we will return): "Thus from the point of view of psychoanalysis, the exclusive sexual interest felt by men for women is also a problem that needs elucidation and is not a self-evident fact based upon an attraction that is ultimately of a chemical nature" (Freud 1905, 11–12). Freud was not, however, the first to consider the origins of different categories of erotic desire.

In his dialogue *The Symposium*, Plato imagines a drinking party attended, as would have been the custom, entirely by men, highly regarded Athenian citizens, some of whom are coupled with each other as lovers, all of whom would have been participants in the Athenian conventions of adult man – youth sex or love. Each attendee is challenged to present a speech in praise of love. Our old friend Socrates is there and, as is usual in Plato's dialogues, gets to give the final, summative speech, arguing for love of wisdom as the highest form of love. But what many readers consider the most memorable of the speeches, and the one most germane to our concerns, is given by a fictional version of the great Greek comic playwright Aristophanes, about midway through the dialogue. Though he warns his listeners that his speech may not only be funny, but even absurd, it is also one of the great stories of what might drive desire and love; the excerpted speech is reprinted in the Appendix.

Aristophanes (as a spokesperson for Plato) uses images and metaphors of bodies in motion to capture the experience of desire. The picture of the "original" humans as multiple beings, melded together and then cruelly (and strategically) riven in order to protect the gods from the power of their love, may very well capture some of the emotional and sensual power of desire for another person. It is also fascinating to note that Aristophanes associates each kind of human with a domain of or object in the greater cosmos: male with the sun, women with the earth, and "man-woman" with the moon. Thus, in this story, humans began as beings who could move throughout the universe, spinning above the ground as well as on it.

From a queer standpoint, the tale is also a reminder of the possibility of variations of sexual desire and romantic love that are inclusive and not hierarchical — that is, all three of these versions of "human" have their own integrity and dignity. There is room, in Aristophanes' speech, for a genuine equality of gay male, lesbian, and heterosexual desire and experience, and for the longing to find the lost "other half" to be given equal dignity and pathos in each case. An interesting side note on the man-woman: while translations vary, the man-woman, before being divided by Zeus, is an image of the hermaphrodite, or, in an idealized way, a being we might today call intersex.

Aristophanes' speech has remained so potent and memorable that it became the inspiration and basis for a very contemporary piece of music in what has become one of the most popular theater pieces (which has also been filmed): John Cameron Mitchell and Stephen Trask's *Hedwig and the Angry Inch*, a musical play in the form of a concert given by Hedwig, a transgender/transsexual person (born Hansel in Germany), whose surgery was unsuccessful — hence, the "angry inch" of the title. One of the songs performed by Hedwig is "The Origin of Love." Its music and lyrics, written by Trask, are based on Aristophanes' speech. The film is available on DVD, and the song "The Origin of Love," as filmed for the movie, is available on a number of sites on the Internet. It is worth watching, not only on its own terms, but also as a modern attempt to comment on and reimagine the original telling of the story in Plato's dialogue. The film, quite apart from its reference to Plato, is a valuable text on desire — sexual, romantic, and other-wise — and on how different kinds of minds and bodies negotiate this experience, always difficult to pin down, that we call sexual desire.

# A FEW THEORIES OF QUEER DESIRE

While the subject of desire, whether in general or in specific reference to queerness (or same-sex erotic emotion specifically), is a huge one, spanning multiple disciplines from philosophy to psychology to politics, it is worth surveying some basic approaches to the topic.

## Psychological and Psychoanalytic Theories

Perhaps the single most influential theory of queer sexual desire (or inversion, as he called it, intending the word descriptively rather than judgmentally) is the childhood sexual development pathway conceptualized by Sigmund Freud. Much of what can be found in parenting and self-help books of the mid- to late twentieth century (and even today) is popularized versions of some of Freud's central theories. Many of Freud's theories have not withstood experimental testing, but they nonetheless remain present in social and cultural consciousness and influence parenting and education in significant ways.

Some of the most important aspects of desire in Freudian theory include the stages of sexual development from infancy to late adolescence and adulthood (oral, anal, latency, phallic, genital) and the three components of the personality (**id, ego**, and **superego**). In addition, Freud's greatest single contribution may have been his conceptualization of the unconscious, that area of mind that presents itself only during our dreams, but which drives much of our waking life. Freud saw human beings as driven by two seemingly conflicting impulses, which he called, using the Greek terms, **eros** (love, desire, sex) and **thanatos** (death, cessation, stillness).

The most central of Freud's theories for queer desire is that of the **Oedipal complex**, which Freud argued occupied the male child on his way to sexual maturity; like most of his contemporaries, Freud focused centrally on male experience as the dominant and "general" one, though he did make some remarks on female sexuality as well, as he did in the case study of Anna, a "hysteric," to use the gendered term of the day. Some of his followers, such as his daughter Anna Freud, Melanie Klein, and Jacques Lacan, have devoted more attention to the specifics of women's experiences, using ideas drawn from Freud.

The Oedipal complex takes its name from the ancient Greek myth and the tragic drama by Sophocles about Oedipus, king of Thebes. In this myth, a prophecy has declared that the child of King Laius and his queen, Jocasta, will slay the king and marry his mother in an incestuous relationship that will curse the city. To try to circumvent the prophecy (never a fruitful move in the culture of the ancient Greeks), Laius gives Oedipus to a servant and commands the babe be left outside to perish or to be eaten by wild animals.

A kindly shepherd finds the child, and Oedipus is raised in the city of Corinth by the king and queen, who have no knowledge of his origins. The exposure he experienced as a child has left Oedipus with a swollen, damaged foot, from which the name Oedipus is derived. Learning of the prophecy, Oedipus flees Corinth, and, on the road to Thebes, he comes upon Laius. In a dispute over who shall pass first on the road, Oedipus kills Laius. He also answers the famous riddle of the Sphinx and arrives in triumph in Thebes, where he marries the recently widowed Queen Jocasta. (He still has no knowledge of his origins and, hence, is ignorant of the taboo he is breaking.)

The city falls into a state of what the Greeks called *pollution* (plague), and Oedipus declares that the person responsible for the pollution must be found out and punished. A blind soothsayer, Tiresias, who has lived as both a man and a woman as a result of a wager between Zeus and Hera, in another legend well known to the Greeks, reveals that Oedipus is himself the source of this pollution, both for having killed his father and for having shared his marriage bed (i.e., having had sexual relations, which led to the birth of a number of children) with his mother. Jocasta hangs herself, and Oedipus blinds himself and goes into exile with his daughters, Ismene and Antigone (the latter being the focus of another great tragedy by Sophocles).

From this legend, which is found in various forms in a number of other world cultures and is explained, anthropologically, as a cautionary tale against incest, consistently forbidden in most cultures, Freud derived a model of how little boys grow from infancy to adulthood as sexually desiring beings. He began by positing that all children (of both sexes, for he wrote and thought in a primarily dimorphic context of sexuality) are born "polymorphously perverse." While most of us are now accustomed to viewing *perverse* as having highly negative connotations, Freud did not intend it that way. By this term he simply meant that all children are born without a singularly directed category of the object of sexual desire (whether based on gender or some other criteria, such as what he called paraphilia — which could be anything from hair color to particular sexual practices). Children, as born, he argued, are open and available to sexual pleasure and gratification by engaging with people of either sex (since sex was understood as binary in his era). Indeed, he argued that, in infancy and early childhood, almost any part of a child's body was available for erotic stimulation; the child is simply a pleasuring, desiring creature at this stage.

Then society takes over. All children who are raised in two-parent heteronormative families are in the presence of a father and a mother, the sources of masculinity and femininity in Freud's theory. Because children, by a natural process, are more immediately bonded with their mothers (through pregnancy, delivery, and breastfeeding), young boys remain emotionally connected more to their mothers than to their fathers. During early childhood — Freud identified the period as lasting from ages three to six) — boys wish (unconsciously) for their father's death, or his symbolic death through absence, which, in the middle-class family on which Freud based his theory, was accomplished through the workplace. To achieve what Freud saw as mature, adult male heterosexuality, the boy shifts his allegiance by identifying with his father's masculinity and separating himself from the world of his mother. In this sense, each boy must become and then surmount the story of Oedipus. It is also during this period, which Freud called the phallic stage, that the boy develops a fear of castration (perhaps in part by viewing the female body) and the girl develops identification with her mother by recognizing their shared body parts (and, in some cases, developing what Freud called penis envy).

Freud did not argue for a genetic or purely medical view of homosexuality, but he looked to environment to explain why some boys (and, by extension, girls) become fixed in homosexual or bisexual desire. Actually, he looked to the environment in which the child was raised; but it is also true that he made no argument in favor of attempting to change or manipulate the environment of the child in an attempt to "undo" the homosexual pathway of such children. Given the young age at which Freud pinpointed the Oedipal complex, the ability of parents to note what was happening in Oedipal terms would be almost impossible to determine. While Freud acknowledged that homosexual desire was, in adults, a minority phenomenon, he was, for his time, surprisingly nonjudgmental about it (given the prohibitions against it legally and socially in many cultures). Indeed, in a famous, often-quoted letter of 1935, Freud wrote to a mother of a young man who was exhibiting homosexual tendencies.

Dear Mrs [crossed out],

I gather from your letter that your son is a homosexual. I am most impressed by the fact that you do not mention this term yourself in your information about him. May I question you why you avoid it? Homosexuality is assuredly no advantage but it is nothing to be ashamed of, no vice, no degradation; it cannot be classified as an illness; we consider it to be a variation of the sexual function produced by a certain arrest of sexual development. Many highly respectable individuals of ancient and modern times have been homosexuals, several of the greatest men among them. (Plato, Michelangelo, Leonardo da Vinci, etc). It is a great injustice to persecute homosexuality as a crime — and a cruelty too. If you do not believe me, read the books of Havelock Ellis.

By asking me if I can help, you mean, I suppose, if I can abolish homosexuality and make normal heterosexuality take its place. The answer is, in a general way we cannot promise to achieve it. In a certain number of cases we succeed in developing the blighted germs of heterosexual tendencies, which are present in every homosexual, in the majority of cases it is no more possible. It is a question of the quality and the age of the individual. The result of treatment cannot be predicted.

What analysis can do for your son runs on a different line. If he is unhappy, neurotic, torn by conflicts, inhibited in his social life, analysis may bring him harmony, peace of mind, full efficiency, whether he remains a homosexual or gets changed. If you make up your mind he should have analysis with me — I don't expect you will — he has to come over to Vienna. I have no intention of leaving here. However, don't neglect to give me your answer.

Sincerely yours with kind wishes,
Freud

Freud's theory of the Oedipal complex as key to the development of sexual desire has had and continues to have significant resonance, culturally if not necessarily scientifically. In the most negative sense, we can see its influence on so-called reparative therapists, who assert that homosexuality is a kind of wound or illness and can be "cured" through various methods, including talk therapy and cognitive-behavioral therapy. Many states (at least fourteen and the District of Columbia, as of this writing) have placed a legal ban on such therapies for minors, though some still permit it for adults if they choose to undergo this form of treatment. This is not to say, however, that Freud's work and his general view of sexual development have been of no use to psychologists and other scholars who view queer desire (and the lives that queer people choose to live) as positive, useful, and healthy. The social and personality psychologist Daryl J. Bem, for example, offered a theory of sexual orientation that he called **exotic becomes erotic**. Bem, who first put this theory forward in the mid-1990s, was writing at least in part in response to the burgeoning interest at the time in genetic and biological explanations for homosexuality. But what Bem, who identifies as a gay man and who lived in a heterosexual marriage for almost fifty years and fathered two children, did pinpoint was genetic predisposition to certain aspects of personality types: that is, the fact that one enjoys certain kinds of and levels of activities is a heritable trait.

This isn't as simple as saying that there is a gene for liking sports and another for liking board games or dolls, but there are genetic markers for enjoying what are often called rough-and-tumble activities and quieter activities. Bem took this genetic evidence and looked at it in social contexts — we live in a society in which rough-and-tumble play is typically associated more with males, and quiet play more with females. If a boy prefers quieter play (dolls, reading, and so forth), he may feel himself different from the majority of other little boys; the same is true for girls, though, in our time and society, girls have often been given more leeway to engage in "boyish" play: perhaps there is some Freudian element, at a kind of social unconscious level, of approval of the masculine over the feminine for all. Bem suggested that the child who views himself or herself as different from others of his or her gender cohort will tend to "exoticize" his or her own gender. He then looked at studies of nonhuman animals, as well as certain human groups (such as kibbutzim, children raised together, though not biologically related, on kibbutzes in Israel), and some large longitudinal (multiyear) data sets of gay people's reportage of attitudes and memories, and found consistently that there was an "eroticizing" of that which is viewed as exotic. Thus, he combined some elements of the traditional Freudian narrative with observations drawn from biology and socialization to explain the varieties of sexual desire and orientation. His theory generated considerable discussion, both for and against.

## Sociopolitical Theories: Freud Meets Marx

We might turn, as we did with Freud, to social and historical conditions. **Capitalism** emerged as a sustained way of life when industrialization became a reality in western Europe and North America in the nineteenth century (thus inspiring Karl Marx to write his critique of it, *Das Kapital*). What is there in queer desire that might be advantageous to capitalism? Some might argue that queer desire, in strictest biological terms, is nonreproductive. The particular kind of sexual desire that has historically been associated with queer people has not been in service of creating new human lives. Hence, if capitalism requires an ongoing supply of new customers to survive, queer desire may work against it. At the same time, an argument can be made that queer desire — and the lives that are built on it — since it has not been centered on the needs of the nuclear family, may provide a set of consumers for various forms of capital and production because of an excess of what is at times called disposable income (money not spent on the staples of housing, feeding, clothing, and educating offspring). Of course, it is necessary to add immediately that the outcomes of queer desire no longer are as clearly nonreproductive and non-family-centered as they have been in the past. But, from a procapitalist perspective, queer desire may in fact lead to greater participation in the capitalist process.

Beyond the economically driven ideology of capitalism, we might also consider how queer desire fits into democratic ideals. Certainly, it is fair to say that democratic ideals focus simultaneously on the rights of the individual and the participation of citizens in the governing and welfare of the country. In historical periods that have placed a great emphasis on the nuclear or even the extended family as microcosms of the democratic ideal, queer desire would seem to work antithetically: again, there has often been an unspoken assumption that queer desire is self-contained and self-directed because it is nonreproductive and therefore has no stake in participatory citizenship. As more and more queer people become visible and are viewed as fully engaged citizens, the specific differences of their sexual desires may move into the background. Thus, queer desire becomes simply another way of being democratic (or American or Canadian or . . . fill in another democratic adjective), which queer theorists label *homonormative*, a concept to which we will return in chapter 11. Ideologies, while in some ways abstractions, are as time- and place-specific in their contextual understanding as anything else.

Historically, certain leftist regimes have viewed queer desire as bourgeois, coming out of a kind of decadent, noncommunitarian impulse in those who engage in the behaviors associated with it. If the goal of a leftist political movement is to create a society of equals, some have suggested that those people focused on queer desire and its satisfaction may be less likely to work for the common good; of course, this could also be because queer folk have often been pushed to the margins of any group and might indeed be suspicious of calls for them to sacrifice their desires and pleasures for the "greater good," when their "greater good" is considered insignificant. And it is also the case that, for some people whose political ideologies are radically leftist, any "private" relationship (which may be the outcome of queer desire) has the potential to threaten the goal of an egalitarian society in which property (which desire and relationality may be seen as forms of) belongs to all and to no one. Current leftist ideologies tend to be less anti-queer or homophobic in their attitudes than ones that emerged in the twentieth century.

## SPOTLIGHT ON HISTORY: 1968 AND BEYOND

In 1968 there was considerable unrest in various countries (including the famous protests at the Democratic Convention in Chicago in the United States). One set of riots that had particularly important intellectual outcomes for those who wished to theorize about the nature and importance of queer desire was the student protests in France (in Paris in particular). University students, faculty, and staff, particularly at Paris's (and France's) intellectual ground zero, the Sorbonne campus of l'Université de Paris, staged protests about the organization of the university and working conditions. (There were broader wildcat strikes by workers in France, as well).

Two writers and activists whose work on queer desire may be seen as emerging from the socialist ideologies underpinning the protests of May 1968 are the French philosopher Guy Hocquenghem, whose *Homosexual Desire* is a slim but dense critique of both Freudian psychoanalysis and capitalist ideologies of production and property, and Mario Mieli, an Italian activist and theorist whose *Homosexuality & Liberation* made important claims for what he called homosexual desire as critical to revolutionary goals and aims. Hocquenghem questioned Freudian and bourgeois concepts of desire itself, seeing in both a kind of privileging of individual property and the capitalist promotion of heterosexual normativity. Where Hocquenghem *does* find value in Freud's theories and thought is in Freud's characterization of "polymorphous perversity" as the normal state of sexual desire in human beings until socioeconomic constraints take over and force all but the most resistant into heterosexuality. Hocquenghem focused positive attention on Freud's concept of the anal stage, as opposed to the phallic, the latter of which he saw as reinforcing the imbalance of power relations in a society driven by capitalism. In Freud's theory, the anal stage, which comes at about age eighteen months and lasts until the onset of the phallic stage (about three years), the primary challenges the child faces and the skills acquired involve knowing and controlling the body as an individual. Until that point, the child has not had a stable sense of self as separate from the mother. Freud and Hocquenghem argue that if children successfully pass through the anal stage, they come out of it with a more secure sense of boundaries, of the care of the body itself, of what they can do with the body — and when and where.

Hocquenghem called for a celebration and greater understanding of the anus as a cite of pleasure, knowledge, and activity. While sex in or at least around the anus has been recorded since the time of the Greeks, as our brief excursion into history reminds us, it is also true that in the twentieth century children (and the adults they grew into) were often made to feel disgusted about their anuses, ashamed about what came out of them, and forbidden to allow anything to go into them. Part of the liberatory psychosociopolitical message Hocquenghem intended was to make conscious and public the ways in which homosexual desire was frequently associated with anal sex. Whether all or even most gay men engage in anal sex or whether few heterosexual couples do is less the point than the role of anal sex as a public symbol of transgression and, once again, of nonreproductive sexual desire. In addition, Hocquenghem argued for a kind of "polymorphous promiscuity," calling for society to acknowledge the non-proprietary natural state of sexual desire, suggesting that (at least the perception of) the nonmonogamous yearnings (and practices) involving sexual desire and its fulfillment were themselves part of a disavowal of capitalist ideologies and practices.

Mario Mieli was also deeply influenced by the actions and thinking that emerged from the May 1968 student riots, and his one major book, *Homosexuality & Liberation*, was, like Hocquenghem's *Homosexual Desire*, a call to move beyond the constraints of normatively directed sexual desire as a way to engage in revolutionary, radical practices. Like Hocquenghem's, his work is a response in part to Freud's Oedipal narrative of normative sexual development; he, too, calls for a return to the almost utopian "polymorphous perversity" Freud saw as the child's state of natural being. And like Hocquenghem, Mieli viewed homosexual desire and actions as providing a road map for genuine social and political revolution, going so far as to title the first section of his book "Homosexual Desire Is Universal," a strong statement meant to jolt readers out of the complacency of their embedded assumptions.

Mieli bravely stands by this statement, and it is obvious that he does so *because* its rhetorical force draws such attention to itself. Now, try to think about the ways in which such a statement could be true. Like Hocquenghem, he uses Freud and the spirit of leftist, liberatory political philosophy to suggest that, if we could somehow remake society so that it rejects Freud's seemingly necessary Oedipal narrative, we could have a world in which sexual desire, including homosexual desire, was available to all, and that would be the most revolutionary world of all. He goes even further than Hocquenghem in some respects, as he imagines a world in which queer people (he focuses on men in his book) would also not restrict their desire or their ability to be desired to their own gender. In a sense, he is calling for homosexual desire to be the first step in a broader move in the politics of desire: in the world he imagines, terms like *homosexual*, *bisexual*, and *heterosexual* would no longer be necessary. Indeed, he suggests that the whole deconstruction of gender will be effected by the call to homosexual desire. He describes himself with pride (and some self-directed but nondisparaging humor) as a "queen" and glories in his femininity, seeing it as a way to connect with women and, indeed, as an opening for being someone who can desire women and be desired by women.

## SEXUAL FLUIDITY: DESIRE AND ROMANCE

Both Hocquenghem and Mieli were writing during the late twentieth century, in a period when both Freud and Marx still had considerable force as representatives of almost scriptural "truths" of psychology and political theory (though both were beginning to be questioned and critiqued), and in the wake of such social revolutionary moments as the May 1968 riots, as well as feminism, civil rights activism, and Stonewall and the birth of gay liberation as major social movements. They were questioning "received" concepts of Freud and Marx (and other thinkers), while also trying to find ways to use them to explain their own experiences and their observations about the societies in which they lived, as well as the new societies they hoped to participate in creating. One of the problems that even such visionary thinkers as Hocquenghem and Mieli had was working within what were then accepted binaries of homosexuality-heterosexuality, and we have noted that their use of the term *bisexuality* was an attempt to broaden the scope of sexual desire.

The lesbian psychologist Lisa Diamond, at the University of Utah, did an ongoing longitudinal study of women and their sexuality, following approximately one hundred women over about a decade, including qualitative data (gleaned from interviews, lengthy e-mails, and so forth), as well as quantitative data. She noted, as have other researchers, that a significant number of the women reported narratives that included both female and male partners over time. The conventional wisdom might be to label such women as either bisexual in their sexual desire or "in formation," not having reached a state of permanence in terms of what Freud called sexual "object-choice," but Diamond found, in the ways in which these women talked and wrote about their desire and the couplings that resulted from desire, something different from and less linear and singular than that. These women had a greater degree of what was already being called **fluidity**, but what this fluidity encompassed was something different from simply moving between male and female partners over time.

From the data Diamond arrived at a different conclusion: many of the women she studied — and the number allowed for a reasonable degree of generalization, following the conventions of social science research — described having two dimensions of "feeling" in this larger, sometimes messy area we call sexuality: the first was sexual desire itself; the second she called **romantic attraction**. Without introducing even more complex, hard-to-agree-on specialized terminology, one might say the former (sexual desire) is what we have been focusing on in much of this chapter — feelings of physical attraction to a person or to a category of people. (The category is often defined by the gender of the people, but it does not have to be — one could have sexual desire for people with red hair, people who are tall, and so forth, regardless of their gender.) Romantic attraction is the equivalent of those feelings of "being in love," which may or may not involve sexual desire. It is a desire to be with a person, to do things — some physical (such as holding hands or cuddling or, even for some, kissing), some social and domestic — to bond with that person as part of a couple.

What Diamond concluded from close analysis and follow-up interactions with these women is that it would be more useful to think of sexual desire and romantic attraction as two separate phenomena, accompanied, if one wanted to follow Alfred Kinsey's concept of a continuum or scale, by two separate sets of degrees or places on a line, which sometimes match up (called **concordant**) and sometimes do not (**discordant**). A woman who found herself sexually desiring primarily other woman *and* attracted romantically primarily to other women would be seen as having a concordant set of attractions or emotions; a woman who felt sexual desire for men but romantic attraction only to women would be seen as discordant (and vice versa — a woman who feels sexual desire for women but romantic desire for men would be similarly discordant). It is important to keep in mind that such terms as *concordant* and *discordant* are meant to be not evaluative or directive, but descriptive and explanatory. These concepts also may explain why some of the women Diamond studied described a history of moving between male and female partners over years: at times, sexual desire may have been the primary motivator for pair-bonding for them; at other times, romantic feeling may have ruled the day.

While Diamond's research has looked exclusively at women's sexuality, her hypothesis certainly could serve logically for men who report variations in the gender of their partners over time. It may also explain the often-challenging lives that such people, male or female, lead in societies and cultures that place a high premium on pair-bonding (coupling) as a social and moral good. We have often had an image of the closeted married gay man as a hypocrite, and at times, especially during the height of the AIDS epidemic, this image has been inflated into a monstrous figure. But for many men this may simply be an attempt to make a life when sexual desire and romantic attraction do not match up. The assumption that such men just need to "admit" that they are gay, divorce their wives, and set up housekeeping or another kind of domestic relationship with a man in order to be "true" to themselves and "honest" with the world is reductive and simplifies what may very well be a more complex issue. This is not to say that there aren't men who, bowing either to social pressure or to homophobic messages they have internalized through family, church, or culture, marry women for the sake of social appearance and acceptance, while actually feeling both sexually and romantically attracted to men; rather, it is to call on all of us not to assume that scenario as the only or obvious one. The same, needless to say, is true for women who remain in long-term romantic and familial partnerships with men but feel and perhaps act on sexual desire for other women.

What is true is that, going back to Hocquenghem and Mieli, if the worlds in which we live were less homophobic, there might be less turmoil over the differences between sexual desire and romantic attraction. But this would also call for a dismantling of the exclusivity that monogamy, at least as it is practiced in most parts of society today, insists on. In that sense, the Greeks and the Romans may well have had greater understanding, even if in terms we would find good reason to critique (as both were highly patriarchal societies, which seriously devalued women outside the spheres of domesticity and reproduction), that sexual desire and romantic attraction may follow different pathways. Even in our much more queer-positive society of the twenty-first century (which is far from universally accepting of queer lives and arrangements, to be sure), there is often an implicit expectation that sexual desire and romantic attraction *should* match, in order to maintain the boundaries a monogamous couple is expected to maintain, though, of course, not all people, queer or otherwise, subscribe to the idea that monogamy is the ideal way for people to live their sexual and romantic lives.

## ISSUES FOR INVESTIGATION

### 1. The Origins of Love

This chapter has introduced both psychoanalytic and political theories of desire, as well as some examples of hybrids of the two. What do you think about these ideas concerning where desire begins and how it is located and, some would say, manipulated socially? Consider this first with various kinds of desire (not necessarily sexual or erotic desire). Can you recall instances in which you are aware, if only retrospectively, that you experienced a desire that you could pinpoint as having been produced by forces outside yourself? Often this experience can be connected to material goods and products. Were there toys you desired to own? Experiences you felt as if you "had to have"? See if you can find similar instances with sexual or erotic desire. This may be more difficult initially, as we are accustomed to thinking of desire as "natural" — that is, coming out of a place inside ourselves and, when directed toward a particular person, a result of that person's "pure" being. Nonetheless, see if you can identify the pathway of desire in those instances. Ultimately, you may decide that more sociopolitical and economic accounts of desire are limited, or useful in talking about some areas of desire and not for others. The main goal is to try to do some self-reflection about an area most of us take as a given.

## 2. Sexual Fluidity in Your Community

Consider doing an inventory of the people in your life (other than relatives) who are important to you emotionally. Some will no doubt fit in what is commonly called the "friend zone" — does this mean that your feelings for them do not have romantic or sexual components? Similarly, when you think about the people in your life, can you describe their own reports of attraction or their social arrangements (such as whom to date, how they spend time, whom they feel comfortable having physical contact with) in the terms Diamond uses? How do traditional gender divisions fit into these patterns? If you or any of the people in your life identify outside binaries of sex or gender, how does this play a part in their sexual fluidity (or lack thereof, as the case may be)?

SUGGESTIONS FOR FURTHER READING AND VIEWING

Cavanaugh, Sheila, ed. "Transpsychoanalytics: Special Issue." *Transgender Studies Quarterly* 4.3 – 4 (2017).

Dean, Tim, and Christopher Lane, eds. *Homosexuality and Psychoanalysis.* Chicago: University of Chicago Press, 2001.

D'Emilio, John. "Capitalism and Gay Identity." In *Making Trouble: Essays on Gay History, Politics, and the University,* 3–16. New York: Routledge, 1992.

Floyd, Kevin. *The Reification of Desire: Toward a Queer Marxism.* Minneapolis: University of Minnesota Press, 2009.

Glassgold, Judith M., and Suzanne Iasenza, eds. *Lesbians, Feminism, and Psychoanalysis: The Second Wave.* Binghamton, NY: Harrington Park Press, 2004.

*Hedwig and the Angry Inch.* Directed by John Cameron Mitchell. New Line, 2001.

Watson, Eve. "Queering Psychoanalysis/Psychoanalysing Queer." *Annual Review of Critical Psychology* 7 (2009): 114 – 139.

# CHAPTER 3

# QUEERING IDENTITIES
## From "I" to "We"

*Identity* is one of the most dominant terms in public discourse today: some observers would argue that we live in a time of **identity politics**, wherein issues of power, justice, and experience center on how we define ourselves as members of groups, including the name or names we or others use for such categories. Depending on one's convictions, such a central issue is either a sign of positive affirmation of diversity or a negative sign of divisiveness — and, of course, there are many positions between these polarities. Identity is the name or set of names we use to describe ourselves or others use to describe us, both to ourselves and to others. Notice a few things about this definition that might merit additional clarification or expansion: first, "name or set of names" — identity is always by its very definition **intersectional**, multiple, contingent, requiring that it acknowledge different aspects of any given person, though, depending on the context, one part of identity may be more salient or significant than another.

In this sense, the complexities of intersectional identities may echo some of the findings discussed in Lisa Diamond's theories of sexual desire and romantic attraction in the previous chapter. Even for those individuals who can state with a degree of self-certainty that, for example, they are men who have sexual desire exclusively for other men and romantic attraction only for women, it is doubtful that they could, if they were trying to be completely honest with themselves and with others, simply say, "I am gay" or "I am straight." We are now in a time in which such terms may not suffice for the multiple identities we may possess even in the realm of sexuality (or desire, understood more broadly) itself.

The second phrase in this definition of identity that needs a bit more elaboration is "we . . . or others use." Let's break it down a bit more. Those raised in the United States, especially middle-class, cisgender, straight, white people, tend to put a high premium on individual identity (except, of course, when such individuality seems to threaten the social order) and to believe that all persons have a right to express and enact their individual

Henderson, Bruce, *Queer Studies: Beyond Binaries*
dx.doi.org/10.17312/harringtonparkpress/2019.09.qsbb.003
© 2019 by Harrington Park Press

identity, within reasonable limits — or at least that is what is claimed, until such individual self-definition threatens the dominant social order. In other cultures, which may be based on more communitarian ideologies, the idea of identity may be more focused on what it means to belong to a larger group and to put the needs of the group first. In some cultures, the idea of having an individual identity may be foreign in and of itself.

In the next sections, we will look at two models of identity formation, developed by two psychologists, one of whom focused most of his attention on life-span studies, the other who works on social and cultural dimensions of identity.

## ERIK ERIKSON'S STAGE MODEL OF IDENTITY DEVELOPMENT

The first of the models of identity development we will consider is one with which you may be familiar if you have taken any psychology courses: Erik Erikson's **stage model**. We hasten to add that there are many other theories of personality development, too many to compare and contrast: Erikson's, while open to and the recipient of critique, is one that has become as much a part of the way most people think about life-span psychology as Freud's theory of psychosexual development. Erikson's language has entered into our everyday conversations.

Erikson's theory is founded on the belief that personality develops dynamically throughout life. Erikson assigned an age range to each of the stages of psychosocial development, and he tied them both to biophysical growth and change within individuals and to their social and psychological journeys. He saw each of the stages as dominated by a particular conflict or challenge, a kind of choice point (though willful, conscious choice may not have been operative at each transition).

1. Hopes: trust versus mistrust (birth–two years)
2. Will: autonomy versus shame (one or two–four years)
3. Purpose: initiative versus guilt (three–five years)
4. Competence: industry versus inferiority (five–twelve years)
5. Fidelity: identity versus role confusion (twelve–eighteen years)
6. Love: intimacy versus isolation (eighteen–forty years)
7. Care: generativity versus stagnation (forty–sixty-four years)
8. Wisdom: ego integrity versus despair (sixty-four years–death)

Critics of Erikson's stage model point to an implied sequentiality of each stage — that is, that the individual passes through each stage and never returns to it. Many have noted that the stage central and critical for our interests, Stage 5, "identity versus role confusion," is by no means limited to the period of adolescence, but is probably a crisis that we revisit throughout our lives. Similarly, Erikson's model can be viewed as reinforcing binaries that, applied rigidly, limit a person's identity to "success" or "failure." In Stage 4, for example, does the individual experience only either industry or inferiority — feeling success at accomplishing tasks or a sense of being lesser for having failed at them?

Erikson's stage model takes as its final period Stage 8, "ego integrity versus despair," which he calls late adulthood. Ego integrity refers to older persons' reflections on their lives as having been a success — that is, their strength of ego (in a good sense) remains integrated; if the end of life consists of reflecting and viewing one's life as having been a failure or a disappointment, then despair has won the battle in that crisis. Because medical science has succeeded in extending life expectancy (absent a calamitous accident or an inevitably terminal illness) considerably beyond what it was when Erikson developed his theory, some psychologists have called for a Stage 9 to account for the experiences of the increasing population (among those in societies or socioeconomic classes with access to health care) living into their eighties, nineties, and even beyond one hundred: the Jungian psychologists Lee Roloff and Russell Lockhart have explored this topic in their book *The Final Interlude*. Roloff was a gay-identified analyst and teacher and was interested in the potential for people of all sexualities at each life stage of identity.

There is research on LGB youth and adults, using Erikson's stage model as a framework for conceptualization; such studies tend not to include individuals identifying or identified as transgender or intersex, as the milestones for individuals living with issues of body integrity and gender expression move in different, though, of course, not entirely independent ways from those living with same-sex desire and romantic attraction. The myriad life experiences of people who identify as transgender or intersex will be the subject of the next chapter. As might be expected, for LGB individuals the emphasis has been on Stages 5 through 7; considerable attention should be given, as it is in many Eriksonian studies, to the "identity crisis" of adolescence and early adulthood — that period when people, whatever their sexuality, begin to articulate, for themselves and typically for those around them, "who they are." Social pressures for conformity to heterosexuality may intensify the crisis for LGB youth, and they may also experience what Erikson called "role confusion," in which they find roles that are approved of by society (achieving student, "good" son or daughter, member of a religious community and adherent to a faith system) are in conflict with an emerging sense of a sexual identity. To be sure, not all LGB youth experience their emerging named sexual identity as a crisis, and, for them, depending on their individual personality and familial or social support system, may be able to integrate their minoritized sexual identity into a more complex, intersectional set of identity "nodes." We will return to some of Erikson's stages in chapter 8, when we examine domestic and familial arrangements and experiences of queer people. In that discussion, we will consider how the kinds of psychosocial challenges Erikson observed intersect with social structures and cultural attitudes and experiences of queer people beyond the central crisis of identity versus role confusion.

## GILL AND INTEGRATION IN IDENTITY DEVELOPMENT

Carol J. Gill, who is a disability studies scholar and professor, as well as a clinical psychologist, has posited a theory of types of identity integration that she sees as representative of how disabled people "come" to their sense of identity as a person with disabilities and as a member of a culture of disability. She has repeatedly underscored that her model is not a stage or phase model (i.e., it does not have a linear or necessary pathway), but is instead a "type" model, meaning that different individuals may come to their identity in any one of these "typical" ways, and they may not necessarily experience all of them. Her model is a useful one for queer identity as well.

Gill is not, in her model, interested in specific individual types of people with disabilities; rather, she is concerned with the possible ways in which such people may come to the **integration model** Erikson writes about. Interestingly, she uses the language of *coming* (as in *coming out*), most familiarly associated with queer identity processes, as the central term in her model. It suggests a kind of dynamism, negating any sense that people with disabilities simply have an identity that is "given." Another similarity to the processes of queer people might be the fact that, for the majority of queer people and for the majority of people with disabilities, this part of their identity (queer, disabled) distinguishes them from the majority of their family, and especially from their parents and, more often than not, siblings. There are, of course, queer parents whose children also identify as queer, just as there are disabilities than can be heritable or families where parents and children have different disabilities. Nonetheless, as opposed to many other categories of identity such as race, ethnicity, and religion, identifying as queer or as disabled typically involves looking beyond one's family of origin for ways of learning how to integrate this sense of self into one's identity.

Gill divides the types of identity integration into four categories:

1. "Coming to feel we belong" (integrating into society)
2. "Coming home" (integrating with the disability community)
3. "Coming together" (internally integrating our sameness and differentness)
4. "Coming out" (integrating how we feel with how we present ourselves)

**"Coming to Feel We Belong" (Integrating into Society)**
The first type, "coming to feel we belong," addresses issues of exclusion and isolation in the larger society in which an individual lives. People who acknowledge their minoritized sexual identity often feel as if they are no longer entitled to the same rights and privileges as their fellow citizens who happen to be straight. They may feel that they have suddenly become "less than," and, as has been true for other minoritized identities (such as those based on race, religion, and economic class), the structures of society have given them good reason to regard themselves this way. This type of integration may be seen as one of experiencing empowerment as an equal citizen and may also serve to remind individuals that they have (or should have) the same rights as people who constitute the majority.

An example of this in queer identity might be the kinds of identity integration that come with the legalization of marriage equality. It is not unusual, though still worthy of note, to see detailed wedding announcements for same-sex couples, along with photographs commemorating the occasion, in a newspaper such as the *New York Times* (often considered the national paper of record), mixed in among those doing the same work for heterosexual couples. Such announcements do not use differentiating language for same-sex nuptials: the same standard tropes and clichés may well be present, such as the educational and employment history of each member of the couple, their parents' names, occupations, and locations, and the previous marital status of each member of the marrying couple.

Similarly, it is not uncommon to see "Mr. X's first marriage ended in divorce," or "Ms. Y was a widow." Words like *divorce* and *widow* are part of a larger set of social meanings, until recently used in quotation marks when describing queer people (such as a surviving partner of a man who died of HIV-related illness being referred to as an "AIDS widow"). Now they are simply integrated into the news of the wedding announcement. Norms of etiquette may currently dictate that no more detail is required or desired than the information that this may not be the first marriage for one or both of the parties. The newspaper has, as best as can be inferred, not drawn legal distinctions between marriage and other forms of long-term commitment and, typically, cohabitation. The newspaper has been including same-sex wedding announcements since 2002, more than a decade before the 2015 Supreme Court decision that determined that bans on same-sex marriage were unconstitutional and therefore opened up marriage as a legal right on a federal level.

Can people engage in the work of "coming to feel we belong" without explicitly acknowledging their queer sexual identity to this larger society to which Gill refers? Some would say no, that keeping this sexual identity hidden or closeted is inherently counter to the development of a "healthy" (a word that itself is value-laden, needless to say) queer sexual identity. Others would argue: it depends. In recent decades, there has been an increasingly rich and powerful body of interviews and writings of men and women who have served in the military, in part because of the major (and now successful) push to overturn the Don't Ask, Don't Tell policy that permitted queer people to serve in the military as long as they did not express their sexuality in any recognizable way. Scholars such as the late Allan Bérubé, author of a moving and stirring book, *Coming Out under Fire*, have documented what might be seen as the double heroism of such soldiers, who felt committed to serve their country in its time of need. They knew that if they made their sexuality known they would be either classified as 4-F (unfit to serve) or, if already enlisted, discharged, very frequently with the adjective *dishonorably* which had serious consequences in the latter half of the twentieth century for future employment and opportunities.

Does this mean that such soldiers took a vow of celibacy during their tours of duty? If their memories are even remotely accurate, the answer would be a resounding "No!" An individual memoir you may find interesting in terms of what it was like to be a gay soldier during World War II is James Lord's *My Queer War*. Lord recounts his experiences serving in the military and fighting the Axis forces in Europe during World War II. He describes the ways in which queer soldiers found each other, how they navigated their sexual identities among their straight fellow soldiers, many of whom became deeply warm and supportive friends, and why these soldiers, who would have been viewed as second-class or even criminal in the eyes of society had people been aware of their sexual identity, nonetheless wanted to join the military because it was intrinsic to their identity as patriotic Americans. Their queerness may have remained silent to anyone but themselves or to other queer military personnel, but there was an important kind of identity integration taking place, of the sort Gill classifies under the first type.

## Coming Home (Integrating with the Community)

One characteristic both queer people and people with disabilities share is what might be called a discordance between their families of origins and central parts of their identity. Gill suggests that people with disabilities may experience a sense of "coming home" when they have opportunities to interact and bond with other people with disabilities, and that this may be true even in cross-disability situations: wheelchair users may regard visually impaired people as "kin," even though their physical disabilities are different. What may be shared is a sense of oppression by those who have not experienced disability themselves, a special kind of humor that may have meaning only to those people who have found themselves required to navigate a world that does not provide accommodations for them (or does so in ways that the people with the specific disabilities could have told them would not serve the needs of the people they were designed for), a general sense of "shorthand," a shared history and daily experience that does not always need to be explained to be understood.

This is also the case for many queer people. While there are, of course, as many ways of living out a queer identity as there are queer individuals, there is frequently a sense in which queer people, in the process of engaging in social, cultural, and other kinds of interactions with other queer people, may say they have found their "true family." Sometimes, the phrase used is *family of choice*, to distinguish this sense of family from a *family of origin*. It should go without saying that the family of origin (or members of it) may be included in the family of choice, but the family of choice typically consists of those people who support an individual's identity. It may also be the case that we all have multiple families of choice to whom we turn for very different needs and to share different histories and experiences. In high school, for example, queer students may find more of a sense of family among some of their activity groups, such as drama clubs, musical ensembles, or even, increasingly, sports teams, than they may with their family of origin.

Our geographic homes may change over the years, to be sure, but we also may feel we have a sense of "home" by virtue of the people with whom we have made these important connections — Gill has referred to this, conversationally, as people "you have in your pocket," not in the sense of controlling them, but in simply having the knowledge that they are there in the world for you, and that their regard and affection for you helps you know who you are.

## Coming Together (Internally Integrating Our Sameness and Differentness)

The third type of integration Gill notes is one that involves balancing the ways in which disabled people experience themselves as similar (sameness) to other people while feeling pride and value in the ways in which their disabilities make them different from other people. This can be one of the most difficult aspects of identity for nondisabled people to comprehend, since they typically view their own bodies, minds, and experiences as normative, or that which is to be desired by all people. Given the stigmas and degrees of oppression and barriers people with disabilities experience, it can certainly be a challenge for many nondisabled people to imagine why a person with a disability might consider themselves fortunate to have a specific impairment. This idea has been central to a group of people who feel so strongly that what society usually views as a "defect" is a difference that offers opportunities and experiences worth maintaining and cherishing that they often reject inclusion among the ranks of disabled people: Deaf people. People who identify as "culturally Deaf" (note the capital D) describe Deafworld not as a deficit of sound, but as a place filled with the meanings and pleasures of silence, motion, visuality, and other kinds of ways of relating to the physical, intellectual, and social world. Debates about treating deafness through technological developments, such as cochlear implants, are complex, and there are passionate proponents and critics on each side.

The integrating of sameness and differentness is equally applicable to queer identity. A pathological or "sickness" view of nonheteronormative desire, experience, and identity usually works from a basic assumption that queer people, all things being equal, would (or should) prefer to be heterosexual, and it may be that, for some people, both social and familial pressures make this seem a desirable aspiration; it is also true that, like any other group with a minority identity, queer people usually do not have access to the often invisible (or unremarked-on) forms of privilege heterosexuals have, so there might be a logic in asking, "Why might you prefer to be queer?"

A question that used to be posed so frequently that it became a cliché was something like this: "If you could take a pill that would turn you heterosexual tomorrow, would you do so?" Some queer individuals answered "yes," usually going on to say that being queer was difficult in society and that being heterosexual would allow them to have children and raise a family (these are responses from many years ago), but many people answered "no." When pressed about why they would choose to remain in an identity that had so much working against it, many people said, quite simply, "It's part of who I am — I would not be me if I were not queer" (or gay or lesbian or whatever term had been used). While this may elide some of the complexities of "what it means to be me," there is a confidence and self-knowledge that is important to note in such a statement.

We might consider what queer people might find positive about their differentness. The answers will vary, to be sure, from one person to the next, but some that are frequently offered include the following: queer people may believe their sexual identity makes them more open to and less judgmental of differentness in other people; it may permit them greater empathy with other people; it may free them from certain social role expectations. For older generations, freedom from expectations of being parents is often cited. The freedom to pursue career paths other than the ones prescribed to them is sometimes cited. The opportunity for various kinds of intimacy with other people of their same sex is often considered a kind of gift.

Of course, someone wishing to play devil's advocate might assert that many of these experiences or qualities are hardly unique to queer folk, nor is being queer a necessary requirement for them (such as empathy for others, for example). That, of course, is true. What may be fair to say is that the fact of identifying as queer and living one's life in whatever way it means to an individual to be queer may mean having to acknowledge or being free to acknowledge (which are probably two different things) one's own individuality and specificity. Perhaps what this comes down to is a self-acceptance of ways in which we are each individual and different and not trying to "repair" what need not be viewed as broken in ourselves and others, and recognizing that a world of pure sameness would be neither functional nor interesting, but a world of nothing but differentness would be incomprehensible and totally isolating. In that sense, perhaps, we all need to get in touch with our own "queerness," whatever our sexual or gender identities may be.

## Coming Out (Integrating How We Feel with How We Present Ourselves)

The fourth of the identity integration types Gill identifies is one that may be the most familiar to students of queer studies: coming out. While Gill does not order her types either hierarchically or necessarily chronologically, it may well be that coming out feels like the logical "last" type, as it involves presenting a sense of ourselves to the world, or (perhaps it is better to say) to particular worlds. There is a popular saying: "You are always coming out" or "You never stop coming out." What this means is that the work of presenting yourself to the world never ends and is never complete, in part because we encounter new people and new situations almost daily, but also because as human beings we remain dynamic and always changing. Psychologists have successfully presented evidence both that there is coherence to our personalities across time and that our attitudes change in some ways but not in others; each day, each year shifts the "who we are," sometimes in minute, undetectable ways, sometimes in ways that feel like earthquakes.

The term *coming out* has a disputed set of historical origins, but what is certainly true is that at one point in the upper-class social world of the United States and countries in the United Kingdom, it circulated as a verb referring to a ritual by which, in a particular season, an eligible young woman would make her debut in society through a series of formal parties and dances. Similar rites of passage continue to exist in non-Anglo-Saxon cultures as well, such as the tradition of the *quinceañera* in Latino families and communities. Such rituals meant that the young women were now able to attend adult events and to be considered figures in society. During the period when such balls were held, women were still, particularly in the upper echelon of the moneyed classes, expected to live primarily in the domestic sphere, moving from the conclusion of their schooling to marriage to motherhood, so such coming-out events were one of the few ways for women of this class to have any public presence. Men typically attended college or entered the workforce.

**Coming out**, as used in queer culture, refers to an act or process that declares the sexual identity of an individual. It has been hypothesized that the term is a humorous, somewhat campy appropriation of the society term, suggesting a kind of acceptance of the image of the gay man as a feminized identity. As George Chauncey has suggested, in its earliest use it was not phrased as "coming out of the closet" (which is the use more familiar today for many), but rather referred to being introduced as a gay man. The term was originally used about men, though it has now, of course, passed into more general use and describes lesbians, trans folk, and intersex people as well. Its feminine association may even hark back to the drag balls of the period, which began in the 1930s and continue to this day, when men would dress in often fabulous, expensive women's gowns and make their entry into gay society. There does not seem to be a single answer.

Gill uses the term in her discussion of disability identity integration to describe the process by which disabled people, particularly those with what are commonly referred to as invisible disabilities, which can range from psychiatric disabilities to less apparent physical disabilities and some sensory disabilities, make their disabled identity known to the world. Some argue that identity categories such as queerness and some disabilities are fundamentally different from race and ethnicity in that the former typically involve people who have the ability to "pass" — that is, not reveal their minority status — whereas the latter do not. Others argue that queer people frequently do not have the ability to pass, depending on their own gender expressiveness, and that even if there is the "luxury" of having the option, passing still produces definite negative effects on health, mental and physical, and political and social power.

*Choice* is a fraught word in queer studies, particularly in the subject of identity. Most researchers and queer individuals today would argue that sexual orientation is not chosen, though how to live one's life within that orientation may be (insofar as people have freedom to live in ways that feel true to themselves). Others, usually those who are anti-queer, argue that sexual orientation and, hence, identity involve choice, though there is no good science to back this argument in any broad or consistent way. A third perspective, worth noting, is that of some (primarily) lesbian feminist thinkers, especially the psychologist Carla Golden and the sociologist Vera Whisman. Both make intriguing arguments that sexual identity can involve choice, particularly when viewed at particular moments in political history, but also simply as part of individual life journeys. Golden cites the work of Barbara Ponse, who, in studying a southern community of lesbians, distinguished between what she called "primary lesbians" (women who felt they were always lesbian, from their earliest memories of sexual desire) and "elective lesbians," who, in Golden's words, "felt that they had chosen their lesbian lifestyle and identity" (8). Such theories may make some queer people uncomfortable, as they may seem to add fuel to the notion of choice and change that they feel pressures them to abandon their sense of a sexual identity. Neither Golden nor Whisman is advocating for that, nor does either suggest a "procedure" for such a choice. Rather, they are attempting to keep open and alive the possible routes to sexual identity. Such voices remain important, as they remind us to consider as many different implications of theories of sexual identity as possible and to acknowledge that there is no "finished" narrative that will account for all individuals who identify as queer.

In a sense, all Gill's types of identity integration may be subsumed in a longer, broader process of coming out if one thinks of the actual declaration or presentation of self to others (whether individual others or public groups of others) as the culmination of the other types. The act of understanding, acknowledgment, and presentation of one's identity is powerful, usually empowering, sometimes risky and, because of that, often involving bravery and a sense of knowledge gained about oneself. Other types of identity integration are equally important and, whatever our multiple identities may be, we all continue to move between the four types throughout life, as new events occur in our lives and worlds, as we gain experiences and insight, as we make contact with others we may not have known we shared sameness and differentness with.

# COMING OUT AS LGB

Coming out is, as we noted in the previous section, the process by which an individual acknowledges and gives name to an identity until that point kept hidden, sometimes from themselves. In the past few decades, there has been much research devoted to identifying and analyzing the process of coming out, including describing the steps typical of the process. It is important to keep in mind that most of this work has been done in Western societies (especially in the United States and Canada), and the majority of participants, whose narratives and interviews constitute the available data or case studies, are middle class and white.

Most theories of queer coming out focus on the adolescent and early adult years. **Adolescence** itself is, in historical terms, a comparatively recent concept, generally considered to have been put into popular usage by the psychologist G. Stanley Hall, who, in 1904, published a book titled *Adolescence*. This does not necessarily contradict the testimony of those individuals who declare that they knew they were gay when they were five, or that they were attracted to members of their own sex as early as kindergarten or first grade. Childhood memories are complex things, neither to be entirely trusted nor to be dismissed. The adult recalling this younger self is engaging in a very natural process, attempting to find continuity across the life span.

In ways analogous to Gill's type model of cultural identification, some argue that the first person queer individuals must come out to is themselves — there must be an internal acknowledgment of same-sex desire in order to be able to articulate such an identity to anyone else. Others would argue that sometimes the feelings associated with queer identity may begin in an inchoate or felt but not intellectualized way; those feelings become part of a conscious identity only when there is a context, whether interpersonal or social, in which to articulate this sense of self. There are countless anecdotal instances of people saying that their friends or family knew they were queer before they did. Such stories may lack scientific validation per se, but they have an emotional and psychological reality for many people. Nonetheless, whether one is using a stage model of coming out or something less linear or chronological, the ability to see oneself as queer or gay or lesbian or bisexual and to begin to name oneself in language is powerful and important.

In this sense, then, the queer person, in coming out, must, at some point, come out to themselves — it is possible to be closeted from one's own consciousness of desire, through denial or other forms of deflection or misattribution. Eve Kosofsky Sedgwick, one of the founders of queer theory, wrote a fascinating if dense scholarly study, *Epistemology of the Closet*. Sedgwick argued that **the closet** as a metaphor and as a phenomenon — the state of being queer but disguising it or denying it to other people and sometimes to oneself — has historically been a homophobic construction, a way of confining sexuality and sexual identities that various societies (she focuses on Europe and America in the late nineteenth and twentieth centuries) have erected to contain that which they would choose to ignore or deny. The closet, then, becomes a way of regulating identity: it may be a place where there is much queerness going on, but which has a door to shield such queerness from the eyes of those who live outside it. Sedgwick analyzes literary texts by such major writers as Henry James, Oscar Wilde, and Marcel Proust to demonstrate how the closet both becomes a way of silencing queer voices, bodies, and experiences and carries with it what she calls "the spectacle of the closet" — often exaggerated, even parodic depictions of queer sexuality and identity that allow the rest of "proper" society to mark off the door between themselves and the queer other. Indeed, she suggests, queer people may, both consciously and unconsciously, participate in such policing of sexual identity and in such "spectacularizing" of it. Another scholar, Joseph Litvak, elaborating on and responding to Sedgwick's theory, suggests that the "success" of the closet as a structure and as a system of behaviors depends critically on what he calls "not-knowing," which can be a literal, authentic ignorance of someone's queer sexual identity or a kind of mutual and implicit "performance" of "not-knowing" (by which he means the people involved know but act as if they do not know, in order to maintain the social order). In everyday terms, this may occur, for example, in families in which an individual has a "roommate" who has been included in family gatherings for decades, but remains not-known as a romantic or sexual partner. Sedgwick and those who have used her theory suggest that the homophobic function of the closet in such an example is to negate the reality and, hence, the value of the person's sexuality and of the relationship between the family member and the roommate. Many queer people speak of a period in their lives when they believed their parents "knew," without acknowledging (or even admitting to themselves at a conscious level), that their offspring was queer.

Historically, the closet has been for many people a necessary place for survival, and, just as the saying "one is always coming out" has a kind of fundamental truth, so it is that people sometimes find themselves "recloseting" themselves for purposes of safety or social strategy. Though in an ideal world no queer person should ever feel compelled to live in the closet (whether they choose to is a more complicated matter), given the variable and often-shifting attitudes toward and treatment of queer people in various times and places, it may be that a person who considers themselves fully out in their town and their place of work will, if they go home or travel to certain places, feel the need to retreat to the closet. Some might argue that "recloseting" or "selective closeting" (say, keeping queer identity unspoken or hidden when visiting family) is dishonest, but it may be a necessary dishonesty at times. What Sedgwick and others have pointed out in their discussions of epistemology (i.e., the way in which "the closet" is known and knowable) is that queer people and others can use the closet as a way of regulating other queers. The threat of either outing someone who, for whatever reason, is in the closet by someone who knows the person is queer, or using such knowledge as a way of controlling them, is certainly one of the darker corners in which the closet has been used.

Social scientists have also examined the concept of the closet, often using such qualitative methods as oral histories, interviews, and autoethnographies, the last a kind of discourse that places the perspective and the experience of the researcher in a kind of dialogic relationship with the people whose stories are being recorded and told. Tony E. Adams's *Narrating the Closet: An Autoethnography of Same-Sex Attraction* is a clear and detailed text in which Adams moves between his own experience of coming out of the closet and those of others to find patterns of similar experiences, without losing the specific experience of individuals. Adams divides the experience of the closet into three stages: coming in, being closeted, and coming out. One aspect of his conceptualization especially worthy of note is that he finds, in the accounts of the closet he has collected and in his own reflection on their relation to his own experience, a stage of coming in that is notably different from a state of simply not knowing one's queer desires. It is an important stage, in that it is itself a kind of act — an act of recognizing, even if initially in diffuse or inarticulable ways, a queer sense of self and coming to be able to name it for oneself, but making the decision to enter a state of closetedness. This leads to Adams's second concept, the state of being closeted, in which a private sense of erotic and sexual identity is more or less in place, but in which the various kinds of strategies Sedgwick and others note are in play because the individual does not yet feel ready (or, in some instances, safe) to come out. Adams's study is accessible in that it is grounded in the lived experience of queer people as individuals, but it offers, as does most good autoethnography, ways to situate individual experiences in larger, shared contexts.

## SPOTLIGHT ON LITERATURE: JANE HAMILTON AND *THE SHORT HISTORY OF A PRINCE*

A dramatic literary instance of the individual's own exploration of sexual (and gender) identity in a space that has many of the characteristics of the closet is Jane Hamilton's novel *The Short History of a Prince*. In the novel, Walter, the adolescent protagonist, is coming to know his own queer sexual identity, both through the emergence of desire he feels for his best male friend and through his participation in the performing arts, specifically the world of ballet, in which he aspires to dance, though he is aware of his lack of sufficient talent to make it as a professional. Still, the ballet provides an opportunity for him to explore a world of people and an art form often associated with queerness, especially with gay men. In the excerpt, which can be found in the Appendix, Walter has waited for others to leave the ballet studio where he is taking lessons, so that he can experiment with his emerging sense of queerness through performance and costuming. He is confronted by Mr. Kenton, who runs the studio and teaches classes, and who lives as a married man. The novel leaves open-ended whether Mr. Kenton is simply a homophobic straight man, perhaps defensive about the queerness assumed about men in ballet, or whether Walter's appearance so threatens the containment of his own comfortable place in the closet that he must throw him out into the streets of rush-hour Chicago.

## MODELS OF COMING OUT

Some theorists, following in Freud's and Erikson's traditions, do see a kind of stage model as appropriate for mapping the common processes of coming out. Richard Troiden proposed a four-stage model, which Frank Floyd and Roger Bakeman extended beyond adolescence to the entire life course. Troiden's model consists of the following steps:

1. An early stage of sensitization to same-sex attractions marked by first recognition of attraction, usually in childhood or early adolescence

2. A stage of identity confusion in adolescence during which sexual experimentation occurs with both opposite-sex and same-sex partners

3. A stage of identity assumption, marked by the event of first self-identifying as gay, lesbian, or bisexual, usually in late adolescence or young adulthood

4. A final stage of identity commitment during which the individual becomes more deeply connected to the identity

5. And begins to disclose to others, usually first to a friend or sibling, followed by disclosure to parents, usually mothers rather than fathers (Floyd and Bakeman 287)

What strengths and weaknesses might there be in a linear approach such as this?

A similar, though somewhat different, model for both gay men and lesbians has been proposed by Vivienne Cass. She designates six stages of coming out:

1. Identity confusion

2. Identity comparison (includes feelings of difference and isolation)

3. Identity tolerance: "characterized by a desire to overcome the isolation of the incongruity of identity"

4. Identity acceptance: the resolution of the incongruity between having thought of oneself as heterosexual and now identifying as queer

5. Identity pride: "characterized by feelings of anger at the oppression of lesbians and gays and embracing of activism"

6. Identity synthesis: a rejection of activism and anger; personal and public sexual identity become fully integrated, and homosexuality is now viewed as only one "aspect of total identity" (222–235)

Margaret Rosario and her colleagues have proposed, on the basis of data they collected from a primarily urban set of participants in their study, the following as elements of the coming-out process for gay men, lesbians, and bisexual individuals:

- Involvement in gay or lesbian activities
- Attitudes toward homosexuality
- Comfort with homosexuality
- Self-disclosure of sexual identity to others
- Sexual identity (Rosario et al., 134)

This is not a prescriptive list, but an extrapolation from self-reports of queer people. Some people named their queer identity to themselves and perhaps to others before engaging in any kind of same-sex behavior. Others may have had same-sex sexual or romantic experiences, but they did not disclose they had such experiences or immediately name their identity, to themselves or to others, as something other than heterosexual. It is certainly possible for someone to develop positive attitudes toward homosexuality before feeling comfortable with identifying as homosexual. Rosario and her colleagues begin with this model of coming out to move on to the central research question they explore: the relationship between coming out and what is referred to as sexual health (including risky behaviors that can expose queer youth to HIV/AIDS, sexual violence, and STDs). Their research looks at potential pathways in coming out, in terms of how some paths may raise the likelihood of risky behaviors and some may help individuals refrain from or be more thoughtful about choices they make.

Are there differences between typical coming-out processes for gay men and those for lesbians, as well as for bisexual people? And do other nodes of identity, such as race, region, ethnicity, and so forth, add different layers in terms of coming out? These are valid and valuable questions, and there has been some research conducted on such differences. Ritch C. Savin-Williams analyzed the coming-out stories of young men, primarily college students, and published his findings in his 1998 book *"... And Then I Became Gay": Young Men's Stories*. Though he found much individual difference, some of the milestones he found common to many of the stories are not unlike those found in the more generalized models of queer identity presented above.

1. In childhood, boys who grew up to identify as gay or bisexual felt different from other boys, seeing themselves, in the words of the gay psychologist Richard Isay, as "more sensitive and [having] more aesthetic interests" (quoted in Savin-Williams 28). They recall being more gender atypical.

2. At or during puberty, these boys found "preexisting thoughts and feelings [becoming] associated with sexuality" (48). In other words, these feelings from childhood started having object targets, whether general or specific.

3. "Sexualization of attraction but not of identity": the hormonal developments that come with puberty did yet lead to a named, conscious identity.

4. Boys may have had girlfriends in the traditional adolescent romantic sense and often strong emotional friendships with girls, but little or no sexual desire for them.

5. Boys had their first gay sexual experience within a year of labeling themselves as gay; for this cohort, labeling the self as gay preceded acting on it. Interestingly, gay virgins had generally later onset of puberty.

6. The majority of these boys also had heterosexual sexual experiences, approximately around the same time as their first homosexual experience.

7. The period during which they identified themselves as gay broke down as follows: 40 percent during high school; 20 percent during childhood or early adolescence; 40 percent after high school. This was self-labeling without necessarily disclosing to others, though a number acknowledged that friends helped them come to this ability to label themselves.

8. Their first gay romance occurred on average at about age eighteen; they met their partners in such places as gay bars, gay organizations, at school, through college, public places (restrooms, malls), through friends, on the computer, and in counseling and support groups.

Actual disclosure to others — the milestone we usually see as the culmination or confirmation of coming out — happened most frequently during their first year of college. The age for this average may well be dropping, as gay men (and other queer folk) gain more public and popular visibility than they had in the media and everyday life in the 1990s, when Savin-Williams gathered his data. Nonetheless, there may still be a sensible correlation between such a declaration of identity and what is for most young men their first opportunity to live outside their home of origin and to feel the freedom to speak of their sexual identity without as much fear that the information will be shared with those they feel it might be most risky to have such knowledge, given the financial and emotional dependence they may still have. Of these young men, 60 percent made their first disclosure after high school. It is interesting to note to whom they made their first disclosure: 50 percent (fully half) of them first told a female friend, 30 percent a male friend (usually heterosexual), and only 20 percent to a family member or supportive adult (such as a teacher, counselor, or other leader). The first family member to whom young gay men disclosed their sexual identity was almost always a female, more often a sister than a mother; some told brothers, and fathers were usually the last to be told — and sometimes fathers were told by an intermediary, such as a mother.

There is considerably less research on the specific milestones and experiences of lesbians' coming out, no doubt a reflection of the general gap between the attention given to men's and women's issues. Nonetheless, some common features found in the coming-out experiences of lesbians are not unlike those for men, though there are important differences to note. First, as a rule, lesbians may come out as lesbian (rather than as bisexual or in an unnamed sexual identity) later than gay men by a few years — more often in early adulthood. In the research that supports this, it is often hypothesized that this is because of differences in sex-role expectations and historical differences in the rigidities of gendering of men and women. What this means is that because women were held to less rigid sex roles in terms of expression of affection and physical contact in general than were men, the social scripts that led men to identify their erotic and romantic desires as queer often came earlier. This does not mean that the desire of the women was somehow "less queer"; rather, the social apparatuses that allow (some might say require) desire and attraction to become named in a specific category were less confining for women.

The research conducted during this period also confirmed some of what Golden and Whisman hypothesize in their "queer by choice" theories: for many young women, identifying as a lesbian was often meaningfully connected to a way of embracing feminism, "women-centered" and "women-valuing" philosophy and activism. In narratives written and told by self-identified lesbians, it was more often the case than it was for men that an acknowledgment and commitment to a queer identity came about as a result of belonging to or attending political and activist organizations and events and, as a result, connecting such work to their desires and attractions. It is not as simple (or as directional) as saying women came out *because* they went to feminist groups, but it is the case that numerous women describe the solidarity of being with other women in such environments as a catalyst for self-identification and participation in what could be called either lesbian consciousness or lesbian culture. Of course, not all women who identified as lesbians during what is usually called second-wave feminism came to their sense of identity and community through overtly political or academic venues; as we will see in chapter 5, working-class lesbians, particularly in some large urban areas or within professions that had significant populations of lesbian workers, created their own sense of communities in different ways, often social and recreational, as well as professional and, yes, political.

It is also the case that, in some of the studies conducted, there was more variability in naming their sexual identity among women than among men, which is in some ways perhaps tied to Lisa Diamond's notion of fluidity. There was often, and still is to some extent, an assumption that a man's identification as bisexual either was a way of avoiding the stigma that came with being identified as a "full-on gay" or was a "stop" along a path to full gayness. While one of these two scenarios was certainly true for some men, neither has by any means been demonstrated to be the whole picture or even true for the majority of bisexually identified men. But what has been true is that women simply did report more fluidity in naming their sexual identity — sometimes calling themselves lesbian, sometimes bisexual — and that such shifts were not as singular in direction as they seemed to be for men who may have first come out as bisexual and then "progressed" or reidentified as gay.

There is much less research on coming out as bisexual, though more is beginning to emerge as consciousness of the neglect of this identity category (what is often called "bi-erasure") has begun to emerge. Statistics indicate that people in younger generations are currently more likely to identify as bisexual than those in previous ones; hence, the important and specific research remains to be done. Some inferences are probably fair to draw, if only at the level of speculation. The naming of stable sexual identities is itself a comparatively recent invention: before the end of the nineteenth century, in Western cultures there were homosexual acts but no sense of people whose identity might be called homosexual per se: thus, we return to Foucault's notion that "the homosexual" as human type was invented in the age of industrialization. The forays into the philosophies of the Greeks and other distant historical moments suggest that there were many individuals who, by today's definition, would be called practicing bisexuals in terms of their acts and behaviors, and, in complicated ways, of their romantic affections and attractions. In some sense, particularly for the men of Plato's time, the term *bisexual* as an identity would have had little distinctive meaning (as would *heterosexual* and *homosexual* as well), as men of Athens were assumed to participate in erotic activities both with men (granted, under some very specific conditions and with limitations in terms of age and class) and with women; women were sufficiently relegated to the domestic sphere that depictions of whatever same-sex desire and attraction they may have acted on are lost, but for the fragments of Sappho and other occasional references classicists may unearth.

For some people, coming out as bisexual may indeed pose different and significantly harder challenges than coming out as gay or lesbian. In general, humans seem to feel a cognitive need or desire for certainty, and they don't always do as well with ambiguity or multiplicity as they may think they do. Of course, for a bisexual person their identity is indeed very stable — or at least, as stable as identity is for their homosexual or heterosexual peers: they are attracted (sexually, romantically, or both) to men and women (and sometimes they do not view themselves or other people through this binary). Their domestic choices (such as whether to pair-bond in a monogamous relationship) are, from their perspective, not contingent on their bisexual orientation. So, for a man to come out as bisexual may make him seem suspect to the gay men with whom he interacts and to whom he might be attracted, as gay men may assume that it is only a "matter of time" until he either comes out as gay or returns to a heterosexual identity. They may be concerned that the bisexual man is trying to hold on to some degree of heterosexual privilege or may not be a person with whom it is wise to get involved, given that his orientation may lead him to want to "cross back" to women. Of course, any of these conditions *can* occur with bisexual men, but there is no compelling reason to assume that bisexual men are by definition less self-aware, morally and politically. While Diamond's concept of sexual fluidity may explain why lesbians tend to be more accepting of bisexual-identified women, the same sets of assumptions and concerns about whether a relationship with a bisexual woman has the chance of stability may obtain. Again, there are no data to suggest the likelihood of these kind of "retreats" into heterosexuality on the part of bisexual men or women, but that does not necessarily prove persuasive for those people whose sexual orientation is **monosexual** (i.e., directed at either members of the same sex or members of the "opposite" sex — in the binary system most people still use psychologically and socially). Because more recent studies suggest that members of the millennial generation (and beyond) are more likely to identify as bisexual than did previous ones, and to claim this identity as their stable one (insofar as any sexual identity can be said to be stable over the course of a lifetime), this narrative of coming out as bisexual as a "stage" on the way to an "authentic" homosexuality no longer is as pervasive it once was, and bisexual identity is less likely to be viewed as a temporary way station (https:www.google.com/search?q=mil lennials+and+bisexuality&oq=millennials+and+bisexuality&aqs=chrome.. 69i57.3806jOj4&sourceid=chrome&ie=UTF-8).

## ASEXUALITY: AN EMERGING IDENTITY

To say that asexuality is an emerging identity is not to suggest that it has suddenly been "invented" as a way of desiring (or not desiring) erotic connections with other people; it is more accurate to say that asexuality has emerged as a shared naming of both a spectrum of experiences involving sex and sexuality and a shared set of political and activist concerns and activities. Just as same-sex desire and behavior surely existed before anyone gave name to them as a stable way of being, so the absence of sexual desire and accompanying myriad ways of expressing and behaving that way of being have existed.

Nonetheless, the growing use of "**ace**" (the umbrella term for asexuality and its related sexual identities, such as aromantic and so forth) has resulted in some confusion on the part of many people who are not asexual; there is a relative paucity of research about people who identify as asexual. Some of the confusion may be terminological: if you have ever taken a biology class, you no doubt studied living species that reproduce asexually (i.e., without need of sexual contact with another member of the same species), and that is a perfectly accurate use of the word. The result, though, is that when the term is applied to human sexual identity, some people, quite understandably, think claiming asexuality is claiming either a different kind of body from humans who reproduce sexually or that the identity is centrally about reproduction, neither of which is the case.

Anthony Bogaert estimates that approximately 1 percent of the population identify as asexual; this estimate seems to be agreed on by some of the activists in the field, who find Bogaert's explanation of this number persuasive. It may be that, as asexuality as something other than a "default" or "defective" identity becomes more understood and represented, we will see an increase in people claiming that identity. Julie Sondra Decker's *The Invisible Orientation: An Introduction to Asexuality* serves both as an informational and a self-help/other-help book. She points to characters in media such as Sheldon Cooper on the very popular CBS situation comedy *The Big Bang Theory*, whose asexuality began as a kind of variation of a "nerd" or "geek" joke. (In recent seasons, however, Sheldon has moved from asexuality to a heterosexual identification, if one that still has a kind of nonnormativity to it.)

Asexuality, in the purest sense of the word and as used in discussing orientation and identity, refers to an absence of sexual desire in an individual. Only people who claim that their sexual identity is asexual can determine how they would measure or detect a complete absence of desire. Some people would go so far as to say it requires *never* having had the experience of wanting to have sex with someone else. Again, such a determination as *never* can be asserted only retrospectively and subjectively. This definition, by the way, does not mean that asexual people don't engage or have never engaged in sexual behaviors with other people: some have in the past and some continue to, often as a way of pleasing a partner with whom they share a romantic or other kind of relationship.

Given social assumptions and expectations, claiming and sharing an identity as an asexual person can be challenging indeed. It is true that it may be more difficult to find other asexual people, since there has, up to now, been no or very few specially designated spaces or cultural activities through which asexual people can find each other. Perhaps the most accessible and successful has been and continues to be the online community space called **AVEN** (Asexuality Visibility and Education Network, www.asexuality.org), established by David Jay, perhaps the most recognized asexual activist in the United States. The site provides both information for those people who identify as asexual or for "sexuals" who wish to know more about the lives of asexual people.

There is considerable stigma toward people who identify and come out as asexual. Some view and talk about asexuality in terms of illness, just as homosexuality and bisexuality have been discussed at various times in history (and, in some places, continue to be discussed as such); some deny the existence of asexuality as a legitimate and authentic identity category, often implying various forms of denial on the part of people who identify as asexual. Bogaert indicates that some people view asexuality more negatively than LGB sexuality, as such people characterize asexual people as "less than human." As is true of homosexuality, some people insist there must be medical, biological, or genetic explanations for asexuality: if this is the case, there has not yet been evidence to indicate that this is so and what the "cause" is. Others look to psychological causation, suggesting that there must have been some childhood sexual violation, perhaps repressed, that has led to denial of sexual feeling. There is no evidence to support this claim, either. Still others suggest that asexuality is a passing phase on the way to becoming sexual: while this may be true for some individuals, it is unlikely to explain all people who claim "ace" identity.

Bogaert, somewhat tongue-in-cheek, but at the same time genuinely respectful of the lives, experiences, and values of people who identify as asexual, offers his own explanation: "just because." By this he means that, just as it may not matter *why* some people are heterosexual, some are homosexual, some are bisexual, and so forth, we would do well to accord people who claim asexuality as their own sexual identity the same degree of respect and dignity. I couldn't agree more with him, and I think we do well to follow Decker's advice that sexuals should enter into conversations with asexuals about their sexuality with the same degree of openness, affirmation, and acceptance that they would want in return.

Decker offers the following statements as a kind of what she calls "Asexuality 101."

1. Asexuality is a sexual orientation.
2. Asexuality is a mature state.
3. Asexuality is a description.
4. Asexuality is a healthy state.
5. Asexuality is a reasonable possibility.

Decker is asking us to take (at least hypothetically) each of the statements as true about asexuality: hence, the *is* is equivalent to the equal symbol (=) in an equation. So "Asexuality 101" begins by asserting the "is-ness" of asexuality as a sexual orientation. What this statement is putting forward is that there is no real gray area in terms of whether asexuality exists as a sexual orientation in the way that other sexual orientations exist. Probably few people reading this far in this book would argue that heterosexuality, homosexuality, and bisexuality *aren't* sexual orientations. Decker asserts the same for her (and others') asexuality: it is as much a sexual orientation (recall that the word *orientation* means where we are in the world and how we direct ourselves or find ourselves directed toward other phenomena in the world) as any other. Consider the four other axioms similarly: What does each mean and what is at stake in the assertion of each?

## ISSUES FOR INVESTIGATION

### 1. What Is/Are Bisexuality/ies?
Ritch C. Savin-Williams, in his 2005 book, *The New Gay Teenager*, summarizes "types of bisexuality," as presented and imagined, in a chart. His chart is not intended to be either definitive or scientifically valid, but it is useful in capturing how many people account for, explain, or regard bisexuality. Look at the chart and then discuss each of the types with your classmates.

**Types of Bisexuality**

| Type | Definition |
|------|------------|
| **Situational** | Heterosexuals engage in same-sex behavior given extenuating restrictive circumstances (e.g., prison). |
| **Chic** | Heterosexuals engage in same-sex behavior for social acceptance (e.g., swingers' group). |
| **Transitional** | Individuals use bisexuality as a bridge to change from one identity to another. |
| **Historic** | Sexual histories include behaviors or fantasies opposite to current identification. |
| **Sequential** | Consecutive relationships with different genders over time so that at any one point individuals are involved with only one gender. |
| **Concurrent** | Individuals maintain relationships with both genders at the same time. |
| **Experimental** | Individuals try out relationships with more than one gender as a test for which gender most appeals to them. |
| **Technical** | Individuals have sex with both genders but prefer to be lesbian or gay. |
| **Cop-out** | Individuals want the "best of both worlds" without having to commit themselves to a particular partner or lifestyle. (Savin-Williams 2005, 171) |

What kinds of attitudes or biases does each type display? Do some seem more neutral in their descriptive language than others? What attitudes toward sexuality, queer sexuality, and personhood undergird each? Do you know people who identify as bisexual (you might be such an individual yourself)? If so, does one or more of these types seem to you to characterize how they express or enact their bisexual identity? To what degree does such a chart help us think about our assumptions about sexual identity? Are there ways in which the chart interferes with or does negative work in regard to bisexuality? If you think so, try to explain why. How might you revise Savin-Williams's typology to be more positive and to represent people you may know who identify as bisexual?

Savin-Williams continues to explore the nuances of the sexual identities of young adults, particularly men, in his recent book, *Mostly Straight: Sexual Fluidity among Men*, in which he follows the experiences of and gives voice to a number of individuals who would find even *bisexual* too constraining a term to capture their own sense of openness to the possibilities of nonheteronormative sex.

## 2. Applying Eriksons's Stage Model of Identity to Queer Life

Can you think of other ways of applying Erikson's stage model to the experiences of the lives of queer people you know (or to your perceptions of them)? If you know older queer people, do integration and role confusion still seem important, ongoing parts of their own sense of self? In what ways? Have you talked with older queer folk about their sense of intimacy and/or isolation? Might the social changes of the past several years, in which we have seen the federal legalization of queer marriage and greater visibility of and participation in the raising of children by same-sex couples or extended "queer" families, change the developmental pathways of identity for queer people? This is not to suggest that identity development for queer people will simply become the same in its specificities as it is for nonqueer people (and all such pathways have individual components for each person), but the two paths may begin to share more common features than they might have in the past.

SUGGESTIONS FOR FURTHER READING AND VIEWING

*Big Eden.* Directed by Thomas Bezucha. Chaiken Films, 2000.

*Desert Hearts.* Directed by Donna Deitch. Samuel Goldwyn, 1986.

Kaufman, Gershen, and Lev Raphael. *Coming Out of Shame: Transforming Gay and Lesbian Lives.* New York: Doubleday, 1996.

*Moonlight*. Directed by Barry Jenkins. A24, 2016.

Ochs, Robyn, and Sarah Rowley, eds. *Getting Bi: Voices of Bisexuals around the World*. 2nd ed. Boston: Bisexual Resource Center, 2009.

Signorile, Michelangelo. *Outing Yourself: How to Come Out as Lesbian or Gay to Your Family, Friends, and Coworkers*. New York: Random House, 1995.

*Word Is Out: Stories of Some of Our Lives*. Directed by Nancy Adair et al. New Yorker Films, 1977.

# CHAPTER 4

# QUEERING BODIES
## Transgender and Intersex Lives

A trans woman identified as Diane suggests the following: "One of the things that strikes me is this sense of being suspect. I think about what it means to be a *body* that's suspect" (quoted in Shultz 123). While in some ways it might seem that the word *body* should be one of the easiest and most obvious words to define, it actually has a complex and layered set of possible meanings. In a sense, all queer people live in "queer bodies," in physical entities that typically enact sexualities and sexual behaviors that stand outside the norms of heterosexual assumptions and expectations. For trans people, it is gender, rather than sexuality (or sexual desire), that is most queered.

So what is a **body**? At the simplest, most everyday level, most people would probably respond with what might be called a "materialist" definition, one grounded in the physical substance of the term: the physiological container for life and existence, including its actual components, such as water, protein, calcium, flesh, and so forth. So far, so good. But what, then, if someone were to ask if prosthetic devices that had been implanted on, grafted to, or added and removed from this combination of organic materials should be considered as part of the body, such as the increasingly sophisticated prostheses developed for amputees. Consider what is at stake in such an answer: What do different responses privilege as inherent in different concepts of body?

Another way of getting at the complexity of what may seem like such a simple term would be to try to answer the question, "What must a body have in order to qualify as a *body*, as we understand human bodies?" Again, most people probably begin with lists of "parts" (including life-sustaining organs): torso, head, arms, legs, eyes, ears, fingers, toes, heart, lungs, brain, and so forth. Indeed, there are philosophers and bioethicists who do engage in passionate and sustained arguments about the meaning of *human body* that are based on a kind of inventory of bodily parts. If a person is born

Henderson, Bruce, *Queer Studies: Beyond Binaries*
dx.doi.org/10.17312/harringtonparkpress/2019.09.qsbb.004
© 2019 by Harrington Park Press

with one arm or one leg rather than two, do they still have a *body* that possesses integrity (wholeness sufficient to warrant considering them human)? What if they lose (an awkward verb for this situation) some of their limbs, as in the example of the military veteran? Does the fact that they at one time had the "complete" body earn them a "pass" in this regard?

What becomes trickier is the value placed on the presence and functionality of these parts. The ethicist Peter Singer, for example, has raised considerable wrath among disability activists by suggesting that some humans with particularly low intellectual capabilities (as determined by traditional if contested tools of measuring IQs) should have fewer legal and deserve fewer "natural" rights than some nonhuman primates. For Singer, a human body (and life) has sufficient value to be preserved only if it meets particular intellectual criteria: he advocates legalization of ending the lives of certain intellectually disabled children if their parents wish it (up to a certain age).

What Singer raises is another layer of complication in defining a *body*: Is the materialist definition sufficient to define a *body* and its worth? Some, like Singer, might argue that it is not, that the body is not simply the sum total of the chemicals and organic materials, but involves something philosophers and neuroscientists continue to struggle over: the relationship of the body and the mind. Some philosophers and neuroscientists argue that there is a gap between *brain* (the organ with its many parts) and *mind* (the intellectual and affective actions that may or may not be restricted to the brain or to the physical body itself).

So the body, even at its most empirically observable, is not a simple concept. It becomes even more complicated when the discussion expands to consider all the different ways bodies get discussed and valued. Judith Butler, for example, is a literary and queer theorist whose theorizing of the body as a cultural and philosophical concept has had considerable influence in queer studies. Butler argues that it is necessary to think of the body as not simply its material components, but as a site (or meaningful intellectual and social construction) of always changing meanings. Thus, as she argues in books such as *Gender Trouble* and *Bodies That Matter*, while certain material elements are of course present in the bodies humans inhabit, how they are named, valued, and made meaningful is a product of the various "performances," by which she means conscious and — probably more important — unconscious "scripts" humans enact in terms of such dimensions as gender, sex, and sexuality. For Butler there is no essential "normal" body, but a series of always changing, often socially reinforced or socially oppressed ways of "performing" in bodies.

The philosopher Sara Ahmed has offered some particularly useful ways of bringing together both the grounded lived experiences of queer people and the theorizing about the social and political constructions of body represented by Butler in what Ahmed calls "queer phenomenology." **Phenomenology** is the branch of philosophy that is concerned with how consciousness relates to lived experience and to the world in which minds exist. One of its central interests is *intentionality* (how consciousness reaches out toward objects and experiences), and, depending on which branch of this field one adheres to, it is less concerned with establishing a commonly shared sense of reality as a final, determinable "truth," and more interested in both individual and shared perceptions and experiences. Its founding principle is something called *bracketing* — the action of putting aside all prior assumptions to understand how consciousness of the world operates. Ahmed's work focuses on what there is about queer conscious-ness and perspective that may provide valuable ways of understanding how people orient themselves to experience and to their worlds: how queer lives are lived — and, hence, how queer bodies experience the world.

What might a queer phenomenology suggest? Another way of asking the question might be: What does a queer body do when it enters a space that is or is not necessarily marked as queer? The body may decide to ignore its sense of self as queer for the purposes of the particular world in which it finds itself at a specific moment, or it may find its focus on some elements of a place being heightened on the basis of what such philosophers might call the "queer horizon," which the queer subject (or experiencing person) brings to any encounter.

Consider classroom spaces as an example. Over the course of teaching queer studies classes for a number of semesters, I have noticed some repeated patterns. During the first week the students who most often sit near the front, almost to the point of forming a bit of a *U* shape, are women whom I "read" as possibly queer in their self-presentation (admittedly on the basis of my own experiences and internalization of social images of queerness). Some of these individuals may eventually identify or self-present as transgender or nonbinary within the space of the class. The men (insofar as they identify as such) in the class whom I read as gay may sit in the second row or closer to the back, but still in a way that makes them "available" to the class as a whole, or near the other women in the class. Women who do not read as queer in conventional or stereotypically visual ways (and who often do not identify as queer or who disclose that they do not) tend to sit in the middle of the room — close enough to participate but, usually, far enough away not to seem to "take space," almost as if they are giving the most prominent "ori-entation" in the room to the queer-identified. The non-queer-identified men in the room sit either in the back or among the non-queer women. It might be useful for me to make this observation at some point in the class, to see if there is any shared consciousness of this use of space and to what degree any self-regulating is at work.

Whereas queer bodies may, at least in the past, have oriented themselves in heterogeneous and hetero-dominated spaces by mixing with other students without thought to their own queer bodies or identities, in my queer studies classes the queer and non-queer students seem to orient themselves in different ways. In my own long-ago college days, as a first-year undergraduate, I enrolled in an upper-level course in women in American literature. I recall walking in the first day to find myself one of two men in the room. Though I might typically have sat in one of the first two rows, I found myself placing my body two-thirds of the way back, as if I knew I needed to orient my body in a less prominent way. The teacher called me over at the end of class and encouraged me to stay in the class (perhaps she could read my own body disorientation), and I did, though always sitting in the back half of the classroom.

Now imagine different kinds of spaces, some that may be marked as queer, some definitely marked as not queer, and some that seem ambiguous or fluid. How do you approach these spaces in bodily terms? In mental terms? How conscious is your mind of what your body is doing? Do you have a sense of "attraction" (or lack of same) in these spaces? For some students, the attraction may be felt when entering a queer social space, such as a bar, or a co-curricular space, such as an LGBTQ+ support or discussion group. If you do not identify as queer, can you recall the physical, emotional, intellectual senses you had when entering this kind of space?

Notice that it has been impossible to try to exclude social, political, or cultural considerations from the phenomenological analysis, and more recent scholars, such as Ahmed, have worked to integrate such concerns into their philosophical work. A queer studies classroom is still a space that is marked differently in some ways from other kinds of classrooms — this is almost certainly true of other courses in which identity is the focus of study, such as critical race theory, feminist studies, and disability studies, to name a few. It is not the physical classroom itself that is marked differently as an objectively described space but how the people using it for a queer activity make it into something different — and perceive it as such.

So bodies are not simply collections of material, nor are they only entities that move through the world in consciousness. Bodies are also social, political, and cultural subjects and objects: this is so powerful a notion that the term *the body politic*, the idea that nation is a kind of body, can be traced back to the Renaissance. It follows that all bodies are "political" — whether willingly or not, they are forced into having political meaning and power (or lack thereof) in the work of nations and states. This is true both about individual bodies and about groups of people viewed as a kind of "corporate" body: they live within individual and shared consciousness, but are also surveilled by and controlled by external forces. The remainder of this chapter focuses on two categories (neither of which is uniform even within itself) of queer bodies, bodies whose materiality, phenomenology, and social/political/cultural dimensions have been central, sometimes contested, and continually rewritten, remade, and reviewed: transgender and intersex bodies and lives.

## TRANS* BODIES: SEX, GENDER, EXPRESSION, SEXUALITY

The earliest term of those under the trans* umbrella to be used was *transvestite*, which literally means "cross-dresser," and it has been used simply descriptively to indicate a person whose attire, either temporarily or habitually, was that of what was considered appropriate to the "opposite" sex. The habitual transvestite became a category of pathology in the development of modern psychoanalytic theory, such as Freudian readings of transvestism as a sexual fetish, which often carried a diagnosis of mental disorder with them. This was followed by the policing of socially gendered roles, such as laws that required women to wear three items of "female clothing" or risk arrest, which was true in the early part of the twentieth century. There was, until research findings were made accessible to the public, a fairly widespread assumption that cross-dressers were also homosexual, and, hence, in a homophobic place and time, to be such a person was to be doubly dis-eased. Sociologists and psychologists have found that the majority of men who cross-dressed in European and American societies in the twentieth century were actually heterosexually identified. Women (or those assigned as female at birth) cross-dressed for myriad reasons, ranging from safety issues (when having to travel or work in places where their female identity might have put them at risk) to pleasure, adventure, and play: for some women, being able to pass as men permitted them to conduct both public and private lives with less scrutiny — if, say, they were living with a more traditionally feminine-appearing woman. Nonetheless, girls in the past century in the United States and the United Kingdom were given more latitude (especially in preadolescent years) to wear boys' clothes: girls who wore boys' clothes often were simply considered tomboys, and there was a conventional belief that boys' clothes were better suited for certain kinds of play and other activities in which girls were engaged, such as athletics. Such latitude ended with adulthood and especially with regard to women who were viewed sexually nonnormative in their desires. During the Victorian and Edwardian eras, adult women who dressed in formal male attire were often assumed to be pursuing other women (usually more traditionally feminine in attire and self-presentation) sexually and romantically: such women were sometimes called *toms*, and they were often castigated and even arrested for such behavior. Some of the toms had successful stage careers as male impersonators: Sarah Walters's novel *Tipping the Velvet* gives rich insights into this cultural moment.

The male transvestite was more consistently considered aberrant and socially unacceptable, except in some kinds of comic celebrations and holidays, such as Halloween and college frat parties where the contrast between the hypermasculine body and the delicacy or hyperfemininity of the lacy lingerie or the formal ballgown was part of the humor. If the football player wore a dress and wig at the end-of-year night of skits, it showed he was comfortable in his masculinity and, in more ways than one, a good sport. If he wore that outfit to go shopping the next day, the social order was upset and he was, as Diane put it at the beginning of this chapter, "a body that's suspect" — and, hence, a suspect person.

Before leaving this now primarily outmoded term, it is important to acknowledge that a distinction is typically made between the term *transvestite*, which is now viewed as outmoded and has more generally been replaced by *cross-dresser*, and a pair of terms that do continue to have ongoing usage: **drag queen** and **drag king**. In most common usage, each refers to a performer or entertainer whose art involves wearing the clothes and otherwise taking on, through voice, gesture, movement, and attitude, characteristics of the "other" sex, often in exaggerated form. The most famous current drag artist is probably RuPaul (birth name: RuPaul Andre Charles), whose television series *RuPaul's Drag Race* is popular across diverse audiences. RuPaul is an artistic (and some would say cultural) invention, based on the extreme hairstyles and larger-than-life outfits from haute couture (high fashion), and the man who performs her acknowledges he is a man — though he passes in the moments of performance, he does not dress as a woman to try to pass as a woman in his offstage life. The same is true with the more recently emerging popular performers who call themselves drag kings, women who not only wear men's clothes, but often choose to wear men's clothes that exaggerate codes of masculinity, as well as to fashion their hair and facial and bodily appearance to accentuate masculinity (such as adding prosthetic facial hair, choosing clothes that deemphasize the kinds of bodily shapes more associated with femininity). Lea DeLaria, an actor and comedian, is notable for her performances of what Jack Halberstam (who has also written earlier works under other names, including J. Halberstam) calls "female masculinity." DeLaria does not try to pass as a man, but she does enact traditional physical and other kinds of masculinity in her roles as a butch lesbian. Part of the enjoyment for both performer and audience in drag performances is the mutual acknowledgment of the "both-and." All "believe" in the cross-gender performance when it is done well, at the same time that they know that the performer is male or female. The drag artist is using cross-dressing as a painter might use oils or a musician sound; the cross-dresser tends to have nonaesthetic reasons for choosing gender-nonconforming clothing.

This leads to a second term that also has fallen out of common usage: *transsexual*. Like *transvestite*, *transsexual* was used to describe something physical, with the desired outcome to be the ability to pass as a member of a sex or gender different from the one assigned at birth. Beyond that, the terms map out different aspirations and beliefs about self. Cross-dressers do not necessarily desire to become a sex different from the one they currently occupy: even if they pass, they retain the sense that they are the sex they were "born into." Transsexual individuals more typically believed that they had been born into the wrong body—that there was a mismatch between their anatomy and their gender identity. The term *transsexual* is less frequently used today because it often seems to restrict the transition to a purely physical set of changes. The term *transgender* is the term most frequently used, both by those who claim a trans identity and by people who study them. The abbreviations AMAB (assigned male at birth) and AFAB (assigned female at birth) are often used to map out the status of having been categorized as male or female when born and gender experienced as an ongoing, presumably permanent state of self and identity.

## MEDICAL, SURGICAL, AND MENTAL HEALTH INTERVENTIONS FOR TRANS PEOPLE

Medical treatments and surgeries for trans people take many different forms, depending on the status and desires of the patient. Much depends on what they wish such surgery or other medical treatments, such as hormonal therapies, to accomplish, as well as other individual issues such as the general state of health, physical and psychological, of the person, financial resources, and plans for future life. ***Standards of Care for the Health of Transsexual, Transgender, and Gender Nonconforming People (SOC)*** is a document published by the World Professional Association for Transgender Health, an advocacy and professional group, that outlines recommended (but not legally or necessarily ethically required) protocols for doctors, health providers, and clients involved in medical and surgical treatment of individuals who wish to transition from one sexual identity to another. Some transgender health clinics have established and use their own protocols, so the *SOC* (as it is frequently referred to) is highly recommended and widely used but not absolutely required for what is considered ethical practices. This document was originally referred to as the *Benjamin Standards of Care*, named after the doctor Harry Benjamin, who was a pioneer in such surgeries and who developed the earliest set of recommendations. The most recent version (2011) of the *SOC* is available online at https://www.wpath.org/publications/soc.

Here are some of the most important elements of it. First, it is concerned with the *health* of individuals who fit into one of the three groups named in the title (transsexual, transgender, and gender noncomforming): this is the single most important characteristic of such a set of guidelines. The Hippocratic Oath, taken by all doctors, begins, "First, do no harm," a reminder to the health provider that the primary obligation is to the individual seeking assistance, not to society as a whole or to political or religious groups that may or may not support the lives of queer people as "healthy" or otherwise positively contributing to the larger social body—and perhaps not even to the parents, if the individual is a child or adolescent.

While the document does make reference to other organizations' taxonomies of illness or pathology, the *SOC* is not itself transphobic in its view of the identities and experiences of trans people. It is *not* arguing that trans (or nonconforming) feelings or behaviors are in and of themselves illnesses; rather, it is making the important point that such dysphoria, literally "dysfunctional or negative feelings," in this case about their gender, may result in psychiatric or psychological disorders if not treated in ways that are respectful and address the individual's experience and desires. It is not the trans experience itself that is "sick"; rather, it is the social and medical refusal to assist the individual who experiences a disconnect or mismatch between anatomy and inner experience of sex or gender that causes whatever pathologies (such as depression or anxiety) that are present. Hence, the *SOC* gives as much weight to mental care and social support as it does to medical and surgical practices. The *SOC* also distinguishes between different life stages and different variations of gender dysphoria, mapping out different treatment and interventional pathways that are dependent on the specific status and history of the individual seeking intervention.

### Sex versus Gender or Sex = Gender: Some Problems

What, of course, complicates all this is a more recent tendency to conflate the terms *sex* and *gender*. In her book *When Sex Became Gender*, the feminist scholar Shira Tarrant traces the history of feminist theory and scholarship from the middle of the twentieth century to the beginnings and development of what is called second-wave feminism (the mid-1960s to the 1990s). Tarrant argues that feminist scholarship was not stagnant during this period, as some historians have argued, but, rather, important work on gender studies—including the foregrounding of *gender* as a term beyond grammar—was being done, often in some of the traditional academic disciplines. She points in particularly helpful ways to the work of women like the anthropologist Margaret Mead, who argued, with controversial responses, that sex roles emerged and developed much more from social conditions and needs than from biological determinism, grounding her findings in her work in Pacific Island cultures such as Samoa.

For Mead and others, *gender*, then, was to be kept distinct from *sex*, the latter being the domain of the natural sciences, such as biology and chemistry, and their applications in medicine. Gender was viewed as primarily socially constructed, a nonnatural category of experience and social arrangements, changing over time and variable from one culture to another. While many scholars agreed that there are certain immutable connections between sex and gender that are probably not simply attributable to social constructions, there was a dominant assumption that there was a biological sexual binary of male and female. Genetic testing confirmed some of this binary thinking regarding the sexual body: as you were no doubt taught, biological men have XY chromosomes and biological women have XX chromosomes — and, when a genetic record showed something beyond this binary, rather than problematizing the either-or thinking of the binary, medical personnel preferred to try to fix the anomaly as far as surgeries and hormones could "turn" such individuals into men or women, though it is as yet impossible to change the sex chromosomes themselves.

The sex-gender distinction has become complex within the past few decades, as biologists and other scientists have indeed begun to question the neatness of the genetic XX-XY binary and the other assumptions about bodies that would seem to follow from it. Such scholars as the biologist Anne Fausto-Sterling and the psychologist Cordelia Fine began to argue that claims about "male brains" and "female brains" were greatly overstated and in many instances specious, and that the data gathered were compromised by methodological errors. The same has been true with some of the search for "gay genes" and "gay brains," the most influential instance of the latter being carried out in postmortem analyses of the brains of men who died from HIV, which created a set of confounding variables that call into question the conclusions, such as that there were measurable differences between the brains of gay and nongay men. Fausto-Sterling's book *Myths of Gender* critiques studies that argue for distinct neurological differences between male and female brains. Her more recent book, *Sexing the Body*, argues that the XX-XY binary does not begin to capture "biological exuberance," to use the biologist Bruce Bagemihl's phrase about homosexuality and diversity in the animal kingdom, of human sexuality; Fausto-Sterling suggests that we would do better to consider at least five categories of sex for humans (including distinct categories for individuals usually clustered together as intersex or anomalous). Thus, scholars such as Fausto-Sterling and Fine have built a foundation for deconstructing even the sex (biology)–gender (society) binary, suggesting that the traditional male-female distinction is also a social construction.

### Nonconforming People: Separate Category?

The third set of people whose health the *SOC* is meant to address is **gender-nonconforming** people, which includes people whose gender identity as well as social presentation and behavior may be viewed as contiguous to the groups covered by other trans words. These are people who may experience and name themselves as either males or females but whose ways of expressing gender and participating in social or cultural activities somehow mark them as "different from" (**nonconforming** to) the stereotypical persons of the sex whose bodies theirs match or the gender they were assigned at birth.

This set of gender-nonconforming people covers a wide spectrum of identities and attitudes toward their own sex, gender, and sexuality and the expectations society places on them. Some of them may identify as genderqueer (i.e., moving along a spectrum of masculinity and femininity as defined by the society or culture in which they live), some as gay, lesbian, or bisexual (either attracted to their own sex or gender or attracted to multiple sexes and genders), and some as heterosexual. Some gender-nonconforming people do not identify with either category of the gender binary; this identification can confound the categories (such as gay, lesbian, bisexual, or straight) we typically associate with the gender of their object of sexual or romantic desire.

The spectrum of individuals who may be viewed (or view themselves) as gender nonconforming is broad, and, of course, dependent on whatever is considered "gender conforming" in any period. In the 1980s and 1990s, when queer theory began to emerge, both to challenge and to interrogate socially dominant views of sexuality and gender, psychiatrists, such as Richard Green and others, published studies that, on the one hand, seemed to advocate for acceptance of gay people (and the studies focused almost exclusively on males), but, on the other hand, reinforced negative valuing of the "sissy" or "effeminate" boy (terms less in use today). In a sense, while such therapists and scholars seemed to be arguing for acceptance of gay males, they simultaneously advocated for kinds of psychotherapeutic treatments or interventions that might reduce the gender-nonconforming behavior of such boys. More research continues to be done, but longitudinal studies suggest that the most likely outcome for gender-nonconforming boys is growing into gay male adults. Green and others suggested, sometimes overtly, sometimes less so, that, if there were to be homosexual people, it would be better (in terms of individual happiness and social order), if such people were more gender conforming.

The literary scholar, teacher, and queer rights activist Eve Kosofsky Sedgwick wrote a smart, impassioned, accessible, and very forward-thinking essay in 1991, with the simple but powerful title "How to Bring Your Kids Up Gay," in which she took on the writings of such psychiatrists as Green. She argues that the subtext of such writers as Green is a desire for erasure of the visibly gay (and, in her use of the term at the time, by extension lesbian, bisexual, and other sexually or gender "suspect") bodies. She writes about the pervasiveness of what she terms *effeminiphobia* and calls for a rethinking of what is "natural" in the gender-conforming if nonetheless gay bodies Green and others advocate for. Again, note that sexuality and gender identity are coupled in intersectional ways in the language and ideas promulgated by some psychiatrists of the time. While Sedgwick is by no means conflating sexuality and gender, she is pointing out how society tends to impose policing and implicit and explicit forms of surveillance and desire to control both in a broad, somewhat amorphous category of identity and experience that it views as nonnormative.

Indeed, much more recent research, led by Colt Keo-Meier and others, provides facts and suggestions for working on "gender diversity and transgender identity in children" ("Fact Sheet: Gender Diversity and Transgender Identity in Children," www.apadivisions.org/division-44/resources/ advocacy/ transgender-children.pdf). This document clarifies just how myriad such variations may be, from children who describe themselves as "half" boy and "half" girl (sometimes more specifically "a boy on the bottom, and a girl on the top," for example) to those who consistently describe their gender identity as different from their bodily anatomy, to others whose "gender diversity" lessens or disappears over time. Keo-Meier and his coauthors suggest that some of the disappearance of gender diversity (a term they prefer to gender dysphoria) may be accounted for by peers or by a shift from a child's focus on gender identity and expression to a pubertal or postpubertal focus on sexual orientation. As Green argued, some of these gender-diverse children do indeed become self-identified LGB adults. And, contrary to Green's reports, many gender-diverse children *persist* (the authors of the study use this term descriptively, not judgmentally) in their gender diversity: such children typically identify as transgender through adolescence and into adulthood.

Keo-Meier and the coauthors of the research acknowledge that it is too early in the research on the lives of trans people to draw conclusions that firmly establish accepted "facts" or point to a consistent set of particular practices. Like the authors of the *SOC*, they identify a similar set of areas for providing positive health care for such children (and for the adolescents and adults they eventually become). Like others, they do not advocate for any kind of medical (i.e., hormonal or endocrinological) treatments or interventions until a child is nearing puberty — to do so is to be premature. At that point, health providers, in consultation with the child and the child's parents, may begin, first, to administer hormonal therapies designed to block the onset of puberty, and then to add hormones that will provide the now-adolescent with more of the physiology and blood chemistry associated with the gender they affirm themselves to be.

The timing is recommended for both optimal physical and psychological benefits: just before or as puberty is beginning is when the body and the mind undergo the kinds of developments that such therapies can serve. To give pubertal blockers or such hormones as testosterone or estrogen earlier than this window of opportunity is premature for the developing body, as well as for the developing psychological sense of self. The available research points to some degree of reversibility of pubertal blockers: if an individual decides, at some point, that they wish to resume living in the gender they were assigned at birth, stopping the pubertal blockers will permit this, though it is not entirely clear whether there will be some lasting effects, such as a micropenis for a trans girl who has taken hormone blockers and decides to return to a male identity. Conclusions are still being drawn about the hormones that affect secondary sexual characteristics (such as the growth of breasts a trans girl may experience under the effects of estrogen or the growth of hair in places not traditionally seen on women, such as chest and face, in a trans boy), and doctors caution that the administration of some of these hormones may require surgical or other medical interventions if reversal to the previous gender is desired.

Perhaps the single most important recommendation Keo-Meier's document makes involves ways in which health providers, especially therapists and other psychological or psychiatric personnel, approach what they call "psychological interventions." They map out three principal approaches, some better for the overall health of the client (and gender and sexual health does have implications for other aspects of health). The least recommended, as you might imagine, is an approach that they call "actively discouraging" a child's expression of gender identity. This can include everything from the sometimes subtle (sometimes far from subtle) messages that parents, teachers, and others may send to the child that their expression of gender is wrong, to medical professionals' classification of their client's gender identity as pathological. A second approach is the "wait and see if these behaviors desist" approach, assuming the child will eventually adopt more traditional and appropriate gender identity and expressiveness. Some have called this the desistance model of approaching gender diversity. While not as harmful in all likelihood as the discouragement model, it still almost inevitably carries with it an unspoken sense of parental disapproval or disappointment and a silencing, implicitly or explicitly, of the child's need (and right) to express who they experience themselves to be.

The most preferred approach is what the authors call "gender affirmative," which in its simplest sense means responding positively to a child's declaration of and request to live in the gender they identify as theirs. Such affirmation does not necessarily preclude having age-appropriate conversations with a child about the kinds of challenges and resistance they may face among peers or in school, but it challenges parents and others to frame such conversations in ways that resist temptations to promote shame, disappointment, or, except when necessary to a child's physical safety, secrecy. What they advocate is open, empathic, and reflective listening, not a bad way to treat anyone at any time of life!

## TRANS LIVES: CHALLENGES AND ADVANCES

Trans people, as a set of individuals and communities who live among others in society, have gained greater visibility in recent years, thanks in part to their growing presence in mass media. The global coverage of the former Olympian Bruce Jenner's transition to Caitlyn Jenner is perhaps the most famous of such presence, not least because Jenner's narrative is woven into another family narrative that was lived in reality television for some years before Jenner decided to transition — the infamous Kardashian dynasty. Another reality television production that has chronicled the ongoing lived experience of a trans teen is the series *I Am Jazz*, which has followed the story of a Floridian trans girl, her family, and friends, showing both the generally happy and positive life of this young woman and the support provided by her parents, siblings, friends, and community. In the arts, the acceptance and success of the trans actress Laverne Cox, best known for her ongoing role on the Netflix series *Orange Is the New Black*, in which she plays a trans woman inmate, has been important, and Cox has become an articulate spokesperson for trans issues in society. Similarly, the cisgender actor Jeffrey Tambor has had great success as a late-in-life trans woman in the series *Transparent*, winning an Emmy for his performance; he has also stated that he now believes the role should have been played by a trans performer, opening up a dialogue about visibility and opportunity for trans people to find success in a business where gender and sexuality are highly visible. Complicating this is the ensuing development in which Tambor was fired from the series amid charges of sexual harassment by some of the trans women who appear on the series, a charge he has denied.

But it would be a disservice to the lives of trans people to simply suggest that we are now in a posttransgender era, in which transgender identity is simply accepted and has been "normalized." Indeed, a relatively new journal, *Transgender Studies Quarterly* (*TSQ*), called its first issue "Postposttranssexual: Key Concepts for a 21st Century Transgender Studies." The editors' (Susan Stryker and Paisley Currah's) use of the somewhat cumbersome word *postposttranssexual* seems deliberately designed to draw attention to a kind of discourse that acknowledges the cultural moment in which this journal emerges: we are, they seem to be saying, beyond *transsexual* in the sense in which all instances of disconnect between biological sex and gender identity and expression might have been viewed as a longing to change the body to match interior life and "solved" (note the problematic nature of such a term in this situation) by medical or surgical means (or both). Thus, in the strictest sense, *transsexual* no longer exists, and in their introduction to the issue, they acknowledge the work of the scholar Sandy Stone in earlier decades to devise a "posttranssexual manifesto."

Then they add another "post-" to the formation of their word, suggesting that Western society is now in a moment even beyond that of "posttransexuality" (so to speak), in which the relationship between biological sex and gender identity are once again put into dialogue and relationship with each other, and continually so. If a "posttransexual" era is one in which gender would seem to be a more dominant concept in self-definition than sex, the editors are saying, now may be a time when that hierarchy needs to be reexamined once again, not to return to previous essentialist concepts (i.e., assumptions of fixed categories, in this case binaries), but pushing boundaries further and opening up conversations even beyond such binary terms as *cisgender* (identifying with the gender assigned at birth) and *transgender* (not identifying with the gender assigned at birth), which, while they do some work toward dismantling biological categories, may reinforce the "either-or" thinking that continues to dominate Western philosophy.

To symbolize and illustrate this postposttranssexual era, Stryker and Currah discuss and place on the cover a photo of one of the more compelling figures in the trans movement: Chelsea Manning, the U.S. soldier who was imprisoned after a court-martial conviction for her participation in the WikiLeaks revelations led by Julian Assange. Manning has, throughout the whole drama of WikiLeaks, been a complex cultural figure, viewed by some as a traitor to the United States, viewed by others as a subversive hero, an individual who violated one of the most secretive and regimented public institutions, the intelligence branch of the U.S. military, for what Manning believed were the best interests of the country — and, hence, to some people a patriot. While in custody, Manning announced her identity as a trans woman, asked to be addressed and referred to as Chelsea, and requested medical treatment supporting this gender identity. For Stryker and Currah, Chelsea Manning is emblematic of how the cultural politics of transgender life are inextricable from the bodies politic of our nation (and our world) as a whole.

What are some of the challenges less famous trans people report about their lives? In a thoughtful and rich book published in 2015, *Trans/Portraits: Voices from Transgender Communities,* the scholar Jackson Wright Shultz profiles over thirty Americans, all of whom identify in some way as transgender; Shultz provides a very useful and detailed set of glossaries at the end of the book, in which he defines both terms of identity that cover the spectrum of possible ways of naming oneself within transgender (the word he uses throughout) identity and communities and medical terminology used in describing transition and ongoing treatment. As a preface he includes a time line of transgender history in the United States, stretching back before colonization by Europeans. What emerges from the interviews is a series of topics, which Shultz helpfully breaks into categories and to each of which he devotes a chapter.

Some of the most consistent and powerful issues that his participants identify include the following:

1. Lacking a vocabulary: many of those interviewed indicate that they initially did not have a name or a way of talking about their trans identity with others (or even to themselves). Note how difficult this has been for us within this chapter.

2. The difficulty of almost all aspects of transitioning, whether medical treatments (expensive, lengthy, sometimes painful), social and psychological facets, and interactions with family, including partners or spouses, children, parents, siblings, and friends.

3. Isolation and lack of social support: finding and sometimes having to make communities, a particular challenge for those individuals living outside urban areas, who may experience particular isolation.

4. Lack of acceptance, sometimes by those in mainstream sexual communities (i.e., non-queer society) and sometimes within various segments of queer society or societies. (I will discuss an example in more detail below.)

5. Violence, employment issues, and poverty: many of those interviewed report being subjected to physical and emotional violence, not always being believed and respected by law enforcement and the judicial system when they have had the courage to report attacks, and heightened policing of their bodies and actions within workplaces.

6. Complexities of navigating both intersectional identities (the challenges of being trans and nonwhite, for example, as well as other permutations of "living on the hyphen") and nonbinary identities (being expected to live *within* a category that fits comfortably into such pairs as man-woman, male-female, gay-straight, masculine-feminine, and so forth) when the lived reality for such individuals may well not fit into such categories.

The National Gay and Lesbian Task Force (NGLTF), working with the National Center for Transgender Equality, published the findings of its own most recent survey in 2011. In addition to some of the challenges Shultz found in his study, the NGLTF survey found some others, including:

1. Harassment and discrimination in education, particularly among K–12 students; such students also experienced poorer health outcomes in general, often directly attributable to harassment and discrimination.

2. Employment discrimination and economic insecurity: trans people reported twice as much unemployment as the U.S. population as a whole; a significant number (over 25 percent) reported loss of job owing to their trans or gender-nonconforming identity, and more than 15 percent reported that they had been forced to work in what the survey called "the underground economy" (often illegal and dangerous work, such as sex work and drug sales) in order to support themselves.

3. Discrimination in public accommodations: this included not only the perennial bathroom problem, but access to public transportation and to social services, as well.

4. Barriers to receiving updated ID documents: a majority reported difficulties in receiving identification documents (such as drivers' licenses) that accurately reflected their gender identity; in an era in which access to voting has been obstructed for many populations (such as racial minorities) because of the difficulty many have in obtaining identification cards in general, the problems reported by trans and gender-nonconforming people in this area may have the effect of disenfranchising them, another way in which they become "less than" citizens ("Injustice at Every Turn: A Report of the Nation Transgender Discrimination Survey, Executive Summary," www.thetaskforce.org/injustice-every-turn-report-national-transgender-discrimination-survey-executive-summary/).

One piece of good news the survey provided was that those participating in the survey did report a higher degree than might have been expected, given all the challenges, of what the report clustered under the heading "resilience" — the ability, despite the barriers, to insist on access to health care, to find employment even after being fired from a previous job for reasons related to gender identity, to pursue education, and to feel more comfortable at jobs after transitioning. It would of course be better and more just for trans people not to have to face any of these barriers, but it is important to note that they find ways to summon strength and not allow themselves simply to be cast aside as victims.

The LGB community is not immune to creating barriers for trans people. The Michigan Womyn's Music Festival (Michfest), held in a rural part of the lower peninsula of Michigan, began in 1976 and was organized by two women, Lisa Vogel and Mary Kindig, as a women-only event. It was held over the course of a week each summer and was originally designed to feature women musicians and other artists; attendance was restricted to women as well. As the years went by, the festival became known as a place for **womyn** (their preferred spelling) to enact cultural performances and activities that celebrated the experience of being female, and it was far more than a series of concerts.

Though there was always debate about the status of trans women at the festival, it was only in its later years that the issue came to a head. Trans men were generally accepted without much question; the majority of trans men, while they may present as male and may have had top surgery, which removes female breasts, in general have not had bottom surgery, and had grown up being viewed and treated by society as female — they had a common bond of "girlhood," in the language of the festival. Trans women became more of a dilemma and a source of discomfort for many of the organizers and attendees: in the eyes of many, such individuals were still men in some important ways — they had been born into boyhood, had grown up, presumably, with some of the privileges that being marked as male provides, and, in some cases, had not had the bottom surgery that would remove the male genitalia. As the festival was importantly a place to celebrate the female body and allowed for considerable nudity, a growing set of voices called for a ban on the admission of trans women to the festival.

Some trans women countered, asking if there were perhaps important distinctions to be drawn between those trans women who had had both hormonal and surgical treatments (specifically, removal of the penis and testicles) and those who remained pre-op. Those opposed to the presence of trans women at the festival responded by calling for a ban on all people who were not "womyn-born womyn" — which would include post-operative trans women. Yet a counterargument pointed to the potentially dangerous assertion that "girlhood" is itself a unitary experience and not one experienced through different cultural-, national-, and class-based lenses. The festival was last held in 2015; its founders decided to end the annual event at that point. In 2014 Vogel issued a statement apologizing for the decision, twenty years earlier, to ask a trans "womon" (in Vogel's language) to leave the festival, but she reaffirmed the validity of a "womyn-only" space as not inherently transphobic in its aims. Indeed, many participants noted that trans women had regularly attended the festival. By articulating a desire for a space open only to those born into biologically labeled female bodies, was the festival participating in the intent to exclude trans women or trans men? Much depends on the definition of terms, and the example is presented less to advocate for, let alone judge, the actions of any of those involved, but to illustrate the complexities of lives and situations faced by trans people and the rest of the population, including those who support their rights and goals. We will return to the Michigan Womyn's Music Festival in chapter 12.

The debates will continue to go on, and not simply within the circles of women's culture. The U.S. academic psychologist J. Michael Bailey, building on the work of the Canadian psychologist Ray Blanchard, wrote a book, *The Man Who Would Be Queen: The Science of Gender-Bending and Transsexualism*, in which he argues that transsexualism (the term he and Blanchard use) among "men-born men" is **autogynephilic** in its foundation: that is, it is based in erotic desires and emotions men have in imagining themselves to have female bodies. Many trans women who criticized and protested Bailey's work asserted that Bailey's thesis devalues and contradicts their own interior experience and, given his status as a cisgender male, is suspect in its value in describing the authentic experiences of trans women. This runs counter to their own determination that they are and have always been women in their truest selves; their anatomy is an obstacle in most cases to living what is to them an authentic life.

In her book *The Riddle of Gender: Science, Activism, and Transgender Rights,* Deborah Rudacille quotes the biologist Milton Diamond: "Nature loves variety. [Unfortunately,] society hates it" (xxiii). While this statement may itself fall victim to the kinds of binary thinking this book aims to respond to, its rhetoric is useful in challenging us all to consider to what degree our own perspectives — and our own inner, personal experiences, for that matter — are inextricably influenced by external, constructed forces. Rudacille advocates for respect for and among all people, regardless of sexual or gender identity, but especially among those different groups who have traditionally been marginalized and viewed by the majority as just variations on the "unnatural" or "abnormal."

# INTERSEX: BETWEEN/BOTH/BEYOND

There is yet another category of queer bodies to consider, those which in one or more ways trouble the "accepted" binaries of male and female from birth. These are bodies that present either atypical genitalia (or other secondary sexual characteristics) or what are sometimes called anomalous features — bodily or genetic elements that do not fit easily recognizable or consistent patterns found in the majority of human populations. Throughout the twentieth century, when presented with such babies, doctors tended to try to "repair" the anatomy and, in so doing, assign a gender to the child. Today, depending on the actual appearance of the baby and perhaps following physical development through early childhood, doctors might question the actual sex of the person and run more sophisticated batteries of tests, including genetic ones. With greater scientific sophistication, it is possible doctors may discover genetic anomalies that coincide with physical appearance, such as XXY chromosomes or other mutations, to use the scientific term.

Even today, though, it is important to say, doctors and, even more so, parents are eager to be able to announce a newborn's sex or gender: the announcement after the delivery — "It's a boy" or "It's a girl" — is probably second in priority only to the answer to the question "Is the baby alive and well?" Many accounts by the parents of such babies describe the confusion and fear they felt when a doctor or a team of doctors pulled them aside, as soon as the delivery was completed, to say they could not tell whether the child was a boy or a girl. The descriptions of such moments often feel as if they are out of a horror movie or an account of contagion and failure, as if either the parents believe they have created a monster or done something wrong or the doctors have been stymied in their charge to deliver a "healthy" and "normal" baby.

Knowledge of the existence and the experiences of intersex people has grown considerably over the past hundred years or so, in large part because there is much more development of what the philosopher Michel Foucault called "the clinical gaze." Of course, there can be no question that there have been intersex people since *Homo sapiens* emerged as a species and began reproducing, but because, until industrialization and the growth of cities that came with it, most births occurred at home, usually attended by midwives (or their cultural equivalent), and because infant mortality rates were much higher, such anomalous children may not have been exposed to such a normalizing examination as they have been in the last century. And because some anomalies are linked to health issues, such infants may have been neglected and died or, to put it grimly, killed or left exposed to the elements because of their seeming "monstrosity."

The term used most frequently in Western traditions until the twentieth century was *hermaphrodite* (sometimes qualified by scientists as *pseudoher-maphrodite* to indicate that such people were not literally equally male and female), which is derived from the Greek myth of the son of Hermes and Aphrodite (the former the messenger and trickster god, the latter the god-dess of love), whose name combines the male and female aspects of his parents and who, the story goes, fused bodily with the naiad (sea nymph) Salmacis, as a result of Salmacis's rape of him: thus was created a single being with the attributes of both a man and a woman. Salmacis, by the way, is traditionally seen as an aberration herself, vain and disobedient, turning away from the duties expected of her by the hunter goddess Artemis. So there is an association of the unnatural female with the weaker male, per-haps the only victim of rape by a female in classical traditions. The word also implies, if only indirectly, a kind of madness within such a creature, who is not of a single mind. Actual intersex people (called hermaphrodites in these traditions) were thrown into the sea (in Greece) or the Tiber River (in Rome) and drowned.

Another hermaphrodite character in the classical tradition is the blind seer Tiresias, who was transformed into a woman by Hera as punishment for killing sacred snakes, and then, some years later, turned back into a man, having served Hera as a sacred priestess in the meantime. As a result of his taking Zeus's side in an argument between the god and his wife, Hera, over who gets more pleasure from sex, Tiresias was blinded by Hera, but he was given the gift of prophecy (or "inner sight") by Zeus.

Tiresias is, then, a complex figure and may or may not be viewed as a hermaphrodite, depending on the definition of the term. He is never both man and woman at the same time in the classical tradition, though he car-ries memories and experiences of both. His blindness places him as dis-abled, but his prophetic ability puts him somewhat closer to the divine. His warnings to Oedipus go unheeded, so, though he has special powers, they do not produce any positive results.

The term *intersex* also has its own potential problems, as some people may assume that people who are identified as such are truly "between" the two sexes. It is nevertheless the term most familiar to the general public, used to identify a wide range of people whose bodies push the boundaries of sexual identification. While the possible anomalies are as variable as individual human bodies, some of the more typically identified ones include the following:

1. Underdeveloped genitals, of either one or both of the traditional sexes, whether internal, external, or both

2. Hormonal conditions, such as congenital adrenal hyperplasia (CAH), a genetically based condition affecting people who present primarily as female but who, because of the hormonal disorder, may have ambiguous genitalia and may grow hair in body areas more typically associated with males

3. Other chromosomally based conditions, such as Klinefelter's Syndrome, in which otherwise male-presenting people have XXY rather than either XX or XY chromosomes, as is typical; such individuals are considered male, but the extra X chromosome produces such symptoms as larger breasts and wider hips than are typical in males, smaller testicles, and sometimes sterility, as well as higher incidence of illness associated with women (such as breast cancer and osteoporosis)

4. Hypospadias, the placement of the urethral opening on the underside rather than on the tip of the head of the penis

Some of these conditions can be treated surgically, hormonally, or through other therapies. A legitimate question raised, when life and physical health are not at stake, is: Should they be? That debate is by no means over.

The medical terminology remains equally fraught. For several decades, beginning in 1968, the **DSM (Diagnostic and Statistical Manual of Mental Disorders)**, the "Bible" for classifying psychiatric disorders, called the psychological conditions associated with intersex people Gender Identity Disorder (usually abbreviated as GID or G.I.D.). In the recent revision (*DSM-V*), the name of the condition was changed to DSD, which most frequently is intended to stand for disorders of sex development, though some people prefer such variants as "disorders of sex differentiation" or "differences of sex development" (in the case of the latter, the term *differences* is viewed as less pathologizing and value-laden).

What some activists and other people who identify as intersex or who have close relationships with intersex people question is whether there is a necessary reason to assume that such people have a psychiatric condition that requires classification and inclusion in such a handbook in the first place. While such leaders of the intersex movement as Cheryl Chase, who founded the Intersex Society of North America, do support the primary name and the abbreviation DSD, many (including Chase herself) argue that the fact that a person has atypical or anomalous genitalia is not in and of itself an illness in need of cure or "fix." It is, as Anne Fausto-Sterling argues in her book *Sexing the Body*, at its simplest level, another way of being in the world.

But to return to that crucial moment, soon after delivery, when doctors and parents identify and begin to make decisions about what (if anything) to do to or with the bodies of such infants: for reasons that may be similar and different, both medical professionals and parents typically feel a need to move to choices that will "sex" the child as soon as possible. Much depends on the particular anomaly or anomalies, needless to say, but throughout most of the twentieth century, the decision, absent any compelling physical reason to do otherwise, was typically to assign such children as female and begin to provide treatments that would "shape" the child's body as that of a girl and to socialize her in ways that would promote feminine identification. John Money, whose research is described in John Colapinto's book, discussed below, who for decades was viewed as the leading authority on such cases, claimed that, because gender was completely socialized (as he and many others believed), assigning the child whichever sex was easiest to reassemble through surgery and hormones posed no potential problems, as the child rearing would lead to the child's identifying with the gender they had, quite literally, been assigned.

This assumption became disproven in rather tragic ways, ironically, the most well-known case being of a child not born intersex at all: the story of John/Joan, recounted in the book *As Nature Made Him: The Boy Who Was Raised as a Girl* by the journalist John Colapinto, published in 2000. The child given the pseudonym of John/Joan was one of a set of twin boys born in 1967 and the victim of a botched circumcision, during which so much of his penis was removed that the child would never have a functional one. Money's recommendation was to remove the penis and testicles and eventually fashion a vagina and raise "John" as "Joan" (alongside John's twin brother). From childhood on, Joan had a difficult and troubled life, always feeling at odds with her body. Money's assumptions, that socialization would provide sufficient "gender shaping" and that hormonal therapy would do the rest of the work needed to make Joan a girl, were clearly mistaken. Ultimately Joan transitioned back, as an adult, to John, but the story ended tragically: too many decades of feeling out of sync with his body led to severe depression, and John (whose real name was David Reimer) committed suicide by shotgun at the age of thirty-eight.

John/Joan was not, of course, intersex in any of the ways in which we and scientists and activists use the term: the sexual (re)assignment was a decision made on the basis not of naturally occurring anomalies, but of a technical mistake. By today's standards, Money's advice seems not only misguided, but bordering on criminal, and reflects a then-popular belief that all aspects of gender are based purely on socialization. But the John/Joan case should serve as a stark reminder that medical and particularly surgical interventions on children's bodies that present as intersex should not be made hastily, if at all. The obvious exception, of course, would be in the situation in which such a child's body poses dangerous risks to the child's health or life: in those cases, some radical decisions need to be made, but they also need to be followed up with counseling and therapies and work by teams of parents, physicians, and mental health professionals to help the person as they grow up and, like everyone else, begin to explore and feel a desire to name their sexual identity.

In recent years, there has been a growing body of research and writing about intersex bodies and lives, including histories, such as Alice Dreger's *Hermaphrodites and the Medical Invention of Sex*, a well-researched and in-depth study of how the hermaphrodite as a medical subject came into being—as opposed to simply being yet another private person, whose body was not necessarily known outside the domestic sphere and not necessarily viewed as abnormal because there was no simple "norm" in many more isolated geographical areas and socially organized towns or villages. Dreger also edited a volume of essays called *Intersex in the Age of Ethics* (1999), which crucially includes writings not only by philosophers and other scholars, but by intersex people, their parents and loved ones, and others with personal investments in expressing the lived experiences of their bodies and minds and of articulating what they want their standards of care and their options to be regarding their own sense of body integrity. Similarly, Suzanne J. Kessler's *Lessons from the Intersexed*, published in 1998, is a pioneering study of what its title suggests: what we can learn *from* intersex people.

A more recent work on developments in thinking and acting ethically about the lives, bodies, and choices of intersex people and their caregivers (particularly doctors and parents) is Ellen K. Feder's *Making Sense of Intersex: Changing Ethical Perspectives in Biomedicine* (2014). Feder begins her discussion of the topic by acknowledging with candor and humility her initial lack of experience in this topic and how she became involved, at the behest of other scholars and intersex people themselves, in exploring in particular what ethics as a field might bring to the actual practices of doctors and parents. She is particularly interested in how medical professionals might reconceptualize what their role and responsibilities in providing guidance for parents of such children might be. She counsels against the quick-fix approach and advocates for a much more parent- and child-centered method of dealing with issues of treatment, early surgeries, and the perceived need to assign a permanent gender identity to the child. She calls on medical professionals to adopt a primarily nondirective approach to counseling parents, especially when neither life nor physical pain or illness is at stake.

This approach is congruent with the emerging voices of intersex people themselves. A landmark documentary was filmed in 1996, called *Hermaphrodites Speak*, by the Intersex Society of North America. The ISNA was founded in 1993 by the intersex activist Cheryl Chase, who was born with ambiguous genitalia and was subjected to a clitoridectomy before she turned two years old, which resulted in lifelong diminishment of sexual feeling. This procedure was not uncommon for babies born with what is considered an enlarged clitoris and to whom doctors and parents decided to assign female gender. The ISNA did important informational and advocacy work for fifteen years, closing in 2008, and was succeeded by other organizations, such as the Accord Alliance. The documentary, which is simply made in terms of technical and directorial qualities, consists of a conversation held among a handful of people who identify as hermaphroditic (probably intersex in their own lives), and it is powerful and informative. It, too, is available for free viewing on the Internet.

What is striking about the documentary is how varied indeed the bodies themselves are. Some of the participants do not appear to the casual eye any more remarkable than people who pass by unnoticed on the street on a daily basis: were they not there to identify themselves as intersex, you would have no way of knowing that some aspect of their bodies is anomalous. Other bodies may carry signifiers, whether physiological (hair, body structure or form, expressive gestures) or assumed (such as clothing) that might read as queer or at least gender nonconforming. Still others may stymie the viewer to assign them to one or the other of the traditional binaries. It may not be that such individuals appear to be "masculine women" or "feminine men" — what may genuinely be the case is that they have bodies that seem "undecidable." In some cases, as their stories indicate, they were simply born into bodies that have led them to identify more as male or female for any number of reasons, and that is the socially gendered way in which they feel most comfortable presenting themselves; in others, they have made a decision to adopt a particular look, accompanied by specific clothing and other items that allow them to identify as one gender or the other. And the third group may genuinely feel nongendered, genderqueer, nonbinary, or polygender in identity and present themselves to the world in a way that asserts that identity.

Similarly, there is variety in terms of these individuals' identification of sexual orientation. Some, even though they live in their anomalous bodies, nonetheless find heterosexual a comfortable description of their desires; others may experience themselves as homosexual or bisexual; and still others may find such labels for sexual desire irrelevant to who they are and how they experience themselves. Even if they were indeed assigned a specific gender (all those interviewed were) and had medical treatments to "confirm" the assignment, their own complex experiences of body, mind, and society no doubt make them consciously aware of their place in the world of queerness. For some, the documentary is an opportunity to reclaim their intersexuality, perhaps to announce it or name it aloud publicly for the first time.

More recently, other intersex individuals have begun to put forward a national and often international presence in the media and other public forums. Tiger Devore, a clinical psychologist and sex therapist born in 1958, who was named Howard and assigned male gender at birth, had extreme hypospadias; by the time he was nineteen, he had already been through twenty surgeries, all of which he claims were failures. Though he presents himself visually as a fairly traditional male in terms of clothing, hairstyle, and so forth, he argues forcefully against the kinds of surgeries to which he was subjected, especially before a child has reached the age of adult consent. Devore has appeared on television, maintains a website, blogs, and writes an advice column, bringing intersex issues and lives much more into the open than was possible in previous generations: www.tigerdevorephd.com.

While most people who would either identify or be labeled as intersex still probably use one of the two binaries as a foundational description of their gender (i.e., even though intersex, they probably think of or refer to themselves as male or female, or a man or a woman), if for no other reason that they have been raised in that identity, Devore and others imagine an emerging identity that is firmly and primarily intersex and eschews the either-or base seemingly forced by the binary. Indeed, we may be seeing the claiming of identity of people who are neither male nor female nor transgender nor cisgender, but genuinely either "both" or "between," as the root *inter-* suggests.

Intersex lives have begun to be represented in popular culture and art, as well. The American novelist Jeffrey Eugenides won the Pulitzer Prize for his 2002 novel *Middlesex*, which tells the story of and from the point of view of an individual who starts life as Calliope, a Greek-American girl, and as an adult becomes Cal, a male, through natural (i.e., nonsurgical) changes to his body, produced by a genetic mutation as a result of the circumstances of his conception. In addition to winning awards, it was a selection of the Oprah Book Club, ensuring it high sales to readers who might not otherwise have been aware of it, and the novel is also now part of many high school and college curricula.

Another novel, published in 2010, by the Canadian writer Kathleen Winter, titled *Annabel*, is set in the remote area of Labrador and uses the rural, hunting-centered milieu of the area to explore the simultaneous presence of the male and the female (as well as the masculine and the feminine) in the child who bears the name Wayne when interacting with his father and Annabel only when with his mother and the mother's close friend Thomasina. Like *Middlesex*, the novel gained national attention: it was a finalist for three of Canada's top literary awards and was promoted by the Canadian actress Sarah Gadon, who helped it become the national selection for the Canada Reads program. It was dramatized for BBC Radio, has been optioned for film, and was the inspiration for a song by the British pop singer Alison Goldfrapp. It has not been wholeheartedly accepted by intersex groups, some of whom see it as reinforcing stereotypes and misconceptions about intersex. Nonetheless, its prominence makes it worth examining.

Even more recently, intersex has entered other literary venues. Abigail Tarttelin's *Golden Boy* uses the rape of an intersex boy and what follows as the basis for a traditional kind of story of parenting and school dilemmas and crises, such as *Ordinary People*. In 2015 *None of the Above*, by I.W. Gregorio, a novel aimed at the young adult (YA) market, was published; it combines the popular format of the identity-discovery novel found in many YA works with a consideration of the bullying of an intersex teen. No doubt by the time you read this textbook, even more novels and perhaps memoirs will have been published, raising awareness of and insight into the lives of intersex people. Other media have also begun to include story lines that depict intersex characters, either centrally or as part of a broader narrative spectrum. Such television series as *Children's Hospital, Freaks and Geeks, House*, and even *Friends* have brought intersex to the small screen. Theatrical films have been slower to do so, perhaps because feature-length films require larger budgetary investments and, hence, may be driven more by expected audience numbers. Nonetheless, there has been a handful, virtually all produced in countries other than the United States. Some are based in realistic drama, such as the Argentinian film *XXY*; others use intersex in such genres as science fiction, historical intrigue, and even musical comedy! Perhaps most notable is the 2005 U.S./Peruvian film *Both*, which, in addition to focusing on an intersex protagonist, is the only film known thus far to have been directed by an openly intersex person, Lisset Barcellos.

If the visibility of an identity is one measure of growing understanding and, perhaps, acceptance, then intersex seems to be having a "moment." It may be that intersex lives, perhaps because they unsettle human desires to categorize and to decide, provide opportunities not only to understand the complexities of those who claim such identities, but for people in general to consider the ways in which they may experience their own identities as more complexly "inter," in sexual, gender, and other domains of selfhood and social roles.

## SPOTLIGHT ON HISTORY: FROM EINAR TO LILI AND FROM GEORGE TO CHRISTINE

Two specific individuals in the recent history of queer bodies were self-identified transsexuals (the term in use when the more recent of the two became known in the public eye), assigned male at birth, both of whom transitioned to female identities and, in complicated ways, female bodies. Interestingly, they were both, to borrow from the title of David Ebershoff's novel (and subsequent film) about Elbe, "Danish girls": Lili Elbe (born Einar Wegener in 1882), of Denmark, and Christine Jorgensen (born George Jr. in 1926), of Danish heritage. Elbe's surgeries were performed in Germany, Jorgensen's in Denmark, though she returned to and lived most of her life in the United States. Their life stories suggest the differences only a few decades can make in both the care and treatment options available and the degree to which people with trans or anomalous or atypical identities or bodies are either stigmatized or celebrated in their respective countries and cultures. Based on the somewhat fragmentary autobiographical and biographical writings that exist by and about Elbe, the "origin story" of Wegener's discovery of and transition to a female identity seems almost accidental or serendipitous, though of course none of us can know what was going on inside Elbe's mind during the first few decades of her life.

Elbe and her wife, Gerda Gottlieb, were both painters. One day, when Gerda was scheduled to have a model sit for a portrait, the model did not appear. Gerda asked Einar to fill in, assuming the clothing set out for the female model. Einar felt comfortable in this traditionally female clothing and continued to model for Gerda. Eventually, Einar, with the support of Gerda, began to appear in public, passing as a woman in women's clothing. Very few people were privy to the fact that the young woman they met as "Lili Elbe" was also the well-regarded male painter Einar Wegener. Though sexual-reassignment surgery, today referred to more often as gender-confirmation or gender-affirmation surgery, was still in its infancy and carried considerable risk, Elbe traveled to Dresden, Germany, in 1930 and began to undergo a set of surgeries, first to remove the male genital organs, and then to have female ones implanted. When the surgeon opened Elbe's abdominal area, he discovered that she had always had what were described as "rudimentary ovaries." Elbe died in 1931 as a result of organ rejection. Nonetheless, by the time of her death, Elbe had managed to get her name changed legally to reflect her female identity and her marriage dissolved in keeping with the law that did not allow marriage between two members of the same sex. Elbe's death at a comparatively early age is sad, but her courage in pursuing a life whose goal was to work to have her body and mind match is undeniable.

Christine Jorgensen was born in the Bronx forty-four years after Lili Elbe's birth. In her fascinating book, *Christine Jorgensen: A Personal Autobiography*, she described growing up in a warm, loving family as a small, somewhat timid child who avoided gender-typical rough-and-tumble play and preferred the company of her sister and other little girls. Nonetheless, she gained popularity with other high schoolers and was drafted into the U.S. Army in 1945. After being discharged, George (as he was still known and as he still identified) trained as a photographer and worked for a number of agencies. During the postwar years, Jorgensen became increasingly concerned about her sexual identity and her actual sex: while the proprieties of mid-twentieth-century America kept Jorgensen from writing more explicitly about it in her memoir, some of this concern was spurred by what was later revealed to be atypical male genital development. This, coupled with an inner sense of being wrongly gendered, led George to seek out both medical and psychiatric treatment. Jorgensen is very adamant in the memoir in declaring that the sexual desires she experienced were not "homosexual" — she did not have fantasies of herself as a man engaged in erotic relationships with other men, and rebuffed the occasional passes made at her by other men.

While some of her confidantes suggested to Jorgensen that she (when viewed as a man) might be homosexual, she resisted this characterization and decided to explore options for living her life as the woman she genuinely experienced herself to be. In 1951 Jorgensen began a transatlantic trip to Sweden, where sexual-reassignment surgery was being performed. Stopping in Denmark, she discovered that there she could receive both hormonal and surgical treatments that would allow her to transition from a male to a female identity. As was typically the case, she first had her testes removed and then, the following year, still in Copenhagen, had a penectomy. After returning to the United States, she had a vaginoplasty. Throughout her process of transition, she also had care provided by Dr. Harry Benjamin, the endocrinologist whose name was associated for many decades with the widely accepted *Standards of Care* for transsexual individuals, which we discussed earlier in the chapter.

Unlike Elbe, whose life after transition was a comparatively quiet and private one, Jorgensen emerged as a woman during a time when the mass media were truly flourishing and expanding, in terms of print journalism and the rapidly developing presence of television, newsreels, and other forms available to millions of people. Jorgensen's return to the United States as a woman made newspaper headlines, and she was savvy enough to recognize that she needed to prepare to be a public figure and to manage, as much as she could, public impressions of her. She presented herself in a number of different female roles, all of which served to normalize her in the gendered terms of 1950s American culture, while also allowing herself to exploit the more glamorous aspects of what it meant to be a woman during this period. While there were, as might be expected, some media and other groups that denounced her as "unnatural" (and, hence, un-American), she was able to use her status as an ex-GI and as the daughter of immigrants to validate her patriotism; this culminated in her being named Woman of the Year by the Scandinavian Society, a heritage organization in New York City.

As time went on, Jorgensen, a clever woman, began to provide news-worthy quips for newspaper columns and magazines, and she became a popular guest on television talk shows. She parlayed what could have been notoriety into a kind of cheerful and wry persona. She acted in summer stock theater and worked up a nightclub act, offering a playful, self-know-ing patter and the occasional good-natured wink at her own gendered life, singing songs such as the popular "I Enjoy Being a Girl"; she did impres-sions of female stars whose own relationship to gender play and gender bending was part of their appeal, such as Marlene Dietrich, who could shift from a highly feminized style of presentation to a that of a tuxedoed male in what seemed like a split second.

Naturally, there was always speculation about her love life, even though it was usually articulated indirectly or through innuendo, and a few times it was announced that Jorgensen was engaged to a man, but because her birth certificate classified her as male, she could not legally marry a man. She remained circumspect in talking about her sex life and spent most of the rest of her life enjoying her celebrity and being a spokesperson for transsexual rights and for other sexual minorities. Her public image was always that of a glamorous woman, aiming for the robust, full-figured look of such movie sirens of the time as Lana Turner and Marilyn Monroe (you can find many photos of her on the Internet). Jorgensen died in 1989 at age sixty-two, as a result of causes not linked to her sexual surgeries.

There are a couple of things to note about both Lili Elbe and Christine Jorgensen. First, both adopted, one might say almost unreflectively, the gender norms of femininity of their times and places: Elbe became the long-haired, somewhat demure young woman who could pass in Euro-pean circles characterized by modesty and politeness; Jorgensen became a kind of "dame," a good-hearted, friendly woman who enjoyed all the trap-pings of being the next-closest-thing to a movie star or screen idol. Both desired to pass as the women they truly believed themselves to be.

Second, by some definitions there are those who would not consider either Elbe or Jorgensen to be trans people at all. Rather, the facts that Elbe, during surgery, was discovered to have rudimentary ovaries and that Jor-gensen, it would seem, had atypical male genitalia might lead us to conclude that they were incorrectly gendered: they were assigned a single gender, drawn from the male-female binary, when they were actually intersex, possessing either genital features typical of both men and women, or organs otherwise not easy to classify.

## ISSUES FOR INVESTIGATION

### 1. Queer Spaces: Your Experiences

Imagine different kinds of spaces, some that may be marked as queer, some definitely marked as not queer, and some that seem ambiguous or fluid. How do you approach these spaces in bodily terms? In mental terms? How conscious is your mind of what your body is doing? Do you have a sense of "attraction" (or lack of same) in these spaces? Are there residence halls that are marked, usually informally, as queer or queer-friendly? Think also about spaces that society marks specifically in gendered terms — such as bathrooms, locker rooms, fitting rooms in clothing stores, and even sections of college residence halls, which, at some schools, may be divided by floor or section along gender binary lines. Do you have memories — intellectual, emotional, or sense — of being in spaces that are marked as inappropriate for your sexuality or gender identity? Can you describe or name these memories?

### 2. Who Decides — and When, What, and How?

You have now read material about ways in which individuals and larger institutions as well as societies have either queered the body or had the body queered for them by external forces. As noted, more and more individuals are identifying as some version of trans at earlier ages, sometimes as young as preschool age. Similarly, medical protocols for the care of intersex people (which covers a wide range of atypical or anomalous anatomical, endocrinological, or genetic conditions) have changed from an assumption, at least in Western medicine, that immediate assignment of an infant to one of the two traditional binary categories of male or female is in the best interests of the child, family, and, by extension, society.

So we now see cases in which there are parents who have children who very clearly identify as trans at a young age, even if they do not have the identity label for it — they may say, "I am a boy" (even if they have a vagina and were gendered as a girl when born), or they may express discomfort or dislike of their gendered anatomy ("I hate my penis and I wish I could get rid of it"). Parents and others who provide care and education for such children have sometimes difficult decisions to make. Should they respond by agreeing to refer to these children by the language they prefer (i.e., pronouns, relational terms such as *son* or *daughter*, alternative names more traditionally associated with the gender with which the children identify)? Should they assist the children by helping them adopt the clothing, cosmetics, and hair length associated with their gender identity? Though preteen children cannot benefit from standard interventions, such as hormones or surgery, should parents work with medical personnel to block the onset of puberty? What about older adolescents (though still not of legal age) who request irreversible surgical interventions, such as mastectomies or vaginoplasties?

Now, consider the situation of parents and other adults who have responsibility for the care and well-being of children born intersex in some way or another. Most of you would probably agree that if the anomalous or atypical sexual condition poses a genuine threat to the life or physical health of a child, it is probably necessary for parents, in consultation with medical professionals, to make decisions that may alter the child's body, even in radical ways.

But what about intersex children whose anomalies do not pose a threat to life or health? Those advocating intervention at an early age also point to social comfort — issues of belonging, stigma, and so forth. Are these legitimate issues to take into account in making decisions about surgery and other irrevocable medical procedures?

Who should decide — and when and how much? Intersex activists are arguing more and more that, with the exception of life-threatening or pain-producing situations, parents and medical professionals should not be permitted legally to "surgically shape children," as the scholar Erik Parens calls it. What do you think? Do trans children's and intersex children's bodies call for different philosophies of care, support, and transitioning, in the recognition that no single approach will be responsive to each individual child's body, mind, or life situation? What kinds of social support should public schools be required to provide, and why? Can you identify and articulate what kinds of values or assumptions are guiding your thinking?

## SUGGESTIONS FOR FURTHER READING AND VIEWING

Dreger, Alice Domurat, ed. *Intersex in the Age of Ethics*. Frederick, MD: University Publishing Group, 1999.

Enke, Anne, ed. *Transfeminist Perspectives in and beyond Transgender and Gender Studies*. Philadelphia: Temple University Press, 2012.

Erickson-Schrath, Laura, ed. *Trans Selves: A Resource for the Transgender Community*. Oxford: Oxford University Press, 2014.

Gregorio, I.W. *None of the Above*. New York: Balzer + Bray, 2015.

Hillman, Thea. *Intersex (For Lack of a Better Word)*. San Francisco: Manic D, 2008.

Jenner, Caitlyn, with Buzz Bissinger. *The Secrets of My Life*. New York: Grand Central, 2017.

Kergil, Skylar. *Before I Had the Words: On Being a Transgender Young Adult*. New York: Skyhorse, 2017.

Kessler, Suzanne. *Lessons from the Intersexed*. New Brunswick, NJ: Rutgers University Press, 1998.

Martínez-San Miguel, Yolanda, and Sarah Tobias, eds. *Trans Studies: The Challenge to Hetero/Homo Normativities*. New Brunswick, NJ: Rutgers University Press, 2016.

McBride, Sarah. *Tomorrow Will Be Different: Love, Loss, and the Fight for Trans Equality*. New York: Crown Archetype, 2018.

Meyerowitz, Janet. *How Sex Changed: A History of Transsexuality in the United States*. Cambridge: Harvard University Press, 2002.

Mock, Janet. *Redefining Realness: My Path to Womanhood, Identity, Love & So Much More*. New York: Atria Books, 2014.

Stryker, Susan. *Transgender History: The Roots of Today's Revolution*. 2nd ed. New York: Seal Press, 2017.

Stryker, Susan, and Stephen Whittle, eds. *The Transgender Studies Reader*. Vol. 1. New York: Routledge, 2006.

*TransAmerica*. Directed by Duncan Tucker. Weinstein/IFC Films, 2005.

Viloria, Hida. *Born Both: An Intersex Life*. New York: Hachette, 2017.

Woolf, Virginia. *Orlando: A Biography*. London: Hogarth Press, 1928.

*XXY*. Directed by Lucia Puenzo. Cinefondation/Ministry of Culture (Spain), 2007.

# CHAPTER 5

# QUEERING PRIVILEGE
## Whiteness and Class

### CONCEPTS OF WHITENESS AND PRIVILEGE

In discussions of racial and ethnic identity category, **whiteness** has very often been viewed as a "noncategory," as the normative, often universalized one against which all others are defined by contrast and comparison. In the last few decades, this has begun to change, as scholars have begun to study whiteness as every bit a way of classifying and valuing individuals and groups of people as any other racial or ethnic grouping. It is often tied to the concept of **privilege**, conscious and unconscious benefits people accrue simply by being a member of a group that has historically had social and economic power. The next chapter examines in more detail the intersections between minority racial or ethnic identities and queer identity. This chapter focuses on how whiteness, privilege, and queerness both intersect and sometimes contradict each other.

What does it mean to be *white*? For some, it may be based in skin color, as well as certain biological features of appearance (what geneticists call *phenotypes*) that make one recognize oneself as white. Geneticists now state that the genetic differences between people of different heritage are much smaller than might have been supposed before the human genome was mapped. Are some ethnicities considered "whiter" than others in social hierarchies? Why? Is it simply a matter of skin tones, or are other elements at work? Changing demographics of intermarriage and parentage in the United States may be making the "science" of race, insofar as there is one, less important than the social and political values attached to it.

So, how is whiteness more complex than what it is not, as the default category for all those people and groups who do not fit easily into one of the historically racial and ethnic categories of differences? Complicating the question is the concept of *class*, the cultural and socioeconomic dimensions of identity; class itself is tied to the notion of privilege, conferring various material and other advantages by virtue of membership in a category.

Henderson, Bruce, *Queer Studies: Beyond Binaries*
dx.doi.org/10.17312/harringtonparkpress/2019.09.qsbb.005
© 2019 by Harrington Park Press

Though we use the word *privilege* in any number of ways, the specific emphasis in this chapter (and throughout this book) is on forms of opportunity and often power that one group, often the majority, but sometimes quantitatively a minority (as in the case of economic privilege, what in contemporary American discourse is sometimes referred to as the "1 percent"), has over other groups in a category. In this chapter, privilege based on socially and historically constructed categories of race is placed in intersection with sexuality, but you may consider other categories in which privilege obtains, such as gender, occupation, education, and so forth. Privilege may vary for an individual, depending on different contexts in which they find themselves: maleness may provide privilege in many contexts, but if the male is a person of color, he may find himself experiencing less privilege than white women in some contexts. The same is true for other categories. While it is not universally true, it is also the case that many think of privilege, as we are using it here, as something that individuals do not necessarily have to earn by merit, but which is simply assigned to them by dint of groups into which they were born or to which they belong by some other process.

The communication scholars Thomas K. Nakayama and Robert L. Krizek contributed an important set of lenses through which to consider whiteness in their 1995 article, "Whiteness: A Strategic Rhetoric." They identified six strategies central to what they called "the discursive space of 'white'" (291):

1. White as majority: the authors noted that in this strategy, *white* was not equated with the universal, but with the majority, suggesting a statistical power that whiteness conferred.

2. White as default: this corresponds to our discussion of whiteness as an unmarked category.

3. White as "natural": this strategy defines whiteness in "purely" biological terms of appearance and differences from other groups, effectively suggesting an ahistorical depoliticized use of the term.

4. Whiteness as synonymous with nationality: this may seem hopelessly outdated to us, but it is worth recalling that the ability to vote was for centuries offered only to white men in the United States (and in this sense, *whiteness* was analogous to *maleness*).

5. Whiteness as all-encompassing: the authors suggest that this is the strategy used by those who argue that labeling by race or ethnicity is counter to their sense of either identity or philosophy of what it means to be human — that by refusing to name themselves as *white*

they maintain the unmarked status of whiteness as a universalized position, not needing to be identified.

6. White as European: At a certain point, *white* simply became a blanket term for people of ethnicities who traced their origins to European nations — reinforcing the nineteenth-century anthropological division of humans into four geographically named "races" (American, European, African, Asian — ironically, in this schema, "American" was not synonymous with "European-American"). (296 – 302)

Come up with examples of uses of the word *white* that fit each of these "strategic rhetorics." To what degree do these examples demonstrate conscious or unconscious associations of whiteness with positive values? Do any carry negative ones (such as "white supremacy")?

There are many kinds of privilege, of course, and they typically are named by groups that have less access to power and opportunity: male privilege, heterosexual privilege, ableist privilege, just to name a few. This does not mean that every individual who belongs to (or is assigned to) one of these groups always "wins out" over people outside the group; rather, theories of privilege usually assert there are automatic benefits people belonging to these groups typically have by virtue of their membership in the group, and that many of these benefits may be psychological (such as feeling more confident because of the privilege bestowed on them in many, if not most, parts of their lives) or unconscious, even to those benefiting from the privilege or those responding to the person whose identity places them in a position of privilege.

The concept of white privilege has a long history, even predating the term itself. Race theorists such as W. E. B. Du Bois wrote about the ways in which white people did not have to think of their own whiteness or, except when it was immediately relevant, the lives of people who were not white. More recently, the cultural and pedagogical scholar Peggy McIntosh introduced the concept of "unpacking the invisible knapsack," in which she used the metaphor of a knapsack white people carried around with them in their daily lives that contained various "items" that contributed to their white privilege. McIntosh's point, which has been very influential, was that it wasn't even the case that white people use every item in their knapsack every day, but that their possession of it and their knowledge that each "item" was there at the ready if needed, was itself an important enactment of privilege. In one paper about the "invisible knapsack," McIntosh identified more than forty different kinds of items in the white-privilege knapsack, which she described as "special provisions, assurances, tools, maps, guides, codebooks, passports, visas, clothes, compass, emergency gear, and blank checks," the burden of which were "weightless" for white people (www.collegeart.org/pdf/diversity/white-privilege-and-male-privilege.pdf).

## DIFFERENT SHADES OF WHITENESS (AND OTHER HUES): QUEERING SOCIAL AND ECONOMIC CLASS

One of the familiar clichés of American exceptionalism (the shared belief that the United States is different from and superior to other countries) is that it has been, from its founding, a classless society, in which merit and industry determine success and status. While it is true that social mobility has been promoted as one of the founding ideals of the country (for white, male property owners), it is also true that, from the very first contact white English-speaking Europeans had with the continent, class played important roles. The historian Nancy Isenberg, in her 2016 book, *White Trash: The 400-Year Untold History of Class in America*, argues that those who left England were not, as our national myths would have it, primarily upright folk in search of religious freedom and opportunities for self-governance. Rather, Isenberg suggests, the colonial enterprise served as a kind of "weeding" of individuals and groups of people Great Britain preferred not to have to deal with — one way she describes the processes is of "thin[ning] out its prisons . . . a way to remove vagrants and beggars" (10).

The question of what constitutes **class** in the United States has become even more complicated as more nonwhite people rise to positions of power, status, authority, and economic privilege (though still very much the minority in terms of numbers). During the mid- to late twentieth century, social class was typically divided into such categories as upper class and upper middle class, middle class, working class, and lower class. The last two categories, working class and lower class, by the way, have often been sticking points in discourse on class — for some, *lower class* carries connotations of moral stigma and aesthetic ugliness and lack of taste (hence, Isenberg's use of the offensive "white trash" in the title of her book); for others, *working class* and *lower class* both denote people on the lower end of the economic scale. For still others, *working class* tends to connote people who have entered the workforce without any education beyond secondary school, and whose professions focus on skills and trades, rather than abstract bodies of knowledge.

For people who use *working class* in this way, a college graduate could still be lower class, depending on their life: economics, while often quite central to such stratifications, does not tell the whole story. For example, the Kennedys, often considered today the closest the United States has to a royal dynasty by dint of political and social involvement and status, are only a few generations from being working-poor Irish, and there are corridors of society that would not admit them to upper-class status; similarly, while the Kardashians have fabulous amounts of economic wealth at their disposal, part of the fascination they seem to hold in current American popular culture is the very dissonance between extraordinary amounts of money and "lower-class" taste and behaviors (such as sex tapes, ostentatious marriages followed by quickie divorces, and so forth). At the same time, there are once-wealthy families whose fortunes no longer place them at debutante balls or charity parties at Newport houses, but who nonetheless hold on to their "upper-class" heritage as part of their self-definition. And as the gaps between the haves and have-nots widen, is very common to talk about the "1 percent" and "the rest of us," a distinction that turns economic class into a political meme.

So, if class isn't simply who has the most money and who "dies with the most toys," what is it? Lisa Henderson suggested the following attributes in her study *Love and Money: Queers, Class, and Cultural Production* (2013):

1. A relatively and potentially unstable economic position in a social system committed to economic hierarchy and exclusion

2. A form of social power over others and vulnerability to discrimination, prejudice, stigmatization, and pain

3. Recognizable in the cultural practices of everyday life . . . [such as] speech, taste, the ways in which we can and do attend to our bodies. (33)

Notice that, in Henderson's schema of class attributes, there is always a contrastive feature, a kind of opposition of those viewed as "in" and those viewed as "out." There is, at least in appearance, a sorting and a kind of conscious and, no doubt, unconscious set of benefits necessary to maintaining class distinctions. (And it is important to note that this chapter focuses on class experiences and LGB people; the experiences of class for trans people are somewhat different, as issues regarding coming out, passing, and status pose different sets of barriers and challenges for those whose gender identity is queered.)

But my queerness (and, I guess I would add, my choice to make it a public part of my identity, though, admittedly, it does not manifest itself automatically to everyone the way my race and gender do) does place me socially in yet another category that is not unrelated to class. By always experiencing my whiteness and my maleness within the intersectionality of my queerness, I am aware that, in the terms Lisa Henderson uses, there is a potential for instability of class "capital" always present: at various time in my life, economic hierarchy and exclusion have felt themselves to be real possibilities, as I have wondered if my queerness would bar me from various kinds of professional opportunities and entrée into upwardly mobile groups, as the academy is typically viewed as being among (in status, if not always in economic terms).

If we take class, as Lisa Henderson does, beyond its economic characteristics, it is true that being queer has its own elements of social power and vulnerability, the second of the major attributes she assigns to class. If part of a class hierarchy is that it implies or asserts that some people's (by virtue of their social status and position) "discrimination, prejudices, stigmatization, and pain" matter more than others, then one could say that historically and socially within the United States, non-queer people have been in a "higher" class than queer people. Similarly, turning to Henderson's last set of class attributes, there are often "recognizable . . . cultural practices of everyday life" that mark people's queerness. If nothing else, the constant historical fight for civil and legal rights by queer people, rights often assumed and therefore unmarked (and unremarked on) by those who do not identify as queer, has created a kind of class system that on the one hand is binary (queer vs. non-queer) and on the other hand, depending on who is doing the evaluating, may within queerness create a class system (historically, with gay, white men at the higher end and trans people of color at the lower end), thus perpetuating systems of injustice and differences in access within the queer nation.

Class systems have typically focused on different stratifications among white people (though there is a growing body of historical, sociological, and economic study of class differences within nonwhite populations and in demographics that are not sorted by race). This is, of course, due to the long history of oppression of nonwhite people in the United States, and the effects of those histories will be taken up in the next chapter. President Lyndon Baines Johnson, who lived most of his life in Texas, famously said, "If you can convince the lowest white man that he's better than the best colored man, he won't notice you're picking his pocket. Hell, give him somebody to look down on, and he'll empty his pockets for you" (quoted in David Frum, "The Real Secret to Trump's Success," *Atlantic*, January 4, 2016, https://www.theatlantic.com/notes/2016/01/the-real-secret-to-trumps-success-contd/422544/). While this is a sad and somewhat cynical statement, Johnson was trying to get at the ways in which race and class coexisted and asserting that racial prejudice allowed some white people to reconcile themselves to the class status that political and economic forces assigned them. For that reason, the focus here is on white people, whose "class trouble" (to alter Judith Butler's "gender trouble") has intersected in complex and often very divergent ways with their queerness.

## Upper-Middle-Class Queers: White-Collar Professionals

Those whose class position is firmly in place and has been for at least a few generations often find that their queerness can either be a kind of nonissue within their social world (insofar as family name and accomplishment can trump what some may view as a comparatively minor aspect of their lives from a social perspective) or something simply not to be discussed. There may be some pressure to marry and produce the next generation in the family, and, if so, sometimes such marriages are understood as part of a social role to be played, rather than as a genuine attempt to "correct" or "cure" queerness as a category of desire, in the same way that, in previous centuries, marriage was often considered less about love than about the merging of successful families.

These are broad generalizations, and the landscape may be changing as social approval of same-sex marriages is now rising and such marriages are legal in the United States. But one of the many luxuries that comes from belonging to such social milieus is a high regard for domestic privacy: because people with inherited wealth, who may or may not have jobs, can, in a sense, claim a greater "given" privacy, the stakes of being outed may be less serious and there may be ways to ameliorate the results.

While it is something of a stereotype, there has been a long tradition, in places such as New York City and Washington, D.C., of gay men (particularly ones in or approaching middle age) serving a useful social function as "walkers": intelligent, well-schooled, nicely dressed single men who can accompany socialites and the wives of wealthy men to parties, charity events, the opera, and other occasions that women of this class traditionally do not attend alone, but which their husbands either may prefer not to attend or may have time conflicts with. That these walkers are gay is usually understood but rarely discussed, except in the most intimate of situations among close friends. While there is no exact correlate for queer women who come from moneyed and older families, there may be what are sometimes called *bearding* situations, in which two people, neither of whom is in or desires to be in a heterosexual relationship, find it useful to become social partners. These sometimes lead to very companionable and permanent relationships, including marriages that not infrequently produce children, and sometimes one or the other in the couple does identify as heterosexual but, either for monetary or for other reasons, finds contentment in the benefits of such a relationship. Some such couples have agreements, either explicit or tacit, that seeking sexual or romantic fulfillment outside the couple is acceptable, particularly if the veil of privacy is maintained.

Of course, there are cases in which the standard of benign neglect, supported by privacy as a kind of social capital, can be violated, intentionally or not. Particularly with gay men — in ways going back as far as Oscar Wilde's scandals with "boys from the dangerous classes" and even earlier — the very crossing of class barriers in making erotic and romantic relationships can be cause for "alarm." When Anderson Cooper, the scion of the Vanderbilt dynasty, which goes back to the nineteenth century in U.S. history and arguably the most famous gay newscaster currently working in the broadcast media, came out to the public at large, some of the gossip focused on his relationship with Ben Maisani, a French-born bar owner (whose family has been described as upper-middle-class), a man whose public persona has been defined by his non-WASP (white, Anglo-Saxon, Protestant) ethnicity and his love of nightlife, working out, and other activities or venues not associated with the class traditions of the Vanderbilts and Coopers. Though he is a college graduate, his degree is from Hunter College, a fine but nonetheless nonelite institution in New York City, a bit of a distance from Cooper's years at the Dalton School (a prep school in New York City) and Yale. To his credit, Cooper never rose to the bait of suggestions that he somehow "betrayed" his class in his choice of a mate. His parents, Wyatt Cooper and the heiress Gloria Vanderbilt, made it clear that he would not inherit their fortune, as they wanted him to make his own way in the world. (One could argue that his lineage has given him advantages that are worth more than money itself.) Cooper has maintained that he is grateful for this.

It is interesting that, when Cooper decided to come out, he identified the issue of privacy as one of the sources of conflict for him, saying, "I've begun to consider whether the unintended outcomes of maintaining my privacy outweigh personal and professional principle. It's become clear to me that by remaining silent on certain aspects of my personal life for so long, I have given some the mistaken impression that I am trying to hide something — something that makes me uncomfortable, ashamed or even afraid. This is distressing because it is simply not true" (https://en.wikipedia.org/wiki/Anderson_Cooper). In interviews Cooper said the issue of privacy had a certain amount to do with the fact that in his profession he often found himself in countries or regions where being an openly gay man might put him at physical risk. Nonetheless, what his statement suggests is an acknowledgment that he had the luxury of privacy as a bonus, as a part of being in the "protected" class of those from old and wealthy families. His ethical reasons for coming out are compelling and admirable, and his success as a journalist has not diminished since he came out.

The same cannot always be said for those who constitute the other set of queer people under the subheading we are considering: white-collar professionals, who may or may not come from distinguished families and who are indeed dependent on continued employment in their chosen fields for such everyday needs as housing, food, transportation, and clothing, as well as for a sense of what the humanistic psychologist Abraham Maslow called "self-actualization," the maintenance of an identity that is satisfying for them in work and home life. While some people who would identify as members of this class might also describe themselves as having a degree of personal privacy that may put them in closer alignment with upper-class or "heritage" families, a significant number do not. We can only hope that we are somewhat beyond the very rigid requirements of the *Mad Men* era, but it would be far from accurate to say that all the professions or even all the businesses within a particular profession have reached anything like a model of inclusivity. Employment laws have made it generally illegal to ask personal questions that would force job candidates to state their sexual identity, but there are always ways potential employers can find out such information, should they desire it.

In various studies, queer professionals or white-collar workers have described sometimes elaborate, often heartbreaking and angering strategies they have had to use to maintain a professional profile while keeping their normative appearance intact, such as working long hours as an excuse for not having time for a home life, sometimes bringing willing "beards" to events that span professional-social roles, such as annual dinners, holiday parties, and weekend outings, and keeping their private lives "out of town," compartmentalizing the emotional and domestic parts of their identities literally and figuratively. These people describe a degree of exhaustion that goes above and beyond what their traditionally heterosexual peers experience in fields that are highly competitive to begin with. They also make the compelling argument that the time and psychic energy they must invest in maintaining such facades could be better spent both in committing that labor to their actual jobs and in working to balance work and life, a problem facing all professionals in today's world.

John Browne, the former head of British Petroleum (BP), one of the leading oil companies in the world, experienced the effects of such compartmentalization firsthand and has used his experiences to devote himself to helping come up with ideas and strategies for making the work and home lives of queer professional and white-collar workers more productive and satisfying. Browne studied physics at Cambridge University in England and later pursued a business degree at Stanford University in California. He worked his way up at BP, spending time in Alaska as a young man. He described years of recognizing and living with his own desires as a gay man but acting on them only occasionally, surreptitiously, and often anonymously. He lived with his mother for a number of years when his home base was in Ohio, which he acknowledges provided what seemed at the time like a cover for his lack of heterosexual partnership; but, in retrospect, this may have been a fairly "glass closet." After his mother died and he returned to the United Kingdom, he began a relationship with a young man whom Browne describes as an escort, someone who provided sexual and personal companionship in return for financial support. Though the relationship came to an end after some years, Browne continued to provide the man some financial support, but he decided ultimately that he did not wish to continue to support him so long after their relationship had ended. The escort announced he was going to expose Browne's sexuality to the tabloids (and did), and Browne decided to resign from the position as CEO of BP, as he (and, it would appear, his employers) believed that the story about his sexual orientation, as well as his involvement in what was an illegal enterprise — paying for sexual services — would be detrimental to the ongoing health of BP as a business.

Browne used this set of events, which though calamitous at the time to his sense of professional self, did not put fulfillment of his own everyday needs at risk, as an opportunity to try to do some good for queer professionals. He studied and interviewed a wide range of self-identified queer people in various walks of business, some out, many closeted, some male, some female, and some even trans (the last being the most challenged of the group), to learn from them what difficulties they faced and continued to face and to try to develop some strategies by which businesses could be more inclusive and supportive of their queer employees. His mantra throughout the resulting book is found in its subtitle: "coming out is good business" — not just for the queer employees but for the businesses themselves. He argues that businesses are recognizing more and more that much of their success rests on the labor of people from what are increasingly called the "creative economies," those workers whose gifts and skills allow them to *create* in the broadest sense — to think expansively, imaginatively, innovatively, and inclusively — and that many of the most talented "creatives" are queer. Forcing them to remain in the closet diverts them from bringing their best, fullest selves to the workplace, and may, in many instances, simply lead them to seek employment in other professions that they see as less oppressive and restrictive.

Browne offers an action plan for business to break down the glass closet, a set of steps that he believes will help businesses and their queer employees avoid the kinds of situations he found himself in and which he readily admits he helped reinforce and support through omission and evasion. His plan consists of seven pretty straightforward components:

1. Actively set direction from the top: as he says in another section of his book, "Bias begins in the boardroom." The leaders of the company

need to provide models of inclusion and support that make it clear that the board members and CEO can articulate and apply a queer-inclusive tone and set of policies.

2. Create and support LGBTQ+ resource groups: by doing so, companies take an affirmative step to recognize the specific needs and challenges of their queer employees. This, in a sense, removes queerness from the closet of "grapevines" (i.e., the informal communications among queer employees about how to handle certain situations that might put their jobs at risk, should employers find out about their sexual orientation in any formal or public way), and workarounds and the sense of "exceptions" (when and with whom it is okay to be open about queer sexual identity in a particular company).

3. Encourage straight allies: by providing programming and opportunities for straight employees to become active allies, the company affirms that LGBTQ+ issues are relevant not only to people who identify as such.

4. Set concrete goals and measure against them: this is where the scientific and social scientific knowledge of professions can be put to use. If a company has a vague, overarching "commitment to LGBTQ+ inclusion," but nothing specific in mind and no way of determining whether the goals have been met, it is simply empty talk. Browne includes a brief, accessible section on statistics in his book to help illustrate how measurement provides powerful social and cultural capital.

5. Get LGBTQ+ people to accept individual responsibilities: by this, Browne means that some of the most important work is done at ground levels at the instigation of individual people, gay or straight. Conversations between individuals can lead to larger initiatives. Social scientific studies have shown time and again that the single most powerful factor in reducing homophobia is a straight person's knowing even one LGBTQ+ person with whom they feel comfortable.

6. Identify role models and tell their stories repeatedly: as we all develop, both as people and as workers, we need narratives and figures that can inspire us, show us successes, and provide symbolic courage when we hesitate or feel as if we can never move forward. Though stories of people such as Browne himself (and Anderson Cooper) may be exceptional, there are many other stories and individuals who might serve as "lower-hanging fruit," models whose lives and achievements we can reasonably emulate — and why not aspire to doing what Browne and Cooper have done? It's not failure

not to achieve their level of success — it's failure not to imagine what you *can* do.

7. Set clear expectations for those working in conservative countries: Browne, working in the oil business, of necessity found himself working for stretches of time in regions where homosexuality and living queer lives were either stigmatized or criminalized (sometimes death being the ultimate penalty). Browne argues that it is simply realistic for queer employees to know and adapt for reasons of safety to the norms of their posting — not that they cannot be out within the "walls," as he calls it, of the company, but to be aware that what happens outside the company may be at odds with their inner authentic lives. He also adds that companies should never post someone, especially against their will, in a place where their safety is known to be at risk. (159–160)

If you have worked in organizations, consider the degree to which any of these elements have been present, either implicitly or explicitly. How might they be implemented in the profession to which you aspire?

## Middle-Class Queers: Growing or Disappearing?

The line between *upper middle class* and *middle class* has become less distinct in recent decades, particularly as college education has become the norm, whether leading to a completed undergraduate degree or an advanced degree, for many more people than in the mid-twentieth century. Similarly, in light of frequent financial crises, who the middle class comprises is more and more open to question. Whereas once the middle class might have been viewed as the "unmarked" class — that is, you are middle class unless you clearly *know* you are not — there is a kind of self-contradictory way in which the middle class is both broadening its scope and becoming more and more marginalized — the center is not holding, so to speak, and more people on one end of the middle class are finding themselves economically part of the working poor and, at the other end, finding themselves economically advantaged but lacking the social status often attributed to the upper classes.

Ironically, it may be that this dilemma places middle-class queer people in a potentially positive position. As acceptance of marriage equality, same-sex parenting, and visibility in everyday life grow, there is a sense in which queer middle-class people are being viewed as and perhaps experiencing themselves more as "just folks." While it is never entirely wise to draw generalized conclusions about actual lives from fictionalized and constructed narratives, the growth of situation comedies that feature middle-class queer lives may suggest that the trajectory of "middle-class respectability" has changed or is changing.

The NBC series *Will and Grace*, which ran from 1998 to 2006 and returned in 2017, marked a milestone in the depiction of middle-class queer (and what might be called "queer-adjacent") lives. Will Truman and Grace Adler, the protagonists of the series, are a deeply bonded gay man and straight female who met in college, flirted quite briefly with romance, and then became close friends and, throughout much of the series, roommates. Each is a member of a white-collar profession, Will a lawyer and Grace an interior designer.

Each, in his or her own way, works to maintain a respectable, "mature" approach to life — and much of the humor emerges from violations of this middle-class view of life — such as the times when Will tries but fails to maintain the virtually asexual but familiarly masculine role his workplace "normed" for him; similarly, Grace's profession as an interior designer is rarely depicted as anything beyond an excuse for a situation to arise that shows her in usually farcical conflict with her dilettantish assistant, Karen Walker, the wealthy, complexly upper-class trophy wife who treats the office as a place to spend her idle hours. Will's own foil, Jack McFarland, is clearly intended to be a kind of queer id to Will's ego; Jack is the childish, sex-driven, and usually superficial "gym bunny" who nonetheless also is totally comfortable with his nonnormative and somewhat feminine way of being a gay man — and as his professional life is usually depicted as something artistic (his hilariously bad theatrical piece, "Just Jack") or practically nonexistent, so his need to conform to professional normativity is conveniently absent.

In later seasons, class issues become more complex, as Will gets involved with a very working-class as well as ethnically Italian (hence, non-WASP) police officer with whom he has an on-and-off relationship. One of the complex narrative issues is the sense in which Vince, Will's boyfriend, is depicted as more authentically emotional and at home in himself than Will's uptight, buttoned-down lawyer. Similarly, while Karen is wealthy and often shows disdain for everyone else's sense of taste and style, she also takes great pleasure in acting out "trashy" playful scenarios with Jack and battles, often unsuccessfully, for power over her immigrant maid, Rosario. The latter's position in the Walker household places her in a lower-class status, but emotionally and in terms of her own sense of self-worth, she is often the victor, and her offscreen death in the reboot is a moment of deep and authentic emotional loss for Karen. Jack learns he is a father in later seasons, in some ways moving him from one class (the queer class) to another, as he takes on a more middle-class sense of parental responsibility. Most tellingly, Karen's wealthy husband, Stanley, never appears on-screen and is described only in terms of the material goods he can offer Karen, his weight and insatiable appetite, and his baggage of children from a first marriage — even his name, Stan, carries with it connotations of the self-made man, not cultured or raised among the elite. *Will and Grace*, which is open to critique on a number of levels, nonetheless served to queer middle-class assumptions and representations in ways it may not itself always have been aware of. When it was rebooted in 2017, the characters, a decade or so older, also reflected shifts in class status: Will has given up his job as a lawyer to work with Grace in her decorating business, which places him in the same workplace as Karen — her sense of entitlement and work as simply another form of recreation contrasts with his ethic borne of years of billable hours.

In recent years, more and more television series have featured middle-class queers, and we will consider one that has been consistently popular for ten seasons (sometimes among the top-rated), on ABC, which has also added situation comedies featuring African American, biracial, Asian American, Latinx, and other kinds of middle-class (and working-class) families not seen with any frequency before the advent of shows such as *Will and Grace*. The most successful in terms of ratings and longevity is *Modern Family*, whose title suggests its aspirations in terms of representation and inclusive vision of what makes a "modern family." It follows the parallel and interwoven lives of three branches and multiple generations of the Pritchett family, presided over by paterfamilias Jay, who has two grown children, a stepson by a much younger wife, and a baby son. His daughter, Claire, works on and off in the family business, closet construction and installation, the kind of company that probably started with Jay as a working-class, blue-collar carpenter and has become a successful enterprise under Jay as its middle-class boss; Claire is married to a real estate salesman, Phil, and they are raising three children, two daughters and a son.

The queering of the middle class is in the other branch of the Pritchetts, Jay's son, Mitchell, a gay lawyer, and his long-term partner, Cam, a former farm boy, large in body, delicate in sensibilities, and artistic in aspirations. Mitch and Cam are raising their adopted Vietnamese daughter, Lily, who has assimilated into middle-class U.S. culture all too well. While Mitch and Cam's status as a queer couple is the source of humor and of situational opportunities, it is not remarkably different from or subversive of what most viewers would recognize as middle-class American values, attitudes, and experiences. The very ordinariness of their life has been a source of criticism by some queer viewers, who find the couple too "Uncle Tom"–like in their adherence to fairly normative aspirations and experiences; some find the character of Cam too "queeny" and hence a kind of reinforcement of the effeminate stereotype of gay men, though, to be fair, there are many cases in which Cam's youth as a rural boy and his love of sports and his use of his excessive body break that stereotype.

It may be the very ordinariness of the queer dimensions of *Modern Family* that is most disruptive and powerful. Whereas the worlds of children, school events, and family vacations were introduced into *Will and Grace* only in later seasons and typically as the sources of comic angst and conflict, on *Modern Family*, for better or for worse, queerness is no more remarkable than the juxtaposition of white and Latinx cultures, than the efforts to revitalize a midlife marriage gone a little stale erotically, than being a STEM-smart girl in a world that often marginalizes such talents. If Mitch and Cam have become boring after ten years — well, isn't that what narratives of middle-class life are often about? Why shouldn't they become as boring as Claire and Phil? Or as any other couple who have nested for a long enough time to fall into recognizable patterns?

It is important to keep in mind that the discussion of these situation comedies focuses on series that take amusement — and laughter — as one of their primary purposes. But each episode points to more serious aspects of middle-class queerness, such as coming out, fitting into "the middle," facing rejection, sometimes within the family, sometimes within social circles, determining how to navigate work, home, and dating. For many middle-class queers, a central dilemma in the past might have been: To whom do I disclose my sexuality, and what are the risks and benefits in doing so? Many saw the risks of rejection from family and friends, of finding professional or social mobility limited by public knowledge of this part of identity; they had to wonder if being queer meant giving up the often-unarticulated benefits and privileges of being in the middle class. The decision to remain closeted may have felt motivated by the sense that there was much to lose by coming out and by the fear of not knowing what the positive results could be.

But for others, the act of coming out and living out, both professionally and personally, may ironically be central to a middle-class identity, whether individuals would have or could have named it as such: middle-class ideology and experience, while it places a high premium on respectability, also tends to absorb the idea of self-actualization and the right to self-determination. In the same way that many middle-class people, of any sexual orientation, believe it is their birthright (or their class-right, so to speak) to own a house, buy a new car every four or five years, go on a vacation each year, and have children if they wish, so may middle-class queers, now that being queer is more frequently being viewed *not* as a disqualification from respectability and class exclusion, believe that there is no good reason for them not to have the same rights as their straight counterparts — including the right not to have to hide their domestic and romantic selves.

## Working-Class Queers: Communities of Labor, Sites of Isolation

Just as the terms *middle class, upper middle class*, and *upper class* may be seen as having contestable and sometimes permeable borders with each other, so it is with terms like *working class, working poor*, and *lower class*. In the case of these latter terms, it is reasonable to draw distinctions between those people who are employed, even if the employment may put them in precarious positions financially — dealing with ongoing worries about sustenance of family, payment of bills, and saving money — and those who are often more dependent on government support or whose employment is inconsistent and frequently turns over. There are theorists who include some white-collar workers among the working class, especially when wages for such jobs are low. Others point to discordant class differences within occupations: public school teachers are often used as an example — their educational level certainly qualifies them to be considered middle class, but the salaries most teachers receive place them in situations that may be closer to working class or lower middle class. Similarly, laborers without college degrees may indeed make more money than teachers, but their educational level and their social and cultural values and concerns may well be closer to those of factory workers. And it is important to remember that part of traditional U.S. ideology is a narrative of social mobility, even if the moves sometimes take a generation or more to occur, if at all.

If privacy is a supreme concern for upper-class people and respectability is one for middle-class people, one might identify *community* and *cohesion* as central terms of importance and identity for working-class people. Jobs typically associated with working-class life might include factory work, mechanical assembly and service, food service, and retail. In each of the examples, a significant part of the ethos (or character) of the work is that of communal, even at times communitarian, labor. Unlike the artisan, who is viewed as responsible for the entire creation of an object, working-class laborers often have a specialized set of tasks and are expected in a sense to downplay their individuality while at work. Variation in procedures and individual approaches to duties are not only frowned on, but may be viewed as reason for firing an employee, as they disrupt the orderly production of goods (as Marxists would put it).

Marxists would also add that this approach to the production of profit (i.e., the goods or services for sale) leads to what they call "alienated labor," a lack of affective or emotional commitment to the labor being performed, but it is also true that such a work climate can lead to a sense of community, albeit one often as fraught as the most dysfunctional family. Working-class laborers, or blue-collar workers, an analogous term, are expected to leave their private lives at home for the sake of efficiency and productivity in the workplace, but they also often cannot make an entire or neat separation between work life and home life — in part because they become inter-twined in the lives of people with less access to money and the privileges that make such distinctions easy to maintain. For example, if a worker is having to work overnight shifts for a few weeks because it is their turn to be on that rotation, and their partner or spouse is on daytime shifts, the lack of freedom to make choices about consistent times to work may put strains on the relationship, which, given human nature, are impossible to keep separate from mood and concentration when performing repetitive tasks; similarly, a sick child may make a parent have to call in to work and miss a day's pay, as there may not be money or arrangements for child care in such a circumstance. The employee may experience worry about lost wages and about performance reviews.

At the same time, many of the white-collar managers who are respon-sible for the performance of the workforce may recognize that it is also in the best interests of the company to foster a sense of belonging and friend-liness among workers, as their cooperation with each other is critical to the company's success. Thus, they may encourage things such as company sports teams, occasional picnics and outings, and a limited degree of social-ization among workers in the workplace. Some of this sense of communal membership may also come about from needs within the workforce: if a family has only one automobile (if that), workers may form carpools. They may work out among themselves ways of helping each other out, as in trad-ing shifts with the worker who has a sick child and needs to ensure that there is an adult home at all times. Management tends to prefer to control the kind and degree of communal life among the workers, as managers recognize that the deeper the personal bonds, the more likely it may become that the workers start advocating for themselves and each other.

The separation of work life and home life from communal culture that defines much of working-class experience has complex and often varied influences on the lives of its queer workers, and there are many variables at play. Historically, many working-class jobs and sites have had a large degree of sex segregation, as particular tasks are considered men's work (such as auto mechanics and electronics) and others women's work (clothing man-ufacture and the hair and beauty service industries). On the one hand, this could lead to extreme forms of closeting (and it has), whereby queer folk who might experience themselves as gender nonconforming have to work to compensate by performing a normative version, or "script" in Judith Butler's terms, of the gender they are classified as. On the other, working-class jobs can sometimes become havens for some queer folk. Sometimes this is because sex segregation, in the case of women, may allow for a greater acceptance of variability; working-class women have often not had quite as much investment in policing a kind of male-dictated normative femininity on other women, though this is not to say it does not happen. This is less the case for men, though their option may be to enter working-class occupations where male femininity is not only not stigmatized, but welcomed and even assumed, to the point where there have been "lavender" professions, such as hairstyling, interior decoration, and floral arranging; popular humor, such as it is, suggests that men in those work spaces are queer unless they prove themselves otherwise. Straight men have also sometimes shown more tolerance for "female masculinity" in traditionally male jobs as long as the women are adept and skillful at their work: indeed, even though some of these work spaces were initially slow to open to women, once they did, "butch" women were probably viewed more favorably than traditionally feminine women as auto mechanics, construction workers, and similarly "male" occupations.

Elizabeth Lapovsky Kennedy, a historian, and Madeline D. Davis, a librarian, chronicled the experience of working-class women in creating work and life communities in the Buffalo, New York, area in the mid-twentieth century in a deeply moving book, based on in-depth interviews, titled *Boots of Leather, Slippers of Gold: The History of a Lesbian Community,* published in 1993. These interviews revealed a number of phenomena of the lesbian community in that urban manufacturing center, some of which may be surprising, given stereotypes about the time period and the geographic location. They were able to identify a relatively large number of lesbian social spaces in Buffalo, including as many as twenty-six different ones at various time in the decades they studied, though not all existed at the same time. There were areas where some of these spaces were concentrated, but there were also outliers, some in neighborhoods that were racially segregated. In addition, they found that equally popular, particularly among African American working-class lesbians, were house parties, large gatherings in private homes, where there were various ways of charging admission, or charging for drinks, the food often provided, music and dancing available, and the safety of being with like-minded women a foremost attraction. Bars were always subject to police raids and graft, and there was some exploitation even by other queer people who owned the establishments, but they nonetheless provided places where these women could be who they were and with whom they wanted to be.

Not unexpectedly, given the history of gender, particularly among queer women during this period, the *butch-femme* conventions of role performance were prevalent, sometimes more rigidly, at other times more fluidly. It is interesting to note that racial segregation does not appear to have been as prevalent among these women as among the population at large. The African American lesbian writer and activist Audre Lorde observed, "Lesbians were probably the only Black and white women in New York City in the fifties who were making any real attempt to communicate with each other" (quoted in Kennedy and Davis 113). Kennedy and Davis don't make as strong a claim as that, but their interviewees suggest that color lines were much less strongly enforced than in straight society. Similarly, while gay men were a distinct minority in such spaces, some of the interviewees report their presence in lesbian-dominated bars as often quite welcome, especially by women who viewed themselves as upwardly mobile, who might appreciate some of the cultural interests of gay men; in turn, gay men acted respectfully and understood that they were guests in a women's space. In sum, Kennedy and Davis make a strong case that the working-class lesbians of Buffalo "pioneered ways of socializing together and creating intimate sexual relationships without losing the ability to make a living" (3). Were there challenges, defeats, lonely women? Of course, as there are at all times and in all places, but the examples of the women Kennedy and Davis interviewed remind us that the historical past is not always regressive and that the resourcefulness of brave people allows them to resist and adapt to the times and places in which they live, and that this ability is hardly unique to those with more formal kinds of education.

Anne Balay, a queer literary and cultural scholar, has studied the lives of queer steelworkers in northwest Indiana, near Gary, one of the midwestern centers for this kind of work. Like Kennedy and Davis, she used in-depth interviews with many workers as the source for her observations about what it means to be queer and working class in this traditionally male occupation. Having worked in the mills herself, she brings a degree of self-reflection to her work, a perspective often described as autoethnographic, in which the subjects the interviewer is studying get a chance to make their voices heard and the ethnographer (Balay) reflects on her own engagement with and difference from her subjects. Her study was published in *Steel Closets: Voices of Gay, Lesbian, and Transgender Steelworkers* (2014).

Balay includes transgender people in her study, which in itself breaks stereotypes about the identities of working-class people in this environment — a surprising number of her male interviewees identify as transgender, though most keep as clear a separation as possible between their presentation as male in the workplace and their gender expression as female at home or in their social worlds, which are usually many miles away from the mill. Conversely, trans men, because of the nature of steelwork and the clothing and equipment required, are able to pass more easily in the mills, though few of Balay's subjects make a point of revealing their trans identity to coworkers.

Balay's study is an important counterpoint to that of Kennedy and Davis, as a reminder that notions of progress over time always need to be kept in check and are always contingent on context, such as the kind of work being done and the conventions and protocols assumed or attributed to it. Balay acknowledges in the very opening pages of her book that steel-workers function as "those archetypes of working-class masculinity" (1), and that her study is intended to explore how this class and occupational identity "overlaps" with the interior and private lives of queer people. She identifies steelworking as part of "old-school macho culture" and notes its "resistance to progress of many kinds" (3). Thus, whereas the kinds of working-class spaces Kennedy and Davis identified in their study provided possibilities for expansion of opportunities for lesbian-identified women, steelworking, even though part of a larger labor movement that is usually depicted as progressive in U.S. political terms, is invested in maintaining masculine-centered characteristics and heteronormative practices.

As noted previously, *community* is a powerful concept in working-class culture, so the descriptions of isolation and compartmentalization of life many of Balay's interviewees report are especially wrenching. Mills tend to be isolated from whatever urban life there is in a community, even if they are situated near small towns, so the geographic isolation of the work space fosters social isolation: there is little to encourage workers to form bonds that extend beyond the shift. Though this may help queer steelworkers protect their identities in a job that is filled with actual physical danger and risk, and where homophobic violence can go unchecked or be disguised as the result of "accidents," the psychological costs can be enormous. Balay notes that many of her interviewees report experiencing what might be called a "damned if you do, damned if you don't" approach to social bonding in the workplace: to reveal personal information may be to make oneself vulnerable and at risk; to conceal large parts of non–work life may lead the worker to be viewed as not a good team player and therefore "ineffective" at one of the central skills of the kind of cooperative work such industries prize. As Balay suggests, the rotating shift work, in which a worker may for three weeks work one time shift, then be moved to a different one, often precludes or obstructs the development of deep bonds of friendship among queer steelworkers.

Hence, many queer steelworkers opt for secrecy, which is different from *privacy*, one of the hallmarks of upper- and upper-middle-class people. Privacy is a privilege and a luxury; secrecy carries with it risk of exposure and what follows from that. But for many steelworkers, it is a necessary choice; Balay notes that George Alan Appleby, a scholar of working-class queer men, asserts that secrecy is a matter of survival (Balay 65). For queer women (and in some ways for queer men), such secrecy can lead to sexual violence: women are raped by straight men in the workplace, and both queer women and queer men are sometimes coerced into unwanted sexual interactions for fear of exposure. For queer women and queer men, the stakes may be different: queer women are forced into sexual acts that are outside the spheres and objects of their desire, having to enact a heterosexual act that feels like a violation of who they know themselves to be at their core.

For queer men, there is an intricate and ugly cycle of desire and disgust — if they engage in sexual practices with straight men who have threatened to expose them, they have found a category that they desire (men), but they are denigrated for enjoying the acts themselves and also lose the agency of deciding with which men they choose to have sex. Such acts of secrecy devalue queer experience as anything other than a struggle for control, power, and rejection of the queer self as worthwhile and valuable — as anything other than an object for heteronormative exploitation.

The nature of steelwork provides a particular and somewhat unusual challenge for queer men. Because steelwork involves frequent, everyday contact with toxic materials — steelworkers average life spans at least ten years shorter — it is necessary for all workers to shower before they leave the mill. Because locker rooms and showers are sex-segregated, the necessity of women's showering does not produce a lot of risk: there are few women to begin with, and women's changing and cleaning areas have traditionally provided more privacy, such as separate stalls, because of social views of women's "natural modesty" about their bodies. This is not the case for men, however, who typically shower in communal spaces that offer no provisions for private space. Queer men in the mills, then, must pass through a daily gauntlet, in which they not only expose their naked bodies in communal spaces, but are exposed to others', with all the vulnerabilities such an experience may produce. Balay devotes an entire section to "the shower," so central a part is it of queer male experience in the steel mills. On the one hand, it is the queerest possible space, in which male-male interaction of naked bodies is mandated, and all kinds of desire may be felt or produced and sometimes acted on; on the other hand, the shower room also becomes a place where masculinity and normativity are constantly being tested, and those who "fail" (an uncontrolled erection? a "just-too-long" lingering glance at the body of another man? a script of ridicule and suggestion by other, presumably straight men?) are subject to derision and potential physical violence. For trans men, a communal shower would be unthinkable, as most do not have bottom (genital) surgeries — not only would such a space automatically out them, it would break conventions and protocols and make them even more vulnerable to physical violence — another way in which workplace issues regarding class play out differently for LGB people and trans people.

Some of the queer women report that they gain some acceptance, even if they are out, by their fellow male steelworkers: in the illogical algebra of such mind-sets, because lesbians are attracted to other women, some of the straight male steelworkers accept them as "one of us," though the nature and experience of the desire are often quite different. Some of the queer male steelworkers, those who have made the brave decision to be out in the mill, sometimes acknowledge that being out may allow them opportunities for sexual pleasure, which sometimes has the appearance of and may actually indeed qualify as consensual. Once out, these men report being sought by other men, who usually identify as straight, for unidirectional sexual satisfaction, the queer men inevitably "cast" as the bottom for oral sex, which, in practical terms, is the most manageable sexual act. Such encounters are kept surreptitious; there is always the implicit or explicit threat of violence should the queer man tell anyone about the encounter. Hence, considering this kind of interaction as consensual in the broadest sense is questionable. Some queer men report using humor, a kind of wit that defuses the potential for danger, often through a kind of sassiness and defiance that mix masculinity and femininity. But conditions continue to be grim within the workplace.

No wonder, then, that most of the steelworkers decide to live in places that, while within commuting distance, are as far from the mill as possible. This adds the hardship of spending extra time going to and from work, but it does afford some sense of a safe place where they can more authentically live out identities that have been made risky in their workplace. Though Balay interviews some men who do identify as trans, and one or two even acknowledge their identity in the workplace (sometimes to straight men they have observed elsewhere in the nearby Gary and Chicago "gayborhoods," where the straight men have traveled for their own sexual release with other men, while maintaining a domestically heterosexual life), for most of these men, their trans identity is their most secret piece of their selfhood, which undoubtedly adds to the stress that trans people experience even in the most welcoming and accepting areas of society.

A question arises: If the lives of working-class queers are so oppressive, why not seek other avenues of employment? To be certain, some do. But class mobility, whatever the favorite myths of U.S. history may be, is not so easily accomplished and may not even be desired. Many of the steelworkers describe pride in doing their work well and take pleasure in the nature of the work itself. For some, family and economic conditions, as well as lack of access to other options, keep them in their positions. It is itself a classist position to assume that everyone should aspire to a higher social, economic, and occupational class—just as much as it is homophobic to assume that all queer people would, if they could, opt for the more socially advantageous status of heterosexuality. Nonetheless, it is also the case that, given the deindustrialization of the United States (including such jobs being moved to foreign countries), as well as reductions in health care and other traditional benefits, working-class people, while they may enjoy both their work and the communities in which they live, may feel increasingly pressed to rise economically, if not socially.

## Lower-Class Queers: "Everybody's a Little Bit Gay"

Some scholars prefer to use phrases like *working poor* as a substitute for *lower class*, and it is true that most of the people about whom this section is written do indeed hold jobs or find other ways of making livings. *Lower class* is a more capacious term, including people who, for whatever reason, do not work and may be largely or completely dependent on either government aid or other forms of support. The term *lower class* has accumulated negative social and ethical connotations, as well: there is usually some sense of reference to people who are burdens or lazy, judgments that are often superficial and simply reductive in terms of the economic processes and occupational barriers these people face in today's society.

As Nancy Isenberg repeatedly and powerfully argues in her book *White Trash*, the concept of *white trash* has historically served a number of purposes, as "our class system has hinged on the evolving political rationales used to dismiss or demonize (or occasionally reclaim) those white rural outcasts seemingly incapable of become part of the mainstream society" (xiv). In other words, white trash or "lower-class whites" serve as a kind of convenient "Other" against which both white and nonwhite people can measure their own worthiness. As long as you can identify as anything other than lower class, there is someone you can feel superior to.

Lisa Henderson suggests that "working-class people . . . are imagined as physically just *too* much" (35), a kind of nightmare of excessive corporeality (bodied-ness). The phrase "honest working-class people" is an easy one for most people to conceptualize; "honest lower-class people" does not fall so easily from the tongue, as the descriptor *lower* feels inevitably bound up, to most of us, with moral judgments. Isenberg turns to the classic American novel *To Kill a Mockingbird* to show how these class hierarchies work even among children: while there are poor people in the Maycomb of the novel, Jem Finch, the older brother of the narrator, Scout, is able to express the stratification of the town, placing the Ewell family, the antagonists, as even lower than other people without much money.

What is excessive about the bodies of lower-class people, as imagined by those who identify outside their sphere? In a literal sense, lower-class bodies may be imagined as either too big or too small, and different scenarios and moral judgments are attributed to them. The obese lower-class body is typically viewed as the product of poor food choices, greedy and insatiable consumption, laziness and indolence — all of which, of course, lead to assumptions about the characters of the people who inhabit such bodies. If pushed further, people may also engage in language about diseases, such as diabetes, that are associated with the too-large body. Conversely, the too-thin lower-class body is suspect in its own way, never viewed as the product of someone monitoring their health or engaging in physical fitness in a positive way. In the story of the too-thin lower-class body, drug use is often inferred (especially such substances as methamphetamines, sometimes regionally referred to as "hillbilly heroin"), poor dental and skin hygiene is assumed, along with poverty that makes food difficult to obtain — the implication being that the too-thin lower-class person has inverted, deviant priorities about what to spend money on (and where to spend it).

Of course, the excessiveness of the lower-class body as a material symbol of a lack of adherence to good practices becomes aligned with various other moral failings, and nonnormative sexuality can all too easily become one of them. For generations, people categorized as lower class have also often been the targets of jokes about such practices as incest, bestiality, infidelity, and overworked libidos (perhaps because they have so little access to more refined forms of entertainment). The eugenics movement in the twentieth century in the United States sought to "thin" or "right" the human species, and its primary targets, in addition to people of color (to be discussed in the next chapter), were poor white people, especially recent immigrants from such European countries as Ireland and Italy. Though there was not necessarily a lot of attention paid to homosexual poor white people in terms of plans for sterilization, perhaps because it was assumed that in those cases, homosexuality was nature's way of stopping reproduction, the projects of forced sterilization were almost always aimed at either lower-class people or people with disabilities — who, both by extension and by economic deprivation, were often elided as one "class" — the class that did not have the right to continue to "breed" (notice the language of animal husbandry). No doubt many felt the same way about lower-class people in general (who were and sometimes still are assumed to be mentally inferior to people from other classes) and about queer people, whose sexual identities could be cast as either disabilities or inappropriate class behaviors.

Where does that leave people who identify as queer and who either identify or are identified as lower class? Such people may find themselves either lacking any kind of queer community that welcomes them, as more "respectable" queers may not wish to be associated with them, or cast out from their own communities and families of origin. In the United States, lower-class people often have less access to broad educational options, so it is also possible to imagine that the kinds of opportunities to understand diverse lives may be limited by circumstance and by some religious or political affiliations that are homophobic. This is by no means to suggest in a sweeping way that all people who fit into the socioeconomic lower class *are* homophobic: one could even imagine they may be more accepting of diverse lives — if one comes from a maligned class, one might be more sympathetic to others whose lives are judged by outsiders. It can certainly go either way, depending on the contexts and experiences.

One of the more visible examples of a queer-positive lower-class popular narrative is that provided by the TLC series *Here Comes Honey Boo Boo*, which ran for fifty-two episodes over a period of four seasons. The series followed the adventures and fortunes of the Thompson-Shannon family, who lived in McIntyre, Georgia, a town of under one thousand. Honey Boo Boo was the family nickname for the youngest daughter, Alana Thompson, who originally came to public attention on the series *Toddlers & Tiaras*, which documented child beauty pageants and on which Honey Boo Boo competed. The nuclear family was composed of two adults, who were not married, and various offspring, who did not all share the same set of parents.

What queered this lower-class family (whose fortunes rose economically because of the series) was the introduction of Honey Boo Boo's uncle Lee "Poodle" Thompson. The series depicted Uncle Poodle as an openly gay man, loved by his niece, who pronounced her position on his sexual orientation in the last episode of the first season, saying, "Ain't nothin' wrong with bein' a little gay. . . . Everybody's a little gay" ("Honey Boo Boo Declares, 'Everybody's a Little Bit Gay," *Huffington Post*, September 27, 2012, www.huffington post.com/2012/09/27/honey-boo-boo-uncle-poodle-gay_n_1919874.html). Many might contest Honey Boo Boo's declaration of the universality of gayness, but it is also true that this was a different way of seeing and hearing a lower-class body and voice comment on queerness. It emerged that the nickname Poodle for her uncle came from Honey Boo Boo's habit of referring to any gay person as a "poodle" (including Anderson Cooper).

Uncle Poodle was depicted as a sympathetic member of the family, not an outsider. He also not long after revealed that he was HIV-positive. He told a complicated story about how he became infected, which involved a former lover who had not disclosed his serostatus to him before they had sex, and he also claimed to have had the lover sent to jail (Mark S. King, "The Strange Case of Uncle Poodle," *Plus*, May 27, 2013, www.hivplusmag. com/opinion/guest-voices/2013/05/27/op-ed-strange-case-uncle-poodle). This led a number of journalists, especially from queer media, to question the time line and facts of the story, which somewhat tarnished Uncle Poodle's status as the face of queer redneck culture. But Uncle Poodle returned to a somewhat heroic stature when he and Honey Boo Boo's mother, June, got into a conflict because June was dating a registered sex offender who had been found guilty of molesting another one of June's daughters. Uncle Poodle then was rehabilitated for a while as the responsible uncle who wanted to protect his nieces from the very sexual offenses that are all too often assumed to be associated with lower-class values and practices.

However problematic the various contradictory aspects of the series as a whole and of Uncle Poodle's character were, the openly gay lower-class individual had a name, a face, and agency. In this sense, the series might have done positive work in outing lower-class culture (in this case, southern rural) from a closet of invisibility. Indeed, as part of a Pride issue, *Creative Loafing*, an online Atlanta newspaper, published a list not unlike one of the comic Jeff Foxworthy's routines, called "You Might Be a Gay Redneck If . . ." Here are a few lines from the catalog of experiences and characteristics that complete the title sentence:

> You met your last boyfriend in the Waffle House restroom.
> You root for the NASCAR driver with the cutest jumpsuit.
> You go commando in your overalls.
> Your mullet has frosted tips.
> Your Pride float spends the rest of the year on cinder blocks in your front yard.
>
> (*Creative Loafing*, September 29, 2006, http://clatl.com/atlanta/you
> -might-be-a-gay-redneck-if/Content?oid=2153749)

Such jokes serve a useful purpose for the people who read the newspaper and for the culture of gay men who may have felt excluded from the queer middle class and above: they are a kind of folklore, a "knowing" shared by people who regard each other as kin. Yes, they can also evoke laughter from outsiders, who may see such a feature as an opportunity to look down at another class, but they also allow members of the "gay redneck" class a way to see each other and to speak out of common experiences of the intersectionality of queerness and class experience. That is not a function to be undervalued.

## SPOTLIGHT ON LITERATURE: DOROTHY ALLISON, QUEER "BASTARD OUT OF CAROLINA"

Perhaps the greatest speaker for the queer lower class is the writer Dorothy Allison. Allison is a writer, born in 1949 in Greenville, South Carolina, probably best known for her 1992 semiautobiographical novel *Bastard Out of Carolina*, which was made into a TV film by the actor and director Anjelica Huston. It is a novel that chronicles the abuse and poverty Allison herself experienced, with a depth of insight and characterization and a fineness of style that made readers and critics take notice. Allison herself came from what we have been calling the lower class, and she was the first member of her family to graduate from high school. Her intelligence and determination earned her a National Merit Scholarship, and she graduated from college and did graduate work in anthropology in Florida. She has also written openly and proudly not only about her lesbian identity, but about other aspects of sexuality, such as BDSM (which stands for bondage-discipline-sado-masochism), that are important to her. Tellingly, she named a book of short stories *Trash*, embracing that class epithet with a kind of defiant pride in her roots and in those parts of herself that she would not ever erase, even if she thought she could. Her experience of growing up both queer and lower class gave her a grit, made her vision unique and authentic.

She also writes with painful honesty about the tensions between her life as a writer, artist, and sometime academic, who now is a recognized and honored member of the "creative" class and her origins and loyalty to her family. In an essay in her book *Skin: Talking about Sex, Class and Literature* (1994), she writes about the complicated and intense feelings she experienced in bringing her girlfriend at the time, a more traditionally middle-class woman, home to meet her family. Another essay, "A Question of Class," is worth reading in its entirety, but we will end this chapter with a brief excerpt from it, to try to suggest how interconnected the various issues we have explored in this chapter are for Allison — and for all queer people, in their own ways, as they are born of individual experiences and class positions. She recalls listening to an army recruiter referring to foreign people as an othered "They," which leads her to consider her own identity:

> When I was six or eight back in Greenville, South Carolina, I had heard the same matter-of-fact tone of dismissal applied to me. "Don't play with her. I don't want you talking to them." Me and my family, we had always been *they*. Who am I? I wondered, listening to that recruiter. Who are my people? We die so easily, disappear so completely — we/they, the poor and the queer. I pressed my bony white trash fists to my stubborn lesbian mouth. The rage was a good feeling, stronger and purer than the shame that followed it, the fear and the sudden urge to run and hide, to deny, to pretend I did not know who I was and what the world would do to me.
>
> My people were not remarkable. We were ordinary, but even so we were mythical. We were the *they* everyone talks about — the ungrateful poor. I grew up trying to run away from the fate that destroyed so many of the people I loved, and having learned the habit of hiding, I found I had also learned to hide from myself. I did not know who I was, only that I did not want to be *they*, the ones who are destroyed or dismissed to make the "real" people, the

important people, feel safer. By the time I understood that I was queer, that habit of hiding was deeply set in me, so deeply that it was not a choice but an instinct. Hide, hide to survive, I thought, knowing that if I told the truth about my life, my family, my sexual desire, my history, I would move over into that unknown territory, the land of they, would never have the chance to name my own life, to understand it or claim it.

Why are you so afraid? my lovers and friends have asked me the many times I have suddenly seemed a stranger, someone who would not speak to them, would not do the things they believed I should do, simple things like applying for a job, or a grant, or some award they were sure I could acquire easily. Entitlement, I have told them, is a matter of feeling like we rather than they. You think you have a right to things, a place in the world, and it is so intrinsically a part of you that you cannot imagine people like me, people who seem to live in your world, who don't have it. I have explained what I know over and over, in every way I can, but I have never been able to make clear the degree of my fear, the extent to which I feel myself denied: not only that I am queer in a world that hates queers, but that I was born poor in a world that despises the poor. (13–14)

## ISSUES FOR INVESTIGATION

**1.** In an elaboration of the "invisible knapsack," McIntosh identified dozens of different kinds of items in the white-privilege knapsack, which she described as "special provisions, assurances, tools, maps, guides, codebooks, passports, visas, clothes, compass, emergency gear, and blank checks," the burden of which were "weightless" for white people. McIntosh discusses both the list of the knapsack's contents and her analysis of them at www.collegeart.org/pdf/diversity/white-privilege-and-male-privilege.pdf. Are there some items that you think no longer exist in McIntosh's knapsack (have they "expired"?), some that have been transformed? Are there others you would add?

Do the same for heterosexuality. Whatever your sexual identity, try to brainstorm, both individually and as a group, about what is in the "heterosexual knapsack"?

**2.** Dorothy Allison and class: Closely reread the passage at the end of the chapter with your classmates. How does Allison create a kind of dialogue between her queer and class identities? In what sense are the two parts of her being inextricable from each other? Which words in Allison's essay stand out for you as markers of the priorities, values, and desires of Allison's "people," the poor, lower-class white folk in her family and in her home communities? Are there one or two terms that also serve this definitional purpose for queer people of each class?

## SUGGESTIONS FOR FURTHER READING AND VIEWING

Allen, Samantha. *Real Queer America: LGBT Stories from Red States*. New York: Little, Brown, 2019.

Balay, Anne. *Semi Queer: Inside the World of Gay, Trans, and Black Truck Drivers*. Chapel Hill: University of North Carolina Press, 2018.

*Beach Rats*. Directed by Eliza Hickman. Cinereach, 2017.

Cuomo, Chris J., and Kim Q. Hall, eds. *Whiteness: Feminist Philosophical Reflections*. Lanham, MD: Rowman & Littlefield, 1999.

Forster, E. M. *Maurice*. New York: Norton, 1971. (Note: A film version of this novel is available.)

Ma'ayan, Hadar Dubowsky. "A White Queer Geek at School: Intersections of Whiteness and Queer Identity." *Journal of LGBT Youth* 8.1 (2011): 84–98.

Mock, Janet. *Redefining Realness: My Path to Womanhood, Identity, Love, & So Much More*. New York: Atria, 2014.

Waters, Sarah. *Tipping the Velvet*. London: Virago, 1998. (Note: A BBC miniseries is available.)

Williams, Anthony J. "A Black Queer Man's Syllabus to Whiteness." *Medium*, December 27, 2016. https://medium.com/anthoknees/a-black-queer-mans-syllabus-to-whiteness-c21d851b6016.

# CHAPTER 6

# QUEERING INTERSECTIONALITY
## Race and Ethnicity

In the previous chapter, we examined the concept of *whiteness* as what might be called a hegemonic position of identity, against which, consciously and unconsciously, other categories of race and ethnicity are contrasted or evaluated. This chapter examines four other categories of racial and ethnic identity, ones that have historically not had as much access to power or opportunity in the United States. In particular, our focus is on how queerness and racial and ethnic identity intersect to produce a more complex sense of identity than any single category can, an approach imported from critical race theory, which began by examining how categories of race (specifically blackness) and gender (women in particular) created experiences and practices different from those of either node of identity looked at individually.

## QUEER NATIVE AMERICANS: TWO-SPIRIT PEOPLE

Terminology used to name and categorize the indigenous people of North America, particularly in the United States, has varied and continues to change, reflecting various views of history and power over time. For those of us who grew up in the twentieth century as outsiders to the cultures of these people, the dominant term for many decades was *American Indian* or sometimes simply *Indian*. The term *Indian* misrepresents history and geocultural presence in many respects, a by-product of Columbus's navigational errors and misconceptions about the people with whom he made contact. From the 1960s forward, a term that gained favor and eventually became the U.S. government's official designation was *Native American*. Yet that also, some activists noted, flattens all indigenous peoples into one category. In recent years, some people who claim indigenous identity have reembraced *American Indian*. Still others suggest that the most meaningful

Henderson, Bruce, *Queer Studies: Beyond Binaries*
dx.doi.org/10.17312/harringtonparkpress/2019.09.qsbb.006
© 2019 by Harrington Park Press

way to identify these longtime inhabitants of North America is by tribal affiliation, when known, such as Cherokee or Sioux, using the language of the tribe when possible. In Canada, the overall term has been *First Nations*, and it includes northern indigenous people, such as Inuits.

For about a century, the term for the variations from heterosexual relations among Native Americans was rooted in the word **berdache**, a French term (passed down from Persian) that translates as "catamite," an equally outdated term, but one that historically referred to a boy who had sex with a man: there was almost always a generational and power differential inherent in the term, and it was always gendered in referring to someone with an anatomically male-appearing body. The term *berdache* was clearly problematic because its origins suggested the stigmas and devaluing that were then dominant in sexual or erotic relationships between men: it reduced one partner to a childlike status (the "boy" in the relationship, harking back to classical Greek traditions, which were utterly foreign to Native cultures), and assumed the same binary that had been operative in European-based cultures.

What was most notable to Westerners was that such people, the berdaches, were not, as best as they could see, viewed as transgressive or "sinful" within the community, though there was often humor at their expense. There was also an attempt to construct a corresponding category for biological women, "female berdaches," who often took biological women as wives and participated in warrior culture, which in most Native American tribes was a masculine domain.

Queer Native Americans have generally called for an end to the use of the term *berdache*, not least because it was a term that was imposed on them by outsiders. In its place, they prefer the term *Two-Spirit people*, which, though still an English term, has a history across a number of Native cultures. While *Two-Spirit* acknowledges male/masculine and female/feminine as distinct and discernible positions in human experience, the term also imagines and validates a third domain, whose inhabitants live "between" and "within" the two realms. It is not the same as bisexual, which implies sexual attraction to multiple sexes or genders; or transgender, which implies a fairly unidirectional movement from one gender to another; or even genderfluid, whereby an individual may move back and forth between genders over time, even within a day or an hour.

**Two-Spirit** is something different from any of these, and, hence, it is important to recognize that it is useful only within Native American culture and within Native American systems of spirituality and communal experience. Qwo-Li Driskill (who identifies as Two-Spirit) and the other editors of the important collection *Queer Indigenous Studies: Critical Interventions in Theory, Politics, and Literature* suggest that a Two-Spirit concept of identity places emphasis on the spiritual dimensions of identity and sexuality without "losing the function of the erotic." Thus, Two-Spirit as an identity does not focus on the social organization of labor (as did the term *berdache*) or the mechanics of sexual activities, but allows for an understanding of gender and sexual identity as tied to a sense of being in the world that spans the seeming bridge between polarities of gender. In the words of Brian Joseph Gilley, Two-Spirit is a "personal subjectivity consisting of two spirits, one male and one female" (quoted in Bishop-Stall, 127).

A number of scholars point to the queer Latinx scholar José Esteban Muñoz's concept of **disidentification** as useful for understanding Two-Spirit sexual identity and gender identity expression: Muñoz argues that people who belong to minority groups engage in a practice by which they neither ignore nor fully reject majoritarian practices or majority images of the minority, but work and play resistantly within them. In this sense, Two-Spirit people do not reject either masculinity or femininity but trouble the binary opposition that on the surface seems inherent in them.

Native American scholars point to the ways in which Native American spirituality and existence have been importantly rooted in their relationship to the land, to the permeability of human, animal, and spiritual (i.e., nonmaterial) existences as part of what it means to be Native American. While it is certainly true that non-Natives have also been tied to the land, they have often, in the case of North America, been focused on how to use the land for human profit; in Native American spirituality, the land is viewed as a living entity, and people as emergent from the entirety of the land. Mark Rifkin writes of "placemaking" as inherent to Native American identity and suggests an "erotics of place" that is tied to how Two-Spirit people experience themselves as spiritual and physical beings (xii).

Because Two-Spirit people have been viewed as different kinds of people in Native tribes, but not as outsiders, they have often been provided honored places within the community. Viewed as embodying the spectrum of gender identities and experiences, some have adopted the role of *shamans*, or holy leaders, who in Native American culture have access to the spirit world and to worlds we associate with medicine and psychology. They may learn from or be trained by other Two-Spirit people or others designated as shamans, and they are often considered even more spiritually gifted than non–Two-Spirit shamans, conduits between the material and the spiritual realms.

It important, however, not to assume that Two-Spirit people do not face homophobia and transphobia, both within their Native communities and from society at large. Qwo-Li Driskill writes about the devaluing of Two-Spirit sexuality within some Native communities, focusing in particular on the case in 2004 of two women, Dawn McKinley and Kathy Reynolds, who initially were able to get a tribal marriage license from the Cherokee nation. This was quickly rescinded, and a tribal law was passed banning same-sex marriage. Because only Congress has legal authority over Native tribes, the protections currently in place outside Native territories do not apply. At the same time, as of this writing, at least twenty-seven nations do permit legal marriage between same-sex members, a right that was first passed by the Coquille tribe of Oregon in 2009. In many tribes, there is no specific edict either allowing or forbidding marriage between same-sex couples, and there are eleven tribes where it is explicitly legally forbidden.

What is the basis for opposition to marriage equality in some Native tribes? The effect of Christian missionaries in the eighteenth, nineteenth, and twentieth centuries on Native attitudes, particularly those of conservative Christianity, which opposes same-sex relationships and marriage equality today across the country, may account for some of the opposition. In an op-ed piece published on the site *Indian Country Today Media Network* in 2015, Steve Russell sums up the complexity of the situation this way: "Those who would take the side of the missionaries against their own tribal citizens, on the other hand, enjoy the same protection from state or federal interference. This is so even when what is being protected is the sovereign right to swim against the current of history" (Steve Russell, "The Headlines Are Wrong! Same-Sex Marriage Not Banned across Indian Country," *Indian Country Today*, April 23, 2015, https://newsmaven.io/indian countrytoday/archive/the-headlines-are-wrong-same-sex-marriage-not -banned-across-indian-country-5OSYm8SPYU6M8r9JsaUj6A/). Russell's point is that the nature of tribal law allows individual communities or nations (a word that has often replaced *tribes*, which carries colonialist historical connotations for many) to maintain practices that forbid same-sex marriage, even though, as Russell suggests, not only does this go against federal law but it also is in contradiction to the growing support of same-sex marriage nationally. Of course, what complicates this more is that *marriage*, as conceived and surveilled by federal and state governments, was often a Western and colonialist imposition on peoples who had other ways of defining and establishing formal and informal unions and kinship, as the scholar J. Kēhaulani Kauanui points out was the case with Hawai'i.

Sociologists began to observe, after about 1950, that Native men who identified as attracted to the same sex began to leave reservations and move to more accepting urban areas, such as San Francisco. The scholar Beatrice Medicine recalls hearing that homophobic comments were made at traditional Native American gatherings in such urban areas, which suggests that the influence of outside attitudes traveled to the reservations and then back again into the off-reservation communities within cities. Nonetheless, the growth of contemporary Two-Spirit identity, as a reclamation of Native

traditions that both predate and resist Western contact and Christian proselytizing, continues, whether it goes under the name of Two-Spirit or some
other marker of identity. Artists, including writers, performers, and filmmakers, have been instrumental in giving voice to celebrations of Two-Spirit
identities and experiences, and to what might even be called an epistemology
(a way of knowing) that comes from the intersection of Native and queer
lives. Some of these artists identify as queer or some variation of this term.
Individual writers, such as Paula Gunn Allen, provide testimony to the rich-
ness of living on the particular hyphen of queer and Native American. Beth
Brant has used the Native American figure of Coyote, a trickster hero, to
explore queer Native life, with humorous, sly, and thought-provoking results.

Non-queer-identified Native American writers have also integrated
queer material and characters into their works. For example, the Ojibwe novelist Louise Erdrich has, throughout her career, written narratives that constantly contest and question gender and sexual roles, among both Native and
non-Native people. One of her most complex and fascinating novels is *The
Last Report on the Miracles at Little No Horse* (2001), in which she tells the
story of a Catholic nun who goes to an Ojibwe reservation as a missionary,
transforms herself into a priest (thus living out a kind of asexual but Two-
Spirit gendered life), and lives to the age of one hundred and may become a
saint. Erdrich's novel suggests the ways in which two very different cultures —
Ojibwe and Catholic — may work together to produce good works.

**Spotlight on the Arts: Queer Native American Writers**
"Some Like Indians Endure" by Paula Gunn Allen, a mixed-race, Pueb-
lo-identified lesbian feminist writer and activist, presents the histories and
complexities of queer Native American lives. These lives embody the intersectionalities Allen lived and celebrate both the sorrows and the power
involved in them. Her strategic use of vernacular terms, such as *dykes* and
the lower-case *indians*, to reclaim and honor her people, with whom she
shared histories of containment and confinement, effectively places *dykes*,
*indians*, and queer lesbians in spaces that remain invisible to and separate
from the larger United States. At the same time, these terms also acknowledge that such people, when they move, by choice or necessity, into diaspora, often feel excluded or marginalized. Allen nonetheless asserts their
strength and resilience, both tied to their connections to land and spirit as
inextricable sources of power.

Though Allen identified as a dyke, that is, a lesbian, there are other
important queer Native American writers who identify as queer by virtue of
their gender identity and expression. As is true of any other racial or ethnic
group, there is variation in terms of language, concept of identity, and sense

of self. Max Wolf Valerio wrote a memoir titled *The Testosterone Files*, published in 2006, in which he documented his transition from female to male. As the magazine the *Advocate* points out, he is probably the only man to have an essay published in the classic anthology of feminist scholarship, *This Bridge Called My Back* (Diane Anderson-Minshall, "Eight LGBT Native Americans You Should Know," the *Advocate*, November 23, 2012, https://www.advocate.com/politics/2012/11/23/eight-lgbt-native-americans-you-should-know).

Nonetheless, in an article he wrote with the provocative title "Why I'm Not Transgender," Valerio asserts that he prefers the word *transsexual* to describe his process and his identity: "I did not change my core gender identity. I changed my biological sex. True, I cannot entirely alter it, but I decisively shifted the rudder of my biology from female to male, most importantly through the use of testosterone, but also through surgery and the unequivocal daily living in the world as a man." He eschews the word *transgender* for himself, adding, it "doesn't remind people of the cutting and sewing of flesh during sex change surgery. It doesn't conjure up images of the regular injection of potent hormones that have lowered my voice, altered my distribution of body fat, made my bones more massive and enabled me to grow an Adam's apple." He argues that, for him, *transgender* is too vague a term, one that does not address the lived experience of his body-mind. He argues for the utility of *queer* as an umbrella term. Obviously, his position is not intended to generalize, but what is useful in thinking of how that position might emerge from the intersections of race and sex/gender is its focus on embodied (or, to use another term, *enfleshed*) experience as central to his being in the world, reminding us of the traditions in Native American life, culture, and spirituality that are always grounded in the experience of the material, animated world.

There are many Native Americans (and many individuals who identify as mixed-race or multiracial, but whose Native American heritage is an important element) who fit somewhere between Allen and Valerio in terms of emphasizing sexual orientation and sex or gender identity as central to their sense of queerness. Sources at the end of the chapter will point you to collections where you can explore this spectrum (or kaleidoscope?) further.

## QUEER AFRICAN AMERICANS

If the history of queer Native Americans as a group has focused on containment, invisibility, and loss of land and, hence, power and identity, the experience of African Americans and, thus, by extension, queer African Americans has inversely focused on themselves being turned into property — and property through theft at that. The more than three centuries of enslavement of people of African descent have a legacy that remains present today, a legacy whose effects include the lives of queer African Americans.

As the scholar Charles I. Nero suggests, the historical work of discovering and examining the intimate lives of enslaved people is still in process and much remains to be done, but there is no reason to assume that there were not meaningful same-sex relationships between black men and between black women, but the ways in which such relationships (or even short-term interactions that had erotic dimensions — the equivalent of hookups) were carried out and what they meant to the people involved remain to be read and articulated. What is emerging, according to recent scholarship, is a degree of reasonable certainty that white men (and probably women) did engage in same-sex relations with enslaved black people and that such relations were, by definition, nonconsensual, as a slave did not have the status to consent. The scholar Vincent Woodard has chronicled, by piecing together existing materials — literature, chronicles, legal accounts, and memoirs — the ways in which what he called "the delectable Negro" became a repeated trope or pattern in nineteenth-century accounts. Woodard subtitled his book "Human Consumption and Homoeroticism within U.S. Slave Culture," suggesting an intertwining, intersectional relationship between various ways of regarding the black body as property, whether for literal cannibalistic purposes (i.e., actual eating) or more figurative consumption, through sexual use.

Woodard traces the history of the consumption of black bodies back to such historical events as the wreck of the whaling ship *Essex*, which was the basis for Herman Melville's novel *Moby-Dick*. As Woodard points out, cannibalism occurred after the wreck, and such acts, though not widely publicized, were hardly unique to this boat and this accident. What remained underemphasized and underanalyzed was the fact that the first four individuals eaten were black men: Woodard points out that there is still no satisfactory historical documentation that determines whether the men were already dead by the time the decision was made to eat their bodies or they were murdered. From this starting point, Woodard traces, in often painful and gruesome detail, accounts from slave memoirs and narratives of literal and symbolic cannibalism that took place on plantations. Often the punishment of black (usually) male enslaved people involved flaying their bodies; this punishment included rituals that treated the bodies in ways that aligned them with food, such as "spicing," the pouring on of substances that were intended to preserve the "meat" or enhance its "flavor." Woodard is led to draw connections to queer performances involving black slave bodies through language that suggests, often indirectly or through euphemism, homoerotic emotions and, no doubt, acts on slave bodies. Because black people were not viewed as having the same rights as white people, those engaged in slave ownership (and their white employees) had erotic access to the bodies of enslaved people.

It is important to keep in mind that, at the time, there was no fixed identity that would be recognizable as the present-day one of the homosexual or gay man or lesbian, just as there was no concept of the heterosexual or straight person. There was the figure of the sodomite, always viewed as someone unnatural and outside society and the law, and whose actions could be and were frequently punishable by death. But it is also not necessarily the case that all men who engaged in sexual acts with other men, whatever their race, would have identified in a stable, ongoing way as a sodomite, and this seems particularly true if the object of their same-sex desire and activity was not white. This behavior probably would have been viewed as only slightly transgressive, not even worthy of comment or policing, as the slave would not be viewed as a person who could have a legitimate say in participating in such acts.

One of the results of this form of consumption by white men of black male bodies was the diminishment of the black man's masculinity. Since he was the object of rape — the person whose anus or mouth was violated, to put it in graphic terms — he was thus equated with being a woman and, hence, feminized. Such men were placed in a double bind: they had no choice about whether to participate in such acts, but they were nonetheless viewed as less than men and less than masculine for being a kind of substitute for women in various forms of intercourse. Ironically, this text of diminished masculinity runs in contradictory ways alongside an equally offensive and inaccurate depiction of and attitude toward black masculinity: the stereotype of the hypersexual, overmasculine "buck," the phantasmic image white supremacist groups have used, from the origins of the Ku Klux Klan through the present day, as a way of maintaining anxiety about whether black men are "safe" to include in society and as citizens.

In the second half of the twentieth century this legacy of slavery and homoerotic consumption continued to affect the lives of queer black men and, by implication, women, as well. Just as black people moved to major urban areas, particularly the northern ones identified in studies of "the Great Migration," the historian John D'Emilio argues there was a similar pattern of migration by people who would identify in some way as queer in general. Queer black people who wished to make their domestic or erotic lives with other queer people could find some degree of anonymity in such cities; they thus found spaces — not always entirely welcoming and by no means devoid of racism — in places like Harlem in New York City. There were enclaves where such individuals could lead queer lives, as much as people from the dominant white queer population could. Accounts from the period, roughly spanning the end of the nineteenth to the middle of the twentieth centuries, suggest that there were even some spaces for black people who today might claim trans as an identity. There were also popular shows and cabarets featuring drag queens, as well as singers such as Gladys Bentley and Ma Rainey, who included lyrics referring to lesbian desire and life in their acts.

Outside these closed communities, however, the most dominant social institutions that supported black people remained resolutely heteronormative, at least in their public presentation: the family and the church (most significantly at the time, various forms of Protestant Christianity, often evangelical). Because occupational and professional opportunities remained by and large limited for the vast majority of black people during this period, the family, including its extended members sometimes not related by blood ties, and the church were places where black people could belong, show respect for each other, and achieve status and validation.

How does "black queerness" fit into this familiar history of economic disparities, urbanization, and scapegoating of black people? Just as the containment of Native Americans on reservations and in residential schools (typically established and run by Christian, especially Catholic, clergy, designed to "beat the Indian" out of the "boy") frequently led to a kind of containment of their capacity to lead positively queer lives, except when they could claim Two-Spirit identities within their own cultures, so the heteronormative pressures of family, church, and community for black people may be seen as tied to crises over gender, sexuality, and sexual identity. Openly queer black men were liable to be viewed as having "sold out" their masculinity in order to follow their erotic and emotional desires: some Afrocentric thinkers continue to insist, contrary to historical and anthropological evidence, that homosexuality is a purely white invention and that only blacks who are willing to abandon their "blackness" participate in queer relationships, culture, and community.

Other social factors, such as the overrepresentation of black men in the prison system, where homosexual acts (if not homoerotic desires and queer identities) are frequent and also many times violent and coercive, may account for the ways the larger, non-queer society may view queer black people (especially men) as having a problem of being "too" sexual and in ways that are not properly contained or containable, either by self or by society.

Until the last few decades, queer black people who lived openly queer lives often found themselves marginalized, made invisible, or policed, as an embarrassment to a kind of theoretical idea of "proper blackness." Thus, the writer James Baldwin, who courageously did depict black queer lives in his fiction and his essays, nonetheless had an ambivalent relationship to gay politics throughout much of his life, and when he wrote his first novel to include representations of gay life, *Giovanni's Room*, he deliberately did not include queer black characters, but set the story among white expatriates in Paris; he did not believe he could write about queer black lives without issues becoming muddled in the minds of the readers. In later writings, he did represent queer black lives in complex and rich ways.

Similarly, the important political figure Bayard Rustin is now being given the attention that, were society less homophobic, he would have received in his lifetime. Rustin was a significant participant in the Civil Rights movement of the 1960s and is usually credited with arranging and strategizing the March on Washington in 1963, which pushed Martin Luther King Jr. into the national spotlight. Rustin was an openly gay black man who made no effort to hide his sexual identity and, no doubt further inflaming an already homophobic segment of the black community, tended to choose white men as his romantic and sexual partners. He had a police record for his homosexual acts, and this was sufficient for him to be excluded from visibility. He barely appears as a character in the film *Selma*, but, with growing interest in the history of "invisible lives," there is a resurgence of attention to his life and work.

It is also important to recognize the historical and ongoing racism performed in gay white male social spaces. The queer scholar Charles I. Nero published an insightful and historically grounded essay titled "Why Are All the Gay Ghettoes White?" (2005). In this essay Nero uses social and urban theories of neighborhoods, along with the concept of **racial formation**, a term he imports from the work of the sociologists Michael Omi and Howard Winant, which refers to the ways in which individuals and groups of people use race as a category of organization and association. Tracing the development of "gay ghettoes" (neighborhoods populated primarily by gay men, sometimes with a significant population of lesbians), Nero argues persuasively that historical conditions, particularly in post–World War II America, led to gay white men, often drawn together by a segregated workforce, creating communities that were almost exclusively white in their demographics. In many cases, such racial segregation was not conscious; it happened because of friendship and workplace affiliations that as a rule discouraged white men from socializing and organizing with nonwhite men. No doubt there were instances when such racial segregation was indeed conscious, and, given the range of individuals who came to live in such communities, it is probably impossible to specify how much of this was conscious or unconscious, and that is not Nero's project in any case. Even unconscious racism is still racist in its outcomes and effects. Though many, if not most, of the white men who were drawn to live in these neighborhoods worked in what might be called blue- or pink-collar occupations, their residence in white enclaves of queerness reinforced power structures by exclusion of more diverse populations; this led to a continued lack of opportunities for nonwhite gay men to make wider choices about where to live and how to enter or build communities: this was a form of power imbalance as much as those that might seem more obvious.

The problem of continued, systematic racism in gay ghettoes (or, to use the more current term, *gayborhoods*) has not ceased to exist, as much as we might wish to think queer white people have become more enlightened and welcoming. In an essay published in 2016, the queer urban anthropologist Zachary Blair, who "reads" visually as white, studied Chicago's most famous gayborhood, an area on the North Side known for several decades as Boystown because of the density of gay, (primarily) white men who reside there and the presence of the greatest concentration of gay male–centered bars and other places of business (it was previously known as Lakeview and, for a time, Newtown). As Blair notes, Boystown is surrounded by racially and culturally diverse neighborhoods, in some cases economically lower-class white enclaves populated by people who are often from impoverished rural areas, Native Americans, Latinx, and immigrants from South and Southeast Asia. So Boystown, while situated in the complexly diverse human geography that is the North Side of Chicago, remains in important ways as "white" as the neighborhoods about which Nero wrote in an earlier decade. Because Blair reads as white to other white men, he was privy to some of their unmediated acts, spoken and otherwise, of racism, such as the use of stigmatizing and offensive language that many might not use in the presence of nonwhites. Blair also observed groups of gay white men harassing nonwhite queer people, including transgender people of color (some of whom appeared to be sex workers), on the streets of Boystown, sometimes shouting epithets and telling individuals to "go home" or ordering them to leave, suggesting a kind of proprietary status assumed by the white men (many of whom, no doubt, were themselves "tourists" in the neighborhood, living elsewhere and coming to Boystown to play). Chicago's Boystown is hardly likely to be unique in this respect.

In the 1980s and 1990s, there was considerable anger about and protests against a number of predominantly white-identified gay male bars and dance clubs, where there were different unwritten and rarely acknowledged policies for admission of nonwhite gay men. Whereas white gay men might be asked for an ID at the door, to prove they were of legal age, men of color would be asked for multiple IDs, no explanation given for why one would not suffice. This became an effective way of segregating spaces the owners wished to keep as white as possible. Some people have suggested that owners of such establishments believed that the whiter the space, the "higher-class" it was likely to be perceived. When this issue was raised to public consciousness within queer communities, there were often threats from white queer people to protest and boycott the business until such policies were changed.

There may be a present-day equivalent of this in racial or ethnic "sorting" on dating and hookup sites, such as Manhunt, Grindr, and Adam4Adam (to name a few), where profiles written by members seeking either short-term sexual partners or long-term relationships may include, often in very offensive language, preferred racial or ethnic categories, which are most often specified by stating exclusions. This racial sorting also extends to other kinds of products involving erotic desires and sexual attraction, including pornography. The racialization of gay male pornography results in the fetishizing of black men, including stereotypes of brutality, violence, and the repeated image of the outsize black penis as a cliché of queer black sexuality. Even when the fetish is presented as something desirable, it has the effect of dehumanizing and reducing the possessor of this symbol of masculinity. Pornography does not, as a rule, deal in subtleties and nuances, and, in that regard, it is probably an "equal-opportunity" medium in its reduction of individuals, but it does contribute to the reinforcement of stereotypes and, more often than not, is produced by companies owned by white men, some gay, some not.

For black lesbians, the 1960s provided different but parallel challenges. Black lesbians have had to fight to make their presences known and their voices heard. Second-wave feminism was hardly utopian, even if many of its goals aimed at an ideal, gender-fair world. In retrospect, it is clear that it would have been more accurate to call the movement "white, middle-class, heterosexual feminism," and some of the major movers and shakers, such as Betty Friedan, wanted desperately to dissociate lesbianism from feminism, calling it "the Lavender Menace." (Friedan later recanted and apologized for this position.)

If feminism was not initially welcoming to lesbians, it certainly was not going to be an ideal space for queer black women, whose racial concerns would further complicate this white version of feminism and might even, to some minds, disrupt it from its goals. Those goals, it can be argued, unconsciously or not served the maintenance of the racial status quo over acknowledging the intersections of racial oppression, queer oppression, and the oppression of women. The writer Jewelle Gomez, in her 1993 essay "Imagine a Lesbian, a Black Lesbian," recalls how, when she approached the black lesbian poet and activist Audre Lorde about appearing in a documentary, Lorde asked whether she would be the only woman of color; Gomez realized she would be, and Lorde appeared in the documentary on the condition that she be filmed in conversation with another black lesbian. In her essay, Gomez called on feminism and on scholarship to acknowledge and investigate the lives of black lesbians, asking, "How much of a lesbian subtext exists within the Black community despite attempts to conceal it?" (263). She added, "Black lesbians survived within the context of the legacy of slavery and racism" (266). She suggested that the black community needed to do better and more nuanced work on inclusion and self-evaluation, to acknowledge "the contrast between the response to homosexuality by the traditional Black working poor and that of the striving, Black middle class" (266).

**Spotlight: Audre Lorde, Poet, Activist, Black Lesbian Feminist**
More and more openly black lesbian feminist writers have emerged in the past several decades. Two examples are Jacqueline Woodson, who specializes in writing for children and young adults (though not exclusively), and whose book *From the Notebooks of Melanin Sun* (1995) was a breakthrough in depicting a young black boy being raised by a single mother who comes out as a lesbian and becomes partnered with a white woman; and Alice Walker, whose writings include the Pulitzer Prize–winning novel *The Color Purple*, made into a film by Steven Spielberg (with most of its lesbian or bisexual content diminished), and then into a Tony-winning musical that restored much of the same-sex love between its hero, Celie, and her lover Shug Avery (who is depicted as bisexual, perhaps even pansexual). Audre Lorde stands as a slightly earlier pioneer in so many arenas of black lesbian arts and activism.

Lorde was born in New York City to West Indian parents; she began writing poetry at a young age and was published while still a teenager. Many of her poems are love poems and were radical at the time (and today) for addressing romantic and erotic feelings between women. She also wrote overtly political poems, often invoking matriarchal traditions and perspectives as part of her heritage as a black woman: again, that her writings used the experience of being a mother alongside her identity as a lesbian brought out complex dimensions of queer experience, especially as they intersect with blackness. She also wrote powerfully and openly about women's bodies and the challenges women face regarding health access, and she drew from her own experiences in writing *The Cancer Journals* (she lived with breast cancer until her death in 1992), which has become a classic in personal writing about health that is infused with social and political meaning and activism. Similarly, she pushed genre boundaries in such books as her 1982 novel *Zami: A New Spelling of My Name*, which was described as a "biomythography," a blend of memoir and imagination that draws on both individual experience (the realm of the novel and the biography) and the collective oral traditional realms of myth and legend.

In an interview conducted by Karla Hammond and published in *American Poetry Review* in 1980, Lorde made the following statement, which sums up her position on the role of lesbianism in the lives of all black women: "While Black sisters don't like to hear this, I would have to say that all Black women are lesbians because we were raised in the remnants of a basically matriarchal society no matter how oppressed we may have been by patriarchy. We're all dykes, including our mommas" (quoted in "Audre Lorde on Being a Black Lesbian Feminist," *Modern American Poetry*, www. english.illinois.edu/maps/poets/g_l/lorde/feminist.htm). Note that Lorde is making the rhetorical and ideological move of shifting the margin to the center: in her words (and her world), to be a black woman is by definition, in some important way, to live somewhere on what Adrienne Rich called the "lesbian spectrum." Lorde makes this claim particularly for black women because of the historical, social, and economic conditions of enslavement that often placed women (mothers, specifically, but also other female kin) as the head of families; though she was not a separatist, it was important to her to speak out about the specific life conditions of black lesbians as part of working for global social justice.

## THE "DOWN LOW" AS RACIST AND HOMOPHOBIC MYTH

The first demographic hit hard by HIV/AIDS in the United States was gay, white men. As the epidemic progressed, epidemiologists tracking the virus found sharp increases in illness within populations of black women. In trying to explain why these groups might be engaged in particularly risky behaviors, they found some common, predictable factors: some of these individuals were intravenous (IV) drug users who had shared needles, and some of them were involved in sex work, as was true of some infected white people, particularly white women. This accounted for some of the infected women of color. But researchers also found that there was a puzzling number of traditionally middle- or working-class black women who did not report either of these risky behaviors.

Investigating further, they found that some of these women had male sexual partners who, when pressed to be tested, came up positive for the virus as well. Typically, these were not men who identified themselves as either bisexual or gay. Though some of the men did acquire the virus either from a sex worker or through needle sharing, it also turned out that many had been having sex, often unprotected, with other men. These men did not view themselves as anything other than heterosexual, and they somehow managed to compartmentalize their same-sex activities as "something else." Indeed, because of those men's reluctance to claim a queer, gay, or bisexual identity, public health workers developed a term for them that they wanted to be as judgment-free as possible and that would allow them to think about ways to offer educational and service outreach to this group of men: they called them MSM — "men who have sex with men." This gives health workers the ability to focus on strategies for behavioral change rather than forcing social or political identities on men unwilling to be labeled with more stigmatizing terms.

Unfortunately, thanks in part to some media outlets, this led to a scapegoating narrative of the **down low** (often abbreviated DL). On daytime talk shows, in grocery store tabloids, and even in the language of some of the individuals involved, this led to what we might call a *meme* or a *trope* of the dangerous bisexual (usually though not always black) DL man, someone who lacked responsibility, was deceitful, and, as in earlier images of black male hypersexuality, could not contain his sexual urges — now with fatal consequences. J. L. King wrote a briefly popular book, *On the Down Low: A Journey into the Lives of "Straight" Black Men Who Sleep with Men* (2004). Stop for a moment and think about this title. What about the placing of the word *straight* in quotation marks? What is implied by such a marking of the word and by its placement next to the racial identifier?

Keith Boykin, a queer black activist and writer who served on Bill Clinton's White House staff, wrote a book in response to King's book, which Boykin titled *Beyond the Down Low: Sex, Lies, and Denial in Black America* (2005). In the book Boykin argues a number of points with thoughtfulness and reason. First, he exposes the entire concept of the down low as a specifically black phenomenon: he points out that the down low is actually infidelity, and that infidelity has a much longer history than anything involving late twentieth-century sexuality and epidemics, and a wider range of participants than black men who have sex with other men. He further argues that the use of the term is homophobic in general, but specifically within mainstream U.S. black culture, it has led to some of the behaviors and lack of honest communication that have been constructed as specifically black and specifically produced by the AIDS epidemic.

### Spotlight on Culture: Queer Black People in Family, Church, and Entertainment

While the majority of the discussion of queer black identity has focused on struggles, oppression, and issues of loss, anger, and trust, there is also much to celebrate in queer black lives and culture. The family and the church, as central and important institutions, can be sites of repression and oppression, but they have also proven to be powerful spaces for important and meaningful opportunities for queer black people. Queer black people, because they have been raised in these spaces, have often found ways to resist the negative messages or respond to them in ways that grow out of the challenges they have faced in their intersectional positions.

One example can be found in the career and work of E. Patrick Johnson, who grew up in a very small town in North Carolina and was the first person from his town to earn a Ph.D. A scholar of performance, he wrote his dissertation on the oral history of his grandmother, a woman who never attended school. From his relationship with her he developed a theory of black queer studies that he named **quare studies**, in acknowledgment of her pronunciation of the word *queer*, particularly when she was using it to denote sexual queerness. He traces the historical significance of this pronunciation, shared by some Irish speakers of English, and the possibilities for a "different" queer studies, one that engages both blackness and queerness at the same time. Johnson acknowledges that his grandmother's attitude toward homosexuality was not entirely positive, but that he learned much from her about how to view and live in the world "quarely." His essay "'Quare' Studies, or (Almost) Everything I Know about Queer Studies I Learned from My Grandmother" demonstrates how what could have been viewed as an adverse environment provided him with experiences and insights that only his identity would have offered him. Indeed, Johnson's ongoing artistic and scholarly work seems to be a testament to this "quareness" of perspective he got from his grandmother: his book *Sweet Tea* is a profound work of oral history in which he collected and provided commentary on the life stories, as told by the people who lived them, of black gay southern men, ranging from young adults to a ninety-something drag queen/transgender person who survived Hurricane Katrina, living in the French Quarter of New Orleans. He has recently published a corresponding oral history of black queer southern women.

Another example comes from the black church. Christopher House, a self-identified heterosexual black scholar of rhetoric, who is also an ordained minister, has studied AIDS and LGBTQ+ ministries within Christian churches in the African diaspora (Africa, the Caribbean, and the United States, specifically). He has identified Christian worship communities, some tied to traditional, established Protestant sects, such as the United Church of Christ (UCC), one of the first Christian denominations to welcome openly queer members and celebrate their lives, and others independently developed. Some of these, such as the Vision Church in Atlanta, are led by self-identified queer ministers (in this case, the Reverend O. C. Allen III); some are led by affirming heterosexually identified ministers, such as the Covenant in Washington, D.C., led by Drs. Dennis and Christine Wiley; some grew out of shared spaces with other denominations, such as a UCC church in Oakland, California, City of Refuge, which was originally given the opportunity to worship in a United Methodist church. All these came out of the experiences of queer African American people and the non-queer people who loved and cared for them, some of whom lost relatives and friends to the AIDS epidemic, to violence against queer people of color, and to the rejection by families and churches in which many of their adherents were raised. The City of Refuge, under the leadership of Yvette Funder, has a commitment to social justice as a necessary part of their spiritual practices (http://www.cityofrefugeucc.org/about.html).

Finally, the experiences of queer black people who push and question the boundaries of gender and normative expression are worth noting. From the 1920s to the present day, queer black (and blacktino, people who identify as a mixture of black and Latino heritage) men and women have produced joyous, "fierce" trans performances that, while in the spotlight of drag, nonetheless have brought to the larger society important and complex issues of how we witness, observe, and experience the queering of what it means to be a man or a woman. Perhaps the single most visible figure is the entertainer RuPaul, whose *RuPaul's Drag Race* has been a popular cable series for many years. RuPaul does not identify as a trans woman; he prefers the term *drag queen*, to specify his gender work as a form of entertainment. The questioning of what makes someone a man or a woman is present in RuPaul's work and, even if one feels this inquiry has been made palatable to a mass media audience, the show became a point of entry for many people to think and talk about queerness, gender, and race and ethnicity.

Two transgender women of color have emerged in recent years as visible, vocal, and acclaimed artists and activists. Janet Mock, who is biracial (African American and Hawaiian American), is an accomplished journalist who wrote her memoir, *Redefining Realness: My Path to Identity, Womanhood, Love, & So Much More* (2014), for which she received the American Library Associations' Stonewall Book Award; she has become one of the most visible and articulate spokespersons on trans lives. Laverne Cox, mentioned in chapter 4, is an actress, the first trans women to be nominated for an acting Emmy for her role as the trans woman Sophia Burset on the popular Netflix series *Orange Is the New Black*. She, too, uses her public visibility to enact activism on trans issues. She has raised awareness of employment difficulties for trans people, and of the particular challenges for trans woman of color, who are the group at highest risk for homicide.

## QUEER *LATINIDAD*

In 1985 the scholar Felix Padilla used the word **latinidad** to describe a set of experiences, histories, and practices by people of Latin American descent that were not restricted to any one specific nation. The terms *Latino* and *Latina* refer to men and women, respectively, but more recently the term **Latinx** has come into usage as a gender-inclusive term; it also offers terminology for people who do not identify with binary systems of gender or who identify with more than one gender.

There are important ways in which the history of Latinx people in the United States runs parallel to that of African Americans, in that both groups have become sizable and influential parts of U.S. culture, but both have been treated at times as outsiders (and, by extension, not belonging) or as inferior to their white counterparts. Latinx also share with Native American people a history of dispossession of land and diaspora, such as *Tejanos*, who trace their lineage to the border areas between Mexico and the state of Texas. Similarly, the experience of Puerto Ricans (who sometimes call themselves Boricua) is geopolitically different from that of Cuban(o) Americans, though the geographical distance between the two islands is smaller than the distance between Puerto Rico and Florida, its closest mainland U.S. neighbor. Puerto Rico was colonized and claimed by Columbus in 1493, but it previously had an indigenous population, consisting primarily of Taíno people, and it became a U.S. territory in 1898 as a result of the Spanish American War. In 2017 it was ravaged by Hurricane Harvey, and it was indicative of its position in the U.S. imagination that some people, including President Donald J. Trump, questioned the degree to which such disaster groups as FEMA have an ongoing obligation to it and its people.

The "in-between" space that Latinx people often inhabit, between white, Native American, and black, has led to a wide range of ways of knowing the self and others in the world that some scholars and activists group under the heading *brown*. (Note that some Asian American scholars and activists use *brown* as an adjective for people whose heritage is from South Asian countries, such as India.) The growing body of scholars of queer Latinx history have pointed to the phenomenon of in-betweenness as one of the significant definitional aspects of queer brown lives; as the scholar Hiram Pérez puts it, it is important "how bodies are situated outside white/black or white/Asian binaries to consolidate cosmopolitan, first world identities" (103). What Pérez means by this statement is that the fact that Latinx people can be viewed as neither white nor black (nor Asian, for that matter) has served majoritarian white desires to remain powerful. Latinx people can be used, ideologically and materially, as a kind of bridge (to borrow a metaphor from the Chicana writers and activists Cherríe Moraga and Gloria Anzaldúa) between hierarchies of race, ethnicity, and social value.

A specifically Latinx experience has involved language and the role of language in creating and defining identity, both from within experience and imposed from without. Chicana lesbians in particular took this set of challenges and attitudes as an opportunity to explore how queerness and bilingual identity might produce different, valuable experiences rather than simply restrictions. Gloria Anzaldúa wrote an important book, based on language and theories of female queer sexuality and Latinx ethnicity, titled *Borderlands/La Frontera: The New Mestiza*. (The word **mestiza** refers to people of mixed indigenous and European descent.) In this book Anzaldúa, a Tejana born in Texas near the border with Mexico, broke with traditional literary forms and created a new kind of text, one that is arguably an embodiment of the intersectionality of her identity as a lesbian and a mestiza. The book combines autobiography, myth and folklore, poetry, and political and cultural rhetoric: its power lies in its multiplicity, its in-betweenness, and its simultaneity, all part of the notion of intersectionality. Anzaldúa refuses to allow her readers to slot the book into one category, one recognizable identity, anymore than her identity can be captured in any single binary. The book is always queer, always multicultural, always multigenre.

One of its most radical and, from some perspectives, queer features is its bilingualism. As the title suggests, Anzaldúa does not "decide" between English and Spanish in choosing what or how to name her book, and that is true throughout the book: it contains passages in English, passages in Spanish, and passages that move, within a single page, even within a single sentence, between English and Spanish, thus creating a complex experience of language and cultural positionality for readers. Bilingual readers can access a text that matches their own experience of language as never a single experience, always turning and twisting, and, by implication, requiring them to move neurolinguistically and culturally between the two languages — one of which is probably more dominant or primary because of when they learned it, just as queer folk must move between identities imposed on them by society and identities that they experience as genuine and authentic. It is equally powerful, in different ways, for readers who are not fluent in one of the two languages, as it places them in the position of knowing and not knowing at the same time, an in-betweenness Anzaldúa is describing in the content of the book.

In this sense, Anzaldúa's rhetorical choice of using two languages in a single text mirrors the experience of being queer and, equally important, *becoming/coming out* as queer, no doubt especially challenging for people of Anzaldúa's generation, who knew that coming out as queer might separate them from their families of origin and might segregate them even more from some abstract notion of "American mobility." All queer people "speak" multiple languages, as chapter 1 of this book argues; all Latinx people "speak" multiple cultures. And, in both cases, they must experience this intersectionality in conscious and unconscious ways. Anzaldúa wrote not only about queerness as an abstract metaphor for the experience of *mestizaje*, the term for the social experience of being mestiza in the Americas, but also about the actual conditions of being a queer woman who identifies with and "disidentifies" with both the English of the United States and the Spanish of her kin. So she turns to stories and legends of women whose lives and experiences place them in this in-between or both-and relationship to ethnicity, gender, sexuality, and language. This space, geographic, psychological, cultural, and erotic, is "*la frontera*," the frontier, where borders are only emerging, usually arbitrary, and continually contested.

In chapter 5 of *Borderlands/La Frontera*, Anzaldúa identifies what she describes as eight different languages (or variations) that Chicanas and Chicanos "speak," to trouble the binarism of English-Spanish that she sees as just as paralyzing as the binarism of heterosexual-homosexual. Her language lesson lists these categories:

1. Standard English
2. Working-class and slang English
3. Standard Spanish
4. Standard Mexican Spanish
5. North Mexican Spanish dialect
6. Chicano Spanish (Texas, New Mexico, Arizona, and California regional variations)
7. Tex-Mex
8. *Pachuco* (slang associated with the zoot suit culture of the 1940s; the slang or dialect was called *Caló*, and was a blend of many ethnicities)

Think about the labor, the intelligence, and the fluidity required to speak in all these languages! The point Anzaldúa is making is that to be Chicano means having to move between multiple social and cultural spaces and roles, signified by the languages required for each — and also to acknowledge that multiple languages may be spoken in the same space at one time. As it is with the ethnic experiences of *latinidad*, not restricted to Chicanos (though that was Anzaldúa's emphasis), so it is for queer people, though there are contexts in which the analogy is not equivalent (such as in income discrepancies, for example, as Latinx people do not as a group earn salaries as high as those of queer people, especially gay men). Think about other ways in which the analogies explored throughout this chapter between race and sexuality and gender identity do produce useful correspondences, and when they do not.

## Spotlight: Cherríe Moraga

One of the most important pioneers in queer Latinx studies is the self-identified lesbian Xicana (initially spelled *Chicana*) poet and activist Cherríe Moraga. The words *Chicana* and *Chicano* were originally terms of derision used by people of European descent in the United States, as they referred to people of Mexican American heritage, more often than not with a mix of indigenous ancestors (including parents). During the 1960s and later, it became a term of identity and pride, claimed by people with such histories and who live "on the hyphen," finding both great strengths and, as is always the case, considerable challenges in living in ways true to their identities. Like Anzaldúa, Moraga did important artistic and scholarly-activist work in establishing and making much more publicly visible the lives of Xicana lesbians. Moraga has written, taught, and been politically active for more than fifty years; with Anzaldúa she edited a breakthrough anthology of writings by women of color, *This Bridge Called My Back*, mentioned earlier in this chapter.

Moraga, like Anzaldúa and others, combined what most readers would identify as "creative writing" (poetry, personal narrative) with political and cultural analysis, quite memorably in her collection *Loving in the War Years: Lo que nunca pasó por sus labios* (1983). (She does not combine languages in her work in the way that Anzaldúa does.) In autobiographical sections, she sometimes uses her birth name, Cecilia, to indicate a younger self, one raised in a family of mixed parentage. As is true of many other Latinx writers, Moraga stresses the importance of family as a place both of self-discovery and of challenges. Her mother is clearly the dominant figure in her development, to the point that, when her mother questions her about her lesbian identity, Moraga she tells her, with love and conviction, that it is her mother's strength and nurturance that have enabled her to claim such an identity with pride and certainty. She is compassionate in writing about her white father's absence from much of the family's life, seeing in him a potentially unacknowledged sexual queerness that, given the time and place, may have made impossible his own ability to navigate family life and the rest of his existence in knowing and effective ways.

Importantly, Moraga addresses a number of issues related to Xicana lesbian existence that had been left unspoken or underexamined. She writes with thought and depth about the meaning of brownness, particularly in communities populated by mestizos and mestizas, including the color range within her own extended family, in which, she says, "my brother's sex was white, mine, brown." She writes with candor and without defensiveness about the various forms of internalized homophobia and racism Xicanos and Xicanas must confront in themselves and in others. She looks to cultural and mythic forebears like the figure of Malinche, the alternative goddess to the Catholic Virgin Mary, a figure based on a Nahua woman maligned for her open and unapologetic sexual engagement with conquistadors, literal and figurative, in the legends that surround her.

In terms of both her work as an artist and her work as a cultural activist, one of her hallmarks is her willingness, even insistence, to write directly and graphically about her erotic love and sexual relationships with other women, and especially from the standpoint of a self-proclaimed *butch* (a lesbian whose self-presentation performs texts drawn from traditional masculinity, including the problematic elements of machismo). Moraga was writing at a time when the butch-femme dynamic was beginning to come under criticism from second-wave feminists, who saw it as a reinscription or reinforcement of stereotypical and patriarchal gender roles. (*Patriarchy* refers to the privileging of the male and the masculine in history and in society at large.) Moraga argued for a distinctly Xicana power of the butch-femme relationship, not seeing it in any simple way as a mere imitation of heterosexual or heteronormative arrangements.

More recently, Moraga created controversy in an essay titled "Still Loving in the (Still) War Years/2009: On Keeping Queer Queer." In this essay Moraga makes two seemingly unrelated but ultimately, for her, inextricable rhetorical moves. In the first part of the essay she offers a critique of the move toward legalization of queer marriage, seeing in it a regressive, even betraying process, undoing the radicalness of queer as a way of thinking of and living in the world. Not unlike the authors of the collection *Against Equality*, which will be discussed in chapter 11, she sees such initiatives as counter to the kinds of social and political interventions that were at the heart of what was in her earlier days known as Gay Liberation Front politics. There is certainly a spectrum of agreement and disagreement on this issue, even among those who worked for marriage equality, but it is the second part of her essay that generated criticism and, in some quarters, outrage.

In it she critiques what she says she witnesses and perceives as a move to erase nonconforming gender styles among those people who might otherwise identify as gay, lesbian, or bisexual. In place of what she sees as the liberating acceptance of and pride in the feminine gay man and the masculine (or butch) lesbian as representatives of authentic and genuine ways of being and acting, she observes what she describes as a kind of essentializing pressure to identify as transgender and, in many cases, to take physical and medical steps to make gender experience and physical body conform. She recounts conversations with young women who, in another day, would probably have identified as butch lesbians and who now, during adolescence, express a desire to have surgeries and other medical treatments that will align their gender (and especially their gendered bodies) with one different from the one assigned at birth. Though Moraga does not foreclose the assertion that there are indeed people whose physical body and gendered subjectivities are trans, she fears for a kind of extinction of the noncon-forming homosexual or bisexual self as a legitimate and authentic way of being in the world. In other words, Moraga suggests, the greater push for trans identification has been a kind of return to gender polarization and an effort, whether intentionally or not, to reinstate heteronormativity (by way of gender conformity) as something desirable.

As one might imagine, such a stance provoked pushback from a num-ber of writers who viewed Moraga's position as itself a form of erasure, itself regressive in its statements that too many people were being encour-aged (or, more strongly, pressured) to view themselves as trans because they did not identify with the gender norms associated with their bodies. For Moraga's critics, her position was itself regressive in seeing a kind of "trans conspiracy" at worst and "trans preference" at mildest. Ironically, it might be fair to say that both sides of the argument fear a kind of sexual or gender genocide, an extermination of a population. To draw an analogy to Deaf cultural politics, it is not entirely unlike the debate over the spread of cochlear implants, which can give deaf or hard-of-hearing people access to some version of hearing — there are proponents and opponents to this pro-cedure, the opponents arguing that along with such procedures will inevi-tably come an effort to make deafness and, inevitably, Deaf culture extinct.

You may find it interesting to read Moraga's essay in its entirety; it is listed in the Works Cited section and readily available.

## Queer Latinx Experiences

When one reads accounts by queer Latinx people, a number of experiences stand out as common. One is that these individuals identified first and for many years as Latinx, rather than as queer, sometimes not coming to self-awareness of their queerness until adulthood, very often only after the end of a marriage and sometimes after having become parents. The latter circumstance is especially prevalent in the narratives told by queer Latinas, whether they identify as lesbian, as bisexual, or in some other nonhetero-normative way. In this sense, the importance of family and kinship is not unlike that reported by queer black people. Because family is so central to *latinidad*, there is often pressure, conscious and unconscious, to conform to traditional heterosexual roles and to engage in what have traditionally been heterosexual domestic institutions, such as marriage and parenthood.

Many individuals, particularly from generations earlier than the current college-age youth, describe themselves as becoming politicized by issues of race, ethnicity, employment equity, and — especially for Latinx people — immigration. It is not that such people report feeling that they had to choose between queer identity and Latinx identity, but that their consciousness focused, as an outgrowth of the social groups and communities in which they lived, on those issues centered on the situation of Latinx. They may describe being able to identify retrospectively queer desires, and sometimes, especially for young Latinx men, they identified them as such even when children or adolescents, but the immediacy of social injustice for Latinx people took priority.

Interestingly, a number of those individuals indicate that it was while gaining political consciousness in Latinx contexts that they began to discover or come out about their queer sexual identity. The collection *Queer Brown Voices: Personal Narratives of Latina/o LGBT Activism*, edited by Uriel Quesada, Letitia Gomez, and Salvador Vidal-Ortiz, contains interviews with and essays by fourteen queer Latinx individuals, from multiple specific Latinx regions, occupations, and generations, and suggests that, though each experience has its own integrity and authenticity, the process of coming out as a politically queer person was preceded by an identity and consciousness as Latinx. Thus, queer Latinx people have had long-standing commitments to issues that remain pressing today, such as immigration and the vulnerability of queer undocumented people, economic disparities, language wars (such as English-only movements), and employment discrimination.

For some women, it was a raised awareness of the double discrimination against women and against Latinx people that led to an understanding of their own same-sex desires. For some men and women, queer identity emerged not only out of recognition of erotic desires, but out of a determination to work to dismantle the oppressive gender politics associated with **machismo**, a valorization of heightened, single-minded masculinity that is often seen as characteristic of *latinidad*. Machismo as a cultural and political entity is oppressive in its various forms for all women and men, but particularly for queer Latino men, who, like queer black men, have already been typically viewed as "less than" full men because of their desire for other men. (It is important to keep in mind that forms of heightened masculinity are by no means unique to Latinx cultures, as current concerns about "toxic masculinity" attest in the broader context of the United States and other nations and cultures.) Machismo was harmful for queer Latina women because it provided a kind of script that simply reiterated a single way of being powerful. Some scholars trace the roots of the term to historical periods and cultures (usually pre-Columbian) when the notion of heightened strength and power was not necessarily oppressive; but over the centuries the term has become more negatively associated with cultural values of behavior (often depicted as the root of domestic violence, sexual double standards, and so forth). Its defenders suggest that there can be "positive machismo" that stresses responsibility and care providing.

Nonetheless, for queer Latino men especially, machismo can create a double bind: because it is almost always originally tied to heteronormativity, such queer men may be placed in lower-status positions and be subject to derogatory terms like *mericón*, which roughly translates as "faggot," and *loca*, which may refer to a woman or a gay man, always in a negative way, the equivalent of "queen" or "whore." They may feel pressured to adopt extreme codes of masculinity that can be restrictive; they may repeat cycles of violence and devaluing of others and may feel inauthentic. In some cases, the dominance of machismo as a kind of warped ideal may lead to skewed, nonreciprocal ways of understanding male homosexuality — some Latino men consider as queer only those men who are penetrated in anal sex or provide (not receive) oral sex.

A second context that many who write about the emergence of their queer Latinx consciousness mention is the AIDS epidemic. Indeed, even today, Latino men account for about 23 percent of newly diagnosed cases of HIV infection, and, of those, seven of ten occur in gay and bisexual men (Centers for Disease Control and Prevention, "HIV and Latinos/Hispanics," October 3, 2018, www.cdc.gov/hiv/group/racialethnic/hispaniclatinos/). According to a number of governmental and nongovernmental agencies, Latinx both were and are one of the demographics less likely to be tested regularly and, hence, all too often go untreated until the disease has progressed to what is now considered full-blown AIDS, often untreatable and terminal. There are also systemic and cultural explanations for the reasons Latino men in particular are so overrepresented in the percentage of new (and ongoing) cases of HIV infection. (The percentage has remained relatively stable for more than a quarter of a century.)

The queer Latino psychotherapist Rafael M. Díaz did an important and insightful study of what he calls "Latino gay men" and HIV that was published in 1998. Its explanatory power remains relevant today, especially given the continuity of infection rates among Latino MSMs (men who have sex with men). Díaz uses the term *gay men*, rather than the more sociologically based behavioral-descriptive *MSM*, because he wants to focus on explanations for infection among Latino men who identify as gay and, thus, are intersectionally multicultural, whereas *MSM* includes men who would resist identification as gay and therefore might engage in risky behavior for different reasons; the figure of the MSM is not unlike the "phantom image" of the black man "on the DL," which we critiqued and deconstructed earlier in this chapter. For Díaz, identification as gay is significant because of its cultural meaning within Latino culture.

Machismo, Díaz argues, is the basis for much homophobia in the Latinx community because it assumes a particular way of being a man, one based on specific attitudes toward sex itself and toward sexual partners (of whatever gender) and on specific sexual behaviors and acts. For the Latino man raised in a culture dominated by machismo, his sense of being a man is rooted in power and dominance (even if, or perhaps especially if, he does not have power in the white-centered economic and political sphere of mainstream U.S. life) and in proving his manhood by engaging in risky and dangerous behavior. Another facet of machismo Díaz identified was a conscious belief that men do not have strong capacities for self-regulation, one explanation for the acceptance of infidelity and cheating in both straight and gay situations: the belief that men, by nature, can't help themselves when it comes to sex, passion, desire, and acting out.

In its positive forms, machismo can lead a man to take responsibility for his life and for the welfare of those to whom he is bonded (power) and to put his own safety and life on the line for his family. The heroes of many novels by the writer Ernest Hemingway, for example, who spent a good deal of his adult life in or near Hispanic cultures (both in Spain and in Cuba), show such men as heroic in their willingness to sacrifice themselves for a woman, a family, or a nation. But, of course, such a view of what it means to be a man has a destructive, negative potential, as well, and this is where Díaz focuses his attention. Because such men have been raised to have both a conscious and an unconscious regard for machismo as the ultimate way of maintaining a sense of male or masculine identity, this can lead to a view of rigid, polar sex roles, even between men who are involved in a sexual and sometimes romantic or domestic relationship. Hence, there are Latino gay men who view themselves as more entitled to being considered macho if they take on the exclusive role of the penetrator (or *top*, to use slang from gay male language) in anal sex in particular and as the one who is "serviced" in oral sex. Some of these men may use this set of practices as a way of not identifying as gay or queer, but those who do identify as gay may retain this role rigidity.

Conversely, this attitude places the Latin "bottom" outside full acceptance, by himself and by others, as a man, which may lead to psychological attitudes and conditions that make him more vulnerable to demands or requests for unsafe sex. If he has essentially been placed as a woman (or at least as a "non-man"), some ways of practicing machismo are likely to lead him to feel that he can make fewer decisions about his own body and its safety. Díaz found that, for some of these men, the reception of their partner's semen in their body was an important part of feeling intimate and feeling that the relationship was authentic. Similarly, the "tops" may believe that spreading their seed, even if it is not going to lead to reproduction, is important to their sense of manhood. Such attitudes are hardly unique to

Latino men, but the culture of machismo, Diaz argues, intensifies the willingness for such men to engage in risky behavior, especially because risk taking is one of the qualities of masculinity in machismo-based culture.

In Latinx culture, there is a strong sense of what Díaz calls family loyalty, which leads, for its queer-identified members, to a corresponding sense of what he calls "sexual silence" — a lack of talk within the family about safer sex practices and about matters of affection, love, and responsibility for those who live in a world of same-sex desires. The kinds of talk a father may have with a son about showing respect for women, about protecting the health and well-being of both partners, but especially the woman's, are simply less likely to occur between Latino gay men and their fathers.

Poverty and racism, to which Latinx people, like African American people, are particularly subjected, can lead to a sense of fatalism, according to the interviews and other sources of data on which Díaz built his thesis — and so an alarming number of gay Latino men surveyed indicated that they believed they would eventually become infected. Though there may be no immediate causal basis for such a connection, the correlation Díaz found suggests that discrimination and devaluing of life in one or more set of life issues (such as economic and sociopolitical) can contribute to a more generalized worldview that may lead to risky decisions.

Díaz proposed a "psycho-cultural model of sexual self-regulation," designed to reduce the likelihood of engagement in risky behaviors by gay and bisexual Latino men. Critical to the success of such a model, he suggests, is understanding the different inner and social lives of gay Latino men who are acculturated (i.e., integrated into mainstream gay culture beyond Latino subgroups) and those who are unacculturated, who remain entirely within linguistic and value spheres associated with *latinidad*. Díaz argues for improvement of cultural competency and work within the gay Latino community in places such as bars and dance clubs where gay Latino man gather and where dialogue between gay Latino men can occur.

### Spotlight: Richard Blanco, Gay Cuban American Poet

For his second inauguration, in 2013, President Barack Obama invited a rising American poet, Richard Blanco, to compose and perform a poem for the occasion, as a number of previous presidents had done. Blanco, in addition to being the son of immigrants from Cuba and the youngest poet ever selected for such an honor, also identifies as an out gay man, a part of his life he includes in his poetry, often in intersectional ways with his ethnic heritage. Blanco grew up in Miami, studied civil engineering as an undergraduate (a "practical" major), but then studied creative writing and earned an MFA from Florida International University.

In his moving memoir, *The Prince of los Cocuyos: A Miami Childhood* (2014), Blanco recalls a generally happy childhood in a family working to become part of the mainstream middle class without losing the heritage they brought with them from Cuba. Blanco depicts himself as a likable, dutiful, occasionally mischievous child, a good student, but always under the watchful eye of his *abuela*, his somewhat stern grandmother, who frequently engaged in a kind of familial "policing" of Blanco's sometimes gender-nonconforming behavior and attitudes (such as discouraging him from playing with dolls and engaging in expressive behaviors that she viewed as girlish). Blanco expresses a love for his grandmother, at the same time acknowledging the ways in which her attitudes provided an obstacle for his development of a healthy and positive sense of the gay boy who would grow into a proud gay man. He writes about these attitudes in a poem, "Queer Theory: According to My Grandmother," which can be found in the Appendix. As you read it, notice how the poem is written in the imperative mood (a "command" form), a series of directives from a voice presumably speaking to the silent, listening stand-in for Blanco. Think about the title of the poem: Is there something potentially ironic or critical in Blanco's choice of "Queer Theory" as the heading for the poem? How does the word *queer* function in this context? Knowing that Blanco indeed identifies very positively as a gay man and mentions his husband in the acknowledgments for his memoir, the doubleness of *queer* as having both negative and positive meanings seems present here.

For some queer Latinx, especially men, there has been a shift from being oppressed by a culture defined by historical codes of machismo to resistance to and playing with gender roles — that is, to viewing gender and sexuality as Judith Butler does, as a series of performances, in which there is no originating fixed, "true" script. For some queer Latinx people, this also involves reclaiming terms and categories from an abject and oppressive cultural past (which remains in the present, of course), that a number classify under the broad term *jotería*. Roughly translated, *jotería* means "faggotry," a way of living out a nonnormative (in the case of this term, male, if not masculine) gender identity. English words such as *sissy, homo,* and, yes, *queer* have a similar painful past, but, for some gay men, they can be rehabilitated by being used both as insider language and concepts and as a way of honoring brave, "fierce" people who lived out their own sense of sexual and gender identity in public ways, despite being subject to violence or ridicule. For some women, it is the adoption within closed circles of terms like *dyke* and *lezzie*: one equivalent in some Latina lesbian culture is *tortillera*, which means "bread maker" and is considered by some to be vulgar (as *cocksucker* and *fudge packer* are in queer U.S. white gay male culture).

The term *jotería* has been used to encompass an approach to queer Latinx culture in general.

For some queer Latino men, it is a celebration of that which has been ridiculed — a femininity that can be associated with queerness, whether through the expressive style of cisgendered gay men or through the enactment of "womanhood" of trans women; for some queer Latinas, it can be through an adoption, in a kind of parodic but nonetheless "authentic" way, of some of the performative elements of machismo — whether in clothing, the affectation of facial hair, a way of walking and moving, or playing with social scripts involving cisgendered women. The communication scholar Shane T. Moreman has written powerfully about his journey, as he says, "from queer to joto." For him, this shift is a way of integrating (not simply assimilating) the intersections of queerness and *latinidad* in his lived experience as a man. In narrating the response of another Latino scholar to a call for papers on the subject, Moreman notes: "When I read Carlos' response, I was reminded of how deeply distressing the term joto can be. . . . Carlos demonstrated how this word, in particular, reached a visceral emotional depth, so as to function as code for Latino masculinity." Moreman goes on to argue that "as a Latino male, the joto is displaced of a rightful home in the United States while he is also displaced of his rightful belonging to Latino culture. He betrays both US culture and Latino culture with his enactment of same-sex desire and becomes homeless within the discourse of US citizenship, Latina/o culture and even Communication academic writing" (Shane T. Moreman, "Rethinking Conquergood: Toward an Unstated Cultural Politics," *Liminalities* 5.5 [2009], http://liminalities .net/5-4/moreman.pdf).

Other scholars, writing from places of resistance, also note the in-betweenness in which many queer Latino men in particular find themselves. The literary and cultural scholar Hiram Pérez recalls a conference titled "Gay Shame" held at the University of Michigan in 2003, at which he was the only scholar of color invited to give a formal presentation. Pérez noted that bodies of color were used, ideologically, verbally, and iconically, as convenient objects on which this room of primarily white academics could project their sense of shame, a shame the conference was meant in its own way to celebrate as a form of resistance by acknowledging it, but which was shame nonetheless. For Pérez, the climax of the conference came in a presentation by the gay white male scholar Ellis Hanson on queer pedagogy, during which he accompanied his verbal remarks with a series of visual projections of a Latino gay porn worker, Kiko, dressed (and undressed) in the colonialist uniform of a British schoolboy. Pérez, in his account of this event in his book *A Taste for Brown Bodies: Gay Modernity and Cosmopolitan Desire* (2015), discusses how uncomfortable his own response was to the exploitation of the queer brown male body and also to the reactions of a number of the attendees, who, much to Pérez's surprise, felt it appropriate and felt themselves entitled to comment on the size and "ability" of Kiko's sexual organ.

Nonetheless, scholars and activists in queer Latinx communities continue to explore how to bring together the lived experience of their members with the kinds of scholarly analysis that can illuminate what the late performance scholar José Estaban Muñoz called "affective differences," which help define and make visible and legible queer Latinx culture. By "affective differences," Muñoz meant that different cultural groups (including ones defined by such intersectionalities as sexuality and ethnicity) participate in the realm of experience that extends beyond the purely intellectual, such as the emotional, the physical, the kinesthetic (the realms of movement and space, for example), and the temporal (how people experience time), in ways that vary from group to group, and that what feels one way in one group may have a very different affective quality in another. It can be difficult to put such affective differences into the kinds of language we are taught to use in the classroom and in academic essays, which is all the more reason to continue to push ourselves to do it.

Muñoz's concept of disidentification may be a way to understand the charged aspect of the moment Pérez describes. Disidentification, Muñoz suggests, means that minoritized groups do not simply work to identify with dominant groups of people, but neither do they entirely discard the images, assumptions, and expectations imposed on them by mainstream popular culture. Rather, Muñoz suggests, they "disidentify": they move between acknowledging and to some extent participating in the work the image or characteristic imposed on them, while also resisting, subverting, and rewriting it. It may be that what Pérez experienced and felt betrayed by in the work of his fellow academics was an act of imposition of an image on Pérez's fellow queer Latinos.

Scholars also note how important a space the nightclub and quite specifically the dance floor has been for queer Latinx people in the decades since the Stonewall Riots (which were led in significant ways by queer Latinx and queer African Americans, as well as queer white men and women). As the dance scholar Ramón H. Rivera-Servera, who has studied the social and erotic dimensions of such dance and musical forms as salsa within queer Latinx culture, as a place for individuals to claim their specific queer Latinx identity and to enter into communal sharing of traditions, heritages, and creativity, remarks, "The dance floor may be one of the most vivid examples of the material conditions from which queer latinidad emerges" (149). In this regard, the mass killing on Latin Night at the Pulse nightclub in Orlando in 2016, whatever its actual motivations, because it was an attack on an "affective performance" of queer *latinidad* as experienced by many who identify either with the queer Orlando community or with queer *latinidad* in general, was an attack with specifically painful meaning and feelings for queer Latinx.

The queer Latinx scholar Bernadette Marie Calafell has written about the Pulse nightclub attack, in which forty-nine people were killed and more than fifty people injured, as a complex instance of the uneasiness with which white America perceives and understands brownness. As the work of Moraga and others suggests, there is a set of cultural differences between brownness and blackness in the discourse of those in power in the United States, but there are also instances when they are conflated. Calafell extends this to a cultural (and, one might add, national) confusion or complication of the very meaning of *brownness* in contemporary Western, particularly North American, usage and perception. As she points out, the killer, Omar Mateen, while born and raised in the United States, was the child of Afghan immigrants and, therefore, brown, though in culturally and historically different ways from the majority-Latinx victims of the shootings on June 12, 2016. That Mateen was reported to have been incensed by seeing two men kissing (before the night of the attack) and that he may have engaged in same-sex activities (though he was married and publicly identified as heterosexual) complicates the narrative even more. Calafell by no means condones or excuses Mateen's horrific act; what she does ask for is a nuanced, thoughtful analysis of the various levels of race and ethnicity (particularly Latinx and Middle Eastern identities) and sexuality in this event.

Some experienced the shooting and its victims in even more specific ways than the broad category of Latinx, such as an attack on queer Puerto Ricans, as Louie A. Ortiz-Fonseca wrote in an op-ed piece in the national LGBTQ+ newsmagazine the *Advocate*, in the week after the murders (Louis A. Ortiz-Fonseca, "Queer Latinx: Tired of Being Targets," *Advocate*, June 15, 2016, www.advocate.com/commentary/2016/6/15/queer-latinx-tired-being -targets). Others may see the shooting as an attack on queer Latinx people in general, as 95 percent of the victims were Latinx, and the killer may have had past experiences with queer Latino men (and quite possibly Puerto Rican men specifically) that led him to this horrifying act. An initial response, in the immediate wake of the shootings, the suggestion that the fact that it was Latin Night at Pulse was perhaps incidental and not key to the killings, no longer seems to be the case. Even if it were, the tally of dead queer Latinx bodies (as well as those of the other individuals sharing the space and the culture that evening) is, whatever the motivation, still another instance of the disregard for queer Latinx people. And still, in a spirit of *jotería*, which suggests other ways of being men and women, outside norms and binaries, the people dance.

## QUEER ASIAN AMERICANS: SILENCES AND MODEL MINORITY MEMBERS

For queer Asian Americans, the histories and shared challenges are yet again somewhat different from those of other queers. In reading scholarly accounts of queer Asian American identity, it becomes clear that there is a kind of tension between what Yen Le Espiritu calls a move to articulate a "pan-ethnic Asian American identity" (quoted in Han, 4), that is, one that is inclusive of all the different national and ethnic experiences that emerge from the various Asian cultures whose descendants now live in the United States, on the one hand, and, on the other, an acknowledgment that there is a considerable range of and difference between the lives and values of people who may identify first with the country from which their families came, and as Asian only secondarily.

For Asian Americans, identifying what is shared can be more challenging than for the other minority groups we have discussed: the descendants of Chinese people who came to California to build the railroads, and who were treated by white businessmen as barely above the status of enslaved people, may not feel quite the same kinship with Japanese Americans, who live with the history of internment in concentration camps during World War II, who may feel very different from Korean Americans, who may have left their home country as a result of the Korean War in the 1950s, and from Philippine Americans, whose country has a long history of occupation by other nations besides the United States, such as Spain. Yet another category of more recent Asian Americans consists of the various groups of people who left Vietnam after the end of the war in the 1970s, and that include mountain people, such as the Hmong (who also emigrated from Laos and Thailand), and the Kinh, who came from the river deltas.

A whole other set of South Asian countries and cultures are represented by such peoples as Indians (and the many ethnicities that populate that large country), Pakistanis, Nepalese, and Afghanis. Yet another set of people claim Asian heritage as residents or descendants of people who lived in what we usually call the Middle East: Israel, Iran, Iraq, Syria, and others.

Thus far, more scholarly attention by sociologists and other scholars of group cultures in the United States has focused on the lives of Asian Americans descended from Eastern and Southeastern Asian populations, though there is growing and rich work on South Asian and Middle Eastern queer identities, particularly because of the growth of those populations in the United States, not just statistically (the number of people), but because of the presence of these ethnicities in everyday, mainstream U.S. culture. The Asian American (Chinese) queer scholar C. Winter Han suggests a familiar position for queer Asian Americans, describing "present gay Asian American men as being outside of both gay America and Asian America"; the same appears to be true for gay Asian American women and for those queer Asian Americans who do not fit neatly into a binary gender system (7). Just like queer members of the other racial and ethnic groups considered in this chapter, queer Asian Americans must navigate what it means to identify as marginalized not only in white heteronormative America, but as marginalized within their ethnic group(s) and their sexual or gender identity group. For many of those writing about their identities as queer Asian Americans, both their sexuality and their race or ethnicity become "problems" that other groups have with them and which they internalize themselves. It is not uncommon for non–Asian Americans to ask individuals they visually identify as Asian in heritage where they come from or where they were born, often insisting that "the United States" is a wrong answer.

If one of the discriminatory dilemmas queer African American and queer Latinx men in particular must encounter is hypersexualization, the assumption that they are defined by an excess of sexual desire and inability to practice self-control, queer Asian American men (and, in somewhat different ways, queer Asian American women) find themselves in the opposite situation, defined sexually by absence, on the one hand, and by silence, especially within their families and within Asian American cultural groups. Han titles the first chapter of his book "Being an Oriental, I Could Never Be Completely a Man," a line from the Chinese American playwright David Henry Hwang's 1988 Tony Award–winning play, *M. Butterfly*, a dramatization based on an actual case of espionage in which a French diplomat carried on a sexual affair for many years with a Chinese actress who was physically a man. The speaker of this line, Song Liling, uses the word *Oriental* with all the irony it carries today — as a way of being defined by Westerners as "other," and, hence, not entirely a man in this limited vision. It is Song's ability to use his "Oriental" identity that allows him to succeed as a spy for the Communist government in getting information from his French lover.

This statement by Song, that, because of his racial identity, he is excluded from normative masculinity in Western eyes, repeats a pattern in the discourse written by queer Asian American men about their masculinity. Han points to the familiar stereotypical physical and expressive characteristics associated with Asians and with Asian Americans in particular, their "delicate features and smaller size" (23). Delicacy and smallness have typically been equated with the realm of femininity, not for any "essential" (i.e., necessarily innate) true reason, but because of the history of relationships and gender arrangements across many cultures. Han points to the history of Chinese immigration during the nineteenth and twentieth centuries in the United States to suggest how economic and occupational issues get conflated with this physical gender stereotype: many Chinese men came to the United

States, unmarried, living together in crowded spaces, because of poverty and racism, and "bachelor societies" emerged in urban areas. The comparative absence of women in these situations, as well as miscegenation laws that made it illegal for Asian men to marry non-Asian women, intensified either a kind of asexuality ascribed to Asian men in the United States or a kind of feminization, in which men took on, out of necessity, many of what have been considered female domestic tasks, such as cooking, cleaning, and serving. The figure of the Asian houseboy became a staple of many popular novels and films, which often depicted such figures as childlike and even girlish in their expressiveness.

The feminization of Asian men in mainstream U.S. culture remains today. Representation of the queer Asian American man in social discourse and popular media as "girl" or "woman" is so common as to require virtually no explanation within the contexts in which it appears. For example, the Filipino American actor and stand-up comic Alec Mapa plays on the stereotypes of gay Asian American men in his act, referring to himself as "America's Gaysian Sweetheart." Mapa often depicts himself in ways that make him seem like the kind of middle-class "princess," demanding of material gifts and services, that the main characters of his television shows regard as their birthright. For some, Mapa's performances may feel uncomfortably aligned with stereotypes of the feminized, almost asexual Asian American, but he typically includes some degree of political defiance and verbal irony to remind his audience of how constructed their stereotype of him is: if he is repeating a script that is familiar and constraining, he is doing so at least in part with a critical eye. Mapa comes across as charming, funny, and nonthreatening — until the moment when he makes it clear that he does not suffer fools well and that his own experience as a bullied, somewhat feminine gay Asian American man has helped him develop skills of survival, defiance, and resistance.

Gay male pornography, particularly film and video work, has provided material for scholarly consideration of the feminization of queer Asian men. Richard Fung, born in Trinidad, ethnically Chinese, and for much of his life a resident of Canada, has used both video and scholarly writing to investigate the masculinity and sexualities of queer Asian American (or Asian Canadian, in his case) men. Beginning his career just as the AIDS epidemic was emerging into public consciousness, Fung worked on issues involving both HIV and the invisibility of Asian American men in homoerotic spheres, such as pornography. *Steam Clean* (1990), a public service short video he made on commission from the Gay Men's Health Crisis and the AIDS Committee of Toronto, while somewhat low-tech in its production values, does important work regarding HIV education and also in making gay Asian bodies visible in sexual situations. The short depicts —

without dialogue — a scene that would have been familiar to its target audience: a young man, dressed only in a white towel covering his lower half and a baseball cap placed jauntily on his head, cruising through the hallways of a bathhouse, looking for a sexual partner. In its brief narrative, the unnamed protagonist receives a rejection, simply through a shaking of the head, by a typical white man in one cubicle and then an invitation to join another man in a different cubicle: this man appears to be Asian, but South Asian (perhaps Indian or Pakistani), rather than Chinese. The two men embrace, kiss, and then proceed to have protected anal intercourse, with the Asian man as the "top," and his partner the "bottom" (though physically positioned on top).

A condom to protect against possible exchange of fluids that might contain HIV is visible, and the scene is a success in showing both men experiencing pleasure. At the end, the words "Fuck safely. Use a condom" are flashed on the screen in multiple languages, including English, Chinese, Vietnamese, Tagalog (the language of the Philippines), and Tamil (a language spoken in India and Sri Lanka), suggesting the target demographics for the film. The work sexualizes the Asian men, while also distinguishing, even for the less discerning eye, different ethnicities, and shows in graphic, nonexploitative terms how to eroticize safer sex practices. It acknowledges that gay men at the time were still engaging in anal sex and does not discourage it, but it also shows how to make it work. Another video by Fung, made a decade later and one of his best known, *Sea in the Blood*, depicts his sister Nan's experience with thalassemia, a blood disease, and his partner Tim McGaskel's experience as an HIV-positive man. That both illnesses involve blood is important, as it suggests a continuous line between various kinds of blood disorders and works to remove HIV from a segregated, wholly stigmatized condition.

Fung is perhaps best known among queer scholars for his essay "Looking for My Penis: The Eroticized Asian in Gay Video Porn" (1991). In this groundbreaking essay, Fung builds an argument that the production, distribution, and accessibility of gay male porn, particularly video, has rendered gay Asian men not only as undersexed, but as essentially lacking in any sexuality; he says, "If Asian men have no sexuality, how can we have homosexuality?" (148). He goes on to argue that "Asian and anus are conflated" in gay porn (153), by which he means that, at the time he was writing, virtually no gay porn represented Asian men as anything other than the recipient (or bottom) in anal sex. This, by implication, essentially erases or removes the gay Asian penis from the imagination (or suggests it was never there at all, a slightly different kind of racist construction of the body) and aligns the gay Asian man with womanhood. As Fung further adds, this absence suggests that the "gay Asian viewer is not constructed as sexual subject" (158) — the producers of standard gay porn do not, he suggests, consider that there may be gay Asian men who view and consume pornography and who might desire to see bodies like their own in positions of phallic or dominant power or pleasure.

That terms like *rice queen* (to designate non-Asian men who are especially attracted to Asian men) still have currency suggests that the conscious and unconscious devaluing of queer Asian men is by no means over. Perhaps it is a sign of some minor progress that there is now a slang term for Asian men attracted to white men (*potato queen*) and one for Asian men who prefer to be involved sexually or romantically only with other Asian men (*sticky rice*). Such terms almost always have a derogatory connotation, but there is at least a kind of "coming out" about cross-racial or cross-ethnic same-sex desire in these terms.

There seems to be considerably less research on people we might cluster under the heading of trans Asian Americans (though they obviously exist); more attention has been paid to "third gender" categories in Asian countries, such as the *kathoey*, or "ladyboy" in Thai culture. There has been a long tradition of Asian American drag performers, such as Kim Chi, a popular performer on the series *RuPaul's Drag Race,* about whom C. Winter Han, whose work we have cited in this chapter, was interviewed by Spencer Kornhaber for the *Atlantic* magazine. Han's comments on Kim Chi are the source of this section's "Spotlight."

## Spotlight: Kim Chi

Few *RuPaul's Drag Race* fans could have been surprised Monday night when the show crowned as champion the 29-year-old New Yorker who goes by the name Bob the Drag Queen. Over the course of Logo's cult-beloved competition's eighth season, the personable and funny Bob so skillfully met the expectations for what a *Drag Race* winner should be that, during the finale, RuPaul asked her just how much she'd studied the show before joining it.

But the most memorable moments of the night belonged to a runner-up, Kim Chi, as had many of the most memorable moments of the season. A 28-year-old Chicagoan and first-generation Korean American, Kim Chi's fantastical outfits had frequently impressed the judges even while her physical clumsiness had become a running joke.

In the finale, Kim Chi's original song, "Fat, Femme, and Asian," performed partially in Korean, took direct aim at three labels frequently treated as undesirable in the gay male mainstream. Breaking with a typical narrative of the show — "*Drag Race:* bringing families together," RuPaul likes to say — Kim Chi revealed she still hadn't told her mom she does drag and doesn't plan on doing so. And when asked about which of the chiseled male models in the show's "Pit Crew" she'd like to lose her virginity to, she deadpanned, "I'm not trying to catch anything, so I'm going to say none of them," sending the theater into shocked laughter. Moments like these contributed to the sense that Kim Chi was doing something novel on *Drag Race*, even though the show has long been concerned with self-love, non-conformity, and playing with stereotypes.

Interested in the wider context of Kim Chi's performance, I spoke with C. Winter Han, an associate professor of sociology at Middlebury College. His book *Geisha of a Different Kind: Race and Sexuality in Gaysian America* features a chapter about Asian American drag queens, including past *RuPaul* contestants Manila Luzon and Jujubee. While Han hadn't watched Season 8 in its entirety, he had kept up on Kim Chi.

*This interview has been edited and condensed.*

**Spencer Kornhaber**: What did you make of Kim Chi?

**C. Winter Han:** My previous thoughts on the show were actually pretty critical of the way it presented the Asian contestants. Particularly it was problematic in the sense that Asian men in general are presented in the gay community as being more feminine in order to present white men as being more normative and acceptable to the mainstream audience.

Now the whole purpose of *RuPaul's Drag Race*, of course, is present yourself as more feminized; it's a little difficult to say, "Well, the Asian contestants are being more feminized than others." But until this season, the Asian characters were heavily racialized in ways that the other contestants weren't, and more importantly, the show rewarded the Asian contestants the more they Orientalized themselves, particularly with [Season 3's] Manila Luzon.

In that season, all the contestants were told to be newscasters for a challenge, and Manila Luzon did this incredibly racist performance where she spoke with a really thick stereotypically Asian accent and suggested that the guest star for that show should marry her brother because her brother needed a green card. She won that challenge. And when [the contestants] had to make over a straight jock, Manila Luzon put chopsticks in the jock's hair and had them walk with a little tiny shuffle steps, like this bad version of the Mikado. And the judges again rewarded her for that.

Embedded in that is the trope of the East being feminized, which has a long history. Part of it is this larger narrative of what we think about when we think about Asian men in general. *Details* magazine used to have a column that said "gay or something else." Usually it was like, "gay or firefighter," "gay or socialite husband," "gay or boy-band member." They had one where it was "gay or Asian." Asians were the only group that were ever marked racially as easily mistaken for being gay.

The joke of it is that it's a dichotomy where you're either gay or Asian — you're not both, even though you are easily mistaken for both. So it's not surprising that gay Asian men are not just marginalized in the gay community but in the Asian community. The drag queens that I talked to for my book were actively challenging that notion, making sure that they were embedding themselves in both Asian America and gay America. They were marking what it meant to be gay and marking what it meant to be Asian as not being peripheral to their identities, but essential to them.

That's what Kim Chi does. The show does follow a larger racial trope of this quiet Asian guy who also happens to be a virgin who also has a lisp. It's almost an immigrant story that unfolds in this 10-episode arc where she goes from being this very quiet, insecure, relatively submissive person into clawing her way to the top without complaint. But she does it in this way that she doesn't marginalize herself. . . .

I was really impressed in the finale when she takes that theme and turns it on its head. Something that is seen as being a deficient within the gay community — being fat, femme, and Asian — becomes just the thing she uses in order to propel herself forward. Some of the comments I've read online say they respect her because she takes a weakness and then overcomes that. But that's really a misinterpretation of what she's doing. She's not "rising above" being fat or femme or Asian. She's saying, "fat, femme, and Asian is in fact attractive. I'm going to prove to you that it's attractive because I'm going to perform and all of you are going to love it. And in loving it you have to question what is it means when we go into the gay world and mark these things as unattractive — when clearly someone has demonstrated to you that it is something that you actually love. (Spencer Kornhaber, "The Fierceness of 'Femme, Fat, and Asian,'" *Atlantic*, May 19, 2016, www.theatlantic.com/entertainment /archive/2016/05/kim-chi-rupauls-drag-race-femme-fat-asian-c-winter-han-interview-middlebury/483527/)

Less has been written about queer Asian American women, perhaps in part because of the more general pattern of relative inattention to women's sexuality overall, but also because of what a number of Asian American lesbian and bisexual women note as a double bind in how their own genderedness as women is constructed and viewed, outside Asian American culture and even sometimes within it. Fung, in his comments on Asian American femininity, observes that, in popular culture, Asian American women are usually viewed as fitting (or needing to fit) into one of two character types: Lotus Blossom or Dragon Lady (147). The Lotus Blossom is the delicate, hyperfeminine Asian woman, typically subservient, usually passive with respect to expressing any kind of desire or agency other than to fulfill the desires of the men in her life: the Madama Butterfly of Puccini's opera is perhaps the best-known exemplar — self-sacrificing, ornamental, almost a kind of still image of the ultimate in femininity. The Dragon Lady (the term is probably drawn from the mid-twentieth-century comic strip "Terry and the Pirates") is equally beautiful and erotic in her presentation, but she often uses her femininity for evil, deceptive purposes. While the Dragon Lady may have more agency than the Lotus Blossom, she is amoral or immoral in her use of her femininity.

Even a stereotype that has agency (such as the Dragon Lady) provides a kind of static, unchanging, and unreal way of experiencing self and other. While the Lotus Blossom and the Dragon Lady are Western clichéd inventions, they are also based on some cultural behaviors and values that Asian American women acknowledge they have been raised to internalize. In an essay with the intriguing title "Why Suzie Wong Is Not a Lesbian: Asian and Asian American Lesbian and Bisexual Women and Femme/Butch/ Gender Identities," the scholar JeeYeun Lee expands on the limiting effects of such polarities for queer-identified Asian American women, posing the question: "How does this construction of Asian women as models of heterosexual femininity par excellence impact on Asian lesbian and bisexual women?" (note: Lee includes Asian American women when she writes *Asian* in this context) (119).

One answer Lee provides is that the **hyperfemininity** assumed of all Asian-identified women is limiting for many lesbian and bisexual women. Lee, as the title of her essay indicates, is particularly interested in exploring what has historically been called the **butch-femme** binary, in which lesbian or bisexual women (of whatever race or ethnicity) were assumed to adopt either a more masculine-identified way of expressing gender (the butch) or a more feminine-identified style (the femme). The butch-femme binary is a complex one, as we discussed earlier, but it has come and gone and then returned at various times in twentieth and twenty-first centuries. The whole notion of a kind of static and essential identity of being either a butch or a femme, with accompanying role expectations, erotically, domestically, and professionally, has at times been critiqued as providing politically disadvantageous fodder for a continuation of antifeminist ways of viewing womanhood: for such critics, the "sorting" of lesbians and bisexual women into these two categories is a kind of reinforcement of stereotypical and typically heterosexist (and heteronormative) behaviors and attitudes that often privilege maleness and masculinity over womanliness and femininity.

Lee argues that more generalized views of Asian femininity have significant negative effects on Asian American queer women, using the butch-femme binary as a theoretical construct of extreme ways of "doing" gender. For the Asian American butch, Asian femininity acts as a kind of erasure or a precluding in the imagination of even the possibility of existence. If to be an Asian woman (including Asian American) is to be "feminine" in a culturally (and racially) specific way, there is no space for the Asian American butch to exist in a way that society can read or understand. There is a sense in which, in the peculiar gender algebra in which many people engage, there can be no Asian lesbians.

Lee finds femme Asian lesbians in a similar double bind. Traditionally feminine women are often especially vulnerable to harassment and unwanted sexual attention from men: this is true whether a woman identifies as heterosexual or nonheterosexual. (And Lee notes that nonfeminine women, such as butches, are vulnerable because they violate norms of femininity.) Femme Asian lesbians, because the stereotype of subservience and passivity is so pervasive, may be viewed as indistinguishable from feminine heterosexually identified Asian American women. While the feminine Asian American lesbian may not be viewed as quite so contradictory a set of intersections as the butch, not as "impossible" a creation, if you will, she becomes homogenized with all Asian and Asian American women. She, too, is viewed as having no agency, no power, no will to her own desire.

A word that comes up with some frequency in the writings of both queer Asian American men and women is *silence*. Certainly one of the ongoing qualities stereotypically associated with Asian culture is one of silence, of speaking as little as possible, either out of a kind of humility born of cultural norms or out of a clichéd "inscrutability," reinforced in various racist texts in popular culture (and some would say in geopolitical styles). Many queer Asian American writers mention silences in their families and within their traditional cultural gatherings and spaces, often as part of showing respect for elders and others in positions of authority. But they can also lead to alienation or separation from families and other kinfolk. Han suggests that perhaps we need to rethink what coming out means and how it is performed within Asian-based cultures, given that it is unusual for typical Asian American families to discuss sexuality of any kind.

This is a useful reminder that cultures communicate in different ways. Whether Han's argument that Kim Chi may not "need" to come out in the way Western societies conceive of the act is true for her or for all or many Asian Americans is not as important as is the understanding that some of the silences that Asian American scholars have noted in this section may not be "empty."

Yet another shared conflict many queer Asian Americans identify is that of their sexual or gender identity with their own identification with (or expectations by others that they will fulfill) the image of Asian Americans as the "model minority." The **model minority** myth suggests that Asian Americans, as opposed to other racial or ethnic minorities in the United States, have typically been viewed as a kind of model to emulate. Asian Americans are viewed generally today as engaged and responsible citizens, who establish useful, well-run businesses, participate in civic volunteerism, and place a high premium on education and upward mobility, earning their way into a kind of quasi whiteness. This stereotype assumes a kind of exceptionalism that ends up diminishing the individual accomplishments of such people — it implies that it is unusual for racial or ethnic minorities to strive and to take their lives in the U.S. community seriously. It can also create added pressure, both internal and external, for Asian Americans who may not meet all the expected criteria of the model minority.

This myth of the model minority can be especially hard for queer Asian Americans because their queerness often means, either to themselves or to those from the Asian American community, especially parents, families, and relatives, that they have somehow failed the community — they are living deficits to the sustenance of the model minority status. As Han notes, there is often an "internal conflict between the collective nature of Asian identities and the individual nature of western identities" (160–161); queer Asian Americans may find themselves experiencing their queerness as a Western quality and therefore a betrayal of their heritage, which places great emphasis on worship of (or at least regard for) ancestors. It also, no doubt, obstructs open communication both between queer Asian Americans themselves and between them and those with whom they wish to and may be expected to share familial events and values.

Finally, another piece of the puzzle can be the effect of Christianized families within Asian American society. As you may be aware, Christian missionaries had remarkable success in converting Chinese people from the mid-nineteenth century through much of the twentieth, often against opposition from governmental and other forces. You-Leng Leroy Lim writes about his own family, which encouraged him to change his Chinese name (Leng), which means "dragon," when they converted to fundamentalist charismatic Christianity because they viewed the dragon as a satanic figure:

My parents' subconscious message in the name change was not lost on me: "There is a part of you that we have given you that we think is completely evil, and we want to absolve ourselves of it." Dragon = gay = devil. Eventually, after more than a decade in the United States, I returned to Singapore to come out to them. Having set aside a year from Harvard to accompany them through the process, I was met by prayers, the laying on of hands, and the casting out of demons. One night I found myself sleepless, my body racked by incredible pain. At bedtime, they had asked if they could pray for me "because we love you" — how can a child say no to that? As they prayed for my healing, I was gripped by a fear unlike any I had felt since my teenage evangelical Christian days. I thought, "What if my homosexuality is a curse from the devil?" As I felt myself disintegrating, five years of gay activism and months of therapy went down the drain. I was fourteen again, fearing my passions and hoping that Father God or Mother Church would rescue me. Now my previously estranged parents had finally come to the rescue, and we could all be a happy family! And then a thought came to me: "You are thirty, not fourteen! The pain is not the devil — it's Mom and Dad. You are being possessed by their shit." Getting out of bed, I lit my sage stick and started cleansing my room. "Take back your shame, guilt, and pain. I no longer carry your load or accept your prayers. May everything coming from you return to you." I collapsed onto my bed, sobbing and exhausted. (325)

## ISSUES FOR INVESTIGATION

**1.** Choose one of the nonwhite races or ethnicities discussed in this chapter and look for images of queerness in media depictions of them. Television series, films, advertisements (particularly in queer-oriented publications) are particularly good sources. To what extent can you identify intersectional elements, and how is the intersectionality represented? What is foregrounded — the sexuality or the race or ethnicity? To what extent do these media texts reinforce problematic stereotypes? Do any complicate queer nonwhite experience in ways that are productive?

**2.** If your college or university has clubs or organizations centered on membership in or interest in nonwhite identities, attend a meeting or set up an opportunity to speak with a member. Are the norms of the group heterosexist? Neutral? Inclusive? How do you determine this? How might the groups be more queer-inclusive? Similarly, make contact with an LGBTQ+ student organization. Is it dominated by white students? In what ways, if at all, does it work to include people of color, as well as to build coalitions with non-white groups. (Depending on your school, it may not be dominated by white students — this is also worth noting and exploring.) If you embark on this exercise, be sure to be respectful of the group's members, its policies and procedures, and to let the people involved know that you are asking for information and for acceptance at the meetings as a way of learning and building understanding. And if they ask that you not attend as an outsider, respect that, as well.

## SUGGESTIONS FOR FURTHER READING AND VIEWING

Arrizón, Alicia. *Queering Mestizaje: Transculturation and Performance.* Ann Arbor: University of Michigan, 2006.

Boykin, Keith, ed. *For Colored Boys Who Have Considered Suicide When the Rainbow Is Still Not Enough: Coming of Age, Coming Out, and Coming Home.* New York: Magnus Books, 2012.

*Brother Outsider: The Life of Bayard Rustin.* Directed by Nancy D. Kates and Bennett Singer. American Documentary, 2003.

*The Business of Fancydancing.* Directed by Sherman Alexie. FallsApart, 2002.

*The Death and Life of Marsha P. Johnson.* Directed by David France. Public Square Films, 2017.

*Happy Birthday, Marsha!* Directed by Reina Gossett and Sasha Wortzel. 2017.

Hwang, David Henry. *M. Butterfly.* New York: New American Library, 1988. (A film is also available.)

Johnson, E. Patrick, ed. *No Tea, No Shade: New Writings in Black Queer Studies.* Durham, NC: Duke University Press, 2016.

———. *Sweet Tea: Black Gay Men of the South.* Chapel Hill: University of North Carolina Press, 2008.

*La Mission.* Directed by Peter Bratt. 5 Stick Films, 2009.

Mock, Janet. *Redefining Realness: My Path to Womanhood, Identity, Love, & So Much More.* New York: Atria Books, 2014.

*Pariah.* Directed by Dee Rees. Chicken and Egg Pictures, 2011.

Rifkin, Mark. *The Erotics of Sovereignty: Queer Native Writing in the Era of Self-Determination.* Minneapolis: University of Minnesota Press, 2012.

———. *When Did Indians Become Straight? Kinship, the History of Sexuality, and Native Sovereignty.* Oxford: Oxford University Press, 2011.

*RuPaul's Drag Race*, Seasons 1–, 2009–.

Snorton, C. Riley. *Nobody Is Supposed to Know: Black Sexuality on the Down Low.* Minneapolis: University of Minnesota Press, 2014.

*Two Spirits*. Directed by Lydia Nibley. SayYesQuickly, 2009.

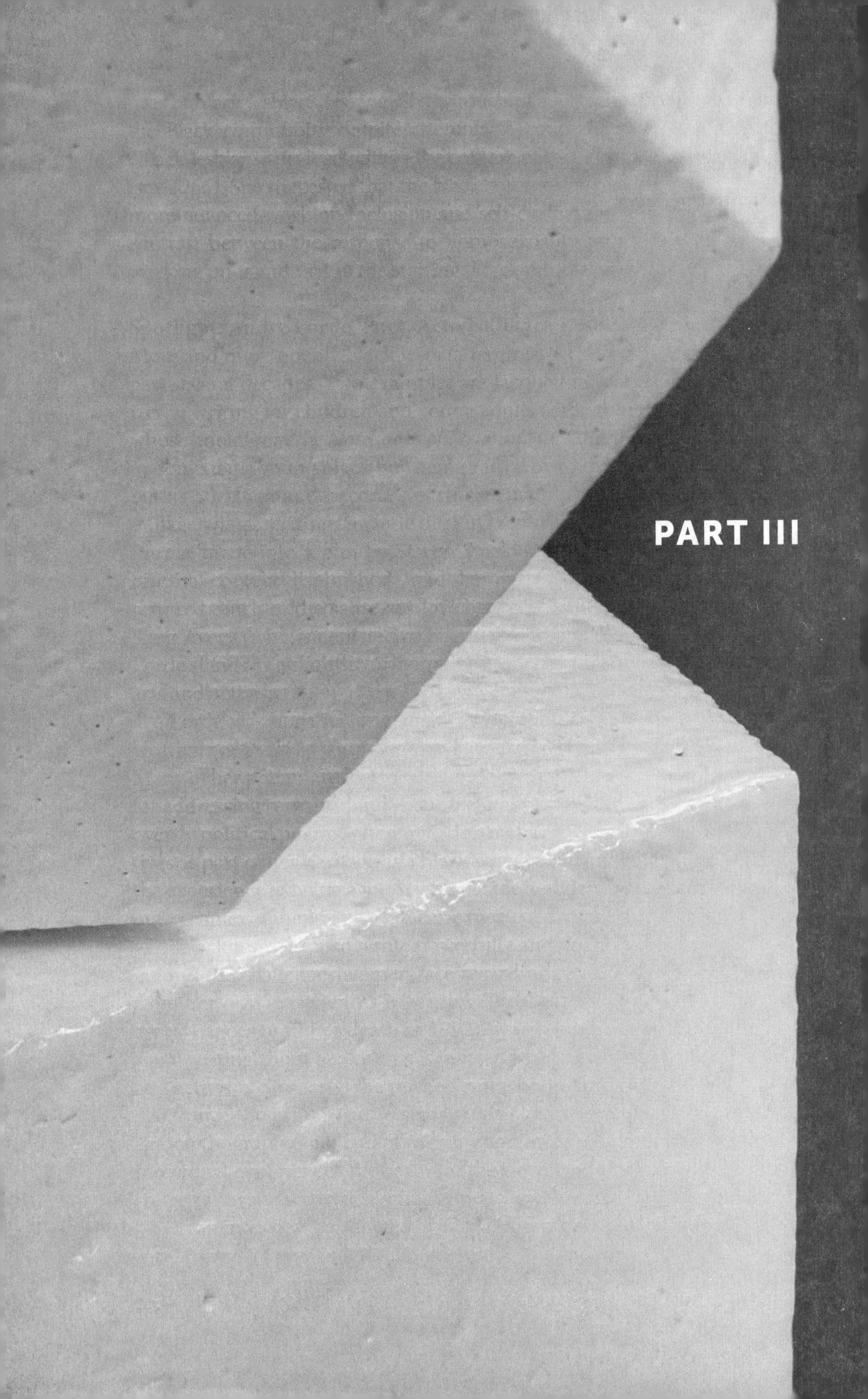

# PART III

# QUEERING CONTEXTS

# CHAPTER 7
## Queering School

The sociologist C. J. Pascoe, in her book *Dude, You're a Fag: Masculinity and Sexuality in High School,* persuasively argues that even when used without any conscious intention to label the addressee's actual sexuality, there is a homophobic subtext at play in the middle and high school use of such words as *gay* and *fag.* Pascoe explores various kinds of "performances" centered on verbal acts that reinforce proper ways of being masculine and ways in which female athletes either profit from assuming masculinity or are derided for it. In the realm of collegiate sports, male athletes who participate in non–contact sports are often named into realms of queerness (soccer becomes "fairy football"), and, inversely, female athletes who play contact sports are often labeled as lesbians (or, in less polite terms, *lesbos* or *lezzies*). Though what seems to be at stake is adherence to gender scripts, it is impossible to distinguish categories of and assumptions about the sexual identities of children and adolescents that are based on rigid binaries of male and female, masculine and feminine, queer (usually lesbian or gay in the typically dualistic thinking of pre-adult minds) and straight (or "normal" or "good").

The bullying that led to the suicide of Tyler Clementi, the undergraduate at Rutgers University, who, after having been spied on and filmed by his roommate while having a romantic encounter with another male in his dorm room (and the video shared with many others on campus), is but one example of how much sexuality remains schooled — indeed, what the French philosopher and social critic Michel Foucault would call "disciplined and punished" through surveillance and other means — even past secondary school. Residence halls are filled with stories, both from the past and probably still occurring as you read these words, of queer folk (or even non-queer folk simply perceived as queer) being subjected to such "learning."

This schooling is by no means confined to the residential realm of college life. Students report classrooms where faculty and other students regularly feel empowered to devalue and diminish the experiences and lives of queer people, through such strategies, sometimes unconscious, sometimes

Henderson, Bruce, *Queer Studies: Beyond Binaries*
dx.doi.org/10.17312/harringtonparkpress/2019.09.qsbb.007
© 2019 by Harrington Park Press

quite deliberate, as omission of the existence and contributions of queer people to the disciplines being taught and studied. This sometimes is done by imposing personal or socially negative attitudes toward queer lives, which is especially inappropriate in institutions that are not linked foundationally to belief systems that have prohibitions on same-sex relationships as part of their creed—though derogatory language that devalues the worth of any student is unacceptable.

Here is an example that illustrates how even well-meaning college faculty may reinforce binaries and boundaries and send messages to a spectrum of students about the nature of queerness, gender, and value. An out lesbian sociology professor who, for many years, taught a course with the title "Sociology of Women's Health," focused on sociological issues surrounding the bodily experiences of women born as biological females (or assigned female at birth). The course's content reflected its time, which was before greater knowledge and visibility of trans people in the college classroom. In her course description, included in the brochure issued in advance of registration, she included a note that said that, while enrollment was open to anyone meeting the course prerequisites, she requested that men consider the value of allowing the course to remain an all-female space and that they look elsewhere for courses that might include similar material. No men enrolled during the period in which it was taught.

This professor was very supportive of both male- and female-identified students, and she deservedly won awards as a campus advocate for them and for education about HIV/AIDS. At the same time, the opportunity for all students to explore and grow to understand experiences aligned not only with their own lives (and bodies) but also with those of others was precluded by her message. The desire to create a space that was women-only outweighed the instructor's responsibilities to the students at the school in general; it may well be that students identified as trans women (but who still had male anatomies) or trans men (but who still had female anatomies) would have been welcome as "women," but the course description did not invite them in explicitly—in other words, it maintained the male-female binary.

Precollege education in the United States remains in a general state of tension, not simply because of conflicts over the role of queer educational issues and the treatment of queer students and teachers. Rather, queer issues are but a few of many complex parts of what most observers, whatever their political positions, would agree is a challenging time in education, both public and nonpublic, in elementary and secondary schools. What does an *inclusive* education mean, both in terms of content taught in classrooms and in terms of pedagogical approaches for a wider spectrum of students in the student body as a whole?

While it is true that there has been a greater push to include diversity in curricula from prekindergarten through college levels, schools have been selective about what counts as diversity and what is most critical. Here's an example from race and ethnic studies. As recently as 2015, the state of Arizona passed a ban on courses in Mexican American history in its public schools, and Mexican Americans constitute one of the largest populations in that state; the law would also have banned the teaching of African American studies, and any other subject that critics viewed as either promoting "ethnic solidarity" or "resentment toward a race or class of people." This law was blocked by a judge in December 2017. The state said it might appeal the judge's decision; as of this writing, it does not appear to have done so (Terry Tang, "Judge Blocks Arizona Ethnic Studies Ban He Found Was Racist," *U.S. New and World Report*, December 28, 2017, www.usnews.com/news/best-states/arizona/articles/2017-12-28/judge-blocks-ban-on-ethnic-studies-in-tucson-school-district). Though it may seem to be comparing apples and oranges to place African American and Latinx educational subjects in the same category, the controversy is a mark of how politically motivated curricular decisions are. Note that Arizona's bill came about during the same time the Republican candidate for president Donald Trump called for a wall to be built to keep undocumented immigrants from Mexico and Latin America beyond the borders of the United States.

The same set of issues can be posited to general arguments about queer education — that it is marginal in terms of the demographics of students represented and the population at large; that there are more central content areas that need priority; that inclusion of queer issues is inherently political and, therefore, inappropriate as requirements in public schools (which neglects to acknowledge that all curricular choices are inherently political). Indeed, in 2014 Florida State Representative Charles Van Zant, speaking at an educational conference in Orlando, argued that the **Common Core** standards themselves were an attempt to "attract every one of your children to become as homosexual as they possibly can." His logic was that the Common Core aimed to teach students to be open-minded about and learn to assess arguments in favor of varied life experiences and identities. Charges of queer folk as "recruiters" of the young has a long and insidious history, but Van Zant's comments demonstrate that such a history is far from over.

While Van Zant's offensive assertion that the Common Core is designed to turn children into homosexuals is a specious claim at best, what is more true is that rethinking curricular objectives throughout the span of public education has led brave and tireless teachers and others committed to education to work to make the lives and experiences of queer and trans people more visible and integral to education. For example, in November 2017 California became the first state to approve LGBT-inclusive textbooks in history curricula in elementary grades (Michael Schaub, "California Will Be the First State to Use LGBT-Inclusive History Textbooks in Schools," *Los Angeles Times*, November 13, 2017, https://www.latimes.com/books/jacketcopy/la-et-jc-lgbt-textbooks-20171113-story.html). That this is happening in California is of special importance, if for no other reason than that the state is heavily populated and textbook content is typically driven by what publishers think will convince school districts to adopt (i.e., purchase and use) a particular textbook. With this mandate from California, inclusion of LGBTQ+ history will become an important feature of books from any publisher or author wanting wide adoption in that state.

## ELEMENTARY EDUCATION: THE "WONDER YEARS"

The first years of formal education are foundational and critical. It is in the years from prekindergarten and kindergarten through the beginning of middle school that children are brought into systems of knowledge and also socialized into values that they will interact with — whether accepting or rejecting them or even working to change them — for the rest of their lives. It is also during this period that parents and family set standards and practices for coteaching outside the classroom. There is no single national curriculum for public schools, let alone parochial and private ones, and so the experience of elementary education can vary quite widely, depending on such things as the tax base of a community, the demographics (race, ethnicity, class, nationality, religion, among others) of a population, and the shared or contested predominant social and cultural values.

As of this writing, there are standards only in language arts and mathematics for kindergarten through twelfth grade in the Common Core; there are also standards in history and social studies and in science and technology for grades nine through twelve. A program called the "Next Generation" has articulated suggestions for social studies and science. Of course, even these four areas do not cover all the curricular areas students are exposed to in elementary school, but there is a kind of logic to the chronology of the development of what is officially called the Common Core: the abilities to read (both in the technical sense and in critical and analytic senses), write, speak, and listen are essential to any learning in other subject areas. Similarly, the ability to perform basic arithmetical or computational skills (such as addition, subtraction, multiplication, and division), as well as to think quantitatively (i.e., to understand such concepts as fractions, decimal systems, probability, and other, more advanced-order aspects of mathematics), is also necessary to understand transactions in everyday life (such as those in shopping, budgeting, working on the mechanics of home life, as well as in many professions) and to understand abstract questions that require thinking in numbers and other forms of quantities. A number of states are resisting or backing away from some of these mandates, so the future of the current iteration of specific standards in subject and content areas is no doubt in flux.

## Language Arts and Literacy

The potential for queer inclusion is very much present in the Common Core Standards in language arts and literacy and in curricula expanding beyond traditional heterocentric content in general. School districts could very well decide that one of the texts to use for kindergarteners or first graders would be Justin Richardson and Peter Parnell's picture book *And Tango Makes Three*, based on the true story of two penguins, Roy and Silo, who lived in the zoo in New York City's Central Park. These birds engaged in what ornithologists identified as behaviors found in male-female penguin couples (who bond for life): they built a nest together and seemed to be trying to "hatch" a rock, in the way that heterosexual penguin couples hatch an egg. A female penguin laid an "extra" egg (male-female penguin couples in nature tend to only one egg at a time), which the zookeepers gave to Roy and Silo. The pair was able to serve as foster or adoptive parents to that egg in a critical way — otherwise, Tango might never have hatched.

Many teachers have used this book for a number of purposes, and its informational value as well as its artistic qualities make it useful in fulfilling several of the goals of literacy at the primary level and in getting young students to see more diverse representations of the central concept of *family*, something crucial to their own experiences and development. A number of school districts, however, have had considerable battles about the inclusion of this book in their formal curricula: some opponents claimed the book was inaccurate, which is not the case, as all observable evidence shows; others claimed that the book sent the message to children that homosexuality was natural, which, as animal behaviorists point out, it is — meaning it occurs in nature, without needing the encouragement of picture books. Along the same lines, some claimed the book furthered a political agenda, and some called for it to be removed from libraries or to be placed under restricted use. Courts have consistently found in favor of the schools and their rights to use books such as this one, but often teachers and administrators, under considerable pressure from vocal parents or other interest groups, have given up the fight.

So, while the Common Core Standards in reading call for the use of diverse texts as foundational to acquiring literacy, their very neutrality in terms of specifying diversity creates openings for those who would erase queer and trans lives and experiences from the curriculum. The effect of such conflicts extends beyond the language arts curriculum per se: one can easily imagine an elementary schoolteacher wanting to use a book like *And Tango Makes Three* to teach lessons in social studies (what makes a family?) and in science (what are different ways nonhuman animals parent?). Curriculum (what is taught) is inseparable from pedagogy (how it is taught and why) — the book's content may be used to help students further their ability to understand words and narrative sequence (time, cause and effect, and so forth), but it may also be used to further students' ways of thinking about nature or social arrangements. It might also, depending on teacher, students, grade, and community, be used to ask students to consider diversity beyond the nonhuman world.

## Mathematical and Quantitative Literacy
It is true that most of the years until middle school involve students' mastering basic computational skills and beginning to understand numerical concepts in more abstract ways. In this sense, to speak of "queering math" may seem either an oxymoron or an unnecessary distraction from gaining skills. But how might mathematics be queered?

Algebra may itself be queered in terms of its pedagogy — looked at in a nonnormative sequence to be optimally available for learners. The education scholar Sarah D. Sparks suggests that beginning with "story problems" or "word problems" may actually help reticent or mathphobic learners find their way into more abstract concepts with greater success. Queering the algebra classroom would be to devise such problems (and math teachers distinguish between narrative problems, which we think of as story problems, and nonnarrative ones, where, presumably, the element of time or cause and effect is not central or relevant to determining the outcome) in ways that include a broader set of characters and situations. Just as such simple things as use of names or objects from diverse racial communities or national cultures can help students from those populations enter the world of the practical roots of mathematical thinking, so the inclusion of details of same-sex pairings or queer families might help students recognize themselves in these story problems.

## Other Areas of Learning
Both social studies/history and science are importantly tied to the queering of education. Leaders in social studies education, for example, agree that a central goal of such curricula is "preparation for civic life." Given this emphasis, the discussion of the status of queer people and the rights and responsibilities of such individuals to act as citizens is critical and encompasses other areas, such as economics, geography, and history, all of which finally point back to civic life — whether through the distribution of goods and money, which we traditionally associate with economics; through the

characteristics and distribution of natural and produced materials, which is tied to geography (itself a field that can include such subareas as human geography and cultural geography, as well as more traditional issues of natural resources, maps, boundaries, and so forth); or through the ongoing narrative of people living together in the world, in nations, and in communities, which we call history. At what point do schools and teachers have the right, some might say the obligation, *not* to provide equal time for those who hold or wish to express homophobic or transphobic worldviews? To what extent are educational institutions, as sites of what we will call School-world(ing) in an ensuing section of this chapter, under an obligation to ensure the physical and psychological safety of their students?

Before leaving the realm of social studies, it is important to consider what and how history is taught in the early years of education. In many schools, history was (and is) not taught in any systematic way until middle school or high school, but more as a series of commemorative events or individuals, often tied to commonly shared holidays or commemorative months. While it is probably true that anything like an in-depth study of the role of queer lives in various historical narratives is best deferred until more formal historical study is part of the curriculum, it is nonetheless possible to lay some groundwork earlier on. Depending on the community and the location of a school district, events like Pride Week may already be part of some children's lives, and the historical origins of it can be discussed in ways that make sense to children. Historically important individuals who have connections to queer life can be featured, and the nature of their domestic and private lives emphasized or deemphasized as makes the most sense for the age of the children in the class.

Science education may seem more like mathematics in that much of the early education in the area may appear to be objective and a matter of learning a set of facts about the natural and technical worlds and their processes. Indeed, like the social studies standards, the science standards are divided into four main areas: physical science, life science, earth and space science, and engineering, each subdivided into separate topics with grade-appropriate knowledge and methodological instruction. Observation, collection of evidence, and building of and understanding of theories are central to all study of natural phenomena. In a sense, one could argue that what is being reinforced throughout is students' growing knowledge of and sophistication with the scientific and experimental method as a form of scientific literacy, starting with very basic observations about the natural world around the child and progressing through more challenging experiments in later years.

But here, too, there is a space where queer education may be not only of value but of necessity. When children start to study theories of heredity, for example, which begins in very elementary, nontechnical ways in first and second grades, questions of what the concept of *natural* is may well crop up. Given the diversity of the people with whom children at all ages come into contact, children may well begin to have questions about why some people (parents, aunts and uncles, siblings, family friends, or neighbors) like or love (the words children at the elementary school age probably use as synonyms for what we as adults would name as sexual orientation) some categories of people but not others. They may also have questions about why some people's gender changes, which is of general importance as trans people become more and more visible in students' everyday lives — whether a teacher, a relative, a neighbor, or another student they interact with who may be transitioning. If a child has been given information regarding sexuality at home that is different from what the scientific community agrees on (such as whether sexual orientation is a choice) and that is not congruent with the materials taught in the classroom, the child must be presented with information that reflects scientific methods and theories. The science teacher may need to distinguish between the social or personal values a family may assign to nonheteronormative sexualities and the ways in which scientists go about making arguments, using evidence and data. This is not a suggestion to undermine the values of a family, but a call to introduce students to the experimental approach as the cornerstone of science as a field of study.

## The Schoolworld and Other Subjects

The preceding discussion of queering elementary education, which focused on only four (albeit the four most common) subjects taught to young people, is of necessity limited. From the time children walk into a prekindergarten or kindergarten classroom, there are always other subjects taught that, depending on the school district, may include various forms of art, such as visual art, music, drama, and creative writing; health, often focused on hygiene and personal safety in the primary grades; modern and classical languages; physical education and dance (disciplines of the body); "practical" arts, such as home economics and consumer education; industrial arts, no longer quite as segregated by gender as they once were; and so forth.

But there is another dimension we have thus far touched on only indirectly, and that is what can be called the **Schoolworld**, the whole environment of school as a physical, social, and cultural site. The sociologist Erving Goffman, in his classic essay, "On the Characteristics of Total Institutions," defined **total institutions** as places where groups of people are separated from the larger world for a time, their needs met within the institution (e.g., food, medical care, shelter). For Goffman, such total institutions could be either benign or quite oppressive. While few schools today serve the function of being total institutions, other than boarding schools or residential schools for, say, disabled children or children or youth in the juvenile justice system (all of which serve a small percentage of the general school-age population), it is true that schools serve as something not entirely unlike total institutions in that they are the space where most children spend a large percentage of their waking time, particularly if they live in families where parents work or where there is only one parent and the school day extends beyond classes into after-school programs.

Thus, the world that includes time spent in formal instruction in classes, as well as what happens outside these rooms, forms the Schoolworld. This might include restrooms, hallways between classes, cafeterias, playgrounds for recess, school buses, and the pathways some children walk to and from school. Some of the most important and powerful lessons are those that take place in the interstices of the Schoolworld, the "in-between" spots. Some of those lessons are very positive ones — cooperation during recess, in a game of four-square or jump-rope; kindness in the cafeteria when a child shares her lunch with a fellow student who may not have enough to eat; empathy when helping another child who has fallen or who looks lonely in a corner of the playground. But the Schoolworld also offers too many opportunities, often unmonitored, either by design or by accident, in which negative or damaging actions can occur: verbal bullying, physical attacks, devaluing of the self or another.

Gender-nonconforming children, who often sense their difference from the majority of other children in their classes, are particularly vulnerable to such actions, and these actions can sometimes be enabled, either implicitly or explicitly, by teachers or other adults. Most recently bathrooms have become highly contested spaces. In 2016 the legislature of the state of North Carolina passed a bill that required that all individuals use public restrooms that matched the gender or sex listed on their birth certificates. Though issues of public safety, particularly for women and children, were the reasons supporters of the law articulated, children (and others) who identify as trans have been affected. Indeed, the noted trans teen Jazz Jennings, known for her television series and picture book, *I Am Jazz*, spoke out against a similar law proposed in Florida that would have made it a criminal act for her to use a girls' restroom. Such children go through considerable efforts to be able to live a life that matches their internal sense of who they are, and they are more likely to be victims of sex-related violence than to be perpetrators of it. North Carolina made their experience of the Schoolworld even less safe and more exclusionary.

What are other elements of the Schoolworld that may teach negative lessons to children, both LGBTQ+ and non-LGBTQ+, about queerness?

Playgrounds can be joyful places where children have opportunities to explore and exercise their physical expressiveness and to create worlds of play and of healthy competition, but they can also be devastating stages on which oppressive scripts are enacted. Though less so now than in the past, recess activities can be designated as for girls or for boys — though "boys' play" is often acceptable for either boys or girls. The boy who prefers to jump rope or play a game of make-believe (such as playing house or enacting a story based on a Disney princess movie) is often told to join the boys, usually by a teacher who senses or fears they may have a potential "queer kid" on their hands. Sometimes recess can feel like a daily stint in a kind of prison for a child who might otherwise succeed in the classroom — it is the site where gender-nonconforming little boys first hear themselves called such terms as *sissy* or *fag* — the latter often not associated with any understanding, either by the bully or the bullied, of sexual orientation per se, but a nasty policing and surveillance of traditional or, all too often, toxic masculinity.

Implicit or explicit messages about what constitutes a family or what is appropriate behavior can become part of the Schoolworld, both inside and outside the classroom. Inside the classroom, they can be imparted by what may feel like unconscious curricular choices of which book to read to a class, or by class discussions in which a teacher assumes that all parents are male-female couples (or, if a child has a single parent, that the parent is heterosexual). School policies, such as who may pick up a child after school, who may sign a permission slip for a field trip, who is allowed to attend PTA conferences, can either help make the Schoolworld a welcoming space for queer students or confirm or reinforce negative messages the world may already have begun to deliver to them.

## Teachers (and Other Adults)

The influence of individual teachers and other administrators who make decisions about the Schoolworld is impossible to overstate. Because children, especially during elementary school, spend so much of their day with their teachers, often with a specific individual teacher, their significance rivals that only of parents. What are the responsibilities of teachers to queer students or to students whose lives are importantly connected to queerness (such as having same-sex parents or guardians)? All teachers should provide respect for the lives of their students and their families and reserve any expression of judgment for nonpublic arenas.

What about queer teachers themselves? Do they have an obligation to be out in their classrooms, even if they teach children as young as prekindergarten or kindergarten, where the majority of the students will not have anything remotely close to an understanding of what sexuality means? The answer is always a contingent one, again based on community, comfort, and context. Teachers often seem somewhat unreal to students, particularly to young ones, who frequently express surprise when they see a teacher at a mall or in a restaurant — as if they assume that, once school is over, the teacher either goes into the classroom closet (literally or figuratively) for the night, only to emerge in the morning, or disappears into thin air.

Nonetheless, it is also true that sometimes teachers do choose to share some aspects or details of their non-Schoolworld lives with their students — sometimes simply spontaneously and nonstrategically, as in mentioning a spouse or a child or a birthday of a loved one. Heterosexually identified teachers do so without much conscious monitoring, one suspects, as their personal dramatis personae fit into conventional structures and expectations of heteronormativity. For the queer teacher, the stakes and the possibilities are somewhat more highly charged. The truth is that in some communities, revelation of a queer identity or, even more so, a queer relationship can put a teacher at risk for loss of employment; this is especially true at many religious-based schools, where the "open secret" of a teacher's queerness becomes the basis for firing once the secret is revealed publicly. At the same time, the more possible it is for queer teachers to acknowledge their own lives and the people who matter to them, in the same way that parents, friends, and others matter to their students, the more continuity there can be between Schoolworld and the rest of the world.

It is important for queer and non-queer students alike that the Schoolworld provides places of safety and visibility. It is important to any queer (or questioning) students because this safety and visibility allow those children, who may not even have the language for their sense of attraction, identity, or difference, to know in a tangible way that they are not alone, that they are not "bad," that they can imagine growing up. And it is equally important for the non-queer students in the room because they also can see, in living, interactive presences, queer individuals they can respect, admire, and wish to be like in many ways (if not necessarily sexually). Such disclosures on the parts of teachers may take time, may require consultation with other teachers and administrators, and may involve moving along a spectrum.

There are many resources online and elsewhere if you are interested in pursuing more in-depth research into queer issues in elementary education. Two particularly valuable resources were both produced in the 1990s but still raise relevant issues for today: a book, *Queering Elementary Education,* a collection of essays edited by William J. Letts IV and James T. Sears, and a documentary, *It's Elementary: Talking about Gay Issues in School* (and its sequel, *It's STILL Elementary,* which provides an update on the earlier documentary): both continue to have much to teach all who care about the education of children in the primary grades.

## MIDDLE AND HIGH SCHOOL: MOVING TOWARD ADULTHOOD

Middle school and high school are different countries of sexual identity and gender expression from elementary school, though the foundations for queer identity may be present before these grades. We will consider middle and high school as a somewhat continuous set of experiences, in part because people vary in terms of when they begin puberty, which is when recognizably erotic feelings that are associated with adult sexuality begin to emerge, and also because there is considerable variance from locale to locale in terms of the separation between elementary, middle, and high schools. In addition to physical, cognitive, and sociopsychological developmental differences from the tween to the late teen years, many educators note that there are different emphases within the larger Schoolworlds of middle school and high school. Some experienced at both levels have suggested that to be successful as a middle school teacher, one has to be more focused on and rewarded by helping students at that age develop certain elements of intellectual and emotional maturity, and to be less focused on in-depth study of subject matter, as is more the case in high school.

Middle school is frequently the time when polarization in reaction to such binaries as gay-straight and masculine-feminine become, at least temporarily, sedimented in the minds of students and, subsequently, the basis for both physical and psychological violence. It is the time when students really seem to learn the power of stigmatizing language, group exclusion, and physical attacks against people they view as different, especially where sexuality and gender are involved. Examine these two phrases, common to middle and high school boys especially: "Dude, that's so gay" and "Dude, you're such a fag." While there are those who argue that they are not necessarily, at least in the speaker's mind, accusations of homosexuality, there is, nonetheless, an undeniable homophobic subtext to each. Girls may use these phrases; my students have also reported that they have heard girls use words like *dyke* and *lezzie* in parallel ways. Again, there is a conflation of sexual orientation and gender expression here — sometimes both are involved, sometimes it is primarily directed at perceived or disclosed sexual orientation, and sometimes the homophobic term stands in for gender identity and expression. In any case, the language is always a form of social and psychic violence and can be as devastating as physical bullying — and sometimes more so.

Sadly, the kinds of homophobic violence in the Schoolworld of middle schoolers is by no means confined to the spoken word. Bullying, teasing, threatening, both in face-to-face interactions and on social media, have led to many terrible incidents with tragic outcomes. One of the most notable occurred in 2008 in Oxnard, California, when Brandon McInerney, a fourteen-year-old student at E. O. Green Junior High, shot a fellow student, Larry King, ostensibly because King had been engaging in what might be described as flirting behavior, such as asking McInerney to "be his valentine" and calling out phrases like "I love you, babe" in the weeks preceding the incident. King was on life support after the shooting and eventually died; after a mistrial, McInerney accepted a plea deal and is currently serving a long sentence. It is important to note that the California justice system decided to try McInerney as an adult because of the severity of the crime; that was within the rights of the court, but it may have added to the dissension among the jury that led to the original mistrial. Even those who believed McInerney should have been pronounced guilty and receive a sentence tend to think the courts made a decision that was not in keeping with our understanding of psychosocial stages of development.

The King-McInerney case is particularly vexing because there were so many different aspects to it that point to the need for better and more thoughtful education about queer issues and their complexities for students of that age. Complicating any consideration of McInerney's acts is evidence that he was becoming interested in white supremacist ideologies and gangs. Indeed, sketches of swastikas and other neo-Nazi symbols and images were introduced during the trial to build a case for the murder as a hate crime. King was biracial, but the hate crime charge focused entirely on sexual and gender issues; it is true that, while white supremacy is squarely centered on racial issues, such ideologies also tend to demonstrate hostility to various other forms of difference, including sexuality and gender. Evidence suggests that Brandon's display of hatred of Larry and of gay and trans people in general was not an isolated incident, nor was the decision to enact violence on Larry a spur-of-the-moment impulse.

Larry King's own behavior was characterized by some of those involved in the trial, especially McInerney's defense team, as "bullying," in that he persisted in paying unwanted attention to McInerney, though *bullying* typically implies the person doing it has some power over the bullied. King exhibited gender-nonconforming expressive behaviors ("acting girly"), and had come out as gay at age ten. He had begun to wear makeup to school, which was supported by the school administration, which, in fact, issued a memo to the student body, not naming King specifically, but calling on students as a community to support the choices of their schoolmates, whatever their own levels of comfort and discomfort were. A supportive teacher even gave Larry an old prom dress her daughter had worn, to show that she wanted him to view his own gender identity as acceptable and not something to feel shame about. He had also recently adopted the name Leticia, which suggests that he might have been moving toward identifying as a trans girl.

What emerges is how complicated and varied the attitudes of those living in the Schoolworld of the junior high were, which returns us to our focus on the queering of public middle school education. Joy Epstein, one of the assistant vice principals, who supported King's behavioral choices regarding his gender and sexuality, is a lesbian; her openness about her identity provided fodder, if inappropriately so, for those who would say that King may have deserved his fate and that the school created a climate where it was likely to happen. Other teachers, such as Shirley Brown, were very vocal in their disapproval of Larry's gender expressions and suggested that they, like the boys in the school, would have wanted to turn to violence; though Brown conceded that murder was not the answer, she did not rule out good, old-fashioned peer violence as a way to regulate Larry's behavior. It seems fair to ask: If the environment in which these teachers and administrators worked was so conflicted and incoherent (and, at best, ambivalent as a whole) in its own discourse about queer lives, what hope could there be for Larry (and other students like him) to find justice and safety? And what hope could there for students like Brandon, raised in a home filled with violence, drug abuse, and lack of consideration for difference, to have an education that would provide them with ways to think and act about difference? Sadly, there are ways in which the two boys shared a narrative of familial neglect and abuse and a chaotic set of "lessons" in the school. In a sense, one might say that the educational system failed both these adolescent boys.

HBO Pictures produced a documentary called *Valentine Road*, in which many of those involved in the case are interviewed — including teachers, fellow students, lawyers, and law enforcement officers (though not McInerney). The gay clinical psychologist Ken Corbett followed the trial and was present for each session. His account of the case, which builds both on testimony and on his own expertise as a psychologist who specializes in studying the psychology of boys, has been published as a book, *A Murder over a Girl*.

High school is typically marked as yet another turn in precollege education, whether it begins in ninth grade, as is most common, or in tenth grade, as is the case in districts that group seventh- through ninth-graders together in middle school. Until the last decades of the twentieth century in the United States, high school was considered the cap for the majority of students, who would then enter the world of work, during a time when a much smaller percentage of students (usually either from financially well-off families or possessed of such strong intellectual promise as to receive financial support from colleges) continued their education beyond high school graduation; this is less true today, when some college is often required for even entry-level jobs in businesses.

Discussion of queer sexuality and lives remains a contested issue at the high school level. In 2011 a bill known as "Don't Say Gay" was proposed twice, both times unsuccessfully, to the Tennessee Senate by the extreme conservative Stacey Campfield. That bill would have made it a legal violation to mention anything regarding homosexuality, including its very existence, in a public school up through eighth grade. Consider what such a law would do to even the most basic elements of middle school (and, by extension, high school, if such a law were eventually expanded to include grades nine through twelve) education. Health classes would have had to omit any discussions of safer-sex guidelines that provide information about protection from STDs for those who engage in sex with a member of their own gender. History classes would have to omit such important social events as the Stonewall Riots and could not include any of the recent scholarship that considers whether there is evidence for queer relationships engaged in by such figures as Abraham Lincoln or Eleanor Roosevelt; even a class session devoted to the difficulties of trying to look at primary evidence from an earlier century to make determinations that use modern concepts of identity would presumably have been criminalized. Discussion of important, time-honored literary texts would be censored or at the very least limited.

The concept that high school is a time when students become more involved in defining who they are can be tied to corresponding elements associated with the Schoolworld. It is generally true that middle schoolers may indeed begin to develop and, as in the case of Larry King, make their queer sexual and gender identities public, but they are less likely to engage in actual sexual activity beyond masturbation, though the age of first sexual encounter with an age peer is dropping, so that middle school is the place where students learn lessons of identifying and naming the sexual. High school is often the site of first forays into sexual activity and, increasingly, of a firmer declaration of sexual identity as something continuous and permanent. It may also be the period when students seek out cohorts of people with whom they feel kinship, affiliation, or simply comfort and safety. What are some of the "queer spaces" in high schools, whether overtly acknowledged as such or not? Clichéd or stereotyped as it may sound, many students report that cocurricular or extracurricular activities associated with the performing arts, such as drama club, speech and forensics, or musical groups, often provide places where young people can discover who they are and feel free to express this sense of self, even if they sometimes remain closeted elsewhere. A growing number of student-athletes are finding arenas of support within their team sports, though this is by no means universal, and it may still be gendered, in that young LBT women may be more accepted on their teams than young GBT men. Are there other groups, such as those dedicated to social justice, politics, philanthropy, and service where being queer or being around queer people becomes an important component of education?

One phenomenon that has seen much growth over the last twenty to twenty-five years has been the development of what are variously called LGBTQ+ support groups or gay-straight alliances, depending on the purpose and composition or membership of the group. The latter has been particularly helpful, in that membership in one does not necessarily out an individual: the hyphen suggests what its name intends — a coalition to support justice and safety and visibility for people committed to fairness to people of any sexuality. One such group, founded over twenty years ago, in what at the time seemed like an unlikely region of the United States — central Nebraska — is the subject of our Spotlight for this chapter.

**Spotlight on School Clubs: John Heineman and GLOBE**

John Heineman, who taught high school for several decades, writes about the process of establishing a gay-straight alliance in the high school at which he taught in Lincoln, Nebraska, a state not known for its widespread support of queer issues, though Lincoln and Omaha as major cities have larger and more progressive populations than stereotypes of the plains states may paint. His essay on the Gay and Lesbian Organization for the Betterment of Everyone, or GLOBE, can be found in the Appendix and will give you an idea of the challenges faced a few decades ago, challenges that have by no means disappeared today in many parts of the country (and the world, for that matter).

Heineman's story — and it is only one of many — is indeed, to use the language of President John F. Kennedy, a "profile in courage." It also suggests what a group of students, teachers, and administrators, working together in the interests of the *complete* education of a school as a community, can accomplish together.

Of course, not all experiences of LGBTQ+ teachers have such positive outcomes as does Heineman's. His essay, "Building a GLOBE in Nebraska," is included in Kevin Jennings, *One Teacher in Ten: Gay and Lesbian Educators Tell Their Stories* (1994); Jennings has edited a follow-up, *One Teacher in Ten in the New Millennium: LGBT Educators Speak Out about What's Gotten Better . . . and What Hasn't* (2015). Both volumes contain a wide spectrum of accounts written by LGBTQ+ teachers in widely different situations (sometimes written under pseudonyms, itself a powerful indictment of the continuing homophobia in education). Heineman grew up in Nebraska, attended Nebraska colleges, and has been an active speech and debate coach and drama director throughout his career. In a state not typically known for its acceptance of sexual difference, he has been an out figure in education for more than a quarter of a century.

# QUEERING COLLEGES AND UNIVERSITIES: "HIGHER" (?) EDUCATION

The very acts of reading this book and taking the course for which it is required are acts of queering college. The expansion of courses and, in still rarer cases, entire major or minor programs in queer studies (under various names, including LGBTQ+ studies) at the college level has been an important step in that direction. While, as is true of queer issues in high school curricula, there has been content about queer people and phenomena in courses for as long as education has existed, it is really only in the decades after the Stonewall Riots that teachers and institutions began to feel either the need or the possibility of offering courses that center on queer lives and knowledge as such. Previously, queer issues came into play, for example, when an English class tried to puzzle out the identity of the individual addressed in many of Shakespeare's sonnets — whether a young man or the "dark lady" (or both, depending on which sonnet the class is discussing). The emergence of stand-alone courses in queer studies would not have come about without the precedence of similar kinds of courses focused on racial and ethnic populations, such as black studies courses that emerged during the 1960s and women's or feminist studies, which were offered from the 1970s onward. Queer issues were sometimes folded into women's or feminist studies courses, sometimes focusing exclusively on the lives and political positions of lesbians (and, more rarely, bisexual women), though the history of feminism is a reminder that lesbians were not universally welcomed in some quarters of second-wave feminism, which emerged in the late 1960s. The lives of queer men may have been acknowledged in such courses, but typically only in ways that raised questions of whether there was any place in feminism for men.

There were courses in the study of queer men's lives and, in broader terms, the study of queer people's lives in the 1970s and early 1980s, but the developments sparked by the Stonewall Riots and the growth of what was then usually referred to as gay liberation, as well as the urgency to become more vocal and visible that the AIDS epidemic raised, were central to what is even now still forming as a "queer curriculum." In some instances, the impetus for such courses came from students themselves — and at institutions where students were encouraged to form student-led courses and where there were concentrations of out students.

In others, faculty and students may not have necessarily been aware that courses they were offering and enrolling in were indeed part of anything that might be categorized under such a name as "queer studies," though students often sought out multiple courses where queer issues and figures were included. A course in literary modernism, for example, may attract students interested in studying such writers as Virginia Woolf and E. M. Forster, who are now viewed as writers engaged in queer work, though neither published explicitly queer novels in his or her lifetime (Woolf's work has been successfully read through lesbian and bisexual lenses in recent decades, and Forster's "homosexual romance," *Maurice*, published after his death, has led modern-day critics to reread his less overtly gay novels, such as *A Passage to India*, through eyes that acknowledge the closeting of some of its central characters, while also identifying openings for homoerotic and nonnormative gender expression in many other texts central to the Western canon). "Uncloseting" figures like Woolf and Forster has led to rereading and rethinking many important literary figures and texts, until recently not taught through queer lenses. For example, Eve Kosofsky Sedgwick has reexamined Willa Cather's story "Paul's Case," long a staple of high school textbooks and anthologies, as a text that reveals different meanings and experiences when attention to codes of queerness and masculinity of its time are applied; similarly, Cather's own never-named but widely assumed lesbianism becomes part of the discussion in ways it may not have before the advent of queer theory and queer studies (Sedgwick 1993, 167–176).

Similarly, students may find a "hidden curriculum" in a history course, looking in the interstices of "great men (and women)" for the queer people whose lives were either diminished, made invisible, or lived in "sideways" fashion. Such courses may welcome these "resisting" (to use Judith Fetterley's term) readers (and students), as may the instructors; sometimes such classes can be sites of debate and contestation — as well as transformation, for teachers and students alike.

What continues to emerge and to be under construction is what an LGBTQ+ curriculum might look like, at the microlevel of, for example, an introductory survey course, for which this book has been written, or across disciplines and departments. Questions similar to those posed about queering the elementary and secondary school curricula can be asked about the more stratified departments and disciplines and subdisciplines of higher education. As always, competing opinions and perceived needs play significant and variable roles from institution to institution and even within departments at specific institutions. Questions of who teaches such courses may be ideological: there are those who firmly believe that only self- and openly identified queer or trans academics should teach courses involving queer studies; others argue that, if a subject is worth teaching, then the personal sexual or gender identity of the instructor should not be a determinant, only that individual's scholarly knowledge.

How is the Schoolworld of higher education different from most elementary and secondary schools? At residential colleges, the structure may be closer to Goffman's concept of "total institutions," places (literally and figuratively) self-contained, where residents have all their daily needs met within the institution. Indeed, for many students and for many of their parents, the appeal of residential colleges is that they provide an experience in learning to live outside the family circle in the safety of the campus. Of course, it is important to acknowledge that many students do not attend residential colleges, often for financial or personal reasons, such as the need to make the college experience economically feasible or a sense of commitment to family members (often driven by a need to provide care for them), so the point is not to valorize one over the other. In those cases, moving simultaneously through Schoolworld and through the outside or home world is complex in different ways.

For some students, living with age peers can be one of the most important avenues for learning during college years, but such a residential arrangement is not without its potential challenges, and this is especially true for queer students. Most residence halls are run, on a day-to-day basis, in a fairly self-regulating way; other students, such as resident assistants, and one or a small number of staff members, are in charge of a whole building or a set of buildings, or, in a really large residence hall, one area. Such arrangements are not by any means wholly self-regulating, in that there are always policies and guidelines by which residents must abide, as well as professional staff who oversee student welfare and the residential culture of the college as a whole.

Because none of the staff can be everywhere twenty-four hours a day, tensions and conflicts can build, and the age and developmental stages of students during college years can create related but sometimes intensified variations of the kinds of conflicts and problems we have noted at earlier ages. Conflicts between roommates can arise naturally, as, very commonly, roommates are likely to be comparative strangers, at least when they enter college. Learning to work through such conflicts can be a very valuable part of moving from adolescence into adulthood, but issues about privacy, homophobia, transphobia, and bullying can arise, and residential life employees, however well-meaning they may be (and, of course, they vary in quality and in their own openness to queer lives among their residents), sometimes cannot foresee or succeed in addressing these issues.

Probably the most famous recent incident involved Tyler Clementi, who was a freshman at Rutgers University's campus in Piscataway, New Jersey. Clementi was a quiet, somewhat reserved young man, who was not particularly well-matched with a more outgoing roommate: the two viewed each other with benign neglect at best — until the roommate moved into the realm of cyberbullying. Clementi was, by all accounts, beginning to come into his identity as a gay man, though he was by no means out in a universal way. He began exploring ways of meeting other young gay men through social media, and he made a date with one for a time when he knew his room-mate would be out. Dharun Ravi, his roommate, learned about this date, set up a camera with the help of his hallmate Molly Wei, and watched the date progress; he then used Twitter to announce a "viewing party" for a second date he learned Clementi had set up. Clementi learned of this, requested a room change, and decided to bring Ravi up on college and legal charges. Clementi ended his life a few days later, jumping off the George Washington Bridge. Ravi received a light sentence for invasion of privacy and Wei received a plea deal in exchange for turning state's evidence against Ravi.

It is important to note that it is impossible to state with certainty that the acts of Ravi and Wei were the immediate and sole cause of Clementi's decision to commit suicide. Clementi had recently come out to his parents and, according to his own report, his father had accepted the news well, but his mother's initial response was not what Clementi had hoped for, though later his mother stated that she and Clementi did have an affirming and loving relationship. His older brother James was an out gay man, which might have led Tyler to think his parents would both respond positively; for his mother, it might have been the shock of learning that two of her sons were gay that caused the less-than-ideal response. All this is to say that Tyler, like many queer youth going off to college for the first time and living among strangers, may not have had the support network, or not have known how to find it, that would have helped him handle what had happened to him. Whether the cyberbullying was indeed the straw that broke the camel's back or not, it demonstrates the degree to which the depersonalized world of much of college residential living, combined with an intensely personal vio-lation of individual privacy, can put queer college students at risk.

The example of Tyler Clementi is representative of the most tragic kinds of challenges residential college life can present. It is true that many students attend nonresidential colleges, such as most community colleges and urban or local undergraduate institutions. The challenges to students attending these institutions may be different, but equally challenging, and they include such issues as how to find and participate in a queer community when stu-dents may not have either designated physical spaces to meet each other or find themselves moving between emerging queer identities in their school (and, frequently, work and social lives), while often continuing to live in their family homes. Since we know from many studies that the most suc-cessful way of diminishing homophobia is typically through ongoing con-tact with queer people, colleges, whether residential or not (or whether having some students in residence and some who commute), need to con-tinue to work to make these institutions welcoming and supportive.

People involved as professionals in student life in higher education are, more often than not, student-centered and strive to find ways, such as programming, discussions, and other activities, to help students mature outside the classroom. But they cannot regulate attitudes or control even the casual daily encounters that enact homophobia, remarks, gestures, and actions that the psychologist Derald Wing Sue calls **microaggressions**: such microaggressions can range from teachers and students making automatic assumptions about pronoun use, about family relationships, as well as about who may use which restrooms and who may room with whom.

An additional development that has only recently begun to be addressed in open and direct ways is the self-identification by college-age students as transgender. The age for such identification is growing younger and younger, but many still wait to come out as trans until college, when they have the comparative autonomy that college offers. Needless to say, this can lead to conflicts and challenges within residence halls. While it is possible that college-age students display less of the fear and anger about gender-neutral bathrooms than do parents of young children, there can still be resistance to or discomfort with sharing such facilities with people whose bodies are anatomically different from their own. For some students, issues regarding physical safety can in some instances reflect real dangers, particularly as college students often also experiment with alcohol and other substances that can diminish capacity for making intelligent choices, though trans students are by far more likely to be victims of violence than they are to be perpetrators.

Many colleges are working thoughtfully and imaginatively to come up with various options for students, including making all bathrooms (which include shower stalls) gender neutral, with private areas so that students can determine their own level of modesty and display. This enables trans students to bathe and take care of other bodily functions in a context in which their anatomy need not be viewed or even specified. Such colleges typically still retain single-sex bathroom options as well. Colleges are beginning to be more savvy in establishing procedures that allow students to express preferences or needs in terms of which residence will best serve their sense of self.

Some colleges are even moving to gender-neutral options for rooming. In the same way that, many decades ago, students could often express a preference for either a single-sex or a coed residence hall, some colleges are now offering students the choice of rooming with a student whose gender does not necessarily match their own. Typically, such programs require, of course, that both parties agree to such an arrangement and such roommate matches are between two people who have become acquainted with each other at least online before agreeing to become roommates. This option is a way of leveling the playing field in terms of different students' comfort and preferences regarding whom they live with, and it also can have the effect of destigmatizing people whose gender identity or sexual orientation might make living with a member of the same sex even less comfortable than living with someone else. Such programs are forward-thinking not because they preclude the possibility that roommates will ever experience conflicts — space, sleep habits, noise, neatness versus sloppiness will remain eternal issues, no matter what the gender configurations — but because they allow individuals to decide to what degree gender-concordance is an important factor in sharing an always-too-small space by two young, unrelated adults. An excellent collection of essays addressing myriad issues is *Trans\* Policies & Experiences in Housing & Residence Life*, edited by Jason Garvey and others, which examines numerous issues that those involved with residential life face in trying to serve trans students; the book features work being done at a wide spectrum of institutions, from urban universities with smaller numbers of residential students to large public institutions, which have their own sets of challenges. Similarly, Z Niccolazzo's *Trans\* in College* looks at student and academic life from the perspective of trans students.

Finally, the college's policies and procedures dealing with sexual identity and gender expression in the realms of work tell you much about the Schoolworld — including how the college treats its employees, all of whom, whether directly or indirectly, are working toward the education of the students. Despite the temptation to stereotype, it is important to note that some religious colleges do indeed have antidiscrimination policies and provide benefits for same-sex partners. Though there will no doubt be test cases in the next few years, the ruling by the U.S. Supreme Court in *Obergefell v. Hodges*, the landmark 2015 decision that made same-sex marriage a legal right at the federal level, would seem to dictate that all institutions that receive any kind of public funding — and most private institutions do, in the form of such things as Pell Grants for their students — must honor the legal status of same-sex marriages; this is under fire at the time of this writing by the reintroduction of so-called religious freedom bills.

The issue of bullying, not only of queer youth, which can happen as early as prekindergarten and continue through graduate school, but of anyone who is perceived as different, whether because of race, ethnicity, class, or disability, and who is thus somehow viewed as inferior to the majority, is pervasive today; some have argued that the distancing that cyberspace permits (some would say encourages and enables) intensifies this bullying. In a powerful and moving article, "Seeking Care: Mindfulness, Reflexive Struggle, and Puffy Selves in Bullying," the queer scholar Keith Berry reflects on a long-ago incident from his childhood, in which, as a fifth-grader, a self-described "chubby bowl-haircut wearing boy . . . said to be my mother's angel, someone known to behave and stay out of trouble," he nonetheless "on the same playground where, just a few weeks before, with full music and make-shift costuming . . . spun as Wonder Woman for my friends and teachers," engaged in an unprovoked (is there such a thing as provoked bullying?) act of bullying of a fellow student, Norman, "a petite, polite, and soft-spoken Pakistani American boy . . . [who] carries himself beautifully and speaks with a gentle voice."

After recalling this incident, Berry considers his experience teaching a course on bullying, in which he uses the It Gets Better Project as a model text to lead college students to create active anti-bullying projects. What is important about Berry's honest reflection is not only the pedagogical value of the class, as well as his advocacy for mindfulness and an ethics of caring, but the significant, painful point he makes that those who engage in bullying have often been bullied themselves. There are many possible explanations for such a cycle of bullying and being bullied, which Berry explores at greater length and in greater depth in his book *Bullied*. Certainly one factor may be that such acts can serve to deflect attention from ourselves as potential targets of bullying. In that sense, they may be a form of what Kenji Yoshino calls "covering," in which the behavior serves to minimize the potentially stigmatized identity of the bullier and lessen the odds that they will be bullied. Yet there are prices to be paid for enacting these rituals that we may think lead to acceptance. In a sense, it is not unlike the coming-in stage of the closet that Tony Adams identified: such bullying maintains the seeming safety and security of the closet by distracting the others on the playground from the dangerous and risky femininity of the boy who only a while ago played Wonder Woman. The line between bully and bullied is often more blurry and fragile than we would like to think. Bullying is not unique to any one level of Schoolworld and, indeed, its lessons linger long after most have cleaned out their lockers for the final time.

## ISSUES FOR INVESTIGATION

**1.** See if you can come up with a lesson or activity for an elementary or middle school social studies class that would bring a recognition of queer issues to each of the four areas spotlighted by the College, Career, and Civic Life (C3) Framework — can you adapt the idea to different age levels? The in-depth program developed by the C3 is available at https://www.social studies.org/c3. New York State has also developed its own set of guidelines in social studies that provide ample opportunities to introduce concepts about queerness that are appropriate to the cognitive and social stages of development of children. For example, for Level K (kindergarten), here are some of the "concept understandings" the Board of Education suggests:

— My physical self includes gender, ethnicity, and languages.
— Each person is unique and important.

— My family and other families are alike and different.

— People have responsibilities as members of different groups at different times in their lives.

**2.** What are some curricular and Schoolworld strategies the school might have enacted that could have led to a different outcome in the Larry King case? Where could issues that might have helped the school avoid this incident have found their way into classrooms, in which specific subject areas (by middle school, students typically take separate courses in various disciplines, which become even more specific and specialized in high school and then in college)? What kinds of interventions in the larger sphere of the Schoolworld (hallways, playgrounds, school activities, parent-teacher conferences) might have helped?

**3.** How might queer perspectives be added to the kinds of curricula you experienced in high school. Imagine, if you will, what would be an "ideal" inclusion of queer content, as well as queer perspectives and, I might suggest, "queer pedagogy," one that asks students to look from the margins at what is traditionally considered the center. While a handful of schools may have the luxury of offering courses in LGBTQ+ history or a more general one in LGBTQ+ studies, this is probably not feasible for most average high schools, given the competing needs in various subject areas. So imagine ways to bring queerness into traditional subject areas — you may have had teachers who did so. How did teachers present the material? How was such material received and discussed by students?

## SUGGESTIONS FOR FURTHER READING AND VIEWING

Block, Francesca Lia. *Dangerous Angels: The Weetzie Bat Books.* New York: HarperCollins, 1998.

Fierstein, Harvey. *The Sissy Duckling.* New York: Simon and Schuster, 2002.

GLSEN. *The Experiences of LGBT Middle School Students: Findings from the 2007 National School Climate Survey.* https://www.glsen.org/learn/reasearch/national/middle-school-brief.

Guy, Rosa. *Ruby: A Novel.* New York: Viking, 1976.

Hartinger, Brent. *Geography Club.* New York: HarperTempest, 2003.

*I Am Jazz.* Seasons 1–. TLC, 2015–.

Newman, Lesléa. *Heather Has Two Mommies.* Boston: Alyson Wonderland, 1989.

Nutt, Amy Ellis. *Becoming Nicole: The Transformation of an American Family.* New York: Random House, 2015.

Sayre, Justin. *Husky.* New York: Grosset and Dunlap, 2015.

Sue, Derald Wing. *Microaggressions in Everyday Life: Race, Gender, and Sexual Orientation.* Hoboken, NJ: Wiley, 2010.

*Valentine Road.* Directed by Marta Cunningham. Bunim-Murray Productions, 2013.

# CHAPTER 8

# QUEERING SOCIALITY
## Friends, Family, and Kinship

Words like *family* and *kinship* can be both frustrating and healing for queer people, sometimes evoking tensions and even rejections on the one hand and developing new and rewarding connections on the other. In recent years, there has been increased scholarly attention to the area of queer sociality — the ways in which queer people form and sustain attachments to each other, and the structures in which they do this. Joshua J. Weiner and Damon Young, in their introduction to an issue of *GLQ* devoted to "queer bonds," point to the need to address eroticism as an important and central defining element of such bonds; they ask, "In what ways do our erotic lives contribute to legible sociality? And how is sexuality both driven and riven by [our] sexual being?" (223). The anthropologist Elizabeth Povinelli points to sexual pleasure as a fundamental form of such bonding, what she calls the "social bond of shared enjoyment" (288). For trans people, social bonding may be grounded in other forms of pleasure and enjoyment than the erotic (though they may include the erotic), such as shared gender identities and other experiences, as well as the general human desire for friendship and connection.

Scholars in other disciplines point to various ways in which queer people may create bonds. The art historian Whitney Davis suggests that, in ways not unlike the currently popular "scrapbooking," "family resemblances among objects in a queer collection of art and visual or material culture might sometimes serve as a way to create an *actual alternate family*" (2011, 310) What Davis is suggesting is that the kinds of items found in queer material culture can represent the kinds of bonds that scrapbooks also represent in more traditional families: they may tell a story of connections and kinship that reflect family dynamics. Scholars of race provide critical perspectives on the tendency to generalize analyses of sociality, kinship, and bonding in terms of whiteness, as when Juana María Rodríguez, a Latina feminist, asserts, "The inability to recognize the alternative sexual practices, intimacies, logics, and politics that exist outside the sightlines of cosmopolitan gay white male urban culture is never benign" (334). Similarly, the queer black male scholar Roderick Ferguson has developed, in his book

Henderson, Bruce, *Queer Studies: Beyond Binaries*
dx.doi.org/10.17312/harringtonparkpress/2019.09.qsbb.008
© 2019 by Harrington Park Press

*Aberrations of Black,* what he calls a "queer of color critique." So it is important to keep in mind that the dynamics by which queers form bonds and units of affinity and affection are always mediated and complicated by the intersectional elements at work within individuals and between group members.

Some scientists have made evolutionary arguments across cultures for the function of queer members within traditional family and community units. Some suggest that the presence of queer people has been one rein on overpopulation, a concern especially in nonindustrialized societies, where food and other resources are frequently scarce. More recently, arguments have been made that queer relatives often play altruistic roles within families, providing care, counsel, and other kinds of support that allow members of the next generation to flourish more fully than they would have without their presence. In a sense, such scientists would argue, what queer family members may do is reproduce values, traditions, and opportunities.

Today more queer people are themselves choosing to become parents. Sometimes they become parents before they have realized or acknowledged their queer sexual identity: in particular, there are many instances of women who, after living in a heterosexual marriage and having given birth during that marriage, realize that they are either lesbian or bisexual. Though the coming out of a parent has led in the past and still today in some cases leads to custody battles in which queer sexuality or transgender identity is used to assert parental unfitness, it is now more common for parents to work together to try to come up with solutions that serve the best interests of the children. The child whose parent(s) comes out as queer is also likely to experience a set of processes of "revising" family stories and roles that is similar to those experienced by family members when one of them comes out or transitions.

If a child is raised from infancy with same-sex or trans parents, that is their "normal." Children bond early on with adults who provide them with nurturance and safety, and the gender of that caregiver does not appear to make much difference — continuity and security do. For the children of queer parents, the greatest challenges may come from outside the family unit — from schools or religious organizations that view the family structure as "unnatural" or contrary to their values, and from other children (and their parents) who are quick to pick up on difference and to view difference as either confusing or "wrong." Children of interracial adoptions can face similar stigmas because they frequently don't look like their adoptive parents or siblings.

## FAMILIES WE CHOOSE: KINSHIP BEYOND BIOLOGY

Since the publication in 1997 of Kath Weston's book of the same title, the phrases *families we choose* and **family of choice** have been widely used to acknowledge the existence and describe the composition and function of families not defined purely by biological links. For queer people, families of choice may serve particularly critical, even at times lifesaving functions. Queer individuals were often rejected or cast out by their families of origin in the past, which is considerably less common today, though ostracism still occurs regularly and the consequences can be serious, both materially and emotionally. What was probably even more true in the past was that queer people might have kept their sexual identity hidden from many or all their family members of origin and, hence, needed other people to whom and with whom they could be "themselves," in a fuller way and a way that did not require masking.

Naturally enough, many queer people turn, as they often have, to other queer people of their own age or other social cohort to take on some of the roles often played by siblings or cousins in traditional blood families — confidants who share similar experiences and who have themselves comparatively recently gone through some of the same benchmarks of experiencing and of formation of sexual orientation or gender identity — or both. In past decades, these queer sibling relationships may well have been formed during college or early work years, times when people start to assert a kind of individuality and independence in many cultures, whatever their sexuality. Today such familial formations may happen at earlier ages.

Older queer folk can serve familial roles as well. Certainly, back in the eras when initiation into queer life often centered on such gathering places as bars, clubs, and other kinds of organizations (such as community theater, amateur athletics, and so forth), young queer people could find people who might serve as mentors, "aunts" and "uncles," who could provide advice and sometimes simply a sympathetic ear as the younger person navigated some of the challenges of living most of their time in a heterocentric and gender-normative world. For many older queer people, taking on these familial roles was in and of itself rewarding, connecting them to new generations of people more like themselves than some of the families into which they were born; occasionally, of course, blurring of social and romantic emotions could and does take place, but no more so than in cross-generational heterosexual friendships.

A particularly interesting example of these constructed queer families is found in the drag-ball culture that flourished especially in the 1980s and 1990s (though such balls have been in existence since the 1930s) in such urban centers as New York, San Francisco, Chicago, and Detroit. Drag balls, elaborate events that featured men (and women) outdoing each other, both in costumes and performances, to depict over-the-top and sometimes very detailed and realistic representations of gender, have a long history, going back as far as the Harlem Renaissance, and continue to this day.

In 1990 the queer documentarian Jennie Livingston directed and coproduced the film *Paris Is Burning*, which attempts to be an ethnographic representation of various aspects of the drag-ball culture. (*Ethnographic*, a term drawn from cultural anthropology, here means working as much as possible to let the subjects speak and present themselves without excessive mediating commentary or judgment by the filmmaker.) It is in this film that you can get as clear a sense as anyone living outside the culture can of how powerful family of choice can be, especially for those queer people often marginalized and stigmatized by their birth families and by society in general. One of the most notable and moving aspects that the film highlights is the existence of "houses," which are sometimes physical places but are, more important, emotional and familial structures. These structures provide these typically young people, who might otherwise be homeless and certainly lacking in psychological and social support, with a sense of a *place* in which they are loved and embraced. There are usually adults who take on traditional kinship roles (as in "I Am Angie the Mother of the House of Xtravanganza"). There is often a genealogy for each "house" (and *house* here represents both house as a home and house as a "fashion house," such as the House of Chanel, with an associated sense of style and history), and figures who are viewed as legendary, which creates a sense of family history. These "houses" often provide safe havens for young trans people, some of whom have no other options but to live on the streets and engage in risky activities, such as sex work.

### Spotlight on a Father and Daughter: Alysia and Steve Abbott and Their Blended "Fairyland"

Memoirs that focus on queer family lives have become a subgenre of their own. In the section on queerness and aging that concludes this chapter, we will look at an example of a memoir written by the adult, middle-aged daughter about her relationship with her elderly father, who, late in life, transitions to identify as a woman. Similarly, there are memoirs written by parents who come out as queer at some point and who give us a sense of what it was like to do so in terms of their relationships with the parents of their children and with their children, who range from toddlers to adults. The children of queer families have also written powerful and informative memoirs. Zach Wahls, who was born in Wisconsin and then raised from age nine in Iowa, is the son of two lesbians, conceived through artificial insemination. He has written a memoir of his experiences, *My Two Moms: Lessons of Love, Strength, and What Makes a Family* (2012), and has testified in front of Congress in behalf of LGBTQ+ rights. He has weathered quite a few public storms for someone of his age, including his public criticism of the Boy Scouts of America for its ban on gay males; as an Eagle Scout, identified as heterosexual, his words carried the weight of someone who lives in multiple communities at the same time and finds value in them. He put his own position with eloquence and strength when he said, "To be clear, I don't consider myself an ally. I might be [a] straight cisgender man, but in my mind, I am a member of the LGBT community. I know the last thing that anyone wants is to add another letter to the acronym, but we need to make sure as a movement we're making a place for what we call 'queer-spawn' to function and to be part of the community. Because even though I'm not gay, I do know what it's like to be hated for who I am" (Reese).

Alysia Abbott's 2013 memoir, *Fairyland: A Memoir of My Father*, tells the story of her relationship with her father, who, after her mother's death, was Alysia's sole custodian. Steve Abbott was one of the leaders in the underground entrepreneurial queer literary scene that emerged in the decades after the Stonewall Riots. By the time of her mother's death in a car accident in 1973, Alysia's parents had already begun to live separate lives, after Steve had announced that he was primarily homosexual in his orientation and wanted to live life as a gay man.

Steve Abbott combined elements of family of birth and family of choice in the structures and environment in which he raised Alysia. He not only felt an obligation as Alysia's birth father to take responsibility for her upbringing, but also loved her deeply — their bond went beyond any legal obligation. How to raise her in what was his fairly haphazard series of domestic arrangements was challenging for him, for her, and for those in their extended social and domestic circles. Steve craved dyadic intimacy, the coupledness with one other man that is part of the tradition of pair-bonding, but he also saw as part of the new consciousness that gay liberation brought a refusal to be bound by any kinds of social pressures to live monogamously.

This led, at times, to rather complex emotional and domestic situations, for Steve and Alysia, as well as for the others in their orbit. Steve had some partners with whom he was involved for longer periods than others, but rarely did these relationships produce the kind of stability that most people assume is secure and comfortable for children, who typically need continuity and dependability. Yet the majority of Steve's partners, aside from some one-night stands, took their role in Alysia's life seriously, sometimes remaining available to her and involved in her welfare even after the relationship with Steve had moved into something less or nonsexual and nonromantic. Steve also worried that his primarily gay male cohort might keep Alysia from having close, ongoing domestic interaction with female role models, so for a time he advertised for a female roommate, perhaps with children of her own, to join their household. While these attempts were serial in nature and none of them seems to have been terribly successful, they were well-intentioned. Such reinventions of family are bound to be bumpy, precisely because they cannot help being haunted by values and histories inherited from existing society and because there are no clear road maps for making them work. Just as Steve and his fellow artists were making new kinds of art, so he and Alysia were making a new kind of family. Steve included Alysia in both.

Their shared lives became even more complicated when Steve was diagnosed with AIDS, while Alysia was across the country at college, and she was torn between returning to San Francisco to care for him and finishing her degree at New York University. She eventually decided to complete her degree at an accelerated rate and return to the West Coast to be with her father. Steve died in 1992, not yet fifty years old. Alysia, now herself middle-aged, wrote her memoir of her life with her father several decades after his death, perhaps feeling that she needed both distance from the lived experiences and the perspective of herself growing into adulthood and early middle age (and parenthood) to make the most thoughtful and understanding sense of what her bond with her queer father meant to her.

## FROM STRANGERS TO FRIENDS TO LOVERS TO FAMILY: DATING, MATING, AND BEYOND

Forming romantic bonds is challenging for all people, whatever their sexuality. How do we develop attraction, how do we express it, what are the steps through which people come together and "try out" each other socially, romantically, and sexually? What leads a more casual dating relationship to feel like (and even be named) something we might call *mating*? It is also true that, particularly in the past, queer people have typically had the extra challenge of trying to determine, in ways that are physically and socially and emotionally safe, whether a person to whom they are attracted is open to a queer relationship or even a brief sexual encounter.

Queers found and in some cases created shared spaces that provided safety for and with each other. "Bar culture," as it may be called, has a long history, both in the United States and in other countries, and this culture has received study as an institution. A number of studies of individual towns, even of individual bars, have been done by historians and sociologists. Two of specific interest historically are Elizabeth Lapovsky Kennedy and Madeline Davis's *Boots of Leather, Slippers of Gold: The History of a Lesbian Community*, mentioned in the discussion of class in chapter 5; and Ricardo J. Brown's *The Evening Crowd at Kirmser's: A Gay Life in the 1940s*, a memoir written by a man who grew up in St. Paul, Minnesota, in a working- or middle-class family, joined the navy, received an "undesirable discharge" for being homosexual, and then returned for a time to his hometown. He discovered what he describes as a dive bar, Kirmser's, run by a heterosexual married couple of that name, but understood as a meeting place for queers. Brown became a member of the "evening crowd," men and women who often communicated through the kinds of codes we discussed in earlier chapters, formed relationships, sexual, romantic, and platonic, and created support for each other, while always having to work hard to avoid the law and straight people (usually men) who felt entitled to enact violence on this community. Kirmser's did not advertise itself as a queer space for "family" to gather — you had to know someone to learn about it or, in some instances, hear about it secondhand and summon up the courage to enter, being vigilant not to be seen entering. In some smaller towns or rural areas, there are bars or clubs that have "queer night," where it is understood that the place is welcoming not only of queer patrons, but of openly queer displays of affection and friendship. One example was a rural bar located in far upstate New York in the mid-1980s, which, one Saturday night each month, placed a sign in its window that indicated that the bar was closed "for a private party." (It was always the same Saturday night of the month.) That was code for "queer night," but you had to be in the know — and some people drove two or more hours to be there on that night.

It is also true that, as in the past, queer people may find, either through deliberate investigation or simply by a congruence of interest, social or recreational or other kinds of spaces where queer and queer-friendly people may congregate in ways that make the revelation of queer identity a nonissue (other than as an occasion to welcome another "family member"). Arts organizations such as theater and music groups have often provided safe havens for young queer (or questioning) people; in some communities and schools, athletics has been another place for young queer women to find kinship, though, because of the stereotypes of female athletes, these spaces can be hyper-policed.

While many assume that queer youth are more likely to be drawn to each other than to their non-queer counterparts for the purposes of sexual activity, the sociologist Lisa Wade, in her 2017 book *American Hookup: The New Culture of Sex on Campus*, argues that "hookup culture is primarily a heterosexual phenomenon." In her study, which builds both on journals and in-depth interviews of college students at different kinds of institutions, as well as on large data, she found that queer undergraduates tend to feel excluded from the *hookup culture* that defines many campuses. She is concerned less about the frequency with which students actually have sexual contact with each other than about the perceptions that students have regarding the frequency with which their peers have sex and to what degree nonheterosexual students are encouraged to engage in nonverbal activities, such as "grinding" in public dance areas. Wade found that it is socially acceptable for two female students to make out, especially if they are viewed as doing so (a) when drunk and (b) for the viewing pleasure of the heterosexual men nearby. The same is not true for two men, who are immediately consigned to being "irretrievably" gay at that moment. Two men who do not otherwise identify as gay may be given a pass if they hook up after a night of drunkenness, but public performances are forbidden.

What Wade finds particularly problematic about **hookup culture**, for college students of any sexuality, is its tendency to depersonalize and remove emotional connectedness from either the sexual encounter or its aftermath. She argues — and the students who participated in the study validate this — that the culture of hooking up seems to require some degree of distancing, especially to keep the clear distinction between a hookup partner and an actual boyfriend or girlfriend. This can lead to various forms of unhappiness, particularly isolation and loneliness, which are often hallmarks of college life for many students, particularly in their vulnerable first semesters.

She describes one such example in analyzing the journal of an Asian American gay male student she calls Lincoln. After a night of parties, Lincoln returns to his residence hall, where what Wade describes as a "giant pajama party" seems to be taking place. Lincoln finds himself flirting with another young man, Terrell, who, in his words, he had "always gotten the gay vibe from." Lincoln does not describe in any detail what the two men did sexually, but he does describe their interaction afterward: "He got out of bed to show Terrell to the door and they hugged goodbye. This — the hug — gave him pause. It was 'something I've never done after a hookup before,' he noted, adding the all-important caveat, 'although I obviously didn't have feelings for the guy'" (138). Wade notes that this was Terrell's first sexual encounter with another man, a fact he had made clear to Lincoln before they began to have sexual contact. While Wade concedes that Lincoln's journal does make it clear that he acknowledged that this was an important moment for Terrell (i.e., he wasn't totally callous about it), it is understood that "feeling something for others is against the rules and so he made sure to specify that no feelings were involved. In hookup culture, there are no tender initiations, even when there are" (138).

Wade is sympathetic to the effect of distanced emotionality in hookup culture on queer people (in terms of either sexual orientation or gender identity — or both), who may have challenges of the closet, of being outed, and of needing to pay special attention to their emotions because of what may be at risk, socially, culturally, and psychologically — an effect felt more by queer persons than their straight or cisgender peers. She finds that relative isolation, particularly at schools that do not have large visible queer populations, can make issues of making friends, dating, and mating even more difficult for queer students. And even once students have left the "bubble," as Wade calls it, of college culture, the remnants of hookup culture may linger as they encounter more challenging logistics in finding people with whom to be genuinely intimate, especially if they live beyond urban areas and ones that are queer-friendly and queer-visible.

Of course, it is also true that many LGB and trans youth do not go to college and indeed find themselves homeless or living in shelters (when and where they are available). One such space is the Ali Forney Center in New York City, named after a homeless gender-nonconforming teen who did much social, political, and outreach work among queer youth, advocating for safer sex and better police protection for vulnerable youth, before he himself was murdered on the streets at age twenty-two (https://www.aliforneycenter.org/alis-story/). And it is crucial to keep in mind that such shelters are by no means prevalent even in major cities, and so it often falls on such queer youth to create bonds and family relationships in other ways. Making matters more difficult, for some of these youth, is that sex work is one of the few ways of earning the money it takes to meet basic needs of food and clothing. This is not to place a judgment on sex work itself, only to highlight the problems that can arise when young persons feel it is their only option. The emotional and relational bonds between such youth can be powerful and deep, which makes the emotional alienation that some hookups (often with adults who pay for sex) create more at odds with a sense of selfhood, belonging, and positive self-image.

On the one hand, greater visibility and earlier identification as queer might lead people looking for friendship with other "family" members more possible and likely; on the other hand, the popularity of social media sites that draw people with multiple motivations has the potential to complicate relational roles in different ways. Granted, some of these sites are known as expressly aimed at hookup culture — for gay or bisexual men, an app like Grindr functions in this way — but others may draw people with a spectrum of reasons for using the applications. The potential for misunderstanding why people make contact with each other (and thus for mismatch) is not necessarily lessened in digital culture — it may just take a different form.

It is probably still the case that men and women approach the family-building dimensions of potential, current, or past romantic or sexual partnerships in different ways, though this too is likely to be changing as gender roles become less rigidly defined. In the mid- to late twentieth century, men were often quick to move to a sexual encounter with others, frequently briefly following an exchange of basic information and desired sexual interaction; while it would be wrong to say that there are no women who did this, the numbers simply point toward differences. And, of course, there are many men who prefer to get to know a potential romantic or sexual partner over time before engaging in sexual contact — this is probably as varied for gay and bisexual men as it is for their heterosexual counterparts. "Friends with benefits" exist on all points of the sexual spectrum.

One difference between queer people and their heterosexual or cisgender counterparts is often the post-romantic place of partners, whether long-term or not, in the "chosen" family. For many queer people, the decision not to continue either a romantic or a sexual relationship with another person does not necessarily result in the end of any kind of social and emotional relationship, as is more likely with heterosexual couples. Gay men, if they have originated a relationship on a purely sexual level, may decide sooner or later, for any number of reasons, that the relationship would be better off in the "friend zone," and they add the individual to the extended family of people with whom they socialize and share important feelings and experiences. In some cases, there may even be intermittent sexual contact, but, by then, with an understanding that such encounters are recreational rather than a commitment to a romantic future.

A book that tries to capture the complexity of friend-kin-lover networks among gay men is *Very Recent History: An Entirely Factual Account of a Year (c. AD 2009) in a Very Large City* by Choire Sicha (2013). Sicha adopts a somewhat disinterested or objective tone for his narrative and, while he may have done some editing and rearranging to create a narrative that serves his purposes, he does strive to give the sense that what he is reporting did indeed happen, more or less in the way he describes. The book has the feel of a documentary, of reportage of what can be observed or stated by the men involved. The network of gay men is a very specific one, all living in what is never named but clearly is New York City, fitting into a fairly narrow socioeconomic and educational demographic, a variation of what Rodríguez and Ferguson critique as a kind of class-determined depiction of queer bonding — but Sicha does not claim to be trying to generalize beyond that demographic.

It is and has been statistically less common for women to hook up on a first date than it is for men. Women generally focus on relationality more, at least initially, than men, and thus they may be slower to move to a level of sexual interaction with other women, though they may start to form emotional bonds earlier. Women, of course, have the capacity to have as much interest in sexual activity as men and can also desire as varied a set of partners, but they have not been as likely to act on them as quickly or with as much frequency as have men. It may be that biological and social pressures to "nest" have played a role in this difference. Women are more likely to be serial monogamists, that is, to live in a relationship in which there is a set and closed boundary for sexual interaction with other women; men have been more likely to have either explicitly or implicitly open relationships, in which sexual monogamy is not a determining factor. Lesbians who come to the end of a romantic relationship are also likely to remain on friendly terms with their ex-partners, often including them in an extended family circle. Because of the way men and women are taught to "do" emotion and sociality in Western cultures, gay men and lesbians may experience different struggles in maintaining these familial bonds, and some choose not to maintain any kind of relationship with ex-partners after the end of the romance: they are no longer family to each other. For trans people, the complications of finding potential romantic or erotic partners may be increased, given the need to find possible mates whose gender identity and sexual desires complement their own (insofar as there is ever a perfect match on such dimensions for any two people).

Once a couple has made some form of commitment to each other, the work of mating is hardly finished, any more than it is for their straight counterparts. Again, historical patterns and social norms often make the kinds of issues that queer couples must work out and agree on more complex, simply because there is a shorter legal and cultural history regarding the assumptions on which such coupledom rests. In most places, for example, sex outside a heterosexual marriage is usually legal grounds for a divorce, though one or both of the married couple need to institute a suit based on this. While there is no reason to assume that the same would not be true legally for queer couples, it is also true that a higher proportion of queer couples may also have stated or unstated expectations about the importance of sexual monogamy, even once the couple has been legally married. While plenty of gay male and lesbian couples (as well as those in which one or both identify as bisexual) also assume and practice monogamy, even without legal marriage, it is probably reasonable to say that there are more couples, particularly gay male couples, which have a looser or at least more variable definition of what sex with another person to whom one is not married might mean in terms of either violating or being within the couple's expectations and understandings. In addition, there is a growing acknowledgment of and visibility for heterosexual couples who identify as "consensually nonmonogamous" (often abbreviated as CNM): both partners agree, as one of the founding and defining attributes of their relationship, that nonmonogamy is acceptable.

Couples that do not believe sexual monogamy is necessary for a marriage or other committed relationship to be successful or authentic often work out, before they either consider themselves committed or decide to go through the legal procedure of marriage, which, if any, conditions of sex outside the relationship are permitted (i.e., accepted as not violating the commitment), and which ones are grounds for considering the couple's agreements to have been violated. These conditions are highly contingent and are based on what the two people can agree to; they sometimes involve compromises of individual preferences and may change over time. For some, any sex outside the relationship is grounds for reconsideration of whether the couple is still genuinely a couple and, if they are legally married, whether divorce is appropriate. For others, conditions may vary: some couples decide that occasional recreational sex is acceptable if the nonparticipating partner is told about the event, and other couples feel just the opposite, establishing a kind of "don't ask, don't tell" policy, often because one or both would prefer not to know about such experiences. For still others, factors such as context ("out of town" may be acceptable) or the pool of possible sexual partners (no dipping into the kinship pool, for example) or the frequency (no repeats with the same person) are critical. Some make space for threesomes or other variations; some put limits on which sexual acts may be engaged in outside the primary relationship.

Such specific negotiations are found more often between men than between women. The picture may change for both men and women as gender roles evolve over time. What is also true is that there are couples that do not have explicit agreements, and they find they have to adapt to changes in their relationships over time. Almost all couples, queer, non-queer, or somewhere in between, report a diminution of sexual ardor over the course of a long-term relationship, as they move into what scholars call **companionate** situations, in which there is greater emphasis on emotional intimacy, social interaction, and, in many instances, coparenting. Interestingly, couples at this stage typically report a higher degree of satisfaction in their relationship than those in the earlier, more sexually and romantically passionate stages.

There are also people, queer if simply by virtue of abandoning the normative notion of pair-bonding, who opt for noncoupled arrangements altogether. They may find structures involving three people (a triad) satisfying, and sometimes a couple may invite a third party into a relationship that is considered familial and romantic. Sometimes three or more people form a romantic and domestic bond that does not involve a preexisting couple (or dyad). Such individuals often identify as *polyamorous*, romantically and sexually involved with multiple people at the same time, or *polygamous*, in a domestic or marriage-like structure involving several parties, or *polysexual*, where there may be sex involving multiple partners, but no romantic attachment, at least as the members of the unit understand it.

Those who find such arrangements rewarding and useful suggest that the challenges are well worth the rewards of having more diverse and multiple connections — a larger and more expansive sense of connectedness to others. Certainly, one obvious challenge is the likelihood of a lack of complete symmetry among various members — and this, of course, is true even in dyads: becoming part of an "us" is itself a change from an "I." The film

*Love Is Strange* dramatizes a crisis experienced by a long-term couple who, after being married, find that one of the two men has lost his job for formalizing the relationship legally. It includes a touching and honest scene between the two characters in which the men celebrate the anniversary of their meeting, their first date at a restaurant, and they discuss how one character has remained monogamous throughout their relationship while the other has not. It is a conversation in which there are no recriminations because of the asymmetry in the question of sexual fidelity, or even a questioning of whether such an arrangement was "fair": both men implicitly agree that they knew about this difference in each other's sexual desires and behavior and affirm the authenticity of the love and commitment they have felt for each other and which they chose to make public through their wedding.

## TO MARRY OR NOT TO MARRY?

In the era after the Stonewall Riots, more and more same-sex couples devised what were typically referred to as commitment ceremonies, non-legally-binding rituals, usually witnessed by friends, family, and other kin, sometimes presided over by a clergy member, sometimes by a close friend. They took the emotional and social, if not legal, place of more traditional wedding ceremonies and were often as elaborate and celebratory as those heterosexual traditions were. Same-sex couples often enjoyed writing their own vows, composing poetry or music, and inventing bonding rituals that were as culturally meaningful for them as were legal weddings for heterosexual couples.

Though such commitment ceremonies became much more visible in the last four decades or so, there is historical evidence that such rites of commitment have a longer history. The historian John Boswell made headlines with his 1994 book, *Same-Sex Unions in Premodern Europe*. In a previous book, *Christianity, Social Tolerance, and Homosexuality* (1980), he makes the argument that the Roman Catholic Church did not initially condemn homosexuality, but that such proscription came about as part of its historical development. In the second book, Boswell argues that in ancient Greece, romantic and sexual relationships between men were given as much value, if not formal legal status, as those between men and women. Tracing the history of Western Europe, he further argues that the early Christian church did not itself place much value on any form of sexual marriage, preferring its members practice celibacy in general, and that there is evidence of rites solemnizing romantic relationships between men in early church documents. Though scholars continue to argue over Boswell's work, what it did, at the very least, was to raise questions about what marriage meant in different Western cultures at different points, a reminder that *marriage* itself, as a word and as a concept, has not been singular or stable across periods and cultures.

Weddings are examples of performative speech acts by which the speaking of particular words and the performance of specific actions make something "happen." At the end of a wedding, there is a change in status and relationality, if not legally, then at least culturally, socially, and interpersonally. When the officiant speaks words such as "I now pronounce you spouses," the verb *pronounce* (along with the submission of the marriage license to the proper authorities) causes all to acknowledge that something new (the marriage) has been created. To that end, same-sex couples who have chosen to marry vary considerably in how they choose to frame and celebrate this action, just as their heterosexual counterparts do. Some couples prefer a very private enactment of wedding vows: going to a secular public office, speaking their vows in front of a judge or clerk, signing the paperwork, paying the nominal fee, and then going out for a meal or about their usual business. Others want more elaborate ceremonies, in places of worship that welcome same-sex couples (not all do, of course), followed by receptions as large and festive as any other. Some couples very much want the most traditional ceremony, in part because they, no less than their heterosexual friends and relatives, have been raised in cultures where such celebrations are part of what makes them happy and makes a marriage feel real.

This is all based on the assumption that people in general *want* to get married, but there are many people, queer and not, who do not wish to. Reasons for not wanting to marry can include not wanting to make a commitment to one other person or not believing that the state should have any business in the private, domestic arrangements between two people who love each other. Some queer people oppose same-sex marriage because they believe it uses heterosexuality as the model for conducting one's romantic or domestic life — that, in a sense, it is "aping" heterosexuality. Some politically radical activists and thinkers argue that same-sex marriage is a form of "homonormativity," of looking for acceptance as a queer person by being as much like the dominant heterosexual society as possible. Some argue that participating in legal same-sex marriage works against unmarried opposite-sex couples, in some respects disconfirming the status of those couples who choose to make commitments to each other outside the regulatory eye of the legal system; this is similar to those who resist marriage for "anti-governmental" reasons — they believe that, by participating in the civil act of marriage, they are disconfirming other committed relationships, including heterosexual ones, that exist outside civil registration (typically by choice). Still others argue that same-sex marriage can be a way of heightening discrimination of trans people, whose legal gender status can be hard to navigate and may not fit into the traditional binaries that legal marriage underscores. Sometimes trans people appear to be in a heterosexual marriage, and then one partner transitions (of course, it is entirely possible for both partners to transition). Such marriages often end in divorce, though there are also instances where a couple remains married, as their sense of commitment to each other is not predicated on their gender identities (or such a criterion may have become less central during the marriage). Conversely, until the legalization of same-sex marriage under the Supreme Court's *Obergefell* decision, some states did not recognize the new gender of the trans person, which made legal marriage impossible. Under current marital law, because marriage is no longer defined as restricted to "one man and one woman" (though it is still restricted to couples), the legal complication of marriage for trans people is not an issue, whether or not a state chooses to acknowledge the new gender of an individual.

## KINSHIP AND AGING: OLDER LGBTQ+ PERSONS

Aging is a natural part of all life; all organisms move through stages that lead toward the end of life. At the same time, different people, including different groups of people, experience aging differently, and these differences are often contingent on such elements as identity, attitudes toward groups of people, and the presence or absence of social structures to support people in what is called "successful aging." *Successful aging* is a term originally coined as far back as the 1950s, but which became popular around the 1980s: it includes physical, mental, and social well-being; it is understood that the criteria by which well-being is measured can vary and that one person's successful aging may not be the same as another's.

As the scholar Jesus Ramirez-Valles points out in his 2016 study, *Queer Aging: The Gayby Boomers and a New Frontier for Gerontology*, the experience of older queer people has been understudied and undertheorized. The reasons for this are numerous. The "normative" older person studied remains white, middle-class, male, cisgender, and heterosexual. Considerable progress has been made in terms of visibility and safety over the past few decades, but many people who make up various cohorts that Ramirez-Valles calls "the gayby boomers" (LGB people who were born between the end of World War II and approximately 1965 — analogous to baby boomers), and who are now entering the age range most gerontologists consider "old" or "older," may still carry memories or live with current experiences of stigma and prejudice that make them less likely to disclose nonheternormative identity.

It is also the case that a disproportionate number of gay and bisexual men of this generation did not live to experience old age, owing in large part to the AIDS epidemic; trans women also have a high rate of HIV infection. Though this is not the case for queer women, there are some notable health disparities that may lead this population to live shorter lives or ones that do not provide such things as financial security, social support, or affordable housing, all aspects of successful aging: statistics indicate that older lesbians tend to have higher rates of physical illness (as well as mental and social conditions) connected to drinking, smoking, and obesity than their heterosexual counterparts. Smoking- and drinking-related physical illness are often tied to social conditions of this generation of queer women (and men), which frequently centered on bar culture, where such habits were promoted and viewed as ways of sharing experiences that could promote friendship and other forms of kinship.

Social aspects of queer aging are also important, particularly those that are associated with the elements of kinship foregrounded earlier in this chapter: ways of understanding, defining, and practicing family and friendship. There are significant contrasts in kinship dimensions for queer and non-queer older people. The 2011 documentary *Gen Silent* provides the somewhat dramatic statistic that, though around 80 percent of older people (usually defined as people fifty-five years and older; sometimes the minimum age is sixty or sixty-five) live with someone, about twice as many older LGBTQ+ people live alone. This is a stark difference and suggests how important establishing and maintaining a sense of kinship can be for older LGBTQ+ folk.

For many older LGBTQ+ individuals, the existence of families of choice is life-enhancing and, in many cases, lifesaving. There are patterns in queer people's relationships with families that are, if by no means universal, found frequently enough to be worth considering. First, older queer people may have experienced estrangement from their families of birth. This phenomenon seems to be changing as society has become more accepting of queer people in general and as queer people come out earlier and, hence, are more visible *as* queer throughout the adult life span. Nonetheless, queer people, whether LGB or trans (or some combination), still find, more than their heterosexual and cisgender peers, greater difficulties in acceptance within their families of origin and may have fewer networks of family relationships as they grow older. While queer people have always been parents, there has historically often been conflict between the traditional family role and identity as a queer person. For example, parents who come out as queer, often after living for decades within the traditional heteronormative roles assumed in the contemporary nuclear family, are often rejected, not only by their spouses but by their children. Sometimes the heterosexual parent discourages contact between the queer parent and the children, and, if the children are adults when the parent comes out, they may themselves decide to cut off contact with their queer parent.

In the past, courts have often sided in custody battles over minor children with the non-queer parent, limiting or blocking custody or even visitation, sometimes putting rather harsh strictures on such contact, such as insisting that the queer parent not discuss their sexuality or bring their own partners into coparenting. Unfortunately, even queer couples have not been immune to using such social restrictions when a queer domestic relationship (including marriage) has been dissolved: in some cases, the biological parent has sued for sole custody and often won. Movements toward second-parent adoption, along with laws ensuring parental rights, are making headway, but this is happening on a state-by-state basis. This can lead to older queer parents losing the emotional and other kinds of kinship supports that we as a society associate with the parent-child relationship.

The dynamics can be even more extreme in cases where a parent transitions to a sex or gender other than the one in which they lived when they became a parent. If the coming-out process is a challenge for the children of a queer parent, the stakes tend to be even higher when a parent comes out as transgender and begins to live in a different gender from the one assumed or assigned at birth. In some cases, the trans parent has been denied custody or visitation rights after transitioning.

A fascinating memoir, written from the point of view of an adult child of a trans person who transitions late in life, is Susan Faludi's *In the Darkroom*. Faludi, a feminist journalist, was contacted by her father, from whom she had been estranged for several decades, when, late in his life, he had transitioned to living as a woman; his transition included having the surgeries associated with the process. Faludi writes about the complex web of national and ethnic affinities (her father was born in Hungary and returned there to live as a woman), history, and gender and sexual identification her father, Stefanie, had lived within, and her own ambiguities and tensions in reestablishing a relationship with her.

What emerges from Faludi's memoir is a network of kinship structures on which Stefanie builds and in which she participates. The social and biological bond between parent and child was of sufficient importance that Stefanie sought to reestablish a relationship with Susan (Susan's mother had died some time before), but Faludi also describes the relationships her father had built with other trans women and queer people with whom Stefanie could share similar experiences, both of transitioning and of living as a woman. Faludi acknowledges the importance such friends had in her father's life (they may indeed even be family of choice, though her father never used language quite like that), even as she is frank about her own challenges in navigating the differences and, sometimes, the frustrations of what she perceives as a lack of difference between the father she experienced as a tyrannical man and the woman who assumed stereotypical attitudes toward her own femininity while retaining the masculinist performance of entitled authority.

For the children of parents who come out as LGB, the shift in perspective may be an existential one that raises the question "Who am I?" Does this coming out call into question the legitimacy of the heterosexual union that produced the child? This may be especially critical for those adult children whose parent(s) come out during middle or old age. For the children of parents who come out as trans, whether or not they go through surgery and hormonal therapies, the questions may be equally existential; the parent's coming out may feel like a rejection of a past that includes whatever the narrative of family has been. Such "revisions" are not necessarily bad things, though to the (sometimes adult) child they may seem to be evidence of intent to deceive or to disavow the parental role — in the case of the Faludis, the transition served to clarify some past negative experiences of kinship. But the rethinking and "re-feeling" of personal and kin narratives can lead to ruptures in the relationships, thus isolating the older individual even more than aging tends to do in general. A complex and moving narrative of such a family is Alison Bechdel's graphic memoir, *Fun Home*, which she subtitles *A Family Tragicomic*. Bechdel has identified as a lesbian since college and as gender nonconforming (though she does not use the word *trans* to describe herself). In the memoir she tells not only her own story of coming to her queer identity, but that of her father, who was a closeted gay man (at least functionally bisexual, though it seems clear that his greatest attraction was to other men, often younger than himself) and whose experience of the closet was the source of considerable unhappiness to his wife, his children, and himself; he committed suicide in middle age — or that is how Bechdel herself depicts it, as her father left no note of explanation, but stepped in front of a truck. *Fun Home* was adapted into a stage musical, which won the Tony Award for Best Musical on Broadway. In the book and the musical, there are moments during Bechdel's first year at college when she and her father "almost" discuss his sexuality, but both book and play are as much about the silences between two queer family members and what those silences foreclose.

The narrative would probably play out differently if the child grew up with a parent or parents who, from the birth or childhood of their offspring, identified and lived as queer, and one might reasonably predict maintenance of social and emotional kinship support for the queer parent in old age. Today we are seeing the first generation in which there is any critical mass of aging parents who have raised their children in a same-sex household or one in which one or both of the primary parents is trans. Continuity is probably the key; also, the presence of social structures that provide support — and some would say, pressure, for offspring to provide support, emotional and material — to aging parents will becomes the default rather than the exception for queer parents.

Similarly, older queer people continue to struggle with their kinship relationships of origin in terms of their roles as daughters, sons, aunts, and uncles — all the typical roles in Western kinship (the nuclear and extended family as understood in North America and Western European cultures). Some of these individuals have anticipated the possibility of rejection and chosen to live either closeted or selectively closeted lives within their families of origin, especially if they have lost a partner to death and therefore feel alone and are concerned that coming out might lead them to lose a family that, for better or for worse, has provided them some sense of belonging — albeit one that remaining in the closet may have compromised.

For many older queer people, however, kinship may, either by preference or by necessity, focus more on families of choice — or, if not family, on meaningful networks of friendship. In the research that exists on queer aging, the importance of having a secure sense of others to depend on and interact with is paramount. Loneliness is one of the elements that obstruct successful aging, and that is true for heterosexual people as well as for queer people. But the history of invisibility, stigma, and oppression has sometimes had the effect of building different kinds and sources of resilience for queer older people. Because many have not been able to depend on their family of birth for support throughout much of their lives, they have learned to create and turn to other kinds of systems. One organization that works for the concerns of older queer people is the LGBT Aging Issues Network (LAIN); their website contains much useful information and a number of resources (https://www.asaging.org/lain).

Queer women, who, because of systems of patriarchy and sexism, have often had to make their own way and imagine diverse ways of building associations that are not dependent on men, have been proactive in forming their own networks of caring. Nancy C. Nystrom writes about an initiative that took place in a city in the Pacific Northwest (she does not specify which, in order to maintain confidentiality of those women she studied), in which a community of older lesbians formed a network that provided financial and labor support to enable older lesbians to remain in their homes — which, along with health, was one of the most important priorities these women identified. By the time the study was completed, three years after the initiative began, over 550 women had become involved. On a national level, Older Lesbians Organizing for Change (**OLOC**) has also been in existence for some time, working locally and nationally to imagine ways for queer women to remain connected with each other in meaningful ways.

Older gay men may find it more difficult to reach out for kinship support; in part, this may have something to do with gendered socialization of men in general, as men are taught that being independent is one of the hallmarks of masculinity. Another factor is that the current generation of aging gay men was disproportionately affected by the AIDS epidemic in its first decades. Certainly, there are many kinship groups of older gay men, as well as gay men and women, that provide support for each other in ways that fit into the concept of families of choice. Generally speaking, however, it is probably fair to say that older gay men are more likely to experience isolation and loneliness unless they have been consistently engaged in social groups or close circles of friends. Groups like Prime Timers, founded in 1987 and designed for aging gay and bisexual men, which, like OLOC, has both national networks and local chapters, continue to grow. Still, gendered scripts make it more difficult psychologically for some queer men to reach out and take advantage of the services and fellowship such organizations offer.

Aging trans people face similar challenges, as well as ones more particular to their history and issues of gender identity. The Transgender Aging Network is an organization created specifically to address such concerns, including the role of what it calls "trans/SOFFA" (significant others, friends, family, and allies) people in the lives of older trans people (http://forge-forward.org/aging/). The organization works under the umbrella of the transgender antiviolence organization FORGE. It sponsors a number of listservs, as well as such projects as a blog called "Gray Pride Parade." Similarly, SAGE (Service & Advocacy for GLBT Elders), as its name suggests, works to improve quality of life for all people who identify in some way as LGBTQ+ or queer. They have outlined a number of ways in which, in their words, "aging poses unique challenges for transgender older adults" (https://www.sageusa.org/about-us). These include the following:

- Lack of services, such as meals, transportation, education, and legal assistance
- Lack of cultural competence (i.e., understanding of and knowledge of how to implement services) by providers of services to transgender older adults, which frequently leads to bias and discrimination, especially in the critical domain of physical and mental health
- Poor health outcomes: transgender older adults report higher rates of disability, depression, anxiety, and suicidal ideation, often as a result of isolation and neglect
- Barriers to employment and to the ability to get necessary identification papers, which makes support harder to access

Older people in general tend to have greater experiences of invisibility and devaluation in modern developed cultures; the effects of such attitudes toward LGB and trans elders are greater because of the intersectionality of multiple identities that are frequently stigmatized.

## Spotlight: Retirement Communities

As modern medicine has found ways of extending the average life of people who live in developed countries and who have access to affordable health care, gerontologists and business professionals have seen the need for (and an opportunity to profit from) either communities that focus on older people or institutions, such as nursing homes and assisted-living residences, that address the changing and increasing need to support successful aging. In general, such residential structures have assumed, if only implicitly, a fairly homogeneous population — usually white (often because of economic disparities), middle class, and heterosexual. Indeed, as various studies and other kinds of data attest, some of these places can be overtly homophobic. In some cases, housing directors openly indicate that there are no queer (they are more likely to use *LGBT*) residents in their facilities or communities and, even worse, that their facilities do not welcome LGBTQ+ people — often for religious reasons or for fear that the presence of LGBTQ+ folk will discourage "normal" people from choosing their facilities.

In nursing homes and assisted-living facilities, queer couples may have to live in separate rooms, and their desire for physical, sexual, and emotional intimacy, which could be even more critical to well-being and a continued sense of family and kinship, may be thwarted. Some older queer people have told stories of workers in these facilities who preach against homosexuality on religious grounds and who are transphobic. Indeed, for such older people, these facilities feel far from safe, and they may add to the kinds of depression and anxiety that often come with deteriorating physical and mental health. These elders may feel that their lives are regressing, moving backward in quality from periods when they could be out about their sexuality. They may feel they must return to the closet. Trans folk may find their gender identities disconfirmed in myriad ways in residences that have little experience in working with gender-nonconforming people.

Therefore, it is gratifying to be able to spotlight an organization that takes as its mission offering different options for older queer individuals, couples, and families: GLARP, the Gay & Lesbian Association of Retiring Persons. It is interesting to note that GLARP uses the word *retiring*, rather than *retired*, which may be to distinguish it from AARP; but it may also serve to acknowledge that retirement is an ongoing process and that people who may have retired from their primary professional position need not view themselves and should not be viewed as having "stopped" — they may have moved into different spheres of *occupation*, as more broadly understood than a job or a profession.

GLARP, which has been in existence since 1996, and was founded by Mary Thorndal and Veronica St. Claire, focuses primarily, though not exclusively, on housing options for older LGBTQ+ people. As of this writing, it is still working to make a senior LGBTQ+ retirement community a reality with a focus on the Palm Springs area of southern California, and it continues to help older queer people imagine what a welcoming community, populated primarily by people whose sexual identities parallel their own, could offer.

There have been efforts to create both communities and specific residences (such as homes or assisted-living facilities) for the aging queer population. The Palms of Manasota, in Florida, is typically acknowledged as the first retirement community aimed at queer seniors (https://palmsof manasota.net). There are other, more recent communities in such places as Los Angeles and New Mexico, as well as apartment complexes in Oregon and what has been called the first queer retirement home, Triangle Square, in Hollywood, California, designed as affordable housing for queer seniors, including a percentage of units reserved for seniors living with HIV/AIDS.

Neither retirement communities nor retirement homes are choices all queer seniors wish to make, any more than all heterosexual people in this age cohort wish to live in such spaces. Some argue that such communities "ghettoize" aging populations, with the unintended consequence of helping make such people invisible to larger queer communities and warehousing them. They argue for more integrative ways of offering places for aging queer people, and for social and other kinds of support that acknowledges the changing needs of people as they grow older, such as specific kinds of medical care, and emotional and psychological support for caregivers as well. Certainly, the solution is not to force people to live in such communities, but to offer options as varied as aging LGBTQ+ people themselves are. Just as younger queer people need to feel safe and happy wherever they live, whether in their small hometowns, rural areas, or large urban areas with dense concentrations of "gayborhoods," so do older people. At this moment, there are no publicized or visible communities designed specifically for transgender older people, though Triangle Square welcomes trans people as residents. Rent at Triangle Square is determined by a sliding scale that is based on income. A project such as Triangle Square is a good, well-intentioned start, but more advocacy and creation of services remain to be done.

### Witnessing Our/Their Stories: Some Final Thoughts on Aging and Queer Lives

In his book *Queer Aging*, Jesus Ramirez-Valles writes the life stories of eleven "gayby boomers" from the Chicago area, using the first-person voices of the men he interviewed. The men included in the book are racially diverse (white, black, Latinx, and some mixed-race) and represent a range of professions and class backgrounds. About half of them are living with HIV. They describe lives filled with struggles and with joys and with both a realistic and optimistic view of their current and future lives. Some of them remain connected with their families of origin, whether as out gay men or as selectively closeted; some depend on friends and other kinds of kin; still others report relatively solitary lives, which for some is a source of unhappiness and for others is what they are used to and prefer.

Similarly, the documentary *Gen Silent*, referred to earlier in this chapter, presents a range of ways of experiencing aging and queerness; it focuses on people living in Massachusetts, from a long-term couple now separated physically by the need for one to live in assisted care, to a lesbian couple continuing to live in their home and remaining vitally connected to their Boston-area community, to a trans woman who is dying of cancer and has a complicated relationship with her adult son. The documentary shows different challenges. In the case of the long-term couple, one of whom has advanced Parkinsonian dementia and is now living in an assisted-care facility, we see the effects on his partner, who, though twenty years younger, is also over sixty and feels the effects of providing care as well as the need for companionship. KrysAnne Hembrough (her full first name, adopted when she transitioned to female, was KrysallisAnne, referring to the transformation of the caterpillar into the butterfly), a trans woman who, as a man, had served in Vietnam and fathered four children, finds support from local social service agencies that focus on LGBTQ+ clients when she is dying from lung cancer. She had chosen not to enter a nursing home for fear that she would be discovered to be a woman who still had a penis. She found support and comfort from local LGBTQ+ groups — an extended group of volunteers that created a sense of kinship for her. There are triumphs in these stories, among the inevitable sorrows that cannot be avoided, but what remains articulate and inspiring is the commitment of the people whose lives are shown, both the aging individuals and those around them: that the aging queer folk remain fully human and vital, that they remain sexual and romantic, and that they remain present as members of a community or set of communities.

## ISSUES FOR INVESTIGATION

**1.** Whatever your sexual orientation or gender identity, consider what would be an ideal wedding for you (understanding that its format is likely to change, depending on whom you marry and their own preferences and desires). Where would you want it to take place and whom would you want to attend? Would you want standard wedding vows (you can find them in many places online) or would you want to write your own? Is there particular music or poetry you would like performed? A number of same-sex couples are now registered at stores, as has been the tradition of heterosexual couples. How do you feel about that? What would be an ideal reception for you?

One of the standard traditions in heterosexual weddings has been wedding announcements, typically published in one or more newspapers (usually hometown ones for one or both of the people being married). In particular, newspapers in cities with large LGBTQ+ populations have become more welcoming of detailed announcements of same-sex weddings, and they may feature in prominent places those of celebrities or well-known citizens, as well as of people who pay for such announcements to be placed. Perhaps the most prestigious location for wedding announcements is the Sunday edition of the *New York Times*. Search their online archive and compare and contrast some same-sex and some opposite-sex (to use a binary for the purposes of this exercise) weddings. What are some features that are common to all of them? Are there differences between them? What are the standard formulas involved (such as how the couple met)? Try writing your own — even if your potential marriage partner is, for the moment, imaginary.

**2.** Consider your own kinship connections. Do you have a family of choice — people you consider "relatives," even though there is no blood or marital connections? Is there a clear line between friend and family in the way you think of these people? Trace your own family of origin: Are there people either who were openly identified as queer or whose sexual identity was speculated about or simply left as a blank, given the times in which they lived? Is there a queer lineage in your family? If it is appropriate or comfortable, speak with other family members about their perceptions. Can you draw a family tree that makes unspoken or not-legally-acknowledged relationships present? Can you draw one that situates people you consider family of choice in parallel or analogous roles to those traditionally labeled (brother, sister, aunt, uncle, cousin, even mother and father)?

## SUGGESTIONS FOR FURTHER READING AND VIEWING

*Beginners.* Directed by Mike Mills. Olympus, 2011.

Galvin, Sarah. *The Best Party of Our Lives: Stories of Gay Weddings and True Love to Inspire Us All.* Seattle: Sasquatch Books, 2015.

Moore, Mignon. *Invisible Families: Gay Identities, Relationships, and Motherhood among Black Women.* Berkeley: University of California Press, 2011.

Peck, Richard. *The Best Man.* New York: Dial Books for Young Readers, 2016.

Rosswood, Eric, and Greg Berlanti. *The Ultimate Guide for Gay Dads: Everything You Need to Know about LGBTQ Parenting but Are (Mostly) Afraid to Ask.* Coral Gables, FL: Mango, 2017.

*Transparent.* Amazon, 2014–2019.

*The Wedding Banquet.* Directed by Ang Lee. Ang Lee Productions, 1993.

# CHAPTER 9

# QUEERING HEALTH
## Well-Being, Medicalization, and Recreation

In 1972 St. Martin's Press published a book called *Society and the Healthy Homosexual*, whose title challenged many previous assumptions that to be queer was to be by definition unhealthy. The author, George Weinberg, focused on mental health, and his purpose was to argue that the "illness" most prevalent among homosexuals was that of an unaccepting society. He is generally considered to have coined the word *homophobia*, an important conceptual addition to queer studies. It is worth noting that the title of Weinberg's book, while an important step forward in how nonheteronormative sexuality was viewed in the mental health community, continued the invisibility of both bisexuality and trans identity, and, indeed, emphasized same-sex orientation and cisgender identity in its reclamation of *health* as an appropriate word to use for the homosexual as a generalized type or category of person. Steps forward are often thus: incremental and sometimes oblivious to what is omitted.

The word **health** is itself a problematic and difficult term to define, and certainly a word whose definition is changeable, depending on the historical and cultural contexts in which it is used. The psychiatrist and educator Norman Sartorius, who served as the head of the World Health Organization's Division of Mental Health, wrote an essay in 2006 in which he defined three principal types of health: (1) "the absence of any disease or impairment"; (2) "a state that allows the individual to adequately cope with all demands of daily life (implying also the absence of disease and impairment)"; and (3) "a state of balance, an equilibrium that an individual has established within himself [*sic*] and between himself and his social and physical environment" (662). The first definition is exclusively medical in its boundaries and puts the determination of health in the hands of medical professionals, such as physicians and nurses.

Henderson, Bruce, *Queer Studies: Beyond Binaries*
dx.doi.org/10.17312/harringtonparkpress/2019.09.qsbb.009

Sartorius's second definition moves beyond the purely medical realm to one that situates people in the social arena — health, by this definition, is a way of being in which people can carry out everyday activities with reasonable success. This definition acknowledges the "situatedness" of *health* as a description — there is no health that is separable from the conditions of everyday life for an individual within a context of activity. Sartorius's third definition focuses in even more complex ways on self-concept and engagement with an individual's world and worldview. In this sense, it seems the most useful one for us to adopt in looking at queering health — in the multiple senses of health issues that affect LGBTQ+ people in particular, though by no means exclusively, as we will argue.

## THE MEDICALIZATION OF (HOMO)SEXUALITY: THE NINETEENTH CENTURY

The queer French philosopher Michel Foucault located what he saw as a paradigm shift in discourse about health in what he called, in the title of his 1963 book, *The Birth of the Clinic*. As a development of Enlightenment philosophy, particularly that branch called empiricism (represented by such writers as Locke and Hume), the "clinic" presupposed that scientific observation could lead to better and more detailed and precise understanding of the health, illnesses, and diseases of the body. Such observation led medical professionals also to make diagnoses of the mind, though often on the basis of physical appearance and actions, both verbal and nonverbal. Foucault dubbed this way of "seeing" the **medical gaze**. He went on to argue, using what he called "archeological" and "genealogical" approaches, that the belief that medical science, through its clinical procedures and practices, had achieved something more "objective" (and therefore "true") was itself a subjective perspective, with as many potential pitfalls and areas of bias as any other. Importantly, this concept of the medical gaze put all the **biopower** or *biopolitics* (terms Foucault also coined) in the hands of people classified as professionals in medicine, and very often gave them power over the bodies of their "subjects" (patients). Foucault tied this ideology to the treatment and containment of those viewed as insane (or mad) alongside those society viewed as criminal, and his larger point was that people (including non-pathologized or non-criminalized citizens) were subject to such surveillance — a process he encapsulated in the title of one of his books, *Discipline and Punish*, which focuses on the "birth of the prison," and suggested that society used some of the same instruments and methods of surveillance as formal prisons did.

Perhaps the single most significant shift in medicine regarding homosexuality came during the nineteenth century, with the development of psychology as a scholarly and professional field. It was during this period that homosexuality began to be seen first and foremost as an illness, rather than as exclusively a moral flaw or criminal act. It remained officially classified as such by the medical community until its removal from *The Diagnostic and Statistical Manual of Mental Disorders* (*DSM*), the "Bible" for psychological and psychiatric professionals in terms of illness and health. As Foucault pointed out in a number of works, there was an important shift from a set of activities associated with nonheteronormative sexuality (grouped under the term for the person who participated in them, "the sodomite") to a more fixed category of identity ("the homosexual," as in Weinberg's title, with which we began the chapter). The former (sodomite) carried religious connotations of sin, whereas the latter was more strongly associated with medicine and pathology. Even within ostensibly heterosexual activities, Foucault argued, purpose and excess become associated with illness — as in the "habitual" masturbator, for example, who was seen as both legally and medically outside the normative bounds of heterosexual purposes (procreation, in the dominant European Christian view of the time).

## "TREATMENT" AND DEPATHOLOGIZATION IN THE TWENTIETH CENTURY

Throughout much of the twentieth century, it was common for a physician or psychological professional to recommend or even prescribe therapy, including psychoanalysis, for patients who raised the issue of homosexuality with them. During this period, many believed that sexual orientation could be changed and, hence, homosexuality could be "cured." In Freudian analysis, a standard narrative was imposed: an overbearing mother, who encouraged the male child to remain erotically attached longer than was acceptable, combined with a distant father, either ineffective or emotionally withholding (and, conversely, sometimes overly masculine in the terms of the era, brutal in his demands on his usually less masculine son), became a staple of such treatment. In the case of lesbianism, the Freudian also attached "blame" (cause) to a prolonged overattachment between daughters and mothers, so that the female child then shifted her feelings about her mother to other women. In other words, mothers — and by extension women in general — were the root cause of homosexuality.

Various forms of "cure" were used, often with tragic results and rarely with a genuine erasure of homosexual attractions. **Aversion therapy** had its followers, whereby homosexual "patients" were exposed to erotic imagery and either rewarded or punished, sometimes with electrical shocks, depending on the response of their bodies to the stimuli. Even more extreme was the use of such barbaric methods as electroconvulsive therapy (ECT) and lobotomies as "solutions" to homosexual impulses: they may have been successful, insofar as the patient no longer acted on queer desires, but the result was more often to remove all sense of personality and will from the person; this was true as well of these treatments for such mental conditions as schizophrenia and bipolar disorder.

As the gay liberation movement began to pick up steam, professionals in the mental health field took on more activist roles in working for change in how homosexuality was viewed and treated at the highest levels. Many of the professionals who worked for change themselves identified, either quite openly or in private, as gay, lesbian, or bisexual; there were also many non-queer professionals who worked side by side with them, simply because they believed the pathologization of queer people, merely on the basis of their queerness, was medically and ethically wrong.

The *DSM*, mentioned earlier, in its initial publication, in 1952, classified homosexuality as a "sociopathic personality disturbance," which placed it squarely among myriad other mental disorders. Ironically, this first edition of the manual was published within a year or so of the groundbreaking work of the sex researcher Alfred Kinsey, who provided data (albeit since challenged conceptually) that made the case that U.S. males had had a much higher incidence of male-male sexual contact leading to orgasm than had previously been thought. Progress was made along the way: the second edition of the *DSM*, published in 1968, still used the language of *deviation* to describe and classify homosexuality, but at least it no longer placed it among the sociopathic disorders. This was a step forward for its time, even if the field was still not where activists and many professionals wished it to be. Two major figures provided a public impetus for the complete removal of homosexuality from the *DSM*, and they deserve a closer look.

## Spotlight on Dr. Evelyn Hooker: Bringing Experimental Method to Homosexuality

Dr. Evelyn Hooker, a Colorado-born, lifelong heterosexually identified psychologist, was a pioneer in gay-affirmative psychology almost by accident or serendipity. As an instructor of psychology at UCLA in 1944, she found herself interacting with one particular student in her lecture course, who often had questions after class and with whom she struck up a friendship, a friendship that included introducing him to her husband and visiting him and his friends at their homes. Her husband identified the student as "a queer" (and Hooker notes that the language was of its times and not the language she would herself use decades later). This had not occurred to Hooker, as she had grown up in a fairly homogeneous rural area and had not been conditioned to "read" for sexual orientation in people. Once she discussed this with her student and his friends, they asked her to study them — essentially, they were calling on this bright and friendly and — especially for the time — accepting woman to bring her psychological insights and experimental acuity to analyze the lives of gay people, a population that had been studied only under what was then called "abnormal psychology" and was assumed to be "disordered" by virtue of being homosexual.

Hooker took on this assignment, and one of the first things she did indeed discover was that the existing scientific and medical literature had based its findings on gay people solely on a subject pool of individuals who had already been in therapy or treatment — in other words, people who either had self-identified or had been referred because they were experiencing more than typical psychological distress. This distress might have been linked to their experience of being homosexual in the mid-twentieth-century United States, and they might have sought therapy to deal with (even in hopes of "curing") unhappiness they attributed to their homosexuality, or their homosexuality might have been simply one part of a more complex profile that included family history, neurological conditions, or any of a number of other factors that contribute to someone's seeking psychological treatment.

So Hooker devised a study to compare homosexual and heterosexual men to see if there was any significant difference in psychopathology between the groups. She eventually found thirty homosexual and thirty heterosexual men who volunteered to participate. One requirement for her experimental design was that none of the men who served as subjects could have either been in therapy or analysis or been disciplined by the military for their homosexuality. To ensure privacy, Hooker conducted the experiment in a small cottage on the grounds of her home.

Hooker's experiment consisted of administering a series of very reliable and highly validated personality tests, such as the Thematic Apperception Test, to each of the men. She then "blinded" the identity of each participant, including his identification of his sexual orientation, and had three experts in testing analyze the test results, particularly to see if they could determine from them the sexual orientation of the individual. One of them was so confident he could do so that he went through the entire data set twice. All three failed to make any kind of correlation between the individuals' performances on these tests, any personality traits, and an implied or inferred sexual orientation. Hooker's hypothesis was thus validated: sexual orientation, as a variable, could not by itself account for neurosis. Gay men were, by the gold standards of the time, scientifically as healthy as their straight counterparts. Hooker presented her findings at the American Psychological Association (APA) convention in 1956, and the results were earth-shattering within the world of scientific, scholarly, and professional psychology.

**Spotlight on Dr. H (Henry) Anonymous: Revealing through Masking the Face of Homosexuality**

The story of Dr. H is very different from that of Evelyn Hooker, but no less fascinating. John E. Fryer was a psychiatrist best known for his work on death and dying. At this point in his life, Fryer was in his mid-thirties and had been the victim of homophobia in his professional life — he lost a residency at the University of Pennsylvania simply because he was gay and then a job at Friends Hospital, a mental hospital also in Philadelphia, not simply because he identified as gay, but because he was viewed as "flamboyant" (i.e., overly theatrical, feminine). In an odd but somewhat predictable catch-22 of the times, the administration indicated that if he had been "gay but not flamboyant" or "flamboyant but not gay" (presumably meaning if he had been to able to "perform" heterosexuality by having a wife and children), it would not have fired him, but the combination was too much — and, of course, there were no protections against such discrimination at the time. As of this writing, Pennsylvania still has no statewide law that protects people from job discrimination based on their sexual orientation, though there is an executive order protecting government employees (Movement Advancement Project, "Non-Discrimination Laws," www.lgbt map.org/equality-maps/ non_discrimination_laws).

Fryer found a new job at Temple University, where he was not yet tenured and where he was not out as a gay man. When a plan to confront the APA about its stance on homosexuality was being organized in 1972, he felt called to participate, and one of the organizers of the protest, Barbara Gittings, came up with an ingenious and powerful solution: they would devise a disguise that would allow Fryer to appear without any way of visually identifying him. He wore a mask, a wig, and an outsize tuxedo, a kind of parodic comment on the "formality" of making such a speech at the gathering of top scholars and professionals in his field. There are a number of images of Fryer disguised as Dr. H, including the ones at the following link: https://www.google.com/search?q=john+fryer&client=safari&rls=en&source=lnms&tbm=isch&sa=X&ved=0ahUKEwjNu-jcmPzaAhVLjlkKHR6hBIYQ_AUICygC&biw=1594&bih=1019#imgrc=ZCbKkEN63WExrM:. His brief speech was powerful in its eloquence and forcefulness; it is reprinted in the Appendix.

Judd Marmor, a prominent and influential psychiatrist who would later be president of the APA, had been working with Evelyn Hooker to destigmatize homosexuality in psychiatry for years. He described himself as having been "privileged" to be in the audience for Fryer's speech, and he saw the speech as an important watershed moment in activating the movements he, Hooker, and many others, gay and straight, had been building toward. (And, like Hooker, he identified throughout his life as heterosexual.) It is a sign of how long stigmatizing, painful attitudes linger that it was only in 1994 that Fryer acknowledged formally that he was Dr. H.

## "CURING THE GAY": REPARATIVE AND "EX-GAY" THERAPIES

*Ex-gay* therapy, which is also sometimes referred to as **reparative therapy** or *conversion therapy*, emerged from multiple motivations and systems of belief, some of which follow in scientific or pseudoscientific traditions that were variations of Freudian psychoanalysis and behavioral conditioning, as well as religious (usually Christian) evangelical faith traditions.

Virtually all ex-gay therapies share a common premise: being queer is a choice, and, while having queer desires may never entirely disappear, there are ways to contain them and to resist acting on them. Ironically, social conservatives are more likely to view sexual orientation as a choice, whereas social liberals view it as inborn—the one area where choice is more dominant among conservatives than among liberals. For those who follow some variation of Freudian psychoanalysis, homosexuality comes about as the result of flaws in the family dynamics of early childhood. Many such analysts view homosexuality as a **misadaptation** and argue that scientific behavioral methods can "correct" this misadaptation. The most notorious organization in support of such therapy is NARTH (National Association for Research and Therapy of Homosexuality), founded in 1992 by Charles Socarides, Joseph Nicolosi, and Benjamin Kaufman.

For Christian evangelicals, questions of obedience to God and to his received word are of primary importance, though they share some of the same beliefs about how sexual orientation can be changed as their more "scientific" colleagues. Using some of the behavioral and cognitive therapies that such reparative or conversion therapists as Charles Socarides and Irving Bieber developed, they combine science with faith traditions and practices that will, they claim, lead homosexuals to the way of God and to happiness. Though the majority of such organizations in the United States are Christian, there have been a few in other faith traditions, such as JONAH (Jews Offering New Alternatives for Healing—note the use of the medical term *healing* in its name), which ceased operations in 2015.

Ex-gay therapists have used forms of conditioning, in which individuals are exposed to stimuli that are combined with rewards and punishments (such as electric shocks or nausea-inducing medications), depending on an individual's response to the stimuli. Viewing heterosexual erotic images and being rewarded for doing so, they contend, will eventually lead the patient to associate heterosexuality with positive feelings (and vice versa). This often involves electrostimulating equipment attached to a person's genitalia, so there is a great potential for trauma and even physical danger in this approach. Such behavioral therapy typically is accompanied by some form of talk therapy, whether it is psychoanalysis or religious counseling. For the latter in particular, centers were set up where homosexual individuals were often housed as inpatients (or residents) and essentially subjected to ongoing forms of mind control. Both authoritarian leaders (counselors) and peer pressure (others in the institution with the same goals) were used to reinforce, at an ideological level, the kinds of physical and behavioral conditioning being performed simultaneously. The largest and best-known of such ex-gay ministries was Exodus International, which was founded in 1976 and ceased operations in 2013, though Exodus Global Alliance continues this ministry today.

Very few of these organizations are still in existence. There are a number of factors involved in their closure. Social change and pressure, as scientific scholars and more progressive faith traditions themselves began to conclude that fundamental sexual orientation cannot be changed, led to diminished support for such places. Some scientists did believe in the possibility for change, though not necessarily advocating it as a method of improving mental health, but most have not. Even those scientists and physicians who believe change may be possible find themselves asking whether providing therapy for such changes might violate the founding bedrock of the Hippocratic oath: First, do no harm.

The other central reason these organizations began to shut down is that, over time, their failure rate, both long- and short-term, began to become public, often in ways that the organizations found embarrassing. Such was the case when John Paulk, who founded the ex-gay ministry Love Wins Out (sponsored by the conservative think tank Focus on the Family) and who married another ex-gay member, Anne, was spotted in a gay bar in Washington, D.C. When confronted, he gave a false name and then disputed that he was in the bar seeking the company of other gay men. Eventually, after six months or so, he left the organization, announced he was ending his marriage and that he no longer identified as ex-gay, and apologized for his participation in furthering the process of reparation therapy.

A recent memoir of one individual forced as a young adult to undergo such therapy is *Boy Erased* by Garrard Conley, who, as a teenager in 2004, entered Love in Action, only to discover that a number of its members had lived in its facilities for many years, as they were still viewed as "uncured" or "in danger." Conley's father was a newly ordained minister, so his son's homosexuality was even more threatening to his status and to his sense of leadership of his very traditional, patriarchal family. The memoir provides a detailed depiction of a faith-based ex-gay therapy, which has probably been the dominant one in the last few decades. He struggled with the competing and perhaps conflicting experiences of selfhood, desire, and spirituality that are put into opposition by such a therapy. He notes that the charismatic leader of the organization, John Smid, has also since renounced ex-gay therapy. Conley's memoir has been adapted to film, with Lucas Hedges (who also played Saoirse Ronan's closeted boyfriend in the film *Lady Bird*) in the role of Conley as a teenager. As of 2018, ten states have banned conversion therapy for minors (Movement Advancement Project, "Conversion Therapy Laws," www.lgbtmap.org/equality-maps/conversion_therapy). Even pro-queer scientists sometimes find themselves in the awkward position of having their work used to advocate for the possibility of a "cure" for queerness or for parenting that is clearly homophobic. The social and personality psychologist Daryl J. Bem's theory of sexual orientation, which he called "exotic becomes erotic," argues, on the basis of responses by queer people in large data sets, that children who see themselves as fundamentally different from their gender peers (i.e., they view their gender peers as "exotic") may transfer such exoticism into adult eroticism. The theory also builds on observed patterns of behavior in nonhuman species—animals are not attracted to littermates, but to those outside their "family." Ex-gay therapists tried to use Bem's theory to suggest that raising children to participate in activities that are more gender conforming would be a solution to the "exoticizing" aspects of queer identity development. Bem's response was that he believed that attempts to do this would fail because such identities are grounded too early in childhood—by the time parents noted the differences, sexual identity was probably fixed—and also because gender-nonconforming behavior did have an innate, heritable aspect, even if the search for a "gay gene" was unsuccessful. Forcing gender-nonconforming children to participate in gender-conforming activities would simply lead to unhappiness and isolation, not change of sexual orientation.

Though the APA depathologized homosexuality itself in 1973, it added the condition known as "gender identity disorder" in 1980. One potential and harmful effect of this addition is providing a kind of "stealth" approach to conversion therapy. Parents who noted gender-nonconforming behavior in their children could, using this category, have their children undergo therapies designed to try to keep them from "becoming" gay, lesbian, or bisexual or, in other cases, to eliminate those aspects of the child that might lead them to identify with a different gender from that assigned at birth. As Bem suggests, there is no good research to suggest that such interventions have any lasting or genuine effects on an individual's sexual orientation or gender identity—they simply contribute to the kind of policing Foucault describes in his critique of biopower.

# MIND MEETS BODY: HEALTH CHALLENGES FOR QUEER PEOPLE

There are a number of health disparities between queer people and non-queer people. They are founded in social conditions that promote unhealthy or risky behaviors, rather than in any innate aspect of being queer.

## Bar Culture

In urban and even parts of the rural United States, Canada, regions of the United Kingdom, and Western Europe, much of the social world of queer life has, since early in the twentieth century, revolved around bars and clubs. While such spaces have many positive attributes, such as providing places for interaction and socializing, they also can enable and even promote behaviors that work against healthy queer lives. In some respects, they are no different from heterosexual spaces, but because of their centrality in queer culture, they have typically been viewed as having greater effects.

### Alcohol and Other Mind-Altering Substances: Their Function and Consumption in Queer Cultures

One of the principal business functions of almost any bar or club is to sell and serve alcoholic beverages. Though some bars began having "juice nights" starting around the 1980s, in an attempt to cater to underage youth, the appeal and availability of alcohol, particularly as a disinhibiting substance, led queer people into habits of drinking at an early age. In 2002 Tonda L. Hughes and Michele Eliason published what is called a meta-analysis of "substance use and abuse in lesbian, gay, bisexual and transgender populations." (A meta-analysis is a scholarly work in which multiple studies are compared, contrasted, and, when appropriate, collated to make broader statements, either across time or across different groups of subjects.) Hughes and Eliason noted that they encountered a number of complex variations in such studies, especially in the case of comparisons of lesbians and heterosexual women (there were few bisexually identified women in the study, so their responses were not included). In some cases, issues regarding variations in the amount of time considered was a variable, such as the amount of alcohol consumed in the past twelve months under study versus longer patterns of drinking, as well as such phenomena as lesbians reporting greater frequency of considering whether they had drinking problems. In summarizing studies done up to about 2000 (the approximate end point of their analysis), they said: "Despite methodologic limitations to many of the . . . studies . . . the following patterns seem to hold generally true: 1) fewer lesbians than heterosexual women abstain from alcohol, particularly when recovery is controlled; 2) even when rates of heavy drinking among lesbians and heterosexual women are reasonably comparable, lesbians report more alcohol-related problems; and 3) the relationships between some demographic characteristics [such as race and socioeconomic class] and drinking behaviors differ for lesbians and heterosexual women" (272). They note that there is a difference between decline in drinking as lesbians and heterosexual women age, the decline being smaller among lesbians.

In similar studies of gay men during the 1970s, rates of alcohol abuse were about the same as for lesbians. As was true of their lesbian counterparts, rates of alcohol abuse dropped in the 1980s and beyond, but more gay men than either heterosexual men or all women reported consistent use of illegal drugs or other kinds of substances (some legal or in vague status) across their adult life spans: these include marijuana, cocaine, methamphetamines, and various substances often nicknamed "poppers" (such as amyl and butyl nitrites). Gay men have been found to continue use of such substances longer than straight men and lesbians. Their use can result in impaired judgment, and this may in part account for continued HIV infection among young gay men. Studies have also indicated that transgender youth experience higher-than-typical rates of substance use, no doubt as ways of self-medicating their own mental health challenges that result from social stigma and pressure and, in some cases, because LGBTQ+ social spaces often center on alcohol and other mood-altering substances (National Institute on Drug Abuse, "Substance Use and SUDs in LGBT Populations," www.drugabuse.gov/related-topics/substance-use -suds-in-lgbt-populations).

*Tobacco Use: "Smoking Guns"*
Just as drinking alcohol has long been viewed as a rite of passage into adulthood in U.S. culture, so has tobacco use. While tobacco use across ages and populations is at all-time low in the United States (since officials started keeping records of it), it still remains disturbingly high among adolescents and particularly among queer adolescents. There have not been any long-term studies of queer smokers across the life span, so it is impossible to draw conclusions, but it is also true that a large percentage of teenage and young adult smokers quit by about age thirty or so.

In a meta-analysis of studies done of smoking among queer people between 1987 and 2007, Lee, Griffin, and Melvin found that 18 percent of the general population of heterosexual women identified as smokers, whereas lesbians (ones not enrolled in college at the time) self-identified as smokers at a rate of between 25 and 37 percent (depending on the time of the study and the specific population). They also found that queer adolescent women were 6.3 times more likely to smoke than their heterosexual counterparts.

Among men, the numbers were closer: 24 percent of heterosexually identified men were smokers, and 24–33 percent of gay men reported habitual smoking; and the numbers among adolescent gay men were twice that of their heterosexual counterparts. There are few data currently available about tobacco use among transgender populations.

What explains these differences in rates of tobacco smoking? Lee and his colleagues suggested the following possible links between smoking and queer populations: the nature of queer social spaces (though today smoking is banned in many bars); stresses due to threats and incidents of violence toward queer people; other forms of mental and emotional distress; general barriers to health access among queer people (especially adolescents); and targeted marketing — the advertising industry's recognition that queer people are an identifiable, contained, if vulnerable market. Tobacco for many generations served, like alcohol, as a kind of social lubricant — calming in its physiological effects, and bonding in its opportunities for social exchanges.

## Food: The "Other" (Potentially) Abused Substance — Eating Disorders among Queers

We all *have* to eat, it is true, so it is necessary for all of us to consume food. At the same time, it is also true that the consumption of food — especially the extremes of deprivation and overeating — has psychological, social, and, many would argue, political dimensions: a popular book in the 1970s and beyond by the psychotherapist Susie Orbach was titled *Fat Is a Feminist Issue*, and it styled itself as a weight-loss self-help book that also raised consciousness about the ways in which women have been oppressed by cultures of dieting.

The fact that we all must consume food to remain alive makes our relationship to it even more complicated. There have been studies that compare eating disorders among queer people to those of heterosexually identified people. Even though anorexia has traditionally been associated with adolescent and young adult women, some recent studies have identified adolescent and young adult gay men as being at risk for anorexia as well. There are complicated scripts of gender and sexuality that may go some distance to explain the vulnerability of gay men to this generally female disorder. First, gay men have often been equated with women (or at the very least, with the female), so there may be a feminine identification for some gay men that means they could be prone to the same (or similar) set of risk factors or motivations as heterosexual women. It is also possible that gay men recognize, if even unconsciously, that they are as much subjected to the "male gaze" as their female counterparts. Gay personal ads and online hookup sites display many profiles with the same kinds of dismissive, stigmatizing, or exclusionary language a straight woman might be likely to find. Hospers and Jansen found that "body dissatisfaction," not generalized self-esteem, was a better predictor of eating disorders in gay men, but that peer pressure from other gay men contributed to this dissatisfaction.

On the basis of a feminist-inflected psychological reading of anorexia, one might reasonably assume that lesbians are probably exempt from this risk, as they presumably do not, at least in their erotic and romantic dimensions, look to men for body approval. Karen Heffernan, who has studied eating disorders and what she calls "weight concern" among different categories of queer people, has not found this to be the case. Her interviews and surveys found that lesbians are "not immune from the effects of not meeting societal ideals of thinness" (127), though she did find that greater involvement in lesbian social and cultural groups was associated with fewer weight concerns for these women.

In a more generalized sense, eating disorders among queer people may be connected to a wide range of dissatisfactions with self, both bodily and otherwise, to which they are prone because of social stigmas. It may be that queer people feel that by disciplining their eating and minimizing their weight, they are gaining a kind of agency and are acting in ways that heterosexual hegemony might find praiseworthy. In his memoir, *My Thinning Years: Starving the Gay Within*, the psychologist Jon Derek Croteau writes about how the homophobia of his family upbringing and social background led him to associate food with his father's disappointment in Croteau's self-described femininity. His father forced him to participate in athletics, which contributed to a mind-set that associated overexercising and food deprivation with being a "good man" (and a good son). Even before he finished high school, his behavior had become so pathological that a school counselor took him to a psychiatrist, whose attempts to get him to talk about his eating disorder led to Croteau's retreat from communication.

**Fat: Also a Queer Issue**
There is almost always, in our current culture, a certain degree of implicit acceptance of negative talk about fat people — including implicit suggestions that their weight is an indicator of lack of control or of moral defects — that one does not find with very thin people. This can be particularly true in some groups within queer culture. While there is a stereotype that lesbians (and women in general) do not place as strong an emphasis on an idealized body shape and size as do men, both queer women and men can be objects of ridicule and exclusion for having what their peers view as too large a body. This can certainly be true in terms of how attractive they are viewed as by potential romantic or sexual partners (and the question of what leads each of us to find some bodies erotic and others not is too multifaceted and not adequately researched for us to

draw conclusions), but it can also be true simply in their realms of friendship and community. There are some gay men who balk at even associating with fat gay men as friends, rarely articulating their reasons publicly but privately stating that they do not wish to be associated with "those" types of gay men. It is as if there is a fear of contagion — that fat is "catching" (and some psychologists and health promotion specialists have suggested that there may be ways in which having fat partners and friends can lead to weight gain — but this is a matter of behaviors, not innate epidemiology!). Might it not be better to address the issues of food and eating within culture and devise models of mutual support than to close off otherwise positive friendships across body types?

Both lesbians and gay men who either themselves identify as fat or are attracted to fat women and men have worked in various ways to try to raise awareness about such stigmas and to create organizations and opportunities for socializing and sexuality for fat queers. Many such groups simply bracket the issue of fat and physical health, seeing it as a domain perhaps best discussed between the individual and a professional health-care provider. There is an association for fat lesbians, which has been in existence since 1998, called NOLOSE, which stands for the National Organization of Lesbians of Size Everywhere, which advocates for "lesbians of size" and which creates a space for celebrating the bodies of women who identify as such and for those who love and find them attractive (http://nolose.org/about/). The fat studies scholar Stefanie Snider in an essay titled "Alternative Publications and the Visualization of Fat and Queer Eroto-Politics," analyzes two 'zines that had relatively short but memorable runs, *FaT GiRL: A Zine for Fate Dykes and the Women Who Want Them* and *Size Queen: For Queen Size Queers and Our Loyal Subjects* (223). Both publications included erotic images and stories and played proudly with the possibilities and realities for sexual pleasure for fat women and their "loyal subjects."

Jason Whitesel, a sociologist who identifies as a "chaser" (a notfat gay man who is attracted to fat gay men), wrote *Fat Gay Men: Girth, Mirth, and the Politics of Stigma* (2014), in which he studies the gatherings and interactions as both an "insider" (a chaser) and as an "outsider" (a scholar). He compares the Pan-Girth & Mirth convention that was held in Oklahoma City (a yearly event whose location changes) with the Labor Day Convergence, held in 2007 in Minneapolis. He notes, with keen insight, the very different characteristics and features of each gathering — the former more akin to a kind of raucous carnival, the latter a more commodified and consumerist performance of middle-class fat male queerness. He does an excellent job of withholding judgments about the values each kind of gathering represents, and he allows the lively, companionable, and thoughtful voices of the men at each event opportunity to speak.

Whitesel also examines the ways in which the "splintering" of identities of men of size can cause divisions and stigmatization that are certainly part of any depiction of mental and social health. Large men who are also hairier than average (or who admire or find such men attractive) have for some time constituted an identity category and a culture that emerged from it — that of "bears." This has led to books being written (such as guidebooks and manuals) about "bear life," erotica aimed at this population, and activities, events, and products (tattoos, clothing, decals, and so forth) celebrating the bear as a position of identity and as an object of desire. Subsequently, other allied categories of identity have emerged, also named for forest animals, such as "cubs" (shorter or younger variations of bears), "otters" (thinner but just as hairy body types), "panda bears" (bears of Asian descent), and "wolves" (alpha-type men, hairy and muscular). Ironically, there has sometimes been a kind of stigmatizing of fat gay men who do not possess the requisite hairiness (a subjective judgment, to be sure) to fit into the ideal of bear identity.

## Suicide and Self-Harm: Myths and Realities

For many years, the implicit or explicit assumption among many mental health professionals was that queer youth were at significantly greater risk for suicide and other forms of self-harm. For homophobic mental health professionals, the very disordered nature of homosexuality was their link to suicidality. For more supportive mental health researchers, queer youth's suicidal ideation (whether accompanied by actions) was a function of an oppressive society that gave queer youth no alternative models or narratives for living healthily and happily as queer adults. The psychologists Ritch C. Savin-Williams and Kenneth Cohen, who have worked with college-age populations for several decades, made the counterargument that, much as Evelyn Hooker found in her 1956 study, the seeming overrepresentation of suicidal thoughts or actions among queer youth was an error in gathering data; the numbers were skewed by who was counted and how. Youth who make use of mental health personnel or facilities (usually the primary pool for information) are more likely to have expressed distress that would lead to thoughts of self-harm.

The British scholar Elizabeth McDermott and Norwegian scholar Katrina Roen, working as a team, suggest a socially and economically inflected explanation for queer youth's suicide and self-harm. They locate the kinds of distress associated with youth's suicide and self-harm in what they argue is a fairly unpathological response to the social attitudes and stigmas to which they are exposed, quoting the queer theorist Eve Kosofsky Sedgwick, who wrote that "all queer youth must, to some extent, finds ways to cope with symbolic violence, misrecognition and being positioned as shamed subjects" (quoted in McDermott and Roen 51). In other words, according to McDermott and Roen, it would be somewhat surprising were queer youth not to experience pain and thoughts of self-harm, given the ways in which the larger society tells them to think about themselves.

One of the biggest problems for queer youth, they suggest, building on some of the work of queer theorist Judith Butler, is that of "intelligibility": queer youth often feel that those around them can't make sense of or "read" who they are. Lack of intelligibility (or Sedgwick's term, *misrecognition*) can lead to a psychic state where queer youth may feel invisible, then, and suicide or self-harm could be viewed either as a way of "embodying" their desire to be recognized or as a way of making the invisibility real and permanent. So, for McDermott and Roen, the solution to the problems of suicide and self-harm is to promote a social health of queerness in which such youth can flourish. In practical terms, that can include providing services, shelter, and spaces for voices and lives to thrive.

A study published in the *Journal of Homosexuality* in 2006 by Clements-Nolle, Marx, and Katz found significantly higher rates of attempted suicide among transgender persons than among queer people who identify as cisgender and LGB. As the authors note, this is not necessarily in itself surprising, as trans people have typically experienced even more of the kinds of social stigma and misrecognition or invisibility that McDermott and Roen note as possible factors leading to suicidal ideation or attempts by LGBTQ+ populations in general. Clements-Nolle and her colleagues found that one-half of the transgender youth in their study had either contemplated or attempted suicide. Queer youth, for both developmental (where they are in identity and cognitive maturity) and social (lack of economic resources and access to nonjudgmental health care) reasons, are at elevated risk in general for suicide and other forms of self-harm; these risks are compounded for gender-nonconforming youth.

In addition, Clements-Nolle and her colleagues identified a number of risk factors frequently encountered by trans people that were correlated with attempted suicide. Some of them overlap with those pertaining to queer people in general, but a few others seem particular to or heightened for trans people: struggling with both sexual and gender identity (the double whammy alluded to already) and a history of forced sex are also factors for transgender people. The latter may be particularly enmeshed with social forces that make life difficult for trans people. As adolescents, trans youth are be more likely to find themselves homeless and part of street cultures in which sex work is one of the few economic options available to them. While there are arguments to be made positively for sex work as a potentially legitimate and socially acceptable form of labor, it puts the workers at significant risk of crime, including forced sex (or rape, to use a blunter term), often accompanied by other kinds of physical danger. A client, or john, who thinks he is having sex with a biological woman but who discovers that the worker is biologically male may turn to violence. Such conditions can lead to other factors that place trans people at risk for suicide and self-harm, such as substance abuse, as a way of coping with depression and other psychiatric challenges, and sexually transmitted infections, including HIV/AIDS, especially since trans people often do not feel empowered to insist on forms of disease prevention.

## AIDS: HIV — FROM GAY MEN'S HEALTH CRISIS TO GLOBAL PANDEMIC

What we now call **AIDS/HIV** or, as it is increasingly called, *HIV-infection-related illnesses*, was first noted in the early 1980s, but most scientists (particularly those who study epidemiology, the pathways by which various illnesses and diseases begin, spread, and, sometimes, disappear) agree that it existed long before it was conceptualized as something shared by enough people to constitute more than an idiopathic (individualized) condition. Even once it began to be conceptualized as something with common features and for which there were likely to be common causes, each case brought with it the history of the body and health of the individuals affected, making generalizations initially difficult. In particular, the populations first affected most by it in the United States played a role in the slowness of official medical bodies (and, particularly, executive leaders, such as President Ronald Reagan) to give it the attention it warranted. In the early years of its visible presence in the United States (the early to late 1980s), the shorthand of the "4Hs" was used to describe the risk groups: homosexuals (male), heroin users (standing in for all IV drug users), Haitians, and hemophiliacs. Even though this was more than ten years after the Stonewall Riots heralded the growth of gay liberation, gay men still remained a stigmatized group, and the presence of AIDS within their population intersected with what we might call a "moral model" of illness — even today, some fringe groups still view AIDS as a disease visited on a "sinful" group of people (conveniently omitting its presence among other populations).

The physician and medical anthropologist Paul Farmer concluded in his study *AIDS and Accusation: Haiti and the Geography of Blame* (1992), that the epidemiological path by which Haiti became an early and notable center of AIDS was probably white U.S. travelers taking the virus with them when they traveled to Haiti and engaging in what is often referred to as "sex tourism" (having sex with locals, whether sex workers or other available men and women). It seems far more likely that HIV traveled *from* the United States and, if Haitian immigrants brought it to this country, it was as a result of a circular path rather than a unidirectional one. Part of what made the puzzle of origins difficult to discern is that many of the HIV-positive Haitian men did not identify as either homosexual or bisexual (the groups of men in which the disease showed itself first in North America), even if they occasionally had sex with other men or particularly if they had sex with men for pay. In other Caribbean countries, such as Jamaica and the Bahamas, AIDS first presented itself primarily among heterosexual populations and, hence, did not carry the same gay stigma it did elsewhere (as is true in many African countries today) (Boxill et al.). Eventually, medical professionals and government officials shifted the language from *risk groups* to *risky behaviors*, which not only served to remove some of the stigma from groups previously cast as villains in the AIDS pandemic, but also brought to consciousness the medical truth — that any human being is at risk for infection.

So where and how did AIDS begin? The simplest and shortest answer is that we don't have a single explanation, despite various theories that have been put forward. Medical anthropologists have argued that "ancestors" of AIDS can be found in archeological remains that would date some variation of it back many centuries. As people tend to feel more comfortable with a single cause, a kind of urban legend emerged that gained a certain credibility because of its inclusion in Randy Shilts's history *And the Band Played On,* published in 1987, which isolated a "**Patient Zero.**" Shilts identified Patient Zero as Gaétan Dugas, a French Canadian flight attendant who in many narratives is depicted as traveling down dark corridors of bathhouses, infecting other gay men, and then announcing that he had "gay cancer" and prophesying that the man he had just had intercourse with would probably develop it. It is only recently that the Patient Zero identification of Gaétan Dugas has been authoritatively and officially debunked for the homophobic and xenophobic legend that it is and always was. An interesting and thoughtful recent book on the process by which the Patient Zero urban legend emerged and the effects it has had is Richard A. McKay's 2017 scholarly book, *Patient Zero and the Making of the AIDS Epidemic.* Chapter 6, titled "Locating Gaétan Dugas's Views," is an especially important rebuttal of Shilts's irresponsible demonizing of an individual, a throwback to the days of Typhoid Mary, when modern epidemiologists know that the spread of such viruses cannot be reduced to the actions of a single person.

Yet another answer, which is intended to be somewhat political (and, one might add, ethical) to the *how* and *why* might be "What difference does it make?" From an ethical standpoint, all infected people deserve the best health care available, and the *how* is probably relevant only insofar as it can help inform responses to future infections. This latter consideration is a legitimate one and parallels issues of prevention of other "sinful" illnesses (ones that may have a behavioral dimension that is viewed negatively by some populations), such as cancer (which can be linked to such things as tobacco and alcohol use) and diabetes (which, while not "caused" in a simple sense by consumption of sugar, is exacerbated by it).

What follows is a very selective chronology of AIDS, based on the much more thorough document "A Timeline of HIV and AIDS," published by the U.S. government (https://www.hiv.gov/hiv-basics/overview/history/hiv-and-aids-timeline). In this section, I move from the scholarly voice to the personal (printed in italics), in order to provide an individual counterpoint to the movement of large groups of scientists, activists, and workers.

## A Highly Selective Chronology of AIDS
### First Years: The Early to Mid-1980s

**July 3, 1981:** New York Times story: "Rare Cancer Seen in 41 Homosexuals."

**End of 1981:** 270 cases reported of what was then referred to as GRID (gay-related immune deficiency).

**January 1982:** Founding of Gay Men's Health Crisis (GMHC) by Nathan Fain, Larry Kramer, Lawrence D. Mass, Paul Popham, Paul Rapoport, and Edmund White.

*On June 5, 1981, the Centers for Disease Control issued an article in their publication* Morbidity and Mortality Weekly Report *describing the incidence of PCP (*Pneumocystis carinii *pneumonia) in "young, previously healthy gay men in Los Angeles" (all quotes come from the government website listed above). Though the story made its way into the New York Times, it did not appear on the front page and was a small item on an inside page, no more significant in importance than the opening of a play or a baseball score. By the end of the year, the first poster boy for what would become known as AIDS "came out" — Bobbi Campbell, a gay male nurse.*

**September 24, 1982:** The CDC begins to use the term AIDS and provides a definition for it: "a disease at least moderately predictive of a defect in cell-mediated immunity, occurring in a person with no known case for diminished resistance to that disease."

**June 1983:** PLWAs (People Living with AIDS, which would soon become known more simply as PWAs) takes over the plenary (main) stage of the National AIDS Forum in Denver.

*Naming matters; activism begins. Note that the new name for the condition does not include any demographic identification of those most* affected by the illness, which at least reflects an effort to destigmatize the condition and its primary targets, an effort that was unsuccessful. The Denver event — particularly the takeover — was one of the signal moments that would help define the different ways science and the public approached the illness: those living with the condition demanded a say in all aspects of treatment, research, and policy. This was no doubt a queer move, as many of those affected and involved in this demonstration had earlier become activated politically by gay liberation tactics and interventions.

*By this time, as a gay man in my mid-twenties, I begin to hear about this mysterious condition, though not sufficiently to have an opinion about it or even to think clearly about how to modify my own behavior. I have a conversation with my closest friend from high school, Gary, who lives in Brooklyn. He has a close friend, Darlene, who is a medical writer. Gary tells me Darlene has said that she has been doing some reading and that she wants Gary and his gay male friends to know there is something very bad "going around" among gay male populations — and he tells me she said it is being called GRID.*

### First Breakthrough: Discovery of the Virus

**April 23, 1984**: Announcement from the federal government that the cause of AIDS has been discovered, a virus then called HTLV-III. Health and Human Services Secretary Margaret Heckler states that there will be a vaccine within two years.

**August 27, 1985**: Ryan White, an Indiana teenager, infected with the AIDS virus through blood product used to treat hemophilia, is refused admission to his local middle school. He becomes a public spokesperson about the disease.

**October 2, 1985**: The actor Rock Hudson becomes the first celebrity to be identified as dying from the disease. Hudson, a closeted gay man, essentially announced in July his sexual orientation and diagnosis simultaneously, probably to avoid being outed by tabloid publications.

### Ramping Up and Going to the Streets (and to Government Offices)

**February 1987**: Cleve Jones creates the AIDS Memorial Quilt.

**March 1987**: The playwright, novelist, and activist Larry Kramer founds ACT UP, an overtly radical queer activist and educational group dedicated to working with the numerous populations affected by AIDS (queer people in general, people of color, IV drug users, sex workers).

**May 31, 1987:** President Ronald Reagan makes his first speech about AIDS, six years after its discovery.

**May 26, 1988:** Surgeon General C. Everett Koop, a Reagan appointee, mails copies of an informational booklet on AIDS to all 107 million U.S. households. He comes under conservative criticism for this act.

**December 1, 1988:** First World AIDS Day observance.

**December 20, 1988:** Max Robinson, first African American news anchor (for ABC), dies of AIDS-related illnesses. Robinson had been married three times and denied being either gay or bisexual.

*In 1988 I move from my teaching position at an isolated college in rural Nebraska, where AIDS is a news item about which I hear as if it were from a foreign universe, to my current position in Ithaca, New York, a town upstate but with a vocal and liberal gay and gay-supportive community. I serve for a period on a local grassroots AIDS education and service board, AIDSWORK, which provides testing, advocacy, education, and support for those affected by AIDS. I also join various emerging committees, student, faculty, and staff at Ithaca College committed to AIDS education. One of these, the AIDS Working Group, sponsors a yearly "Living with AIDS" panel, bringing in people with AIDS to tell their stories; another, The Prevention Network, formed by Susanne Morgan, a sociology professor, and some student activists, provides in-class and residence hall informational sessions at the college. This kind of work is beginning to happen at many campuses and in many towns across the country.*

*I find myself personally affected by the move because I had felt the need to be closeted when I lived in rural Nebraska, in a town that was quite conservative and dominated by evangelical Christian religion; nonetheless, despite my best (or worst) efforts to present myself as "neutral" about my sexual orientation, I came back to my office one night to find the word "AIDS" scrawled on my door in permanent black marker. I spend time with my friend Gary in New York City, where the presence of AIDS is more visible in the bodies of many gay men in such densely populated areas as the Village and the Theater District, and in posters and other kinds of mediated and street depictions of the illness and calls for political action.*

**July 26, 1990:** The Americans with Disabilities Act goes into effect, and it includes protections and accommodations for people with AIDS as a "disabled" class.

**November 7, 1991:** Earvin "Magic" Johnson, a star professional basketball player, reveals that he is HIV-positive. He asserts that he acquired the virus through heterosexual contact. (As of this writing, he is still alive, though long retired from pro sports and now a businessman.)

This summer I become alarmed when I lose contact with Gary; all I get is his answering machine. After close to a month, I finally hear from him. The last time I saw him was at the end of April, when I went down to New York City to celebrate his thirty-fourth birthday. He was feeling unwell the whole weekend, barely able to get out of his bed to go out and celebrate. When Gary finally calls me in early summer, he tells me that he had to enter the hospital, as the fever and fatigue he had been experiencing his birthday weekend had not abated. The good news is that he is on the mend and is now back at home in Cobble Hill; the bad news is that he has indeed been diagnosed as HIV-positive and the presenting illness is toxoplasmosis. Gary returns to work at Macy's, where he is a senior copy editor, and he finds a new boyfriend. His boyfriend is HIV-negative, but he has had a relationship with a positive man earlier. Nonetheless, Gary does not reveal his serostatus to his new partner, but, in our conversations, he indicates that he practices only safer sex with him.

Labor Day weekend 1992, I visit Gary in Cobble Hill, the neighborhood in which he lives and where he has bought a co-op after many years of moving from one railroad flat to another. He shows me a lump on the side of his neck. I brush off his fears, reminding him that as kids we all were subject to this kind of lymph node infection — our mothers simply called them "swollen glands," and they usually disappeared after a few days. We spend a weekend around the city, visit a former "friend with benefits" of Gary's, who also has a house near Ithaca and whom I have met. The friend also notices the lump on Gary's neck and comments on it. Gary decides he will have it looked at after the holiday weekend. Gary calls me with the news that he has been diagnosed with non-Hodgkin's lymphoma, a cancer highly, though by no means exclusively, associated with HIV infection. Gary begins intensive chemotherapy and radiation treatment and takes a leave from his job at Macy's, which, nonetheless, continues to pay him while he is going through the treatment and does not move his status to disability pay or ask him to relinquish his job. His regimen includes treatment several days a week in which a stent is inserted into his skull for eight hours at a time. He emphasizes the sense of camaraderie he has developed with the other men with whom he is spending time in the clinic where he is being treated.

Gary has not shared his positive status with his family back in suburban Chicago, perhaps in part out of some sense of denial himself, and also because he does not want them to worry about him, particularly when there is nothing they can do about the illness. Now that he has a cancer diagnosis, he feels he must tell them SOMETHING about his health, so he simply tells them he has Hodgkin's lymphoma. When I ask him why he altered which cancer he has in disclosing to them, he says that Hodgkin's disease has a higher survival rate and isn't as frequently associated with AIDS.

His partner, Bruce (the same first name as mine), who at the time is commuting between Washington, D.C., where he has taken a job after one on Wall Street ended, and New York City, devotes all his free time and energies to making sure Gary has care, takes his meds (it is crucial that he follows up the intense chemo with "rescue" medications to counteract the toxic effects of the chemo), and has food prepared; many of Gary's circle of friends, from college and from his years in New York, rally and provide him company and cooking while Bruce is out of town for work. Bruce asks me to come down to the city for a weekend when he cannot make the trip, to make sure Gary takes his medications when he is supposed to; left to his own devices, he can become forgetful about them at times. I go and am somewhat shocked to see how much Gary has declined — he is experiencing some hair loss, and his tall, svelte figure has become emaciated — a development that he tries to disguise with layers of clothes, suitable for the chilly December weather. We walk the block and a half it takes to go to the local movie theater, where we view Home Alone 2, a movie we would never have chosen to see. But it is the only one neither of us has seen — and, hence, it is a treat for Gary. It takes close to half an hour for us to walk less than two blocks. We stop for dinner at a restaurant across the street. Gary takes a few bites of his hamburger and then stops eating.

We both fly home to Chicago to spend the holidays with our families. I drive to Gary's home and spend time with him and his family. His mother takes me aside and expresses her worry that Gary will lose his job at Macy's because of his illness; she is also worried about his insurance. I explain that he is protected by the ADA as a cancer patient, which seems to allay some of her fears. Later, Gary confides in me that he thinks he may have "mucked it up," because his mother said to him, "I hope you and Bruce [his partner] are being careful, because it would be awful for you to get AIDS on top of the cancer!" He does not feel he can take this opening to be more forthcoming.

I remain in touch by phone with Gary throughout January and February — the weather in upstate New York makes travel difficult and I am in the thick of a new semester. The therapies are not reducing the tumor spotted in Gary's brain. He is able to remain somewhat upbeat, describing the daylong sessions in the clinic, sitting, strapped to the infusion IV, almost as a social event, where he manages the small talk between the disparate people. "The ones I feel the most for," he says one time, "are the mothers. . . . They always have such a sad look." When we learn that one of the men, who was a cabaret critic for the New York Times, has died, Gary says, "You meet a lot of nice people there — they just don't stay around very long."

Then, late one Sunday night, after eleven (in those days, the time when long-distance rates went down), my phone rings. It is Gary, and his partner, Bruce, has just left to attend to some business at his Manhattan apartment for a few hours; Bruce will be back, but Gary is feeling lonely and depressed. He sounds restless, though he tries to maintain a chipper voice, quoting campy lines from our favorite films. After a while, I hear him begin to cry, something in our two decades of friendship I have never heard him do. When I ask him what's wrong, he says, "It's just so discouraging. It doesn't seem to be making any difference. I know how my mother and Aunt Betty feel." His mother has been living with multiple sclerosis for some years; his Aunt Betty, a dignified professor of Victorian literature at a college in Indiana and Gary's travel companion in Europe on a number of occasions, is living with breast cancer, which she has thus far successfully beaten back, but which will return and claim her life in a few years.

"I was listening to 'Selected Shorts,'" he goes on, "and there was a story by M. F. K. Fisher, about a woman who is ill, and she goes out in the middle of the winter and dances around on the dunes at her beach house. And I feel like I wish I could do what she does. At least she can be free for that moment." After a while of fecklessly trying to comfort Gary, I agree we should hang up, as I can hear him starting to drift into sleep, but I find ending the call difficult. I tell him how brave he is and how much I admire him. I stop short of saying, "I love you," because, well, after all these years, and we are midwestern boys . . .

On Wednesday, I receive a message from Bruce, asking me to call him. When I finally get him at Gary's house, ten minutes before I am scheduled to teach a class, he abruptly tells me, as if having to rip a Band-Aid off quickly, "Gary went into cardiac arrest this morning as we were waking up. He passed away." The words make no sense to me, and I say, "But I just talked to him Sunday night." I ask if Gary's parents have been told. "Yes," his partner says, "I called Paul and Jill [his younger brother, to whom he was especially close, and his wife at the time] and let them know. He went over to the house on Thatcher and told Carol and Jerry." Paul will tell me later that when he walked in the door, on a Wednesday morning, his parents knew something was wrong. His mother said, "But I don't understand — the treatments for Hodgkin's are supposed to be effective. Did they do something wrong?" Paul has to tell his parents that Gary's cancer was non-Hodgkin's, and, in fact, that he had AIDS.

Bruce and I fly to Chicago for the funeral, where we serve as pallbearers. It is a closed casket and Gary will be cremated. His mother is quick to say to me, "We chose cremation just because we thought it was what Gary would have wanted." I think she was afraid that I would have thought they were doing it out of shame of the illness — there had been a time when funeral homes would not take care of the bodies of people with AIDS, out of the ignorant belief that the virus was still active. The service is lovely and dignified. A few months later there is a memorial service in New York City, *attended by hundreds of Gary's friends, where all his male colleagues from Macy's wear bow ties, in tribute to their friend, whose sense of taste and style they all loved.*

*Several months later I receive a call from Bruce, with whom I have stayed in touch from time to time, though we had not ever become close friends, simply because of the conditions and timing of our interactions. "I need to ask you a question," he says to me. "How long was Gary HIV-positive?"*

*"Why do you want to know?" (This is a conversation I never wanted to have.)*

*"Well, I know more about HIV than most people," he says. "Cancer is just not usually the presenting illness."*

*"I will tell you," I say, realizing I am about to violate the privacy of one person to set the mind of a living one at peace, "but realize that once I tell you, I can't untell you, and you will not be able to undo the knowing."*

*"Just tell me," he repeats, not impolitely, but firmly.*

*"He had been positive for about three years before he died. His presenting illness was toxo. He was afraid to tell you because he hadn't been sick since the two of you met and by the time he was diagnosed with the cancer, he loved you so much and he was afraid he would lose you."*

*"No, he wouldn't have lost me."*

*"I know. I begged him to tell you, but I finally left it alone — I was afraid I would alienate him myself. I'm sorry. He did tell me you two were always safe."*

*"We were. No, I'm fine. I was tested after Gary died, at the advice of my doctor, as, when Gary was seizing, I did give him mouth-to-mouth. My doctor also gave me a month's supply of AZT to take just in case. I'm still negative. But I just needed to know."*

*Not a day goes by that I do not think of Gary. And I also think often of Bruce, now happily married to a film scholar, whose specialty is the Hollywood actress Bette Davis, Gary's favorite — indeed, in our last conversation, we reenacted by phone some of the dialogue from our favorite film, Davis's masterpiece* All about Eve: *he would be happy for them. His illness is long over — our lived experience of AIDS is not and probably never will be. And I still miss him more than words can convey.*

### From a Death Sentence to a Managed Chronic Illness

**December 23, 1994:** The FDA approves an oral AIDS test, making testing easier and more accessible.

**October 31, 1995:** According to government figures, 500,000 cases of AIDS have been reported in the United States.

**1995:** Protease inhibitor combination therapies — "drug cocktails" — are introduced as approved treatment. They are less toxic and far more effective, lowering many people's viral loads to a status described as "undetectable."

**October 1996:** The AIDs Memorial Quilt is displayed in full for the last time. It has become too large to be shown all in one space.

**1997:** HAART (highly active antiretroviral therapy), an advance on earlier drug cocktails "becomes the new standard of HIV care."

**1999:** The World Health Organization announces that HIV/AIDS is now the fourth-biggest killer globally and the number-one killer in sub-Saharan Africa.

**2005:** The Nobel laureate and former president of South Africa Nelson Mandela announces that his son has died of AIDS-related causes.

**March 10, 2006:** First National Women and Girls HIV/AIDS Awareness Day.

**October 30, 2009:** President Barack Obama announces that his administration will lift the travel and immigration ban for visitors with HIV. (Bill Clinton had allowed it to be lifted on a temporary basis for athletes and other participating in the Gay Games.)

**July 16, 2012:** The FDA approves Truvada as a form of pre-exposure prophylaxis — a pill taken daily to prevent HIV infection.

**November 21, 2013:** Obama approves the HOPE (HIV Organ Policy Equity) Act, which allows HIV-infected patients to receive and to donate organs from and to other HIV-infected individuals. Before this, there was a ban on such transplants, even when the alternative was certain death.

**December 6, 2015:** The CDC announces a 19 percent drop in new HIV diagnoses; while this is good news, it is also necessary to note that there has been a rise in new HIV diagnoses among gay and bisexual men between 2005 and 2014, particularly among men between thirteen and twenty-four and among African American and Latino men.

**January 28, 2016:** Research reports that HIV resistance to certain antiretroviral drugs (specifically tenofovir) is increasing.

I have devoted this much space to a single health crisis in queer lives because it seems to me one of the most important periods in queer history and because it is far from over. The conservative queer writer Andrew Sullivan, himself HIV-positive, wrote an article published in the Sunday *New York Times Magazine* in 1996, titled "When Plagues End," in which he discussed the successes with the kinds of antiretroviral therapies listed in the chronology, and indeed, the incredible progress toward making AIDS an illness that for thousands, if not millions, of people may be a chronic but manageable condition should not be underestimated or undercelebrated. At the same time, Sullivan rightly came under criticism for the impression the article left many readers with that somehow the pandemic was over, and that it was simply a matter of taking daily medications.

Sullivan also writes from the position of a cisgender, middle-class white gay man (as do I, I hasten to add), which is, in some sense, all he can do, but that does mean that his sense that AIDS is "controllable" or "manageable" cannot help being inflected by those experiences and his sense of inclusion in a generally privileged racial or ethnic class. The homophobia, transphobia, and racism that have been endemic to non-queer persons (and sometimes subsets of queer populations, in the case of transphobia and racism) have not magically disappeared, and the rates of new infections, both among younger gay men, who still may not have access to knowledge, support, and good counseling, either at home, school, or in their friendship communities, and among men of color, where homophobia and transphobia may continue to be systemic and socially enabled, speak to the urgency with which we must continue to view this crisis. Statistics bear this out: currently, estimates indicate that around one-quarter (somewhere between 22 and 28 percent) of transgender women are living with HIV and more than half (an estimated 56 percent) of black or African American transgender women are living with HIV (Centers for Disease Control and Prevention, "HIV among Transgender People," www.cdc.gov/hiv/group/gender/transgender/index.html).

This health crisis brought together queer people, not always in harmony or agreement — that would be asking too much, given the "epidemic of meanings" to which Paula Treichler refers (263), as well as the "epidemic" of conflicting information at different times regarding the epidemic — but with the common cause of making sure that people with AIDS got as much access to treatment as possible and that the dignity and the worth of their lives were maintained.

A very important point in this regard needs to be made about the role of lesbians and other queer women during the height of the epidemic. Statistically, women who have sex exclusively or primarily with other women have been at lowest risk for HIV infection (putting aside other factors, such as IV drug use or having partners who more frequently have sex with men), and it might not have been unreasonable to expect that their involvement in the research, caregiving, and politics of AIDS would be comparatively smaller than that of other groups: after all, most of us assume some degree of self-interest in taking up causes (even in utopian worldviews of mutual support). Nothing could be further from the truth. Lesbians were and continue to be among the most passionate and hardworking fighters in the AIDS crisis — from participating in the many political actions of ACT UP to providing care and shelter and comfort for the primarily gay men first hit hardest in urban areas of the United States.

## LGBTQ+ ATHLETICS: FROM THE GREEKS TO THE GAY GAMES

In turning from the ongoing AIDS epidemic to queer athletes and athletics, we also turn from perhaps the largest threat to queer health (especially queer male health) in recorded times to a realm designed to promote health from early civilizations to the present day — sport and athletics.

In Western culture, perhaps the most famous premodern forms of athletic competitions were what we now refer to as the Ancient Olympics, which were first recorded in 776 B.C.E. Any free male Greek citizen was eligible to compete in the various events. Even as far back as these competitions, there were elements of the homoerotic (as well as the sexism of the time, which kept married women from competing in or even attending the events). This "queer history" of the Ancient Olympics was reinvoked in 2016 when Vladimir Putin made clearly homophobic comments about gay athletes who might attend the Winter Games in Sochi, declaring that they would not be subject to harassment unless they approached children, thus reinscribing the harmful stereotype of queer people (particularly gay men) as pedophilic predators.

**Queers, Sports, and the "Healthy Body": An Uneasy Relationship**
The valorization of "physical culture," out of which such groups as the YMCA began in the nineteenth century, led, in the twentieth century, to the institutionalization of physical education. It is difficult to generalize about the experience students have had with physical education, given how widely and variously it has been constructed and how different individuals are in terms of ability and interest in the world of sports and physical activities in general.

Ironically, there are two seeming opposing stereotypes about gay men and gym class. On the one hand, for many decades, there was the assumption that gay men, who as a group have been imagined as "less than masculine," dislike physical education, are poor at athletics and sports, and will do whatever they can to avoid participation in them. When true, this may be because they have found such classes to be places of exposure, display, and bullying by fellow students, teachers, and coaches alike, often in the complex realm of the locker room and shower areas, where naked male bodies circulate. The other stereotype builds on the phantom image of the predatory gay male (parallel to the "predatory dyke," discussed below), using the locker room as a site for viewing and, perhaps, making physical contact with other males, including straight ones, who, in this narrative, are seen as vulnerable and exposed to the "queer gaze."

Lesbians often find themselves in a kind of reversal of stereotypical assumptions by their straight female peers and by some of their coaches and teachers: there is often an unspoken assumption that any girl *too* interested and skilled in sports — and some sports in particular — are sexually suspect. Many female athletes who identify as heterosexual recount instances in which they have been called "dykes" or "lezzies," because of their participation and achievements, either in school-based physical education or in competitive athletics, especially in specific contact sports. Studies have shown there is an overrepresentation (in terms of percentages of general, non-queer populations) of queer women in sports, so some of this labeling by association is probably a product of that, but it is certainly not a good reason for using slurs and stigmatizing terminology. And it is easy to imagine how much more stressful and psychologically unhealthy it is for lesbian athletes to be called out for their identities, not simply for associations with presumed queer women, for which straight female athletes are criticized. Just as the gay male phys ed student or athlete is chastised and policed for a seeming lack of traditional masculinity, so the lesbian athlete is similarly judged for an excess of masculinity, as sports and athletics have traditionally been defined as realms of masculinity. It is useful to note that this is not a challenge simply for lesbian athletes, but for many women in athletics in general, especially those engaged in sports not exclusively or traditionally thought of as "feminine" (such as figure skating or synchronized swimming). Serena Williams, to pick just one example, has had her performance (or presentation) of "womanhood" or "femininity" critiqued and surveilled because of her highly developed musculature (which, of course, accounts in no inconsiderable part for her success on the tennis court). Can you think of other examples?

**From Classrooms to Arenas: Queering College and Professional Sports**
David Kopay, who played for a number of NFL teams in the mid-1960s and early 1970s, is generally credited as one of the first professional male athletes to come out. Significantly, he came out only *after* he retired from professional sports, and that pattern has been followed ever since by the majority of high-profile queer athletes. From today's perspective, this may seem to be a less-than-forthright kind of timing (and, to be sure, it is), but it is also understandable, as even now out athletes have a more difficult road to travel, both within the culture of their teams and as professional figures. Especially since pro athletes make a good deal of their income

from endorsements and working for advertising campaigns, both during and after their pro careers, coming out even after retirement from sports can involve a sacrifice of significant amounts of money — and make them high-profile objects of homophobic discourse.

Pat Griffin, whose 1998 book, *Strong Women, Deep Closets: Lesbians and Homophobia in Sport,* remains a classic study of this phenomenon, one Griffin traces back to such figures as Babe Didrikson, who many consider the greatest all-round athlete of the twentieth century, who was described in the media as "mannish," not-so-coded language of the time for *lesbian,* just one example of many forms of gender policing of appearance and demeanor Griffin identifies. She writes of the phantasmic figure of the "predatory dyke" in women's sports and argues persuasively that much of the homophobia comes from within the sports world itself: Griffin identifies softball and basketball as the college sports where unease about lesbian presence was typically most notable, and tennis and golf as the professional sports where there were assumptions of the presence of these "predatory dykes."

Griffin created a model of different attitudes toward and treatment of lesbians in sports:

- Hostile: discrimination and harassment are accepted and even promoted.
- Conditionally tolerant: there is a "glass closet," and lesbian presence is accepted so long as it is silent and restrained.
- Open and inclusive: nondiscrimination is practiced, and sexual identity is affirmed. (92)

Griffin notes that women who choose to come out as lesbian while participating in college athletics may experience numerous challenges, such as pressure from religious groups. (Both male and female sports often have a Christian evangelical mind-set, even if the supporting institution is public or nonreligious, so prayer circles are not uncommon before a game, which, even for non-queer players who do not share the faith traditions of the coach or the captains of a team, would clearly be uncomfortable). Also, lesbian — and gay male — athletes are frequently on scholarship and any threat to their eligibility may pose a serious and genuine threat to their ability to continue to pay for schooling. (College athletes can be cut for many reasons, which are rarely contestable, usually at the discretion of coaches, who can simply claim the individual isn't playing well enough.)

In international sports, the definition of the category *woman* has been the subject of controversy. In 2014, for example, the International Association of Athletic Federations (IAAF) raised the issue of whether a higher level of testosterone would disqualify some athletes who identified as women (in their noncompetition lives, as well as in competition) from being allowed to compete. Such women as the Indian sprinter Dutee Chand and the South African runner Caster Semenya were challenged in their bids to compete in international races, as the IAAF decided to classify them as *intersex*, rather than as *women*. In trying to make its arguments, the IAAF not only created discriminatory discourse and regulations, but also engaged in faulty logic and poor science. Especially since there is, as yet, no competitive category for intersex athletes (if any commission could agree on what the parameters defining an intersex person would be), these athletes were faced either with competing with a cohort with which they had no identification (i.e., men) or with not competing at all. Studies on the assumed advantages of elevated testosterone levels produced no significant results, so the entire episode seems to have the result only of once again invalidating gender identity for these individuals and, by extension, for a spectrum of potential athletes (Karkazis and Jordan-Young).

### Amateur and Community Sports: A Few Words

Many large urban areas, such as Chicago and San Francisco, have elaborate and extensive queer sports leagues, often involving particular sports. In these cities, the amateur queer sports scene has grown so large that queer athletes, if they so desire, can find opportunities to compete year-round; football, basketball, hockey, wrestling, volleyball, and softball are the most popular and prevalent sports. They tend to remain gender-segregated, though the role of transgender players is still an issue under construction.

The increasingly widespread notion of gender and sexual fluidity has posed some complicated questions of membership and eligibility for a number of these leagues. The balance has probably shifted in ways that reflect changes in openness about sexual identity in society. In the mid-twentieth century, women's amateur softball teams and bowling leagues probably had a fair number of lesbians on them (particularly during periods when such teams were formed by coworkers at factories and other companies), and this caused little concern, as long as lesbianism was left unmentioned. "Roommates" may very well have been understood to be something more than two people splitting rent, but they didn't need to be named as anything more than roommates, and there were no doubt social ways of welcoming these players (who often were instrumental to team success) without acknowledging their sexuality. Because of different gender role expectations, this may have been easier for women than for men during this period, but that is a history yet to be written.

Initially, as openly queer sports teams and leagues were created, the default assumption was that all players identified as queer (in some category or other, whether gay, lesbian, or bi), as the reasoning would be that it was highly unlikely a non-queer person would *want* to be on a queer team and risk being labeled "by association." As social attitudes began to change and as such leagues became more competitive, some of the expectations began to change again. For many players on queer teams in queer leagues, winning was first and foremost the goal — which makes them no different from other athletes who take their sport seriously — so, for some, getting the best players on the team, whatever their sexual orientation, was paramount. Also, in some cases, there may not have been enough queer-identified individuals to form a team. Yet another reason straight players sometimes joined queer leagues was that they had queer friends or relatives involved, and the social connection was a drawing point.

**Spotlight on the Gay Games: Performing the Olympian Queer Body Today**

The **Gay Games**, which began in 1982, continue to be held every four years, with greater visibility and participation. The Gay Games have, from the start, been devoted to promoting queer health in the broadest and most inclusive sense, whatever criticisms are directed at them in any given year (and there have been some, in many cases justified). In a book of this scope, we can't hope to capture all the complexities of the Gay Games phenomenon, and, fortunately, there are a number of excellent sources. The most complete and detailed one is Caroline Symons's book *The Gay Games*, which traces the development of the games in painstaking and illuminating detail from their inception up until the 2006 Gay Games, when there was a splintering that caused some dissent between various nations.

The Gay Games were the brainchild in particular of the former Olympian athlete Dr. Tom Waddell, a military medical officer and paratrooper, who represented the United States in the 1968 Summer Olympics in the decathlon. Though he already identified privately as gay, he remained closeted while in the army. After his discharge (he received an honorable one, which was standard for most personnel) at the end of his term of duty, he completed medical residencies, specializing in the study of infectious diseases, particularly viruses — which would carry a certain irony, as he was one of the most public individuals to die from AIDS in the early part of the epidemic in the United States. He fathered a daughter with a fellow athlete who was a lesbian.

Also quite progressive for the time was his vision that the games should be a an event at which people of varying degrees of skill and ability would be allowed to compete. While it is true that the Special Olympics, founded by Eunice Kennedy Shriver, had been in existence since 1968, some four-teen years before the first Gay Games, the Special Olympics were a kind of cordoning off of disabled athletes and restricted to those with intellectual disabilities: as much good as they do, it is not inaccurate to say that they had some of the same functions as sheltered workshops, where intellectually disabled people are "protected" and given useful work to do. Waddell developed different arenas for people of different ages and skill levels and set up separate events for men and women (and at the time, the blurring of genders was not as much on the national or international radar as it is today).

The history of the Gay Games and rival competitive organizations is a complex one, involving both individual conflicts and international cooperation and opposition. Many things have changed about the competition since Waddell and his fellow athletes devised it, in some ways adapting both to the changing myriad faces of queerness across the world and to the always shifting geopolitics of countries. It remains, despite occasional setbacks and controversies, a highly visible site of queer physical and body health — including healthy HIV-positive competitors — for queer and non-queer spectators alike.

## QUEER/CRIP AND CRIP/QUEER: DISABILITY AND QUEER SEXUALITY

The final intersections to be considered under the rubric of queer health are two positions often viewed synonymously: queer sexuality and disabled body or mind. In some contexts, to be *disabled* was often to be viewed as outside qualification as capable of heternormativity — indeed, the idea of disabled sexuality was viewed as monstrous. One way of saying this might be that all queer sex is in some social sense *cripped* (to use the parallel to *queer* more and more adopted within disability activist and cultural circles), and that all sex involving disabled people is by some reckoning queer, as it involves bodies and minds that are viewed as not wholly qualified for heteronormative status or citizenship.

Before we proceed further, it will be useful to define the term *disability* itself, along with two terms often associated with it, *impairment* and *handicap*. The three are often used interchangeably, and there is certainly nothing inherently wrong in doing so (and you are likely to see this if you do any reading on the subject), but considering the differences in what each focuses on may prove valuable in connecting it to queerness.

*Impairment* is used to identify the aspects of what Eli Clare calls the "body-mind" that deviate from what Rosemarie Garland-Thomson terms the "normate" individual (8). *Handicap* moves the impairment into the area of functionality — and that functionality can be in the private realm, the social realm, or the professional or occupational realm. *Disability* goes even further in situating the person's impairment in a social and cultural (and psychological) world. It looks at the various barriers, physical and otherwise, that society places on the person.

This phenomenon of the intersection between queerness and disability has begun to produce rich and provocative theoretical and critical work. The theater and performance scholar Carrie Sandahl coined the word **queercrip** to describe just such a point of intersection. The queer feminist disability scholar Alison Kafer situates the study of the intersection of queer and crip identities and experiences as a social and political site of understanding of self and of the self in larger social groups. Kafer also looks historically at how the AIDS epidemic forced queer people in particular to rethink such concepts as "life expectancy" and what it might mean to think of a "whole life" from a temporal perspective.

What about the actual lived experiences of those people who inhabit and experience queercrip life? Of course, each individual has their own experience, and, in the case of this intersection, specific experiences will prove even more variable, as disability can range from such invisible (or less visible) conditions as learning disabilities, such as dyslexia, to very visible conditions (such as physical impairments that require wheelchair use or personal assistants). Nonetheless, there are some common experiences queercrips writing about their everyday lives report.

Perhaps the most overarching one is what Robert DeFelice, a teacher and performer, describes. DeFelice, who lives with cerebral palsy and, in his performances, talks about having been a poster child (a disabled child used for fund-raising campaigns), remarks: "Young able-bodied college students often seem surprised to discover that disabled people are sexual beings, let alone that we can flaunt our sexuality. . . . Initially, . . . their laughter is uncomfortable, as though I wasn't expecting or wanting it" (quoted in Sandahl 33). So, perhaps more than anything else, "normate" people are likely to assume that disabled people are asexual, either by nature or by necessity — that the realm of sexual desire and identification is not part of their experience. Because many societies have viewed disabled people as equivalent to children, particularly if the impairment is cognitive or intellectual, there can be an unacknowledged sense of unease if such people become viewed as sexual beings with rights to pleasure and satisfaction.

When a queer person also becomes a crip, there may remain challenges, as the state still maintains control (though it is variable) over who gets to make decisions for disabled people. One of the most famous cases, which went on for eight years, bears the legal title "In re Guardianship of Kowalski" (the Latin phrase *In re* means "In the matter of"). Sharon Kowalski was a high school physical and health education teacher in St. Cloud, Minnesota, living with her partner, Karen Thompson. Though her sexuality was known within the lesbian community of the town, Kowalski was closeted from her family. In 1983 Kowalski was hit in a car accident by a drunk driver and suffered severe brain injuries, leaving her both with physical disabilities that required her to use a wheelchair and, more significantly for the law case, with considerably diminished intellectual capacities. Both Thompson and Kowalski's father petitioned the court to be her legal guardian. The court initially granted her father control, as the legal next of kin, and eventually he moved her five hours away from her partner and had the court cut off visitation rights.

The homophobia of this initial finding and the Kowalskis' treatment of Thompson continued over the years, to the point that, when the father in 1988 requested a new guardian be named, as his health was beginning to fail, and Thompson petitioned again for guardianship, he and his wife (and family friends) worked actively to oppose Thompson. This time, Sharon was deemed able to participate in her own decision making, and Thompson was able to call sixteen medical witness to testify to the benefits of Thompson's presence in Sharon's life. The parents remained stubborn in their statement that they would no longer visit their daughter if she were living with Thompson, and the judge once again denied Thompson's petition, awarding guardianship to a friend of the Kowalskis, who had testified against Thompson. In a final appeal in 1991, Thompson was at last granted guardianship, as the Minnesota Court of Appeals ruled in her favor. By then, Thompson had become partnered with another woman, and Sharon joined the household in what has been called a "family of affinity." LGBTQ+ activists viewed this verdict as an important watershed in gay rights, as indeed it was. It is also an important moment for the rights of people with disabilities, who often have not been granted autonomy or agency in making life choices after they have acquired a disability, particularly one that affects cognition.

As the Kowalski case demonstrates, queer people with developmental or cognitive disabilities may find special barriers, as too many people, including some social workers and mental health workers (who should know better), assume, if not asexuality among this population, the opposite — a kind of childish, unregulated, uncontainable sexuality that may be equally "dangerous" to the social order and to the safety of people with whom such individuals live in adult group homes, as they often do. Forced sterilization, lack of privacy, and social barriers continue to occur, though sterilization, under the name of *eugenics*, is far less prevalent than it was at the height of its prominence, in the early to middle twentieth century. Fortunately, professionals like John D. Allen have in recent years done more research about best practices and strategies for working with LGBTQ+ populations with developmental disabilities.

Though queer women have, over time and as a group, been more activist and successful in building communities that support physical and other kinds of disabilities, queercrip men and women report loneliness as one of the biggest challenges to their quality of life. Disabled gay men in particular point both to problems of accessibility — the ability not simply to enter a physical space, but to navigate it socially and emotionally — and to ideals of male physical attractiveness as barriers for them, whether they are looking for a life partner or simply a short-term hookup. Some, like Carmello Gonzalez, talk about the raised risks disabled gay men may face as they enter the dating or cruising scene; Gonzalez discusses his own sexual molestation as an adolescent by an able-bodied man (quoted in Guter and Killacky 54). Even in spaces that have been developed to celebrate physical difference within queer culture, there may be gaps that isolate. Robert Feinstein, a blind man, writes about his experience at one of the two annual events designed to celebrate gay fat men (discussed earlier in this chapter): "Walking down Castro Street, I felt both invisible and conspicuous. Invisible because no one cruised me and conspicuous because I was so different. In the Castro, I am disabled first, gay second" (quoted in Guter and Killacky 139).

For others, the nature of specific disabilities becomes a crucible for rethinking what their sexuality is about. John Killacky, who experienced a spinal injury that left him with no sensation below the waist, including the genital area, reveals that "as someone who was quite phallocentric, I have been forced to reorient my sexuality" (57). Given the premium on normative masculinity that is often central to gay male sexuality (as it is to heterosexual male sexuality), the disabled gay man can experience both physical and psychic wounds to his masculinity, to his sense of being a sexual man. For Killacky, as for a number of other men, there was an opportunity to refashion a new sexual self, one that could provide equal, if different, forms of pleasure and celebration.

Some queercrip folk have also experienced the attentions of individuals who are called either *festishists* or *devotees*, typically able-bodied people. Alison Kafer writes, in an essay titled "Inseparable: Gender and Disability in the Amputee-Devotee Community," about able-bodied men who have a specialized erotic attraction to women amputees. Bob Guter interviewed Alan Sable, a psychotherapist, about the phenomenon of gay men who fetishize disabled gay men. Sable makes the interesting initial observation that "ability is a socially-approved fetish" (Guter and Killacky 66). In their discussion of what might be both positive and negative about the fetishizing of disabled gay men by able-bodied gay men, Sable offers the following, as a way of rethinking a concept that is typically viewed as a sign of pathology: fetishizing disability may be "a way to care for someone, a way to approach someone vulnerable. Which is also saying it's a way to see someone as approachable" (67). While a word like *vulnerable* may raise some red flags, Sable is suggesting that the fact that the devotee may at the very least see the disabled gay man as someone worth approaching could be an improvement over invisibility or rejection. As Guter asserts, more often, "those body parts [the physically disabled features that may be the object of fetishistic gaze and fascination] become emblems of shame and disgrace, never badges of erotic power" (72). Both Guter and Sable are trying to imagine the conditions under which interactions between disabled gay men and nondisabled gay men (who may or may not identify as fetishists) could become legitimate, mutual opportunities for shared erotic power.

## Transgender People and Disability

One of the difficulties in speaking about transgender people and disability is that such identification has often been pathologized as a disorder in and of itself. That the *DSM V* has shifted its terminology from "Gender Identity Disorder" to "Gender Dysphoria," including a statement that gender nonconformity is not in and of itself a mental disorder, is a step in the direction of asserting that trans people can indeed be viewed as mentally healthy and that, if they are not, it is not simply because of the trans identity they occupy, but because of the *dysphoria* (or distress) they experience as a result of this difference between gender assigned at birth and gender experienced.

The writer who has written most consistently about the experience of physical disability, trans identity formation, and the social factors involved in living in the intersections of these two axes is Eli Clare. Clare was assigned female gender at birth and raised as a girl; at age two and a half she was diagnosed as mentally retarded, to use the term in place at the time, and then ten years later rediagnosed with cerebral palsy. Growing up in the culture of the lumber industry in Oregon, Clare witnessed the destruction of the environment; she also experienced forms of physical and sexual abuse. In recent years, Clare has claimed identity as genderqueer and writes poetry, essays, and memoirs that articulate the individual and political experience of these identities and their relationship with the body politic. Clare's 2017 book, *Brilliant Imperfection: Grappling with Cure*, is a hybrid of polemical essays and poetic observations that are instances of resistance to a philosophy and the practice of "curing" — curing disability, curing trans identity, and curing (in an ironic sense) the environment (which should never have needed to be cured in the first place). Clare's writings are testaments to the inseparability of multiple commitments to identity and to social justice — and how the health of the body, mind, and world, both physical and social, is intimately interlinked.

## ISSUES FOR INVESTIGATION

**1.** As a class, you may wish to spend some time reading Dr. H's (Fryer's) speech together. Consider the specificity of his observations about the conditions of being a homosexual psychiatrist, and the more general conclusions about power and oppression and the debilitating effects such imbalances and stigmas have on the psychological health of both psychiatrists and their clients. He is unafraid to use confrontational, even offensive language — such as the phrase *Nigger Syndrome* — in order to model a tough style of confrontation by self of other that he believes is necessary if his profession is to serve gay people ethically and humanely. Imagine if you had been in that audience in 1971 — whether you identify as gay or not, whatever your own professional aspirations may be. What do you think your reactions might have been?

**2.** A question you and your fellow students might address is "Why change?" If people could change sexual orientation, why might they choose to? What do you think of such reasons? As we discussed in chapter 3, an old question that used to be posed was, "If you could take a pill that would make you wake up tomorrow morning permanently heterosexual, would you?" You might be surprised at the range of answers — what are the social, historical, and personal conditions that might lead to different answers? We often assume that change is always progressive — that the future we head into, with more technological and scientific knowledge, necessarily leads to better lives and better ways of making choices. Can you think of changes that have not been for the good? (Try to come up with some that do not easily become reduced to the wishes of whichever political party you may wish to see in power.) Some might argue that the change from *homosexual acts* to *homosexual identities* has brought with it some negative elements, as well as positive, personally affirming ones. Take this thought experiment one step further: Can you imagine a situation in which a person who identifies (in the deepest part of their being) as heterosexual might find it beneficial to change to homosexual (imagining such a thing were possible). It is often easy to come up with reasons to change to a more majoritarian identity (as in racial, ethnic, class, and gender categories), but what might a change to a minority category do that might be desirable?

**3.** For this exercise, I'd encourage you to be imaginative, creative, and hopeful. Get together with a few of your classmates and design a physical education building (or whatever spaces you would need within a high school building) that would be inclusive and queer-friendly. What design features of the physical facilities would allow all students to feel comfortable? How might you lay out the locker rooms (assuming most schools still maintain gender divisions — though it is worth considering how physical education might be handled comfortably for trans students, of whom there are more and more)? What kinds of activities, course options, and goals would you set for all students? Why? Consider all the possibilities — even ones that might seem playful or beyond the reach of most school budgets. After all, the verb we use for athletics and physical education is *play* — how could you create a world of sports and athletics where all can play?

## SUGGESTIONS FOR FURTHER READING AND VIEWING

Brownworth, Victoria A., and Susan Raffo, eds. *Restricted Access: Lesbians on Disability.* Seattle: Seal Press, 1999.

Clare, Eli. *Exile and Pride: Disability, Queerness, and Liberation.* 2nd ed. Durham, NC: Duke University Press, 2009.

Fagan, Kate. *The Reappearing Act: Coming Out as Gay on a College Basketball Team Led by Born-Again Christians.* New York: Skyhorse, 2014.

France, David. *How to Survive a Plague: The Inside Story of How Citizens and Science Tamed AIDS.* New York: Knopf, 2016. (A documentary of the same title is also available.)

Kafer, Alison. *Feminist, Queer, Crip.* Bloomington: Indiana University Press, 2013.

Kopay, David, and Perry Deane Young. *The David Kopay Story: An Extraordinary Self- Revelation.* New York: Arbor House, 1977.

Louganis, Greg, with Eric Marcus. *Breaking the Surface.* New York: Random House, 1995.

*Personal Best.* Directed by Robert Towne. Geffen, 1982.

Symons, Caroline. *The Gay Games: A History.* New York: Routledge, 2010.

Thompson, Karen, and Julie Andrzejewski. *Why Can't Sharon Kowalski Come Home?* San Francisco: Spinsters Ink, 1988.

Tuaolo, Esera, with John Rosengren. *Alone in the Trenches: My Life as a Gay Man in the NFL.* Naperville, IL: Sourcebooks, 2006.

*We Were Here.* Directed by David Weissman. Docurama, 2011.

Woog, Dan. *Jocks: True Stories of America's Gay Male Athletes.* Los Angeles: Alyson, 1998.

# CHAPTER 10

# QUEERING SPIRITUALITY
## Religion, Belief, and Beyond

Though many people use the words *religion* and *spirituality* interchangeably, many do not. When pressed, many draw a distinction between spirituality, which for them involves a belief in and a quest for that which is beyond the purely observable or empirical dimensions of life and existence, and religion, which they more often associate with specific traditions, with histories, often directive dogmas, and some degrees of literalism and systems of reward and punishment for "sins" (which may be defined quite differently by various organized religions).

In what follows, particularly in the first three religions we will consider, the so-called **Abrahamic faiths**, much about homosexuality and other forms of queerness hinges on the reading of scriptures (holy books) and commentary on them by scholars. There are comparatively few verses in any of the scriptures of these religions specifically about homosexuality (and, by extension, other nonheteronormative sexual identities and activities), given how much debate has been had and, in some cases, how much blood has been spilled over the issues. Language about gender identity tends to focus on what various religions prescribe as appropriate to the binary of male and female and rarely addresses the kinds of issues transgender people face in their lives.

## THE ABRAHAMIC FAITHS: MONOTHEISM IN THE DESERT (AND THE GARDENS)

**What They Share in Common: Lot/Lut and What Happened in Sodom**
One thing all three of the Abrahamic faiths — Judaism, Christianity, and Islam — share, especially with regard to issues involving queerness, is the story of Lot (Lut in Islamic tradition) and the city of Sodom. It is from the name of the city, Sodom, that the English terms *sodomy* and *sodomite* are derived. Because of the sins of its people, this city (along with some others) was destroyed in fire and brimstone by a vengeful God.

Henderson, Bruce, *Queer Studies: Beyond Binaries*
dx.doi.org/10.17312/harringtonparkpress/2019.09.qsbb.010
© 2019 by Harrington Park Press

But what *is* the story of Lot (we will use this form for consistency in this discussion) and his escape from the city of Sodom? Here are the relevant passages from the book of Genesis:

19 *And there came two angels to Sodom at even; and Lot sat in the gate of Sodom: and Lot seeing them rose up to meet them; and he bowed himself with his face toward the ground;*

² *And he said, Behold now, my lords, turn in, I pray you, into your servant's house, and tarry all night, and wash your feet, and ye shall rise up early, and go on your ways. And they said, Nay; but we will abide in the street all night.*

³ *And he pressed upon them greatly; and they turned in unto him, and entered into his house; and he made them a feast, and did bake unleavened bread, and they did eat.*

⁴ *But before they lay down, the men of the city, even the men of Sodom, compassed the house round, both old and young, all the people from every quarter:*

⁵ *And they called unto Lot, and said unto him, Where are the men which came in to thee this night? bring them out unto us, that we may know them.*

⁶ *And Lot went out at the door unto them, and shut the door after him,*

⁷ *And said, I pray you, brethren, do not so wickedly.*

⁸ *Behold now, I have two daughters which have not known man; let me, I pray you, bring them out unto you, and do ye to them as is good in your eyes: only unto these men do nothing; for therefore came they under the shadow of my roof.*

⁹ *And they said, Stand back. And they said again, This one fellow came in to sojourn, and he will needs be a judge: now will we deal worse with thee, than with them. And they pressed sore upon the man, even Lot, and came near to break the door.*

¹⁰ *But the men put forth their hand, and pulled Lot into the house to them, and shut to the door.*

¹¹ *And they smote the men that were at the door of the house with blindness, both small and great: so that they wearied themselves to find the door.*

<sup>12</sup> *And the men said unto Lot, Hast thou here any besides? son in law, and thy sons, and thy daughters, and whatsoever thou hast in the city, bring them out of this place:*

<sup>13</sup> *For we will destroy this place, because the cry of them is waxen great before the face of the Lord; and the Lord hath sent us to destroy it.*

<sup>14</sup> *And Lot went out, and spake unto his sons in law, which married his daughters, and said, Up, get you out of this place; for the Lord will destroy this city. But he seemed as one that mocked unto his sons in law.*

<sup>15</sup> *And when the morning arose, then the angels hastened Lot, saying, Arise, take thy wife, and thy two daughters, which are here; lest thou be consumed in the iniquity of the city.*

<sup>16</sup> *And while he lingered, the men laid hold upon his hand, and upon the hand of his wife, and upon the hand of his two daughters; the Lord being merciful unto him: and they brought him forth, and set him without the city.*

<sup>17</sup> *And it came to pass, when they had brought them forth abroad, that he said, Escape for thy life; look not behind thee, neither stay thou in all the plain; escape to the mountain, lest thou be consumed.*

<sup>18</sup> *And Lot said unto them, Oh, not so, my Lord:*

<sup>19</sup> *Behold now, thy servant hath found grace in thy sight, and thou hast magnified thy mercy, which thou hast shewed unto me in saving my life; and I cannot escape to the mountain, lest some evil take me, and I die:*

<sup>20</sup> *Behold now, this city is near to flee unto, and it is a little one: Oh, let me escape thither, (is it not a little one?) and my soul shall live.*

<sup>21</sup> *And he said unto him, See, I have accepted thee concerning this thing also, that I will not overthrow this city, for the which thou hast spoken.*

<sup>22</sup> *Haste thee, escape thither; for I cannot do anything till thou be come thither. Therefore the name of the city was called Zoar.*

<sup>23</sup> *The sun was risen upon the earth when Lot entered into Zoar.*

<sup>24</sup> *Then the Lord rained upon Sodom and upon Gomorrah brimstone and fire from the Lord out of heaven;*

<sup>25</sup> *And he overthrew those cities, and all the plain, and all the inhabitants of the cities, and that which grew upon the ground.(King James Version)*

If people remember anything about the story of Lot, it is probably the attempt by the men of Sodom to rape the (male) angels who visit the city in disguise as men and the turning of Lot's wife into a pillar of salt, her punishment for turning around to look at the destruction of the city. What is consistently at stake is how we are to understand what the actual sin that brought about the destruction of the city and its people was. Literalists tend to read the "wickedness" of the men of Sodom as homosexuality itself. More recent and less literalist or fundamentalist theologians argue that the principal sins of the men of the Sodom are ones connected to the cultural conventions of the desert: inappropriate treatment of strangers or guests in the city. In this sense, it is the threat of violence and sexual transgression in and of itself, not the act of homosexual genital penetration that may be the issue.

While it may strike some of us as odd that inhospitality is deemed a greater sin than homosexual activity, that may be a function of history and our own cultural values and inheritances. In cities located in desert climates, inhospitality could mean the difference between life and death for travelers, and there was even an often-implied expectation that one should treat even one's enemies with hospitality while they were in one's city (barring a situation of war). And those who argue against homosexuality per se as the sin of Sodom note that, from today's perspective, there are sexual mores and assumptions in Lot's story that seem greater transgressions than sex between men, such as Lot's offering his virginal daughters to the men of the city as a substitute for the angels, and what amounts to his daughters' "rape" of Lot in order to begin a new line of descendants ("Come, let us make our father drink wine, and we will lie with him, that we may preserve seed of our father"; Genesis 19:32, KJV).

Since the Hebrew Bible is accepted as scriptural in all three of the Abrahamic religions, other stories in it have been marshaled by queer-supportive religious thinkers, such as the relationship between David and Jonathan ("passing the love of women," as the King James Version translates 2 Samuel 1:26), and that between the mother-in-law Naomi and her widowed daughter-in-law, Ruth, who are sometimes read as a romantic, domestic couple, living together after the early death of Naomi's son and Ruth's husband, Boaz. Because all such texts come down through changing cultural norms and meanings, it is probably most accurate to say that the Abrahamic scriptures do not provide definitive religious proof either of support or of condemnation of queer acts and relationships.

## Judaism and the Book of Leviticus

The other major source for those who believe Judaic scripture forbids homosexual relations is the book of Leviticus. The third book of the Torah, Leviticus is primarily a series of injunctions spoken to Moses by God. Among these many rules are two verses that speak to (male) homosexuality: 18:22, "Thou shall not lie with mankind, as with womankind: it *is* abomination," and 20:13, "If a man also lie with mankind, as he lieth with a woman, both of them have committed an abomination: they shall surely be put to death; their blood *shall* be upon them" (KJV). These are, needless to say, strong statements, and, from a fundamentalist viewpoint, they seem to leave no doubt about the Hebrew God's perspective on (at least male) same-sex activity.

A less literalist view tends to look at these verses within historical and textual contexts in which the words were written (or spoken, if you believe God spoke them to Moses). Leviticus also forbids the eating of creatures with cloven hooves (such as pork) and seafood that has no fins or scales (shellfish) and mixing meat with the "milk of its mother" (hence the disallowance of dairy and meat combinations and the need in a kosher home to keep separate sets of dishes). Wearing of clothing that combines more than one material is also forbidden. A reasonable question to ask is why some of these injunctions are viewed as historically or culturally contingent, whereas others are considered by some to be eternal and transhistorical.

## Branches of Judaism and Contemporary Queer Lives

The three major branches of Judaism, Orthodox, Conservative, and Reform, take different stances on the roles of queer people in their moral and ritual worlds. Orthodox Judaism still maintains an official prohibition against women becoming rabbis; similarly, there are only a few Orthodox rabbis who identify openly as gay men. Steven Greenberg was the first publicly gay Orthodox rabbi; he did not come out as gay until after ordination. Though he recognized his desire for men and indeed his romantic feelings for specific men while a student, he kept this knowledge between himself and one of his teachers until 1999. The first Israeli rabbi to identify openly as gay was Ron Yosef, who came out in 2009.

These two men have approached their own homosexual identity in different ways. Yosef still acknowledges that, from a scriptural and *halachic* (relating to the laws passed down orally and through writing) perspective, Judaism is still clear that "a man [lying] with a male as with a woman" is wrong, but he calls on Orthodox Judaism to provide support for its same-sex members and asserts that to live as a gay man need not disqualify him from being a rabbi. Greenberg is more of an activist in arguing that the verses in Leviticus do not prohibit all same-sex activities, just very particular ones.

In his 2004 book, *Wrestling with Gods and Men: Homosexuality in the Jewish Tradition*, Greenberg argues at length that even a literalist reading of the Torah does not preclude sexual relations between women and speaks only to anal sex between men. Here he is taking the literalist approach one step further, viewing "lie with a male as with a woman" as descriptive not of all manner of erotic behavior between men (such as oral sex, mutual masturbation, and so forth), but quite specifically of penetrative sex. The documentary *Trembling before G_d*, directed by Sandi Simcha Dubowski, includes interviews with Greenberg and several other queer Orthodox men and women (including a lesbian couple and an HIV-positive man) in the United States and elsewhere, as they struggle with families, schools, and their religious communities to find a place for their religious beliefs and sexual identities

Finally, while both American Conservative Judiasm and Reform Judaism as a whole are accepting of queer Jews as members, as families, as leaders, and as people of faith and dignity in general, it is necessary to note that the official stances of these branches of Judaism do not necessarily mean that such people do not continue to have struggles that involve their identities as Jews and as queer people. Queer people may find forms of Judaism that not only accept but embrace their sexuality, but they may still find tensions within their families about their sexuality and may experience residual feelings of internalized homophobia.

## Judaism and Transgender and Intersex People
There is a long tradition within Judaic texts, including the Torah and the many volumes of commentary on the Torah, collectively referred to as the Midrash, of drawing distinctions beyond the normative binary of male and female that we often associate with traditional religions. Ancient Jewish texts actually had a broader set of categories and descriptions that included commentary and laws pertaining to people who either by body or by practice did not fit into that binary. A collection of modern-day writings that address both personal experiences and scholarly perspectives on transgender and intersex people is *Balancing on the Mechitza: Transgender in Jewish Community*, edited by Noach Dzmura, whose own life narrative provides some interesting parallels between the processes of coming out as transgender and coming out as a Jew (or converting to Judaism). In a biographical profile (https://www.lgbtran.org/Profile.aspx?ID=384), Dzmura describes growing up as a child sexed as female at birth, whom he identifies under the pseudonym Vickie. At various points in his life, Dzmura identified as a lesbian, initially because she (the pronoun Dzmura uses to describe himself before he transitioned) found herself attracted to gay men, in part through her work with people with AIDS, many of whom were gay men,

and because she could not think of another category beyond homosexuality in which she fit. (She had not yet become aware of transgender as a viable "space" that her body could inhabit.) She lived as a lesbian for about a decade. Eventually, she describes being at a conference on the subject of support for transsexual people, and hearing a speaker who she deduced was transgender — someone who appeared to have been born into a female body but who presented and performed as a male. This eventually led Dzmura to transition to a male identity.

Similarly, Dzmura found himself moving between different religious traditions and faiths, in ways that may be seen as analogous to questioning the authenticity of a sexual or gendered self. After rejecting Catholicism, in large part because of its policies and attitudes toward female reproductive rights, Dzmura found himself drawn to the figure of Christ as a rabbi (that is, a teacher). He began a divinity degree to become a Unitarian Universalist but ultimately found that Judaism felt the most genuine form of theology for him. He eventually earned a master's degree in Jewish studies.

In the same book, Reuban Zellman and Elliot Kukla write about the historical antecedents of present-day thinking of the place of intersex people in Jewish life and practice, drawing on the commentary of Rabbi Yosi, who wrote, "*Androgynos bria bifnei atzma hu,*" which they translate as "The *androgynous*, he is a created being of her own" (Zellman and Kukla in Dzmura 185). This statement contains a very forward-thinking turn of phrase — the coexistence in one body and, hence, one being, of a multiplicity of sexed or gendered elements, which are not viewed as "abominations" or "sinfulness" but simply require their own particular and individual ethics of belief and action within the Jewish tradition: the androgyne has as much right to claim identity as a Jew as anyone else, in this theology. Reform Judaism, probably not surprisingly, has been more progressive and inclusive on issues regarding the place of transgender people in Judaic faith traditions and practices (Commission on Social Action of Reform Judaism, "Resolution on the Rights of Transgender and Gender Non-Conforming People," 2015, https://urj.org/what-we-believe/resolutions/resolution-rights-transgender-and-gender-non-conforming-people). Elisheva Sokolic, in an article in *Forward* titled "Judaism Needs to Be Kinder to Transgender People," argues that even within some forms of Orthodox Judaism (which typically remain opposed to homosexuality and bisexuality in practice, though they are sometimes accepting of people who may identify as LGB but do not live out these identities in sexual practices), such as Modern Orthodox, there is space for inclusion of transgender people and for supporting their living within their gender identities. This is the case especially in those parts of the Torah that speak to the community's obligation to provide support for the mental and physical health of its members.

## Christianity: From "Social Tolerance" to "Queer Theology"

It is important to remember that Christianity is also not monolithic in its beliefs or its practices. At a simple level, it is possible to divide Christianity in two — Catholic and Protestant — but even this binary division quickly creates problems. Within the many different Protestant denominations there are subsets within subsets: the differences between Southern Baptist and American Baptist are more than just regional, as are those among the many different Lutheran synods.

An article of faith among all Christians is that there was a man today referred to as Jesus Christ, a Jew, who was the son of God and a virginal though married woman named Mary; he was sent to Earth to bring a New Testament and to save the souls of mortals through the sacrifice of his own life in crucifixion. His death on the cross (a common form of execution) and resurrection on the third day after his death (Easter Sunday) are consistent parts of the Christian narrative. Most forms of Christianity also see as central to common faith a belief in the Trinity, that is, a "three-personed God," as the Anglican poet and minister John Donne named it: God (the Father), Jesus (the Son), and the Holy Ghost (or Spirit).

Those who believe that Christianity should prohibit same-sex relations often do so, as many Jews do, on the basis of a handful of verses within scripture. In addition, anti-queer Christian theologians point to passages in the New Testament, or Christian scripture, as the basis for their opposition. First and foremost, they find prohibitions against same-sex acts in the writings of Paul, particularly the following verses in the book of Romans, chapter 1:

> 26 *For this cause God gave them up unto vile affections: for even their women did change the natural use into that which is against nature:*

> 27 *And likewise also the men, leaving the natural use of the woman, burned in their lust one toward another; men with men working that which is unseemly, and receiving in themselves that recompence of their error which was meet.* (King James Version)

Like the verses from Leviticus discussed earlier, these two verses can be read as condemning same-sex relations, and they have been interpreted to do so for many centuries.

In more recent times, theologians and historians have worked through them to see if there are alternative, but nonetheless legitimate, ways of understanding what Paul was saying. Some of this movement comes from the observation that nowhere in the four Gospels, which are traditionally viewed as the stories of Jesus during his time on Earth, does Christ make any mention of homosexuality; indeed, if anything, he seems to view marriage as a probably necessary but regrettable practice between men and women. Some add that Christ's own sexuality is never specified, that he never married (unusual for a Jewish man of his time and class), and that he in fact took public stances against the punishment or devaluing of such sexual outsiders as the woman taken in adultery ("Let he who is without sin cast the first stone") and Mary Magdalene, a prostitute.

The queer historian John Boswell made headlines in 1980 with the publication of his scholarly book *Christianity, Social Tolerance, and Homosexuality: Gay People in Western Europe from the Beginning of the Christian Era to the Fourteenth Century* (which was referred to in chapter 8), which argued that Paul's references to same-sex relations (at least those between men) involve complicated terminology that would not necessarily have referred to voluntary same-sex relations between free adult men, but, rather, probably were based on the forms of homosexuality Paul would have known most about — the use of male temple prostitutes — and that the sins committed were those of sexual exploitation. Boswell and other historians and scholars who followed in his path also have made the argument that Paul's theology and much of the theology of the early church followed what were read as Christ's recommendation against any sexual relations outside marriage and not performed with the intention of reproduction. In this sense, any nonmarital sex and any sexual activity simply for pleasure rather than production of more Christians would be equally sinful. Boswell further argued that a careful examination of historical documents, as incomplete as they are, provides evidence that, until around the fourteenth century, queer people had a place in the church. Boswell tried to show ways in which same-sex unions were solemnized and accepted during this period.

Those critical of Boswell's general philosophy of queer history took issue not only with some of the specific details of his reading of primary documents, but also with his conception both of sexual identity and of historical continuity in general. Some found his use of *gay* itself problematic, though the term was still the umbrella word used when he wrote the book.

Why was *gay* problematic? Boswell's critics argued that such a term would not have had meaning as a way of naming a class of people: there were "homosexual acts" but not "homosexuals," in the sense of a shared identity that marked groups of people as belonging to a different category of being. Therefore, Boswell's critics argued, to say that there were "gay people," in any meaningful way, in the early Christian and pre-Reformation European world is to commit an anachronism. That is, it was a misuse of a term that carries a particular meaning regarding identity in modern culture to refer to people who, while they may have felt desire and love for others of their sex and no doubt did have sexual (genital) relations with them, were less likely to identify as part of a distinct identity category, any more than heterosexual people were likely to identify with a category of people we today would call straight: such identity categories remain comparatively recent historical developments.

Even those who took issue with some of Boswell's scholarly methods and philosophies did not necessarily see his goals as invalid or lacking in worth. Mark Jordan, another historian of religion and sexuality, faults Boswell for what he sees as a kind of ahistorical or transhistorical view of *gay* as a category. Jordan makes the argument, as have many others, that we simply do not have sufficient evidence to say that same-sex desire and life in, say, fifth-century Europe is transferable to twenty-first-century New York City. Nonetheless, what Jordan sees at stake in Boswell's work is something we might view as cultural, rhetorical, and even political: a desire to help today's gay Christians see themselves as less isolated from the history of Christianity and from those who also claim Christian faith as part of their core identity.

### "Queer Theologies": Practices, Beliefs, Possibilities

In a provocative essay titled "God's Body," Jordan examines the ways in which Christianity has avoided (and evaded) coming to terms with what it means to speak of the body in Christianity, and, quite specifically, God's body, that is, ways of conceptualizing the body of Jesus Christ. Christianity is founded on an "incarnational" set of premises — of bodies taking shape, form, and flesh as part of the holy and spiritual experience, a phenomenon, as Jordan points out, that is reproduced every time the act of communion is performed. In some Christian traditions (such as Roman Catholicism), there is belief in transubstantiation: when the priest speaks the appropriate ritual and offers the wine and the host, they literally become the blood and body of Christ. In others (often Protestant traditions), the belief is in consubstantiation, that body and blood and wafer and wine all exist at the same time. But in both cases, the materiality of the substances of communion is tied up in the knowledge that we have bodies and that these bodies are not separable from our spiritual existence (i.e., our souls).

Jordan extends this set of beliefs to a queer reading of how Christian iconography, particularly carved crucifixes that are virtually always present in churches, depicts the body of Christ. Inevitably, Jordan argues, the artists, perhaps at the direction of religious leaders, however graphic and detailed they make the body of Christ in his moments of torment, do not represent him as naked, which, historically, would probably have been the case, as part of the shaming and ridiculing of the crucified person. Jordan goes further and indicates that this practice, which includes a loincloth to preserve the "modesty" of the body of Christ, is a neutering of his sexual anatomy.

Another prolific writer on queer theology, himself an ordained Episcopalian priest, is Dr. Patrick Cheng. Cheng's overall approach may be seen as combining elements of queer studies and theory with critical race theory: as an Asian American gay man, he is invested, intellectually, spiritually, and personally, particularly in matters of intersectionality. His theology can be seen as embodied in the title of one of his books, *Radical Love*. Rather than dismissing traditional Christian theology wholesale, he works to reconsider what an understanding of queer theory and queer lives might add to a deeper understanding of Christian theology and life.

He draws on such potentially provocative areas as what might be grouped together as an *erotics* of queerness to provide different perspectives on the relationship among God, Jesus, and everyday humans. He draws on some of the role identities often associated with gay male sexuality to think of the power relationship between God and humans, describing God as the ultimate "top" and, alternatively, David, Israel, and all of us as "bottoms." What Cheng is trying to do here is not unlike Jordan's goal — to get his readers to think relationally and in corporeal (bodily) ways about spirituality. He invokes practitioners of BDSM (bondage/discipline/sado/masochism) similarly, finding some of the relations within that community analogous to the give-and-take involved in God-human relations. As people who identify as part of the BDSM or leather community often note, it is reductive to simply assume that the power or the pleasure always rests in the hands of the dominant; rather, being in roles of service or subservience can have potential for power and dialogue. Similarly, Cheng looks at the Trinity through "queer eyes." He considers the possibility of queer work that the Trinity might do — it is yet another undoing of rigid binary boundaries, and he asks Christian believers to see beyond such pairs as divine-human or even gendered-ungendered.

In *Radical Love*, Cheng helpfully lays out what he calls "four strands of queer theology," four different but interweaving emphases and approaches to considering Christian life and belief from a queer perspective: (1) apologetic theology (apologetics more broadly refers to the branch of theology that defends Christian thought and dogma — here he uses it to mean the theological strategies to view "gay [as] good" within Christian scriptures and teachings); (2) liberation theology, which originated in the late 1960s, principally in Latin American and African American versions of Christianity, and which served to provide ways to understand the meaning of freedom both for social and political purposes and for religious and spiritual ones; (3) relational theology, which Cheng situates as emerging from lesbian responses to their omission from gay male theologies and which focuses on finding spirituality within relationships with other people — specifically, within the one-on-one relationship of lovers, partners, or spouses; such a theology also draws on second-wave feminism, which emerged in the 1960s and 1970s and is associated with what we now call women's liberation; (4) queer theology itself, which is inclusive of bisexual, transgender, and other nonheteronormative identities and experiences. Cheng calls on us to work toward greater intersectionality and to make space for hybridity in our spiritual and religious lives and in the theologies that guide us.

Yet another response to the need to find or make a place for queer Christians is the work of the Reverend Troy Perry, a gay man and former Pentecostal minister, defrocked because of his open identification as homosexual. In 1968, following a personal crisis that led him to attempt suicide, he founded the **Metropolitan Community Church (MCC)**, which remains a nondenominational community for all Christians, but with a special ministry to queer people. The MCC has churches in many regions. Perry tells his story on the church's website, which contains other useful information, including readings about queer spirituality: http://mccchurch.org. There are other, more recently developed stand-alone or networked Christian churches that have queer-positive ministries.

Queer men and women have often felt called to religious life. A fair number, particularly among Catholic clergy, who are bound by vows of chastity or celibacy, have left when they realized, not unlike their heterosexual counterparts, that they could not faithfully remain celibate and live a useful and happy life in service to Christ. Of course, some clergy who either entered orders knowing they had queer desires or discovered them only while in the seminary or some years after ordination also left the priesthood, sometimes having been counseled to do so. (Indeed, the Catholic Church currently states it will not ordain seminarians who confess same-sex desires.) Others chose not to do so for any number of reasons: in some cases, their faith was so critical to them that they could not imagine a life outside the priesthood; for others, the social benefits of the priesthood were such that they were unwilling to sacrifice them to live openly as gay men; still others, sad to say, found that the priesthood offered them a cover or an opportunity to use their authority to gain sexual access, often to younger parishioners or students. The church's sexual abuse scandals, which were depicted in the film *Spotlight*, winner of the Academy Award for Best Picture of 2015, were not in any simple or exclusive sense a "gay problem." The cases involved issues of pedophilia, and it cannot be stressed enough that, though more and more research points to pedophiles as having a preference for targets of their own gender, there is simply no equating homosexuality with pedophilia. The emphasis has been on the role of Catholic priests in such abuses, primarily because these men (as well as nuns, who do not have any statistically significant incidence of sexual abuse of youth) are required to take vows that preclude appropriate outlets for their sexual and romantic desires, but there have been cases of men in other Christian denominations (and other religious traditions) who have abused their positions of authority for sexual gain.

Some Christian leaders and churches found themselves challenged during the height of the AIDS crisis in the 1980s and 1990s. The scholar of religion and sexuality Anthony M. Petro, in his book *After the Wrath of God: AIDS, Sexuality, and American Religion*, traces the role of organized religion, specifically in the United States, during the period in which HIV/AIDS emerged and became an epidemic. Petro discusses groups and churches that took measured and compassionate stances on the epidemic, viewing it, properly, as a biomedical phenomenon that called on people of faith to treat those struck by it with support, love, and an absence of judgment. On the other hand, he provides documentation of meetings and commissions attended by Cardinal John O'Connor, who worked doggedly and with all the power of his position against condom distribution and safer-sex education, as well as the efforts of such televangelists as Jerry Falwell, who used his pulpit to continue to spread disinformation about homosexuality. Petro counters this material with interventionist work with religious content or perspectives by groups like ACT UP, which appropriated traditional images of Jesus Christ to make pro-sex and pro-activist messages.

Some might argue that the AIDS epidemic led more Christian denominations to have to "come out of the closet" about homosexuality within their congregations and within their members' own hearts and souls: sons, brothers, uncles, mothers, aunts, sisters, friends, and fellow worshipers were infected in large numbers, and they often returned home to die or were taken home to be buried. Their churches (and the churches of their families) could not continue to pretend, beyond a certain point, that these people were not members of, raised in, or related to the Christian church. Many churches underwent transformations and found the teachings of Christ to guide them in positive ways; some did not.

## Islam and Queerness: Faith and Reason, Communities of Love

Islam is currently the second-largest organized religion in the world, behind only Christianity, and it is considered the fastest-growing religion globally. Islam has also gained a higher profile in recent decades because of greater interaction between the West and the Middle East, which has, in turn, often led to a conflation of the religion and the politics of the countries where Islam is dominant. There is considerable diversity among Islam's different branches. In looking at the relationship between Islam and queerness, it is important to begin by considering how the religion as a theology views and regards queerness and queer people, and how politics often influences the religion's use for homophobic ends; the same is true of Judaism, Christianity, and other world religions.

Islam is typically dated as beginning in 610 CE, when Muhammad began to receive prophecies from Allah. Until that time, Allah was one of a number of gods in local Middle Eastern (specifically Arabic) religions, which were polytheistic, though Allah was considered the most important of them — the "Father," so to speak. Arab leaders, seeing parallels with the other desert religions, began to view their local polytheism as inferior to the monotheistic religions that had also originated in the desert. The word *Islam* literally translates as "surrender," and the religion is founded on a belief that surrendering oneself to a monotheistic God is the way to a holy and good life. Similarly, because Islam grew out of a somewhat sophisticated urban culture, part of that virtuous life is a concern for *ummah*, the welfare of the community as a whole.

After the death of Muhammad, various factions splintered into groups, most notably the Shi'ite and the Sunni. At the time, the principal difference between the two had to do with lineage and who would be authorized to speak for Islam after Muhammad died in 632. Shi'ites maintained that only those in Muhammad's bloodline were entitled to serve as leaders, whereas Sunnis (who today far outnumber the Shi'ites) believed that any virtuous person could potentially lead the faith. From such conditions, as the historian of religion Karen Armstrong observes, all manner of divisions arose within the faith, as well as wars and battles with those outside the faith.

The subset of Islam that may have the most historical relevance to the place of queer desire and relations within the religion is **Sufism**, which is considered not a separate sect or a variation of either Sunni or Shi'ite Islam, but an approach or a set of disciplines within both, usually centered on esoteric and ecstatic practices. It is both deeply spiritual and deeply physical, and it can involve trancelike dances and repetitions of language that combine poetry and music: in a word, it is a sensual way of embodying the elements of love and being that are central to Islam as a whole. Because Sufism focuses on the revelation of God's truth and love through the heart rather than through rational thought, it has been a place where queer Muslims in particular have found an outlet for their identities, which are founded in important ways on their experience of love and of the ecstasies of the body.

Historically, one of the most significant figures in the history of Sufism for queer Islam is Rumi, the thirteenth-century poet and mystic who many believe had both a female wife and at least one male lover. As has been the case with all historical claims around the queer identity of individuals removed from our own period, there is continuing disagreement over this issue in Rumi's life. What is true and has been documented is that he had a long, intense, and passionate relationship (which may or may not have involved genital contact, and the presence or absence of that is very important to some and less so to others) with another Sufi mystic, Shams, whom he met in 1244, and historians of Sufism and biographers of Rumi agree that this meeting and the relationship that ensued altered the course of Rumi's life, his practice of faith, and his artistic life as a poet. They became close companions, sometimes to the displeasure of Rumi's family, and Rumi devoted some of his most passionate poetry to Shams. Today it is not at all unusual to find collections of Rumi's love poetry in LGBTQ+ sections of bookstores, and the queer scholar Brad Gooch has written about the question of "unknowability" regarding the exact nature of the relationship between Rumi and Shams:

> The greatest and most guarded secret in Rumi's life concerned the nature of his fiery and transformative friendship with Shams of Tabriz, "the sunshine of the heart." Some have explained the torrent of passionate love poems that ensued when Shams disappeared from Rumi's life as fitting into a tradition of devotion of disciple for sheikh [here meaning teacher or mentor]. Yet Rumi and Shams — as well as other witnesses — emphasized the complexity of their relationship, its failure to conform to such a neat teacher-student model. While no evidence exists of an erotic component, Rumi chose to speak of their spiritual love in the mode of Persian romantic love poetry, and from weaving the two came his evanescent message. (308)

Rumi stands with other Persian poets, such as Hafez of Shiraz, who used the classical form of the *ghazal* (not unlike the European sonnet in its traditional familiarity and emphasis on romantic love), and whose poetry can be read on multiple levels, both about earthly, embodied love (whether taken to a level of actual physical interaction) and about spiritual connectedness with the beloved, with Allah, and with the universe itself.

The scholar who has written most extensively and widely about queer perspectives on Islamic scripture is probably Scott Siraj al-Haqq Kugle, whose books *Homosexuality in Islam: Critical Reflection on Gay, Lesbian, and Transgender Muslims* and *Living Out Islam: Voices of Gay, Lesbian, and Transgender Muslims* argue that Islam, as a later religion, tends to be less patriarchal at a scriptural level than some of its predecessors. Kugle sees the heart of the lesson of Sodom as the sin of "using sex as a weapon" rather than as a vehicle of respectful and mutual love (2010, 56). In examining many of the commentaries, which are collectively referred to as the *hadith*, he notes that there is very little mention of same-sex relations in them. (This is especially true of relations between women, which are signified by the Arabic word *sihaq*, which means "rubbing.")

Kugle also asserts that some of the verses in the Quran and statements in the hadith can be read as acknowledging a positive place for queer men in Islamic society, through references to a category of men as "those not reproducing" (66), without any condemnation of them per se, just the commonsensical directive that such men should not be encouraged to enter into a marriage with a woman. (There was no category in the Quran equivalent to *gay men*, as is also true of the scriptural texts of the two religions we have discussed previously.) Two terms used for such individuals are *mukhannathun* and *khanith,* which some scholars view less as what we might think of as cisgender homosexual men and more as either trans women or intersex persons. These terms and commentaries were created at times when there were no stable concepts of either *trans* or *inter* identities, so how exactly these people were conceptualized will probably remain open to debate. We do know that men who were described as effeminate were frequently permitted (or even forced) to live as women and sometimes turned to sex work. In some instances, depending on the country in which they lived they were regarded as a "third gender" or "third sex"; today such individuals may in some places still be regarded as "third gender" or "third sex," and live as such; in a few countries, they are provided support (financial and social) to undergo sex-reassignment surgeries.

There is a move toward forming organizations and associations in support of queer Muslim lives globally today. One such association began in 1996 in South Africa as the Inner Circle, led by the openly gay imam (spiritual leader) Muhsin Hendricks; this was the same year that South Africa passed a law prohibiting discrimination against LGBTQ+ people, so there was newfound freedom for such an association. In Britain, where, somewhat surprisingly, there have been violence against and opposition to queer Muslims, the organization Imaan was formed to serve queer men, women, and people of other genders, to do advocacy work and educate the public. There is currently at least one openly gay imam in the United States, Daaylee Abdullah, born in Detroit and raised in a Southern Baptist family, who converted to Islam at age thirty and has been involved with education, advocacy, and spirituality. On a broader level, the Global Queer Muslim Network is a consortium of queer Muslim groups that grew out of the initial work of the Inner Circle in various parts of Africa and Asia.

## HINDUISM AND BUDDHISM: EASTERN RELIGIONS AND QUEER LIVES

The two best-known Eastern religious traditions are Hinduism and Buddhism. Both originated in Asia, but they have a broader reach than that continent alone. Hinduism is generally agreed to be the oldest organized religion in existence, dating back at least as far as 1500 BCE in its documented presence. Buddhism is younger, though only by about a millennium, usually dated as having originated somewhere between the sixth and fourth centuries BCE. Both were founded in India, and Buddhism then spread to such eastern Asian countries as China, Japan, and Korea. Both Hinduism and Buddhism are usually considered less homophobic and more queer-friendly religious traditions than the more orthodox and fundamentalist versions of the Abrahamic religions, though there is variation within both religions.

**Hinduism and Queerness**

The religious scholar Ramdas Lamb offers the following as clarification of Hinduism's perspective on polytheism and monotheism:

> In Hinduism, polytheism and monotheism coexist in a relationship much like the parts of a wheel. The many deities are like the spokes, emanating from the hub and each playing an important role. . . . Then, there is the Hindu form of monotheism, in which the Divine is formally referred to as Brahman. . . . It is said to be the source, the hub, from which all deities are manifest, it transcends all attempts at defining and describing it. . . . The merging of polytheistic and monotheistic concepts . . . allows people to believe in and pray to their own conceptualizations of the divine in whatever form they choose, while at the same time elevating all of them to their ultimate reality, which is the singular omnipotent, omnipresent, and omniscient divinity, who demands no allegiance, punishes no one for lack of belief, yet provides wisdom, comfort, compassion, and freedom to those who seek it.

The divine (perhaps the equivalent to God in the Abrahamic traditions), Lamb suggests, does not have a personification — or at least not one as immediately graspable as those in other faiths. Rather, it is a state of being toward which one works, through various paths, each of which may be named by a particular *yoga*, a Sanskrit word that can be translated as "discipline," or set of methods, exercises, or practices that move the individual on the path to achieving oneness with the divine.

Hindu scriptures do not contain prohibitions against same-sex love and same-sex behavior. One of the attractions of Hinduism for its early queer Western adoptees was its belief in a "third sex," a category not entirely analogous to our modern conceptions of either transgender or intersex people, but one that acknowledges more than the traditional binary found in the Abrahamic religions that dominate Western theology and systems in Europe and the United States). In India, the **hijra**, a category of people born into what would appear to be male bodies but who live their lives in the roles of women, have had cultural status as a separate gender; they gained legal status as such only in 2014. Some earlier scholars have translated the term into English as "eunuch," but only a subset of the *hijras* either were born intersex or had male genitalia removed. Though in some communities *hijras* experience considerable poverty and social stigma, there are religious tales and legends that pay honor to people who inhabit this category, including ones about such respected figures as Lord Shiva and the fertility goddess Parvati, who come together in yet a third avatar, Ardhanari, who is the patron of *hijras*.

Insofar as Hinduism provides guidance that might seem to devalue queer relationships and desires, it is primarily in the same realm of all desiring, which can be seen as an impediment in the path to dharma, or cosmic wisdom. Homosexuality is no more an impediment than heterosexuality in this regard, or any nonsexual forms of worldly desire or longing. When Hinduism speaks out explicitly against queer acts, it is usually within the complex intersection of faith with history, politics, and culture. In his history of colonialism in India, *The Intimate Enemy* (1983), for example, Ashis Nandy argues that white British men, who were often not initially accompanied by their wives to India, often formed erotic and romantic bonds with Indian men. He further asserts that British women were eventually encouraged to go to India to live with their husbands (or to form marriages once there) to lessen the possibilities that the white British colonialists would engage in what, in the time of the Raj, Britain viewed as sodomy. It was only during this historical period, which spans 1858 to 1947, the year India gained independence from Great Britain, that same-sex relationships and actions became prohibited legally and that, by extension, this legal prohibition led to a group of people who claimed Hindu identity who viewed and talked about homosexuality in negative terms.

Indeed, in Hindu myths and legends, there are multiple depictions of close friendships between same-sex couples. The meaning of *friend* is open to interpretation and speculation, and it carries different connotations in different cultures at different times. Though the representation of such relationships cannot stand as definitive evidence of the acceptance of what today we would probably classify as gay or lesbian relationships, they do attest to the acceptance and even celebration of the value of close, intimate pairings between men and men and between women and women. Such relationships are typically viewed in Hindu literature as "natural" and therefore acceptable as part of the path to enlightenment — at least no less than traditional heterosexual ones are.

The scholar Ruth Vanita has examined such phenomena within a definition of marriage in Indian and Hindu culture that sees marriage as a vehicle for procreation. While same-sex couples may be granted integrity and authenticity within Hinduism as part of a yoga of love, they stand outside the stated purpose of marriage as understood culturally and theologically. Vanita suggests traditions in Hinduism that might provide an opening for same-sex marriage, even if it requires redefining (perhaps renaming) marriage. She looks at Hindu traditions such as the **swayamvara**, a special friend, as an alternative to procreation-centered marriage for queer Hindus. She examines the etymology of the word, drawn (from Sanskrit) from *swayam*, which means "self," and *vara*, which she suggests can mean "boon," wish," or "desire" and has come also to mean "bridegroom" as well as, more generally, "desired one" (114). She argues that *swayamvara* connotes more than just closeness and suggests the kind of singularity of commitment and bonding associated with marriage. Vanita describes such relationships as *janamantara* ("continuing from birth to birth" — recall that Hindus believe in reincarnation until the achievement of oneness with the divine), which she says is "based on reciprocity, selfless devotion, and sacrifice; as in ideal marriage, the partners live and die together" (114).

**Buddhism and Queerness**

Hinduism and Buddhism, as might be expected, share certain terms and ideas, such as *karma*, the acts performed by each human being and the subsequent results (particularly those that are spiritual and what we might think of as ethical), and *dharma*, the sense of reality and duty to that which is true and eternal. Buddhism is different in some fundamental ways from Hinduism. If Hinduism subscribes to a belief in an ultimate divine presence in the universe, one that is obstructed for humans in their lives by the illusions of what they see and sense as imperfect beings, Buddhism tends to put the question of whether there is a divine in an even more atheistic framework, asserting that absolute truth is itself an absence, a nothingness, though not in a way that is intended to foster pessimism or dread. Rather, this emptiness is seen as the greatest achievement to which humans can aspire, as it marks the final cessation of the ongoing cycle of human suffering and pain. Both Hinduism and Buddhism believe that attachment, whether to other humans, to objects, to sensory experiences, or to life and existence itself, is at the heart of suffering.

Similarly, since all existence is ultimately illusory for Buddhists, it has, since its beginnings, viewed gender in a very egalitarian way: there has been a place for both monks (male) and nuns (female) in Buddhism, and there is no gender-based patriarchal system that in significant ways defines the Abrahamic religions. (Buddhism, however, is not without its own instances of gender inequality — women, for example, are viewed as less likely to be reincarnated as lamas than men.) As all human existence is illusory for Buddhists, so one might assume that sexuality is, as well, and, hence, Buddhism has no place for homophobia or heterocentrism. Though there is good reason for this assumption, it is actually the case that Buddhism, while often and not inaccurately viewed as queer-friendly, is not quite as egalitarian as one might think — at least not without some qualifications. Whereas Hinduism does not contain any prohibitions against homosexuality in its sacred texts, Buddhism does identify "sexual misconduct" as one of the hindrances to enlightenment. For monks and nuns, celibacy is required. For lay followers of Buddhism, the question of what constitutes sexual misconduct is an ongoing subject of debate.

Buddhists subscribe to the Five Precepts of virtuous living, one of which prohibits sexual misconduct. Sexual misconduct is itself broken down into subcategories, including sex with an "inappropriate person," which many interpret to encompass homosexuality, especially as one of the other forms of sexual misconduct involves using the "inappropriate organ" (which can include oral and anal sex, whatever the gender of the people involved). In general, sexual misconduct involves any sexual activity that falls outside the standard mores and morals of a given society.

The Dalai Lama's own positions on queer sex have vacillated over the decades. In the 1990s he very clearly asserted that gay sex, whether male-male or female-female, was inherently wrong, on the basis of what the "natural" functions of sexual organs are and how they were intended to be used (an obviously heterocentric viewpoint). Yet, as recently as 2014, he changed his position to some extent and spoke out in favor of same-sex marriage. He took a somewhat less theological stance in making this statement, focusing both on individual agency and on governmental laws and regulations. As long as the relationships and the sex that occur within them are consensual and nonabusive, he said, it is a private matter. That, as of this writing, is the current official stance of Buddhism on *queer relationships and the sex that accompanies them*: I use this phrase rather than *queer sex* because it seems inherent and consistent within the Dalai Lama's teachings that sex is ideally and appropriately located in a relational context, not in simple physical (or psychological) pleasure.

### Spotlight: Issan Dorsey Roshi

The queer Zen monk Daishin David Sunseri wrote about his own teacher, Issan Dorsey Roshi: "In his early life, my teacher, Issan Dorsey Roshi, was a speed freak, a drag queen, a junkie, a prostitute, an alcoholic, and at times a real bitch. My teacher was also a Zen monk, a hospice worker, a friend to homeless people and drug addicts, a loving and compassionate being, and at times a real saint. The dichotomy was actually the foundation for his life and teaching, and was his path to liberation, albeit a somewhat unusual one" (quoted in Leyland 149). Thus begins Sunseri's essay, in *Queer Dharma: Voices of Gay Buddhists*, about his experience learning from and working with a remarkable individual, whose life and actions embody the aspirations of queer Buddhists — indeed, in the hospice he ran in the Castro neighborhood of San Francisco during the first decade of the AIDS epidemic, he was considered by many to embody the qualities of the *bodhisattva*, a figure much admired in Buddhism, an individual possessing great compassion who wishes for enlightenment for the entire world and is, therefore, willing to delay attainment of his own Buddhahood along the way. As Sunseri suggests, a simple listing of the past roles played by the man born Thomas (Tommy) Dorsey in Santa Barbara to a traditional Irish Catholic family scarcely begins to capture the spiritual journey and contributions of this man. An excerpt from a longer article about Dorsey, by Kobai Scott Whitney, which first appeared in the Buddhist magazine *Lion's Roar*, can be found in the Appendix.

## Lesbians and Buddhism

The scholar Valerie Rylance views the concept of *lesbian Buddhism* as a feminist and political issue as much as a theological one, arguing convincingly that Buddhism, while typically depicted as inclusive and accepting, can be as gender-polarized and silencing of women (and sexual minorities, as she refers to queer people) as any other organized religion. She offers the following challenge to what she describes as the silencing and making invisible of lesbian Buddhists:

> Although few people are excluded from Buddhism, many are excluded from Buddhist representations, and if Western Buddhist traditions are to promote egalitarian ethics, they must consider issues of diversity. To be inclusive and welcoming of lesbians, Buddhist attitudes towards sexual orientation and identity should be made known and, if necessary, changed. Buddhist women are being innovative, and, given that lesbians have produced the most radical theologies in Christianity, it is reasonable to assume lesbians are producing the most radical innovations in Buddhism. However, while so little is known about lesbians in Buddhism, this remains speculative. By defining an area in the public domain for reporting and debating previously ignored experiences, the name "Lesbian Buddhism" challenges the status quo and creates an area dedicated to lesbian Buddhists' affirmation and support. (284)

Rylance's argument that naming, acknowledging, and making space in a tradition that describes itself as "promot[ing] egalitarian ethics" as, quite literally, an article of faith, has power as an opening for more conversation — and action.

## QUEER NEO-PAGANISM: EARTH-CENTERED SPIRITUALITY AND GODDESS WORSHIP

To begin with, the word *pagan* itself needs a little unraveling. The original word is derived from Latin and first meant someone who did not follow Christianity; it could also refer to someone who worshipped false (non-Christian) gods or idols. This meaning emerged around the fourteenth century CE. *Pagan* has been reclaimed by its adherents because it carries with it a sense of finding what is holy in what can be called *pantheism* (which finds the spirit of the holy in all existence, including natural and material entities, such as rivers, plants, forests, planets, and so forth) and polytheism (not unlike Hinduism).

This led those who identify in some way as **neo-pagans** to turn to spiritual practices and beliefs grounded in the general notion that the Earth is a living organism itself and that holiness and spirituality must be connected to respect for and a mystical union with all that is part of the life of the Earth, which is typically personified as feminine, whether it is Mother Nature or Gaia or some other divine being. Central to many versions of neo-paganism has been the role of the *shaman*, or holy person. Shamanism places emphasis on the shaman's ability to enter, often in a state of trance or dream, into spiritual and physical ecstasies that are not removed from the sensual and the erotic and that span multiple worlds. For some traditions, it is in those moments of ecstasy that the ritual healing of communal wounds takes place, and such a psychic and corporeal space is far from lacking in sexual energy.

### The Radical Faeries

In 1978 Henry "Harry" Hay, along with two other gay male activists, Don Kilhefner and Mitch Walker, organized a group dedicated to the development and spread of what they called a "gay consciousness," different in its set of beliefs and perspectives from the everyday assumptions of hegemonic heterosexist and heterosexual ways of experiencing the world and the spirit. They called themselves and their association **Radical Faeries** and held their first conference (which they preferred to call Faerie Circles) the following year. Both Hay and Walker were trained in Jungian psychology, from which the Radical Faeries drew a number of precepts for their sense of a different "gay consciousness." The term *Faeries* is a deliberate choice and a deliberate spelling. As you may know, during the twentieth century, the word *fairy* was frequently used as a derogatory term for a gay man, particularly for one who was viewed as (inappropriately) "effeminate" (a word less in use today, though still always intended to devalue a man). The three men decided to reclaim the word as a sign of their pride in rejecting normative masculin-

ity as an indicator of "maleness," adding the adjective *radical* both as a political signpost and as a spiritual (by way of physics and metaphysics) marker of
change. The spelling of the word *faerie* served to hark back to earlier mystical
and legendary traditions — you may have read the Renaissance poem *The
Faerie Queene* by Edmund Spenser. *Faerie* evokes not the everyday putdown
or even the figure out of children's literature, but a being both of and outside
the mundane, capable of great gifts and filled with great strength.

The Radical Faeries saw in Jung's concepts of the anima and the animus,
the two complementary spiritual domains of gender (the anima being the
feminine dimension of men and the animus the masculine dimension of
women), the potential to celebrate the feminine sides of gay men, rather
than the previous widely held belief that the masculine and the feminine
should be rigidly assigned to the binary biological sexes (little was known
and even less written or said about nonbinary bodies and individuals at this
point) and that there was a proper way to be male or female. Radical Faerie
gatherings are composed entirely of biological men (though similar groups,
such as Gay Spirit Visions, have permitted trans men to participate occasionally) and are therefore charged with a sexual energy that is understandably centered on male dimensions of the body and of sexual desire, but the
Radical Faeries work to integrate the feminine into their rituals and their
mindful activities. Thus, drag, understood as costuming and performance
(and separate from the dress of those who identify as transgender), is a spiritual as well as playful element of "worship" at gatherings. In particular,
many Faeries work tirelessly in preparing for gatherings to create the almost
ritualistic outfits and "scripts" for their female/feminine alter egos. For
some, this is an opportunity to honor female relatives, such as mothers and
grandmothers, by creating a conscious and deliberate link to their heritage;
they can thus use the opportunity to heal from what they had previously
experienced as wounding relationships and encounters with the feminine in
their family histories and create a kind of rebirth of matrilineal values.

Toby Johnson, whose book *Gay Spirituality* is an extended "scripture,"
notes that within the Radical Faeries (and other neo-pagan queer spiritual
traditions), gay spirituality can have different attributes, thus providing a
specific example of what Hay, Kilhefner, and Walker described as gay consciousness. Johnson suggests that gay spirituality (as envisioned and experienced within the neo-pagan traditions he practices) has the following
attributes. It is

1. Experienced from an outside perspective

2. Nondualistic

3. Incarnational (sex-positive and not otherworldly)

4. Evolutionary (and, therefore, challenging to the status quo of traditional religion)

5. Insight-provoking

6. Transformational

7. Adaptively virtuous (13–14)

Communality and communitarianism are central to the Radical Faeries, and, it is within this sense of being both one and together that the Radical Faeries do work that spans religion, psychology, and politics. It is no accident, then, that *place* and *space* are also critical to the work of Radical Faeries. One of the goals of the activities of the Radical Faeries is to connect the participants to a sense of the land, of being themselves extensions of the Earth as a macro-organism. In this regard, the Radical Faeries take some of their philosophy from Native American traditions, in which humans are viewed not as dominant over the land, but as inhabitants, like other animals and plants. Thus, there is always an awareness of a kind of ecological and nature-based spiritualism in the gatherings. Some men describe the gatherings as a way of "going home," putting aside the produced materialism of their everyday lives for something that feels more elemental and primal (Morgensen).

A number of rituals or celebrations associated with one of the better-known religions may have either emerged from a neo-pagan observance or belief or, over time, become combined with one. (Such combination of religious traditions is called syncretism.) One example of this can be found in the description in the Appendix, excerpted from an essay by the performance and folklore scholar John S. Gentile, of a gay men's neo-pagan celebration of Ostara, a Wiccan festival marking the vernal (spring) equinox. *Ostara* can be translated from High German as the equivalent of Easter. Read Gentile's description and analysis and consider how it fits Johnson's characterization of gay spirituality.

### Witchcraft, Dianic Wicca, and Women-Centered Neo-Paganism

Just as the Radical Faeries turned to neo-paganism to find a spiritual path that was not grounded in a history of patriarchy and heterocentrism, so women have revived or continued practices and communities focused on the worship of a goddess or of multiple goddesses. There is great variation among groups, some admitting or even encouraging men to join them in their worship, some being open only to women, whether the women identify as lesbian, bisexual, or some other sexuality. The place of trans-identified women remains contested: some groups include them, either simply *as* women (i.e., not drawing a distinction between biological anatomy and personal identification) or as yet another category of being, whose presence is acceptable and honored.

Many women-centered neo-paganist traditions hark back to the history of witchcraft in Europe and North America in past centuries and acknowledge the range of people targeted as witches. There is reasonable evidence to suggest that people identified as witches fell into a number of categories: women who were viewed as nonheteronormative; women and men who today might fit some of the criteria associated with mental illness or other forms of disability; older women; women and men who generally rejected social and political norms. In tying present-day paganism (neo-paganism) to the history of those persecuted as witches in past centuries, it is important to acknowledge that the historical line is neither perfect nor necessarily continuous.

The concept of **Wicca**, as a modern term, was used by Gerald Gardner and Doreen Valiente and is derived from an Anglo-Saxon term used for male and female witches. Because *witch* and *witchcraft* have been so strongly associated with satanism in Western cultures, *Wicca* became a less fraught term for those who wished to be involved in pagan forms of worship.

Wicca is practiced in many different ways. Many Wiccans subscribe to a belief in a centrally duotheistic structure of divinity, combining a Mother Goddess and her male equivalent, the Horned Man, each of whom has dominion over a different part of existence. In addition, some Wiccans believe in many more gods or other supernatural beings. The duotheistic structure may, in some respects, serve as a kind of binary, just as the notion of androgyny (the complementary elements of the masculine and the feminine) has been viewed. At the same time, because of this duotheism, there is no real privileging of one deity over the other (though the Mother Goddess is often viewed as more encompassing, since she is sometimes seen as synonymous with the Earth itself — Gaia in the original Greek).

In her study *A Community of Witches: Contemporary Neo-Paganism and Witchcraft in the United States,* the sociologist Helen A. Berger examines the spread of these forms of spirituality in the late twentieth century. Berger notes that in some women-only Wiccan groups there is an honoring of "the three aspects of the woman: the maid, the mother, and the crone" (37). What this feminist and women-centered approach to spirituality creates is a place to celebrate different ways of being female. The celebration of the maid is particularly central to some branches of women-centered spirituality, which are grouped together under the name "Dianic Wicca." Diana was the Roman goddess of the hunt. In the form of Dianic Wicca first popularized in modern times by Zsuzsanna Budapest in the 1970s in the United States, Diana was herself viewed as the avatar encompassing all goddesses (though not in the realm of fertility). Berger describes a Dianic ritual observed by the scholar Wendy Griffin: "In the ritual of the maid, Diana, the goddess of the hunt, was portrayed by a large woman, whose form would have been intimidating to many in mundane life, and was made more powerful within the ritual. This is no chaste virgin who fears going out in the world; this is an independent woman, who during the ritual appears coming across a moonlit field bare-breasted. She is the goddess, an element of all women, young, strong, capable, and independent" (37–38).

One of the most popular and prolific of queer people to write on neo-paganism in general is the writer and scholar Starhawk. Starhawk, whose best-known book is *The Spiral Dance* (originally published in 1979, and then revised for subsequent editions), identifies as neo-pagan, as ecofeminist, and as bisexual. These three axes of identity are inseparable for her and converge in her practice of goddess worship in Wicca, through which she views the environment as a manifestation of the sacred feminine. Her own identification as bisexual is, she argues, a critical piece of this spiritual practice: "When we hold the erotic as sacred, we say that our capacity for pleasure has a value in and of itself, that in fact it is one of the ways in which we connect with the deepest purpose of the universe. I believe that is a position we as bisexuals need to take. For our struggle is not only about affirming our own right to pleasure, but about affirming pleasure, variety, diversity, fluidity, as sacred values worth struggling for." She is careful not to privilege bisexuality over a "monosexual" orientation, but she does see in the experiences and consciousness of bisexual people a place to lead the world, including lesbians and gay men, beyond a narrow view of existence and possibilities.

## "GAYTHEISM" (AND "GAYGNOSTICISM"): BELIEF IN NONBELIEF

By their very definitions, atheism and agnosticism do not present a unified or singular set of beliefs. In a 2001 survey, known as the American Religious Identification Survey (ARIS), 14.1 percent of respondents described themselves as "without religion," but only 0.9 percent used either *atheist* or *agnostic* to describe their religious identity. Some people use the terms somewhat interchangeably, but there are significant differences worth observing. Atheism typically refers to the position that there is nothing beyond that which, at least in theory, can be observed scientifically or empirically. Christopher Hitchens summarized, in his book *God Is Not Great*, what he views as the four principal arguments against the existence of God and against the value of religion in society: "That it wholly misrepresents the origins of man and the cosmos, that because of this original error it manages to combine the maximum of servility with the maximum of solipsism, that it is both the result and the cause of dangerous sexual repression, and that it is ultimately grounded on wish-thinking." (4) Hitchens is here focusing on those believers whom we might group as fundamentalists or, in some instances, orthodox believers, who take the various scriptural accounts of creation as literal. His third argument, that it is the "cause of dangerous sexual repression," is, of course, of special interest, as it takes on issues connected to queerness and sexuality in general: prohibitions of nonheterosexual sexual and romantic activities.

Agnosticism is different from atheism in some important ways, most centrally in a difference between "absence of God" and "absence of knowledge," the latter of which is sometimes grounded in skepticism. Such skepticism may derive from any number of sources, from philosophical arguments to lack of personal experience of what might be described as the divine. Of course, neither atheism nor agnosticism precludes having an ethical code of conduct and regard for others and for the world. Some atheists and agnostics might argue that their positive and respectful conduct carries greater moral weight, as it is not predicated on a belief in a reward to come in a life beyond this one.

For others — and this is where it may most be useful to introduce the intersection between religion or faith and queerness — atheism or agnosticism may come about as a result not only of personal experience but of observation of social and global events and patterns. Some people who have identified as believers, growing up or through some portion of adulthood, have experiences and observations of the world that play a role in the shift from belief to disbelief. This shift can combine the social and the individual, and this is where the atheism or agnosticism of queer people can come into play. For people who have been raised in or practiced one of the traditional faiths, there can be what psychologists call *cognitive dissonance* between these teachings and their own experience of self and self-worth (as well as their regard for other people, whether they themselves identify as queer or not). They search genuinely to resolve the queer-negative claims (or interpretations) of their religion and the integrity and worth of their own lives. Some queer religious folk may find that the experience of coming out leads them to move away from faith completely and to adopt either an atheistic or agnostic attitude toward the universe. They find that the contradiction between the teachings of their "home" religion and their intrinsic or acquired sense of the positive value of being and living queer is impossible to reconcile.

In this sense, queer atheists and agnostics — as well as queer believers and non-queer nonbelievers — ask the same central question: How is one to live? In *Slouching towards Gaytheism: Christianity and Queer Survival in America* (2014), the literary and cultural scholar W. C. Harris argues, as his subtitle suggests, that Christianity as an organized religion poses serious and real threats to the well-being of queer people — from the ex-gay ministries described earlier to the cultures of "purity circles." He takes a hard line on the importance of queer people being actively resistant to organized religion, including the more moderate, inclusive, and affirming sects of some of the traditional Christian denominations. He doesn't have much use for alternative queer spirituality traditions such as those outlined by Toby Johnson, either. These practices, Harris suggests, retain a reinforcement of codes regarding what it means to be a man or a woman, masculine or feminine, gay or straight — in this sense, they once again divide experience and identity into the very binaries much queer theory and queer activism have sought to dismantle. Near the end of the book, he writes:

> It seems necessary, in closing, to ask what a gay embrace of atheism might mean for the queer individual. Given that the rejection of religion, including deinstitutionalized forms of spirituality, is unlikely to happen on a national level, it's worth considering gaytheism's personal and political implications. . . . The move to gaytheism . . . promotes a more civil standard of debate regarding the worth and dignity of citizens than current political and social rhetoric, which tends either to be directly infused with religious homophobia or invested in paradigms, such as spirituality, monogamy, and child-rearing, that reinforce heteronormative values and preserve invidious moral distinctions hostile to nonnormative individuals and communities. (197–198)
>
> "Gaytheism" also means to connote a project of believing in queerness, in our own subversive, nonnormative ethical cores, believing in it *more than* in the ability of religious authority, extra-mundane beings, or invidious normative valuations to make us whole, to sanction us in ways that queerness's best insights have taught us to question. . . . Being stamped as indelibly given or natural, sacred or elect, is an imprimatur — religious, cultural, or otherwise — whose cost is almost always paid by someone else. (207)

It may be that there is the possibility of a space for religion and atheism or agnosticism to coexist in a productive way. Chris Stedman maps out, in a narrative of his own spiritual journey, ways in which atheism can be part of valuable social and, one might say, spiritual (in the sense of enriching the inner life) collaborative work with faith-based initiatives. In his memoir, *Faitheist: How an Atheist Found Common Ground with the Religious*, Stedman describes his experience growing up in a relatively secular (though not overtly atheistic or agnostic) family in suburban Minnesota in straitened financial conditions. His family was not homophobic, and indeed, welcomed visits from a relative who they understood to be and whom they referred to as lesbian.

His "conversion experience" to Christianity came during middle school. He became involved with a cohort of young people in a local Christian youth program, and they invited him to join them. As he moved into adolescence, he became more and more aware and certain of his homosexual orientation, which was at odds with the teachings of his faith community. This led, as is often the case in such narratives, to a crisis of belief, in which something that felt core to his very being (his sexuality) was in extreme conflict with the form of Christianity he was part of. He describes the disappearance of faith, not only in this particular brand of worship, but in the existence of the God he had believed in during the height of his religious experiences. In his case, there was an overlap between his discovery (or acknowledgment) of his sexual orientation and the turn toward atheism. As a student at Augsburg College, a Lutheran school, he became a religion major, and this proved to be the crucible in which he would affirm his non-belief. In fact, he went on to take a graduate degree in religion at a Unitarian Universalist–based seminary. There Stedman continued his studies of religion, working in urban Chicago neighborhoods, to wed that which he learned to social activism, justice, and welfare: that he did not believe in God did not, for him, exclude doing work he described as "interfaith," working with people from other religions for the commonweal of a beleaguered city and its people. He eventually became the assistant humanist chaplain at Harvard University and served for a time as the humanist chaplain at Yale University. In 2017 he returned to Minneapolis, serving as a fellow at Augsburg, his alma mater.

Stedman is very clear in his claiming of atheism as core to his belief system. He even describes some complex, at times difficult conversations with more orthodox or fundamentalist religious believers, as well as with some of his fellow atheists. He recounts going to a dinner after a presentation by an atheist scholar and entering into a conversation with two people he had not previously met, both of whom also identified as atheist. When he described his own atheism, including a willingness to interact professionally and intellectually with people who were religious, one of the people rather scornfully dismissed him as one of those "faitheists." In an interview published elsewhere, Stedman elaborates on the meaning of the word: "It's one of several words used by some atheists to describe other atheists who are seen as too accommodating of religion. But to me, being a faitheist means that I prioritize the pursuit of common ground, and that I'm willing to put 'faith' in the idea that religious believers and atheists can and should focus on areas of agreement and work in broad coalitions to advance social justice" (Kimberly Winston, "What's a 'Faitheist'? Chris Stedman Explains," *Washington Post*, November 21, 2012, https://www.washingtonpost.com/national/on-faith/whats-a-faitheist-chris-stedman-explains/2012/11/21/5c39 dace-33ef-11e2-92f0-496af208bf23_story.html?utm_ term=.6b733c9e6756).

Christopher Hitchens, who was married to a woman but who was open about past same-sex experiences that lasted long into adulthood, participated in a debate held at Westminster in London in 2009, the topic of which was "whether the Catholic Church is a force for good in the world" ("Intelligence² Catholic Church Debate," December 2, 2009, https://www.amindatplay.eu/en/2009/12/02/intelligence²-catholic-church-debate-tran script/). As his speech moved toward it climax and conclusion, he turned to matters of most relevance to our study; speaking of the influence of Catholicism on African nations, he said:

> I think it will one day be admitted with shame that it might have been in error to say that AIDS is bad as a disease, very bad, but not quite as bad as condoms are bad, or not as immoral in the same way. I say it in the presence of His Grace, and I say it to his face, the teachings of his church are responsible for the death and suffering and misery of his brother and sister Africans, and he should apologise for it, he should show some shame. For condemning my friend Stephen Fry for his nature, for saying you couldn't be a member of our church, you're born in sin. He's not being condemned for what he does, he's being condemned for what he is. You're a child made in the image of God — oh no, you're not, you're a faggot, and you can't go to heaven. This is disgraceful, it's inhuman, it's obscene, and it comes from a clutch of hysterical, sinister virgins, who've already betrayed their charge in the children of their own church. For shame! For shame!

Hitchens's speech claims an ethics of viewing the valuation of lives and the complexities of those lives as not being determined by anything external to what humans can construct (including ideas, systems of thought, and actions) and not dependent on forces or unseeable (in an empirical sense), incomprehensible realms. Like Stedman, Hitchens here argues that the question of what makes the virtuous life is not a question to ask of a deity or of a set of scripts that have been authorized because of their (attributed) sacred validity. In that sense, atheism and agnosticism may indeed be practices of spirituality in the broadest sense.

## ISSUES FOR INVESTIGATION

**1.** As a group, discuss Toby Johnson's schema for gay consciousness. What aspects of gay spirituality are nondualistic? (And how does this either complicate or resolve the questions about the potential to reify binary divisions raised by such concepts as "masculine" and "feminine" in the ideal of "androgyny"?) If "adaptively virtuous" means that virtues themselves are always changing and that new ones emerge for new situations and world conditions, what in gay spirituality might be considered "adaptive virtues"? (Johnson names androgyny, wonder, love, adventure, innocence, transparency, selflessness, and generosity as some of the adaptive virtues of gay spirituality.) In what ways do gay people experience these qualities differently from an imagined majoritarian or everyday straight society? What might "straight society" (assuming such a thing exists) learn from gay (outsider) perspectives?

**2.** If you were raised in or participate in a faith tradition, investigate in more detail its stance on queer people and queer activities. On what does it base its creed? If you were not raised in a religious tradition, can you identify the ways in which that has also shaped your views on queerness? If you identify as queer and continue to consider yourself a believer, how do you reconcile these two parts of your identity?

## SUGGESTIONS FOR FURTHER READING AND VIEWING

Alameddine, Rabih. *The Angel of History.* New York: Atlantic Monthly, 2016.

Curb, Rosemary, and Nancy Manahan, eds. *Lesbian Nuns: Breaking Silence.* Tallahassee: Naiad Press, 1985.

Jama, Afdhere. *Queer Jihad: LGBT Muslims on Coming Out, Activism, and the Faith.* N.p.: Oracle Releasing, 2013.

*A Jihad for Love.* Directed by Parvez Sharma. First Run Features, 2009.

Loughlin, Gerard, ed. *Queer Theology: Rethinking the Western Body.* Malden, MA: Blackwell, 2007.

Pattanaik, Devdutt, comp. *The Man Who Was a Woman and Other Queer Tales from Hindu Lore.* Binghamton, NY: Haworth Press, 2002.

Schneider, David. *Street Zen: The Life and Work of Issan Dorsey.* 2nd ed. Cambridge, MA: Da Capo Press, 1999.

Thompson, Mark. *Gay Spirit: Myth and Meaning.* New York: St. Martin's Press, 1987.

Vines, Matthew. *God and the Gay Christian: The Biblical Case in Support of Same-Sex Relationships.* New York: Convergent Books, 2015.

<br>

# CHAPTER 11

# QUEERING CITIZENSHIP
## Politics, Power, and Justice

What does it mean to be a "citizen," and are there better and worse ways to be one? What does it mean to be a "queer citizen" – and is being a queer citizen different from being a good citizen? The language of citizenship pervades daily life — and it is sufficiently powerful that, at the height of the first wave of the AIDS epidemic, in 1990, four leaders from the HIV/AIDS activist group ACT UP decided to form a broader organization, which they called **Queer Nation**, to address the kinds of physical, social, and structural violence they were witnessing against LGBTQ+ people. The epidemic brought with it a return of the kinds of tactics used during the 1950s by Joseph McCarthy and the "witch hunters" of the Red Scare, which also targeted queer people as being both sexual and political deviants. Just as the Red-baiters used the term **comintern** to designate those involved (or believed to be involved) in an international conspiracy to spread communism in the West, so the term **homintern** was used as early as the 1930s to add the layer of sexual "otherness" to often phantasmic figures.

The term *Queer Nation*, then, was an intentionally provocative one: the word *queer* was only then reentering the vocabulary of LGBTQ+ people as one with potentially positive power, especially when embraced by those who usually heard it as a slur. Queer Nation used the language of nationhood, which has long been central to concepts of patriotism, and also claimed space for queer citizens in the democracy that the United States identifies itself with. At the same time, its foregrounding of *queer* marked a territory — political and social, rather than geographic — with all that goes with territories — boundaries, admittedly shifting and sometimes contested, as well as features that bind citizens together.

What makes someone a citizen, anyway? There are, of course, a number of different ways to answer this question. Someone is usually conferred citizenship automatically by dint of being born in a specific place or to parents who have been identified by rule of law as citizens of a specific place. Thus, the whole "birther" issue surrounding Barack Obama, both

Henderson, Bruce, *Queer Studies: Beyond Binaries*
dx.doi.org/10.17312/harringtonparkpress/2019.09.qsbb.011
© 2019 by Harrington Park Press

during his campaigns and throughout his presidency, was in virtually all respects a red herring, a false issue, about which there was already settled law in place. According to the *Oxford English Dictionary*, the most common definition of the term *citizenship* includes "the rights to live and work in a particular nation state and to participate in its politics while being subject to taxation" (https://keywords.ace.fordham.edu/index.php/Citizenship_and_Queer). The Fordham website from which the *OED* definition is taken goes on to suggest that there are less legalistic and more social understandings of the term: "A citizen is also someone who holds membership in a certain geographic location and one who actively participates in the society of their specific region. Voting, taking part in community events, community service, or working a job are all responsibilities of being known as a citizen, or having citizenship."

It is important to acknowledge that the word *citizenship* should not be assumed to be an absolute and automatic guarantee either of rights (though one wishes that were the case) or of social acceptance. The critical race theorist Devon W. Carbado, in an essay titled "Racial Naturalization," distinguishes between *citizenship* and *naturalization,* as he looks specifically at his experience as a black man born in the United Kingdom and residing in the United States. He recounts various incidents in which police have read his racial appearance as an excuse or explanation for surveillance of various intrusive kinds. Traffic stops, house searches — these may be legally acceptable practices to which citizens, as part of what is often called "the social contract," agree (though the question of how "reasonable" such actions are remains a constitutionally debatable one), but the fact that they are statistically imposed more on nonwhite (particularly black) men speaks to what Carbado calls *naturalization,* which ironically, he suggests, may be granted to white noncitizens. For example, Carbado relates an incident when he and his brothers (all from the West Indies) were stopped by the police in a traffic incident. Their Caribbean accents, he argues, combined with their skin color, served to denaturalize them to the police. He suggests that whiteness, regardless of the national origin of an individual, may confer certain kinds of informal naturalization on individuals — that to be American on various levels is to be viewed and treated with the kinds of respect that, consciously or unconsciously, authority figures and many ordinary citizens grant to most white people (unless a white person does something to violate the tacit expectations of behavior and adherence to social norms). So a white German tourist may be "naturalized" in ways that a United States–born black person might not. One could extend Carbado's argument to suggest that the epidemic of police shootings of young men of color in the United States are acts of denaturalization.

Carbado is most centrally interested in racial naturalization, but his more general distinction between citizenship (which may be a legal status, but it does not necessarily offer social or political protection) and naturalization may be of value in thinking about queer issues in terms of citizenship. Can you think of examples in which queer people, who may possess citizenship, are denaturalized because of their sexual orientation or gender identity? The line between citizenship and naturalization may blur, as it has in recent court battles regarding such questions as whether a baker is required to provide a wedding cake for a same-sex marriage (a case that began in Colorado and has made its way to higher courts; the U.S. Supreme Court found in the baker's favor, but on very narrow terms that were specific to how legal procedure was handled in the case, rather than a broader principle) and whether Kim Davis, a Kentucky county clerk, has the right to refuse to issue marriage certificates to same-sex couples. Carbado might say that Davis's decision to have other employees in her office issue the certificates shows the gap between citizenship and naturalization and the potential dangers of assuming that citizenship in and of itself guarantees fair and equal treatment. While Davis may declare that she has fulfilled her obligation to same-sex couples by not making it impossible for them to get married (thus acknowledging their citizenship), she herself, by refusing to issue or sign the certificates, denaturalizes these couples. For trans people, denaturalization may come in making it difficult or impossible for them to obtain forms of identification that reflect their self-identified gender (probably not the one that is on their birth certificates). Once we start making the distinction between citizenship (a legal concept) and naturalization (a set of social practices), we can see how thorny a concept citizenship becomes.

Key to most uses of the term *citizenship* is another word, *public* (in contrast to *private*), or, more specifically the term, coined by the German philosopher Jürgen Habermas, the **public sphere**. The public sphere is not in its most philosophically resonant sense a literal place of bricks and mortar, but rather an intellectual and what might be called discursive space (i.e., a place where people talk and write): "a virtual or imaginary community which does not necessarily exist in any identifiable space" (Soules). For Habermas, the public sphere, though originating from the rule of "public authority," is a place of possibilities and optimism, and it is through the talk that is produced within the public sphere that, if a government is to serve its citizens well, policies, laws, and values become articulated and realized.

In most Anglo-European countries in the past three or four centuries, the public sphere has been dominated by assumptions of heterosexuality and maleness as norms (even when not named as such), and the discourse created that leads to laws and practices has tended to make queer opinions, beliefs, and arguments invisible or minimized. Eric O. Clarke, whose 2000 book *Virtuous Vice* elaborates on Habermas's theories, argues that hetero-sexism had the power for "defining proper civic personhood" (5) — that is, that to be a proper citizen meant to be or at least act out the social script of being heterosexual. Clarke traces the emergence of queer voices in the public sphere from its beginnings in the early homosexual rights movements in the late nineteenth and early twentieth centuries, centered in Germany, by such leaders as Magnus Hirschfeld. Hirschfeld was a German-Jewish physi-cian who in 1897 founded what is typically credited as the first modern organization dedicated to studying and advocating for the rights of homo-sexuals, the Scientific Humanitarian Committee, which, as its name sug-gests, argued that scientific research would lead to better understanding and improved rights for people who would today be identified as queer. In particular, the committee (and Hirschfeld as its leader) worked for the repeal of the notorious Paragraph 175, which criminalized homosexual acts, even between consenting adults. Hirschfeld was able to reintroduce the subject of homosexuality into the public sphere, first in 1919 by founding the *Institut für Sexualwissenschaft* (Institute for Sexual Research) and then in 1921 by organizing the First Congress for Sexual Reform, which drew researchers and activists from many countries. He continued the work to repeal Paragraph 175, which was not formally removed until 1994.

Clarke views the history of the political discourse of homosexuality as what he calls "visibility politics," wherein one of the central goals is to do just what Hirschfeld continued to do — make the marginal or the oppressed become visible, even if they are not yet fully viewed as citizens in the major-itarian sense of citizenship. Clarke argues that, during the period when he was writing (the beginning of the twenty-first century), the most pervasive problem in the placement of queer life in the public sphere involved the mar-ginalization and devaluing, often within the LGBTQ+ community itself (and more in the LGB than in the T segment, to be sure), of what he cites Ellen DeGeneres as calling the "scary homosexual." This figure somehow stands for all who are most "outside" the public sphere of normativity; they are often identified as the people who those who pine for assimilation wish would not participate in the annual Pride parades: "Dykes on Bikes," men and women representing and performing publicly the costumes, props, and scripts of the leather or BDSM community, trans people who do not pass (some might say, cannot pass) or, conversely, trans people who pass too well and therefore are viewed by some as "deceptive" in their presentation of gender, just to name a handful (68). Such figures, Clarke argues, sit uneas-ily with the public sphere's need to maintain "erotic propriety" (43). These figures (for they are viewed as types or groups rather than as individuals in public discourse) test and create conflict in what are sometimes viewed as oppositional forces between autonomy (which is not simply to be relegated to the private or intimate sphere, but is closely identified with a certain aspect of U.S. citizenship) and conformity, a foundational value of, in particular, middle-class citizenship. Queer people will fully gain what Clarke calls "enfranchisement," he suggests, only at "the point at which all forms of official and unofficial social membership and participation converge" (36).

Membership in groups, especially groups with power, typically leads, whether consciously or not, to some degree of acceptance of the norms, the typical beliefs or practices of the group. It is in this sense that the system of homonormativity also "upholds and sustains" the "assumptions and institutions" of heteronormativity. There are other ways as well. Turning again to education, we might say that when queer people do not question the preponderance of examples in textbooks or classroom lectures that assume heterosexuality as the default position (say, in discussions of domestic arrangements or economic and professional opportunities) — and we are doing so either out of timidity or out of a desire *not* to be viewed as "that queer" who always insists on bringing up queer examples when a "more general" principle is being explored — we are "upholding" and "sustaining" heteronormativity. In this example, it may be that we are participating in "our" own "demobilization" — that we are willing participants in our own silencing in Habermas's public sphere. Either from exhaustion or from a wish to gain approval as a good gay classroom citizen, we simply tell ourselves that it is reasonable for the examples always (or nearly always) to use male-female or cisgender couples as examples, because *they* are the majority and *we* cannot expect our minority experiences ever to become the focus.

## HOMONORMATIVITY AND HOMONATIONALISM

Some people would argue that the goals of being a good citizen or a citizen of a nation-state at all are fundamentally problematic, in terms of advocating for and acting for any semblance of global or universal justice, that notions of citizenship by their very definition involve unequal degrees of power, which often are based on economic inequities or historically determined valuing of some identity categories over others. Two terms have been coined to critique these processes: **homonormativity** and **homonationalism**. The first term was popularized by the scholar Lisa Duggan, who defined it as "a politics that does not contest dominant heteronormative assumptions and institutions, but upholds and sustains them" (179), a process we considered above. In addition to upholding heteronormative standards as the "ideal" for queer people as well, homonormativy also carries with it an implicit agreement to act as what Michel Foucault called "docile bodies": Duggan suggests that such a practice of homonormativity and homonationalism also involves "promising the possibility of a demobilized gay constituency and a privatized, depoliticized gay culture anchored in domesticity and consumption" (179). A less frequently used term, but one that is equally important, is *transnormativity*, which does work similar to what *homonormativity* does, but with respect to gender identity — engaging trans people as socially and politically acceptable so long as they conform to gender norms associated with the gender with which they identify. For this reason, more radical trans activists today place less emphasis on passing than they have in past eras, wanting not to have their own presentation of gender dictated to them as a condition of naturalization, to use Carbado's term again. We should hasten to add that a desire to pass as the gender with which one identifies need not be viewed as regressive; such desires, choices, and possibilities are best looked at through the complexity of individual people's lives and histories.

Workplace behaviors provide examples of both heteronormativity and homonormativity in action. If a queer worker places a photograph of their partner or spouse on their desk, they may fear (or be told directly by coworkers, including supervisors with more power), that it would be better if clients who come into the office did not have to see evidence of the worker's private life, though nothing is said to the coworker who displays a picture of their opposite-sex spouse or partner: the office then becomes a heteronormative space. And even if the queer person internally registers the inequality in such a request or instruction, they may remain silent and simply do as told, because they know from experience that, even if they won this particular battle, it might result in all employees' being prohibited from displaying anything personal in a work space; the queer worker thus earns the resentment of all coworkers. If the office manager allows pictures of same-sex-headed families, but polices them to make sure there is, for example, no trace of queer culture (say, pictures taken at a Pride parade, or images in which one or both parents make their trans identity explicit) appears that might lead viewers to think of the family as anything different from the heteronormative family they are most familiar with and probably comfortable with. Policies of "appropriateness" can mask assumptions about how to be a good LGBTQ+ citizen, worker, or community member in a normative society.

Some of the earliest LGB (almost never T) organizations formed in the 1950s, such as the Mattachine Society and the Daughters of Bilitis, may be seen as operating in somewhat homonormative ways, for reasons that are probably more understandable when viewed in historical contexts. In the first years after the end of World War II, what queers may have wanted more than anything was a kind of benign neglect. Just as some women resisted the imperative to leave jobs they had acquired during the war to make way for returning men, so queers wanted both the right to associate with whomever they wanted, a right guaranteed by the First Amendment (though states were not obliged to uphold that right until a series of cases tested and pushed the question of free association), and to live their private lives as they wanted. Many of the members of these associations believed the best way to achieve these goals was to appear, dress, and behave as "normally" as possible, and to display their badges and behaviors of queerness only in the not-always-safe spaces of private homes and clubs.

Another term associated with homonormativity and essentially a global extension of it is *homonationalism*, a concept most extensively theorized by the ethnic and gender studies scholar Jasbir Puar in her 2007 book *Terrorist Assemblages: Homonationalism in Queer Times*. Puar uses the term *homonationalism* to expand some of the aspects of homonormativity to global and transnational situations and processes, particularly as they involve queer people and a generalized concept of queerness that circulates to other people who are viewed by the majority or the powerful as different or inferior. She begins her discussion of her theory with the commemoration on July 19, 2006, of the International Day of Action against Homophobic Persecution in Iran, on the first-year anniversary of the execution by hanging of two young Iranian men for homosexuality (ix). She uses it as the foundation of her larger argument, which is that some of the West's (particularly the United States') involvement in the Day of Action might well have been motivated by or certainly correlated with a desire to justify a military invasion of Iran. For Puar, this day symbolizes what she will come to define as homonationalism, which involves the "queered darkening of terrorists" (xiii). The West has, she suggests, used the execution of queer bodies that it would otherwise have queered (not in a positive sense) because of their race (i.e., the "darkening" of the Iranian bodies). Puar sees this strategy as morally unsupportable, as she views the United States' involvement as not genuinely interested in the young men themselves, nor does she see the United States (and other Western countries that participated in the Day of Action) as being engaged in what queerness in Iran means or how it works culturally. She sees it as an imposition of Western concepts of queerness on these darkened bodies. The term *pinkwashing* has been used to describe a complementary, but opposite process: countries or cultures describing themselves as queer-friendly as a way of distracting public critique of mistreatment of groups of people subjected to other forms of discrimination; one frequently cited example, controversial to be sure, is the depiction of Israel as queer-friendly, which, some argue, may be a way to try to deflect attention from what its critics see as devaluation of Palestinian bodies. Pinkwashing works by seeming to suggest that being politically positive toward one group (or one issue) obviates negative attitudes toward or actions against people for other reasons, such as race, religion, or ethnicity. Similarly, this tactic can be used to reinforce transphobia; a country or society (or individual, for that matter) can act or speak in positive ways about LGB people, which may shield it from accusations of discrimination against trans people (and vice versa).

She further argues that heteronormative politics pulls queer people into citizenship by rewarding them for supporting military aggression and violence toward non-Western countries, such as Iran, in the wake of 9/11. She suggests that homonationalism permits inclusion of LGBTIQ (the acronym she uses) sexualities at the expense of the antiracism she sees as the core of a radical and socially just performance of positive queer citizenship. She observes: "There is a transition under way in how queer subjects are relating to nation-states, particularly the United States, from being figures of death (i.e., the AIDS epidemic) to becoming tied to ideas of life and productivity (i.e., gay marriage and families). The politics of recognition and incorporation entail that certain — but certainly not most — homosexual, gay, and queer bodies may be the temporary recipients of 'measures of benevolence' that are afforded by liberal discourses of multicultural tolerance and diversity" (xiv). The commitments she identifies are, as might be expected, a tacit or explicit endorsement of a kind of white or at the very least Western supremacy: "This benevolence toward sexual others is contingent upon ever-narrowing parameters of white racial privilege, consumption capabilities, gender and kinship normativity, and bodily integrity" (xiv–xv). In other words, only queer people who fit into what Puar calls these "ever-narrowing parameters" of those who have been traditionally deemed acceptable as citizens in the United States (and many other Western countries) receive the benevolence (acceptance, approval, access to rights) of the hegemonic or authoritative government. Domestically, homonationalism plays out in more complex and in some respects conflicted ways in the ongoing debates about and tensions regarding immigration policies and immigration "reform" (which means quite different things to different factions).

## QUEER POLITICS IN THE UNITED STATES

### Some General Principles and Concepts

In her 2012 book *Gay Rights at the Ballot Box*, Amy Stone makes an important distinction between two broad areas of political change in LGBTQ+ history: **social movements** and **ballot measures** (17). The shape of each and the strategies that succeed most for each are very different, and activists would do well to consider how differences between them lead to different choices and, typically, different outcomes. Social movements, as Stone (and others) define them, tend to be broader and longer in their ambitions:

thus, the fight for LGBTQ+ rights might be viewed as a social movement whose narrative has changed over time. Though a single event or act may be deemed a landmark or turning point in a social movement, a closer analysis will reveal change at microlevels along the way.

Often, such changes that result from social movements are reflected powerfully in the way people begin to behave on an everyday level — what the sociologist Pierre Bourdieu called **habitus** (as in *habit*), a way of performing everyday social life. Such a major event as the Stonewall Riots may stand in the public sphere as a harbinger of change already in motion or about to occur; the habitus may be seen in what then becomes internalized and is viewed as acceptable and (often implicitly) agreed-on by people who might not view themselves as political activists.

But these shifts in practice come about both through the longer time spans of social movements and through individual acts and changes in laws and policies. Stone, then, distinguishes between the processes of social movements, which tend to be more ambitious and wide-sweeping, and such specific individual changes in law or policy as can be effected through balloting, where voters make decisions about specific referenda, such as same-sex marriage. In analyzing many of these instances, Stone concludes that "campaign politics is rarely queer politics," meaning that working to get the electorate to make such large changes through voting tends to end in defeat on the biggest issues (xxviii). This is in part because social movements, being larger and more complex, become blurrier for many voters, and they can thus make voters resistant to what seems like "too much all at once." Such examples as the notorious repeal of gay rights in Dade County, Florida, in 1977 as a result of very visible and active campaigning led by the former beauty queen and archconservative Anita Bryant, is one of the most dramatic examples Stone identifies.

Stone also suggests that working at levels more local than the federal government is more useful and more likely to have queer-friendly outcomes: state, county, even city ballot measures may be more successful. An example is the case of the Briggs Initiative, formally known as Proposition 6, a California referendum that would have banned LGBTQ+ individuals from teaching in public elementary and secondary schools. In examining the successful defeat of this measure, Stone identifies the considerable importance of local activists in making contact with voters and getting them to acknowledge to themselves the LGBTQ+ people in their lives and even some of the braver teachers who were already out and making a difference in the schools.

Stone goes on to examine other ballot measures regarding LGBTQ+ rights that either passed or failed, such as similar same-sex marriage initiatives in Oregon, which succeeded, and Colorado, which failed. She holds the Oregon campaign up as a model for the following reasons: (1) high degree of voter contact (recall that this strategy helped defeat the Briggs Initiative in California); (2) messaging (not just providing a cogent and persuasive content, but being innovative and creative in how to disseminate it); and (3) managing the size and scale of the campaign (knowing how large to make it and how to limit it to something voters would support) (69). She also points to elements that are common to successful social movements and ballot initiatives — fund-raising and increasing professional campaign staff. Both may seem outside the lofty goals of changing society, but labor is inextricable from achieving progress. The campaigners in Oregon were also able to identify central challenges in order to consider whether and how to address them: rural campaigns against same-sex marriage and the widespread use of direct mail (often with misleading or simply incorrect information) by opponents. In this campaign, the LGBTQ+ community did a better job in reaching out to African American voters (and the demographics skewed less evangelical among them in Oregon).

One weakness Stone identifies in many LGBTQ+ ballot-box initiatives is what she calls "the problem of transgender exclusion" (170). This refers not only to the tendency of LGBTQ+ political activists to focus on issues most relevant to cisgender queer people, but also to a hesitation to give transgender people a prominent place in the campaign team — in a sense, creating a strategic invisibility, not unlike the ghost of Ellen DeGeneres's "scary homosexual." Attitudes may be changing, but there may still be the belief that transgender people are too nonnormative to be effective door-to-door campaigners. Indeed, the transgender historian Susan Stryker has argued that this is a form of homonormativity enforced within the queer community itself.

## LGBTQ+ Politicians and Electoral Politics

The first members of the U.S. Congress to identify as openly gay were Representatives Gerry Studds in 1983 and Barney Frank in 1987, both of Massachusetts. Neither was out at the time of his election; both came out publicly as the result of scandal that brought their private lives to the public sphere. Studds was involved in a broader investigation in 1983 of officials' involvement with congressional pages, young — in some cases underage — high school students who serve primarily as delivery persons for congresspersons. Frank's outing was as a result of his involvement with Steve Gobie, a sex worker, whom he initially hired for his professional services. Eventually, he invited Gobie to live with him, and Gobie, without Frank's knowledge, used the home to continue his illegal work. When Frank was informed of this by his landlord, he evicted Gobie. Gobie threatened to take the story to the media and, in response, Frank requested that Congress investigate the situation, an act intended to co-opt Gobie's grab for money and fame. Frank was reprimanded, but he was consistently reelected to serve both his state and the country as a whole.

Space precludes discussion of, even listing of, every openly queer elected official since Elaine Noble (also of Massachusetts) opened the closet door in 1974, but it is worth acknowledging two additional figures, as they have not only served the country with courage, power, and eloquence, but embody the complicated intersectional axes of identity many queer politicians live. Barbara Jordan, an African American, first served in the Texas state senate, the first African American since the Reconstruction period to do so; she then represented Texas in the House of Representatives, becoming the first southern African American woman to do so. The other, Tammy Baldwin, is the first openly gay or lesbian person to be elected to the Senate; she is notable because she was the first woman elected to represent her state, Wisconsin, thus highlighting both her gender and sexual orientation, as well as the first openly gay woman from any state to be elected to the House. While Jordan was not publicly out during her lifetime, those who knew her privately were aware of her twenty-year relationship with the educational psychologist Nancy Earl. The Human Rights Campaign describes Earl as Jordan's "long-time companion, co-owner of their home, executor of her estate, primary care giver and lifesaver." Baldwin has been out throughout her political career, which makes the intersection of identities as woman and queer person, both still greatly underrepresented in national electoral politics, a source of power and evidence of courage.

## Criminalizing Queerness: Sodomy Laws

Of all the laws that have either been explicitly designed to limit the rights of LGBTQ+ people or been implemented unequally with prejudice toward them, the most high-profile and long-lasting have been laws that are referred to under the umbrella "sodomy laws." Sodomy laws (or their equivalent) have existed in many countries for many centuries. What has been consistent about them is their very inconsistency — what is covered by the term *sodomy* itself, to begin with (recall from the previous chapter how much disagreement there was and is over what the story of Lot and Sodom referred to as the city's "evil"), and what kinds of penalties and punishments should be meted out for various acts covered by the laws. Though sodomy laws are typically most strongly associated in the public sphere with consensual sex between men (laws have been more frequently silent on sex between women specifically), they also could include bestiality, sex with minors, and any sexual acts that were not designed for or could not result in reproduction.

Throughout most of the history of the United States, sodomy laws have been handled primarily at the state level, which led to a confusing and somewhat arbitrary set of policies and standards, not unlike the variation in age-of-consent laws, which remain in place today. Illinois was the first state to legally decriminalize sex between members of the same sex, in 1962, and others followed until, in 2002, thirty-six of the fifty states had repealed the laws or seen the judicial system dismantle them, as it often found them unconstitutional.

The constitutionality of sodomy laws, in the last decades of the twentieth century, became the center of the debate that ultimately led to the over-turning of sodomy laws at the federal level, through a series of cases that made their way to the U.S. Supreme Court. What the cases had in common was issues of whether there could be such a thing as a right to engage in sodomy and what the limits or extensions of *privacy* as a right of citizenship meant in private and intimate contexts. The first of the major cases that led to the legal change was decided in 1986, *Bowers v. Hardwick.* (Court cases are typically referred to by the names of the opposing sides, in this instance Michael J. Bowers, then attorney general of Georgia, and Michael Hardwick, a private citizen arrested under Georgia's sodomy law.) Though Hardwick's sexual partner was included in the case, he was referred to only as "et al." ("and others"). Hardwick paid a fifty-dollar fine for the lesser charge of throwing a beer bottle into a bush.

The local district attorney declined to take the case to trial, both for the technical reason that the warrant for the arrest was both expired and incor-rect, given that Hardwick had already paid the fine for the "throwing" or littering violation, but Hardwick sued the state's attorney general on the grounds that the sodomy law was itself a violation of his civil rights as a gay man — that, even if this case was dismissed, he would be vulnerable to arrest at any time. At this point, the American Civil Liberties Union became involved and offered to represent Hardwick in court. The case against the State of Georgia was first dismissed and then, on appeal, upheld, until it finally reached the nation's Supreme Court.

The Supreme Court upheld the sodomy law five to four. The majority opinion centered its argument on the issues of rights and privacy, both of which are at the core of the Fourteenth Amendment. Byron White, writing for the majority, stated that they did not find that the amendment extended to the right to engage in sodomy even in private settings (obviously, other laws criminalized public sex — "lewd and lascivious behavior," or "L&L," as they are commonly called). The majority further asserted that sodomy itself (here referring pretty exclusively to sex between members of the same sex and, inferentially, specifically to anal sex between men) has throughout history been considered against nature (as if nature were an entity with conscious will and opinions), and, therefore, there is no right to violate what they would view as "natural" law — that is, what is acceptable based on normative perceptions of what is natural, either explicitly or implicitly.

The dissenting minority pointed out that the majority opinion focused almost exclusively on homosexuality with, in Justice Harry Blackmun's words, an "almost obsessive focus." Justice John Paul Stevens concurred with Blackmun, writing his own dissent, arguing that the majority decision distinguished between homosexual and heterosexual couples — that, on the basis of previous cases, the Court had ruled that there was no right to violate the privacy of heterosexual couples' sexual activities, which could just as easily fit definitions of sodomy as those of homosexual couples, and it is indeed true that the ruling applied explicitly to homosexual sex.

The case that led to the ultimate dismantling of sodomy laws at the federal level was *Lawrence v. Texas*, decided in June 2003. Like *Bowers v. Hardwick*, this case had its origins in what might be seen as something private being accidently thrust into the public sphere. *Lawrence* arose because three men, two of whom were long-term friends and the third a romantic partner of one, got themselves into a complex interpersonal dynamic that led one to seek revenge by calling the police. John Lawrence was socializing in his apartment with a friend, Robert Eubanks, and Eubanks's date (they had been involved with each other, but would not have been described as a long-term couple), Tyron Garner. Eubanks thought Lawrence and Garner were flirting, and he took the opportunity when he left the apartment to call the police and tell them that there was a black man with a gun acting dangerously at Lawrence's address. The police arrived, entered the unlocked apartment, and found the two men — doing what appears to remain in contention. One of the officers claimed to have seen them having anal sex, another oral sex, and two others present did not say that they saw any sexual activity. Because the arresting officer claimed to have seen them engaged in anal sex, the Texas sodomy law applied. Lawrence and Garner were arrested and spent the night in jail; Eubanks was later charged with filing a false report, to which he pled guilty, but for which he served less than thirty days.

An important LGBTQ+ organization, Lambda Legal, helped bring this relatively limited (in terms of fines and penalties) case to the national spotlight as yet another test case for sodomy laws. Lambda Legal focused its case on three issues: (1) equal protection for homosexuals under the Fourteenth Amendment; (2) violation of liberty and privacy, also guaranteed under this amendment; (3) the whole question of whether *Bowers v. Hardwick* should be revisited and overturned on the violations stated in 1 and 2 (Carpenter 185).

What Lambda Legal did was ask for reconsideration of the earlier decision, in light of the different times, a shift in the membership on the Court, and new forms of evidence, especially expert testimony by organizations ranging from the American Psychological Association to the Log Cabin Republicans (an association of politically conservative gay people, primarily men). While Log Cabin Republicans may well be outliers in typical queer culture, here they could help bolster a kind of "rainbow coalition" of LGBT (if not necessarily queer) perspectives. Conservatives and liberals alike can agree on the importance of the Constitution in establishing and guaranteeing rights, and both groups have strong investments, if different ones, in the guarantee of privacy.

This time the Supreme Court decided in favor of arguments for liberty and privacy—that is, that Lawrence (and Garner) did have the right to engage in whatever sexual activities he agreed to and to the privacy of his intimate space. The decision was not as closely split this time, six to three. Some have suggested that it helped that the opposing side this time did not appear as invested in winning the case and that the oral argument seemed unpersuasive and disengaged. The effect was not only to find in favor of the plaintiffs as individuals, but, in effect, to find sodomy laws in other states unconstitutional (though some of them remain on the books, if unenforceable).

## Same-Sex Marriage or Marriage Equality

Same-sex couples have formed marriage-like arrangements for as long as there have been pairs of people who have wanted to pledge their lives to each other. Couples have found ways, not unlike African American enslaved people, also forbidden by law to marry, to solemnize their relationships in meaningful ways. The push to legalize same-sex marriage in the United States, though it gained momentum and heat in the last two decades, can be traced back to such documents as an opinion piece in the gay and lesbian magazine *One* in 1963, "Let's Push Homophile Marriage." Two men decided to test the legal waters in 1970. Jack Baker and Michael McConnell applied for a marriage license in Minneapolis that year. A sympathetic clerk issued them one, though the marriage was quickly declared invalid. The couple took the case to the Minnesota Supreme Court, where it was defeated, and the U.S. Supreme Court, where it was rejected, but their act began a discourse on what in recent years has been called "marriage equality."

In 1983 a Harvard Law student, Evan Wolfson, wrote a 141-page term paper for a third-year class, arguing for the right of same-sex couples to marry; its title, "Samesex Marriage and Morality: The Human Rights Vision of the Constitution," suggests the terms on which advocates would argue— the constitutional equality and moral values same-sex marriage could promote. The latter, the arguments based on moral values, was the tack taken by such conservative gay proponents of same-sex marriage as Andrew Sullivan and Jonathan Rauch, who argued that same-sex marriage would bring queer people, especially gay men, more fully into the moral universe of citizenship. One of the effects of the growing AIDS epidemic in the 1980s and 1990s was to demonstrate how the absence of same-sex marriage worked in adversarial, often openly cruel ways against the wishes and commitments of queer people, especially gay men, the demographic hit hardest in the United States by the disease at the time. There are countless stories of the displacement and discarding of deeply committed, long-term partners of dying men by their biological families, with whom many of the men had broken and had no contact for years. The law treated them as if their relationships had never existed and were certainly not equivalent to those of either blood relatives or married couples.

During this period, there was some disagreement even among LGBTQ+ people about whether same-sex marriage should be the goal of this activism and advocacy. The conservative writer Andrew Sullivan suggested that queer people should fight for what were then referred to as either domestic partnerships or civil commitments, legally binding arrangements that were "marriage-adjacent." More radical left-wing opponents argued (and still contend) that the expectations of monogamy that heterosexual marriage made part of the traditional wedding vow implied an exclusivity that they found both sex-negative and arbitrary in determining the meaningfulness of the relationship between two people. They suggest that same-sex domestic relationships need not — *should* not — simply reproduce heterosexual assumptions but should be seen as an opportunity for other kinds of approaches to what faithfulness and love might mean.

The collective Against Equality (http://againstequality.org), whose writers fall into either far-left-wing or anarchistic political traditions, make arguments against putting marriage into so prominent a place in queer activism. They further argue that same-sex marriage has a negative effect on those of whatever sexuality who are not involved in legal marital arrangements; they make the point that marriage in and of itself can be critiqued as a middle-class, bourgeois institution, and that individuals or groups of people who do not handily fit into straightforward classification systems that are based on gender binaries and other characteristics may be harmed or at least disempowered by LGB assimilation into the ideological and political assumptions that marriage entails. An essay with the provocative title "Is Gay Marriage Anti-Black?" by Kenyon Farrow makes this argument explicitly. It articulates the ways in which the marriage equality movement, in striving for traditional (i.e., coupled, heteronormative-equivalent) marital structures for same-sex couples, can be viewed as placing black people, especially through such stereotypes of the homophobic black church (which Farrow argues does not represent all or even most of the black people in the United States who identify as Christian, let alone black people of other or no faith traditions) as well as the racist image of the hypersexual black male, in the exploitative hands of the political right on the one hand and the opportunistic hands of liberal white LGB people (whom Farrow sees as the overwhelmingly primary participants in same-sex marriage) on the other. Farrow ultimately answers his question in the affirmative, but he also calls on black people who oppose same-sex marriage to do so not in the name of religious verses (such as Leviticus), but for more secular reasons, such as political and economic inequities and disparities.

Another important intervention in the critique of same-sex marriage came from the organization Queers for Economic Justice, whose executive director, Joseph DeFilippis (now a college professor of social work), in 2006 organized and gathered 250 signatures for a document titled "Beyond Same-Sex Marriage," which argued for the importance of actively working for economic and social justice "for securing governmental and private institutional recognition of diverse kinds of partnerships, households, kinship relationships and families. In doing so, we hope to move beyond the narrow confines of marriage politics as they exist in the United States today." The document argues that such "household & family diversity is already the norm," pointing to census data that indicate that the nuclear family that more conservative views of marriage equality articulate is itself no longer the norm for families, whatever the gender, sexual, racial, or ethnic makeup of the household, if indeed it ever truly was. The document articulates a set of cogent and persuasive arguments for expanding the legal and social definitions of family, especially in terms that affect economic well-being; it is worth noting that the word *economics* comes from the Greek for "management of a household," so the Queers for Economic Justice group is in a sense calling for a return to the origins of the purpose of economics as a field of study and a practice of everyday social and legal life.

A 1991 case in Hawaii, in which Evan Wolfson and Lambda Legal pled a case for a gay couple wishing to marry, used the privacy and equal-protection clauses of the Fourteenth Amendment to argue for the right of same-sex couples to marry. The case gained enough national visibility to lead to the introduction of the Defense of Marriage Act (DOMA) in 1996, which explicitly introduced and codified the legal language used to define marriage as heterosexual in nature. It passed both houses of Congress and was signed into law by Bill Clinton. While the act did not preclude individual states from legalizing same-sex marriage, as Massachusetts was the first to do, in 2004, it invalidated same-sex marriage in federal matters, such as spousal benefits and rights. Hence, anyone employed by the federal government, even if employed in a state that legally permitted same-sex marriage, would not have been eligible for same-sex spousal benefits. It also led to such roadblocks as the passage of Proposition 8 in California, which reversed the legalization of same-sex marriage in that state and nullified those marriages that had been performed.

DOMA led to two cases that ended up before the Supreme Court. The first case, *United States v. Windsor*, centered on a lesbian couple, Edie Windsor and Thea Spyer, who had lived together for several decades and who had married in Canada in 2007 and had their marriage recognized in New York State the following year. Spyer died in 2009 and left her entire estate, which was sizable, to Windsor. Windsor sought to claim the survivor's tax exemption, as provided by federal law, on the basis of her state-recognized marriage to Spyer; in the absence of the exemption, Windsor would have had to pay a large tax on the inheritance. The Internal Revenue Service denied her claim of exemption, on the basis of DOMA, and Windsor took the federal government to court, on the basis of discrimination against her as a homosexual. The attorney general at the time, Eric Holder, announced he would not defend DOMA, and Windsor won the case initially. It was overturned in the court of appeals, however, and thus found its way before the Supreme Court.

In yet another close decision, the Supreme Court found in favor of Windsor, five to four. Justice Anthony Kennedy, who wrote the majority decision, included such issues as states' rights, the equal-protection clause of the Fourteenth Amendment, and the time-honored concept of liberty as foundational to the decision; he also included an important concept that would reappear in another case — *dignity*. He, on behalf of the majority of justices, argued that one of the rights of citizenship is to be treated with appropriate dignity as a human being and that Section 3 (the pertinent section of DOMA) did not ensure such dignity and therefore was unconstitutional. The decision was a moment of triumph not only for Windsor and her advocates, but also for affirming values on which the United States claims to have been founded and putting them into policy and practice.

This decision did not fully nationalize same-sex marriage in the United States, however. That was to come in a case decided in 2015, *Obergefell v. Hodges*. In this case, the argument centered on whether states that ban same-sex marriage should be required to recognize those performed in other states. The plaintiffs in the case were a gay male couple, James Obergefell and John Arthur, who resided in Ohio, a state that did not issue marriage licenses to same-sex couples. The couple married in Maryland, a state where same-sex marriage had been legalized. Arthur was dying of the disease ALS, and Obergefell petitioned to be listed as the surviving spouse, both as an acknowledgment of the legality of their marriage (as performed in Maryland) and for the benefits Windsor had sought in her case. Arthur died in 2013, so the case was decided after his death. Again, after hearings and decisions in lower courts, it ended up before the Supreme Court, where the decision was once again five to four. Once again, Justice Kennedy wrote for the majority, invoking issues of dignity as well as the right to autonomy and, "within legal realms" (and the decision was itself an endorsement of what should be considered legal), "to define and express their identity."

This decision meant, at least in theory and quite generally in practice, that same-sex marriage is legal in all parts of the United States. Nonetheless, several counties in both Alabama and Texas still refuse to issue marriage licenses to same-sex couples; while this violates the federal ruling, residents of those counties can simply go elsewhere to receive licenses. This is not to suggest that such willful disobedience of the law in those counties is acceptable, but, rather, to affirm that it does not stop same-sex couples from getting married. Kim Davis, a county clerk in Kentucky, refused to issue licenses to same-sex couples, and the suits brought against her became a cause célèbre in the wake of the decision in *Obergefell v. Hodges*. She was found guilty of contempt of court and fined and briefly jailed. She gained a degree of notoriety, as the media focused on her own three marriages, all of which ended in divorce, which raised questions about her status to make judgments about who should be allowed to enter into what is presumed to be a permanent state of couplehood.

## Queering the Military

There have been queer soldiers in the U.S. military since its origins, though most have been unnamed as such. Baron Friedrich von Steuben, a Prussian (German) officer who is often credited with turning the tide of the Revolution when he arrived at Valley Forge in 1778, was what today we would recognize as a gay man. Indeed, he escaped arrest in Paris for his acts with other men (and boys, which was especially the sticking point), and he was recommended by Benjamin Franklin to assist George Washington in bringing discipline and strategy to what, by all accounts, was a kind of "rag-tag" group of soldiers (Segal).

By the early 1940s, the military had formalized the policy of not inducting men who acknowledged they were gay and of discharging those who were found out to be. During World War II, nonetheless, gay men and lesbians (the latter assigned to noncombat units, in such roles as medical personnel, administrative employees, mechanics, technicians, truck drivers, and so forth) served — and served patriotically. There is an assumption that they all remained closeted or formed their own small, trusted inner circles, but there is also reason to believe, on the basis of interviews and oral histories, that many of their straight fellow soldiers knew that they were gay (or at least could guess they were). In some instances, there was an unofficial "Don't Ask, Don't Tell" policy, and a number of straight veterans have spoken with admiration and affection about the courage and self-sacrifices these men and women made. Because gay men could have used their sexuality to get out of the draft, and lesbians, as women, were under no obligation to enlist, the service of queer soldiers is particularly admirable.

After World War II, homophobia once again increased in the military, coinciding with the panic regarding the spread of communism that was central to the McCarthy witch hunts. During this period of national paranoia, the focus was less on homosexuals as "diseased" (though that was still the official position of medical and psychological professional organizations), but on their being security risks — the belief that they would be more vulnerable to blackmail by enemy forces and, hence, more likely to engage in espionage for the communists.

In the period from World War II forward, the military stratified "tainted" discharges even further — in the late 1940s and throughout the 1950s and 1960s, there was a distinction between soldiers discharged for *being* homosexual (undesirable discharge) and those guilty of such conduct (dishonorable discharge). By the time of the Vietnam War, the distinction had shifted to general discharge (which could cover a number of ways in which a soldier had not met standards of conduct or performance), given to men and women who identified as homosexual, and dishonorable discharge, for those who admitted to engaging or were discovered to have engaged in gay sex while enlisted in the military.

### Spotlight: Leonard Matlovich and Margarethe Cammermeyer

Perhaps the most famous early challenge to the military's ban on homosexuals and homosexuality was raised by Sergeant Leonard Matlovich, who joined the U.S. Air Force at nineteen and became an exemplary soldier, serving in Vietnam for three tours of duty; after the war, he worked as an instructor on race relations within the military. He came out to himself around age thirty (and subsequently to some of his fellow soldiers, but not to his supervisor or other superiors) and in the following year made contact with the gay rights activist Frank Kameny, who encouraged him to bring a lawsuit to allow him to remain in the air force — he would be a major test case and his suit landed him on the cover of *Time* magazine. The air force was willing to allow him to remain in the military if he would sign a document swearing he would not engage in any additional gay sex while enlisted. When he saw that he would not win his case, he accepted a settlement and an honorable discharge, which the air force was willing to give for his valor in Vietnam and his work on race relations. So, though his suit was unsuccessful, he brought greater attention to the situation of gay men and women in the military, paving the way for others to come. He died of AIDS in his mid-forties and is buried in the Congressional Cemetery in Washington, D.C. On his headstone is the haunting epigraph, "When I was in the military, they gave me a medal for killing two men and a discharge for loving one."

Another high-profile case was that of Margarethe Cammermeyer, a nurse who rose to the rank of colonel in the national guard. Cammermeyer was married to a man for fifteen years and had four children with him. In 1988 she met the women who would become her wife and, the following year, came out to military authorities during a security clearance. She was honorably discharged in 1992 (after Matlovich, it seems that the military decided a compromise that destigmatized the discharge, while still excluding gay personnel, was most advisable) and subsequently brought suit; the judge found the ban on gays in the military unconstitutional, and Cammermeyer returned to service under the Don't Ask, Don't Tell policy and continued to serve until she retired a few years later. She wrote a memoir, *Serving in Silence*, which was then adapted into a highly praised television film broadcast on NBC and which won Glenn Close a Best Actress Emmy for her performance as Cammermeyer and Judy Davis a Best Supporting Actress Emmy for playing her wife, Diane Divelbess. Both book and film are excellent narratives.

The **Don't Ask, Don't Tell (DADT)** policy was written in consultation with a professor of military sociology at Northwestern University, Charles Moskos, who coined the phrase, and President Bill Clinton eventually approved the policy. While asserting that openly active homosexuals (and, by implication, bisexual people, who, for these purposes, were grouped with gay men and lesbians) were deleterious to the military, it conceded that such people could serve the military well and honorably, but only under the conditions that they not reveal their sexual orientation or anything connected to it in their domestic or private life (such as partners, spouses, children, where they went for the weekend) that would even by implication suggest they were homosexual. In other words, they could be homosexual in the military as long as they were not culturally or socially gay. (We will return to this below, but it is important to note that, even under DADT, there were separate policies for transgender members of the armed forces.)

In return for this, military personnel were forbidden to ask, to make any inquiry about a soldier's sexual orientation. (Presumably the greatest concern was asking about anything that would allow the military to determine a soldier was gay — asking questions about pictures of other-sex partners or about family plans for holidays was probably considered acceptable, as heteronormative society considers itself the unmarked and assumed category.) If, however, a soldier disclosed a queer identity or engaged in queer actions, the military could discharge them. What could and did become sticky in the implementation of this policy — and it would have been reasonable to expect the framers of the policy to have anticipated this — was when a fellow soldier revealed another soldier's homosexuality to an officer.

This would be, in many interpretations of the policy, a violation of the policy by the "telling" soldier, but it was highly unlikely that said teller would be discharged. Once the information was out, it was out, and there was no way for it not to be known. The policy also had no way to deal with accidental outings, such as an officer seeing a soldier entering a gay bar or out on a date. After some court cases along the way, DADT was repealed by both the House and the Senate in December 2010, and the repeal was signed into law by President Barack Obama the same month. The armed forces prepared policies and procedures for the transition the following year.

The most famous trans soldier is no doubt Chelsea Manning (referred to as Bradley in coverage predating her transition). Manning was raised as a boy in Oklahoma, but she has said in interviews that she identified as a girl from an early age, even without having a name for her identity or her feelings. She entered the army as a man and served in intelligence, which brought her into the public spotlight, though not initially as a trans or female soldier. She (at the time, *he* in terms of public perception and presentation) had a rough set of stints in boot camp, including breaking her hand the first time around. Men who served with her recall that she endeavored to do her best but seemed inevitably to alienate those around her and disappoint supervisors; as one soldier remembered, she was frequently referred to as a "faggot," which, of course, in the macho culture of the armed services could have literally been intended as a slur on her sexual orientation or a devaluing of her performance of masculinity (Shaer). In 2010, disobeying the regulations on classified information, but feeling a moral responsibility to provide truth about what she saw as unethical actions by the United States, she sent over 700,000 e-mails and other documents to WikiLeaks, which led to her conviction on twenty-two charges under the Espionage Act, one charge carrying a possible death penalty. She was instead given a thirty-five-year sentence. During her time in Iraq, she began to experiment with dressing and going out in public as a woman, as her transgender identity was becoming more central to her sense of self. Her discharge from the army was not based on her trans status, but on her involvement in these information leaks.

In late 2016, in his last days in office, President Barack Obama announced that, as was the custom at the end of the year and particularly at the end of a term of office, he would be commuting or pardoning sentences for a number of individuals. One was Chelsea Manning, a decision that, in the aftermath of the very conservative national election of November, outraged some and provided a moment of grace and compassion to others. Obama was clear, in announcing and defending his decision, that he did not believe that Manning had not committed serious crimes — he was not pardoning her for "being right." Rather, he declared that he felt that, having served a seven-year sentence in military prison, she had done the time appropriate to her crime, and that the initial sentence had been overly harsh for any actual damage Manning may have done to security in the U.S. military and to the country. Manning has been released from prison and is facing the rest of her life, living as the woman she identifies herself to be.

Of course, nothing progressive seems to happen without counter-trends that are discouraging and confounding. In May 2017 a disheartening announcement made its way into national news: two cadets graduating from the Air Force Academy and West Point had identified as transgender. They were not allowed to be commissioned as officers, as their cisgender classmates were, and Donald Trump subsequently announced (though not specifically in response to this development) that he would block the presence of transgender people in the military; though there did not initially seem to be any move on the part of the military to enforce such a ban, in January 2019 the Supreme Court voted 5–4 to uphold the ban as a temporary measure, while cases that challenge the ban moved through the judicial system. A few exceptions to the ban were announced: personnel already serving and out as transgender, as well as people who identify as transgender but who are willing to serve as their "biological sex." This means that no current military personnel may transition (or announce their desire to transition) without risking discharge. The Trump administration requested an immediate hearing of cases that challenge the ban; the Court declined to fast-track such cases.

### Hate Crimes and Hate Speech: "Special Circumstances" and Continuing Debates

The FBI's formal definition of a **hate crime** is a "criminal offense against a person or property motivated in whole or in part by an offender's bias against a race, religion, disability, sexual orientation, ethnicity, gender, or gender identity" (Federal Bureau of Investigation). The highest proportion of hate crimes are based on race and ethnicity, especially those against African Americans, followed by Hispanics (using the FBI's terminology). Second is sexual orientation, followed by religion. Gender identity accounts for a much smaller percentage, which may be explained by sheer numbers. Hate crimes based on gender identity are not necessarily a less serious problem for that population; the population is simply smaller. Also, it is the case that those tracking statistics often conflate sexual orientation and gender identity, so that if an assailant yells an epithet like "faggot" when attacking a trans woman, it may be reported as a hate crime based on sexual orientation (or perception thereof) rather than on gender identity. In the conflation of sexual orientation and gender identity, the fact of transgender identity may get lost in the attribution of sexual orientation; such criminals are not likely to draw such distinctions with any accuracy.

The high profile of the Matthew Shepard case in 1998, which drew attention from far beyond Laramie, Wyoming, brought an increased awareness of hate crimes and motivated politicians to find ways to enact policy to recognize the role of identity and perception of identity in crimes and their punishment. The *hate* aspect revolved around the two killers' attitudes toward LGBTQ+ people and the state's argument that their homophobia was a central motivating factor in the crime; the defense tried to use "gay panic" as a justification. The defense argued that the two men were in fear of sexual attack by Shepard, whose physical build was slight enough to make the argument weak. At the time, Wyoming's hate crime laws did not include homosexuality as a protected category, so there was no formal attempt to charge the killers with a hate crime, though it was certainly viewed and discussed as such in the media and the court of public opinion.

Federal hate crime legislation was enacted in 2009, with the approval of both houses of Congress and the signature of President Barack Obama. Officially, it is known as the Matthew Shepard and James Byrd, Jr., Hate Crimes Prevention Act. Arguments in its favor pointed especially to the documented longer recovery times and increased risk for depression and post-traumatic stress disorder experienced by survivors of hate crimes, as well as, in the case of LGBTQ+ people, increased stigma that can result. And, indeed, those who opposed the legislation at the time (and continue to do so) typically pointed to the "special rights" they saw the legislation granting to queer people, whom their religious beliefs viewed as morally corrupt and sinful.

Judith Butler argues, in her book *Excitable Speech*, that censorship is inevitably involved in attempts to prevent hate speech, even when the goal is to provide safety and security for groups of people (and she writes specifically about homosexuals) who have been victimized by hateful statements and actions. For Butler, this does not mean abdicating any decision making about what practices of speech are acceptable in a given situation, but, instead, it means being fully aware that restricting speech carries with it a set of preconceptions and acts of power (or desire for power) that must be reckoned with.

### Trans (and Intersex) Politics: An Emerging Territory

That less space has been devoted to the issues of citizenship for trans and intersex citizens of the queer nation is by no means to suggest that the challenges and inequalities are fewer or less important, or that trans and intersex people (whom we are grouping together for the purposes of this brief discussion) have not been active and important members of social and political movements throughout history and especially in such groundbreaking events as the Stonewall Riots. Considerably less research has been done on trans and intersex politics, which is not to say that there are not and have not been important issues for as long as there have been trans people. In an anthology of essays coedited by Jami K. Taylor and Donald P. Haider-Markel, *Transgender Rights and Politics: Groups, Issue Framing, and Policy Adoption*, a number of scholars write about various issues and ways of thinking about the challenges and opportunities facing trans people. They make the important and insightful point that one significant difference between LGB rights and T rights is that the former tend to focus on "morality politics" (i.e., getting rights not only on the premise of fairness and equal protection, but also because queer people are just as "moral" as non-queer people), and trans rights tend to emerge from what they call "reinvention pressure," which is the need to have laws that acknowledge and support the trans person's process of affirming or transitioning to their appropriate gender. In recent years, trans activism has shifted its focus even more centrally to deconstructing and challenging gender binaries themselves, as oppressive ways of sorting people into arbitrary and questionable categories. Daniel C. Lewis, for example, finds that trans people who are able to and choose to pass fare better in the public sphere — that there can be both a kind of discrimination toward non-passing trans people and hierarchies of valuing even within trans communities in regard to this issue. This suggests that within trans society there can be forms, subtle or otherwise, of discrimination (quoted in Taylor and Haider-Merkel 122).

Important real-world issues for trans people often center on "identity documentation" — how trans people must navigate systems of validation, such as birth certificates, driver's licenses, social security cards, and other cards of identity, as they fight to affirm their own identity, rather than the ones they were assigned by others. Thus, West Point's refusal, mentioned earlier, to acknowledge the trans identity of a graduate (which it might argue is for legal reasons, as the student was probably both accepted and registered under their birth name and their assigned gender), is an instance of how what may seem to those of us who identify as cisgender as mainly an annoyance (such as standing in line at the DMV if we change our address) becomes a critical matter of equality and justice for trans people, and one they constantly have to fight and which varies from location to location and state to state. For the most up-to-date figures on laws affecting trans people, the best sources are the Movement Advancement Project's maps, which also include information about forms of equality related to sexual orientation and gender identity (www.lgbtmap.org/equality-maps).

Bathrooms, those critical spaces for bodies, have been central sites of political and legal conflict. The concern has been primarily with, once again, the fear of the "scary trans woman," usually imagined as an individual who has not had bottom surgery who will invade women's restrooms, either for voyeuristic or assaultive purposes. Particularly vulnerable to this kind of policing of restroom space have been young people, and it may be that one of the reasons the issue of "bathroom laws" has become so prominent in recent years is the visibility of younger people (including children of pre-school and kindergarten age) identifying as trans (though they may not have that specific word yet) and wanting not only to wear clothing of the gender with which they identify and to be addressed with a different name and pronoun from the one assigned at birth, but also, quite naturally, to use the bathroom other people with whose gender they identify are using. Similarly, as these children reach adolescence and, in more and more cases, are engaged in medical procedures and therapies that stop the onset of puberty or are otherwise designed to assist the teen in transitioning, where to go to the bathroom is not unimportant at all. It can be the source of anxiety, bullying, peer pressure, judgment by authorities and adults, and monitoring, at just the time of life when even people who go through life cisgendered and heterosexual may feel most alienated from their bodily changes and developments.

One solution, which some schools and other institutions have established, is gender-neutral bathrooms, sometimes designed for individuals and sometimes expanded as "family bathrooms," where parents can comfortably take children of any sex or where they can attend to the needs of infants (such as diaper changes and feeding), and sometimes for multiple users. In some cases, efforts are made to reconfigure existing bathrooms, removing urinals and adding stalls, to ensure privacy for those who wish it. In other cases, it may be more a matter of changing signage and deciding on location. Less satisfactory have been such compromise solutions as instructing trans students to use a teachers' bathroom, thus isolating and spotlighting the students' already painful sense of difference from their peers.

As such things typically do, the bathroom controversy began to find its way into legal and political arenas. As we saw in chapter 7, in 2016 North Carolina challenged "guidance" (not a law, but a set of informal suggested guidelines made by the Obama administration) that recommended that students be permitted to use whichever bathroom matched their own self-determined gender identity; the state instead passed a bill that required students to use the bathroom aligned with the gender listed on their birth certificates. This led to significant economic loss for the state, as many organizations refused to do business there as long as the law was in place. Perhaps most famously, the NBA moved its all-star game from Charlotte, where it was scheduled to be played, and the NCAA took similar action with playoff games in a number of its sports. Two months later, the Obama administration issued additional "guidance," which, while again not having the force of law, made clear that schools that did not comply with support of transgender students in their policies and procedures were likely to face lawsuits, based on the interpretation of Title IX, and loss of federal financial support. This announcement became a lightning rod, both for supporters of transgender students and opponents of bathroom choice. The same year, a trans student named Gavin Grimm successfully brought suit in Richmond, Virginia, and won the right to use a male restroom at his school. Throughout the year, other, similar cases came forward in such states as Texas (where the transgender bathroom rights were challenged) and California (where Governor Jerry Brown signed an order that all single-user bathrooms be designated as gender neutral).

## GLOBAL AND TRANSNATIONAL ISSUES IN QUEER POLITICS

### The European Union and Queer Rights

The European Union is the largest association of nations that affirms queer antidiscrimination: to belong to the Union, a country must agree to the EU's policies, which forbid employment discrimination and criminalization of same-sex acts and require that member countries honor same-sex marriages, even if an individual country does not itself permit the legal marriage of same-sex couples in its own borders. Membership in the EU does not ensure same-sex marriage or same-sex adoption as a universal right, so there is considerable variation from country to country on both issues. There are, as of this writing, twenty-eight member nations. Of the Western European EU members, fifteen allow same-sex marriage outright (the one exception being Northern Ireland, where it remains illegal); of the remaining, all but six recognize some form of same-sex civil union or partnership but stop short of using the word *marriage* (or its equivalent in the language of the country). Other than Northern Ireland, the dissenting countries are typically formerly Soviet-occupied countries or ones where queer-negative religious beliefs and practices dominate. Seventeen member countries allow either adoption by same-sex couples or an alternative, stepchild adoption, for a second parent in a couple. (The latter is legal in some states in the United States; some states, such as Texas, have laws that allow private adoption agencies to discriminate not only on the basis of the adoptive parents' sexuality, but on other bases, such as a prospective parent's divorce status.)

The political scientist Philip Ayoub has studied the processes by which EU countries that have joined the association in more recent years have entered into what he calls the "politics of visibility" (3), engagement in transnational movements (across different nations) either to support LGBTQ+

rights or to maintain homophobic laws and policies. His theory, one of diffusion, identifies "first movers" (countries that originate such progressive issues as LGBTQ+ rights), which in a sense "send out" these ideologies and their accompanying policies to what he calls "new adapters," whereby contact between and among these countries "allows new ideas to enter the dominant discourse" (10). In studying patterns among the EU nations, he does not find a necessary correlation between what he terms *modernization* (whether industrial or economic) and progressive laws and policies enacted by these new adaptors (15). "Norm visibility," as he calls, is a necessary component of openness in these countries to greater granting of rights to LGBTQ+ people. Often, new adaptor countries may look to other countries, hence the transnational character of such progress.

What he finds most determinative in this regard is what he calls "religious nationalism," the ways in which the profile and position of the religion(s) of a country moderate "the ways international norms are received and internalized" (11). He compares Poland and Slovenia, two countries occupied by the Soviet Union throughout long periods of the twentieth century, to show how this has played itself out in recent history. Poland, while strong on labor unions and workers' rights, has also had a powerful Catholic presence, one that has dominated (and continues to dominate) social and political discourse and practices. It has been less open to such things as same-sex marriage and adoption by same-sex couples; Slovenia, while still a somewhat Catholic country, has had a weaker religious presence in national politics, and so the antigay attitudes of the Church in this country have been far less important.

### Russia and the Russian Federation

In Russia itself, homosexuality has been decriminalized, but that is about as far as queer rights have progressed there. Same-sex marriage is not permitted and, while adoption is legal for single people, there is no provision for same-sex couples to adopt. Homosexuality is still viewed as a psychiatric disorder by medical authorities (although, no doubt, there are individual doctors whose opinions differ). Two issues have gained significant profile in recent times, having to do with censorship and with "containment." Russia has on its books a "gay censorship" law that makes it a crime to print and distribute any documents that promote homosexuality (or other queer identities) as an acceptable lifestyle for minors. These policies were first passed regionally and then signed into national law by Vladimir Putin in 2013. Included under the propaganda prohibitions are such things as expressing the belief that queer relationships are equal to heterosexual ones; organizing and participating in gay Pride parades; and simply speaking in favor of gay rights. So, while private sexual acts between members of the same sex are legal, anything that could be construed as public support of them is not. The question of what constitutes support is left open enough to make living a daily life as a queer person risky: Wearing a rainbow pin, holding hands with a partner, what are the limits of "speaking in favor"?

In June 2017 the European Court of Human Rights heard a case brought by three gay Russian men who claimed their rights were being violated by Russia's law; these men were activists who had, in defiance of the law, organized small Pride parades and been arrested for this activity. The men initially took their case before the Russian Federation Court, which, as expected, found against them. They then took it before the European Court. The Court found in favor of the men, saying that Russia's law violated the European Convention on Human Rights, which Russia had signed in 1988 (more than thirty years after it was established), and ordered the Russian government to pay the three men €43,000 (about $48,000). The vote was decisive, six to one — the one negative vote came from a judge who is himself a Russian citizen. The government has claimed both that it will not obey the finding, as it says it violates the Russian constitution, and that it will file an appeal.

Perhaps more troubling and still unresolved as of this writing is the revelation that gay men (not women yet; and women have typically, because — ironically — of sexism, often been ignored by such purges) have been gathered in concentration camps in the Chechen Republic, a Russian Federation country in the North Caucasus that has a large concentration of Shi'ite Muslims. Though the Republic is officially under Russian rule, it has maintained some kinds of autonomous control, and one area in which it has done so has been in the recriminalization of homosexuality, with special mention of *sodomy* (which, in the national law, is specifically described as anal intercourse, either between two men or between a man and a woman, though women have not been the targets of the recent wave of arrests). Gay men and men suspected of being gay in the country have been rounded up and placed in concentration camps, not unlike the ones run by the Nazis in World War II and the Soviet Union at the height of the Stalinist era. Men there are tortured and live in brutal conditions, and killings have been reported (not as official penalties, but also not monitored or prosecuted as crimes). The Chechen government takes the official line that the existence of "gay concentration camps" is an illusion — for the reason that, according to the government, there *are* no gay people in the country. This is a double-speak worthy of George Orwell, who first prophesied the dangers of totalitarian rhetoric in his dystopic novel *1984*.

## ISIS, the Middle East, and Conditions for Queer People

The number and variety of countries in the Middle East make it difficult to generalize about queer rights. Other than Israel, the country typically viewed as most progressive on queer issues is Lebanon, not coincidentally the most religiously diverse of the Middle Eastern countries, almost equally populated by Muslims and Christians. Israel, so progressive in many ways, still does not allow same-sex marriage, in part because the right to perform marriage is controlled by the Orthodox branch of Judaism, which forbids such marriages. Same-sex couples who wish to marry must do so in other countries.

It is important to note that the Middle East is no more monolithic in its attitudes and views than any other part of the world, and there is a danger in conflating all nations that are majority-Islam in that part of the world as having the same sets of beliefs, attitudes, and practices, as there is in assuming that all Arab countries have the same relationship between state politics and government and the dominant religion, Islam. Joseph Massad, a scholar of Middle Eastern studies who teaches at Columbia University in New York City, argues in his detailed and complex book, *Desiring Arabs* (and elsewhere), that what we call queer sex has long existed in Arabian countries, and the West's view of it typically carries with it a high degree of what his mentor Edward Said termed *Orientalism*, a kind of exoticizing of "the Other" (sometimes captured in the phrase "the West and the rest"). These views impose Western history and contemporary values on countries and cultures that have had their own histories and practices that are not well served by such lenses. Massad coined the phrase "the Gay International" to describe what he sees as a project by Western gay or queer activists, scholars, and others to turn LGBT or queer identity into a universal and what might be called transhistorical category of identity, thus flattening the alternative ways people in such countries have had sexual activities and relationships with each other. His focus is on Arab sexualities, but his point is one worth considering and keeping in mind. Massad traces, from early Arabic history and literature to the present day, the ways in which same-sex activities have been described, represented, and either valued or condemned, and he points out, as have others, the role colonialism has played at different times. He makes the claim, which his critics contest, that the violence and imprisonment of men who have sex with other men is less about the actual commission of such acts (in the privacy of the domestic sphere) and more about the public claims for identity and for spaces that are marked for identity.

Massad is not without his critics, including vocal and articulate persons who identify as queer Arabs. The self-identified queer Arab novelist Saleem Haddad, whose heritage is both Iraqi-German and Palestinian-Lebanese (he now lives in Europe), published a novel, *Guapa*, in 2016, which represents the experience of a gay-identified young Arab man in an unnamed country over the course of twenty-four hours. The novel shows various ways in which men of Arab descent engage in sexual activities and in relational interactions with other Arab men. While finding value in Massad's critique of Western imperialist moves to absorb Arabic same-sex subjects into this Gay Internationalist perspective, Haddad also finds Massad's own rejection of queer politics equally limiting and monolithic in its claims to generalize about the complex cultures of such countries and the desires — sexual, romantic, and political — of its subjects. As he puts it in an essay that cites Massad's work, "Who owns queer Arab bodies?" (Haddad, April 2, 2016). While Haddad certainly does not suggest that Western "universalizing" of gay or queer identity is the correct answer, he is also careful not to suggest that Massad can or should try to speak for all Arabs who might wish to identify as queer or gay and for whom alignment with queer politics and queer individuals from other countries and cultures may well be what they desire, and not simply out of a kind of cultural brainwashing. So the debates continue, and it is useful to pay attention to the merits and arguments on both sides (and there are, needless to say, more than two sides to consideration of these issues).

Of all the countries in the Middle East, Iran has been particularly in the news regarding queer issues. It is one of the countries with the harshest stated penalty for homosexual activity, but it is also notable for its view of transgender people. Because it views trans identity as a medical illness, rather than an identity category, it actually approves of treatment and surgeries for people wishing to transition, often paying up to half the costs. The argument for this disparity in policies runs thus: living life as an LGB person, and actively engaging in homosexual behaviors, is a violation of nature and of the will of Allah, and therefore, an intentional crime that merits the legal penalty prescribed for an extreme violation, that of the body's purity and sanctity. The transgender person (who is often referred to as transsexual, using the older term), on the other hand, is no different from someone with cancer, diabetes, heart disease, or some other disabling condition, either one present from birth (congenital) or one acquired at some point in life. The goal of medicine, then, is to restore or produce a state of *health* (a term whose problematic meaning we considered in an earlier chapter). When gender transition is complete, the person can truly be a "proper citizen" of the nation and an appropriate adherent of the religion.

That possibility is explored in the young adult novel *If You Could Be Mine* by the Iranian-American writer Sara Farizan, published in 2013. The narrator, a seventeen-year-old girl named Sahar, lives with her widowed father in Tehran. She has quietly but resolutely identified as a lesbian for some years and has had a romance and sexual relationship with her best friend from childhood, Nasrin. When Nasrin's engagement to a man selected by her parents is announced, Sahar investigates the possibility of transitioning to become a man. The plot of the novel takes Sahar into the underground, an often defiant, often terrified world of what might be called "queer Tehran," in part guided by her gay male cousin, Ali, who is slightly older and more involved in the queer community of the city. The novel includes many characters on different points of the queer spectrum, showing the reader the many ways there are to identify as queer and the challenges each group faces in Iran.

Iran has also been in the news for a particularly troubling case involving the execution of men who were found guilty of engaging in homosexual acts. In 2005 Mahmoud Asgari and Ayaz Marhoni, aged sixteen and eighteen, respectively, were hanged in the town square in Mashhad, a city in Khorasan, a province in northeast Iran. They had been convicted of performing forcible anal sex with a thirteen-year-old boy — that is, of raping him. Human rights advocates and LGBTQ+ rights activists decried the execution on a number of grounds. To begin with, both of the executed men were minors at the time of the alleged crime, and their execution violated widely accepted human rights practices. Second, there was some question about whether the sex was consensual or nonconsensual. Under Iran's law, sodomy, as it would have been considered, would have warranted the application of the death penalty, though, were the act consensual, the age of the individuals involved might have been taken into consideration. The Iranian government claimed that the execution was punishment for rape; some, though by no means all, human rights workers asserted that the punishment was determined by the homosexual nature of the acts.

There was and continues to be debate about the sexual identity of the boys in this incident. Some activists and scholars suggest that human rights workers such as Peter Tatchell, who identified the two boys as gay, imposed an identity label on them that they might not (and did not publicly) choose for themselves. They prefer to place the incident in a larger context of human rights violations, particularly of the rights of children. Photographs of the execution made wire services across the world. More than a decade after the incident, there does not seem to be any closure on the motivations for the execution and its meaning for queer people in Iran, and all over the world, other than Iran's continued insistence that it is not a homophobic country because there "are no homosexuals" within its borders.

ISIS, also known as the Islamic State, the extremist terrorist group responsible for countless murders through bombings, suicide vehicle attacks, and myriad other methods of spreading its message, has been an especially virulent source of violence and homophobia against gay men in the Middle East. The mass murder that took place at the Pulse nightclub in Orlando, Florida, was perpetrated by a radicalized ISIS follower — and ISIS was happy to claim him and praise his act. The journalist Tim Teeman wrote a column for the *Daily Beast* in 2016 in which he discusses what he calls "the secret, hypocritical gay world of ISIS," chronicling such acts as the execution (by throwing off a tall building) of a fifteen-year-old boy in Syria who was discovered to be having a sexual relationship with a top commander in ISIS. The commander, Abu Zaid al-Jazrawi, was flogged for his participation in the relationship, but he was then sent to the front in Iraq to continue to fight for ISIS. The age difference between the executed boy and the adult soldier was much more significant than that in the case of Asgari and Marhoni in Iran, and the question of consent is equally unknown. The Iranian government had recommended that Abu Zaid also receive the death penalty, but ISIS decided it had more important uses for him. Think back to the concepts of homonationalism (as coined by Jasbir Puar) and pinkwashing introduced earlier in this chapter: How might the clemency from execution granted to Abu Zaid by ISIS be an example of these tactics?

It is worth noting, in concluding this section on challenges to queer lives and rights (putting aside Massad's argument that *queer* as a category is an imposition on non-Western cultures and people), that both culture and experience carry histories and have opportunities for change — inevitably so, one might argue. Thus, the Iranian American scholar Shadee Abdi's "Staying I(ra)n: Narrating Queer Identity from within the Persian Closet," is an essay that juxtaposes personal narrative and public, official statements erasing or condemning same-sex activities and identities both by political leaders in Iran and from such scriptural sources as the Quran. She explores how assumptions and beliefs about homosexuality migrate from the Middle East into the lives and homes of families such as Abdi's, who live in such more generally queer-visible places as California. Abdi recounts the conventions of queer erasure and denial she encounters among her family and the ensuing pressures to remain in what she calls the Persian closet: her essay is a powerful testimony of coming out, not simply as an individual but as someone whose life emerges from histories and cultures that precede her.

## Africa: A Continent, Not a Country

Given that there are currently fifty-four countries (counting territories regulated by other countries, typically European ones) recognized both by the African Union and by the United Nations, there is nonetheless enough consistency among them to allow generalization and say that the vast majority (by some measures all but South Africa) maintain discriminatory laws that continue to make same-sex activities criminal and forbid same-sex marriage and adoption by same-sex couples. South Africa, despite its own national heritage of racial apartheid, has the most progressive laws and policies with regard to queer rights. South Africa has, comparatively recently (1988), decriminalized male homosexuality and has never had any laws against female homosexuality. It permits same-sex marriage, adoption by same-sex couples, and LGBTQ+ inclusion in the military; it also permits transgender people to change gender legally after medical treatment. While not everything is perfect for queer folk in South Africa (lesbians have sometimes been victims of "corrective rape," that is, forced sexual intercourse with men, the explanation being that this will cure these women of their homosexuality), there is more that is positive than negative in its legal system.

At the other end of the spectrum is Uganda, which has had and continues to have some of the most extreme and draconian antigay laws in the world. In 2009 a bill was introduced that would make homosexual activity grounds for the death penalty; the bill was ultimately defeated, principally on a technicality, but it received both legislative and popular support, especially among the media. Interestingly, unlike Russia, for example, Uganda does not have laws banning "gay propaganda," but, given homosexuality's criminalization, the presence of progay literature, speech, and other forms of expression must be seen as a paradoxical situation.

Many reasons have been suggested for the overwhelmingly antigay positions of African governments and legal systems. One is grounded in the history of colonialism that continues to be present even after liberation and the establishment of autonomy of countries once claimed and exploited by primarily European countries, as well as ones exploited by the United States. There is, among many citizens of these countries, especially those who are descended from indigenous populations, a perception, sometimes expressed as "fact," that homosexuality did not exist before the arrival of colonists. The colonists are viewed as having stolen, without any natural or cultural authority, the lands and their products, and also as having brought their "unnatural" homosexual practices with them. To complicate the circularity of the argument even further, many sodomy laws, codified by colonists, came about because of the conditions of colonialism: men involved in either military or business aspects of colonialism were separated from women, especially their wives or other racially "concordant" women, for long periods. So, one might argue, the attitudes today toward same-sex relations in previously colonized countries are in large part artifacts of the imposition of social and cultural attitudes of the oppressors themselves.

Some of this may be explained, at least in part, by different practices and ways of conceiving of same-sex relations. If fixed categories of identity like *gay* and *lesbian* are, by some reckonings, always at least in some way social constructions, then there might have been countless instances of same-sex activity that occurred among people in these countries that might not have been conceived of as legible or fixed aspects of an identity. The modern homosexual, as understood as a category of selfhood, might have either remained sub rosa (unspoken) or been accepted in limited, sometimes ritual or vague contexts. To claim oneself as gay, lesbian, bisexual, or transgender might indeed have required an epistemological structure that coincided with the presence of Westerners, though even that is far from certain.

One additional factor has to do with another force that came with colonialism and continues to make its power felt: evangelical Christianity, of a particularly heteronormative nature. Former U.S. president Barack Obama made headlines, disappointing many of his supporters, when he announced that the clergyman he had invited to provide the traditional invocation at his first inauguration was Rick Warren, a popular and media-prominent evangelical pastor whose influence was seen as figuring heavily in Uganda's harsh antigay legislation (Michaelson). Indeed, Christian missionaries have exerted strong cultural influences in many African countries, and this was one of the most recent initiatives. In addition to his generally antigay stances and his influence on such policies not only in Uganda, but in other countries, such as Rwanda, he spearheaded an AIDS-education program that stressed an abstinence-only message.

Despite, or perhaps because of, such harsh antigay rhetoric and policies, there are brave and outspoken queer activists in various countries in Africa. An anthology, *Queer African Reader*, edited by Sokari Ekine and Hakima Abbas, published in 2013, provides space for voices of essayists, memoirists, poets, fiction writers, and academics whose work spans a wide range of shared and individual experiences about being queer in various African countries. Its very existence and its inclusiveness of perspectives is itself an important political act.

And there are grassroots political coalitions and interventions, one of which we focus on here

## Spotlight: The Rainbow Project in Namibia

Namibia is one of the poorest and more sparsely populated countries in southwest Africa and, like many other countries on the continent, has no LGBTQ+-affirmative laws (other than decriminalization of sex between women). Though the sodomy law against sex between men remains on the books, it has not been enforced for many years. John Walters, the country's ombudsman (whose charge is essentially to handle complaints brought by citizens against government officials and discriminatory laws), went on record in 2016 as saying that he supported same-sex marriage, observing, "If people of the same sex would like to get married, it is their choice, whether the country, the community, churches and government acknowledge that [is something else]" (Igual). While this statement may not seem to have the same force as advocacy for same-sex marriage itself, it is a step forward in terms of affirming separation of church and state, while recognizing that legalization will not in and of itself protect Namibia's LGBTQ+

population from the kinds of everyday discrimination and violence they encounter — but it would be a start.

Robert Lorway, a Canadian medical anthropologist, did an ethnographic study of Namibia's Rainbow Project, an organization committed to providing education, service, and activism is support of queer issues in the country. One of the challenges to Namibian queer people is, as one might expect, the distances between communities, as well as the lack of resources (xx). The country also faces problems associated with tensions between local concerns and the often well-intended interventions and work done by outsiders. He poses his central question thus: "What are the consequences when international interventions like the Rainbow Project try to save and protect LGBT people from discrimination with programs that treat their sexualities in isolation from the local conditions in which they are embedded?" (3).

These "local conditions" include everything from the conflation of gender-nonconforming persons with sex workers, as embodied in the slang word *moffie*, a term used to refer to both groups and which a number of LGBTQ+ Namibians find devaluing of their sexuality, apart from the stigmas they associate with sex work. This general attitude toward queer people, summed up in the word *moffie*, is also found in what they call "the hate speeches" delivered by the Southwest African People's Organization (SWAPO), the ruling party of the government during the time of Lorway's fieldwork. Such speeches associated queer Namibians with the foreigners who, in the dominant narrative, brought homosexuality to Namibia, contrasting them with the Christians, who, ironically, were also a product of colonialism. But the Rainbow Project persevered, creating the first LGBT Human Rights Awareness Week in 2000 in Windhoek, the national capital. The Rainbow Project, in Lorway's analysis, worked hard, both through its messages and its support activities, to provide a positive set of values for sexual desire itself (51), in contradistinction to the more restrictive views of sexuality and sexual activity articulated by authorities. It encouraged the use of coming-out narratives by those who represented the project and by those coming to it for assistance as what Lorway calls "technologies of the self," empowering tools for understanding and gaining command over their own sense of themselves as sexual beings.

Beyond the emotional and morale issues faced by queer Namibians, there are violence and oppression. For example, lesbians who do sex work with men are vulnerable to violence (as well as the "corrective rape" practiced in such countries as South Africa); while this violence is illegal, it is also not highly policed. SWAPO, the governing party, on occasion has rounded up young men wearing earrings to interrogate them on their sexuality. As is not uncommon in gender-polarized societies (and hardly exclusive to African countries), feminine gay men often hook up, either on a onetime or more regular basis, with straight men—that is, men who do not identify as gay or queer: such straight men often insist on having bareback sex (without condoms), which thus makes these feminine gay men even more vulnerable, not just politically, but medically. Lorway also notes the development of a negative cycle that comes with economic development and opportunities. Some of the gay men found partners in foreigners, often white expatriates, who were willing to support the Namibian men in return for sexual favors. While such wealthier partners often funded education, travel, and luxuries for their partners, these benefits were usually not without a price—domestic violence rose among many of the couples. Even when the gay Namibians were sufficiently established to become somewhat independent—what Lorway describes as an upwardly mobile class of gay men— these usually feminine gay men frequently began to take more masculine Namibian men as lovers (when they did not take white men as lovers), and then were frequently exploited by these men, who often had female lovers and did not identify as gay; the feminine gay men themselves were subject to rape and other forms of violence. At the time Lorway published his study (2015), HIV prevalence in Namibia was among the highest in the world and the leading cause of death in that country.

## Other Continents, Other Countries: "The Rest"

We have not devoted much space in this chapter to South and Southeast Asia, or to South and Central America; it is important to recognize that in countries as vast geographically as China, or as complex in their view of social relationships as Japan, or as divided as North Korea and South Korea, religious beliefs and practices may have very little to do with governmental laws and procedural policies. North Korea's requirement of sexual abstinence for all its soldiers while enlisted in the military is but one example. The lack of visibility of queer voices and faces is hardly proof that there are not thousands, if not millions, of people living out their queer lives privately and, increasingly, in public spaces. More and more films and literature depicting the dramas of queer lives in Asia are emerging, and, thanks to such outlets as Netflix, Amazon Video, and cable channels like Here, they are finding their way to non-Asian audiences and beginning to shed some light on what it means to be queer and living in an Asian country.

Similarly, while Australia and New Zealand are both generally quite progressive about most aspects of LGBTQ+ rights, Australia remains adamantly against same-sex marriage, defining marriage legally as between a man and a woman—though in almost all other ways, Australia is considered one of the most queer-friendly countries and has a large queer-centered tourist and travel trade. Such are the complexities of nations—and reasons for such seeming contradictions are often deeply embedded in their histories, including those of colonization, and in local figures in power at any given time. And while the United States likes to think of itself as the world power most committed to individual freedom, support of liberty, and self-determination, we need look to our northern neighbor, Canada, for a model of early and robust support for its queer citizens—and for those who "come from away" (to use a Canadian expression) seeking them.

## ISSUES FOR INVESTIGATION

**1.** Spend some time with a few of your classmates and try this exercise. First, on your own, try to describe the various places and other units you feel yourself to be a "citizen" of—using the term as broadly as you wish (see the definition taken from the Fordham website at the beginning of this chapter). Is there a hierarchy to them—presumably your national citizenship might be the largest umbrella under which the others fall, though even that may be debatable or variable for some. (There are those who view themselves as "citizens of the world," a term sometimes captured by a particular use of the term *cosmopolitan*, and others who eschew any use of nationality to describe their sense of participation in politics and society.) Is there a kind of sweet spot to any of these—in the sense that one is closest to your identity (as Chicago is to mine, in terms of citizenship); in other domains of identity, there may be different terms that take precedence). Share your list with a few others in your class. Talk about what gives you a sense of belonging in a public sense to the group (or region) with which you affiliate. Former governor Jim McGreevey (New Jersey) described himself as a "gay American" (following the standard pattern of subset— gay—followed by country citizenship); what difference, if any, would it have made for him to say he was an "American gay"? (And would it have been even more different had he called himself an "American gay man"?)

In your group, see how many different rights and responsibilities you can list as citizens, either in general (i.e., probably as citizens of whichever country you hold this status in) or in one of the other communities to which you belong. Is there any connection between rights and responsibilities in any of the instances? For example, some people argue that the right to vote in elections should carry with it the responsibility to vote (and this is the case in some countries). What do you think of this example? Also, is there a difference between responsibility and requirement? Where does one end and the other begin? Do all people who are legally considered citizens in the unit you are analyzing (such as country, state, city, ethnic group, sexual or gender identity) have the same and equal (another term often debated) rights? Can you think of historical periods when some citizens were (or are), to use George Orwell's phrase from his satiric novel *Animal*

*Farm*, "more equal than others"? Specifically, can you think of (or find through research) areas where LGBTQ+ folk have fewer or different rights from non-queer people? Are there any instances where they have *more* than their non-queer fellow citizens? (And if you find any of those, write to me immediately!) Have there been changes in rights and responsibilities — usually viewed as the foundations of citizenship — in the years since you were born or that you can remember? Can you think of what the processes involved in these changes included?

**2.** A useful project, which you might take on individually or in groups of like-minded class members, would be to do more research on either one of the countries discussed in this chapter (other than your own) or one not covered by this survey. Individuals or groups might then have a day or more of your own queer version of "It's a Small World" ("It's a Queer World"?), in which you present your findings to the class, so your classmates have the opportunity to hear more details and in greater depth than the discussions in this chapter can provide. Your teacher might suggest that everyone focus on one or two specific aspects of citizenship — whether the military, adoption, marriage, criminalization, or some other common theme. On the one hand, you might select a country about which you know little (such as some Asian or African countries, about which Westerners, unless they have a personal or scholarly interest, tend to know less well than we ought), or you might choose a country that you have a heritage connection to: it could be an opportunity to imagine what it would be like to be a queer person in one or more of the nations from which your ancestors came. Depending on how much time you have and how ambitious you are, you (and your group, if you decide to make this a collective effort), might choose two different countries, either ones that are geographically related (say, two countries in Eastern Asia, such as China and North Korea) or, conversely, two countries that may, at first glance, seem to share little in common. As you do your research and plan your presentation, look both at official sources (i.e., government documents and legal policies) and at more informal, "on the ground" sources you may find in browsing through online sources.

If you live in an area where you are able to find a person from the country you are studying, it could be worth trying to interview that person, whether they identify as LGBTQ+ or not, to get an insider's perspective on that country's attitudes toward and legislation regarding LGBTQ+ rights: obviously, were you to do so, you would need to prepare very carefully, so that the interviewee does not need to provide a basic education about the country and its culture, and you would need to frame questions and conduct the conversation in ways that are respectful and open to different ways of seeing the world from your own. Keep in mind the gay Ghanaian ethicist

Kwame Anthony Appiah's founding principle of cosmopolitanism: disagreement is not only acceptable, but often necessary, but the ethical road to it is by listening first and engaging in dialogue. Let your work on this activity be an opportunity to put this philosophy into practice—for from such individual conversations can come larger movements to help articulate and, in some cases, reformulate what it means to be a citizen.

**3.** While this chapter has introduced some of the central figures in queer politics, there are many others whose contributions have been considerable. Choose one of the following and do research into their lives, writings, speeches, and actions; some of the suggestions for further reading and viewing provide useful material about them and about their roles in larger movements. What have been their contributions, both as individuals and as members of social movements of their times? You may wish to form small groups to research these people and present your findings to the class.

1. Harvey Milk
2. Barbara Jordan
3. Del Martin and Phyllis Lyons
4. Frank Kameny
5. Barbara Gittings
6. Larry Kramer
7. Bayard Rustin
8. Marsha P. Johnson
9. Evan Wolfson
10. Essex Hemphill

Your instructor may propose others.

## SUGGESTIONS FOR FURTHER READING AND VIEWING

*Call Me Kuchu.* Directed by Katherine Fairfax Wright and Malika Zouhali-Worrall. Chicken and Egg Pictures, 2012.

Corrales, Javier, and Mario Pecheny, eds. *The Politics of Sexuality in Latin America: A Reader on Lesbian, Bisexual, and Transgender Rights.* Pittsburgh: University of Pittsburgh Press, 2010.

Currah, Paisley, Richard M. Juang, and Shannon Price Minter, eds. *Transgender Rights.* Minneapolis: University of Minnesota Press, 2006.

D'Emilio, John. *Lost Prophet: The Life and Times of Bayard Rustin*. New York: Free Press, 2003.

Essig, Laurie. *Queer in Russia: A Story of Sex, Self, and the Other*. Durham, NC: Duke University Press, 1999.

Faderman, Lillian. *The Gay Revolution: The Story of the Struggle*. New York: Simon and Schuster, 2015.

Gupta, Alok. *This Alien Legacy: The Origins of "Sodomy" Laws in British Colonialism*. New York: Human Rights Watch, 2008.

Healey, Dan. *Russian Homophobia from Stalin to Sochi*. London: Bloomsbury, 2017.

Katz, Jonathan Ned. *Gay American History: Lesbians and Gay Men in the U.S.A.* Rev. ed. New York: Plume, 1992.

Lemer, Bronson. *The Last Deployment: How a Gay, Hammer-Swinging Twenty-something Survived a Year in Iraq*. Madison: University of Wisconsin Press, 2011.

*Milk*. Directed by Gus von Sant. Focus, 2008.

Milk, Harvey. *An Archive of Hope: Harvey Milk's Speeches and Writings*, edited by Jason Edward Black and Charles E. Morris III. Berkeley: University of California Press, 2013.

Shilts, Randy. *Conduct Unbecoming: Lesbians and Gays in the U.S. Military, Vietnam to the Persian Gulf*. New York: St. Martin's Press, 1993.

*The Times of Harvey Milk*. Directed by Robert Epstein. Black Sand Productions, 1994.

Tuller, David. *Cracks in the Iron Closet: Travels in Gay and Lesbian Russia*. Chicago: University of Chicago Press, 1997.

**PART IV**

# QUEERING IMAGINATION

# CHAPTER 12

# QUEERING IMAGINATION
## Arts, Aesthetics, and Expression

In an oft-quoted comment made at a symposium held at the New Museum in New York City in 1984, titled "Is There a Gay Sensibility and Does It Have an Impact on Our Culture," the journalist and art critic Jeff Weinstein, after the panel had gone on for some time, summed up the complexity and contradictions inherent in such a question by stating, "No, there is no such thing as a gay sensibility, and, yes, it has an enormous impact on our culture" (quoted in Sherry, 7). Perhaps what Weinstein was getting at in his ironic yet sincere statement was the simultaneity of multiple truths, truths that, on first glance, might seem to contradict each other. So, yes, in Weinstein's phrase, gay sensibility, in its many forms and manifestations, did and does have "an enormous impact on our culture." Given the time period in which Weinstein made his remark — after Stonewall but before *queer* had been reclaimed as a term or concept — we should probably assume he meant *gay* to refer primarily to gay men, though there certainly are examples of what could be called lesbian sensibility (though probably not, in any clear-cut way, bisexual sensibility) and the beginning of an emerging trans sensibility that often was associated with the work of drag queens (and, to a lesser extent, drag kings).

Today we might frame the topic or question by saying that, given the comparative openness in the ways in which queer artists are more willing to produce art that has explicitly queer content, it is also true that some of the common qualities of art produced by queer artists have had an effect on art produced by those who do not identify as queer in the sense of sexual identities. Further, audiences have begun to become much more receptive, and have begun to accept and consume art that is queer in style, form, and perspective. The perspective of the audience was captured by the late gay scholar and theorists Alexander Doty in his 1993 book, *Making Things Perfectly Queer: Interpreting Mass Culture*. In this book Doty presents an over-

Henderson, *Bruce, Queer Studies: Beyond Binaries*
dx.doi.org/10.17312/harringtonparkpress/2019.09.qsbb.012
© 2019 by Harrington Park Press

arching theory of what can be called queer spectatorship, which he then applies to phenomena from mass culture, such as situation comedies from the 1950s, 1960s, and 1970s: queer spectatorship refers to the active sense-making and sense-experiencing done by an audience of people who are self-conscious of their own queer identity and its effects on how and what they view and hear. So "queer aesthetics" or "queer expressiveness" may reside in how a queer person (or an imagined queer culture) might view art and entertainment that does not necessarily have overtly queer content, as well as works produced by people who overtly identify as queer.

## THE QUEER SUBLIME AND THE QUEER UNCANNY: DIFFERENCE/SAMENESS, NEWNESS/REPETITION

While there are many different ways of defining queer aesthetics, including those that stress LGBTQ+ content, two related, some might argue complementary concepts could provide us with a set of lenses through which to consider the implications of both Weinstein's "gay sensibility" remark and Doty's concept of "queer spectatorship": the queer sublime and the queer uncanny.

In everyday conversation, we tend to use the word **sublime** as a term of highest praise, for either an artistic or some other sense-based experience. After a particularly wonderful, intensely chocolate soufflé, for example, we might exclaim, "That dessert was sublime!" It's a word that is often equated with "the best there could be" in some category. While it is true that even in narrower usage, in reference to artistic expression in various media, the sublime always carries with it some sense of elevation, of being beyond the everyday and the ordinary, on a higher plane of experience; it is more complicated than *beautiful*. The Greek rhetorician known as Longinus wrote a treatise on speaking and writing that is traditionally referred to as *On the Sublime*. Within the philosophical and critical tradition, he is credited with introducing and codifying the term.

The word came back into popularity during the Romantic era in Europe (the first half or so of the nineteenth century), in part because that was when non-merchants began to travel to geographically diverse and often dramatic places, such as the Alps, which became the subjects for poetry, as in Percy Bysshe Shelley's "Mont Blanc," and for paintings, such as *Wanderer above the Sea of Fog* by Caspar Friedrich, which shows a traveler, his back to us, staring from a mountaintop into an abyss of white fog. Mary Shelley's *Frankenstein* set scenes both on the tops of the Alps and in the frozen Arctic. As Longinus suggested in his original treatise, the sublime is not merely the highest achievement of that which is "pleasing" in the simple sense in which we often use the word, but it also always creates a sense of terror and an acknowledgment, in the midst of unspeakable pleasure, of the equally unspeakable possibility of death and dissolution in the midst of a universe larger than the individual.

What, then, is the "queer sublime"? The term has come into usage in the last decade or so, and it is fair to say that scholars and critics are using it in both common and variable ways. The Canadian writer Danielle Lewis wrote a study of the queer sublime in her analysis of the Turcot Yards in Montreal. The Turcot Yards are the area underneath the Turcot Interchange, a highly complex and somewhat dizzying set of highways and interchanges; in the Yards there are many derelict objects and materials, instances of graffiti as art and as social protest and expression, and a kind of community space, viewed as a park by many who use it as a place to meet and interact. For Lewis, this "officially" neglected (in some respects, abandoned) place has, by its very neglect, been transformed into something that is both queer, in that it has become a place for interaction among citizens who may be homeless or otherwise marginalized, and sublime, in its capacity to produce pleasure and terror at the same time. For Lewis, both the queer and the sublime, and their intersection in the bringing together of the two, are experiences of place "in which the multiplicity of communal and individual identities of Saint-Henri residents are simultaneously maintained and suspended, but never fully represented, through an experience of longing within the site." For Lewis, neither *queer* nor *sublime*, by definition, can ever be completed, the former because queerness involves fluidity, change, and a lack of final or permanent fixedness, the latter because a fully sublime experience would end in destruction and the disappearance of consciousness and activity — one is always just "this far" away from the finality that the sublime moves toward.

Another discussion of the queer sublime is that published by the communication and cultural scholar Davin Grindstaff in his 2008 article, "The Fist and the Corpse: Taming the Queer Sublime in *Brokeback Mountain*," published in the journal *Communication and Critical/Cultural Studies*. In this essay Grindstaff writes about the popular film *Brokeback Mountain*, based on the short story by E. Annie Proulx, which is about the decades-long love affair between two men, Ennis del Mar and Jack Twist, that began during a summer when they worked as sheepherders, and was conducted periodically and often long-distance until Jack's death through what in the story is left ambiguous but in the film is more definitely identified as an act of homophobic violence by men in the town in Texas in which Jack lives with his wife and child. By the time Ennis learns of Jack's death, he has been divorced from his wife and has had little ongoing contact with his daughters; he makes a final journey to Jack's childhood home, where he meets Jack's stoic parents.

Grindstaff's particular focus is on what he terms "taming the queer sublime" for viewers of the film. For some viewers, the tragedy of the story is in the social homophobia, combined with rural poverty, that makes it impossible for the two men to imagine, let alone embark on, a permanent domestic relationship with each other. For others, it is a tragedy of individuals, especially Ennis, who could not take their own destinies into their hands and make their way from the world in which they have been raised to such outposts as Denver or San Francisco, where gay men from the country often found communities of other queer men.

Grindstaff is more interested in what the film does for its viewers, in terms of providing an example of the queer sublime: he suggests that it "symbolically represents the collective trauma that would otherwise result from directly witnessing homophobic repression and violence; yet because the film aesthetically induces a feeling of pleasure, audiences transcend the terror that would ordinarily accompany such encounters" (223). The Wyoming setting of the idyllic summer when the two young men meet and fall in love has its own real-world sublime resonances. For the viewers, the film both alludes to and provides glimpses into and apprehension about the possibilities of the kinds of violence that are always present in experiences of the sublime; Grindstaff's thesis suggests that some of the fear is ameliorated by the visual and emotional beauty of the scenes of the men in love, physically showing affection for each other, including nonpornographic but clearly defined scenes of erotic interaction between them. For Grindstaff, the queerness of the sublime in *Brokeback Mountain* resides both in its content—the homoerotic relationship between Ennis and Jack—and in the cinematic pleasures of the visual images and the kinesthesis of editing, musical score, and other formal elements.

The concept of the *uncanny*, which, like the sublime, has everyday meanings not necessarily tied to art and expression, is a translation of the German word *unheimliche*, which literally means "unhomelike," or, in simpler terms, "unfamiliar." It took on its specialized usage principally on the basis of Sigmund Freud's 1919 essay, "The Uncanny." Freud, who placed his essay in the context of processes of repression and the unconscious, which were the foundations of his theories, used the term *uncanny* to denote a particular kind of unfamiliarity or strangeness: those experiences or works of art that are "strangely familiar" (and, yes, the shifting use of *familiar* can be a bit thorny at first). What he was trying to identify and analyze were those moments when we feel simultaneously that we are in the presence of something that is familiar, not unknown to us, but that that familiarity has some dimension of oddness or difference from what we might expect. Freud used the fiction of the German Romantic writer E. T. A. Hoffmann as his example, especially a story called "The Sandman," in which there is both a dancing automaton (an early mechanical kind of robot) named Olympia and a frightening figure who steals people's eyes. Olympia is uncanny in a fairly straightforward sense: she has the appearance of being human and can enact certain human movements, but we are aware that she is also not human. That realm of feeling where we are caught between the appearance of the real and acknowledgment of the artificial is the place of the uncanny. The eye thief is more complex, in Freud's analysis, because it is an instantiation of paranoia and the fear of being robbed of something typically thought of as defining of a body (human or otherwise). Freud's essay, one of his more accessible, places both examples in terms of what he believed humans do unconsciously in order to repress that which they would prefer not to have to confront. Thus, the monstrous, which became a central feature of the gothic fiction that became very popular in various European and other literatures in the nineteenth century, is often viewed as a way of coping with the uncanny in ourselves and in our surroundings. (Freud also tied it, in its extreme manifestations, to pathological paranoia.)

If you have studied media or technology, you may have run into the phrase "the uncanny valley." It was coined by a Japanese scholar of robotics, Masahiro Mori, in 1970 and translated as "the uncanny valley" when the work was published in English. Mori suggests that, as robots are fashioned to look more and more human, humans tend to develop more empathy toward them. But at a certain point, he hypothesized, just before the robot reaches a state where human and thing become indistinguishable, we dip into a valley and experience the robot as uncanny, which produces discomfort and some degree of alienation. Filmmakers, particularly those involved in animation, consider whether they have ventured into the uncanny valley in their work — they may wish to provoke frightening or abject feelings, or they may decide to withhold so near a "fit" as to retain sympathy or other positive feelings for their created androids.

How is this related to queerness? The literary scholar Paulina Palmer has written a fascinating book, *The Queer Uncanny: New Perspectives on the Gothic*, in which she addresses this very question, focusing on a set of novels she examines through the lenses of queerness and the uncanny (and the intersectionality of the two). Her overarching thesis is that nonheteronormative sexuality and non-cisgender identity have traditionally been depicted as uncanny realms (for the implied majority readership of the novels, who, though the terms are a bit anachronistic for some of the works about which she writes, were less likely to have conscious same-sex orientations or experiences or to identify as what today we would call anything but their assigned gender). In pre-twentieth-century literature, it was uncommon for either nonheternormative sex or sexuality or transgender identity to be depicted overtly. (There were graphic descriptions of sexual realms in general — much of it deferred to the "spaces" between chapters, itself a kind of repressive move to the uncanny.) So monsters and the monstrous, particularly vampires, ghosts, haunted houses, places where the lines between the living human and the spectral other get blurred, became popular. In some cases, these were realms where lesbian sex, for example, could be introduced indirectly, through the figure of the female vampire who preyed on the bodies of other women, or reproduction without heterosexual sex through manufactured quasi-humans, such as Frankenstein's monster: Dr. Frankenstein could be seen as both father and mother to "the Creature" (as he was referred to in Mary Shelley's novel), and thus as transgressing or spanning gender identities. Closer to our own time, the revival of fascination with vampire novels, films, and television series began during the 1980s, when questions of the dangers of blood (particularly what became thought of as "tainted blood," a particularly homophobic and stigmatizing phrase) arose during the first decade of the AIDS epidemic. To feast on blood or to be made into a vampire because of contact with another vampire had an uncanny relationship with perceptions of how the epidemic was spreading to "innocent" (i.e., nongay male, non–IV-drug-using, primarily white) populations.

Palmer considers the ways in which issues of sameness and otherness and the blurry place in between is queer in the sense of the complicated and often conflicted ways in which queer sex, affection, and attraction are depicted and understood. For non-queer readers and spectators, queer feeling and experience may reside in or near the uncanny valley, as most people have an understanding of their own structures of attraction, desire, and emotion, but the queerness of same-sex relations may provoke a sense of unease or incomprehension. Similarly, most people have an understanding of gender and of their own identity as gendered, and, it is safe to say, they experience that in cisgender terms. Thus, even within a broadening range of what gender itself means (and where it comes from, whether neurobiological, sociocultural, or some combination of factors) and what is typically associated with the two dominant parts of the gender binary, transgender challenging or "disobedience" to the policing of gender may create a sense of the uncanny. Because so little research has been done about people who identify as nonbinary, it is impossible to say with any certainty, but it may be that for some cisgender people, a nonbinary gender–identified person "feels" more uncanny than a trans person: as humans, we are taught to place people in categories, and *trans*, even if foreign to cisgender people's own experience of the self, may feel more comprehensible than either fluidity of gender identity or absence of it entirely.

It may well be that such parts of human experience as sexual orientation and gender have some degree of the uncanny for all people — at different times, in different ways, and to different extents. Puberty and adolescence are typically considered to be difficult times for all people, often because the body is developing in ways that make it feel both familiar and strange at the same time. Even cisgender, heterosexually identified teens, whom we may think of as having fewer (or different) challenges during this period, may find upsetting the growth of pubic hair, the development of breasts (for girls), and the often dramatic changes in size of penis (for boys). The onset of menstruation can be sufficiently strange or upsetting (in making the body feel unfamiliar) that cultures have often developed rituals that bring young women into the realm of adulthood upon this event. (In some European cultures a girl, upon announcing to her mother that she has begun her first period, may be slapped. Some might argue that this act of physical violence is meant to police the young women, a kind of reminder that she now needs to conduct herself in a "proper" sexual way.)

For children and adolescents who either already or will at some point identify as queer (in terms of sexual orientation, gender identity, or both), there may be elements of both the sublime and the uncanny that are different in form or degree from those of their heterosexual and cisgender peers. Interestingly, it is in literature written for these audiences that we find some fascinating and powerful explorations of queer sublimity and uncanniness.

## Spotlight: Learning to Read — Queer Children's and Young Adult Fiction

Though young people's literature occasionally has had memorable characters who stepped outside stereotypical conventions of the gender expectations of their times, such as Jo March in Louisa May Alcott's *Little Women* (who nonetheless becomes a more traditional wife and mother by the end of that book and in its sequels), it was rare, until the 1960s, to see books for young readers that truly challenged assumptions of cisgender heteronormativity. An interesting and until recently rare example of a transgender character in children's literature is that of Tip/Princess Ozma in the Oz series written by L. Frank Baum (and by other writers for later books in the series). Other than Oz fans, few people read beyond the first Oz book. Most memories are based on the 1939 MGM film starring Judy Garland, who was an icon for generations of gay men; the film has been read through queer lenses, especially Dorothy's desire to leave Kansas for a place "over the rainbow" and her camaraderie with her three magical friends and protectors, who stand outside various kinds of normativity. In the second book in the series, most often published under the title *The Marvelous Land of Oz* (1904), the plot is dominated by a young adolescent male named Tip, who has created a living Pumpkinhead (thus continuing the father-mother role of Frankenstein, though in far less malevolent ways). At the climax of the novel, Tip learns that when he was born, he was a girl, the rightful Princess Ozma, but was transformed by the "hag" Mombi into a boy, and Glinda, the good witch, dictates that Tip must now "resume your proper form, that you may become Queen of the Emerald City" (http://gutenberg.org/files/54/54-h/54-h.htm#Page_256).

It is probably wise not to make too much of the author's intentions in placing a transgender character in his magical land. In some sense, it feels like a plot contrivance, perhaps allowing Tip to be a boy for the bulk of the novel in order to attract young male readers, and then transforming the character into a girl in order to set the ensuing social structures of the following novels in place. Nonetheless, for some readers, the "trans-ness" of Tip/Ozma is a powerful and important reading experience, one of value and meaning in their own lives and process of identity formation and transition. The blogger and writer Charlotte Finn, focusing on comic book adaptations of Oz stories, remarks, "But then, I learnt about the character of Princess Ozma, and not long after that, I realized I was transgender — so the path I took into Oz started with her." While aptly critiquing Baum's "beauty politics" in the novel, Finn adds, *The Marvelous Land of Oz* "takes a different path, and postulates a world where the presence of the strange and unusual makes us more tolerant, not less so." So what Freud might call the uncanny in the trans identity and revelation of Tip's female "proper form" can become a vehicle for what might be considered the sublime. At the moment at which Tip must dissolve in order for the Baum-created universe to achieve harmony, there is a kind of joyfulness in what is on the other side, the benevolent, wise, and courageous Ozma, who rules well in her female form.

Other recent writers, such as Geoff Ryman in his novel *Was*, which centers on a gay man dying from AIDS who seeks Dorothy's Kansas and finds himself "over the rainbow" by book's end, and Gregory Maguire's series of books, collectively called *The Wicked Years*, use such tropes as Elpheba's green skin as analogies to various kinds of queerness. Both Ryman and Maguire identify publicly as gay men. A more recent series of riffs on the Oz mythos is the *Dorothy Must Die* series by Danielle Paige, which reintroduces Tip (here called Pete, a variation on Tip's full name, Tippetarius, in Baum's novel) and Ozma, who appears at moments near the end of the novel, when Pete is not present, and speaks a kind of nonsense, suggesting a mental illness brought on by Dorothy and her minions. Paige does not seem to suggest an equation between trans identity and mental illness, but the coexistence of them in the depiction of Ozma raises complex questions.

A relatively recent classic that does an excellent job of exploring gender identity issues for younger readers, without being prescriptive and indeed by being slyly subversive, is Louise Fitzhugh's *Harriet the Spy* (1964), and its sequel (or companion book), *The Long Secret* (1965). Fitzhugh identified primarily as a lesbian and was open about her identity within her cohort of fellow artists and friends in Greenwich Village; she was not out as such in the world of publishing (few writers could afford to be at the time, and certainly not a writer for children). Harriet is a sixth-grade girl who lives with her well-to-do family on the Upper West Side of Manhattan and attends a private school. (Her father works in public relations and her mother is a typical housewife, though she has a housekeeper, which allows her to spend her time doing what "the ladies who lunch," to use Stephen Sondheim's phrase, do with their days.) The parents are pleasant and affectionate, but they do not seem deeply involved in Harriet's life. She is looked after by her childhood nanny, Ole Golly, whose exit to marry provides the first crisis of the novel. From the start, Harriet is depicted, both in the language of the book and in Fitzhugh's illustrations (she was a gifted artist, as well), as gender nonconforming, changing, as soon as she gets home from school, into her "spy" uniform: pants, sweatshirt, tool belt, and her ever-present notebook. She spends much of her free time in solitude, observing neighbors in the blocks near her house, which suggests a life of watching rather than participating. In addition to having dreams of being a spy, Harriet aspires to become a writer. Her two close friends are also gender nonconforming in significant ways: Sport (Simon), who cooks and cleans house for his single father, and Janie, who wants to be a scientist and blow up the world. Neither of Harriet's friends is depicted as potentially trans or gay (though there is fan fiction, stories written by typically amateur authors, that imagine their favorite characters in new narratives, often emphasizing erotic possibilities between characters not explored in the original texts), but Fitzhugh suggests the ways in which modern urban life and the changing nature of families lead to different ways of growing up gendered. Harriet's notebook, filled with observations of her schoolmates, most not flattering, is seized, and she is stigmatized for some time by them. After what is never named as such, but clearly is a nervous breakdown, Harriet sees a child psychiatrist, is given a more useful role as coeditor of the school paper, and apologizes. As Ole Golly writes to her, "Sometimes you have to lie," perhaps a message of strategic self-closeting from a lesbian writer who could not be out to her readers during her lifetime.

In the sequel, *The Long Secret,* Fitzhugh focuses on a classmate of Harriet's, Beth Ellen Hansen, setting her with Harriet in a resort town on Long Island during the summer. The novel is less well known than the first, but in some ways it does even more radical work on sexuality and gender. Beth Ellen, whom Harriet nicknames "Mouse" because of her timidity, is very traditionally girlish in her appearance and behavior. The main part of the novel focuses on the upheaval to Beth Ellen's well-ordered life with her grandmother when her absentee mother, Zeeney, and Zeeney's latest husband arrive in town. In the middle of the novel, Beth Ellen gets her first period, and Janie, who is visiting for the weekend, explains the biological meaning of the process to the two girls. In addition to being one of the first novels for young readers to explain these body issues, it also shows Harriet's revolted response to this body function. While there is never any suggestion that Harriet does not identify as female, the sense of not wanting her body to go through this process has a mild element of gender dysphoria to it. Janie, the ever-practical scientist, simply acknowledges it as a given, but she also declares that she wants to invent a way to avoid it.

The novel takes the reactions of the three girls to their female bodies with seriousness and without condescension. While Harriet's ignorance of how her body works is criticized by Janie, it is also the case that Janie recognizes that it is the gender policing and assumptions about what is proper to discuss that is the root of her disgust, not any pathology on Harriet's part. Many lesbians have adopted Harriet and Janie as, in their (affectionate) terms, "baby dykes." It is not stretching things to suggest that they may possibly also be somewhere under the trans umbrella. Sexual orientation per se does not arise (other than Harriet's thinking about, though not particularly desiring, marriage and what it might be like).

Four years later what is usually considered to be the first novel written for young adults (i.e., middle and high school students, often referred to as YA literature) to depict the possibilities of same-sex romantic and physical attraction between teenage boys was published: John Donovan's *I'll Get There. It Better Be Worth the Trip* (1969). Donovan was a gay man and worked in children's publishing, also holding the position of president of the Children's Book Council for many years. His novel is told from the first-person point of view of its protagonist, Davy Ross, a thirteen-year-old boy who, at the beginning of the novel, has to deal with the shifts in his life brought about by the sudden death of his grandmother, with whom he has been living after his parents' divorce. He moves from Massachusetts to New York City, where he and his dachshund, Fred, must adapt to the smaller space of a city apartment, a new school, and Davy's mother's ambivalence toward being an active parent, which is complemented by her alcoholism, a narcissistic personality, and what today might be diagnosed as borderline personality disorder. An incidental detail may suggest (at least to an adult) the unspoken role of homosexuality in the family: at the funeral of Davy's grandmother is the single, early-middle-aged Uncle Jess from California, who visited his mother only every five years or so, and who works as "some kind of model," in Davy's words. While he feebly offers to have Davy live with him, that idea is quickly squelched, much to Uncle Jess's relief, and he does not reappear. It is likely that young readers, especially in 1969, would not have read him as a possibly coded gay uncle, but adult readers might have been more savvy.

The possibility of homosexuality enters the novel when Davy begins attending a local boys' Episcopal school. One of the first students he meets is Altschuler (Douglas, though the boys are addressed by their last names in the schoolroom), who resents that Davy has taken the seat of Wilkins, Altschuler's closest friend, who, we learn, has been ill with what is not named but clearly is a form of leukemia. Wilkins eventually dies, and it is clear that this loss is for Altschuler more than simply that of a classmate. Nothing sexual or even romantic is hinted at, but the passion that the two friends had felt for each other is clear, at least from the depiction of Altschuler's sense of loss. Though Davy and Altschuler begin as antagonists, they eventually become each other's close and, at least during the period the novel covers, only real friend. One day, the two boys, left alone in Davy's apartment, get drunk on some brandy and tentatively and impulsively "make out." The novel indicates they kiss and embrace: it is clear that there is some mixture of romantic and erotic dimensions to this interaction, though each boy claims he is not queer (and Donovan uses that specific word, another part of his realistic portrayal of boys' talk during that era). Indeed, each claims to have a girlfriend to whom he is "practically engaged," though they eventually admit these relationships are not really serious (as is the case with most young teenage romances, whatever the sexual combination).

Donovan established a trope that would be present in many of the LGB YA novels for the next few decades: the tragic punishment that comes with homoerotic feeling and action. Davy's mother loses control of Fred's leash, and the beloved pet is struck and killed by a car. Though Davy considers whether he is being punished by or is responsible for Fred's death because of his "transgression" with Altschuler, it is to Donovan's credit that Davy dismisses this kind of magical thinking fairly quickly. The novel ends inconclusively, in terms of the boys' view of their own homoerotic encounters and what the future may hold for them, but, as critics have pointed out, it ends with both boys affirming the possibility of respecting each other, whatever their sexual orientations turn out to be. That in itself was radical for its time.

Two novels that depict lesbian experience among adolescents from this period merit consideration as well. The first, *Ruby* by Rosa Guy (1976), is the second in three linked YA novels that follow the lives of a pair of sisters who, with their parents (though the mother has died of cancer), emigrate from the West Indies to New York City, where they live with their traditional and tyrannical father, Calvin, who owns a restaurant and controls the girls' lives. *Ruby* is told from the point of its eponymous heroine, an eighteen-year-old young woman, in her senior year of high school, somewhat timid and submissive, who falls in love with a fellow female student, an African American teen named Daphne, who lives with her single mother in a household that, for the most part, feels more like a sisterhood than a traditional mother-daughter hierarchy. Daphne aspires to attend Brandeis, is unafraid to disclose her sexuality or to confront systems of white and male privilege she encounters in school and on the streets of the city. *Ruby* is generally considered the first book in English written for young adults to depict lesbianism: indeed, the word *dyke* is used by the characters to describe their sexuality. The novel ends with Daphne's decision that her lesbianism was only a phase, and she heads off to Brandeis. It is implied that she may be more an opportunist than anything else; her "return" to heterosexuality seems as much motivated by her desire for the financial and social support of her mother's married, white, well-to-do boyfriend, who may have had a hand in gaining her admission to Brandeis. Ruby, who has become more politicized in the novel (there are references to Malcolm X and Frantz Fanon, the Caribbean psychoanalyst, social activist, and scholar), is crushed by the rejection. The novel, like Donovan's, ends on an ambiguous note, in terms of both the protagonists' life path and their sexual orientation.

A less ambivalent and, therefore, more controversial book of lesbian adolescence is Nancy Garden's *Annie on My Mind* (1982). Indeed, so "dangerous" is Garden's affirmation of lesbian love that the book has shown up consistently on lists of those most challenged by communities. Garden writes from the point of view of a teenage girl, Liza, who meets Annie (of the title) by chance in a New York City museum. (The girls attend different schools, Liza a private one, Annie a public one, in different parts of the city.) The girls develop a romantic and sexual relationship and are eventually outed after they spend time together in the apartment of a closeted pair of teachers for whom they have agreed to housesit while the older couple is on vacation. The teachers are fired from their jobs, and there is talk of expelling Liza; in a plot development that is remarkably optimistic and open-minded for its time (though the novel was written more than a decade after Stonewall, which suggests opportunity for progress), Liza is not expelled. But the girls drift apart and attend colleges on different sides of the country. Nonetheless, at the end, they reconnect and decide to meet during their break, with the implication that they are now free to rekindle their relationship and explore its more permanent possibilities.

That no one dies, no pets are harmed, and the only tragedy is that the closeted teachers lose their jobs at a school dominated by a narrow-minded headmistress (and, hence, perhaps the firing can be a catalyst for the two women to live lives truer to themselves), is probably what those who would keep the book from its target audience found most daunting. Indeed, a minister in Kansas City in 1993 organized a public burning of the book, which drew analogies to the Nazis' burning of books and otherwise destroying what they termed "degenerate" art, which was not simply queer art, but also that produced by Jews, political dissidents, and other groups deemed inferior under the Third Reich (Casey Stepaniuk, "The Burning and Banning of an *Annie on My Mind*," *BookRiot*, March 18, 2018, https://bookriot.com/2018/03/16/annie-on-my-mind/). Nonetheless, *Annie on My Mind* has not been out of print since it was first published and was dramatized by the BBC in 1991; it was adapted for the stage in 1993 and premiered in Lawrence, Kansas, the same year the books were burned in Kansas City.

Other than such anomalies as the Oz books discussed earlier, it has taken much longer for children's and young adult literature to depict the lives of trans children and adolescents, though, as suggested, the growth of second-wave feminism and gay liberation did call traditional gender roles into question, and third-wave feminism has drawn gender fluidity and trans identities into the discussion in more open ways. In the last ten or fifteen years, fiction written for young readers has seen considerable growth in representation of a wide spectrum of narratives that take up not only sexual orientation and gender roles in society, but gender identity and expression in ways that make trans and intersex lives much more visible. One measure of this that you may find interesting to explore is the list of winners and finalists for major LGBTQ+ literary awards, such as the Lambda Literary Awards, which have long had a category for LGBT literature for young readers (https://www.lambdaliterary.org) and the Stonewall Book Awards, presented by the American Library Association (www.ala.org/rt/glbtrt/award/stonewall/honored). In recent years one or more of the books designated as winners or finalists is typically about trans or other non-cisgender identity.

The first book on trans youth experience to receive awards and mainstream attention is probably Julie Anne Peters's *Luna* (2004). *Luna* is told from the point of view of sixteen-year-old Regan, whose older sibling, known as Liam during his daily life, tells his sister that he identifies as a woman and wishes to be known as Luna (hence the title, a play on the metamorphosis of the moth). In recent years, the novel has come under justifiable criticism on a number of dimensions. First and foremost, it uses the point of view of the cisgender sister, rather than that of its transgender title protagonist. Whether this is a marketing move, the assumption being that a wider audience may be able to identify with the cisgender observer, or whether the fear was that trying to represent the inner life of the trans person might be stereotypical or unrealistic (and most writers of these earlier novels identified as cisgender), this has been seen as limiting the sense of authenticity of such stories and as robbing the trans character of agency. Some have also criticized *Luna* for focusing on external actions, such as the siblings going to a local mall with Luna dressed in female clothing, as also limiting what young readers might potentially learn and understand. Nonetheless, the place of *Luna* as a historical moment when transgender youth experience could be represented, even if in an imperfect and flawed fashion, is important to acknowledge.

Recent years have seen novels that work more directly to represent trans, intersex, or nonbinary youth experience; these novels are sometimes written by people who identify with the gender identity they are describing and sometimes by cisgender writers who, as a rule, nonetheless strive to do the kinds of work it takes any writer to write with truth, respect, and knowledge about an identity or experience category they do not share. There remains lively and ongoing debate about who *should* have the right to write about various kinds of identities and experiences, which is hardly limited to queer categories of identity. Some feel that, at least at this moment in queer history, only those occupying particular identity categories should write about them; others believe that such identity positions need not be restrictive, as long as writers listen to, research, and respect identities they do not inhabit.

*Beautiful Music for Ugly Children* (2012) by Kirstin Cronn-Mills is about a teenage trans boy who lives as Elizabeth (Liz) in his family life and at school, but becomes Gabe when he DJ's a radio show, which he calls "Beautiful Music for Ugly Children." Encouraged by John, a next-door neighbor, middle-aged man, and DJ himself, Gabe turns the show into an underground, late-night hit, developing a following of "ugly children" who perform various pranks and what might be called social interventions, identifying as members of Gabe's "family." In an afterword written on the novel's fifth anniversary, Cronn-Mills honestly and thoughtfully indicates that, had she to do it again, she probably would not have written the novel, for the simple reason that she is cisgender and she has come to believe that such stories need, at least first, to be written by trans authors.

*Girl Mans Up* (2016) by M-E Girard is a novel that looks with directness, honesty, and the grittiness of the real language and experiences of adolescents who identify as queer, and perhaps gender-challenging, but not transgender or genderqueer. Pen (short for Penelope) lives with her Portuguese-immigrant family. Pen is masculine-identified in her dress, manner, and interests, deeply bonded with her older brother, Johnny, and part of a gang of teenage males. Pen does not identify as trans — she is reasonably comfortable (as much as most adolescents are) in her female body, even if her performance of dress and swagger seems more typically masculine in presentation. The novel follows Pen's struggles to make her parents understand her experience of her own femaleness, which may be described by J. Halberstam's term *female masculinity*. It is fair to say (without spoiling the plot) that Girard does not avoid such gritty topics as violence against women, both those who present their femininity in traditional ways and those whose performance of gender may be more threatening to some adolescent males, as well as reproductive choice and safety. The language is true to the experience of contemporary teens, and the novel depicts such activities as smoking and drinking and mild drugging, all of which make it feel more real than a more sanitized version would. In addition to the excellence of the writing, the novel is valuable in depicting how a queer adolescent female who performs female masculinity but does not identify as transgender experiences herself and those around her.

I. W. Gregorio's *None of the Above* (2015) is one of the rare novels that ventures into the experience of people who identify as or are labeled intersex. Its narrator and protagonist, Kristin Lattimer, appears to all (including herself) at the outset of the novel as a typical high school girl—indeed, perhaps even more than typical, as she is named homecoming queen! After a painful and traumatic attempt to have celebratory sex with her boyfriend, Sam, she goes to her doctor, who discovers that Kristin has a number of anomalies associated with a particular form of intersex experience, androgen insensitivity syndrome (AIS), one of the consequences of which is a shortened vagina, which is responsible in part for the painful sex. The novel includes considerable information about AIS, as Kristin must learn (or relearn) her body; it also shows the stigma Kristin experiences among her schoolmates until she finds her own set of supporters. Gregorio is a urologist and was inspired to write the book by the experiences of one of her own patients.

Other writers have depicted transgender characters and experiences in different ways. Brie Spangler, for example, turns in *Beast* (2016) to a retelling of the French fairy tale (and subsequent Disney blockbusters) "Beauty and the Beast," but here with a trans boy taking the role of Belle (and not, for a change, the monstrous beast, not the freak so many trans characters are required to be). Spangler identifies as cisgender. Another author, April Daniels, who identifies as a trans woman, has begun a series of novels set in a fictional American city, in a world in which superheroes exist as an everyday part of society. The series begins with *Dreadnought* (2017), and it skips over the typical initial conflict about trans identity and the process of transition by using the sudden transformation characteristic of comic books and superhero movie franchises as its origin story. The narrator and hero of the novel is Danny, who, on the first page of the novel, comes on the dying superhero Dreadnought, who passes his superpowers on to Danny. When Danny receives the powers, she (then a he) also immediately transitions physically into the girl she experienced herself to be even before she met

Dreadnought; as we learn in the course of the novel, the process of conferring such powers (they are passed down from one superhero to another) also makes the recipient become "who they really are." (In one case, this process turns a former mortal heterosexual person into a gay man.) What is interesting and innovative about Daniels's choice of how to set the plot in motion is that, even though Danny's father is depicted as resistant to Danny's gender transition (or transformation, in the magical terms of the genre), it is a given and natural within the order of the world of the novel's terms. As Danny suggests, any attempt to do hormonal therapy or surgical intervention will be for naught. At the end of the first novel, upon defeating the villain responsible for Dreadnought's murder, Danny, at a press conference, declares: "And one more thing. I'm not telling you this because it's important, but because I know you'll hear about it eventually and I don't want anyone to think I have something to hide. . . . I'm transgender, and a lesbian, and I'm not ashamed of that" (279). The novel concludes with Danny's internal addition, "And I think maybe I could be a good person." The second book in the series, *Sovereign* (2017) continues Danny's adventures as a doubly queer (trans and lesbian) superhero.

David Levithan, a gay male writer of books for young adults, has included trans issues in both realistic and fantastic ways. His companion books, *Every Day* (2012), *Another Day* (2017), and *Someday* (2018), tell the same story, but from complementary points of view. *Every Day* follows the experiences of A, a character who wakes up each day in a different self — in terms of body and identity, sometimes male, sometimes female, and so on. *Another Day* tells the same story, but from the point of view of Rhiannon, the girl with whom A is having a relationship. *Someday* continues the story of A and reveals others who live similarly fluid lives, some of whom narrate portions of the novel. His 2013 book, *Two Boys Kissing*, is a highly poetic novel, centered on the efforts of a pair of teenage boys, former boyfriends, to break the world's record for uninterrupted public kissing, and thus make history together for themselves and for LGBTQ+ people, symbolically demonstrating how strong and lasting queer love can be, whatever its form. They have been inspired to do this public act as a peaceful response to an episode of gay-bashing against one of the other gay boys. They become an international phenomenon as their video feed goes viral; they are supported by friends, teachers, and family, and they withstand the occasional jeers and thrown bottles (and are protected by those around them). The novel is narrated by an unseen chorus (similar to a Greek chorus) of the ghosts or souls of men who died from AIDS, who spur the kissing boys on from the afterlife and draw attention to the differences between their lives and those of queer youth today. One of the queer boys in the present day is a trans boy, Avery, who meets a cisgender gay boy, Ryan, at a prom. While Avery experiences some anxiety at the prospect of disclosing his trans identity to Ryan, the novel depicts his trans identity as his true one, the "boy he always was" — he has every right to be part of the community of boys (and their supporters) the book celebrates. The novel introduces Avery with this simple but powerful description: "Pink-haired Avery was born a boy that the rest of the world saw as a girl" (12). No additional explanation of Avery's gender identity is required.

The last book we will consider is a novel written for the youngest readers usually considered ready for chapter books — grades three and up. Interestingly, it is also the source of current controversy, perhaps particularly because its audience is seen by some as unready for these complex topics; such critics may underestimate what children are capable of understanding. It is *George* (2015) by Alex Gino, who identifies as genderqueer, and it is the winner of numerous awards, including both the Lambda and Stonewall awards. *George* tells the story of its title character, a fifth-grader, assigned male at birth, who presents as male to his family and schoolmates and teachers, but who internally identifies as a girl; we see him moving toward a stronger identification as he hides and takes pleasure in looking at images of women's clothing, makeup, and hairstyles in magazines he keeps out of sight. He lives with his single mother and his initially obnoxious (and typical) teenage brother, Scott, who by the end of the novel becomes a strong and sympathetic ally to his younger sister.

The dramatic conflict of the novel centers on a theatrical one in George's life. His teacher has just finished reading E. B. White's classic novel of friendship, acceptance, and belonging, *Charlotte's Web*, and then announces that the two fifth-grade classes will put on a dramatization of it for the school. George decides she (Gino uses the female pronoun for the character throughout) wants to play the role of Charlotte but is shut down by her teacher at the audition: the novel makes it clear that it is not because George is unable to act well, but because wanting to play a female role violates the teacher's sense of propriety and acceptability. George retreats into a kind of depression, refusing to perform at all, opting instead to work backstage, where she is teased for her nonmasculine behavior — not for presenting in girl's clothing (which she does not do until the final chapter), but simply for being a less typically "boyish" boy. In a lovely and even thrilling turnabout, she conspires with her best friend, a very sympathetic classmate named Kelly, who has been cast as Charlotte, to substitute for her, taking everyone by surprise, for the second evening performance of the play, which her family attends. Some of the bullies continue to bully, but many of her classmates, male and female alike, compliment her and tell her how much they admire her. Even her mother, who has said she would be accepting of her if she were gay, but has found her trans identity hard to accept, seems to be moving toward more open-mindedness. In the final chapter Melissa (as George now calls herself) goes with Kelly and her uncle, who has never met George/Melissa before, on an outing at the zoo, during which Melissa dresses in Kelly's female-gendered clothing, and the uncle is none the wiser.

It is a beautifully written novel, providing information about transgender life and processes for transitioning in language accessible to third- through fifth-graders, the target audience for the book. In a section of Frequently Asked Questions (And Things Alex Wants to Say), as the author dubs it, which is now included in paperback editions of the novel, Gino provides young readers with even more information about sources for learning about transgender lives. They (Gino's preferred pronoun) also make the important point that they have regrets about naming the book *George*, explaining that it was initially meant as a nod to Boy George, the lead singer of the genderqueer band Culture Club, but they realize that the title *Melissa* might have modeled a more appropriate protocol for avoiding "deadnaming" (the act of referring to or addressing a trans person by the name they were given at birth, which draws attention to the previous gender they were assigned) the title character. Under whatever title, it is a powerful book and important in providing children — who more and more may be identifying as trans or intersex with classmates, friends, and siblings — and adults as well with ways of understanding and imagining trans lives.

The book became the center of a controversy in 2018, when it was selected by a panel as one of the books for the annual Oregon Battle of the Books, a reading competition held statewide. The principals of the five elementary schools in Hermiston, a small town, decided not to have their schools participate in the competition because *George* was one of the books on the list for the Battle. As reported by the journalist Jayati Ramakrishnan, "The elementary school principals sent a letter to parents stating that the novel *George*, by Alex Gino, was not appropriate for their third- through fifth-grade students, based on their adopted human growth and development curriculum" (quoted in Ryan Harrington, "The Trouble with *George*: A Trans Character Causes Controversy in Oregon Literary Competition," Melville House, May 2, 2018, https://www.mhpbooks.com/the-trouble -with-george-a-trans-character-causes-controversy-in-oregon-literary-com petition). Students in other age brackets, in which *George* was not part of the competition, could and did compete. What is most sad, in addition to the simple fact that students from these schools were denied an opportunity to participate, is that this action shut down opportunities for genuine dialogue and discussion and sent messages of shame and stigma to children at an age at which they may not have formed as sedimented attitudes of transphobia as they might a few years down the road. Nonetheless, *George*, like its equally brave predecessor *Charlotte's Web* (which, when published, some librarians and critics censured for its frank presentation of death), seems destined to become a favorite — and children find ways to get the books they want to read, even if, like George/Melissa, they have to do so in indirect or inventive ways.

## SOME CENTRAL CONCEPTS AND TRADITIONS IN QUEER EXPRESSION

### Aesthetics and "Art for Art's Sake"

In his study of the homoerotic in late Enlightenment and nineteenth-century **aesthetics**, *Queer Beauty*, Whitney Davis makes a compelling argument for the presence of what we might call the undertones, subtextual or sometimes explicit elements of same-sex attractiveness (if not attraction) underpinning what was evaluated as beautiful — even when critic and artist were both what we would classify today as heterosexual. Similarly, men who we know or have good reason to believe were primarily homosexual could admire and find beautiful such representations of the female body as the Venus de Milo or Winged Victory.

The pleasures of the beautiful, then, were viewed as a physical response, but a response first and foremost to elements such as the use of materials, achievement of harmony and balance, closeness to real life (what was called *verisimilitude*); the beautiful was typically seen as manifest in the formal pleasures it produced in the mind and senses of the viewer, rather than in the almost dynamic and kinesthetic experiences and responses associated with the sublime. David Hume, an Enlightenment philosopher best known for his works on empiricism (the belief that reality inhered only in that which could be apprehended through the senses), wrote an interesting and important essay titled "On the Standard of Taste," which considered the problems of trying to universalize and dehistoricize beauty, arguing that what critics and audiences might claim as beautiful was really a matter of taste.

Interest in aesthetics became tied to the emerging identity of the male homosexual during the Victorian period in England, in part as a reaction to some of the moralistic writings by such figures as the poet and critic Matthew Arnold, who argued that the primary function of art was to instill proper notions of good and bad conduct in right-thinking citizens. The primary leader of the movement to queer this form of ethical aesthetics was the writer Walter Pater, who today is commonly believed to have been homosexual, and whose best-known writings on aesthetics are about "art for its own sake," that is, for the particular pleasures the beautiful can provide the spectator (or audience or listener). His views are found in his book

*The Renaissance*, especially in his essay on Leonardo da Vinci's famous portrait, commonly known as the *Mona Lisa* (formally, *La Gioconda*), which has come to stand for what art means, in all its mystery, for the Western world. In his essay on Leonardo's iconic painting, he uses the word *desire* to express what viewers feel when they are in the presence of the painting, but the desire seems neither consumerist (wanting to own the painting) nor sexual (wanting to have physical contact with the woman depicted), but a desire for the beautiful that art can provoke.

This is what is meant by the phrase "art for art's sake," which originated with French writers and artists in the early nineteenth century. For followers of this movement, art needed no justification other than "itself" — that is, its own formal and stylistic qualities and their effects on the "receiver." By removing the necessity of a moral stance from either the artist (and their work) or the audience or viewer, the question of the morality of same-sex desire and same-sex attraction would no longer be relevant to that which is beautiful. The queer writer Oscar Wilde famously wrote, in the preface to his novel *The Picture of Dorian Gray*: "There is no such thing as a moral or an immoral book. Books are well written, or badly written. That is all." It is probably reductive to say that Wilde had no interest in morals, either as an individual or as an artist, but his statement links him to Pater and the "art for art's sake" movement. Wilde also famously titled one of his essays on art "The Decay of Lying," suggesting, using the classical form of the Platonic dialogue, though in the mouths of Victorian men, that the highest art is a form of lying, of making something so convincingly that we believe the fiction.

This separation of the aesthetic from the social and the political remains a point of argument, which became intensified during the post-Stonewall years, especially during the height of the AIDS crisis and the fight for queer rights in a larger sense. Many activists and artists rejected an aesthetics of "art for art's sake," making the point that art has the power to move hearts, minds, and bodies — that art could not, nor should it be, cordoned off from the body politic. Thus, such aesthetically designed performances as "political funerals," in which the dead body of an AIDS victim was carried through city streets so that everyday people would have their traffic and time interrupted by rites of mourning, loss, and anger (rites not contained within the silent or polite spaces of funeral parlors), had both an aesthetics of design and a politics of intervention at work. The work of such groups as ACT UP, which brought together gay men, lesbians, trans people, and people of color, involved both art and politics in productive and powerful ways. Such arguments over the relationship between art and politics have been going on since the earliest writings on and instances of the arts in human expression: they are not likely to end anytime soon, if ever.

## Camp and Irony: Performing the Disguise Openly/Disguising the Performance

### Irony

At the same time that Pater and others were advocating for the aesthetics of "art for art's sake," there was also an emerging depiction of a sensibility that began with the concept of **irony** and then, later in the twentieth century, was named and theorized as **camp**. Irony is, in and of itself, a difficult term to agree on definitionally. While there are many kinds of irony, at the simplest level irony exists when there is a discrepancy or gap between what is said or depicted and what is meant or known to be the true state of affairs. So, when Oedipus, in Sophocles' play, proclaims that there is a pestilence in Thebes, and he will discover its source and punish the person responsible for it, the audience, at least in Sophocles' time — when all viewers would have known the plot of the story — is aware of something Oedipus is not: that HE is the person responsible for the plague because he has killed his father and married his mother (which he does not yet know himself). The scholar Wayne Booth also distinguishes between what he calls stable irony, in which a listener is aware of the contradiction between what the speaker says and what the speaker actually means, and unstable irony, in which the listener or reader is in doubt and the speaker's actual intended meaning remains undefinable or "slippery" — indeed, it may be to the speaker themselves.

Irony can be viewed in the history of modern queerness as one of the strategies both caused by and used for management of a closeted identity in a culture. For example, if a gay man says to his mother, "I'll never leave you to marry a woman," or a lesbian says to a man who is interested in dating her, "I'm not on the market, but I can't think of a man I'd rather go out with than you!" both are using irony as a coping method for avoiding revelation of their queer identities and also deflecting attention from a subject. They are not exactly lies, but they are forms of unstable irony, in that the listener takes one meaning that masks another one.

### Camp

What is key to virtually all theories of camp is that it is a style and an attitude rather than a specific thing: camp is a way of being or making or appearing and crosses all manner of art forms; it can find its way into everyday life, in speech and movement and environments — *habitus*, a habitual way of being and perceiving. It always involves some degree of excessiveness, a kind of "too much" that produces pleasure in the audience. It has traditionally been associated with queerness, from the first serious attempt to codify it by Susan Sontag, in her famous essay "Notes on Camp," published in 1964. Though later scholars and theorists have taken issue with many of Sontag's claims about camp, her essay remains an important statement, an attempt to mark out the territory and function of camp.

Sontag draws a distinction between "naïve and deliberate Camp," suggesting that "pure Camp is always naïve. Camp which knows itself to be Camp . . . is usually less satisfying." She goes on to elaborate, saying that "pure examples of Camp are unintentional; they are dead serious." Some later critics have taken issue with this distinction, suggesting that she does not adequately support her evaluative claims. But what is useful is when she modifies this seemingly equal binary distinction by suggesting that camp as a style and as a process or performance can be dynamic — that what begins as pure Camp can, in responding to or building on the response of the audience, become more self-consciously campy and even more exaggerated — that camp can be fluid in its reception and effects.

Whereas Sontag relegates camp to the realm of the apolitical, in more recent decades writers have contested this in a number of ways. First, with the growth of more openly queer artists and audiences in the public sphere, the degree to which camp sensibility has been restricted to "hidden" cohorts of devotees has lessened. The politicization of camp, especially in its attempts to destabilize hegemonic narratives of gender, identity, and authenticity through simultaneous exaggeration and authentic commitment to emotion and identity, is also part of the various legendary stories surrounding the Stonewall Riots. The image of drag queens taking on uniformed New York City police officers has elements of camp, which does not diminish the bravery and fierceness of the gender warriors using outfits, appearance, and language to comment on images of queerness and gender in that era. Similarly, the traditions of a group of gay men who dressed as nuns and performed street actions under the collective name of the Sisters of Perpetual Indulgence (SPI) have built, with both playfulness and complete seriousness, on the excessive and repressive elements of Roman Catholicism, with its rites and rituals, juxtaposed with the queer community's need to intervene in homophobia in the public sphere, particularly during the 1980s and 1990s. Currently, there are eighty-three "houses" of the SPI on four continents, and their work includes health care and outreach as well as what the scholar Melissa Wilcox calls "serious parody"; her book *Queer Nuns* is an excellent study of the growth and development of their work.

There are other more recent examples of popular and mass culture in which camp — or at least its echoes — has been present. The film career of the director-producer-writer (and occasional actor) John Waters is one of the most interesting to trace. Waters, who grew up in Baltimore, where he still lives and which is the setting of many of his films, was briefly a film student at New York University, but he was expelled for smoking marijuana, perhaps the best thing that could have happened to him, given the trajectory of his career. Returning to Baltimore, he began to collaborate in making experimental, usually short and technically crude films with a group of actors (often nonprofessional people he became friends with and who agreed to appear in his films initially as a lark), including such "tasteless" items as *The Diane Linkletter Story* (1970), which was originally done to test the color film he would be using. The title referred to the sad fate of the daughter of the wholesome daytime television host Art Linkletter: high on psychedelic drugs, she jumped out a window to her death. Diane was played by the "actress" who would become Waters's muse, the drag queen Divine (herself named after a character in the gay novelist Jean Genet's dreamlike homoerotic novel *Our Lady of the Flowers*). Divine was a very large man whose stock in trade was heavy, unrealistic makeup, often form-fitting outfits to accentuate his body shape and size, a vocal delivery in a range not easily assignable to male or female registers, and foul and violent speech. Waters's greatest financial success was the last film he made before Divine died of cardiac arrest in his sleep, *Hairspray* (1988), a takeoff on teeny-bopper movies of the late 1950s and 1960s, which also managed to slip in some mildly subversive commentaries on the racism of that period (which has never been erased, Waters seems to be saying). The film was the basis for the extraordinarily successful Broadway musical, which, in turn, was adapted for film, with the A-list star John Travolta playing Edna Turnblad. Harvey Fierstein played the role of Edna on Broadway, for which he won a Tony Award. The musical comedy is now performed in high schools, community theaters, and on television. So an artistic sensibility that began as camp for a relatively small audience has now become mainstream — some would argue, with a loss of sharpness of critique.

Another strain of criticism regarding camp that developed after Sontag's piece has been what some, especially feminist theorists, have seen as camp as being centrally a reinforcement of sexism, including strains of misogyny in the depiction and use of women. There is legitimate reason to consider this aspect of camp within queer expression, especially as there is often a complicated range of attitudes toward women among different groups of gay men. Though this is less true today, especially among younger generations, one of the results of the kinds of separation often encouraged by the closet has been a mistrust or devaluation of the other sex (in binary systems of thought and society) by both gay men toward lesbians and vice versa. (I hasten to add that there were plenty of gay men and lesbians who worked together on social and political issues and had loving and friendly relationships with each other during the pre-Stonewall period.) Since camp as a sensibility has been associated more with gay men than with lesbians (though we will consider the possibility of lesbian camp shortly), the exaggeration of the feminine and the female in many camp texts has led some feminist critics to view camp as antiwomen, as making fun of the other. Some respond that camp tends to enshrine strong women as heroes to emulate — that in the laughter there is also genuine admiration of what an oppressed class of people (women in the mid-twentieth century) was able to achieve.

This raises a somewhat different question, about which considerably less has been written: Is there such a thing as lesbian camp — camp art or entertainment either produced for or consumed and enjoyed by lesbians? There are those who answer "no," basing their position on the sexual and gender politics out of which camp has emerged since it was first recognized as a phenomenon. They argue that since wanting "to be a man" has never been viewed as anything other than a reasonable and positive desire, since maleness is a privileged position, it is hard to imagine the camp value that might be produced for lesbian consumers by the gender crossing and gender exaggerating that camp typically engages with in queer life. And it is certainly true that there are far fewer obvious examples of lesbian camp than there are of gay male camp. At the same time, one might argue that lesbian camp can be found in those performative and representational instances of exaggeration of extreme (and comically so) hypermasculinity. One example is the growing popularity of drag kings as an equivalent to drag queens. Women who dress as men are not a new phenomenon, and certainly there have been popular entertainers who have had success in this kind of work.

But drag kings today seem to inhabit places where the same appeals men find in feminine-based camp are available. Lea DeLaria, who has had a great amount of success as a singer, comedian, and actor, has presented as an almost over-the-top "butch dyke" since the beginning of her career, and she continues to have a long run as Big Boo on the Netflix women's prison series, *Orange Is the New Black*, where her highly masculine performance of lesbianism is not ridiculed but is a source of her identity, her intelligence, and her bravery — and Big Boo is very successful within the prison in "getting her woman." Boo is a funny, likable character — and the show made a risky choice in placing a persona so easily reduced to a stereotype of predatory sexuality in this narrative, but much credit goes to the writers, directors, and the actor herself for making Boo a character we admire and like, and whom we would want on our side. Her camp is a knowing camp — she is in on the jokes that are always hovering around her butchness, but she chooses to celebrate it rather than hide it.

While much of lesbian camp uses exaggerated masculinity as the basis of its humor, critique, and commentary of gender, there are memorable artists who also consider stereotypical scripts of femininity from a lesbian perspective in ways that fall comfortably and usefully under the heading of camp. One is the performance artist Alina Troyano, a Cuban American woman, who is better known by her self-created alter ego, Carmelita Tropicana (she also has a macho equivalent named Pingalito Betancourt—*pingalito* is slang for "little penis" or "small cock"). Even the name Carmelita Tropicana announces its camp attitude and style: *Carmelita* evokes the Hollywood and popular cultures images of Latin American women, such as the Brazilian performer Carmen Miranda, popular in the 1940s, always dressed in outlandish and exaggerated "native" outfits, borrowing patterns, shapes, and colors from authentic traditions, but raised to a frequently absurd level—Miranda sometimes seemed like a "female female impersonator," wearing wedgies with enormous heels. She wore "drag," but what it "dragged" were images of femininity and Latina presentation. What is particularly interesting and important about the uses to which Troyano puts her Carmelita Tropicana character is that, despite the heightened femininity and knowing use of the theatrical, purposefully inauthentic Spanglish speech style, Tropicana is depicted as an open and often-lovelorn lesbian. That she presents herself as some male-imagined version of the exotic feminine thus plays in both funny and serious ways with an audience's possible assumptions about what a lesbian Latina would look like or act like. Though many lesbians engaged in camp focus on exaggerated masculinity, Tropicana's work suggests that the femme side of the lesbian equation is just as constructed and problematic.

Similarly, Donna Marie Nudd and Terry Galloway, two lesbian artists (and spouses) who for more than a quarter of a century have led the queer-crip cabaret and filmmaking ensemble the Mickee Faust Club, in Tallahassee, Florida, play with and against gender scripts in ways that invoke multiple camp styles. Galloway, who often takes a more central onstage role, frequently presents herself in roles that are drawn from detective film and fiction and inhabits the already exaggerated masculinity of the tough guy. She provides multiple levels of camping—just as Carmelita Tropicana camps on both femme lesbian gender performance and Latina ethnic styles as viewed or produced by people external to the culture, so Galloway, who acquired hearing loss in childhood and has lived most of her life as a hearing-impaired person (she has recently had cochlear-implant surgery), also uses the exaggerated, ironic perspective of crip (disability) culture, sometimes turning her sardonic and witty eye on the clownish, grotesque Jerry Lewis (Scary Lewis in her rendition) and his telethons that exploited the bodies and narratives of children with muscular dystrophy for decades. The pair, along with their associate Diane Wilkins, have made short films, including parodies of *The Miracle Worker*, in which both Helen Keller's wild-child version of untamed feral femininity and Annie Sullivan's hyper-disciplining spinster femininity come in for some serious play. Similarly, the company uses the familiar format of sex education films to suggest hidden opportunities for lesbian desire to find expression, but under the disguise of traditional feminine-populated spaces, such as sleepovers and slumber parties, drawn from the repressed and repressive black-and-white 1950s, where the grays could be seen only by those inside the inner world of same-sex desire and closeting.

Perhaps the most obvious example of someone who embodies the intersection of queer and person-of-color uses of camp is the enormously popular and successful performing artist RuPaul, who identifies not as transgender but as a drag queen—hence the name of the reality game series *RuPaul's Drag Race*. The host always appears on this series in full, "fabulous" female outfit and hair, and he has also made recordings as the character. Part of the series' camp value is in the power that this queer person of color holds as empress of his own universe—he is almost unimaginably popular among audiences, including mainstream ones. RuPaul is the fulfillment of wishes and dreams of the drag queens who stormed the Bastille of the West Village during Stonewall. He has stated that, when he decided to move into drag work and to create the RuPaul character, he was determined to invoke not the clichéd image of the drag star as black hooker, but the drag diva as supermodel or "glamazon." Indeed, the RuPaul we all recognize without needing to have him identified is the height of glamour and celebrity. RuPaul appeared in male dress and played a male camp counselor in the indie film *But I'm a Cheerleader!* in which his role depicted him attempting to instruct a group of teenage boys in lessons in masculinity at a reparation therapy summer camp. Part of the camp pleasure that this performance provides lies in the juxtaposition of our usual expectations of seeing RuPaul dressed as a woman and performing femininity with this role, in which he essentially mimics, with no real attempt to adopt a masculine voice or style, what a man is and does.

RuPaul and his show have come under criticism from some trans activists, in part because such activists argue that the show, and RuPaul's use of the word *tranny* (generally considered a slur within the trans community), blurs the line between drag queens and trans women (and, by extension, between drag kings and trans men). Indeed, we are in a time of social transformation and growth of knowledge about such differences, and RuPaul commented, when asked about the issue: "Drag is really making fun of identity. We are shapeshifters. We're like 'okay, today I'm this, now I'm a cowboy, now I'm this.' Transgender people take identity very seriously—their identity is who they are" (Nick Duffy, "RuPaul Explains the Difference between Drag Queens and Transgender People," *Pink News*, March 2, 2016, https://www.pinknews.co.uk/2016/03/02/rupaul-explains -the-difference-between-drag-queens-and-transgender-people/). Complicating matters is the fact that there have been contestants on the show who eventually have come out as trans. The question of whether these people identified as trans while competing on the show, and, if so, what relationship that might have had to the choices they made as contestants, is complicated and not yet studied. In the house ball scene documented in the film *Paris Is Burning*, some of the participants did use pronouns that were not the ones of the gender they were assigned at birth to describe themselves. In some cases, such language was being used in a campy, ironic, even parodic way, which was in keeping with some of the exaggerated gender performances of the balls. In other cases, the pronouns were being used to state a truly felt transgender experience. Joseph Cassara's recent novel, *The House of Impossible Beauties* (2018), is an intriguing attempt to imagine the range of gender identities — cis, trans, and genderqueer — within the performative and domestic lives of some of the actual participants of the Harlem ball scene, as well as fictional characters. (Cassara identifies as cisgender; literature about and by transgender people from major publishers, such as Jordy Rosenberg's *Confession of the Fox*, is only now emerging in any numbers.)

A number of scholars and commentators have asked whether we are at "the end of camp" (or, indeed, whether it is over), some arguing that camp flourishes or is necessary only when there is a need for the indirect or the closeted to find a way of expressing itself and for people who share queer identities to find "knowing" ways to communicate with each other. There is certainly legitimacy to this view, especially if one chooses to define camp in terms of a reflection of a self and identity that have been socially stigmatized and as a coping strategy for living within an abject category. If, on the other hand, camp can be viewed as a way of bringing to light with visible or legible strategies of irony and simultaneity, and through images held up for criticism and through pleasurable performances, that which is both ridiculous and powerful at once, excessive in ways that reflect on inequalities or simply contradictions in both our thinking and our affective responses, there may be room for new forms and transformations of the camp perspective and Sontag's view of camp as style.

### Expression as Communion and Community: Celebrating "Us"

Thus far in this chapter the emphasis has been on individual artists and, to a somewhat parallel degree, the individual audience member, spectator, reader, or listener. Needless to say, art can also be an expression of a collective or communal experience and identity, which may be created through collaborative processes, performed or produced by multiple people, and viewed or heard by groups of people, all individuals, but gathered together for the purposes of acknowledging, celebrating, sometimes mourning on the basis of some shared characteristics or affinities.

## Marches and Parades

Political marches to protest homophobic laws and practices have long been part of the work of queer culture, a way of expressing dissatisfaction with current policies and treatment and calling for change, all the way back to those organized by the Mattachine Society and the Daughters of Bilitis in the 1950s and 1960s. Similarly, these marches were designed to be as visible but nonviolent or nondisruptive as possible, part of the Cold War mind-set of citizenship. Later marches, especially after Stonewall, have been less normative in their form or style, as groups like ACT UP and Queer Nation took as an article of belief the need for majoritarian, hegemonic America to see and experience a much wider range of queer people, including ones whose appearance might be initially off-putting or confusing to those who believe themselves not to have had any contact with queer culture. The inclusion of people whose presentation disrupted the normative desire to see queer people as "just people," and therefore appealing to more centrist or conservative factions in LGBTQ+ culture, may have seemed unnecessarily confusing or upsetting to the audiences they wished most to target and to gain as allies. On the other hand, those at the other side of the political spectrum, more radical and less assimilationist, wanted to confront straight society (and those parts of LGBTQ+ society that aspired to a performance of "normalcy") and believed that it was only by exposing such spectators to the wide range of people who had citizenship in the "queer nation" could there be any hope for typically marginalized people, such as transgender people and fetishists to gain fair access to wider national citizenship.

Parades designed to celebrate LGBTQ+ identity and folkways have been in existence for more than four decades. Of course, queer folk have been involved in parade traditions that go back further, though in many cases those events were not openly identified as queer. It is probably impossible to try to pinpoint the "first" queer Pride parade, particularly as the line between a *march* and a *parade* has always been unstable and blurry. Nonetheless, around 1970, just a year after the Stonewall Riots, commemorations of this revolutionary moment began to crop up. Over the years, more and more major cities, both in the United States and then globally, began to develop their own traditions and rituals, virtually all culminating in an increasingly larger, more extravagant, and more widely attended parade, each city distinguishing itself by featuring local figures, floats sponsored by local gay businesses (such as bars, stores, even bathhouses), and a more and more expansive panorama of what it means to be queer in a specific place. Though the last weekend of June has remained the unofficial "Pride Weekend" as a nod to history, different cities have sometimes scheduled their activities for different weekends in June (or even other months), in hopes of attracting people from other areas: indeed, if one tries, one can probably find a place to celebrate queer Pride every weekend in June. Over time, local politicians have often found it to their advantage not simply to permit such parades, but to provide positive protection by the police force and even to ride in a car or on a float as a show of solidarity (and as an appeal to an increasingly active and powerful political demographic).

The parade and Pride traditions are not without their challenges, controversies, and conflicts. Originally, the parades were designed primarily for "insiders"; participants knew that by appearing in the parade they were essentially announcing their queer sexual identity, and the vast majority of spectators were also queer or at least queer-friendly, perhaps straight-identified members of the heavily queer-populated neighborhoods where the parades traveled. In many places, there has been a shift in terms of spectators: there are more groups of what would appear, to the casual eye, to be heterosexual couples and more "traditional" families. On the one hand, this could be a very good development, if what it signals is greater support and acceptance of queer lives by the society at large. On the other, some worry, not without reason, that these demographics may actually indicate a kind of "enfreakment" of the queer, that the attendance of some (many?) straight people is an excuse to drink earlier in the day and gawk at the more theatrical of the participants.

At the same time, the parades feature numerous images of the wide spectrum of queer lives. Families, religious organizations, youth groups, arts and performance ensembles are also there, alongside the drag queens and leather daddies and bondage lesbians, as they all should be. That some ostensibly straight-identified people seem, each year, to act on impulse and join the parade spontaneously may be attributable to the effects of alcohol or other less mindful motivations of solidarity, but it may also be the presentation of an opportunity to walk alongside people one may not have thought one had much in common with. Parades have always been and no doubt will always be both conservative, in trying to continue traditions and to embody historical lines of inheritance, and potentially revolutionary, in the possibility of change and transformation they embody and offer to participants and spectators alike.

### The Michigan Womyn's Music Festival
One of the most important cultural-spiritual phenomena has been the annual Michigan Womyn's Music Festival, which was held for close to forty years, beginning in 1976 and ending in 2015; it is discussed from the perspective of issues regarding trans identity in chapter 4. It was established by a nineteen-year-old woman named Lisa Vogel (along with her sister and another female friend), who remained its leader and owned the land on

which it was held in Hart, Michigan. Michfest, as it is commonly known, was not the first musical festival designed to feature the work of female musicians and other performing and visual artists, but it became the most widely known and most successfully sustained. At its height, it was a week-long opportunity for women to be in the company of other women, both to celebrate through art the experience of womanhood (especially lesbian womanhood) and to provide social space where they could interact and experience their bodies without the presence of men.

While musical performance remained the anchor of the entertainment at the festival, over the years other art forms, such as spoken word, also became important features, as did the making and selling of arts and crafts. Breast-casting, for example, the use of plaster to allow women to make replicas of their breasts, was a feature. This was more than simply a leisure-time entertainment; it was an important opportunity for women to celebrate their own bodies. The only men permitted on the land were those providing necessary services, most notably the emptying of the "Porta-Janes" used as toilets. Their presence was typically announced vocally, so that women who did not want to have any sight of them or who, conversely, did not want to subjected to their gaze could take steps to avoid them.

Kath Browne, a British scholar of ecofeminism, has written an interesting analysis of the Michfest as an imperfect lesbian utopia. In the essay she examines both what Michfest accomplished that served lesbian utopian goals and how the festival also fell short of bringing about a perfect utopia, acknowledging that there can never be such a thing. The interviews she did with attendees indicated with overwhelming consistency that the value of the festival experience was a validation of women's bodies. Public nudity was not only permitted but in many respects encouraged, and this allowed women who had experienced **body shame** or trauma in their lives outside the festival to celebrate the various aspects of their bodies, such as shape, disability, and race, that they had felt judged for in a male-dominated system of body valuation.

Similarly, many of the women whom Browne interviewed or who responded to her surveys indicated that the festival was an important place for them to explore and celebrate their lesbian sexuality. The nature of this celebration took many forms. In some cases, women met long-term partners at the festival, finding proximity and opportunity that was more difficult to access in everyday life. In other cases, Browne notes, the festival was also an opportunity to end a relationship — and often in ways that were experienced as more healing and less hurtful than those in the outside world. The ethos of the celebration of female, especially lesbian, sexuality helped support those separating from partners and no doubt provided affirmation that there were many women-loving women in the world. For some women, it may have been the first environment in which they felt they could safely act on their queer desires. And for others, it was a place to heal from sexual abuse and other traumas that made erotic pleasure and romantic trust difficult.

The experience of the festival as a place of community and healing lives on. In 2017 the Artemis Singers, a lesbian feminist chorus in Chicago (open to all women), which performs only music written or arranged by women, founded in 1980 and still going strong almost forty years later, performed a musical theater piece about the festival, titled *Wanting the Music,* with book and lyrics by the writer and chorus member Loraine Edwalds (with collaboration by the chorus itself). In an interview with the *Chicago Tribune,* Edwalds, who attended the festival for twenty-seven years, spoke of the significance of the festival to her and her cohort:

> Having the festival end in 2015 was a deeply emotional experience for women who are part of the lesbian community. . . . With this performance, we honor the musicians who formed the heart of the festival community over the years. . . . Our lives changed so much in the years that we had Michigan. . . . How lesbians are accepted, how they're able to have children, the expectations they have for their relationships are very different now than when the festival started. I hope by creating this fictional story we can remind women of all we've been through. (www.windycitymediagroup.com/images/ publications/wct/2016-12-28/current.pdf)

Excerpts from the script are included in the Appendix.

## Spotlight: Art and the AIDS Crisis

In the following section, we survey the queer responses to one of the most significant phenomena affecting queer people (as well as others) in the last half century: the AIDS epidemic. The majority of artistic works created in response to the epidemic are by gay white men, though there are important works by lesbians (such as the work of Sarah Schulman) and queer people of color (such as the poetry of Melvin Dixon, Assoto Saint, and Essex Hemphill, three of the best-known queer men of color who produced written and performance poetry about the intersectionality of queerness, race, and HIV/AIDS). The explanation for this is as much about the economics and sociology of artistic production and distribution as anything else. The arts have been dominated, at least in terms of who gets published (produced, performed, exhibited), by white men; these men simply have had more access to the means of production and to the publishers, galleries, and music halls where artistic works are exhibited. This is not to place a value judgment on the worth of the works of artists from underrepresented groups — which frequently speak or depict with power, directness, and beauty — but to make visible (or audible) *why* some artists have had more representation than others. Statistics tell us that trans people (especially trans women) have a rate of HIV infection and illness disproportionate to their population numbers, for reasons discussed in earlier chapters; yet the poems, musical pieces, sculptures, and dances by them remain under the radar — in general, but particularly those dealing with AIDS.

When they are represented, like the character played by Jared Leto in the film *Dallas Buyers Club* (2013), it is still most often by writers, directors, and actors who identify as cisgender. The actors Matthew McConaughey and Jared Leto both won Oscars for their performances in this film, which is based on the true story of Ron Woodruff, a working-class man with HIV/AIDS who organized a secret group to purchase unapproved HIV-treatment drugs from Mexico and smuggle them across the border. Though both actors' performances received considerable praise, the script-writers "flattened" Woodruff's character by making him initially homophobic (good, no doubt, for dramatic change, though by all reports he was not antigay) and omitting his own queer experiences (accounts by those who knew him suggest he was fairly open about having had sex with other men). Leto, who played a transgender woman with AIDS, gave a fine performance, including a powerful scene in which he dresses as a man to ask his forbidding father for money; however, it seems that the character was a composite of a number of people. Some were disappointed that Leto's role was not played by a transgender actor.

That this art was produced by cisgender artists does not necessarily make it bad or even by definition inauthentic. (Good, ethical cisgender artists are capable of engaging trans artists in the collaborative processes of art.) But it does mark such work as categorically different from that which is produced under the control or guidance of trans people. There has recently been some progress, as in the recent television series *Pose*, set in the 1987 arts scene of New York City, which has used trans writers in its production. And MOTHA (the Museum of Transgender History and Art), currently a "moving" museum, setting up shows and installations in various cities, sites, and existing gallery and museum spaces, has hopes of creating a permanent home for works that fulfill its mission of insisting on "an expansive and unstable definition of transgender, one that is able to encompass all trans, non-binary, and gender non-conformed art and artists" (www.sfmotha. org/about). In the meantime, the artistic history of HIV/AIDS among transgender people remains to be expressed and heard, read, and viewed.

### Literature: AIDS Narratives and Poetry

As might be expected, gay male writers were among the first to tell their own stories and imagine stories of fictional others affected by the AIDS crisis. From approximately the middle of the 1980s through the late 1990s, there was a growth of writings by gay male writers, typically white, centered on men living with (and dying from) AIDS; there were also works written by people from other groups, including lesbians such as Sarah Schulman, whose novel *People in Trouble* (1990) is about the effect of AIDS on the East Village arts scene. African American writers also began to address the issue of AIDS within their community — and novels like *The Day Eazy-E Died* (2001) by James Earl Hardy took on the silences about the epidemic in African American communities, concurrent with the sharp rise in infection among young gay African Americans. Similarly, the African American novelist Pearl Cleage tackled the topic of HIV infection among heterosexual African American women in *What Looks Like Crazy on an Ordinary Day* (1997). The children's and YA market addressed the effects of the epidemic through young people's attitudes toward older relatives infected with (and, in the first decade or so, almost always dying from) AIDS. A picture book, *Losing Uncle Tim* (1989) by Marykate Jordan, depicts a young boy's grief at the death of his beloved uncle in language that was appropriate to preschool and elementary school children; its illustrations portray Uncle Tim as a man recognizably gay to parents and teachers, but without any overt reference to his sexuality.

Memoirs and poetry also began to appear to reflect the experiences of those either themselves living with HIV or close to those with the virus and its associated illnesses. Paul Monette's memoir, *Borrowed Time* (1988) was one of the first and most prominent, and it was accompanied by a volume of poems by Monette, *Love Alone*. A documentary about Monette's life, *Paul Monette: The Brink of Summer's End,* was released in 1996, a year after his death, and won a number of awards at film festivals.

Of all the writers of narrative who were involved in their lives and their art with AIDS, the most notable was the group of seven gay male writers who dubbed themselves The Violet Quill (sometimes The Violet Quill Society). Their name was taken from a shade of purple associated with queerness. These writers became a kind of support group and workshop for each other, men who were inspired to write about the lives of gay men, but who did not typically find editorial and publishing support for their work. Edmund White, one of the most prominent of the group, imagined fictional characters involved with the epidemic in personal and public ways. His most recent novel, *Our Young Man* (2016), combines the tradition of the Bildungsroman (novel of setting out in the world) with the progress of the AIDS epidemic for a young man originally from working-class beginnings in France who makes it to the world of high-fashion modeling, as he also has to confront AIDS in the lives of his friends and companions.

In the last few years, there has been a resurgence of novels that have highlighted the AIDS epidemic and the experience of survivors. It may be that writers who did not want to address AIDS directly in their fiction (perhaps because they were dealing with it in their own lives) are now, with the passage of time, ready to look back to the most critical days of the epidemic and take stock of what has happened between then and now. In a sense, many of these novels are both current and retrospective in their orientation, expressing the vantage point of those who continue to survive (and who may have indeed escaped infection altogether, but were not untouched by the epidemic in other ways) and their attempts and desires to make narrative sense (or to acknowledge the lack of a coherent story that can yet be assembled) of the last forty years. *Christodora* (2016) by Tim Murphy looks at the effects of the AIDS epidemic on queer and non-queer people alike, giving special attention to Latinx folk; he sets his story in the apartment building in New York City in which many of them lived. John Whittier Treat's *The Rise and Fall of the Yellow House* (2015) returns to the early years of the epidemic in a story set in the Pacific Northwest. Rabih Alameddine's earlier novel *Koolaids: The Art of War* (1998) was a fantastic, somewhat dreamlike meditation on the war in Lebanon (the author's home country), juxtaposed with the effects of AIDS on his adopted city of San Francisco. His most recent novel, *The Angel of History* (2016) takes place during a single night in a psych ward; it is filtered through the consciousness of a Yemeni poet, Jacob, raised in an Egyptian whorehouse and living in San Francisco as a gay man. It deservedly received the Lambda Literary Award for Best Gay Male Fiction, as well as the award for Best Arab American novel from the Arab American National Museum. Perhaps the most acclaimed of the new AIDS novels is 2018's *The Great Believers* by Rebecca Makkai, which was a finalist for the National Book Award for fiction. Like some of the others, it shifts back and forth in time, in this case between Chicago and its suburbs in the mid-1980s and Paris in the 2010s.

## Visual Arts

One of the most familiar artistic *signatures* (i.e., the recognizable style of an artist) during the 1980s was that of Keith Haring, who was born in 1958 in Reading, Pennsylvania, and who, after a few false starts, became a student at the School of Visual Arts in New York City. He was always committed to drawing as an art form with the capacity for the direct and the subtle. At the School of Visual Arts he found like-minded artists, queer and non-queer alike, whose work encouraged him to develop his own form of expression, which was built on the growing popularity and ubiquity of graffiti and cartoon-based art found in subways, on posters, and elsewhere. You may be familiar with his image of the "radiant baby."

Haring's street art about AIDS is often playful and childlike in style, though its messages are direct and as serious as the disease it is meant to raise awareness about. One, advocating safer sex practices, shows a penis with a face on its head, testicles with feet sprouting from them, and arms holding a condom, with the logo "SAFE SEX " in bright red letters above. The ACT UP slogan, "Silence = Death," appears in a number of his images, accompanied by anonymous human figures, not sexed, to illustrate the messages; others show male figures engaged in mutual masturbation as a form of safer sex, but they are abstract enough not to raise any issues of pornographic intent, so they remain reasonably suitable for wider audiences. In the last few years of his life, he was open about his illness and combined his art with other media in a kind of heightened "public service" set of works (Keith Haring Foundation, "Bio," www.haring.com/!/about-haring/bio).

At the other end of the spectrum of popular versus "fine" art we find the American figurative painter (meaning his subject was the human figure, in various positions and contexts) Hugh Auchincloss Steers. He was born and raised in a very wealthy and prestigious family — he counted Jacqueline Kennedy Onassis and the writer Gore Vidal as relatives. He attended both the well-known prep school Hotchkiss and Yale University. The art historian Justin Spring has written of the juxtaposition in Steers's paintings of the ordinary, everyday lives of his gay male subjects, often shown in drab apartments, with the dreamlike images of such men in fabulous dresses and excessively high-heeled shoes. Spring initially found such images too wedded to what he thought were outmoded or clichéd traditions of drag, but he ultimately found a different way to understand Steers's aesthetic, especially as Steers turned to representations of people who were obviously living with AIDS:

> I think that another way to consider these works is as a sort of visual poetry, describing not just what it looks like to be sick with AIDS, but rather the emotional state of a person living with AIDS: what it feels like to be inside that body from day to day, trying to assert one's own personhood as the disease runs its course. What Hugh realized about his situation and captured so brilliantly in his paintings is not the shock of realizing one's own mortality but rather those more immediate, in-between moments of loneliness, bewilderment, and paranoia, as well as outright eccentricity. By portraying the domestic and the commonplace — actions as banal as changing a light bulb or moving from chair to bed — and including some erotically charged detail — a platform wedgie, a satin cape — he

reminds us that disease itself is a secondary concern, a by now long-familiar circumstance rather than the immediate cause of drama. Moreover, he suggests that (whatever his fellows are up to) there's a complex emotional conflict going on here: beyond mere anger, a lingering desire for something transcendent; below the outer layer of bitterness, a core of romantic longing.

By depicting men who, though sick, were still resolutely sexual in the most unexpected ways, Hugh was daring to introduce comedy and absurdity into the story of living a slow death. This seemed to me to be a high-stakes sort of exhibitionism, and as such it created an eerie, brave, and wonderfully idiosyncratic narrative. (159)

Steers shared with his fellow artists with AIDS a desire to accomplish his vision of reality, a reality filled with color and emotions, with lines that sometimes expressed the reality of emotions and even moments of transcendence, evoked by the presence of angelic figures in works near the end of his life.

An artists' collective that emerged specifically to address the cultural politics of AIDS was Gran Fury, an offshoot of ACT UP, founded in 1988 and in existence until 1995. The group's political and aesthetic philosophies, which were inextricable, drew from existing images and icons to call attention to injustices related to AIDS. They often invoked historical genealogies that nonetheless pointed in directed ways at modern figures. Thus, their use of what might be viewed as commodified products, such as decals, pins, and T-shirts, was consciously intended to diffuse images and messages where they would most likely be seen — on the torsos of queer bodies, on billboards, in advertisements. For one project, they opened newspaper vending machines containing the *New York Times* and swapped the papers for their own parodic but informational substitutes, the *New York Crimes*, which contained information about the AIDS crisis. Such an act involved pulling consumers into the transgressive act by tricking them into taking, often initially unreflectively, this alternative source of "the news."

One of the most significant pieces created by members of ACT UP was *Let the Record Show* in 1987 (many of those involved were part of the group that formed Gran Fury a year later). At the invitation of the director of the New Museum of Contemporary Art, William Olander (also a member of ACT UP), these artists, working as an ad hoc committee of ACT UP, created an installation that appeared at the entrance to the museum on Broadway, a spot with high foot traffic, and that used various artistic media and materials to call to judgment governmental and other public powers for their neglect of and discrimination against people with AIDS. The now-iconic SILENCE = DEATH and pink triangle images were placed in neon at the entrance, along with cardboard images of some of the individuals the collective thought most guilty of crimes against the humanity of people living with AIDS: the extreme right-wing talk show host William F. Buckley, who called for all people with AIDS to be tattooed for identification; Senator Jesse Helms, who pushed right-wing bigotry in the Congress; the Reverend Jerry Falwell, whose evangelical television broadcasts were deeply homophobic and who asserted that AIDS was punishment from God against homosexuals; President Ronald Reagan, who did not utter the word AIDS for the first five years of his administration; Cory SerVaas, Reagan's head of the AIDS Commission; and an anonymous surgeon who spoke for the medical authorities who did not advocate for or provide appropriate treatment and research. The work of Gran Fury was vivid, sardonic, and very public. The group marshaled all its knowledge of design, placement, and intervention, and it was unafraid to name names, show faces, and go into "polite" spaces and disrupt the facade of balance and harmony.

Finally, we look at a form of popular folk art, visual and verbal in its origins: the **NAMES Project**, commonly called the AIDS Quilt. Quilts have a long tradition in American folk culture, typically as a feminine activity of bonding and production benefiting needy members of communities. In 1985 the San Franciscan gay activist Cleve Jones, who had been organizing candlelight marches to honor Harvey Milk and George Moscone, both assassinated in 1978, learned of the one thousand or so San Franciscans who had died from HIV/AIDS. He called on marchers to carry placards with the names of those they knew who had died from AIDS and carry them to the end of the march. At the end, they placed the placards on the Federal Building; Jones noticed that, assembled, the placards resembled the panels of a quilt. This inspired him to begin working on a quilt panel in memory of a friend who had died from the illness, and this act gained momentum. In October 1987 the assembled panels ("patches") were displayed together on the National Mall in Washington, D.C. Half a million viewed the quilt that first weekend. The following year, the quilt was sent on a tour of a number of major cities. At each site, local members from the LGBTQ+ and AIDS communities (sometimes they were virtually identical, sometimes not) performed the ritual of the reading of the names. Multiple readers were usually required, both because the physical act of reading the names became exhausting and because the emotional labor was draining. The multiplicity of readers created a chain of supporters, and, indeed, there were also in a number of instances multiple panels created for the same individual by different groups. Whereas Gran Fury's visual and verbal interventions were confrontational, subversive, and even battlelike in their style and intent, the NAMES Project, though equally political in its goals, took an approach that built on traditions of grief and communal mourning in ways that were often emotionally overwhelming, but more "monumental," to borrow the sculptor Peter Lane's term for his own art. The effect of Gran Fury was "nervous" — it jabbed its finger with force and sharpness at those it accused; the effect of the NAMES Project was no less powerful, but it was powerful in the way that seeing a graveyard where soldiers are buried is — a sense of loss that is both personal and communal.

## Music

Popular music is certainly the art form in which we might most readily expect expressions derived from HIV/AIDS to find their way. For one thing, popular music in the United States has generally been dominated by vocal music, so the opportunities for lyric content to address the epidemic are more abundant than they are for instrumental or even choral pieces more strongly associated with classical music. In 1985 the popular singer Dionne Warwick collaborated with a group of other well-known singers to record a choral version of the popular song "That's What Friends Are For," produced as a single to raise money for AIDS research.

Various other popular musicians over the years have written, performed, and recorded songs that, either overtly or indirectly, "sing" to the AIDS crisis, ranging from very personal ballads about specific people in a singer's life to more all-embracing calls to show love and support. In an article in *Slant*, the journalist Sal Cinquemani annotated fifteen songs that are associated with AIDS (Sal Cinquemani, "15 Songs about AIDS," *Slant*, June 5, 2013, www.slantmagazine.com/house/article/15-songs-about-aids). These include such high-profile songs as "Streets of Philadelphia" by Bruce Springsteen and "Philadelphia" by Neil Young, both of which were featured in the film *Philadelphia*; both were nominated for the Academy Award for Best Song (Springsteen's won). Others, Cinquemani notes, come from very specific real-life losses and situations, such as George Michael's song that refers to the death of a lover from the illness, and Madonna's, whose friendship with gay men who died of the illness was the subject of at least one song.

The world of popular music itself was vulnerable to the disease. One of the earliest rock-and-roll musicians to come out was the gay "glam" singer Jobriath, who once called himself a "true fairy" and used makeup and costumes to evoke traditions of feminine and androgynous magic style. His approach was not unlike that of the Radical Faeries, but it was similar as well to such better-known commercial musicians as David Bowie, Lou Reed, and the Velvet Underground. He became ill and eventually died from AIDS complications in 1983. The "Fabulous Sylvester," the African American unapologetically feminine star of disco, had a highly developed falsetto, which was transgressive for its time. His hits "You Make Me Feel (Mighty Real)" and "Do Ya Wanna Funk?" were anthems on dance floors throughout the 1980s and beyond. Sylvester left most of his estate to HIV/

AIDS charities and other causes supporting queer people. Today he is viewed as having been the true and authentic leader of the kinds of disco music that were then commodified in such films as *Saturday Night Fever*. Cultural critics have remarked on the historical line from Sylvester's willingness to perform male femininity to such superstars as RuPaul today. Freddie Mercury, the front man for the group Queen who played with hypermasculinity as well as bold queerness and theatricality derived from glam rock, announced his AIDS diagnosis only one day before he died. His life has been depicted in the recent film *Bohemian Rhapsody* (2018), for which Rami Malek won the Best Actor award for his performance of Mercury. These are but three of the many musicians who have died from AIDS.

Classical music was also hit by the AIDS epidemic, though often less visibly and with less overt acknowledgment. The openly gay, Pulitzer Prize–winning composer John Corigliano wrote his first symphony, the first movement of which is subtitled "Of Rage and Remembrance," as a response to the deaths of friends and fellow musicians. Symphonic music is typically abstract, usually named by the tempo or musical form of each movement, sometimes by a theme. Each of the symphony's three major movements is dedicated to a specific friend who died of AIDS: a pianist, a cellist, and a music executive who developed dementia during his illness, reflected in the musical rhythms and notes (Edward Rothstein, "Themes of AIDS and Remembrance in Corigliano's Symphony," *New York Times*, January 11, 1992, www.nytimes.com/1992/01/11/arts/review-music-themes-of-aids-and-remembrance-in-corigliano-s-symphony.html). Corigliano has indicated that, though he had until that point in his career eschewed writing in large forms like the symphony, preferring to write for soloists and small ensembles, the powerful sense of loss he had, along with his experience of the AIDS Memorial Quilt, inspired him to write the work.

Other classical composers and performers have created expressions of their responses to the epidemic. For example, Robert Savage, a young composer who died from AIDS, wrote a piece for solo piano called *AIDS Ward Scherzo*. In 2010 the composer Alexandra Pajek composed a piece of music called *Sounds of HIV*, in which, on the basis of scientific knowledge now available, she assigned notes to the DNA sequence identified with the virus. The actual art of creating the composition was not as mechanical as it may sound — Pajek had to make decisions about key, rhythm, instrumentation, and so forth.

### Film and Television

One of the earliest full-length televised dramas about AIDS was 1985's *An Early Frost*. The story centered on a closeted gay man, a successful young lawyer, Michael Pierson, living in Chicago, a thousand miles away from his family, who discovers, after becoming ill, that he was infected by his lover, Peter, with whom he believed he had a monogamous relationship. He throws Peter out and flies to see his family and deliver the news that not only is he gay, but he has AIDS (the distinction between AIDS and HIV was not yet firm in anyone's minds). His mother is accepting of his sexuality though, of course, worried about his health; his father initially rejects him, but, by the end of the story has reached a point of openness both to his son's sexuality and to supporting his needs; a wise grandmother speaks public service information and models unconditional love; his sister, who knew he was gay, initially shows fear of contact (both for her child and for the unborn child she is carrying). Michael is eventually reunited with Peter. Along the way, while in the hospital, he becomes friends, at first begrudgingly, with a "queeny," sympathetic, and brave man in an advanced stage of the disease, displaying the signifiers of AIDS death, Kaposi's sarcoma lesions and a persistent cough. Michael helps the dying man write a will and comes to acknowledge his kindness, bravery, and humanity, which help him confront his own internalized homophobia. The film ends on a hopeful note insofar as Michael has not died; but, given assumptions at the time, we as the audience assume he will eventually die. The teledrama was both praised and criticized: praised for bringing AIDS into living rooms, but criticized for implying fault and reinforcing monogamy as the only virtuous way to enact queer sexuality.

Independent film was also taking AIDS as a subject matter around the same time, in films that usually felt much closer to the lived experience of the illness among gay men and their friends and families. The gay director Arthur Bressan Jr. released his film *Buddies* a few months before the broadcast of *An Early Frost*. A year later, the gay director Bill Sherwood made his one feature-length film, *Parting Glances*, which focused on a gay male couple facing separation because of the more closeted member's job opportunity in Africa. It took an Oscar-winning director, Jonathan Demme, and one of America's most popular leading actors, Tom Hanks, to break through to a mass theatergoing audience, with 1993's *Philadelphia*, which was based on an actual case of a lawyer with HIV who had been fired from his firm and then sued the firm (the film fictionalized the characters and events). Again, many members of the AIDS community found much to criticize in the film: it is true, we never see the protagonist interacting with any other people with AIDS, and the unanimous support he has outside his workplace is far from the experience many people with AIDS had to struggle with. Nonetheless, others have noted that Demme's talent and the presence of an actor with Hanks's likeability quotient were of great value, even if this was not the AIDS film the activist community wanted and had every right to ask for. (Hanks won his first Academy Award for his performance.)

Other films began to show faces beyond the white, gay, middle-class ones that were virtually the only ones seen in earlier movies — *Boys on the Side* (1995), in which Mary-Louise Parker plays a heterosexual woman infected with the virus by a former male lover; and *Precious* (2009), the highly successful adaptation of Sapphire's novel, in which the title character, played by Gabourey Sidibe, then an unknown, is a teenage and once-again pregnant mother, a victim of incest, raped by a father, who, we learn, died of AIDS. Marlon Riggs's documentary, *Tongues Untied* (1989), which predated *Philadelphia*, featured a number of gay black men, such as Essex Hemphill and Riggs himself, who were living with AIDS. This documentary was broadcast on PBS, though some outlets chose not to show it, given the explicitness of its frank discussion of queer love and eroticism between men (and between black men, which, in some venues, added to the controversial and taboo nature of the film). A number of documentaries and other dramatic films dealing with the AIDS epidemic have been released in recent years, including *How to Survive a Plague* (2012), which was nominated for the Academy Award for Best Documentary, and the French film *120 Battements par Minute,* titled *BPM (Beats per Minute)* (2017) in English, which moves between a re-creation of the formation of ACT UP Paris and a love story between two serodiscordant men.

## Theater: Staging HIV/AIDS

The 2017 Broadway season included, as one of its critically praised offerings, the first major revival of one of the earliest musical plays to include the AIDS epidemic as a central feature of its plot: William Finn's *Falsettos,* which consists of two linked one-act shows that follow a married man from his coming out through the death of his lover from AIDS. Theater fans and critics wondered whether the show would seem dated and no longer relevant in an age when various treatments make death from AIDS at an early or even in middle age the exception rather than the rule — at least in the Western, developed world, where health care is readily available.

The two best-known nonmusical plays taking AIDS as a central plot element have also had recent revivals. The first, the semi-autobiographical *The Normal Heart*, written by a longtime survivor and activist (one of the founders of ACT UP), Larry Kramer, depicts the formation of the Gay Men's Health Crisis alongside the central character's coming to political consciousness. The second, Tony Kushner's *Angels in America*, which won just about every possible award in its initial run, has been revived by the National Theatre in London and moved to Broadway in 2018; the revival won the 2018 Tony Award for Best Revival of a Play and Tony Awards for two of its actors, Andrew Garfield (for leading actor) and Nathan Lane (for a featured actor). Both Garfield and Lane used their acceptance speeches to speak out on queer issues — Garfield about the political and social attacks on queer people under the Trump administration, Lane, touchingly, in an acknowledgment of his husband and the transformative effect his marriage has had on his life. As both Garfield and Lane are major figures in the entertainment industry, their words provided a drama worthy of the play for which they won their awards.

*Angels in America*, like Kramer's play, has a serodiscordant couple at its center, Prior Walter and Louis Ironson. Kushner weaves together a Mormon family; an African American nurse; Roy Cohn, the closeted gay man who was Joseph McCarthy's accomplice in his reign of terror in the Cold War purges of communism in the 1950s, who is dying (and eventually dies) of AIDS, denying it and his homosexuality from beyond the grave; Ethel Rosenberg, whose execution Kushner accurately depicts Cohen as being responsible for; and some angels.

Off-Broadway, Steve Dietz's play *Lonely Planet*, first produced in 1993, was revived in 2017. It is a two-person play featuring the friendship between two gay men who face (or do not face) the epidemic in very different ways; the play combines a realistic depiction of gay male friendship with techniques drawn from such absurdist playwrights as Eugène Ionesco and Samuel Beckett.

The single most successful theatrical production, in terms of its run and its popularity among general audiences, is Jonathan Larson's musical *Rent*. This winner of both the Pulitzer Prize and multiple Tony Awards opened off-Broadway and then moved quickly to Broadway in 1996, closing in 2008 after more than five thousand performances, making it one of the longest-running musical plays in the history of Broadway. The show takes the basic situation of Puccini's opera *La Bohème*, itself based on a set of linked stories set in the bohemian culture of artists in nineteenth-century Paris. Larson transformed these nineteenth-century characters into late twentieth-century equivalents, including drag queens, rock musicians, performance artists, and sex workers of different races and economic classes. Controversy arose when the novelist Sarah Schulman noticed what she and some others felt were too many equivalences between her novel *People in Trouble* and Larson's show. Larson died the night before *Rent* opened, so a suit brought by Schulman was unsuccessful, as the only person who could really have spoken with knowledge was dead. Schulman's book *Stagestruck: Theater, AIDS, and the Marketing of Gay America* made her own case for what she claimed was plagiarism and expanded to consider the commodification of AIDS by American popular culture in general.

This question of appropriation and commodification of AIDS leads to one last thought, not really relevant to theater per se, but perhaps usefully considered under the "theatricality" of AIDS as a cultural phenomenon with props and costumes (e.g., red-ribbon pins, stickers, and coffee mugs, to name a few, symbols adopted by people to gain a kind of identity within the community of supporters). In 1994 Daniel Harris's article "Making Kitsch from AIDS" appeared in *Harper's*, a monthly magazine targeted at middle- to upper-middle-class educated readers. Harris begins his essay with the attention-grabbing statement, "AIDS may be the first disease to have its own gift shop." From there he proceeds to describe the various objects one may purchase in the Workshop Building of the AIDS Memorial Quilt, called Under One Roof, to help fund AIDS services and show support for AIDS victims. Among those items are "Cuddle With" teddy bears that sport tasteful red ribbons, Keith Haring tote bags, and T-shirts stenciled with the words "We're Cookin' Up Love for People with AIDS."

Harris places these items under the heading "kitsch"; he finds the products inauthentic in their cultural origins and mass-produced. Harris sees this turn to kitsch as an intentional strategy to deflect attention from those aspects of AIDS that tend to be most unsettling or distancing to the general public: "Unlike less controversial illnesses, like multiple sclerosis or leukemia, AIDS is vulnerable to kitsch in part because of the urgent need to render the victim innocent" (56). In a sense, this is something like what Schulman accused Larson of doing in *Rent*, by reversing the fates of the characters from Puccini's plot: allowing the heterosexual female lead to survive and having the genderqueer person of color die "in her place."

## Dance and Performance Art

### *Dance*

Numerous dance communities were hit quite hard by the AIDS epidemic, which is no surprise given the high degree of representation of gay men in them, from classical ballet to musical theater to the discotheque dance floors. Within the world of classical ballet, perhaps the most famous dancer to die of AIDS was the Russian Rudolf Nureyev; both his sexuality and the cause of his death were matters of public knowledge. Of all the arts, dance is so quintessentially about the body as material and medium for expression, and so it is fitting that dancers, particularly those working in modern and contemporary traditions, have created pieces that place bodies in juxtaposition with the epidemic, often with overtly autobiographical use of their own bodies.

One piece by the dancer-choreographer Neil Greenberg is titled *Not-About-AIDS-Dance*, itself a typical queerly ironic nod to the aesthetics of presence and absence, of denial and affirmation, of openness and closetedness. The piece was first performed in 1994, a particularly difficult year for Greenberg and those around him. Several people close to him died from

AIDS, including his older brother Jon, an actor and AIDS activist. Greenberg's website contains this description of the inspiration for the piece: Before these events, and before the dance acquired its name, "Greenberg had conceptualized a work in which the audience would receive extra-dance information about the dancers that usually remains hidden or unspoken, altering the relationship between audience and performers. *Not-About-AIDS-Dance* is a development of this previously planned dance" (www.neilgreen berg.org/naad.html). In performance, this information was presented as slide projections on the back wall of the stage, and it began as information that identified a dancer's nationality or other relatively innocuous, unremarkable facts. The information became more revelatory and emotion-laden, such as that about the death of the mother of one of the dancers, and culminated in a slide that reveals Greenberg's own HIV-positive status. The interplay between the abstract, kinetic movements of the dancers, both as individual bodies and as performers in concert and contact, in which there was no necessary connection to be made between their steps and AIDS, and the slides, which personalized the lives and experiences of the dancers, made the circuitous title, intentionally awkward and twisted in its syntax, an authentic even if contradictory statement. The dance was not "about AIDS," but, through the imposition of the text, which *is* part of the dance as a piece of art, it cannot escape being "about AIDS." Not only does the dance become deeply personal, as it is communally shared by the dancers and the audience, but it also takes on social and political meanings, reminders that even this dance, with its absence of representational movements (i.e., it is trying neither to reproduce social dance forms, such as waltzes, nor to dramatize a narrative, as *Swan Lake* does), has a backstory reflected in the lives of each dancer and in the combined experiences they share and their bodies bear witness to. The 1994 performance can be viewed online at www.neilgreenberg.org/naad.html.

A second dance piece proved more controversial, not necessarily because of its connection with AIDS and queer experience, but because of arguments over whether it even had the right to call itself art: *Still/Here*, by Bill T. Jones. Jones is an HIV-positive dancer-choreographer of color; cofounder, with his late partner, Arnie Zane (who died in 1988 of AIDS), of the Bill T. Jones/Arnie Zane Dance Company; and two-time Tony Award winner for his choreography for the shows *Spring Awakening* and *Fela!* Jones spent months traveling the country, doing workshops in which he interviewed a wide spectrum of people living with life-threatening diseases and helping them learn how to use dance and movement in their lives (most of them had no training or experience in concert dance, they were adults of all ages, and their bodies reflected their lives and experiences with illness). Jones devised both choreography and a verbal text, drawn from the interviews themselves. The production premiered in Lyon, France, at the Biennale Internationale de Danse in 1994, and then had its New York opening at the Brooklyn Academy of Music the same year. Trained dancers performed the piece, which was in two parts, as the title suggests; taped voices and video footage from the interviews were played at various points. By the end of the performance, the audience has gained a degree of intimacy with the people from whom Jones drew his textual material (https://vimeo.com/33288787).

Critical response to the piece was immediate and divided, though most spoke of the power of the performance, even if they had mixed reactions to some of its qualities — so it is with any work of art. The controversy arose when Arlene Croce, the chief dance critic for the *New Yorker*, and generally considered one of the top writers on dance (some, such as Susan Sontag, dubbed her the greatest writer on dance), wrote a broadside called "Discussing the Undiscussable," in which she stated that she refused to attend the performance because she believed it stood outside real art and was instead an example of what she saw as a debased form, which she called "victim art." From her perspective, what Jones had endeavored to create was something that could not fairly be discussed in the traditions of aesthetic evaluation to which she held artistic works. Rather, she said, she felt that either she would be compromised, placed in the position of saying potentially unkind things about texts devised from the actual words of the sick, or she would have to ignore the standards of art she held dear in order to affirm their humanity. Croce cast her net of resentment wide, complaining that she was also expected now to extend her artistic criticism to express sympathy for "dissed blacks," "abused women," and "disenfranchised homosexuals." Response to Croce was equally heated. The novelist Joyce Carol Oates responded in the pages of the *New York Times* with an excoriation of both Croce's argument and her narrow view of the purview of art. That Croce refused even to attend the performance suggests a desire to keep herself hermetically sealed from any possible taint of the social or political in her experience of art. Her nonattendance seems clearly a protest designed to strive to make the piece invisible. And, of course, that invisibility is exactly what Jones's piece was designed to challenge.

### Performance Art

Ron Athey, a **performance artist** who identifies as HIV-positive, challenged audiences with performances such as *Four Scenes in a Harsh Life*, presented at the Walker Art Center in Minneapolis in 1994, in which he used such elements as ritual incision and the presence of blood to disrupt the comfort zone of his audience. Other queer performance artists, such as Tim Miller, have used body, language, and story to comment on both queerness and the experiences, negative and positive, of being part of a community of activists that is working to make information and access to health care for people with AIDS more accessible.

A performance piece that is not, at core, intended to be about AIDS, but which uses the fact of AIDS and the experience of people living in the broadest sense "with AIDS" is Scott Dillard's *Breathing Darrell*. Dillard is a professor of performance and rhetoric at Georgia College and State University. He is also involved in the Gay Spirit Visions movement, mentioned in chapter 10 as a group of men tied in many ways to the spiritual and philosophical traditions of Radical Faeries, who are in turn informed by some elements of Native American spirituality, particularly those parts tied to Two-Spirit people. In his article "*Breathing Darrell*: Solo Performance as a Contribution to a Useful Queer Mythology," he discusses the events that led to his creation of the performance — principally the experience of his partner Darrell Kirk's illness and death from AIDS — and his aims and approach to making a performance piece in honor of him and their relationship. He situates his work within his own responses to the AIDS epidemic, saying: "Trying to respond to the AIDS pandemic often times seems futile. As I struggle as an artist to come to terms with my role in a time of death, I am often overwhelmed and saddened by my inadequate responses. I cannot cure those who are ill. I do not have a magical formula that will take away the pain and hurt of those who are dying and those the dying have left behind. I wonder if my art is of any use at all" (74).

Following this framing of his own identity as an artist and as a gay man, Dillard proceeds to consider the roles he has played and continues to play: partner to Darrell, speaker of stories and of loving words, and, critically, a *maggid*, a sacred Jewish storyteller (a title that requires ordination, as other sacred offices do). The scholar Andrew Ramer is a *maggid* who speaks of the "Stand between People," a Native American identity, often held by people who would be identified in modern non–Native American cultures as gay men, sometimes trans, in the sense of standing *between* worlds and genders, rather than as identifying in a fixed way with the female gender. Dillard's work intends to "creat[e] space for people to contemplate the crossing-over time. What you witness in the performance is me doing this with him. In the performance, you witness me letting go of a partner and how he and I work together to take him to the other side. What is remarkable is not the uniqueness of that crossing but rather the universal nature of the crossing" (77).

Dillard's "breathing" both with and of (in the sense of incorporating the spiritual and emotional presence) Darrell does important work that comes out of the experience of AIDS and may, at this point in history, be yet another way of memorializing the extraordinary courage of and profound care provided for the men and women who lived (and died, though many continue to live) with AIDS. Dillard's text is reproduced below; it seems a fitting conclusion not just to this section on AIDS and the arts, but to the question of what might constitute a "queer imagination" (or, rather, "queer imaginings," plural).

### Breathing Darrell

*[The stage is unadorned. The only set piece present is a straight back chair set at a slight angle as if pulled up to a bed. I start in the chair looking at the imaginary bed. I begin to breathe. Long, deep breaths at regular intervals. I take three breaths.]*

I sat next to you dear, trying to regulate the breath that came so irregularly to your pneumonia-filled lungs: shallow breaths that came at such long intervals. I tried to bring you in synch with me, hoping that you would catch my breath, my rhythm. Like when we would lie together in bed and try to breathe together so that we could fall asleep at the same moment. But you would not be regulated, and so I tried to breathe with you, to feel your pain, to go with you just a little.

Those last few hours in the ICU, you were with me at times. You couldn't talk, tubes separating your vocal cords, but you did your damnedest to let me know what was going on. Writing seemed impossible to you, so, with the help of an angel-nurse who had sadly become proficient in reading the lips of the ill, we communicated our last.

I remember you asked me if I could see all of the people who were in the room waiting for you. I said "no." You laughed and gave me that sweet little grin of yours that could make me follow you anywhere. You pointed around the room to where they were waiting: around the bed, in the corner, at the door, in a chair. You told me they were there to take you with them. I asked if it was a good place you were going to and you broke out into the most magnificent smile I have ever seen. A smile so clear and genuine that your soul could be seen. You were translucent. Then you said, "Oh, yes!" I'll never forget how you forced the air out of your throat to mouth those words. The rush of the sound that had escaped you caught me off guard and I inhaled the most satisfying bit of air ever breathed.

You were so filled with joy at the prospect of your new life that you spilled over and onto me. Then your face looked at me so hopefully and you said, "You come too!" I said, "No, not yet." You nodded your approval, and shut your eyes to sleep.

Later, you told me with great effort that you were going to a place called "Mead." You had to spell it for me, mouthing the letters, "M-E-

A-D." When I finally understood, you laughed and shook your head at me like you couldn't believe I was so incredibly dense. It was later that your friend Sherry told me that mead meant meadow. And, Dear, that is where we laid you down, in a meadow.

Toward morning I told you that I needed to go outside for a cigarette.

*[I stand up from chair in order to leave the room.]*

You tried to tell me something but I couldn't understand. I asked if it was important and you said no. I said that I would be back in a moment. You said okay, which was unusual because you didn't like it when I left. I said, "I love you." You pointed at yourself and then at me and nodded — yes.

*[I move down stage left about five or six feet.]* Outside, in the cool morning air, I stood in the parking lot of the hospital. Taking a moment to breathe freely, to fortify myself with new energy so that I could return to you. And then it happened. Something so magical swept over me. I felt a true peace, a settling, a calm that I had never experienced before. I stood motionless for a few moments and then it passed and I was back in the world. *[I turn to go back in the hospital.]* I turned to return to the hospital and noticed the doctor running out the front door. *[I mime dropping keys.]* I dropped my keys, he noticed me, stopped and returned to the hospital, satisfied I guess that I was returning. *[I say the next line as I make my way back to the chair.]* I told myself that it was nothing, all the way up the elevator, through the halls, by the sad glances turned my way.

I arrived at your room and saw about eight people gathered there. I walked in and froze. The nurse said that you went into cardiac arrest and were gone now. You went peacefully, she said. I didn't believe her. I could see you breathing. I looked there. The nurse, noticing my confusion, said that it was just the machine breathing now. "Oh, yes" was all I could say.

*[I sit in the chair.]*

They cleaned you up my dear and I held you a few last moments but knew you were not there anymore.

*[I speak in a halting, stuttering, out-of-breath manner.]*

I — gathered myself together — and drove — the thirty — miles home — in a — daze. I — made –phone — calls, — I made — plans, — I went — crazy — with — missing — you. I — could not — talk with — out a — stutter — for what seemed — like days. No — intake of — breath — could — satisfy

—my need. No — one — was — breathing — with me. There — was — no — one — to breathe — for.

*[I take several long, deep breaths at regular intervals in order to recover.]*

I can no longer hear your voice and when you came to me once in a dream, we spoke but no sound could be heard. [*I rise from the chair and walk down stage and relive the dream.*] In the dream, all of my friends and yours are there. Everyone says you look great, like you always did. Eventually, you walk to the back of the yard and wave goodbye [*I lift my arm to wave*] to me and are gone. And I am alone now with my breath and yours.

*[I take three deep breaths with my eyes closed. On the last intake of breath I hold it, open my eyes and smile.]*


## ISSUES FOR INVESTIGATION

**1.** The AIDS epidemic has been publicly visible for over three decades. To what degree do you and your fellow students regard it as part of history or part of your present lives (or both)? Which artistic works on the epidemic are familiar to you? You might find it instructive to compare and contrast artistic works created during the height of the epidemic in North America and Western Europe, in the 1980s and 1990s, with those that have been produced more recently. What differences do you note, either in the perspectives of the artists or in the political perspectives of the artworks?

**2.** Irony and camp have been identified as two of the recurring forms of queer creativity and expressiveness, particularly before Stonewall. As suggested, some have wondered if these tropes of indirection and coding will disappear (or have indeed disappeared already) in societies in which the closet is no longer the default public strategy for queer people. What do you think of this hypothesis? Can you identify either popular or fine art that still uses irony and camp as important to its effects? If so, is such use still tied to queerness, or has it expanded to other realms of experience and identity?

**3.** Choose an artistic medium of interest to you — literature, music, the visual arts, theater, dance, or some combination. Create a work of art that touches on some element of queer life or queer studies that has been explored in this textbook or that reaches beyond the specific topics and issues covered. How does using art to embody the imagination add to your understanding of queerness, whatever your own identity is? Present this work to the class — if it is a performance, solo or group, see if you can find an interesting, somewhat queer space for it — and it may be that your classroom may itself feel sufficiently queer as a space for art. If it is a work of visual art, provide a brief comment — not necessarily an explanation or analysis — to accompany its display. How can art engage and express the imagination in ways more traditional academic discourse may not?

## SUGGESTIONS FOR FURTHER READING AND VIEWING

*An AIDS Quilt Songbook: Sing for Hope.* GPR, 2014.

*The AIDS Quilt Songbook.* Harmonia Mundi, 1994.

Blum, John. *Acting Gay.* New York: Columbia University Press, 1992.

Brett, Philip, Elizabeth Wood, and Gary C. Thomas, eds. *Queering the Pitch: The New Lesbian and Gay Musicology.* 2nd ed. New York: Routledge, 2006.

Bullock, Darryl W. *David Bowie Made Me Gay: 100 Years of LGBT Music.* New York: Overlook Press, 2017.

*Common Threads: Stories from the Quilt.* Directed by Rob Epstein and Jeffrey Friedman. Home Box Office, 1989.

Duberman, Martin. *Hold Tight Gently: Michael Callen, Essex Hemphill, and the Battlefield of AIDS.* New York: New Press, 2014.

Gamson, Joshua. *The Fabulous Sylvester: The Legend, the Music, the Seventies in San Francisco.* New York: Henry Holt, 2005.

Harris, Daniel. "Making Kitsch from AIDS." *Harper's,* July 1994, 55–60.

Hodges, Ben, ed. *Forbidden Acts: Pioneering Gay & Lesbian Plays of the Twentieth Century.* New York: Applause Books, 2003.

Jones, Therese, ed. *Sharing the Delirium: Second Generation AIDS Plays and Performances.* Portsmouth, NH: Heinemann, 1994.

Katz, Jonathan Ned, and Rock Hushka. *Art AIDS America.* Seattle: University of Washington Press, 2015.

Koestenbaum, Wayne. *The Queen's Throat: Opera, Homosexuality, and the Mystery of Desire.* 1993. Reprint. New York: Da Capo, 2001.

Kugelmass, Jack. *Masked Culture: The Greenwich Village Halloween Parade.* New York: Columbia University Press, 1994.

Larnach-Jones, Will. *50 Queer Music Icons Who Changed the World: A Celebration of LGBTQ+ Legends.* London: Hardie-Grant, 2018.

Merrill, Lisa. *When Romeo Was a Woman: Charlotte Cushman and Her Circle of Female Spectators.* Ann Arbor: University of Michigan Press, 1999.

Osborn, M. Elizabeth, ed. *The Way We Live Now: American Plays and the AIDS Crisis*. New York: Theatre Communications Group, 1990.

Packer, Renée Levine, and Mary Jane Leach, eds. *Gay Guerrilla: Julius Eastman and His Music*. Rochester: University of Rochester Press, 2015.

Palmer, Paulina. *The Queer Uncanny: New Perspectives on the Gothic*. Cardiff: University of Wales Press, 2012.

Reed, Christopher. *Art and Homosexuality: A History of Ideas*. New York: Oxford University Press, 2011.

Russo, Vito. *The Celluloid Closet: Homosexuality in the Movies*. Rev. ed. New York: Harper & Row, 1987. (A documentary of the same title is available on DVD.)

Saslow, James M. *Pictures and Passions: A History of Homosexuality in the Visual Arts*. New York: Viking, 1999.

Spring, Justin. "Hugh Steers: A Memoir." *New England Review* 22.1 (2001): 155–163.

Tropiano, Stephen. *The Prime Time Closet: A History of Gays and Lesbians on TV*. New York: Applause Books, 2002.

# CONCLUSION
## Imagining Utopias in Queer Studies

### QUEER FUTURE = NO FUTURE

In *No Future: Queer Theory and the Death Drive,* the literary scholar Lee Edelman argues that queer identity and life are fundamentally *not* invested in what he calls "futurity," by virtue of their orientation to nonreproductive sex and the social institutions that help define queer ways of being in the world and knowing the self. Borrowing from Lacan's concept of the **sinthome,** the experience of sexual pleasure (*jouissance*) that is knowingly divorced from any connection to future children who might be produced from queer sexual interactions and relationships, Edelman argues that a more radical and authentic way of viewing the politics, psychology, and philosophy of queerness would be to orient life outside the child as the center of how we organize society. In this sense, his call to replace the centrality of reproductive philosophies of sexuality with what he calls "sinthomosexuality," a play on Lacan's word, creates an equality among different sexual identities that has the potential to foster worlds where each individual can be regarded with as much worth and as many rights as any other. He acknowledges, "It is true that the ranks of lesbian, gay, bisexual, transsexual, and transgendered parents grow larger every day, and that nothing intrinsic to the constitution of those identifying as lesbian, gay, bisexual, transgendered, transsexual, or queer predisposes them to resist the appeal of futurity, to refuse the temptation to reproduce" (17). Edelman does argue, at length, that queer people can resist the foundational centrality of parenting and the needs of the child in society, to the benefit of all. This requires, however, a commitment to a belief in "no future," that is, in not making social or political choices contingent on future generations as the basis for action and justice in the present.

### FAILURE AS QUEER "SUCCESS"

Jack Halberstam (writing under the name Judith Halberstam) offers in the 2011 book *The Queer Art of Failure* a provocative and fresh approach to

Henderson, Bruce, *Queer Studies: Beyond Binaries*
dx.doi.org/10.17312/harringtonparkpress/2019.09.qsbb.00c
© 2019 by Harrington Park Press

conceiving of one of the central contributions he believes queer experience can bring to the way society at large might restructure its worldview of accomplishment and working toward futures. This difference is embodied in the unexpected word in the title: *failure*. Failure is usually considered a negative value, but, Halberstam suggests, it is useful to rethink the positive values of failure, by queering it, as an opportunity for us as individuals and as groups to shift our assumptions about how we know and accomplish things and what the "natural" state of human subjectivity and imperfection truly is.

Halberstam puts forth three maxims for this "queer art" of **failure**:

- Resist mastery (11).
- Privilege the naive or nonsensical (stupidity) (12).
- Suspect memorialization (15).

Halberstam suggests that mastery is itself the road to a kind of dead end — indeed, the "death" of the future. Honoring the second, which essentially says, "Be stupid," goes against who most of us are (or who we aspire to be, as thoughtful, reflective beings), but sometimes not knowing has led to better outcomes: the naïveté of a person can allow a freer flow of possibilities. Halberstam suggests that privileging the naïveté of *not* assuming that heterosexuality is the default position from which to live or to which to aspire may produce a richer set of life possibilities. Finally, Halberstam's call to "suspect memorialization" is an interesting counterpoint to Edelman's "no future": it encourages us to resist valorizing the past as the site of what is "right" and from which we draw our traditions (including the power genealogies hold over us, both in our family lives and in our intellectual lives).

Like Edelman, Halberstam is making a strong argument that, when challenged, may not work for every moment of our lives. But what is worth thinking and talking more about is how Halberstam imports the ways in which queerness has been deemed "failure" (think of such phrases as "Dude, that's so gay," as an often unconsciously homophobic way of dismissing someone's actions as wrong or inappropriate), and he provocatively imagines a future when some of the precepts of this queer art, where failure may be the highest form of success, has as valid a place. The *failure* bound up in messages about queerness may ultimately be more productive than the *success* implied by heterosexuality.

## UTOPIAN PERFORMANCE AND QUEER POSSIBILITIES

It is a truism that all utopias are always fated to be imperfect and, in worst-case scenarios, as suggested above, they devolve into nightmarish dystopias, often the opposite of the ideals on which the society was initially planned. That does not mean, however, that aspiring toward utopia — as the late queer performance scholar José Estaban Muñoz puts it playfully in the title of his book on the subject, *Cruising Utopia* (*cruising* here a play on moving along a path, sometimes diverging from the route, and the sexual cruising that gay men especially engage in, though there is probably a culture of cruising for all sexualities) — is not worthwhile. What Muñoz, as well as the lesbian theater scholar Jill Dolan in her book *Utopia in Performance*, envisioned are those spaces in which queer people "perform" utopian moves — whether dance floors, theaters, drag clubs, or the streets that provide the stages of our lives — and this is one of the reasons the mass murders in the Pulse nightclub in Orlando, until then a kind of queer and people-of-color utopia, was all the more devastating: it had been a place of hope and imagining.

So, a third way of imagining and enacting (or performing) queer futures is through knowing yet stupid (in Halberstam's sense) utopian movements, gestures, and actions. What is *knowing* is being deliberate about making choices and working toward goals for a future where queer life is as valued as all life, and perhaps even imagining a world where such a binary as queer/non-queer no longer makes sense. Kath Browne suggests that the Michigan Womyn's Music Festival was one such queer (in this case, specifically lesbian) utopian effort — and that it ended because it could not accommodate competing demands from different groups; that these demands would cancel each other simply means that it was a human thing. Similarly, while the AIDS epidemic may be the very definition of a dystopia, the sexual liberation of the period preceding it may well have been genuinely utopian in its moment; Scott Dillard's piece, *Breathing Darrell*, while a form of "memorialization," also, in doing that work, is a hopeful move toward a utopia of learning how to grieve, mourn, and continue to live and to celebrate the possibilities of queerness beyond the binaries of either-or.

## ISSUES FOR INVESTIGATION

**1.** Working first on your own, then in small groups, imagine what a queer utopia might be. How is the queerness of the utopia important to your imagining of it? Since virtually all intended utopias become dystopias (at some point, for some people), can you see potential "cracks" in the imagined perfect world? Share your own and your group's ideas with your class.

**2.** You have come to the end of this book and, presumably, the end of the course for which you have been reading it. Take this opportunity to consider what your queer journey has been. How has your understanding of the critical role of language in creating queer lives and realities changed? Has your understanding of identity become more concrete — or, conversely, does it seem more fluid or diffuse? (There is no correct answer to this question.) Which contexts for queer studies (social, psychological, religious, political, educational, artistic) are ones that feel most immediately relevant to you — which ones can you connect with either your major field of study or your career goals?

In other words, what do you know or understand now that you did not when you began this class and this book? What do you still want to learn?

## SUGGESTIONS FOR FURTHER READING AND VIEWING

In a sense, the list for this conclusion (other than the texts cited within its pages) is yours to discover, perhaps even yours to write and to create. Look online, at various sites, to see what new writers, artists, activists, and others have produced since this book was published. That is the future of queer studies, as we all stumble toward, if never quite achieving (for, as the poet Richard Wilbur memorably wrote, "such Edens can't be found"), possible queer utopias.

# APPENDIX
## Primary Texts for Study

**From Plato, *Symposium*, translated by Benjamin Jowett
(Upper Saddle River, NJ: Prentice-Hall, 1956), 30–34.**

The sexes were not two as they are now, but originally three in number; there was man, woman, and the union of the two, having a name corresponding to this double nature, which had once a real existence, but is now lost, and the word "Androgynous" is only preserved as a term of reproach. In the second place, the primeval man was round, his back and sides forming a circle; and he had four hands and four feet, one head with two faces, looking opposite ways, set on a round neck and precisely alike; also four ears, two privy members, and the remainder to correspond. He could walk upright as men now do, backwards or forwards as he pleased, and he could also roll over and over at a great pace, turning on his four hands and four feet, eight in all, like tumblers going over and over with their legs in the air; this was when he wanted to run fast. Now the sexes were three, and such as I have described them; because the sun, moon, and earth are three; — and the man was originally the child of the sun, the woman of the earth, and the man-woman of the moon, which is made up of sun and earth, and they were all round and moved round and round: like their parents. Terrible was their might and strength, and the thoughts of their hearts were great, and they made an attack upon the gods; of them is told the tale of Otys and Ephialtes who, as Homer says, dared to scale heaven, and would have laid hands upon the gods. Doubt reigned in the celestial councils. Should they kill them and annihilate the race with thunderbolts, as they had done the giants, then there would be an end of the sacrifices and worship which men offered to them; but, on the other hand, the gods could not suffer their insolence to be unrestrained.

At last, after a good deal of reflection, Zeus discovered a way. He said: "Methinks I have a plan which will humble their pride and improve their manners; men shall continue to exist, but I will cut them in two and then they will be diminished in strength and increased in numbers; this will have the advantage of making them more profitable to us. They shall walk upright on two legs, and if they continue insolent and will not be quiet, I

Henderson, Bruce, *Queer Studies: Beyond Binaries*
dx.doi.org/10.17312/harringtonparkpress/2019.09.qsbb.00d
© 2019 by Harrington Park Press

will split them again and they shall hop about on a single leg." He spoke and cut men in two, like a sorb-apple which is halved for pickling, or as you might divide an egg with a hair; and as he cut them one after another, he bade Apollo give the face and the half of the neck a turn in order that the man might contemplate the section of himself: he would thus learn a lesson of humility. Apollo was also bidden to heal their wounds and compose their forms. So he gave a turn to the face and pulled the skin from the sides all over that which in our language is called the belly, like the purses which draw in, and he made one mouth at the centre, which he fastened in a knot (the same which is called the navel); he also moulded the breast and took out most of the wrinkles, much as a shoemaker might smooth leather upon a last; he left a few, however, in the region of the belly and navel, as a memorial of the primeval state. After the division the two parts of man, each desiring his other half, came together, and throwing their arms about one another, entwined in mutual embraces, longing to grow into one, they were on the point of dying from hunger and self-neglect, because they did not like to do anything apart; and when one of the halves died and the other survived, the survivor sought another mate, man' or woman as we call them, being the sections of entire men or women, and clung to that. They were being destroyed, when Zeus in pity of them invented a new plan: he turned the parts of generation round to the front, for this had not been always their position and they sowed the seed no longer as hitherto like grasshoppers in the ground, but in one another; and after the transposition the male generated in the female in order that by the mutual embraces of man and woman they might breed, and the race might continue; or if man came to man they might be satisfied, and rest, and go their ways to the business of life: so ancient is the desire of one another which is implanted in us, reuniting our original nature, making one of two, and healing the state of man.

Each of us when separated, having one side only, like a flat fish, is but the indenture of a man, and he is always looking for his other half. Men who are a section of that double nature which was once called Androgynous are lovers of women; adulterers are generally of this breed, and also adulterous women who lust after men: the women who are a section of the woman do not care for men, but have female attachments; the female companions are of this sort. But they who are a section of the male follow the male, and while they are young, being slices of the original man, they hang about men and embrace them, and they are themselves the best of boys and youths, because they have the most manly nature. Some indeed assert that they are shameless, but this is not true; for they do not act thus from any want of shame, but because they are valiant and manly, and have a manly countenance, and they embrace that which is like them. And these when they grow up become our statesmen, and these only, which is a great proof of the truth of what I am saving. When they reach manhood they are loves of youth, and are not naturally inclined to marry or beget children, — if at all, they do so only in obedience to the law; but they are satisfied if they may be allowed to live with one another unwedded; and such a nature is prone to love and ready to return love, always embracing that which is akin to him. And when one of them meets with his other half, the actual half of himself, whether he be a lover of youth or a lover of another sort, the pair are lost in an amazement of love and friendship and intimacy, and would not be out of the other's sight, as I may say, even for a moment: these are the people who pass their whole lives together; yet they could not explain what they desire of one another. For the intense yearning which each of them has towards the other does not appear to be the desire of lover's intercourse, but of something else which the soul of either evidently desires and cannot tell, and of which she has only a dark and doubtful presentiment. Suppose Hephaestus, with his instruments, to come to the pair who are lying side, by side and to say to them, "What do you people want of one another?" they would be unable to explain. And suppose further, that when he saw their perplexity he said: "Do you desire to be wholly one; always day and night to be in one another's company? for if this is what you desire, I am ready to melt you into one and let you grow together, so that being two you shall become one, and while you live a common life as if you were a single man, and after your death in the world below still be one departed soul instead of two — I ask whether this is what you lovingly desire, and whether you are satisfied to attain this?" — there is not a man of them who when he heard the proposal would deny or would not acknowledge that this meeting and melting into one another, this becoming one instead of two, was the very expression of his ancient need. And the reason is that human nature was originally one and we were a whole, and the desire and pursuit of the whole is called love. There was a time, I say, when we were one, but now because of the wickedness of mankind God has dispersed us, as the Arcadians were dispersed into villages by the Lacedaemonians. And if we are not obedient to the gods, there is a danger that we shall be split up again and go about in basso-relievo, like the profile figures having only half a nose which are sculptured on monuments, and that we shall be like tallies.

From Jane Hamilton, *The Short History of a Prince* (New York: Random House, 1998), 271–277.

Walter paused outside the dressing room, considering that remark. Of course he was always going to be a homo. He had already figured out that his kind didn't reach the age of twenty-one and automatically and genuinely become marriageable material. He stuck one fluttering arm back through the door, as _if to say in swan language, So will you too be a cream puff, and he hiked up his skirts and went slapslapping into the studio.

The late-afternoon sun filtered through the clouds over the lake, and in the long bank of mirrors it was hard to see where the gauze of the skirt ended and the glittering dust began. He was no more flat-chested than half of the girls, He looked terrific, he did! He tinkered with the undershirt on his head, tucking the sleeves into the roll of the crown. If only they could wear costumes for class, instead of the drab black tights and the plain white T-shirt. He turned his head to this side, to that, admiring himself. He did a jump step called a pas de chat, one foot to the knee, step, the other foot to the knee, a sideways leap, the step of the cat. The pointe shoes made a pleasing noise as they came to the floor, wood against wood, and the skirt followed him, floating, a beat behind his movements, He sang, bringing his arms over his head, crossing them down to his knees, wavering on his pointes. His every movement, he thought, expressed the agony of rejection and the spell of sorrow. Poor Odette, he danced, who loves so purely and loses her chance of earthly happiness. He brought his trembling arms behind him, threw back his head, the way Odette does in both her passion and her grief. Mitch's words came to him — "You'll always be a homo" — and he thought too of the horrible things Susan had said to him at school. Daniel was lying in a steel hospital bed shoved up against a tiled wall, waiting to go from this world. How could that be real? Walter raised his voice and it cracked. Sinng, dancing, he guessed, was the only way he could ever really communicate. It did cross his mind, as he so poignantly bobbled to his own strains, that he should be careful not to stay too long, one more look, and he'd pitter-patter back to the dressing room.

It was inevitable, he later thought, predictable, that Mr. Kenton flick on the lights and see him clearly. Under the white ball fixture Walter was no longer obscured by the deepening golden afternoon sunlight. He continued to move, shutting his eyes, laughing, as if he were already middle-aged and the scene was a past embarrassing moment. He had escaped the police in the alley, and Mitch, under his bed, had not been found out by Joyce and Robert. Still, it seemed so familiar, this getting-caught-in-the-light business. Mrs. Manka was standing behind Mr. Kenton, peering over his shoulder. Although it was April it was unseasonably cold. She looked like a Russian diplomat in her black-and-white-checked coat, with the big, black, plush fake-fur collar and a black fur hat.

"What in Sam Hill — " she began.

Mr. Kenton did not register surprise. "All right, then," he said simply. He came forward, pulled at the thighs of his trousers with his thumbs and index fingers and sat himself down on the white bench with the blue cushion, where he always sat when he watched their combinations. "We'll have Odile's fouetté music, please, Agatha."

Mrs. Manka seemed to be having trouble taking off her coat, or else, Walter thought, she was removing it reluctantly, stalling. She glanced at him once, shaking her head, pursing her lips, not a look of encouragement or amusement. He understood her to mean that the fouetté turns were difficult and that the man of the establishment did not have a forgiving temperament. There was no little pocket of mercy in Mr. Kenton and maybe he was going to give Walter a lashing he'd never forget, and who was to say that Walter didn't deserve it?

"Come to the center, Odile," Mr. Kenton said, clapping three times.

No, no! Walter was the good swan, Odette, not the bad swan. The wicked one had the hardest variations, the demanding turns. He was much better at expressing pain and misfortune; he couldn't possibly convince anyone, even through the dance, that he was conniving, out to spoil a prince's pleasure and happiness.

"Let's see your thirty-two fouetté turns," Mr. Kenton ordered, "You have two measures for preparation. About like this, Agatha." He hummed the music, setting the speed. It was far slower than the recording, but faster than a novice could manage. Mrs. Manka quickly lit her cigarette and took a sustaining puff.

Walter felt as if he were wearing flippers as he came to the center, as if he were all equipment, suited up for a horrific dive. Fouetté turns are sharp whipping turns, one after the next. He was to do thirty-two of them without stopping, just as Odile does in *Swan Lake*, when she's bewitching the Prince. He could sense the weight of the shoes but he didn't think he could find his own feet. It might be possible to turn around and around on half-pointe, without rising up on his toes. Walter's one strength in ballet was his ability to turn. It crossed his mind, just for an instant, that Mr. Kenton was appealing to his talent, But no, no, how could Walter forget? This was the hunter and his prey, the great big old cat with yellow teeth getting closer, closer, cornering the mouse, the resigned mouse, the I-am-already-dead mouse.

Mrs. Manka played her measures, and he did his preparation, arms to the front, arms and feet à la seconde, arms and feet to fourth position. He got three quarters of the way through the first turn when Mr. Kenton clapped to stop the music, "No, no, no, no. On pointe. You're a swan now, remember? You've got the costume and the shoes, now do the dance, GIRL."

Mrs. Manka again began the introduction. "And one and two and three and four," Mr. Kenton shouted.

It is trying enough for a seasoned ballerina to successfully execute thirty-two fouettés. There was a brittle anger in Mr. Kenton's voice as he counted. It's a long way down to the ground from the twelfth floor, Walter thought, and his sleeves would not have much wing action to slow the fall. He felt as if his feet were laced up in cement blocks; the numbness was rising from his ankles, spreading like dye along his calves. His hands were wet, his skin so cold, and the knocking of his chest was in his ears, overpowering the music. Those irregularities, he thought, meant that he was frightened.

"MOVE," Mr. Kenton ordered.

Walter turned. He went around in a burst, and again, and a third time. His feet were going to snap at the ankle with a few more rotations, he was sure of it, and he'd have to dance on the raw bleeding stub of a leg. He fell after the sixth turn. He lay still in the pool of his skirt. He hardly knew if he was crying, didn't want to feel his face to find out, couldn't in any case locate his cheeks or his eyes, all of him to the top of his head packed into the shoes.

"GET UP," Mr. Kenton shouted, with the force, the venom, of a sergeant. "Take it from the top, DEAR."

"I don't think I can — "

"FROM THE TOP." He was standing, banging the cane against the wall, shouting at Mrs. Manka, and at Walter, shouting, "Faster, faster, faster." Walter's turning foot bent and he skittered across the floor.

"Center, sweetheart," Mr. Kenton said with terrifying enunciation. "Again, lover."

Walter dragged himself, hauled his feet, to the front of the studio. He was preparing for the turns when he saw Mitch at the door, Mitch's right foot crossed over the left, Mitch resting against the jamb, Mitch's lip curling, Mitch sniggering.

"AGAIN," Mr. Kenton bellowed.

Walter looked at his teacher, at his flashing eyes, his red ascot bunched at his throat, that dot of color like a gaping wound. "It's not going to be good," his mother in her infinite wisdom had said the night before.

Why am I here? Walter thought. I need to go to the hospital. I need to see Daniel, my brother.

*It's not going to be good, sweetie.* He picked up his beaten, his quite dead, feet, and made for the door. He brushed against his friend, the one with the fiendishly long and hard winkie, the beauty of which he could only imagine because he had never been allowed to revel over it. He walked from the studio without hearing Mr. Kenton's invective, without listening to the demands to return, the threats, he supposed, and the insults. There were twelve flights of stairs, in the neighborhood of 240 individual steps and the walk around every landing. But he couldn't stand there waiting for the elevator with Mr. Kenton on his tail and he certainly didn't want to explain his girl getup to the elevator man. It was at the fifth floor that he felt his feet, suddenly, briefly, a stab of pain as if the nerves were finally being severed. His feet, he thought, were like two squashed hearts inside of Sonja Marendaz's pointe shoes, shoes that had been made by an old man cobbler across the ocean in England. He went down and down, the bloody pulp sloshing in his slippers. When he got to the last marble flight he sat and scooted on his behind down each stair to the lobby, where many of the girls in his class were waiting for the elevator.

He had a fair idea that he looked like a crippled pigeon. The girls were too startled to squeal or laugh out loud, and he was grateful for the silence, He got himself upright and walked out the door to the street. It occurred. to him as he crossed Van Buren that he couldn't very well ride the el in the costume, and that he also could not go back to the studio to fetch his clothes. He stood on the pavement, the wind blowing his skirt up in the back. It was chilly and the tulle and satin weren't much for warmth. He realized that he couldn't ride the el anyway, because he didn't have his wallet. There were red stains spreading from the pink satin toe on each foot towards the instep. He had no money. It would be the first time in history a person bled to death from a wound to the big toe. He supposed that the newspaper would call it suicide first and murder later, after Mrs. Manka came forward and told the police the truth.

He turned back and hobbled up the block to the Pick Congress Hotel. In front of the porters in their green pants and green vests and green top hats, he walked along the curb and got into the first taxi in the lineup. He had no choice but to lift his skirts modestly and climb into the car. It was perhaps there, outside the row of grand hotels, that Walter found in himself a confidence that was later to hold him in good stead in Otten. There was nothing to do but be a fool in as dignified a manner as he could muster. The driver did not look at him, did not say a word, as if every day a boy dressed as a wili got in his cab. Walter took off the slippers and although he tried to massage his feet, one at a time, both of them remained in the shape of the shoe for the duration of the trip. The nails had come off seven of his toes and he let them bleed on the floor mat of the cab. He couldn't think what would have happened if he'd stayed on, if Mr. Kenton had planned to beat him or make him dance until he broke a leg. He put his head back and tried to find rest in the thought that it was over, he had gotten away.

When they pulled up to 646 Maplewood Avenue thirty minutes later Walter told the driver to wait.

"You bet I'll wait, kid, until I have every penny of the fare."

He limped up the sidewalk and into the house and through the rooms, opening drawers and looking in pots, searching for cash. Joyce had so thought-fully left ten dollars for pizza under the vase. "Bless you," Walter whispered. He found three dollars in small change, and two dollars in Daniel's wallet that had been on the counter for a month. He went back out in his costume and his bare feet. It was when he opened the car door and handed the money to the driver that the man at last took notice. He looked Walter up and down and said, "What's the matter wich-you?"

"Is it extra for analysis, or do you do it for free?" Walter said, slamming the door.

In the following hour, in his living room, he considered killing himself by using a number of different methods. He didn't exactly want to die, but living was not something he wished to continue. He would have liked to go elsewhere, not as a traveler or a runaway — just elsewhere; to sit and wait, until his life was over.

He found he could not walk. He was sitting at the bottom of the stairs in the hall, and he could not move. It would be impossible, then, to climb the three flights to pitch himself off the attic roof. It would be out of the question to get to the medicine cabinet, to the full bottle of aspirin. His parents did not own a gun, as far as he knew. He couldn't warm to the thought of stabbing himself with a butcher knife. It took more than enough effort just to take off his costume and ball it up and stuff it behind the piano. Getting his father's trench coat off the hanger almost did him in, and he collapsed on the sofa before he finished threading the buckle. He would pass out, that's what he would do. He had never fainted, and he didn't know if it was something that could be willed. It would be best, if he was going to lose consciousness, to go slowly, to music. He crawled to the stereo. If he could only manage to get the record on the turntable without standing, he'd have *Tosca*. It was worth doing for Tebaldi, never mind his bloody feet and all the rest of him that was hurt too.

When she came on in the second act singing "Vissi d'arte," Walter, in a pile on the floor, lifted his head and weakly sang along with her, feeling the meaning as he never had before. "Love and music, these have I lived for, nor ever have harmed a living being." He was with her all the way to the end. "Why, heavenly father, why hast thou forsaken me?"

Richard Blanco, "Queer Theory: According to my Grandmother" in *Looking for the Gulf Motel* (Pittsburgh: University of Pittsburgh Press, 2012), 34–36.

> Never drink soda with a straw —
>     milk shakes? Maybe.
> Stop eyeing your mother's Avon catalog,
> and the men's underwear in those Sears flyers.
>     I've seen you . . .
> Stay out of her Tupperware parties
> and perfume bottles — don't let her kiss you,
>     she kisses you much too much.
> Avoid hugging men, but if you must,

pat them real hard
on the back, even
if it's your father.
Must you keep that cat? Don't pet him so much,
Why don't you like dogs?
Never play house, even if you're the husband.
Quit hanging out with that Henry kid, he's too pale,
and I don't care what you call them
those GI Joes of his
are dolls.
Don't draw rainbows or flowers or sunsets.
I've seen you . . .
Don't draw at all — no coloring books either.
Put away your crayons, your Play-Doh, your Legos.
Where are you hot Wheels,
your laser gun and handcuffs,
the knives I gave you?
Never fly a kite or roller skate, but light
all the firecrackers you want,
kill all the lizards you can, cut up worms —
feed them to that cat of yours.
Don't sit *Indian* style with your legs crossed —
you're no Indian.
Stop click-clacking your sandals —
you're no girl.
For God's sake, never pee sitting down.
I've seen you . . .
Never take a bubble bath or wash your hair
with shampoo — shampoo is for women.
So is conditioner.
So is mousse.
So is hand lotion.
Never file your nails or blow-dry your hair —
go to the barber shop with your grandfather —
you're not *unisex.*
Stay out of the kitchen. Men don't cook —
they eat. Eat anything you want, except:
deviled eggs
Blow Pops
croissants (Bagels? Maybe.)
cucumber sandwiches
petit fours

Don't watch *Bewitched* or *I Dream of Jeannie*.
Don't stare at *The Six-Million Dollar Man*.
    I've seen you . . .
Never dance alone in your room:
Donna Summer, Barry Manilow, the Captain
and Tennille, Bette Midler, and all musicals —
    forbidden.
Posters of kittens, *Star Wars*, or the Eiffel Tower —
    forbidden.
Those fancy books on architecture and art —
    I threw them in the trash.
You can't wear cologne or puka shells
and I better not catch you in clogs.
If I see you in a ponytail — I'll cut if off.
What? No, you can't pierce your ear,
    left or right side —
    I don't care —
you will not look like a goddamn queer
    I've seen you . . .
even if you are one.

**John Heineman, "Building a GLOBE in Nebraska," in *One Teacher in Ten: Gay and Lesbian Educators Tell Their Stories*, ed. Kevin Jennings (Los Angeles: Alyson, 1994), 208–211.**

How is it possible for an openly gay teacher to be sponsoring a gay and lesbian support group in the middle of Nebraska? It starts with the word "No."

It was October of 1992 and I had just returned from a year's sabbatical leave to my seventh year of secondary school teaching at Lincoln High School in Lincoln, Nebraska. I had taken the sabbatical leave because I was burning out in my classroom. Although I had many success stories to tell, my commitment to teaching was beginning to fade.

I went off to graduate school at the University of Northern Iowa where I learned about the tragic suicide and runaway rates among gay and lesbian teenagers. It was this knowledge alone that brought back the fire to my teaching. I knew there was still work for me to do.

The other significant event happening for me at this time was finally coming out to my parents. My younger brother had come out to them several years before. By the time I told them about myself, my mother responded with a smile: "We thought so!"

I now knew it was time to make a difference with my teaching. I had to find support for gay and lesbian students at Lincoln High. My first chance for change was National Coming-Out Day. Although I was not ready to come out of the classroom closet, I did want to put an announcement in the daily school bulletin about NCOD. This kind of announcement was common with other cultural and gender issues at my school. There were always announcements about Black History Month and Women's History Month.

The announcement I submitted dealt with the tragedy of suicide and runaway rates among gay and lesbian teenagers. It assured the students that if they were dealing with sexual-orientation issues, there were supportive teachers, counselors, and administrators who cared about them. I knew this announcement would be controversial, so I submitted it directly to one of the assistant principals for approval several days early. She brought it to the whole administration and the answer came back, "No."

She explained, "Only announcements coming from a specific group can be read as part of the daily bulletin." She had even gone back over the previous month's announcements to see if there were any exceptions. There weren't. I then asked, "So if I had a gay and lesbian group, I could put this announcement in the bulletin?" My assistant principal grinned and said, "I guess so."

I ran up to my room, copied my original announcement, and added these words: "If you are interested in starting a gay and lesbian support group, please put your name in my box in the main office." I then resubmitted my announcement to the administration and after a deep breath they said, "Yes."

Announcements at Lincoln High are read every day by any teacher with a fourth-period class. The announcement was read on a Friday and by Monday I had a note in my box from an interested student. I clearly remember being blown away by the first note. The student was a senior and had discovered his sexuality two years earlier. He had come out to his mother at age sixteen and was excited about starting the group. I knew then the challenges ahead would be many. Was I qualified to help students who were out to their parents when it took over thirty years for me to do it? Would I be able to fulfill their expectations of the group? I didn't have long to contemplate these questions, because by the end of the week I had five interested students and we set a date for our first meeting.

I was also delighted that several teachers and counselors approached me to say how very pleased they were that our gay and lesbian students would be getting the attention they needed. One teacher who taught human sexuality commented on how she felt she could never do enough in the regular classroom for gay and lesbian students. She and several others offered their time and support to the success of the group.

The first meeting was exciting. It reminded me of my first day of teaching, when I wasn't sure if I had what it took to be an educator. I was also nervous because we had decided to announce the meeting in the daily bulletin, meaning anyone, including the homophobes, could walk through the door.

When we started the meeting, there were several students attending whom I didn't know. I laid out a few ground rules. First, our group was not going to be a place where we would out each other. If anyone wanted to share their sexual orientation, it was going to be their choice. Only one student objected; she had just moved to Lincoln and was hoping to find a date. The second ground rule was that the leadership and direction of the group were to come from the students. There were no objections.

To be an official group or club at my school there are two basic guidelines: groups must have a name and they must have a constitution stating the mission of the group and stating that the group is open to all students. Our first order of business was to work on the name and the constitution. After much brainstorming and lots of acronyms we settled on GLOBE, the Gay and Lesbian Organization for the Betterment of Everyone. We wrote the constitution, submitted it, and started meeting on a regular basis.

A lesbian teacher, along with two counselors, helps sponsor the group. The typical meeting consists of talking about the latest gay and lesbian issue in the news, keeping a file of newspaper and magazine articles for students' and teachers' use, designing and ordering t-shirts for the group, and watching the latest issues of *Network Q*. It was also not uncommon for us to write our governmental officials about both national and local issues. We were fortunate to have the media's daily coverage of President Clinton's "gays in the military" policy. This gave us the opportunity for many lively discussions and letter-writing campaigns to our congressional representatives.

When April rolled around, I had saved several special-leave days so I could go to the March on Washington. The local TV station came and filmed one of our GLOBE meetings, which they used as a followup to the coverage of the march. The reporter outed me on the ten-o'clock news, but it was all right, because I was also quoted in the local newspaper in a story about Nebraskans who were in the march. When the newspaper reporter asked if he could use my name, I said, "Yes." How else could I be a role model for my students about the importance of being out and proud?

Coming home from the March on Washington was just as empowering for me as the march itself had been. Returning to school, I was met by the members of GLOBE, who wanted to know every detail of the march and to talk about my being on the ten-o'clock news. Some had watched the march on C-SPAN and the national news, and all had their opinions and questions about it. I felt honored that I was the one getting to hear their ideas and to answer their questions.

One week later, when my pictures had come back from the developer, the excitement was back. I had intentionally tried to capture the wonderful diversity of the march. I wanted to be sure that my Nebraskan students knew of the endless possibilities and life choices gay men and lesbians had. Each picture brought a wide range of reactions from my students. Some were impressed with the carnival elements of the march, while many wanted to know the stories of each couple that appeared in the pictures. What was clear from their reactions was the lifting of limitations to their personal possibilities. They could see their hopes and dreams lived out in other gays and lesbians, something often missing from their lives in Nebraska.

At the next several meetings we watched the videotape of the march. The students saw many things they wanted to discuss, but most importantly, they saw gay and lesbian people fighting for their rights. I will always be proud that I was there and proud that I could bring part of the march back to my students.

The group is still going strong. We now meet every Monday after school, and students from the other three high schools in town have also been coming to the meetings. I have received lots of support from my colleagues and I feel good about the fact that many teachers and counselors refer students to the group.

I have been fortunate that my being out has not caused me any serious problems at school. I did overhear one of my sophomores refer to me as *the* gay teacher. I laughed when I realized this student could not imagine more than one gay teacher in the world, but I also smiled, knowing the whispers of a student about my sexual orientation were not a secret but a statement I was proud to make.


"Dr. H"'s Speech at the APA, Dallas, May 1972.
https://web.archive.org/web/20080314224843/http://www.aglp.org
/pages/VolumeXXVIII%283%29.html.


Thank you, Dr. Robinson. I am a homosexual. I am a psychiatrist. I, like most of you in this room, am a member of the APA and am proud to be a member. However, tonight I am, insofar as in it is possible, a "we." I attempt tonight to speak for many of my fellow gay members of the APA as well as for myself. When we gather at these conventions, we have a group, which we have glibly come to call the Gay-PA. And several of us feel that it is time that real flesh and blood stand up before you and ask to be listened to and understood insofar as that is possible. I am disguised tonight in order that I might speak freely without conjuring up too much regard on your part about the particular WHO I happen to be. I do that mostly for your protection. I can assure you that I could be any one of more than a hundred psychiatrists registered at this convention. And the curious among you should cease attempting to figure out who I am and listen to what I say.

We homosexual psychiatrists must persistently deal with a variety of what we shall call "Nigger Syndromes." We shall describe some of them and how they make us feel.

As psychiatrists who are homosexual, we must know our place and what we must do to be successful. If our goal is academic appointment, a level of earning capacity equal to our fellows, or admission to a psychoanalytic institute, we must make certain that no one in a position of power is aware of our sexual orientation or gender identity. Much like the black man with the light skin who chooses to live as a white man, we cannot be seen with our real friends — our real homosexual family — lest our secret be known and our dooms sealed. There are practicing psychoanalysts among us who have completed their training analysis without mentioning their homosexuality to their analysts. Those who are willing to speak up openly will do so only if they have nothing to lose, then they won't be listened to.

As psychiatrists who are homosexuals, we must look carefully at the power which lies in our hands to define the health of others around us. In particular, we should have clearly in our minds, our own particular understanding of what it is to be a healthy homosexual in a world, which sees that appellation as an impossible oxymoron. One cannot be healthy and be homosexual, they say. One result of being psychiatrists who are homosexual is that we are required to be more healthy than our heterosexual counterparts. We have to make some sort of attempt through therapy or analysis to work problems out. Many of us who make that effort are still left with a sense of failure and of persistence of "the problem." Just as the black man must be a super person, so must we, in order to face those among our colleagues who know we are gay. We could continue to cite examples of this sort of situation for the remainder of the night. It would be useful, however, if we could now look at the reverse.

What is it like to be a homosexual who is also a psychiatrist? Most of us Gay-PA members do not wear our badges into the Bayou Landing [a gay bar in Dallas] or the local Canal Baths. If we did, we could risk the derision of all the non-psychiatrist homosexuals. There is much negative feeling in the homosexual community towards psychiatrists. And those of us who are visible are the easiest targets from which the angry can vent their wrath. Beyond that, in our own hometowns, the chances are that in any gathering of homosexuals, there is likely to be any number of patients or paraprofessional employees who might try to hurt us professionally in a larger community if those communities enable them to hurt us that way.

Finally, as homosexual psychiatrists, we seem to present a unique ability to marry ourselves to institutions rather than wives or lovers. Many of us work 20 hours daily to protect institutions that would literally chew us up and spit us out if they knew the truth. These are our feelings, and like any set of feelings, they have value insofar as they move us toward concrete action.

Here, I will speak primarily to the other members of the Gay-PA who are present, not in costume tonight. Perhaps you can help your fellow psychiatrist friends understand what I am saying. When you are with professionals, fellow professionals, fellow psychiatrists who are denigrating the "faggots" and the "queers," don't just stand back, but don't give up your careers, either. Show a little creative ingenuity; make sure you let your associates know that they have a few issues that they have to think through again. When fellow homosexuals come to you for treatment, don't let your own problems get in your way, but develop creative ways to let the patient know that they're all right. And teach them everything they need to know. Refer them to other sources of information with basic differences from your own so that the homosexual will be freely able to make his own choices.

Finally, pull up your courage by your bootstraps, and discover ways in which you and homosexual psychiatrists can be closely involved in movements which attempt to change the attitudes of heterosexuals — and homosexuals — toward homosexuality. For all of us have something to lose. We may not be considered for that professorship. The analyst down the street may stop referring us his overflow. Our supervisor may ask us to take a leave of absence. We are taking an even bigger risk, however, not accepting fully our own humanity, with all of the lessons it has to teach all the other humans around us and ourselves. This is the greatest loss: our honest humanity. And that loss leads all those others around us to lose that little bit of their humanity as well. For, if they were truly comfortable with their own homosexuality, then they could be comfortable with ours. We must use our skills and wisdom to help them — and us — grow to be comfortable with that little piece of humanity called homosexuality.

**Loraine Edwalds and the Artemis Singers, "Wanting the Music: A Choral Musical of the Michigan Festival"**

*Setting: Trees and ferns—a large white wood structure labeled "message board" is off to one side. A large tree, ferns, hay bales, a portion of a tractor, and a striped tent edge create the scene.*

*Drumming begins at the back of the auditorium.*
*The chorus enters singing the first verse of Motherbeat.*

**All Chorus (ALL CH):** Once upon a time, in a very deep Michigan wood, women created a secret land.

**Chorus Member 1 (CM1):** For one week out of every year, music played in the air day and night, the sun shone on the pedestrian pathways, sweet water flowed from underground wells, and the earth of trees and ferns smiled greenly on women of all ages, sizes, and colors.

**Chorus Member 2 (CM2):** Loaves of nut came forth from pits of fire, and all the world was only women.

**Chorus Member 4 (CM4):** Our story begins in 1978.

*Linda, 20, enters awkwardly trying to carry a pup tent, a sleeping bag, a vinyl suitcase with no wheels, and a canvas backpack. She wears a t-shirt, gym shoes, and shorts. She looks puzzled.*

*Sandy, 22, enters from the other direction. She wears a men's tank shirt, cutoff jeans shorts, and Birkenstocks. She looks like she owns the world. She looks Linda over, smiling.*

| | |
|---|---|
| **Sandy:** | Need some help? |
| **Linda:** | Oh I guess I do. I'm supposed to set up next to my friends Jean and Patty. Do you know where they are? |
| **Sandy:** | There's like 5000 women here. And it's not like we're lined up in alphabetical order. |
| **Linda:** | Oh right — I don't know what I was thinking. |
| **Sandy:** | Well first let's check the message board — if they're expecting you they probably left a note. |
| **Linda:** | Yes! They mentioned that, now that I think about it. |
| **Sandy:** | Put your stuff down, it's safe here. The message board is over there. (She walks towards it while Linda puts her stuff down.) What's your name? |
| **Linda:** | Gibbons. |
| **Sandy:** | That's your first name? It's by first name. |
| **Linda:** | Oh no! Linda. How interesting that they sort them that way! |
| **Sandy:** | Well a lot of women on the land don't even use their real names, and a lot more won't give their last names. Just in case, you know, someone would find out. |

| Linda: | So a lot of women here aren't out. But it's open to all women — you don't have to be a lesbian to be here. |
|---|---|
| Sandy: | No, but (she looks Linda over) — chances are pretty good. |
| Linda: | I'm here with some girls — I mean women — from our Women's center at school. |
| Sandy: | A women's center? Is that like — a sorority? for lesbians? |
| Linda: | Oh not at all! We're not all lesbians. We're united by feminism. |
| Sandy | Ah. But your friends here . . . ? |
| Linda: | They're lesbians. Jean is out even to her mother! |
| Sandy: | There's a step I haven't taken. (rolls eyes) There are 3 messages here for Lindas — see if one of them's for you. |
| Linda: | Oh here they are! It says to turn left by the Community Center — I guess I'd better figure out where that is. |
| Sandy: | I'll take you there. I got here on Monday, so I've got it pretty well figured out. |
| Linda: | Oh thank you! (they exit together) |

*The chorus sings the second verse of Motherbeat.*
*(Linda and Sandy enter together)*

| Linda: | I always liked girls, of course. But — |
|---|---|
| Sandy: | You never really thought you could be involved with them. |
| Linda: | Yes that's it exactly! |
| Sandy: | And now you know you can. |
| Linda: | (throws her arms around Sandy's neck) Yes I do! (moves in to kiss her) |
| Sandy: | (has her arms around Linda's waist, but moves her head back) I'm not really free to start a new relationship now. |
| Linda: | You're not? |
| Sandy: | I have a lover at home. |
| Linda: | At home — like in your tent here or like Ohio? |
| Sandy: | Ohio. |
| Linda: | So — she wouldn't really mind about some college girl from Illinois, would she? |
| Sandy: | I don't think so. It's just for the weekend, after all. (they kiss, and during the song, exit amorously) |

*The chorus sings "I Kissed a Girl."*

*(Linda and Sandy enter by the tractor. Sandy is helping Linda load stuff on the tractor. Linda is scribbling an address on a piece of paper.)*

**Linda:**   I know I can't really call you — but you can write sometime.

**Sandy:**   I will. Although I'm not very good at writing.

**Linda:**   I'd love to hear from you. I'll never forget this festival!

**Sandy:**   No one ever forgets her first Michigan.

**Linda:**   But you made this so much more magical.

**Sandy:**   (blushes) It was definitely fun.

**Linda:**   I'm going to remember everything about you.

**Sandy:**   Will you be back next year?

**Linda:**   I hope so! It depends on what kind of summer job I get I guess.

**Sandy:**   Well I'll see you then. I've got to take my tent down. (They kiss goodbye. Sandy leaves.)

**Linda:**   (stares after her) I wish we could be real lovers, in the real world!

### Scene 16

**ALL CH:**   The women remember

**CM2:**   Taking my top off and being bare breasted without fear.

**CM4:**   Our story continues in 2012.

**Linda:**   *(Waves to the tractor offstage)* Bye, Kali! See you in a little while!

**Sandy:**   Did you miss the tractor?

**Linda:**   Oh no, I prefer walking. No that's my grandbaby, Kali!

**Sandy:**   Oh right, Summer's little girl.

**Linda:**   She's almost 6.

**Sandy:**   I guess being a grandmother isn't too bad.

**Linda:**   It's so wonderful! It's like a love bonus that pays all the time.

**Sandy:**   I remember when Summer was that age.

**Linda:**   You do?

**Sandy:**   Sure! I've been here almost every year.

**Linda:**   Yes, it's been a little smile for me every time, seeing you.

**Sandy:**   I was your first, wasn't I?

**Linda:**   You were. And see I'm still a lesbian today! You must be very convincing.

| Sandy: | Like appreciating women was a hard sell. |
|---|---|
| **Linda:** | You appreciated a lot of women, back in the day! |
| Sandy: | Well why not? I like women! I just wasn't maybe as discriminating as I could have been. |
| **Linda:** | Are you seeing anyone now? |
| Sandy: | No. There are a couple of women after me, but they seem a little old. |
| **Linda:** | Ha! Like me, a grandmother already. |
| Sandy: | No, I think grandkids might even keep you young. I like women who get out and do things. It's the ones who stay in all the time that I'm not really into. |
| **Linda:** | I'm not opposed to being your long-distance girlfriend, if you want to keep the suitors at bay. |
| Sandy: | You're not too busy to make room for another person? |
| **Linda:** | I keep busy just because it's a habit. Someone like you I always have time for. (She puts her hand on Sandy's hand) |
| Sandy: | This might be a good idea. (They kiss) |

### Scene 17

| ALL CH: | The women remember |
|---|---|
| CM1: | Holding all our thousands of hands together while we sang. |
| CM2: | Claiming our heritage as powerful women, not for the last time. |
| CM4: | Our story runs to its conclusion in 2015. |

*Kali cartwheels to the hay bale where Summer and Jill are sitting.*

| Summer: | Hi Kali what's up? |
|---|---|
| Kali: | We're doing a display performance in Gaia. |
| Jill: | Really? You have a bunch of gymnasts this year? |
| Kali: | We always have a variety. But some of us are pretty talented. |
| Summer: | Is it a competition? |
| Kali: | No mom! This is Michfest, not school. |
| Summer: | Is it for everybody to watch? |
| Kali: | Yes. We're going to add it to the parade on Saturday night. |
| Summer: | I imagine that will be a little difficult for the girls with fairy crowns. |

| **Kali:** | Well it's mostly us older girls. We have singers and dancers and tumblers. (somersaults) I'm a tumbler. |
| **Summer:** | Tumbler today — Tuba player tomorrow! I've always said you can be anything you want to be. |
| **Kali:** | I know that best of all! |

*Kali sings "You Gave Me a Choice."*

*Sandy and Linda are walking past the tents, admiring.*

| **Sandy:** | Do you remember the old land? |
| **Linda:** | Where I met you? Of course I do! |
| **Sandy:** | Everything was so unpredictable then. |
| **Linda:** | Even the organizers were so young. |
| **Sandy:** | I thought it had all been created just for me. |
| **Linda:** | Maybe it was. Your first bit of magic. |
| **Sandy:** | Ha ha! And I conjured up you, and thousands of other beautiful women. |
| **Linda:** | You really were a bit of a heart breaker back then, weren't you. |
| **Sandy:** | I was. I'm so glad we got together when we did! |
| **Linda:** | It feels so much more real to me now. |
| **Sandy:** | I needed to have a real relationship first. I was just dating back in the day. Even though I always liked you. |
| **Linda:** | I think I wanted you to be more like me back then. I wanted everyone to be like me. |
| **Sandy:** | And if there's one thing I've learned from life it's that everyone's not going to be just like me! |
| **Linda:** | I'm glad you're not like me. I think we're better together because of it. |
| **Sandy:** | I do too. (Summer, Jill and Kali join them) |
| **Linda:** | It looks like the sun's coming out after all! |
| **Sandy:** | What a beautiful festival this is. |
| **Jill:** | You must be sad to see it end. How long have you been coming? |
| **Sandy:** | Since the second festival! I only missed 2 years in there. |
| **Linda:** | And I've been coming since the third. |

| | |
|---|---|
| **Summer**: | For me I've been coming my whole life. |
| **Kali**: | Me too! |
| **Jill**: | I missed a lot of years in there. And it still seems like a big loss to me. |
| **Linda**: | But I'm so glad it's been here all that time. |
| **Sandy**: | Think of all the varieties of women we've seen here! |
| **Summer**: | We won't find anyplace like this again, I don't think. |
| **Linda**: | Probably not. But I know women are thinking about creating new events — on women's land, or public campgrounds even. |
| **Jill**: | I hope we never forget what it was like to be part of a women's community, from all over the world. |
| **Summer**: | Even if we only had it for one week each year! |
| **Linda**: | We'll have it in our hearts forever. |
| **Sandy**: | Do you have your acorns from opening ceremonies? |
| **Jill, Summer & Kali**: | Of course! |
| **Sandy and Linda**: | So do we. Let's go out and create a little Michigan in the world! |

*(They toss their acorns to the audience.)*

*Chorus sings "We Shall Go Forth."*

**From Kobai Scott Whitney, "The Lone Mountain Path: The Example of Issan Dorsey," *Lion's Roar: Buddhist Wisdom for Our Time*, March 1, 1998. https://www.lionsroar.com/the-lone-mountain-path-the-example-of-issan-dorsey/.**

Born Tommy Dorsey in Santa Barbara, California in 1933, he was the oldest of ten children and raised Catholic. Although he contemplated studying for the priesthood, he ended up joining the U.S. Navy, from which he was eventually expelled for homosexual conduct. In the 1950's he then began a long career as a performer in drag shows in San Francisco's North Beach—a district which served as the Castro Street of its era and also hosted such fringy populations as the Beat poets, drug dealers, coffeehouse anarchists and jazz musicians. . . .

During these years he had frequent injuries, overdoses and run-ins with the police. He once said, "Sometimes I'd wake up hung over in jail. The first thing I'd do was feel to see if I had my tits on. This would tell me whether they had locked me up on the men's side or with the hookers on the women's side." . . .

Unafraid to acknowledge his long history of drug use, cross-dressing and prostitution, Issan Tommy Dorsey served as a kind of fringy shaman to the uptight and elitist Zen Center community of those years—a community with an atmosphere that actor and writer Peter Coyote once called "high Episcopal." Tommy had always been comfortable in the borderlands of respectability and could serve to welcome anyone to Zen Center, no matter how odd they seemed to the broader sangha. This benefited individual beginners whom Issan could usher through the sometimes unwelcoming veneer of the Page Street City Center. It also helped the sangha, since Tommy's success in adjusting to the rigors of Zen training proved to them that meditation practice could benefit anyone.

Like a shaman, Issan served in the capacity of healer and what ethnographers call a "stranger handler." He acted as clown, as mediator and, generally, in the archetypal role that Robert Bly has dubbed the Male Mother. Many of his students saw him as an embodiment of Kuan Yin, the goddess of compassion. Like this female manifestation of the Buddha, he learned to hear "the cries of the world" and to respond to them in his own unique way.

Issan Dorsey, as Zen priest at Tassajara and the San Francisco city center, did not see himself as any kind of Buddhist missionary to the gay community: in fact, he made fun of the macho, middle class, consumer values of gay San Francisco. Those were the years when jeans and lumberjack flannel shirts were the official uniform for gay men, when doing drag or using "Miss Names" were not politically correct activities.

Years before the founding of Hartford Street Zendo, when the first meeting of a "Gay Buddhist Club" was announced, Issan scoffed at the idea. "Buddhism is Buddhism, practice is practice," might be a summary of his response. At that time, in those last, pre-AIDS years, his major preoccupation was starting a soup kitchen in San Francisco's Tenderloin district.

Although he made fun of white middle class American culture in all its forms—gay or straight—he never judged or rejected a person because of their social class or values. He had wealthy friends and he had friends who lived on the streets. He spent most of his social time in the seventies with the predominantly straight men and women who practiced at Zen Center. In his role as male mother, Issan had many straight men who were deeply devoted to him as friend and mentor.

"Sometimes," he told fellow priest Shunko Michael Jamvold, "I like to go out with straight men because they treat me like a lady." . . .

## Big Mind and the Epidemic

What happened from there was AIDS. As the health crisis grew in San Francisco, Issan told a friend that, more and more, the epidemic was teaching him what Suzuki-roshi had meant when he talked about Big Mind.

Meditation practice, at least in the Zen tradition of Dogen, is about mind and body dropping away. Small, lively, individual mind and grasping, needful, individual body can recede, if only temporarily, into the background of experience. After twenty years of Zen practice, Issan was able to experience life with Big Mind in the foreground of consciousness; he began to see and express the fact that an individual death, including his own, might not be such a big thing in the light of the steady blossoming of Big Mind experience.

To appreciate Big Mind in the midst of a plague is to know that the seemingly pressing concerns of individual personalities, identities and cravings can fall away in an instant. With mindful practice, the compassion which arises automatically with the experience of Big Mind makes working for the good of all much easier. Big Mind, Issan began to see, presumes that taking care of others is also taking care of self. As co-participants in Big Mind, sufferer and helper are mutually necessary—both help, both suffer. Living and surviving, while someone nearby is dying, becomes like wave and trough on the surface of the sea—each needs the other, both are fleeting.

Regular meditation and mindfulness practice gave Issan the experience of mental balance needed to be with self and others through the losses caused by the epidemic. His street experience added an important dimension in the form of daring, direct action that could get things done, like the founding of Maitri Hospice. Yet he knew that no amount of social action and no amount of time on a meditation cushion could spare us from all suffering and grief. He responded to the needs of survivors in different ways at different times. . . .

## AIDS as God

In the early days of the AIDS epidemic, when the Christian right was describing AIDS as the wrath of God directed against homosexuals for their sins, Issan was asked to participate in a San Francisco Council of Churches symposium called "Is AIDS the Wrath of God?" He was the only Buddhist representative at the meeting, and he was quite emphatic about removing the reality of AIDS from the dualistic good/bad, sin/salvation paradigm being dealt with at the conference. He ended his short presentation with the astonishing (to Christians, anyway) statement that "AIDS is not the wrath of God. AIDS is God."

As Issan was called upon more and more to make sense of the AIDS pandemic, for himself and for others, he was able to teach Buddhism in the context in which it was surely meant to be taught, that is, within the framework of a life-and-death search. The Buddhist teaching of impermanence began to take on new power and immediacy as Issan's work with the founding of Hartford Street Zendo soon turned into the work of founding a hospice for the people dying of AIDS. . . .

### Dementia and Delusion

J.D., the first gay man with AIDS to be taken in by Issan, was virtually at the point of death when he arrived, but the good care he received at Hartford Street helped him live for quite some time. At one point J.D. asked Issan if he could give a dharma talk. Issan had no problems granting J.D.'s request, even though many gay people around the zendo reminded Issan that J.D. had a rather severe case of dementia and would probably embarrass himself and everyone attending the talk.

"We all have dementia!" was Issan's gleeful response to the community's reservations, and despite the discomfort of others J.D. gave his best effort at giving a dharma talk. This lecture, however uncomfortable it might have been for his audience, came to be of great benefit to J.D. and was a major spiritual milestone for him prior to his death.

"We all have dementia" was just another way of reminding everyone of the delusions which make up the fabric of our daily lives. While others around the zendo were caught up with ideas about J.D.'s intellectual competence and the protocols of dharma discourse, Issan made his decisions with other criteria in mind. Status in the sangha, the hidden agenda behind opposition to J.D.'s talk, was not a factor in Issan's decision, just compassion and the true expression of the practice of equanimity. In other words, who is capable of saying who else is accomplished enough to speak the dharma? Who among us is not deluded or demented?

**From John S. Gentile, "Celebrating Ostara: A Ritual Performance by Gay Male Contemporary Pagans," in *Queers in American Popular Culture*, ed. Jim Elledge, 3 vols. (Santa Barbara: Praeger, 2010), 2:259–273.**

On Sunday morning, March 20, 2005, I drove through Atlanta, Georgia, and enjoyed the flowering trees lining its streets that were just starting to burst into blossom. It was Palm Sunday. As I passed various churches, I saw the faithful gathering together and carrying clusters of palm branches. On a usual Sunday morning, I attend All Saints Episcopal Church where I meet my friends for mass and, afterwards, we might discuss the day's sermon while we share a meal. This Sunday was also the vernal equinox and I was forgoing mass at All Saints in order to attend a very different ritual — a contemporary pagan ritual to celebrate Ostara.

"From the 1970s onward the United States," writes Ronald Hutton in *The Triumph of the Moon*, a history of the movement, "has been the world centre of modern paganism [. . .]" (340). Even informal contact with contemporary paganism readily shows that gay, lesbian and bisexual people are welcomed within the movement and that they form a significant presence among its followers. *Voices from the Pagan Census* [H. Berger, E. A. Leach, and L. S. Shaffer] reports that:

> 4.8 percent [are] lesbians, 4.5 percent gay men, and 19 percent bisexual. The large number of bisexual respondents in both studies is an indication of Neo-Pagans' openness to alternatives — including sexual alternatives. (28)

My current research interest is to investigate how gay male contemporary pagans create ritual performance to express their spirituality. Contemporary paganism offers a rich field of study for its creativity: its syncretism of beliefs, its use of folklore, mythology and history (and pseudo-history) to invent a spiritual tradition, and its bricolage of old mythical images and stories. "The characteristic feature of mythical thought," Claude Levi-Strauss writes in *The Savage Mind*, "is that it expresses itself by means of a heterogeneous repertoire [. . .]" (17).

. . .

## THE RITUAL: CELEBRATING OSTARA

My invitation to the Ostara ritual came in early March over the internet via a listserv for Gay Spirit Visions (GSV), a national community "committed to creating safe, sacred space that is open to all spiritual paths, wherein loving gay men may explore and strengthen spiritual identity" (GSV Mission 2). The importance of the internet to create and maintain community is evident in both contemporary)paganism and gay spirituality (in general and GSV in particular), for both movements claim ancient roots while participating fully in contemporary postmodern, late-capitalist American culture and its reliance on electronic forms of communication/community-building. One of the hosts, Jonathan, sent subsequent messages that included driving directions and suggestions for ritual preparation, including ritual cleansing prior to the event in the form of intentional bathing.

His suggestions, like all acts of ritual preparation, were intended to heighten the experience of *separation* discussed by van Gennep in *The Rites of Passage*.

The ritual was held in the home of Jonathan and Eliot in a large apartment complex near Emory University in Atlanta. Being the first to arrive for the 11:00 A.M. gathering, I had the opportunity to talk with the hosts about their background in contemporary paganism, their preparation for the morning's company, and to observe closely the setting the hosts had created for the ritual. Jonathan and Eliot, whom I had not met prior to that morning, warmly welcomed me. Their immediate emotional openness, generosity and trust surpassed what I had already found typical of the men of GSV. From the moment of my entrance into their home to the beginning of the formal ritual, I had entered a heightened *pre*-liminal phase that further separated me from my ordinary profane life into the sacred time and place of the ritual.

An altar table was located within the center of their small living room and served as the focus of the ritual. The images and objects upon the altar demonstrated a striking syncretism of various spiritualities, including European, Hindu, Buddhist, and Native American traditions. A large Green Man tapestry hung behind the altar draped over (and obscuring) an étagère and entertainment unit that held a television and a CD player along with books and photographs. Along with sacred objects, candles, and spring flowers, the altar held images of Eostre, an obscure Anglo-Saxon goddess of the spring. For this reason, contemporary pagan devotional and practical books identify the vernal equinox as *Ostara,* named after Eostre, whose name, the authors argue, the early Christian church appropriated in its naming of *Easter* as the celebration of the Resurrection of Jesus Christ. The books also link Eostre to Eos, the classical goddess of the dawn. Ronald Hutton in *The Stations of the Sun* traces the connection to Eostre back to the writings of Bede and follows other scholars, such as Venetia Newall in *An Egg at Easter: A Folklore Study*, in questioning whether or not the ancient Anglo-Saxons ever worshipped such a goddess.

Whatever her veracity as an ancient goddess, Eostre now represents for contemporary pagans the Goddess in her maiden, or Kore, aspect, and as such is connected to beginnings and openings. The veneration of Eostre by contemporary pagans shows how a spiritual tradition is invented and how belief may be a conscious choice. Other objects upon the altar included eggs, home-baked hot cross buns, and, in a lofty place of honor atop the étagère, a store bought chocolate bunny.

This last ritual object, perhaps more than any other object, embodies the humor and pastiche typical of contemporary paganism.

Along with the ritual objects and altar preparation, the hosts prepared an extensive brunch featuring a variety of egg-based entrees (including many quiches). The guests arrived, bringing with them more flowers and contributions to the brunch meal. The foodstuffs, I noted, were all homemade emphasizing a mutual giving of time and care between guests and hosts. Some of the guests changed into sarongs, which served as ritual costumes, supplied by the hosts. The tone of the morning continued to be joyful and playful. Participation in the morning ritual was highly reflexive and self-conscious. Members of company (a term I will use to include the hosts) shared comments that indicated complex levels of belief. At times, their comments expressed devotion and serious spiritual practice while at other times they expressed a comic distance or humorous perspective on the day's ritual. The emotional dialectic between gentle humor and serious devotion informed the entire morning; all participants seemed comfortable in holding the tension between faith and doubt in an emotional double-distance toward their spirituality without moving to extremes of either skepticism nor uncritical faith. They were able to participate in the ritual's meaning while recognizing it as construct by holding the ritual in symbolic consciousness. "The trick of symbolic consciousness," D. Stephenson Bond [in *Living Myth: Personal Meaning as a Way of Life*] writes, "is in allowing yourself to maintain the distance — I am aware that I'm pretending, gaming, imagining — while at the same time preserving participation" (19). *Voices from the Pagan Census* confirms this understanding of contemporary pagan symbolic consciousness. Its authors note,

> Many Neo-Pagans simultaneously participate in the rituals and stand outside of them to the degree that they can reflect on the rituals as something that they created. Neo-Pagans often joke about their own rituals and seem to be taking themselves and their religious practice with a grain of salt, at the same time viewing their spiritual practices as serious. (7)

At no time did I perceive a naïve or zealous literalist belief, which is in marked contrast to my experience with members of more established religions, especially fundamentalist Christians, who demonstrate a noticeable lack of critical distance from their faith or church.

Jonathan called the company together to begin the ritual, which demonstrated both traditional and emergent qualities in its adaptation of contemporary pagan (especially Wiccan) practice. He scented each participant with burning sage and then invited four guests from among those men more experienced in pagan ritual to call the spirits of the four cardinal directions and to create the ritual circle. Based upon a scripted invocation, each spoke in turn, holding a candle, and called the spirits of the East, South, West, and North. The intent of the ritual circle was to create a sacred emotional space emphasizing protection and mutual caring. In *The Sacred and the Profane*, Mircea Eliade writes, "*the religious man sought to live as near as possible to the Center of the World*"

(43). The invocation moved us into the liminal phase of the ritual and effectively created the sense of being at the *axis mundi* or sacred center throughout its duration.

"Among the most important items found upon a Pagan altar," writes Sabina Magliocco in *Neo-Pagan Sacred Art and Altars*, "are images of the deities" (26). Upon the Ostara altar were images of Eostre and Hyacinth, whom the two hosts then honored as the Goddess and the God, the female and male principles, by telling their myths. The choice of Hyacinth, a beautiful young man beloved by Apollo, as the mythic image of the masculine principle in the morning ritual, is indicative of gay spirituality's mythopoesis. Will Roscoe retells the story of Hyacinth and Apollo in his book, *Queer Spirits: A Gay Men's Myth Book*, which reclaims same-sex myths as sacred texts. Robert Drake includes Ovid's version of the myth in *The Gay Canon: Great Books Every Gay Man Should Read*. By choosing Eostre and Hyacinth, mythic figures from two different traditions, Anglo-Saxon and Greek, the hosts demonstrated the practices of syncretism and bricolage typical of contemporary paganism. Additionally, Hyacinth and Eostre, despite their different cultures of origin, represent male and female images of the archetype of the *Puer/Puella*, which Jung identifies in "The Psychology of the Child Archetype," as concerned with futurity. Thus, they are highly appropriate deities for meditation on the season of spring and its multiplicity of meanings connected to its promise of new beginnings.

Jonathan honored the Goddess principle and offered a telling of a myth of Eostre. Immediately following, Eliot honored the God principle and told the myth of Hyacinth and indicated the hyacinths on the altar. The hosts then passed around a small bowl of hard-boiled white eggs, while Jonathan explained their symbolism as the ovaries and ova of the Goddess. Additionally, he reconfigured the symbolism of the eggs to represent for us the testes and sperm of the God. His discourse affirmed the creativity and generativity manifested in each individual, especially those present. The hosts then passed a chalice of champagne and the plate of hot cross buns among the men to drink and to eat. At this point, the hosts invited the company to the meal and to color the eggs using a variety of dyes. Along with eating, drinking, and egg dying, the remainder of our time together was spent in casual conversation and fellowship.

At the time the first guest indicated his need to leave, the hosts called us together to close the ritual, broke the chocolate bunny to share, invited the four men to thank the spirits of the cardinal directions for their presence, and gave gifts of baskets to each man present. The limen was closed; the circle was opened. The guests were invited to stay for as long as they wished. Those men remaining behind gave warm farewells to those departing as they faced reincorporation into their daily, profane lives.

# GLOSSARY

**Abrahamic faiths:** one or more of the three world religions tracing their lineage back to the patriarch Abraham — Judaism, Christianity, and Islam.

**ace:** an umbrella term, initially derived from asexual, that refers to a cluster of sexual identities that are best described by the absence of a particular set of emotions (such as aromantic), orientation (such as asexual), or gender expression or identification (such as agender). The term may also include various gradations (such as demisexual), which demarcate either particular degrees of sexual or romantic attraction or certain conditions under which sexual or romantic attraction may occur for individuals.

**adolescence:** the social and psychological life stage between childhood and adulthood; analogous to but not synonymous with puberty.

**aesthetics:** the study of art and the artistic; in its narrowest sense, it examines issues of beauty, especially of form and style in art and the pleasure produced by such works.

**agender:** most commonly, an adjective used to describe an individual who does not identify as either masculine or feminine.

**AIDS/HIV:** acquired immunodeficiency syndrome, today more commonly referred to as HIV-related disease (human immunodeficiency virus), in which a virus causes the immune system to be compromised and weakened, which usually leads to the development of opportunistic diseases and other medical conditions.

**androgynous:** having qualities of both the masculine and the feminine.

**aromantic:** an adjective referring to individuals who do not identify as having feelings of romantic love for other people.

**asexual:** an adjective used to refer both to the condition of lacking any sexual organs or bodily features related to sexual functioning and to people who do not identify as having the experience of sexual feeling or desire.

**autogynephilic:** an adjective used by the psychologists Ray Blanchard and Michael Bailey to refer to transgender people whose identity and sexuality are based on their sense of themselves as engaged in sexual relations as the gender not assigned to them at birth; Bailey, in particular, uses this term to refer to a group of trans women. The term remains very controversial and is disputed by many trans people.

**AVEN:** the Asexuality Visibility and Education Network, a social awareness and advocacy group for people who identify as asexual (or any of the other "ace" identities).

Henderson, Bruce, *Queer Studies: Beyond Binaries*
dx.doi.org/10.17312/harringtonparkpress/2019.09.qsbb.00e
© 2019 by Harrington Park Press

**aversion therapy:** a largely discredited approach to "curing" queer or LGBT+ people of their homosexuality or other nonnormative sexuality through the use of conditioning in which rewards are given for positive responses to heterosexual stimuli, and punishments (such as electric shocks) are administered for positive responses to homosexual stimuli — and vice versa.

**ballot measures:** local issues placed on ballots, voted on at the municipal, county, or state level; they are often viewed as more likely to be successful for queer-positive initiatives.

**berdache:** a term once used to describe biological men who live in female or feminine roles in Native American communities; it is no longer used by these communities.

**binary:** any pairing that forces thought into "either-or" categories; here it is most frequently used in discourse that sees heterosexual-homosexual as the two "options" for sexual identity.

**biopower:** a term coined by the French philosopher Michel Foucault to indicate the relationship between biological status and social and political power; those in power make decisions about minoritized bodies, and those whose bodies (and desires connected to the body, such as sexual desire) are viewed as normative are therefore deemed best equipped to make decisions for all.

**bisexual:** in biology, an adjective that refers to any organism that is both male and female. In sexuality studies, the term is used to describe individuals who experience sexual desire for those categories of people traditionally described as male and female; in nonbinary thinking, the term is often replaced by pansexual or some other equivalent.

**body:** a word that has a multiplicity of meanings and uses, from the physical matter that makes up a human organism to social, political, and cultural meanings, often focusing on the values placed on and interpretations made of both categories of bodies and individuals who inhabit them.

**body shame/shaming:** the social process by which groups of people endeavor to make public negative evaluations of both individual bodies and categories of bodies, on the basis of such factors as weight, color, or other feature, which results in feelings of loss of worth by people whose bodies have been subject to such targeting.

**butch-femme:** a term used in lesbian culture to denote relative masculinity (butch) and femininity (femme), often leading (particularly in mid-twentieth-century Western cultures) to assumption of social and sexual roles; in some cases, there was an implicit "regulating," whereby couplings of two butches or two femmes were not viewed as normative within lesbian culture; it is less frequently used today, though it still has some historical and cultural significance.

**camp:** a style of or approach to art and to social interaction, often, though not exclusively, associated with gay men of the nineteenth through twenty-first centuries. It is marked by a blend of satire, often hyperbolic emotion, and deep feeling; it is sometimes used as a way of indirect communication between gay men and others in contexts in which direct disclosure may be unsafe or socially judged. The origin of the term is contested, but it is strongly associated with the writer and social commentator Susan Sontag.

**capitalism:** an economic system based on private ownership of property and the production of goods and services controlled by the owners of property; it is often used to describe the political ideology and governmental practices that accompany such a system.

**cisgender:** an adjective used to describe individuals who experience the gender they were assigned at birth as their authentic gender identity.

**class:** a term used to denote both the economic status of an individual or a group of people and the social status attributed to such people and the shared cultural practices (and often inferred values) of people in these strata.

**closet, the:** a metaphoric image mapping out a social and often psychological space in which people of various typically stigmatized or devalued identities hide such identities and do not disclose them publicly.

**code-switching:** in linguistics, this term refers to changes in language use by members of minoritized groups (such as nonwhite, queer, or working-class people), in which one set of choices of words, dialects, and other features is used when communicating with the public at large or with those outside the minoritized population and another is "switched" to when communicating with insiders in that community or population.

**coming out:** the process or processes by which individuals (sometimes groups of people) who identify as members of a minoritized group, usually one that is not necessarily visible, disclose their hitherto closeted identity. This is often viewed and described as an ongoing process: people may come out in different contexts at different times and may come out multiple times about different aspects of their identity (such as coming out as queer, coming out as disabled).

**comintern/homintern:** terms that were coined during the Red Scare of the McCarthy communist witch hunts of the 1950s. The former abbreviates "Communist International"; the latter comes from the belief that many of those labeled cominterns were also closeted homosexuals. The words are no longer used in common discourse.

**Common Core:** name for the collective curricular and pedagogical objectives agreed to by the vast majority of states in the United States; they have been criticized for their lack of inclusiveness and diversity and for essentially mandating that schools teach students to pass standardized exams.

**companionate:** an adjective used to describe relationships in which companionability (friendliness, warmth, and comfort) defines the strength and priorities of a couple.

**concordant/discordant:** social-scientific terms used to contrast phenomena or qualities that are either the same (concordant) or different (discordant); in queer culture, they are very frequently used to describe HIV status within couples — concordant signifies that partners are both either HIV-negative or HIV-positive; discordant means that one member is HIV-negative and the other HIV-positive.

**diachronic:** literally, across time; it is used in linguistics to refer to features analyzed within a particular time frame, such as "post-Stonewall terminology" or "twenty-first-century pronouns."

**desire:** the state or action of wanting something or someone; in queer studies, the word is most frequently used to mean a state of attraction to another person, or a category or group of people, or a particular erotic attribute or activity.

**discordant:** See concordant/discordant.

**disidentification:** a term most identified in queer studies with the queer Latino performance theorist José Esteban Muñoz, who used it to describe the situations and processes used by minoritized subjects who neither attempt to identify with majoritarian values and experiences nor entirely negate them, but actively move between and within them, pointing out imbalances of power and hidden assumptions about the identities of people who often belong to multiple minority groups.

**Don't Ask, Don't Tell (DADT):** the military policy enacted during the administration of Bill Clinton, whereby military personnel were forbidden by law to ask members or potential members of the military their sexual orientation, and, similarly, members of the military were forbidden to disclose their sexual orientation; in practice, it applied only to nonheternormative enlisted members and officers, and it was eventually repealed in 2010.

**down low (DL):** a slang term used most frequently to describe the situation of black men who have sex with other men (of any race) but who publicly maintain a heterosexual identity and are often involved in heterosexual relationships, including marriage; the term is widely critiqued for its racist implication that such a situation is unique to or definitive of black men.

**drag king/drag queen:** while connotations and usages vary, both terms are most frequently used to name entertainers, frequently professional, whose medium is the performance, often exaggerated and hyperbolic, of a gender to which they were not assigned at birth. For some, the ability to pass is part of their aesthetic; for others, the assumed gender markers are intended to be in visible and vocal contrast to that which they were assigned and may inhabit offstage. The terms are not to be confused or conflated with the now rarely used transvestite, which tended to be used for people who enjoyed dressing in clothes usually associated with a gender different from their own (or different from the one assigned to them at birth) for either sexual or psychological reasons and who do so in everyday life or in private, but not as part of a performance framed as such.

***DSM (Diagnostic and Statistical Manual of Mental Disorders):*** a handbook published by the American Psychiatric Association to create a common set of criteria for diagnosing mental "disorders," for purposes of treatment and insurance coverage; the DSM has gone through several editions and has throughout its history proven controversial in its language and its placement of queer lives and experiences within a medical framework of illness and disease.

**ego (Freud):** the conscious part of the personality, one of three parts hypothesized by Sigmund Freud, which he saw as mediating between the id and the superego, and as the part of the self that is most often presented in everyday life and is closest to the experience of ordinary reality.

**eros (Freud):** one of two central psychological drives hypothesized by Freud, the life force, as exemplified in erotic and romantic directedness.

**exotic becomes erotic (Bem):** a theory of sexual orientation and identity development hypothesized by the psychologist Daryl J. Bem, who argued that, while there is no evidence of a gene that accounts for sexual orientation, there is a genetic basis for personality types and activity preferences, which may lead children, in early stages of identity formation, to view their same-sex playmates as "exotic" (different from themselves categorically), and, when they become sexually aware, they thus find themselves erotically attracted to their own sex.

**failure (Halberstam):** a key term in Halberstam's recent work, in which he argues that various kinds of failure (including the perception or in some cases reality of failure as normative social citizens or members) is a distinctive and potentially positive aspect of queer experience.

**family of choice/family of origin:** while these two groups may frequently overlap, the terms are used to distinguish between those people to whom one is related by blood (including those less literally so, such as adoptees and in-laws) — family of origin — and those whom one experiences as kin by virtue of affinity and preference — family of choice.

**fluidity, sexual (Diamond):** a term popularized by the lesbian psychologist Lisa Diamond and used by her in her research on lesbian sexualities to describe the nonfixed variability of sexual attraction and desire, particularly regarding the binary structure of male or female partners. Diamond extends her concept of fluidity to include distinctions between romantic attraction and sexual desire, which she argues, on the basis of her data, may be fluid and variable, both in terms of gender categories and in the life course.

**gay:** used variously (1) as an adjective to describe homosexually identified men; (2) as an adjective to describe all homosexual people, regardless of sex or gender; (3) used to describe people who identify as part of social groups or cultures centered on homosexuality (this has sometimes included bisexual people).

**gaydar:** a folk belief that people, especially gay (and, by extension, all who fit under the umbrella term queer) people, can identify gay people as such, by voice, appearance, or mannerism; some attempt has been made by social scientists to determine whether the phenomenon has any scientifically verifiable basis, but not enough data have been accumulated to make any valid or reliable conclusions.

**Gay Games:** an international equivalent to the International Olympics; the International Olympics Committee blocked the organizers from using the word Olympics, under copyright infringement laws, though many regarded the IOC's move as motivated by homophobia.

**gayvoice:** a phenomenon, widely disputed, describing a certain set of vocal qualities (pitch, intonation, rhythm, and other parts of what linguists call prosody) that are associated with the voices of stereotypical gay men.

**gender nonconforming:** in sexuality studies, this term is used most often to refer to identification and behaviors of people who reject, ignore, or question the conventions associated with the sex or gender to which they were assigned at birth.

**habitus:** a term popularized by the sociologist Pierre Bourdieu to refer to a habitual way of being and acting in everyday social life.

**hate crime:** a crime whose motivation is attributed in some demonstrable way to the perpetrator's hate, fear, or dislike of members of an identifiable social group, such as queer people, people of color, or people with disabilities; depending on the jurisdiction, hate crimes can carry different and usually more severe penalties, such as longer sentences and, in states that still have the death penalty, capital punishment.

**hate speech:** in speech act theory, especially as elaborated and queried by Judith Butler, speech that expresses hatred toward particular groups and motivates violence and/or discrimination against them and has, some believe, the same force as a physical act of violence toward them.

**health:** a sense of well-being, along dimensions that include the physical, biological, psychological, and spiritual; the word is not to be confused with questions of disability, as disability theorists argue that people with disabilities can still be said to possess health, depending on the nature of their impairments and the social treatment of them.

**hermaphrodite:** a largely archaic term, derived from Greek myth, referring to any organism that possesses both male and female sexual characteristics; in humans, it has generally been replaced by the term intersex.

**heteronormative:** an outlook, implicit or explicit, and put into practice either through individual behavior or social surveillance and policies, that privileges heterosexuality as the standard, "natural" state of being and experience.

**heterosexual:** used as a noun and an adjective, referring to those individuals and groups of people who are primarily or exclusively attracted sexually to people of the gender opposite (in binary terms) to that to which they were assigned at birth and with whom they identify.

*hijra:* in Indian (Asian) tradition, individuals born into biologically male bodies, but who identify with and live as females.

**HIV:** See AIDS/HIV.

**homonationalism:** the phenomenon or process by which people who identify as same-sex attracted demonstrate support for the political, social, and often militaristic values of their country, in order to gain status as "good citizens" and thus be accepted, often in spite of their nonheternormative lives.

**homonormativity:** similar to homonationalism, the word refers to the phenomenon of identifying as homosexual (or some variant, including bisexual or pansexual), but subscribing to and living in ways that reinforce heteronormative values and conventions, in order to gain acceptance as "normal" members of society. It is often used when referring to social norms, to distinguish it from homonationalism, which stresses political aspects of citizenship.

**homosexual:** used as both noun and adjective, with widely varying meanings. It can refer to people who either possess some same-sex attraction or engage in same-sex activities; or it can refer only to those who have (or report having) exclusively same-sex desires or to anyone who has any degree of same-sex desire or experience.

**hookup culture:** used to describe the prevailing attitudes toward arrangements for and interpretation of sexual activity, primarily among adolescents and young adults (college age through late twenties, approximately), in which hooking up, or making decisions to have sex with a partner, is based on sexual desire alone, without any necessary intersection with social interaction, relationship formation, or other elements of sexual romantic relationships; often used pejoratively, though not in and of itself necessarily grounded in moral criticism.

**hyperfemininity:** in lesbian culture, this refers to a kind of gender performance grounded in extremes of acting out social conventions associated with women-as-feminine (including dress, body appearance, passivity or receptivity in sexual interactions, and sometimes extending to professional or occupational choices and behaviors); the term may also be used, though less frequently, to describe the adoption of extreme social stereotypical behavior associated with women by men, particularly gay or queer men.

**id (Freud):** the part of Freud's model of the personality that refers to often unconscious, primitive, and childlike desires, unmediated in their purest state by consciousness or society.

**identity:** a term with wide and variable meanings and usage, generally referring to the structure of characteristics, both individual and social, by which people view themselves as beings in the world, and which may be imposed on them by social groups and cultures. It can include such elements as sexual orientation, class, race and ethnicity, disability, nationality, and so forth. In some contexts, identity discourse may focus on where an individual fits into one domain, such as sexual orientation; in others, it is the intersection of multiple facets or categories that is being described.

**identity politics:** an approach to political thinking and practice that is grounded in one or more categories of identity, rather than necessarily grounded in some other set of commitments or beliefs (e.g., LGBTQ+ identity politics, in which sexual orientation is the principal basis for political work rather than a broader sense of social justice itself).

**integration model (Gill):** a model of personality and cultural development based on the self becoming integrated into a group larger than the individual; Gill's model focuses on how people with disabilities "come to" identify with disability culture. In this textbook, the argument is made that the same model has validity for coming to a culturally queer identity.

**interpellation (Althusser):** in Althusser's Marxist-inflected political philosophy, the process by which individual members of a society are "hailed" (Athusser's verb) as members of the body politic and are in a sense given messages about behavior and attitudes that are appropriate for members of that sociopolitical unit.

**intersectionality:** a term brought to prominence in critical race/law scholarship, originally as part of work designed to describe living simultaneously in multiple identity categories (such as the intersections of race and sexuality) and the historical and judicial (and other) implications of occupying the intersectional position. Initially used specifically to describe the experiences of black women, it has been expanded to address a wide spectrum of ways in which multiple identities intersect to produce complex ways of being in the world and being treated in social contexts.

**intersex:** a term used to describe any organism that possesses biological sexual characteristics of both male and female members of a species; in humans, the term is used to replace the archaic and usually devaluing term hermaphrodite, and it may be used to describe or identify a spectrum of individuals, from those who have identifiable characteristics associated with both men and women to those whose characteristics are either only partially present or difficult to identify as either exclusively male or female.

**irony:** in queer contexts, irony may be seen as a linguistic and communicative strategy of indirection, in which a speaker (or artist or other person) says one thing but means another, sometimes for comic or rhetorical effect, sometimes to engage in coded communicative acts in which only insiders are likely to understand the speaker's genuine intentions.

***jotería:*** a term from queer Latino culture, referring to openly and usually playfully gender-transgressive behavior, speech, and performance (in both an everyday and a theatrical sense) by which queer Latino men subvert gender expectations and policing specific to norms of heterosexual Latino behavior and appearance, especially those grouped under the heading of machismo.

**ladder of abstraction:** a phrase coined by the linguist S. I. Hayakawa as part of the philosophical movement called General Semantics, which distinguishes between different levels, from the most abstract to the most specific, by which various phenomena (including humans) can be named and understood; thus, terms like queer may be analyzed in the context of how abstract or how specific they are (and will vary in their position on this metaphoric "ladder," depending on context and specific usage).

*latinidad:* the set of characteristics and experiences of people either born in, or descended from the various peoples of, Latin America; the term is used to cast a broad net for such experiences, as it recognizes shared life and cultural experiences without attempting to reduce such experiences to an essence or to a prescriptive set of elements.

**Latinx (sometimes Latino/a/x):** an adjective used to denote any individual or group of people who are related by heritage or history to the various peoples of Latin America.

**lesbian (sometimes Lesbian):** in its most specific and singular usage, the word refers to women who identify as sexually and/or romantically attracted primarily or exclusively to other women (sometimes including both trans women and trans men); in wider usage, it may refer to social and cultural ideologies and practices that center on women apart from men (or in resistance to patriarchal supremacist attitudes and policies).

**lesbian continuum:** a phrase coined by the lesbian poet and activist Adrienne Rich that posits that all (or most) women have experiences, whether related to sexual desire or not, that place them within the political and social realm of women-identified culture; the concept of the continuum is to make a space for the range of experiences and identities, from women who wholly identify with a lesbian separatist ideology (whereby women attempt to live lives as separate as possible from men and, in some variations, from nonlesbian women, within economic and cultural constraints) to women who identify as heterosexual in their sexual and/or romantic attractions but who are committed to the lives of women and to the value of women-only experiences and institutions.

**lesbian existence:** a phrase often used synonymously or interchangeably with lesbian continuum, though it tends to denote a realm of women-identified same-sex social and/or sexual and erotic interactions and cultural practices, rather than the gradations that lesbian continuum suggests.

**LGBT (sometimes LGBTQ+ or LGBT\*):** an acronym (sometimes presented as GLBT or other variations) intended to include all people who identify with some nonheternormative experience or attraction or, in the case of the T, share political and cultural commitments with LGB folk, even if they would not describe their sexual orientation as same-sex (as in the case of trans men and trans women who, by nature of their trans identity, may or may not describe their sexual orientation as heterosexual). The acronym still has wide usage, but has come under increased scrutiny and criticism for its ability to maintain rigid categories of sexuality that may not provide space for more fluid or nonbinary people.

**linguistics:** the scientific study of language; it is usually divided into such branches as phonology (sound structures and systems); morphology (word systems and structures); syntax (arrangements of words into sentences and other grammatical units); semantics (systems of word and sentence meaning); and pragmatics (the use of language in utterances larger than the sentence, such as conversations, speeches, and other phenomena). Queer linguistics is a field that looks at how queer people use language and can range from such phenomena as gayvoice (emphasizing phonological elements) to dialects and conventions of such phenomena as Polari.

**machismo:** a term used in Latinx culture to refer to the belief that hypermasculinity is a defining characteristic of what it means to be a man; it is critiqued and rejected by many, especially by gay men who engage in *jotería* as an alternative for queer masculinity.

**medical gaze:** term coined by the French philosopher Michel Foucault to refer to the process by which medical professionals, beginning around the time of the Enlightenment, exerted what he calls biopower by turning their professional "eyes" on human bodies (especially those they diagnosed as diseased, disabled, or abnormal) to devalue or control those outside socially constructed norms.

**mestiza:** a term referring to people whose ancestry combines European and Latin American indigenous heritage.

**Metropolitan Community Church (MCC):** a nondenominational church founded in 1968 by the Reverend Troy Perry, a gay man, that is inclusive of all sexualities and multiple faith traditions.

**microaggression:** a spoken or nonverbal action by which a member of a dominant social or cultural group devalues some aspect or characteristic of a member of a minority group (such as appearance, language, or social practices); microaggressions can be intentional or unintentional.

**misadaptation:** the largely outdated belief that nonheteronormative sexuality represents an individual's failure to develop in ways that lead to heterosexual identification and desire.

**model minority:** a term used in race theory to identify a minority group that is usually held up as exemplary of what it means to aspire, conform to, and achieve the values, practices, and aspirations of the majority group; in the United States, Asian Americans have typically been identified as the model minority.

**monosexual:** an adjective used to describe individuals whose sexual orientation is directed at one of the two traditionally defined binary sexes; someone who is monosexual can be either heterosexual or homosexual — but not bisexual or pansexual.

**NAMES Project (the AIDS Quilt):** both a cultural artifact and a cultural movement, begun by the activist Cleve Jones in 1985 to create quilt panels to honor individuals (of any sexuality) who have died as a result of HIV/AIDS-related illnesses.

**neo-paganism:** a term that serves as an umbrella for various spiritual or religious associations (sometimes formally named and organized, sometimes spontaneous, local, and grassroots) that are queer-inclusive, not affiliated with any of the major world religions (such as the three Abrahamic), and often tied to celebrating and honoring the connections of the human, natural, and spiritual domains; these associations are generally feminine-centered or nonpatriarchal (or both).

**nonbinary (sometimes non-binary):** an adjective that describes something not adhering to the division of phenomena into contrasting, either-or structures; in sexuality studies in particular, it refers to rejection of the heterosexual-homosexual division (and sometimes also of the concept of bisexuality as a term reinforcing the binary, often substituting polysexuality or pansexuality). It can also refer to the identification of individuals as neither masculine nor feminine or neither male nor female.

**nonconforming:** in sexuality studies, the word is used most often to refer to identification and behaviors of people who reject, ignore, or question the conventions associated with the sex or gender to which they were assigned at birth.

**normativity:** in its broadest sense, the belief that there is indeed a "normal" (and therefore preferred) way of being or acting, which often leads to policing of those who act outside normative conventions. It should be noted that normative isn't necessarily synonymous with normal: many social scientists use the term normative nonevaluatively to describe what the majority of their subjects do or are, without the assumption that it would be better for them to follow the norm(s).

**Oedipal complex:** a keystone to Freud's theory of childhood sexual development, based on the Greek myth of Oedipus; in Freud's theory, little boys face a crisis of development in which they are attracted to their mothers and wish symbolically to kill (by erasure) their fathers; in Freud's narrative of normative male sexual development, successful completion involves a shift to identification with the father and to a latency period of sexual desire that eventually leads males to desire females sexually. Freud had less to say about female child sexual development, but he suggested that there is probably an equivalent for girls (often called the Electra complex, also drawn from Greek myth) and that lesbianism typically results from a failure of girls to detach from their mothers as their first erotic connections.

**OLOC:** an acronym for Old Lesbians Organizing for Change, founded in 1989, an association of chapters of women serving both social and political goals in advocating for housing for aging lesbians.

**Patient Zero (Gaétan Dugas):** a French Canadian flight attendant who was identified by Randy Shilts in his book *And the Band Played On* as the vector (or beginning point) of what was identified as the HIV virus in the United States, through Dugas's frequent sexual interactions with men; Dugas's role in the spread of HIV is now widely discredited, and his identification as the singular origin for the virus is viewed as sensationalist journalism on Shilts's part.

**performance art:** an art form present globally under different names since the turn of the twentieth century, which is often characterized by the use such "materials" as the human body, time, space, and technology as the media for the creation of visual and kinetic art pieces and events (often called "happenings" in the 1960s and 1970s); from the 1970s onward, much performance art has been created by queer artists (and their collaborators, some of whom do not personally identify as sexually queer, but who may identify as such aesthetically, socially, and politically) and has become especially visible as an artistic response to the AIDS epidemic.

**phenomenology:** a philosophic approach that focuses less on what positivist philosophers would define as objective reality and more on the structures of consciousness and the experience of various phenomena (objects, emotions, other less tangible elements) as the conscious observer encounters them.

**Polari:** a dialect or form of slang or argot used by queer men, especially in England, during the twentieth century, typically to communicate with each other about topics that were often viewed as taboo or to reveal queer identity publicly in times and contexts when such disclosure would not have been desired.

**privilege:** the position whereby individuals, by their very membership in a group (particularly such dominant groups as the white race, male gender, and heterosexuals), gain power and opportunities; the term is often used to refer particularly to the status of having such benefits simply by being born into and raised in these categories, and not having earned such privilege by merit. Privilege is often viewed as both conscious and unconscious, intentional and unintentional.

**public sphere (Habermas):** a term coined by the German sociologist and philosopher Jürgen Habermas to describe the social and ideological communities in which groups of people carry out and enact social relations and cultural values.

**quare studies (Johnson):** a term coined by the American performance studies scholar E. Patrick Johnson to describe an approach to sexuality and race studies that takes the perspective of people who live at the intersection of blackness and queerness as the standpoint from which social and other phenomena are analyzed and experienced.

**queer:** a wide-ranging term whose meaning and value vary depending on historical period, time and place of usage, and intention; in its defining sense in this textbook it refers to all phenomena that exist outside heteronormativity. In earlier historical periods, it was used to mean such varied things as "odd," "nonnormative" (not necessarily in sexual ways), or homosexual, or as a synonym for LGBTQ+. Today many distinguish it from LGBTQ+ generationally (queer is more commonly used by those who came out at some point after Stonewall) and also frequently by its connotations of activism, celebration of difference, and inclusiveness of nonnormativities that extend beyond sexual orientation itself. It is probably most useful not to assume a hierarchy of valuation of either LGBTQ+ or queer, but to understand how different people use the terms and why.

**queercrip (sometimes cripqueer):** a term originally used by the American performance, theater, and disability scholar Carrie Sandahl, in her study of four performance artists, to identify the intersectional position of being queer and "crip" (disabled and identifying as such in a cultural and political sense) simultaneously.

**Queer Nation:** a political and social activist organization founded in New York

City in 1990 by members of the AIDS activist group ACT UP, designed to focus on confrontation and elimination of homophobia.

**questioning:** an adjective most often used to describe individuals who experience their sexual orientation and identity as still undefined in the sense of having a specific name (i.e., they do not feel it is accurate to label themselves as homosexual, heterosexual, bisexual, pansexual, or in any other way that implies fixedness and "completion" of the process of self-definition). It differs from terms that overtly reject binaries or highlight fluidity, in that questioning people may believe they will eventually come to a more certain sexual identity (though some do not see that as a goal for their process of questioning).

**racial formation:** a process by which people organize social life and perceptions using the category of race as a central principle for such purposes as residence, social affiliation, and identity.

**Radical Faeries:** a neo-pagan group, typically all-male, first developed by Harry Hay and other gay men in 1978, focusing on a return to nature, gender play, and a spirituality that places queer people in roles that have shamanistic (mystical, often acting as conduits between the material and the mystical worlds) elements.

**reparative therapy (sometimes conversion therapy):** discredited by all major psychological and psychiatric associations, this form of therapy seeks to "repair" the "wound" of homosexuality, often by conditioning and religious proselytizing.

**romantic attraction:** attraction grounded in emotional desire and positive feelings, rather than purely sexual, physical, or erotic ones; romantic attraction may align with sexual attraction, but it need not do so, as Lisa Diamond's research on sexual fluidity argues.

**Schoolworld:** a concept of the entire (or gestalt) experience of schooling, not limited simply to classroom instruction and formal curricula, but including social elements, such as athletics, interactions, group memberships, extracurricular activities, and even, in many instances, the family's attitude toward schooling.

***sinthome*:** the Latin way of spelling the French word *symptôme*, for "symptom," this term was used by the French psychoanalyst Jacques Lacan to describe the traces and presence of a person's experience of *jouissance*, or sexual pleasure; the American queer theorist Lee Edelman used it specifically to refer to sexual activities and experiences that have no connection to concepts of reproduction.

**social movements:** distinct from ballot measures, social movements tend to be broader in aim and wider in distribution; the political scientist Amy Stone argues that social movements tend to be less successful in making inroads for queer and LGBT+ liberation and progress.

**sodomy/sodomite:** largely archaic terms, originally derived from the various versions of the story of Lot/Lut and the "cities of the plains" (Sodom and Gomorrah); they are used to refer to different versions of socially forbidden sexual acts in various historical periods.

**stage model (Erikson):** a model of psychological development that views the individual as moving through different stages toward attainment of a full sense of self (usually conceding that any sense of absolute completion is unlikely); Erikson's may be the most familiar and famous, and it argues that individuals all go through the same set of stages, marked as crises between two possible states of being, though when and how each person achieves completion of the stage varies.

***Standards of Care for the Health of Transsexual, Transgender, and Gender Non-conforming People (SOC):*** formerly known as the Benjamin Standards (after Dr. Harry Benjamin), this is a set of protocols and conventions recommended by the World Professional Association for Transgender Health (WPATH), which specifies such things as processes for determining if and when a person is medically and psychologically appropriate for transition (whether surgical or medical).

**sublime:** a concept from the field of aesthetics, going back to classical Greece, that describes an experience of beauty that also carries with it the recognition that, even in the moment of aesthetic pleasure, there is the potential for dissolution of the self and destruction of the world.

**Sufism:** a branch of or form of Islamic mysticism, often associated with same-sex (particularly male) love and desire; the best-known Sufi poet is Rumi, who may have had same-sex erotic and/or romantic experiences and relationships.

**superego (Freud):** the third branch of Freud's three-part model of personality, referring to that part of the self that is constituted from outside regulating social forces and is often responsible for prescriptive moral rules and standards.

***swayamvara:*** a Hindu term that, the scholar Ruth Vanita argues, provides evidence for an acceptance of lifelong same-sex coupling within the religion.

**synchronic:** an adjective meaning, literally, "with time"; it is a linguistic term used to describe analysis of all elements of an utterance at the same time and of related terms, such as all the terms currently in use to describe people who more broadly might be classified as queer.

**thanatos (Freud):** along with eros (q.v.), one of Freud's two principal drives; *thanatos* is Greek for death, and Freud argued that just as humans are always desiring love, they are also always aware of and, at some level, desirous of death or cessation of being.

**total institution (Goffman):** sociological term coined by Erving Goffman to describe those settings that provide for all the daily needs of a population, including, for example, prisons, psychiatric hospitals, and boarding schools.

**trans\* (sometimes trans+):** the * or + symbol is present to indicate the multiple possibilities that the prefix trans- may include (such as those in the entries below).

**transgender:** refers to the interior experience of self as belonging to a gender other than the one assigned at birth and/or which may be customarily associated with a physical body (especially the primary and secondary sexual characteristics).

**transsexual:** less commonly used today, it was widely used in the first several decades of the twentieth century to describe individuals who desired to undergo surgical and/or other medical procedures to create the primary and secondary sexual characteristics of the sex (in the male-female binary) other than the one to which they were assigned at birth.

**transvestite:** also less commonly used today, it literally means "cross-dresser," and has generally been used to describe people who dressed in what was considered the appropriate clothing associated with the gender other than the one to which they were assigned at birth; particularly as standards of dress have changed, the term has fallen into disfavor because it is perceived as prescriptive of gender roles and requirements.

**Two-Spirit:** a term used by many Native American people to describe those members of their community who are understood to be living in multiple genders and are usually accepted as such; they are viewed as neither male nor female, but as belonging to a third category. At many times in history and among specific Native American peoples, they were viewed as having shamanic gifts (i.e., they were conduits between the material and the mystic worlds), and they were frequently partnered with or married to someone of a more traditional gender category.

**whiteness:** not a biological category (though viewed as such during numerous periods in history), but a social state of being, typically associated with a higher position of privilege and status in hierarchies built on skin color and appearance.

**Wicca:** used generally to refer to forms of neo-paganism, especially those that are female-centered, using forms of magic (or magick, as it is sometimes spelled); there are various forms of Wicca, some exclusive to women (and to "womyn-born womyn").

**womyn (sometimes womon, wimmon, and other variants):** an alternative spelling of the noun woman or women, devised and placed in use during second-wave feminism (from the 1960s onward), and especially popular among lesbian feminists and lesbian separatists as a linguistic move to erase "man" as a part of the word; "womyn-born womyn" is a term that gained prevalence during the arguments over who should be permitted to attend the Michigan Womyn's Music Festival; the term distinguished those "born into girlhood" from trans women, either pre-, post-, or non-operative.

# WORKS CITED

Abbott, Alysia. *Fairyland: A Memoir of My Father.* New York: Norton, 2013.

Abdi, Shadee. "Staying I(ra)n: Narrating Queer Identity from within the Persian Closet." *Liminalities: A Journal of Performance Studies* 10.2 (2014): 1–19. https://search.proquest.com/openview/75bc257e21c33eca9fd030ed0c04cb15/1?pq-origsite =gscholar&cbl=2028801.

Adams, Tony E. *Narrating the Closet: An Autoethnography of Same-Sex Attraction.* Walnut Creek, CA: Left Coast Press, 2011.

Against Equality. www.againstequality.org.

Ahmed, Sara. *Queer Phenomenology: Orientations, Objects, Others.* Durham, NC: Duke University Press, 2006.

Alameddine, Rabih. *The Angel of History.* New York: Atlantic Monthly, 2016.

———. *Koolaids: The Art of War.* New York: Picador, 1998.

Ali Forney Center. https://www.aliforneycenter.org/alis-story/.

Allen, John D. *Gay, Lesbian, Bisexual, and Transgender People with Developmental Disabilities: Stories of the Rainbow Support Group.* New York: Routledge, 2003.

Allen, Paula Gunn. "Some Like Indians Endure." *Journal of Lesbian Studies* 1.1 (1996): 9.

Allison, Dorothy. *Bastard Out of Carolina.* New York: Dutton, 1992.

———. *Skin: Talking about Sex, Class and Literature.* Ithaca, NY: Firebrand Books, 1994.

Althusser, Louis. "Ideology and Ideological State Apparatuses." In *Lenin and Philosophy, and Other Essays,* edited by Althusser, 85–126. New York: Monthly Review Press, 1971.

American Psychiatric Association. *Diagnostic and Statistical Manual of Mental Disorders,* 5th ed. (*DSM-V*). Arlington, VA: American Psychiatric Association Publishing, 2013.

Anderson, Benedict. *Imagined Communities: Reflections on the Origin and Spread of Nationalism.* London: Verso, 1983.

Anzaldúa, Gloria. *Borderlands/La Frontera.* San Francisco: aunt lute, 1987.

Armstrong, Karen. *Islam: A Short History.* New York: Modern Library, 2002.

Ayoub, Philip M. *When States Come Out: Europe's Sexual Minorities and the Politics of Visibility.* Cambridge, UK: Cambridge University Press, 2016.

Bailey, Michael J. *The Man Who Would Be Queen: The Science of Gender-Bending and Transsexualism.* Washington, DC: Joseph Henry Press, 2003.

Baker, Paul. *Polari—The Lost Language of Gay Men.* London: Routledge, 2002.

Balay, Anne. *Steel Closets: Voices of Gay, Lesbian, and Transgender Steelworkers.* Chapel Hill: University of North Carolina Press, 2014.

Bechdel, Alison. *Fun Home: A Family Tragicomic.* Boston: Houghton Mifflin, 2006.

Henderson, Bruce, *Queer Studies: Beyond Binaries*
dx.doi.org/10.17312/harringtonparkpress/2019.09.qsbb.00f
© 2019 by Harrington Park Press

Bem, Daryl J. "Exotic Becomes Erotic: A Developmental Theory of Sexual Orientation." *Psychological Review* 103.2 (1996): 320–335.

Berger, Helen A. *A Community of Witches: Contemporary Neo-Paganism and Witchcraft in the United States.* Columbia: University of South Carolina Press, 1999.

Bergman, David, ed. *The Violet Quill Reader: The Emergence of Gay Writing after Stonewall.* New York: St. Martin's Press, 1994.

Berry, Keith. "Seeking Care: Mindfulness, Reflexive Struggle, and Puffy Selves in Bullying." *Liminalities* 9.2 (2013). http://liminalities.net/9-2/berry.pdf.

Bérubé, Allen. *Coming Out under Fire: The History of Gay Men and Women in World War II.* New York: Free Press, 1990.

Bishop-Stall, Reilley. "Re-Imaging and Re-Imagining the Colonial Legend: Photographic Manipulation and Queer Performance in the Work of Kent Monkman and Miss Chief Share Eagle Testickle." *Gnovisjournal: Communication, Culture, and Technology* 12 (2011): n.p. www.gnovisjournal.org/2011/11/21/reilley-bishop -stall-journal/.

Blair, Zachary. "Boystown." In *No Tea, No Shade: New Writings in Black Queer Studies,* edited by E. Patrick Johnson, 287–303. Durham, NC: Duke University Press, 2016.

Blanco, Richard. *The Prince of los Cocuyos: A Miami Childhood.* New York: Ecco, 2014.

———. "Queer Theory: According to My Grandmother." In Blanco, *Looking for the Gulf Motel,* 34–36. Pittsburgh: University of Pittsburgh Press, 2012.

Bogaert, Anthony F. "Asexuality: What It Is and Why It Matters." *Journal of Sex Research* 52.4 (2015): 362–379.

Booth, Wayne. *A Rhetoric of Irony.* Chicago: University of Chicago Press, 1975.

Boswell, John. *Christianity, Social Tolerance, and Homosexuality: Gay People in Western Europe from the Beginning of the Christian Era to the Fourteenth Century.* Chicago: University of Chicago Press, 1980.

———. *Same-Sex Unions in Premodern Europe.* New York: Villard, 1994.

*Both.* Directed by Lisset Barcellos. Solaris Films, 2005.

Bourdieu, Pierre. *Outline of a Theory of Practice.* Translated by Richard Nice. Cambridge, UK: Cambridge University Press, 1977.

Boxill, Ian, et al. *Tourism & HIV/AIDS in Jamaica & the Bahamas.* Kingston, Jamaica: Arawak, 2005.

Boykin, Keith. *Beyond the Down Low: Sex, Lies, and Denial in Black America.* New York: Carroll & Graf, 2005.

*BPM (Beats per Minute).* Directed by Robin Campillo. Les Films de Pierre, 2017.

*Brokeback Mountain.* Directed by Ang Lee. Focus, 2005.

Brontsema, Robin. "A Queer Revolution: Reconceptualizing the Debate over Radical Reclamation." *Colorado Research in Linguistics* 17.1 (2004): 1–17.

Brown, Ricardo. *The Evening Crowd at Kirmser's: A Gay Life in the 1940s.* Minneapolis: University of Minnesota Press, 2001.

Browne, John. *The Corporate Closet: Why Coming Out Is Good Business.* New York: HarperBusiness, 2014.

Browne, Kath. "Beyond Rural Idylls: Imperfect Lesbian Utopias at Michigan Womyn's Music Festival." *Journal of Rural Studies* 27.1 (2011): 13–23.

Bucholtz, Mary, and Kira Hall. "Theorizing Identity in Language and Sexuality Research." *Language in Society* 33.4 (2004): 469–515.

*Buddies.* Directed by Arthur Bressan Jr. Film and Video Workshop, 1985.

Burke, Kenneth. *Language as Symbolic Action.* Berkeley: University of California Press, 1966.

Butler, Judith. *Bodies That Matter.* New York: Routledge, 1993.

——. *Excitable Speech: A Politics of the Performative.* New York: Routledge, 1997.

——. *Gender Trouble: Feminism and the Subversion of Identity.* New York: Routledge, 1994.

Calafell, Bernadette. "Brownness, Kissing, and US Imperialism: Contextualizing the Orlando Massacre." *Communication and Critical/Cultural Studies* 14.2 (2017): 198–202.

Cammermeyer, Margarethe. *Serving in Silence.* New York: Viking, 1994.

Carbado, Devon W. "Racial Naturalization." *American Quarterly* 57 (2005): 633–658.

Carpenter, Dale. *Flagrant Conduct: The Story of Lawrence v. Texas.* New York: Norton, 2012.

Carson, Michael. *Sucking Sherbet Lemons.* London: Victor Gollancz, 1988.

Cass, Vivienne C. "Homosexual Identity Formation: A Theoretical Model." *Journal of Homosexuality* 4.3 (1979): 219–235.

Cassara, John. *The House of Impossible Beauties.* New York: Ecco, 2018.

Chase, Cheryl. *Hermaphrodites Speak!* Video. Ann Arbor: Intersex Society of North America, 1996.

Chauncey, George. *Gay New York: Gender, Urban Culture, and the Making of the Gay Male World, 1890–1940.* New York: Basic Books, 1995.

Cheng, Patrick S. *Radical Love: Introduction to Queer Theology.* New York: Seabury Press, 2011.

Clare, Eli. *Brilliant Imperfection: Grappling with Cure.* Durham, NC: Duke University Press, 2017.

Clarke, Eric O. *Virtuous Vice: Homoeroticism and the Public Sphere.* Durham, NC: Duke University Press, 2000.

Cleage, Pearl. *What Looks Like Crazy on an Ordinary Day.* New York: Morrow, 1997.

Clements-Nolle, Kristen, Rani Marx, and Mitchell Katz. "Attempted Suicide among Transgender Persons: The Influence of Gender-Based Discrimination and Victimization." *Journal of Homosexuality* 51.3 (2006): 53–69.

Colapinto, John. *As Nature Made Him: The Boy Who Was Raised as a Girl.* New York: Harper, 2000.

Colours of Resistance Archive. www.coloursofresistance.org.

Conley, Garrard. *Boy Erased.* New York: Riverhead, 2016.

Conrad, Ryan, ed. *Against Equality: Queer Revolution, Not Mere Inclusion.* Oakland, CA: AK Press, 2014.

Corigliano, John. *Symphony No. 1.* Erato, 1991.

Croce, Arlene. "Discussing the Undiscussable." In *Writing in the Dark, Dancing in The New Yorker: An Arlene Croce Reader*, 708–719. New York: Farrar, Straus and Giroux, 2000.

Croteau, Jon Derek. *My Thinning Years: Starving the Gay Within*. Center City, MN: Hazelden, 2014.

*Dallas Buyers Club*. Directed by Jean-Marc Vallée. Truth Entertainment, 2013.

Davis, Whitney. *Queer Beauty: Sexuality and Aesthetics from Winckelmann to Freud and Beyond*. New York: Columbia University Press, 2010.

———. "Queer Family Romance in Collecting Visual Culture." *GLQ: A Journal of Lesbian and Gay Studies* 17.2–3 (2011): 309–329.

Decker, Julie Sondra. *The Invisible Orientation: An Introduction to Asexuality*. New York: Skyhorse, 2014.

DeFilippis, Joseph. "Beyond Same-Sex Marriage: A New Strategic Vision for All Our Families and Relationships." *Monthly Review Online*, August 8, 2006. https://mronline.org/2006/08/08/beyond-same-sex-marriage-a-new-strategic -vision-for-all-our-families-relationships/.

de Lauretis, Teresa. "Queer Theory: Lesbian and Gay Sexualities: An Introduction." *Differences: A Journal of Feminist Cultural Studies* 3.2 (1991): 1–10.

D'Emilio, John. *Sexual Politics, Sexual Communities*. Chicago: University of Chicago Press, 1983.

Diamond, Lisa M. *Sexual Fluidity: Understanding Women's Love and Desire*. Cambridge: Harvard University Press, 2008.

Díaz, Rafael. *Latino Gay Men and HIV: Culture, Sexuality, and Risk*. New York: Routledge, 1998.

Dietz, Steven. *Lonely Planet*. New York: Dramatists Play Service, 1994.

Dillard, Scott. "*Breathing Darrell*: Solo Performance as a Contribution to a Useful Queer Mythology." *Text and Performance Quarterly* 20.1 (2000): 74–83.

Dolan, Jill. *Utopia in Performance: Finding Hope at the Theater*. Ann Arbor: University of Michigan Press, 2005.

Doty, Alexander. *Making Things Perfectly Queer: Interpreting Mass Culture*. Minneapolis: University of Minnesota Press, 1993.

Dreger, Alice. *Hermaphrodites and the Medical Invention of Sex*. Cambridge: Harvard University Press, 1998.

———, ed. *Intersex in the Age of Ethics*. Frederick, MD: University Publishing Group, 1999.

Driskell, Qwo-Li, et al., eds. *Queer Indigenous Studies: Critical Interventions in Theory, Politics, and Literature*. Tucson: University of Arizona Press, 2011.

Duggan, Lisa. "The New Homonormativity: The Sexual Politics of Neoliberalism." In *Materializing Democracy: Toward a Revitalized Cultural Politics*, edited by Russ Castronovo and Dana D. Nelson, 175–194. Durham, NC: Duke University Press, 2002.

Dzmura, Noach, ed. *Balancing on the Mechitza: Transgender in Jewish Community*. Berkeley, CA: North Atlantic Books, 2010.

*An Early Frost*. Directed by John Erman. NBC Productions, 1985.

Ebershoff, David. *The Danish Girl*. New York: Viking, 2000.

Edelman, Lee. *No Future: Queer Theory and the Death Drive*. Durham, NC: Duke University Press, 2004.

Edwalds, Loraine, and the Artemis Singers. "Wanting the Music." Irish American Heritage Center, January 28, 2017 (unpublished manuscript).

Ekine, Sokari, and Hakima Abbas, eds. *Queer African Reader.* Nairobi, Kenya: Pambazuka, 2013.

Elshaikh, Eman. "Being Queer, Arab, & Everything in Between: Interviewing Saleem Haddad, the Author of 'Guapa.'" *Muftah.* https://muftah.org/queer-arab-an-interview-with-saleem-haddad-the-author-of-guapa/#.WlOmyBiZM3g.

Erdrich, Louise. *The Last Report on the Miracles at Little No Horse.* New York: HarperCollins, 2001.

Erikson, Erik H., and Joan M. Erikson. *The Life Cycle Completed.* Rev. ed. New York: Norton, 1997.

Eugenides, Jeffrey. *Middlesex.* New York: Farrar, Straus and Giroux, 2013.

Exodus Global Alliance. https://www.exodusglobalalliance.org.

Faludi, Susan. *In the Darkroom.* New York: Metropolitan Books, 2016.

Farizan, Sara. *If You Could Be Mine.* Chapel Hill, NC: Algonquin, 2013.

Farmer, Paul. *AIDS and Accusation: Haiti and the Geography of Blame.* Berkeley: University of California Press, 1992.

Farrow, Kenyon. "Is Gay Marriage Anti-Black?" March 5, 2004. http://kenyonfarrow.com/2005/06/14/is-gay-marriage-anti-black/.

Fausto-Sterling, Anne. *Myths of Gender: Biological Theories about Women and Men.* 2nd edition. New York: Basic Books, 1992.

———. *Sexing the Body: Gender Politics and the Construction of Sexuality.* New York: Basic Books, 2000.

Feder, Ellen K. *Making Sense of Intersex: Changing Ethical Perspectives in Biomedicine.* Bloomington: Indiana University Press, 2014.

Federal Bureau of Investigation. "What We Investigate: Civil Rights: Hate Crimes." https://www.fbi.gov/investigate/civil-rights/hate-crimes.

Ferguson, Roderick. *Aberrations in Black: Toward a Queer of Color Critique.* Minneapolis: University of Minnesota Press, 2004.

Fetterley, Judith. *The Resisting Reader: A Feminist Approach to American Fiction.* Bloomington: Indiana University Press, 1978.

Fine, Cordelia. *Delusions of Gender: How Our Minds, Society, and Neurosexism Create Difference.* New York: Norton, 2010.

Finn, Charlotte. "Lost in Transition: Meet the Transgender Princess of 'The Marvelous Land of Oz.'" *Comics Alliance.* http://comicsalliance.com/marvelous-land-of-oz-transgender-ozma.

Floyd, Frank, and Roger Bakeman. "Coming Out across the Life Course: Implications of Age and Historical Context." *Journal of Sexual Behavior* 35.3 (2006): 287–296.

Foucault, Michel. *The Birth of the Clinic: An Archeology of Medical Perception* (1963). Translated by Alan Sheridan. New York: Pantheon, 1973.

———. *The History of Sexuality*, Vol. 1 (1976). Translated by Robert Hurley. New York: Pantheon, 1978.

Freud, Sigmund. "A Letter from Freud." *American Journal of Psychiatry* 107 (1951): 786–787.

————. *Three Essays on the Theory of Sexuality.* Translated by James Strachey. New York: Basic Books, 2001. (First German edition 1905).

Fung, Richard. "Looking for My Penis: The Eroticized Asian in Gay Video Porn." In *How Do I Look? Queer Film & Video*, edited by Bad Object-Choices, 145–168. Seattle: Bay Press, 1991.

Garland-Thomson, Rosemarie. *Extraordinary Bodies: Figuring Physical Disability in American Culture and Literature.* New York: Columbia University Press, 1996.

Garvey, Jason C., Stephanie H. Chang, Z Nicolazzo, and Rex Jackson, eds. *Trans\* Policies & Experiences in Housing & Residential Life.* Sterling, VA: Stylus Publishing, 2018.

Gaudio, Rudolf P. "Sounding Gay: Pitch Properties in the Speech of Gay and Straight Men." *American Speech* 69.1 (1994): 30–57.

Gentile, John S. "Celebrating Ostara: A Ritual Performance by Gay Male Contemporary Pagans." In *Queers in American Popular Culture*, edited by Jim Elledge, 3 vols., 2:259–273. Santa Barbara: Praeger, 2010.

Gill, Carol J. "Four Types of Integration in Disability Identity Development." *Journal of Vocational Rehabilitation* 9.1 (1997): 39–46.

Goffman, Erving. "The Characteristics of Total Institutions." In *Symposium on Preventive and Social Psychiatry*, 43–84. Washington, DC: U.S. Government Printing Office, 1958.

Golden, Carla. "Diversity and Variability in Women's Sexual Identities." In *Lesbian Psychologies: Explorations and Challenges*, edited by Boston Lesbian Psychologies Collective, 18–34. Urbana: University of Illinois Press, 1987.

Gomez, Jewelle. "Imagine a Lesbian, a Black Lesbian." In *The Columbia Reader on Lesbians and Gay Men in Media, Society, and Politics*, edited by Larry Gross and James D. Woods, 262–270. New York: Columbia University Press, 1999.

Gooch, Brad. *Rumi's Secret: The Life of the Sufi Poet of Love.* New York: Harper, 2017.

Green, Richard. *The "Sissy Boy Syndrome" and the Development of Homosexuality.* New Haven: Yale University Press, 1987.

Greenberg, Steven. *Wrestling with God and Men: Homosexuality in the Jewish Tradition.* Madison: University of Wisconsin Press, 2004.

Gregorio, I. W. *None of the Above.* New York: Balzer + Bray, 2015.

Griffin, Pat. *Strong Women, Deep Closets: Lesbians and Homophobia in Sport.* Champaign, IL: Human Kinetics, 1998.

Grindstaff, Davin. "The Fist and the Corpse: Taming the Queer Sublime in *Brokeback Mountain*." *Communication and Critical/Cultural Studies* 5.3 (2008): 223–244.

Guter, Bob, and John Killacky, eds. *Queer Crips: Disabled Gay Men and Their Stories.* New York: Harrington Park Press, 2003.

Habermas, Jürgen. *The Structural Transformation of the Public Sphere: An Inquiry into a Category of Bourgeois Society.* Translated by Thomas Burger. Cambridge: MIT Press, 1989.

Haddad, Saleem. *Guapa.* New York: Other Press, 2016.

————. "The Myth of the Queer Arab Life." *Daily Beast,* April 2, 2016. https://www.thedailybeast.com/the-myth-of-the-queer-arab-life.

Halberstam, Judith. *Female Masculinity.* Durham, NC: Duke University Press, 1998.
———. *The Queer Art of Failure.* Durham, NC: Duke University Press, 2011.
Hall, G. Stanley. *Adolescence: Its Psychology and Its Relations to Physiology, Anthropology, Sociology, Sex, Crime, Religion and Education.* 2 vols. New York: D. Appleton, 1904.
Hamilton, Jane. *The Short History of a Prince.* New York: Random House, 1998.
Han, C. Winter. *Geisha of a Different Kind: Race and Sexuality in Gaysian America.* New York: New York University Press, 2015.
Hardy, James Earl. *The Day Eazy-E Died.* Los Angeles: Alyson, 2001.
Harris, Daniel. "Making Kitsch from AIDS." *Harper's,* July 1994, 55–60.
Harris, W. C. *Slouching towards Gaytheism: Christianity and Queer Survival in America.* Albany: State University of New York Press, 2014.
Hayakawa, S. I., and Alan R. Hayakawa. *Language in Thought and Action.* 5th ed. San Diego: Harcourt Brace Jovanovich, 1990.
Heffernan, Karen. "Eating Disorders and Weight Control among Lesbians." *Eating Disorders* 19.2 (1996): 127–138.
Heineman, John. "Building a GLOBE in Nebraska." In *One Teacher in Ten: Gay and Lesbian Educators Tell Their Stories,* edited by Kevin Jennings, 208–211. Los Angeles: Alyson, 1994.
Henderson, Lisa. *Love and Money: Queers, Class, and Cultural Production.* New York: New York University Press, 2013.
Heselton, Philip. *Witchfather: A Life of Gerald Gardner,* vol. 2, *From Witch Cult to Wicca.* Loughborough, Leicestershire: Thoth, 2012.
Hitchens, Christopher. *God Is Not Great: How Religion Poisons Everything.* New York: Twelve, 2007.
HIV.gov. "A Timeline of HIV and AIDS." https://www.hiv.gov/hiv-basics/overview/history/hiv-and-aids-timeline.
Hocquenghem, Guy. *Homosexual Desire.* Durham, NC: Duke University Press, 1993.
Hospers, Harm, and Anita Jansen. "Why Homosexuality Is a Risk Factor for Eating Disorders in Males." *Journal of Social and Clinical Psychology* 24.8 (2005): 1188–1201.
Hughes, Tonda L., and Michele Eliason. "Substance Use and Abuse in Lesbian, Gay, Bisexual and Transgender Populations." *Journal of Primary Prevention* 22.3 (2002): 263–298.
Human Rights Campaign. "Profile: Barbara Jordan (1936–1996)." https://web.archive.org/web/20081114152344/http://www.hrc.org/issues/3554.htm.
Igual, Roberto. "Namibia's Ombudsman Calls for Same-Sex Marriage amidst UN Report Furore." *Mamba Online,* August 23, 2016. www.mambaonline.com/2016/08/23/namibias-ombudsman-calls-sex-marriage-amidst-un-report-furore/.
Isenberg, Nancy. *White Trash: The 400-Year Untold History of Class in America.* New York: Viking Press, 2016.
*It's Elementary: Talking about Gay Issues in School.* Directed by Debra Chasnoff. New Day, 1996.
*It's STILL Elementary.* Directed by Debra Chasnoff and Johnny Symons. Ground Spark, 2007.

Jennings, Kevin, ed. *One Teacher in Ten: Gay and Lesbian Educators Tell Their Stories.* Los Angeles: Alyson, 1994.

——. *One Teacher in Ten in the New Millennium: LGBT Educators Speak Out about What's Gotten Better . . . and What Hasn't.* Boston: Beacon Press, 2015.

Johnson, E. Patrick. "'Quare' Studies, or (Almost) Everything I Know about Queer Studies I Learned from My Grandmother." *Text and Performance Quarterly* 21.1 (2001): 1–25.

Johnson, Toby. *Gay Spirituality: Gay Identity and the Transformation of Human Consciousness.* 2000. Reprint, Maple Shade, NJ: Lethe Press, 2004.

Jones, Cleve, with Jeff Dawson. *Stitching a Revolution: The Making of an Activist.* San Francisco: HarperCollins, 2000.

Jordan, Mark. "'Both as a Christian and as a Historian': On Boswell's Ministry." In *The Boswell Thesis,* edited by Matthew Kuefler, 88–107. Chicago: University of Chicago Press, 2006.

——. "God's Body." In *Queer Theology: Rethinking the Western Body,* edited by Gerald Loughlin, 281–292. Oxford, England: Blackwell, 2007.

Jordan, MaryKate. *Losing Uncle Tim.* Morton Grove, IL: Concept, 1989.

Jorgensen, Christine. *Christine Jorgensen: A Personal Autobiography.* New York: Paul S. Eriksson, 1967.

Kafer, Alison. "Inseparable: Gender and Disability in the Amputee-Devotee Community." In *Gendering Disability,* edited by Bonnie Smith and Beth Hutchison, 107–118. New Brunswick, NJ: Rutgers University Press, 2004.

Karkazis, Katrina, and Rebecca Jordan-Young. "The Treatment of Caster Semenya Shows Athletics' Bias against Women of Colour." *Guardian,* April 26, 2018. https://www.theguardian.com/commentisfree/2018/apr/26/testosterone-ruling-women-athletes-caster-semanya-global-south.

Kauanui, J. Kēhaulani. "Indigenous Hawaiian Sexuality and the Politics of National Imposition." In *Critically Sovereign: Indigenous Gender, Sexuality, and Feminist Studies,* edited by Joanna Barker, 45–68. Durham, NC: Duke University Press, 2017.

Kennedy, Elizabeth Lapovsky, and Madeline D. Davis. *Boots of Leather, Slippers of Gold: The History of a Lesbian Community.* New York: Routledge, 1993.

Kessler, Suzanne. *Lessons from the Intersexed.* New Brunswick, NJ: Rutgers University Press, 1998.

King, J. L. *On the Down Low: A Journey into the Lives of "Straight" Black Men Who Sleep with Men.* New York: Broadway, 2004.

Kramer, Larry. *The Normal Heart.* New York: Dutton, 1985.

Kugle, Scott Siraj al-Haqq. *Homosexuality in Islam: Critical Reflection on Gay, Lesbian, and Transgender Muslims.* Oxford, UK: Oneworld, 2010.

——. *Living Out Islam: Voices of Gay, Lesbian, and Transgender Muslims.* New York: New York University Press, 2014.

Kushner, Tony. *Angels in America.* Rev. and complete ed. New York: Theatre Communications Group, 2013.

Lamb, Ramdas. "Polytheism and Monotheism: A Hindu Perspective." *Huffington Post,* March 31, 2011. https://www.huffingtonpost.com/entry/polytheism-and-monotheism_b_841905.html.

Larson, Jonathan. *Rent: The Complete Book and Lyrics of the Broadway Musical.* New York: Applause, 2008.

Lee, JeeYeun. "Why Suzie Wong Is Not a Lesbian: Asian and Asian American Lesbian and Bisexual Women and Femme/Butch/Gender Identities." In *Queer Studies: A Lesbian, Gay, Bisexual, and Transgender Anthology*, edited by Brett Beemyn and Mickey Eliason, 115–132. New York: New York University Press, 1996.

Lee, Joseph L., Gairel K. Griffin, and Cathy Melvin. "Tobacco Use among Sexual Minorities, USA, 1987–2007 (May): A Systematic Review." http://tobaccocontrol.bmj.com/content/early/2009/02/10/tc.2008.028241.short.

Letts, William J., IV, and James T. Spears, eds. *Queering Elementary Education: Advancing the Dialogues about Sexuality and Schooling.* Lanham, MD: Rowman & Littlefield, 1999.

Lewis, Daniel C., Jami K. Taylor, Brian DiSarro, and Matthew L. Jacobsmeier. "Is Transgender Policy Different? Policy Complexity, Policy Diffusion, and LGBT Nondiscrimination Law." In *Transgender Rights and Politics: Groups, Issue Framing, & Policy Adoption*, edited by Jami K. Taylor and Donald P. Haider-Markel, 155–188. Ann Arbor: University of Michigan Press, 2014.

Lewis, Danielle. "The Turcot Yards: Community Encounters with a Queer Sublime." Montreal: Concordia University, Department of History, 2009. http://cityaspalimpsest.concordia.ca/palimpsest_II_en/papers/Danielle_Lewis.pdf.

Leyland, Winston, ed. *Queer Dharma: Voices of Gay Buddhists.* Vol. 1. San Francisco: Gay Sunshine Press, 1998.

Lim, You-Leng Leroy. "Webs of Betrayal, Webs of Blessings." In *Q & A: Queer in Asian America*, edited by David L. Eng and Alice Y. Hom, 323–334. Philadelphia: Temple University Press, 1998.

Litvak, Joseph. "Sedgwick's Nerve." *Criticism* 52.2 (2010): 253–262.

Livia, Anna, and Kira Hall, eds. *Queerly Phrased: Language, Gender, and Sexuality.* New York: Oxford University Press, 1997.

Lord, James. *My Queer War.* New York: Farrar, Straus & Giroux, 2010.

Lorde, Audre. *The Black Unicorn: Poems.* New York: Norton, 1978.

Lorway, Robert. *Namibia's Rainbow Project: Gay Rights in an African Nation.* Bloomington: Indiana University Press, 2015.

Lucas, Ian. "The Color of His Eyes: Polari and the Sisters of Perpetual Indulgence." In *Queerly Phrased: Language, Gender, and Sexuality*, edited by Anna Livia and Kira Hall, 85–94. New York: Oxford University Press, 1997.

Makkai, Rebecca. *The Great Believers.* New York: Viking, 2018.

Massad, Joseph A. *Desiring Arabs.* Chicago: University of Chicago Press, 2007.

McConnell-Ginet, Sally. "Intonation in a Man's World." *Signs: Journal of Women in Culture and Society* 3.3 (1978): 541–559.

McDermott, Elizabeth, and Katrina Roer. *Queer Youth, Suicide and Self-Harm: Troubled Subjects, Troubling Norms.* Basingstoke, UK: Palgrave Macmillan, 2016.

McIntosh, Peggy. "White Privilege and Male Privilege: A Personal Account of Coming to See Correspondences through Work in Women's Studies." www.collegeart.org/pdf/diversity/white-privilege-and-male-privilege.pdf.

McKay, Richard A. *Patient Zero and the Making of the AIDS Epidemic*. Chicago: University of Chicago Press, 2017.

Michaelson, Jay. "Rick Warren's Troubling Africa Mission." *Daily Beast*, September 14, 2014. https://www.thedailybeast.com/rick-warrens-troubling-africa-mission.

Mieli, Mario. *Homosexuality & Liberation: Elements of a Gay Critique*. Translated by David Fernbach. London: Gay Men's Press, 1980.

A Mind at Play. "Intelligence2 Catholic Church Debate: Transcript." https://www.amindatplay.eu/2009/12/02/intelligence²-catholic-church-debate-transcript/.

Mizock, Lauren, Effie Mougianis, and Colton Keo-Meier. *Fact Sheet: Gender Diversity and Transgender Identity in Youth*. https://www.researchgate.net/publication/263697096_Fact_sheet_Gender_diversity_and_transgender_identity_in_youth.

Monette, Paul. *Borrowed Time: An AIDS Memoir*. San Diego: Harcourt Brace Jovanovich, 1988.

——. *Love Alone: Eighteen Elegies for Rog*. New York: St. Martin's Press, 1988.

Moonwoman-Baird, Birch. "Toward the Study of Lesbian Speech." In *Queerly Phrased: Language, Gender, and Sexuality*, edited by Anna Livia and Kira Hall, 202–213. New York: Oxford University Press, 1997.

Moraga, Cherríe. *Loving in the War Years: Lo que nunca pasó por sus labios*. Boston: South End Press, 1983.

——. "Still Loving in the (Still) War Years/2009: On Keeping Queer Queer." In Moraga, *A Xicana Codex of Changing Consciousness: Writings, 2000–2010*. Durham, NC: Duke University Press, 2011.

Moraga, Cherríe, and Gloria Anzaldua, eds. *This Bridge Called My Back: Writings by Radical Women of Color*. Watertown, MA: Persephone Press, 1981.

Morgensen, Scott Lauria. "Arrival at Home: Radical Faerie Configurations of Sexuality and Place." *GLQ: A Journal of Lesbian and Gay Studies* 15.1 (2009): 67–96.

Morris, J. F., C. R. Waldo, and E. D. Rothblum. "A Model of Predictors and Outcomes of Outness among Lesbian and Bisexual Women." *American Journal of Orthopsychiatry* 71 (2001): 61–71.

Muñoz, José Esteban. *Cruising Utopia: The Then and There of Queer Futurity*. New York: New York University Press, 2009.

——. *Disidentification: Queers of Color and the Performance of Politics*. Minneapolis: University of Minnesota Press, 1999.

Murphy, Tim. *Christodora*. New York: Grove, 2016.

Nakayama, Thomas K., and Robert L. Krizek. "Whiteness: A Strategic Rhetoric." *Quarterly Journal of Speech* 81.3 (1995): 291–309.

Nandy, Ashis. *The Intimate Enemy: Loss and Recovery of Self under Colonialism*. Oxford: Oxford University Press, 1983.

Nero, Charles I. "Toward a Black Gay Aesthetic: Signifying in Contemporary Black Gay Literature." In *African American Literary Theory: A Reader*, edited by Winston Napier, 399–420. New York: New York University Press, 2000.

——. "Why Are All the Gay Ghettoes White?" In *Black Queer Studies: A Critical Anthology*, edited by E. Patrick Johnson and Mae G. Henderson, 228–245. Durham, NC: Duke University Press, 2005.

Nicolazzo, Z. *Trans\* in College: Transgender Students' Strategies for Navigating Campus Life and the Institutional Politics of Inclusion*. Sterling, VA: Stylus Publishing, 2017.

*Not-About-AIDS-Dance*. Choreographed by Neil Greenberg. 1994.

*Online Etymology Dictionary*. https://www.etymonline.com/.

Orbach, Susie. *Fat Is a Feminist Issue: The Anti-Diet Guide to Permanent Weight Loss*. 1978. Reprint, New York: Berkley Books, 1994.

Ortiz-Fonseca, Louie A. "Queer Latinx: Tired of Being Targets." *Advocate*, June 15, 2016. https://www.advocate.com/commentary/2016/6/15/queer-latinx-tired-being-targets.

Pajek, Alexandra. *Sounds of HIV: Music Transcribed from DNA*. Azica, 2010.

Palmer, Paulina. *The Queer Uncanny: New Perspectives on the Gothic*. Cardiff: University of Wales Press, 2012.

Parens, Erik. *Surgically Shaping Children: Technology, Ethics, and the Pursuit of Normality*. Baltimore: Johns Hopkins University Press, 2008.

*Paris Is Burning*. Directed by Jennie Livingston. Miramax, 1990.

Pascoe, C. J. *Dude, You're a Fag: Masculinity and Sexuality in High School*. Berkeley: University of California Press, 2007.

Pérez, Hiram. *A Taste for Brown Bodies: Gay Modernity and Cosmopolitan Desire*. New York: New York University Press, 2015.

Petro, Anthony M. *After the Wrath of God: AIDS, Sexuality, and American Religion*. Oxford: Oxford University Press, 2015.

*Philadelphia*. Directed by Jonathan Demme. TriStar, 1993.

Plato. *Phaedrus*. Rev. ed. Translated by Christopher Rowe. New York: Penguin, 2005.

———. *Symposium*. Translated by Benjamin Jowett. Upper Saddle River, NJ: Prentice-Hall, 1956.

Ponse, Barbara. "Finding Self in the Lesbian Community." In *Women's Sexual Development: Explorations of Inner Space*, edited by Martha Kirkpatrick. New York: Springer, 1980.

Povinelli, Elizabeth A. "The Part That Has No Part: Enjoyment, Law, and Loss." *GLQ: A Journal of Lesbian and Gay Studies* 17.2–3 (2011): 287–308.

*Precious*. Directed by Lee Daniels. Lionsgate, 2008.

Puar, Jasbir K. *Terrorist Assemblages: Homonationalism in Queer Times*. Durham, NC: Duke University Press, 2007.

Quesada, Uriel, Letitia Golez, and Salvador Vidal-Ortiz, eds. *Queer Brown Voices: Personal Narratives of Latina/o LGBT Activism*. Austin: University of Texas Press, 2015.

Ramirez-Valles, Jesus. *Queer Aging: The Gayby Boomers and a New Frontier for Gerontology*. Oxford: Oxford University Press, 2016.

Reese, Phil. "That Kid from YouTube." *Washington Blade*, May 23, 2012. https://www.washingtonblade.com/2012/05/23/that-kid-from-youtube-grows-up/.

Rich, Adrienne. "Compulsory Heterosexuality and Lesbian Existence." *Signs: Journal of Women in Culture and Society* 5.4 (1980): 631–660.

Richardson, Justin, and Peter Parnell. *And Tango Makes Three*. New York: Simon and Schuster Books for Young Readers, 2005.

Rifkin, Mark. *Beyond Settler Time: Temporal Sovereignty and Indigenous Self-Determination*. Durham, NC: Duke University Press, 2015.

Rivera-Servera, Ramón H. *Performing Queer Latinidad: Dance, Sexuality, Politics*. Ann Arbor: University of Michigan Press, 2012.

Rodríguez, Juana María. "Queer Sociality and Other Sexual Fantasies." GLQ: A *Journal of Lesbian and Gay Studies* 17.2–3 (2011): 331–348.

Roloff, Lee, and Russell Lockhart. *The Final Interlude: Advancing Age and Life's End*. Everett, WA: Lockhart Press, 2015.

Rosario, Margaret, Joyce Hunter, Shira Maguen, et al. "The Coming-Out Process and Its Adaptational and Health-Related Associations among Gay, Lesbian, and Bisexual Youths." *American Journal of Community Psychology* 29.1 (2001): 133–160.

Rosenberg, Jordy. *Confessions of the Fox*. New York: One World, 2018.

Rudacille, Deborah. *The Riddle of Gender: Science, Activism, and Transgender Rights*. New York: Pantheon, 2005.

Russell, Steve. "The Headlines Are Wrong! Same-Sex Marriage Not Banned across Indian Country." *Indian Country Today*, April 23, 2015. https://newsmaven.io/indiancountrytoday/archive/the-headlines-are-wrong-same-sex-marriage-not-banned-across-indian-country-5OSYm8SPYU6M8r9JsaUj6A/.

Rylance, Valerie J. "Lesbian Buddhism?" M.Phil. thesis, SOAS, University of London, 2011. http://eprints.soas.ac.uk/18468.

Sandahl, Carrie. "Queering the Crip or Cripping the Queer? Intersections of Queer and Crip Identities in Solo Autobiographical Performance." *GLQ: A Journal of Lesbian and Gay Studies* 9.1–2 (2002): 25–56.

Sartorius, Norman. "The Meaning of Health and Its Promotion." *Croatian Medical Journal* 47.4 (2006): 662–664. www.ncbi.nlm.nih.gov/pmc/articles/PMC2080455.

Savin-Williams, Ritch C. ". . . *And Then I Became Gay": Young Men's Stories*. New York: Routledge, 1997.

———. *Mostly Straight: Sexual Fluidity among Men*. Cambridge: Harvard University Press, 2017.

———. *The New Gay Teenager*. Cambridge: Harvard University Press, 2005.

Savin-Williams, Ritch C., and Kenneth M. Cohen. "Development of Same-Sex Attracted Youth." In *The Health of Sexual Minorities: Public Health Perspectives on Lesbian, Gay, Bisexual and Transgender Populations*, edited by Ilan H. Meyer and Mary E. Northridge, 27–47. New York: Springer, 2007.

Schulman, Sarah. *People in Trouble*. New York: Dutton, 1990.

———. *Stagestruck: Theater, AIDS, and the Marketing of Gay America*. Durham, NC: Duke University Press, 1998.

Schultz, Jaime. *Qualifying Times: Points of Change in U.S. Women's Sport*. Urbana: University of Illinois Press, 2014.

Sedgwick, Eve Kosofsky. *Epistemology of the Closet*. Berkeley: University of California Press, 1990.

———. "How to Bring Your Kids Up Gay." *Social Text* 29 (1991): 18–27.

———. "Willa Cather and Others." In *Tendencies*, by Sedgwick, 167–176. Durham, NC: Duke University Press, 1993.

Segal, Mark. "Meet the Gay Man Who Actually Won America Her Independence."

*LGBTQ Nation*, July 4, 2017. https://www.lgbtqnation.com/2017/07/meet-gay-man-won-america-independence/.

Shaer, Matthew. "The Long, Lonely Road of Chelsea Manning." *New York Times*, June 12, 2019. https://www.nytimes.com/2017/06/12/magazine/the-long-lonely-road-of-chelsea-manning.html?rref=collection%2Fsectioncollection%2Fmagazine&action=click&contentCollection=magazine&region=rank&module=package&version=highlights&contentPlacement=5&pgtype=sectionfront.

Sherry, Michael S. *Gay Artists in Modern American Culture: An Imagined Conspiracy*. Chapel Hill: University of North Carolina Press, 2007.

Shilts, Randy. *And the Band Played On: Politics, People, and the AIDS Epidemic*. New York: St. Martin's Press, 1987.

Shultz, Jackson Wright. *Trans/Portraits: Voices from Transgender Communities*. Hanover, NH: Dartmouth College Press, 2015.

Sicha, Choire. *Very Recent History: An Entirely Factual Account of a Year (c. AD 2009) in a Large City*. New York: Harper, 2013.

Slagle, R. Anthony. "Ferment in LGBT Studies and Queer Theory: Personal Ruminations on Contested Terrain." *Journal of Homosexuality* 52.1–2 (2006), 310–328.

Snider, Stefanie. "Fat Girls and Size Queens: Alternative Publications and the Visualizing of Fat and Queer Eroto-Politics in Contemporary American Culture." In *The Fat Studies Reader*, edited by Esther Rothblum and Sondra Solovay, 223–230. New York: New York University Press, 2009.

Sokolic, Elisheva. "Judaism Needs to Be Kinder to Transgender People." *Forward*, January 11, 2018. https://forward.com/life/391821/judaism-needs-to-be-kinder-to-transgender-people/.

Sontag, Susan. "Notes on Camp." In *A Susan Sontag Reader*, edited by Elizabeth Hardwick, 105–119. New York: Farrar, Straus & Giroux, 1982.

Soules, Marshall. "Jürgen Habermas and the Public Sphere." *Media Studies*, 2007. www.media-studies.ca/articles/habermas.htm.

*Spotlight*. Directed by Tom McCarthy. Participant Films, 2015.

Spring, Justin. "Hugh Steers: A Memoir." *New England Review* 22.1 (2001): 155–163.

Starhawk. "The Sacredness of Pleasure: A Bi Spirit Classic." *Journal of Bisexuality* 10.1–2 (2010): 18–21.

Stedman, Chris. *Faitheist: How an Atheist Found Common Ground with the Religious*. Boston: Beacon Press, 2012.

Stein, Gertrude. "Miss Furr and Miss Skeene." https://webpages.scu.edu/ftp/lgarber/courses/eng67F10texts/MissFurr.pdf.

*Still/Here*. Choreographed by Bill T. Jones. 1994.

Stone, Amy. *Gay Rights at the Ballot Box*. Minneapolis: University of Minnesota Press, 2012.

Stryker, Susan. "Transgender History, Homonormativity, and Disciplinarity." *Radical History Review* 100 (2008): 145–157.

———. "The Transgender Issue: An Introduction." *GLQ: A Journal of Lesbian and Gay Studies* 4.2 (1998): 145–158.

Stryker, Susan, and Paisley Currah, eds. "Postposttranssexual: Key Concepts for a 21st Century Transgender Studies." *Transgender Studies Quarterly* 1.1–2 (2014).

Sullivan, Andrew. "When Plagues End." *New York Times*, November 10, 1996.

Symons, Caroline. *The Gay Games: A History*. New York: Routledge, 2010.

Tarrant, Shira. *When Sex Became Gender*. New York: Routledge, 2006.

Tarttelin, Abigail. *Golden Boy*. New York: Atria, 2013.

Taylor, Jami K., and Donald P. Haider-Markel, eds. *Transgender Rights and Politics: Groups, Issue Framing, and Policy Adoption*. Ann Arbor: University of Michigan Press, 2014.

Teeman, Tim. "The Secret, Hypocritical Gay World of ISIS." *Daily Beast*, January 6, 2016. https://www.thedailybeast.com/the-secret-hypocritical-gay-world-of-isis.

*Tongues Untied*. Directed by Marlon Riggs. Signifyin' Works, 1989.

Treat, John Whittier. *The Rise and Fall of the Yellow House*. Boston: Big Table, 2015.

Treichler, Paula. "AIDS, Homophobia, and Biomedical Discourse: An Epidemic of Signification." *Cultural Studies* 1.3 (1987): 263–305.

*Trembling Before G_d*. Directed by Sandi Simcha Dubowski. Simcha Leib Productions, 2001.

Troiden, Richard R. "Homosexual Identity Development." *Journal of Adolescent Health Care* 9.2 (1988): 105–113.

Troyano, Alina. *I, Carmelita Tropicana: Performing between Cultures*. Edited by Chon A. Noriega. Boston: Beacon, 2000.

Valerio, Mark Wolf. "Why I'm Not Transgender." *Making Our Lives Easier*, February 9, 2014. http://makingourliveseasier.org/?p=1101.

Valiente, Doreen. *The Rebirth of Witchcraft*. London: Robert Hale, 1989.

Vanita, Ruth. *Love's Rite: Same-Sex Marriage in India and the West*. New York: Palgrave Macmillan, 2005.

*Velvet Goldmine*. Directed by Todd Haynes. Channel Four Films, 1998.

Wade, Lisa. *American Hookup: The New Culture of Sex on Campus*. New York: Norton, 2017.

Wahls, Zach, with Bruce Littlefield. *My Two Moms: Lessons of Love, Strength, and What Makes a Family*. New York: Gotham, 2012.

Weinberg, George. *Society and the Healthy Homosexual*. New York: St. Martin's Press, 1972.

Weiner, Joshua J., and Damon Young. "Queer Bonds." *GLQ: A Journal of Lesbian and Gay Studies* 17.2–3 (2011): 223–241.

Weston, Kath. *Families We Choose: Lesbians, Gays, Kinship*. New York: Columbia University Press, 1991.

Whisman, Vera. *Queer by Choice: Lesbians, Gay Men, and the Politics of Identity*. New York: Routledge, 1996.

White, Edmund. *The Farewell Symphony*. New York: Knopf, 1997.

——. *Jack Holmes and His Friend*. New York: Bloomsbury, 2012.

——. *The Married Man*. New York: Knopf, 2000.

——, ed., in cooperation with the Estate Project for Artists with AIDS. *Loss within Loss: Artists in the Age of AIDS*. Madison: University of Wisconsin Press, 2001.

Whitesel, Jason. *Fat Gay Men: Girth, Mirth, and the Politics of Stigma*. New York: New York University Press, 2014.

Whitney, Kobai Scott. "The Lone Mountain Path: The Example of Issan Dorsey."

*Lion's Roar: Buddhist Wisdom for Our Time*, March 1, 1998. https://www.lionsroar.com/the-lone-mountain-path-the-example-of-issan-dorsey/.

Wilcox, Melissa M. *Queer Nuns: Religion, Activism, and Serious Parody*. New York: New York University Press, 2018.

Wilde, Oscar. *The Picture of Dorian Gray*. www.gutenberg.org/files/174/174-h/174-h.htm.

Winter, Kathleen. *Annabel*. Toronto: Anansi, 2010.

Woodard, Vincent. *The Delectable Negro: Human Consumption and Homoeroticism within U.S. Slave Culture*. New York: New York University Press, 2014.

Yoshino, Kenji. *Covering: The Hidden Assault on Our Civil Rights*. New York: Random House, 2006.

# INDEX

family impact of, 225; gay men and, 161, 289–290, 334; Latinx people and, 172; lesbians and, 270–271; MSM and, 162; older queer people and, 234–235, 238–239; origins of, 260–262; public awareness about, 181, 225; queer education and, 210; queer linguistic history and, 14–15, 28; same-sex marriage and, 329–330; vampire interest during, 363; in young adult fiction, 365, 390. *See also* AIDS epidemic—artistic responses to; HIV/AIDS

AIDS epidemic—artistic responses to: artists responsible for, 388–389; in dance, 400–402; in film/TV, 395, 396–398; Issues for Investigation, 406; literary/poetic, 390–391; musical, 395–396; in performance art, 402–406; theatrical, 398–400; in visual arts, 391–395

AIDS Memorial Quilt, 263, 269, 394–395, 396, 400, 451

AIDS ministries, 163

AIDS narratives, 390–391

AIDS research, 395

*AIDS Ward Scherzo* (R. Savage), 396

"AIDS widows," 64

Alabama, 333

Alameddine, Rabih, 391

alcohol, 253–254, 386

Alcott, Louisa May, 364

algebra, 199

*All about Eve* (film; 1950), 268

Allah, 297, 345

Allen, John D., 278

Allen, O. C., III, 163

Allen, Paula Gunn, 152–153

allies, 28, 128, 209

Allison, Dorothy, 143–146

"Alternative Publications and the Visualization of Fat and Queer Eroto-Politics" (Snider), 257

Althusser, Louis, 45, 449

Amazon Video, 351

American Baptists, 291

American Civil Liberties Union (ACLU), 327

American exceptionalism, 121

*American Hookup* (Wade), 226–228

American Indians, 148. *See also* Native Americans

American Library Association, 370

*American Poetry Review*, 160–161

American Psychological Association (APA), 248, 249, 252, 328, 426–428

American Religious Identification Survey (ARIS), 309

Americans with Disabilities Act (ACA; 1990), 264

amyl nitrite, 254

anal sex, 172, 182, 303, 327, 328, 343, 346

Anderson, Benedict, 15

Anderson-Minshall, Diane, 153

androgen insensitivity syndrome (AIS), 372

androgynes/androgyny, 28–29, 290, 308, 314, 442

*And Tango Makes Three* (Richardson and Parnell), 199–200

*And the Band Played On* (Shilts), 261, 452

"... *And Then I Became Gay*" (Savin-Williams), 76–77

*Angel of History, The* (Alameddine), 391

*Angels in America* (Kushner), 398–399

anima/animus, 306

*Animal Farm* (Orwell), 352–353

*Annabel* (Winter), 110–111

*Annie on My Mind* (Garden), 369–370

anomalous features, 104

anorexia, 255–256

*Another Day* (Levithan), 373

anti-bullying programs, 216

anticommunism, 316, 334, 385, 399

antidiscrimination legislation, 299

antidiscrimination policies, 215

antiracism, 323

antiretroviral therapy, 269–270

anxiety, 340

Anzaldúa, Gloria, 165, 166–167, 168

Aphrodite (Greek deity), 105

apologetics, 294

Appiah, Kwame Anthony, 353–354

Appleby, George Alan, 137

Arab American National Museum, 391

Bérubé, Allan, 65
bestiality, 141, 326
"Beyond Same-Sex Marriage" (petition), 331
*Beyond the Down Low* (Boykin), 162
Bieber, Irving, 250
Biennale Internationale de Danse (Lyon, France; 1994), 402
"bi-erasure," 79
*Big Bang Theory, The* (TV show), 15–16, 81
Big Mind, 436
Bildungsroman, 390
bilingualism, 166–167
Bill T. Jones/Arnie Zane Dance Company, 401
binaries: deconstruction of, 3–4; defined, 443; in gender identities, 99, 205, 289, 330, 339, 363; genetic, 94–95; intersex people and, 104; Latinx people and, 165; in linguistic reclamations, 17; queer/non-queer, 412; queer spirituality traditions and, 311; religion and, 284; school reinforcement of, 195, 205; in sexual orientation, 56, 205; trans marriages and, 233–234; Two-Spirit people and, 150; Wicca and, 308
biopolitics, 245
biopower, 245, 252, 443
biphobism, 24
birtherism, 316–317
*Birth of the Clinic, The* (Foucault), 245
bisexuality/bisexuals: aging, 239; Asian American, 186–187; coming out experiences of, 74, 75–76, 79–80; dating/hookup sites for, 228; defined, 443; Freudian view of, 46, 50; invisibility of, 244; Jewish view of, 290; Latino, 173–174; lesbians identified as, 78; linguistic history of, 23–24; MSM and, 161–162; neglect of, 79; as parents, 410; pathologization of, 81–82; queer theology and, 295; terms associated with, 40; Two-Spirit people vs., 149; types of, 83–84; as undertheorized, 14; use of term, 55, 56, 348–349; Wicca and, 309
bisexual sensibility, 358
Bishop-Stall, Reilley, 150

black church, 163–164, 330
Blackmun, Harry, 328
black studies, 210
blacktinos, 164
Blair, Zachary, 158
Blanchard, Ray, 103
Blanco, Richard, 174–175, 421–423
blue-collar workers, 133–134. *See also* working class
Bly, Robert, 435
*Bodies That Matter* (Butler), 87
body: black, 154–155; of Christ, 293–294; of color, 176–177; dance and, 400; defined, 443; defining, 86–90; dissatisfaction with, 256; docile, 4, 320; female, and gay men, 376; gay Asian, 181–182; healthy, and queers, 271–272; idealized, 256; lower-class, 140–141; queer theory and, 87. *See also* queer bodies
body politic, 89, 100
body shame/shaming, 387, 443
Bogaert, Anthony, 81, 82
*Bohème, La* (Puccini), 399, 400
*Bohemian Rhapsody* (film; 2018), 396
*Bona Drag* (album; Morrissey), 35
Bond, D. Stephenson, 440
book burnings, 369–370
*BookRiot*, 369–370
*Boots of Leather, Slippers of Gold* (Kennedy and Davis), 135, 225
*Borderlands/La Frontera* (Anzaldúa), 166–167
*Borrowed Time* (Monette), 390
Boswell, John, 232, 292–293
*Both* (film; 2005), 111
"bottoms," 294
Bourdieu, Pierre, 324
bourgeoisie, 53, 54, 330
Bowers, Michael J., 327
*Bowers v. Hardwick*, 327–328
Bowie, David, 8, 395
*Boy Erased* (Conley), 251–252
Boy George (singer), 375
Boykin, Keith, 162
Boy Scouts of America, 224
*Boys on the Side* (film; 1995), 398

Cheng, Patrick, 294–295

Cherokee tribe, 151

Chicago, 265, 266, 267, 312; AIDS epidemic in, 396–397; Democratic National Convention in (1968), 53; drag-ball culture in, 222; "gayborhoods" in, 139, 158; "gayby boomers" in, 241–242; lesbian feminist chorus in, 388; queer sports leagues in, 274; racism in, 158

*Chicago Tribune*, 388

Chicanos(as), 165–166, 168

Chicano Spanish language, 167

child custody, 235–236

children: custody battles over, 235–236; of gay men, 124; gender-nonconforming, 252; intersex, "sexing" of, 104, 107–108, 110; queer, 364; of queer parents, 221, 223–225, 235–237, 410; sexual identities of, 194; trans-identified, 340. *See also* education; elementary education/schools; high school; middle school; schools; young adult fiction

Children's Book Council, 367

*Children's Hospital* (TV series), 111

China, 300

Chinese immigrants, 179, 180–181

choice, 70, 78

*Christadora* (Murphy), 391

Christianity: in Africa, 349, 350; African Americans and, 163–164; AIDS crisis and, 296, 436; body in, 293–294; "conversion experiences" to, 312; evangelical, 273, 349; growth of, 296; heteronormativity and, 156; homophobia and, 297; iconography of, 293–294; lesbians and, 304; Leviticus rules in, 288; Lot story in, 284–287, 326; in Middle East, 344; missionaries, 151; Native American attitudes and, 151; as nonmonolithic, 291; queer theology in, 292–296, 304; reparative therapy based in, 250; same-sex relations as prohibited in, 284–288, 292–293; sports and, 273; as threat to queer people, 310–311; Trinity in, 294. *See also* Catholicism; Protestantism

*Christianity, Social Tolerance, and Homosexuality* (Boswell), 232, 292–293

Christianization, 188–189

*Christine Jorgensen: A Personal Autobiography* (Jorgensen), 113

Cinquemani, Sal, 395

cisgender identity, 8, 26, 60, 244, 270, 384

cisgenderism/cisgender people: as actors playing trans people, 98; AIDS art authored by, 389; binaries and, 99; defined, 26, 99, 444; education and, 320; intersex people and, 110; *jotería* and, 176; as normative, 234, 320; as psychologists evaluating trans people, 103; queer people vs., 229, 235; romantic relationships of, 229; transgender exclusion and, 325, 337; the uncanny and, 363–364; as young adult fiction authors, 370–371, 372

citizenship: Cold-War mindset of, 385; defined, 316–317; heterosexuality and, 319; homonormativity/homonationalism and, 320–323; Issues for Investigation, 352–354; middle-class, 320; naturalization vs., 317–318; public sphere and, 318–320; queer, 316, 323; same-sex marriage and, 323, 329; trans/intersex people and, 337–341, 345. *See also* queer politics; United States—queer politics in

City of Refuge (Oakland, CA), 163, 164

civic life, 199–200

civil commitments, 330

civil rights, 123, 327

civil rights activism, 56, 157

civil unions, 341

Clare, Eli, 276, 280

Clarke, Eric O., 318–320

class: defined, 444; distinctions between, 129; Issues for Investigation, 145–146; lower-class queers, 141–143; middle-class queers, 129–132; privilege and, 118–119; queer bonding and, 229; shifts in, 131, 139–140; Spotlight on Literature, 143–145; upper-middle-class queers, 124–129; in USA, 121–122; whiteness and, 118,

disabilities, people with: camp and, 382–383; families of origin of, 66; fetishizing of, 279–280; identity development of, 67; queer people and, 66; queer sexuality and, 276–280; Special Olympics, 275–276

disability studies, 89

*Discipline and Punish* (Foucault), 245

disco, 395–396

discordance, 57, 66, 444–445

discrimination, 101–103

"Discussing the Undiscussable" (Croce), 402

disidentification, 150, 167, 177, 447

dispossession, 165

Divelbess, Diane, 335

diversity, in school curricula, 195–197

Divine (drag queen), 380

divorce, 64

Dixon, Melvin, 388

*Do I Sound Gay?* (documentary film; 2015), 31

Dolan, Jill, 412

domestic partnerships, 330

Donne, John, 291

Donovan, John, 367–368

Don't Ask, Don't Tell policy, 65, 333, 335–336, 445

"Don't Say Gay" bill (TN; 2011), 207–208

*Dorothy Must Die* (Paige), 365

Dorsey, Issan (Thomas), 303–304, 434–437

Doty, Alexander, 5, 6, 358–359

down low (DL), 162, 172, 445

"Do Ya Wanna Funk?" (song; Sylvester), 395

drag: appeal of, 91–92; -ball culture, 69, 222–223, 384; outmoded clichéd traditions of, 392–393; spiritual aspect of, 306. *See also* drag kings; drag queens

drag clubs, 412, 434

drag kings, 91, 358, 381

Dragon Lady stereotype, 186

drag queens, 8; African American, 156, 163, 164; Asian American, 183–185, 188; camp and, 380, 383–384; defined,

91, 445; drag kings as equivalent to, 381; as political activists, 379, 386; transgender women vs., 383–384; trans sensibility and, 358

Drake, Robert, 441

*Dreadnought* (Daniels), 372–373

Dreger, Alice, 108

drinking, 235, 253–254

Driskill, Qwo-Li, 149–150

drug abuse, 141, 161, 435

"drug cocktails," 269

DSD, 28, 106

dualism, 306, 314, 436

Du Bois, W. E. B., 120

Dubowski, Sandi Simcha, 289

*Dude, You're a Fag* (Pascoe), 194

Duffy, Nick, 383

Dugas, Gaétan, 261, 452

Duggan, Lisa, 320

dyads, 231–232

dyke: black women as, 161; "diesel," 39; drag kings and, 381; identification as, 152; "predatory," 272, 273; use of, in school contexts, 205; use of term, 32, 175; in young adult fiction, 367, 369

"Dykes on Bikes," 319–320

dysphoria, 280. *See also* gender dysphoria

Dzmura, Noach, 289–290

Earl, Nancy, 326

*Early Frost, An* (TV drama), 396–397

Earth, 305, 307

eating disorders, 255–256

ecofeminism, 309, 387

economics education, 199

Edelman, Lee, 410

education, 188; abstinence-only, 349; current tensions in, 195; Issues for Investigation, 216–217; middle/high school, 205–209, 210, 211, 216–217; safe-sex, 296. *See also* college/university; elementary education/schools; Schoolworld

Edwalds, Loraine, 388, 428–434

effeminacy, 95, 131–132, 305–306

*Egg at Easter, An* (Newall), 439

ego, 48, 446

Ekine, Sokari, 349

Elbe, Lili, 112, 113, 114–115

electroconvulsive therapy (ECT; electric shock therapy), 247, 250–251

elementary education/schools: Common Core standards for, 197–198; importance of, 197; Issues for Investigation, 216–217; in language arts, 198–199; in mathematical/quantitative literacy, 199; queer inclusion in, 196–197, 198, 199, 200–201, 204; Schoolworld in, 201–203, 215–216; in science, 199, 200–201; in social studies/history, 199–200, 216–217; teachers/adults and, 203–204

Eliade, Mircea, 440

Eliason, Michael, 253

Ellis, Havelock, 50

emotionality, distanced, 227–228

empiricism, 245

employment discrimination, 341

English language, 166, 167

Enlightenment philosophy, 245, 376

E. O. Green Junior High School (Oxnard, CA), 205–207

epistemology, 5–6, 73

*Epistemology of the Closet* (Sedgwick), 72

Epstein, Joy, 207

Erdrich, Louise, 152

Erikson, Erik, 61–63, 74, 84, 457

eros, 48, 448

eroticism, 220, 252

"erotics of place," 150

escorts, 127

Espionage Act, 336

Espiritu, Yen Le, 179

ethnicity, 130, 148, 189–190, 337

ethnic studies, 196

ethnography, 223

Eubanks, Robert, 328

eugenics movement, 141, 278

Eugenides, Jeffrey, 110

Europe, Western, 253

European Convention on Human Rights, 343

European Court of Human Rights, 343

European Union (EU), 341–342

*Evening Crowd at Kirmser's, The* (R. Brown), 225–226

*Every Day* (Levithan), 373

*Excitable Speech* (Butler), 338

ex-gay therapy. *See* reparative therapy

Exodus Global Alliance/International, 251

exotic becomes erotic, 252, 448

extracurricular activities, 208

extramarital sex, 230

*Faerie Queene, The* (Spenser), 306

faggot: machismo and Spanish equivalents for, 172; transgender women and, 336, 337; use of, in school contexts, 194, 203, 205; use of term, 32, 175–176

failure, 410–413, 446

Fain, Nathan, 262

fairy, 13, 305–306, 395

*Fairyland* (A. Abbott), 224–225

*Faitheist* (Stedman), 311–313

*Falsettos* (Finn), 398

Faludi, Stefanie, 236

Faludi, Susan, 236

Falwell, Jerry, 296, 394

familial neglect, 207

*Families We Choose* (Weston), 221–222

family: assumptions about, 214; of choice, 66, 221–223, 224–225, 226, 229, 235, 446; as coteachers, 197; extended, 237–238; *latinidad* and, 170, 174; legal/social definition of, 331; messages about constitution of, 203; nuclear, 52, 235, 238, 331; of origin, 66, 224, 235, 237–238, 330, 446; queer, 223–225; use of term, 220

Farizan, Sara, 345–346

Farmer, Paul, 260–261

Farrow, Kenyon, 330–331

fatalism, 174

*Fat Gay Men* (Whitesel), 257–258

*FaT GiRL* ('zine), 257

Fausto-Sterling, Anne, 25, 94–95, 106

Feder, Ellen K., 108

Feinberg, Leslie, 25

Garvey, Jason, 215
Gary (author's friend), 263, 264, 265–268
Gary (IN), 136, 139
gay: defined, 446; as homophobic insult, 194, 205, 411; linguistic history of, 19–21, 25, 29; parallel terms for, 2; use of term, 292–293, 348–349
Gay and Lesbian Organization for the Betterment of Everyone (GLOBE), 209, 423–426
"gayborhoods," 139, 157–158, 241
gay Buddhist clubs, 435
gay businesses, 385
"gayby boomers," 234, 241–242
Gay Canon, The (Drake), 441
gay consciousness, 305, 306–307, 314
gaydar, 29, 448
Gay Games, 269, 275–276, 447
Gay Games, The (Symons), 275
gay ghettoes, 157–158
Gay International, 344, 345
Gay Liberation Front, 169
gay liberation movement, 14, 56, 224, 247, 260, 370
gay male pornography, 159, 181–183
gay men: African American, 390, 398; aging, 238–239; AIDS epidemic and, 161, 263, 289–290, 334; Asian American, 179–180, 181–183, 294; as athletes, 272–273; ballet and, 74; bars/dance clubs frequented by, 158–159; black, 156–157, 163; bullying of, 194, 212–214; closeted, 263; closeted married, 57; code-switching by, 33; coming-out experiences of, 69, 74–79, 125, 127, 272; cultural icons of, 33, 364; dating/hookup sites for, 159, 228, 255–256; disabled, 279–280; execution of, 346–347; fat, 257–258; female body and, 376; feminine, 169, 255, 256, 350–351, 395–396; hate crimes against, 338; health challenges of, 255; Hinduism and, 301; hyper-masculine, 396; incarceration of, in Chechen Republic, 343; irony as used by, 378; Islam and, 299; Latino, 172, 173–174; lesbians and, 136, 380; lower-class, 142–143; marriages of,

332–333; media representations of, 30; middle-class, 129–132; military service of, 333, 334; as parents, 224–225, 237, 410; politically conservative, 328–329; as politicians, 325–326; psychological research on, 247–250; as rabbis, 288; racism among, 157–159; role identities of, 294; salaries of, 167; secret language of (Polari), 34–38; sexuality of, 279, 294; sociality of, 228–229, 230; as soldiers, 65, 334; stereotypes/misconceptions about, 131–132, 271–272; substance abuse among, 254; terms associated with, 39; upper-middle-class, 124–129; white, and class, 123; working-class, 137–138, 139; in young adult fiction, 365
Gay Men's Health Crisis, 181, 262
gay politics, 156–157
gay rednecks, 142–143
gay rights, 278, 324–325, 327
Gay Rights at the Ballot Box (Stone), 323–325
gay sensibility, 358
"Gay Shame" conference (University of Michigan; 2003), 176–177
Gay Spirituality (T. Johnson), 306–307
Gay Spirit Visions, 306, 403, 438
gay-straight alliances, 209
gaytheism, 311–313
gayvoice, 29–32, 447
gaze: clinical, 104; male, 255; medical, 245, 451; queer, 272
Geisha of a Different Kind (Han), 184
gender: binaries in, 3, 99, 330; Buddhism and, 302; critical race theory and, 148; Hinduism and, 300–301; intersectionality and, 148; intersex people and assigning of, 104, 107–108; Islam and, 299; in Jungian psychology, 306; performances of, 87, 175, 194; policing of, 273, 363; queering of, 16; romantic bonding and, 229–230; sex (biological) vs., 93–95; sexuality vs., 86; "third," 299; Two-Spirit people and, 150
gender dysphoria, 93, 280
genderfluid, 149, 370
gender identity, 220; biblical references to,

Johnson, Earvin ("Magic"), 264

Johnson, E. Patrick, 163, 453

Johnson, Lyndon Baines, 123

Johnson, Toby, 306–307, 311, 314

JONAH (Jews Offering New Alternatives for Healing), 250

Jones, Bill T., 401–402

Jones, Cleve, 263, 394

Jordan, Barbara, 326

Jordan, Mark, 293–294

Jordan, Marykate, 390

Jordan-Young, Rebecca, 274

Jorgensen, Christine (George Jr.), 112, 113–115

*jotería* (faggotry), 175–176, 178, 451

*Journal of Homosexuality*, 259–260

Judaism, 250; branches of, 288, 344; homophobia and, 297; Leviticus rules in, 288; Lot story in, 284–287; queer lives and, 288–289, 344; sacred storytellers in (*maggid*), 403; trans/intersex people and, 289–290

"Julian and Sandy" routines, 35–36, 40

Jung, Carl Gustav, 441

Jungian psychology, 62, 305, 306

Kafer, Alison, 277

Kameny, Frank, 334

Kansas City (KS), 369–370

*Kapital, Das* (Marx), 52

Kaposi's sarcoma, 397

Kardashian family, 98, 122

Karkazis, Katrina, 274

karma, 302

*kathoey* (ladyboy), 183

Katz, Mitchell, 259–260

Kauanui, J. Kēhaulani, 151

Kaufman, Benjamin, 250

Keith Haring Foundation, 392

Keller, Helen, 382

Kennedy, Anthony, 332

Kennedy, Elizabeth Lapovsky, 135, 136, 225

Kennedy, John F., 209

Kennedy family, 121–122

Kentucky, 318, 333

Keo-Meier, Colt, 96–98

Kessler, Suzanne J., 108

*khanith*, 299

Kilhefner, Don, 305, 306

Killacky, John, 279

Kim Chi (drag queen), 183–185, 188

Kindig, Mary, 102

King, J. L., 162

King, Larry, 205–207, 208, 217

King, Mark S., 142

King, Martin Luther, Jr., 157

Kinh people, 179

Kinsey, Alfred, 57, 247

kinship, 235–239, 243

Kirk, Darrell, 403

Kirmser's bar (St. Paul, MN), 225–226

kitsch, 400

Klein, Melanie, 48

Klinefelter's Syndrome, 106

Klub Polari (dance club secret language), 35

*Koolaids* (Alameddine), 391

Koop, C. Everett, 264

Kopay, David, 272

Korea, 300, 351

Korean Americans, 179, 183–185, 188

Kornhaber, Spencer, 183, 184–185

Kowalski, Sharon, 277–278

Kramer, Larry, 262, 263, 398, 399

Krizek, Robert L., 119–120

Kuan Yin (Buddhist deity), 435

Kugle, Scott Siraj al-Haqq, 298–299

Kukla, Elliot, 290

Ku Klux Klan, 155

Kushner, Tony, 398–399

Labor Day Convergence (Minneapolis; 2007), 257–258

labor movement, 137

Lacan, Jacques, 44, 48, 410, 454

ladder of abstraction, 18–19, 22, 449

Lamb, Ramdas, 300

Lambda Legal, 328, 331

Lambda Literary Awards, 370, 374, 391

Lane, Nathan, 398–399

Lewis, Danielle, 360

Lewis, Jerry, 382

Leyland, Winston, 303–304

lezzie, 175, 205, 272

LGB people: class experiences of, 122; coming-out experiences of, 71; as community, 102–103; organizations of, 321; pinkwashing and, 323; trans people vs., 138, 323; youth identity crises, 62–63

LGB rights, 339

LGBT Aging Issues Network (LAIN), 238

LGBT Human Rights Awareness Week (Windoek, Namibia; 2000), 350

LGBT/LGBT people, 4, 5, 450

LGBTQ+/LGBTQ+ people: as activists, 278; culture of, 385; defined, 452; educational materials including, 196–197; ministries, 163; parallel terms for, 2; resource groups, 128; student groups, 189–190, 209. *See also* older queer people; queer people; *specific individual category*

LGBTQ+ rights, 223, 341–342

LGBTQ+ studies, 5, 12–13

liberation theology, 294

Lim, You-Leng Leroy, 188–189

*Liminalities* (journal), 176

Lincoln (NE), 209, 423–426

Lincoln, Abraham, 208

"linguistic reclamation," 17

linguistics, 12, 452–453

*Lion's Roar* (Buddhist magazine), 304, 434–437

literacy, 198–199

literature courses, 210–211

*Little Women* (Alcott), 364

Litvak, Joseph, 72

*Living Myth* (Bond), 440

Livingston, Jennie, 223

lobotomies, 247

*loca* (queen; whore), 172

Locke, John, 245

locker rooms, 138

Lockhart, Russell, 62

Log Cabin Republicans, 328–329

loneliness, 238

*Lonely Planet* (Dietz), 399

"Lone Mountain Path, The" (Whitney), 434–437

Longinus, 359

*Long Secret, The* (Fitzhugh), 366–367

*Looking* (TV sitcom), 30

"Looking for My Penis" (Fung), 182–183

Lord, James, 65

Lorde, Audre, 135–136, 159, 160–161

Lorway, Robert, 350, 351

Los Angeles, 241

*Los Angeles Times*, 196–197

*Losing Uncle Tim* (M. Jordan), 390

Lot, biblical story of, 284–287, 326

Lotus Blossom stereotype, 186

*Love Alone* (Monette), 390

*Love and Money* (Henderson), 122–123

Love in Action, 251–252

*Love Is Strange* (film; 2014), 231–232

*Loving in the War Years* (Moraga), 168

lower class, 121, 133, 140–141

lower-class queers, 141–143

Lucas, Ian, 36–37

*Luna* (Peters), 370–371

Lut, Islamic story of, 284–287

Lutheranism, 312

Luzon, Manila, 184

Lyon (France), 402

machismo, 171–174, 382, 451

*Madama Butterfly* (Puccini), 186

Maddow, Rachel, 32

Madonna (singer/actress), 395

*maggid* (sacred Jewish storyteller), 403

Magliocco, Sabina, 441

Maguire, Gregory, 365

Maisani, Ben, 125

"Making Kitsch from AIDS" (D. Harris), 400

*Making Sense of Intersex* (Feder), 108

*Making Things Perfectly Queer* (Doty), 358–359

Makkai, Rebecca, 391

male gaze, 255

male impersonators, 91

Malek, Rami, 396

mental health professionals, 258

Mercury, Freddie, 396

*mericón* (faggot), 172

mestizaje, 167

mestizos(as), 166, 167, 168, 451

meta-analyses, 253

methamphetamines, 141, 254

Metropolitan Community Church (MCC), 295, 451

Mexican Americans, 168, 196. *See also* Chicanos(as)

Miami (FL), 175

Michael, George, 395

Michaelson, Jay, 349

Michigan Womyn's Music Festival, 102–103, 386–388, 412, 428–434

Mickee Faust Club (Tallahassee, FL), 382–383

microaggression, 214, 453

Middlebury College, 184

middle class, 133, 160, 330

middle-class queers, 129–132

Middle East, 343–347

Middle Eastern immigrants, 179

middle school, 194, 205–207, 208, 216–217

*Middlesex* (Eugenides), 110, 111

Midrash, 289

Mieli, Mario, 54, 55–56

military: DADT policy in, 333, 335–336; homosexuality banned in, 334; queer soldiers in, 333, 334–335; trans soldiers in, 336–337

military aggression, 323

Milk, Harvey, 394

Miller, Tim, 402–403

mind control, 251

mind vs. brain, 87

Minneapolis, 257–258, 311–312, 402

Minnesota Court of Appeals, 278

Minnesota Supreme Court, 329

Miranda, Carmen, 382

misadaptation, 250, 451

miscegenation laws, 181

misogyny, 380

misrecognition, 258–259

"Miss Furr and Miss Skeene" (short story; Stein), 20

Mitchell, John Cameron, 47

*Moby-Dick* (Melville), 154

Mock, Janet, 164

model minority myth, 453

*Modern Family* (TV sitcom), 30, 131–132

modernization, 342

moffie, 350

mollies, 19–20

*Mona Lisa* (Leonardo da Vinci), 377

Monette, Paul, 390

Money, John, 107

monogamy, 79, 229–231, 330, 397

monosexuality, 80, 453

Monroe, Marilyn, 114

"Mont Blanc" (poem; Shelley), 359

Moraga, Cherríe, 165, 168–170, 178

morality politics, 339

*Morbidity and Mortality Weekly Report* (CDC), 262

Moreman, Shane T., 176

Morgan, Suzanne, 264

Morgensen, Scott Lauria, 307

Mori, Masahiro, 362

Morrissey (musician), 35

Moscone, George, 394

Moskos, Charles, 335

*Mostly Straight* (Savin-Williams), 84

Mother Goddess, 308

Mother Nature, 305

Movement Advancement Project, 252, 339

MSM (men who have sex with men), 161–162, 172

Muhammad, Prophet, 297

*mukhannathun*, 299

multiculturalism, 166, 172

Muñoz, José Esteban, 150, 177, 412

*Murder over a Girl, A* (Corbett), 207

Murphy, Tim, 391

Museum of Transgender History and Art (MOTHA; San Francisco), 389

music, 395–396

musicals, 398, 399

*My Queer War* (Lord), 65

*My Thinning Years* (Croteau), 256

"not-knowing," 72
nuclear families, 52, 235, 238, 331
Nudd, Donna Marie, 382–383
nudity, 387
Nureyev, Rudolf, 400
nursing homes, 240
Nystrom, Nancy C., 238

Oakland (CA), 163, 164
Oates, Joyce Carol, 402
Obama, Barack, 174, 269, 316–317, 336–337, 338, 340–341, 349
Obergefell, James, 332
*Obergefell v. Hodges*, 215, 234, 332–333
obesity, 140–141, 235, 256–258
O'Connor, John, 296
Oedipal complex, 48–51, 55, 454
*Oedipus Rex* (Sophocles), 378
off-Broadway plays, 399
Ohio, 332
Ojibwe tribe, 152
Oklahoma City, 257–258
Olander, William, 393
Older Lesbians Organizing for Change (OLOC), 238, 239, 452
older queer people: children of, 223–225; defined, 234; familial roles of, 222; health disparities among, 234–235; housing options for, 240–241; kinship support for, 235–239; life stories of, 241–242; scholarship on, 234; successful aging and, 234, 235, 238, 240
Olympic Games, 271, 275
Omi, Michael, 157
Onassis, Jacqueline Kennedy, 392
*One* (gay/lesbian magazine), 329
*One Teacher in Ten* (ed. Jennings), 209, 423–426
*One Teacher in Ten in the New Millennium* (ed. Jennings), 209
*On the Down Low* (J. L. King), 162
"On the Standard of Taste" (Hume), 376
*On the Sublime* (Longinus), 359
oral sex, 139, 172, 173, 303, 328
*Orange Is the New Black* (TV series), 98, 164, 381

Oregon, 241, 280, 324–325, 375
Orientalism, 180, 344
"Origin of Love, The" (song; Trask), 47
Orlando (FL), 177–178, 346, 412
Orthodox Judaism, 288–289, 290, 344
Ortiz-Fonseca, Louie A., 178
Orwell, George, 343, 352–353
Ostara (Wiccan festival), 307, 437–441
othering, 140, 180, 316, 344, 363
otters, 258
*Our Lady of the Flowers* (Genet), 380
*Our Young Man* (E. White), 390–391
overpopulation, 221
Ovid, 441
*Oxford English Dictionary*, 13, 19, 20, 317
Oxnard (CA), 205–207

*Pachuco*, 167
Padilla, Felix, 164
paganism, 305, 308
Paige, Danielle, 365
pair-bonding, 79
Pajek, Alexandra, 396
Pakistani Americans, 179
Palestine, 322
Palmer, Paulina, 362–363
Palms, The (Manasota, FL), 241
Palm Springs (CA), 241
panda bears, 258
Pan-Girth & Mirth convention (Oklahoma City), 257–258
pansexual, 24
pantheism, 305
parades, 385–386
Paragraph 175, 319
paraphilia, 49
parental rights, 236
parenthood, 170
parents: as coteachers, 197; queer people as, 221, 235–237, 410; same-sex, 203
Paris (France), 53–54, 398
*Paris Is Burning* (film; 1990), 223, 384
Parker, Mary-Louise, 398
Parnell, Peter, 199–200
Parvati (Hindu deity), 301

queer people: Christianity as threat to, 310–311; of color, 388; devaluing of, 194–195; disabled, 277–280; health challenges of, 253–260; lower-class, 141–143; middle-class, 129–132; as parents, 221, 223–225, 410; as politicians, 325–326; social acceptance of, 235; sociality of, 220–221; as soldiers, 333, 334; stereotypes/misconceptions about, 271; upper-middle-class, 124–129; utopias "performed" by, 412; working-class, 134–140. *See also* older queer people; *specific queer type*

queer phenomenology, 88–89

queer politics: in Africa, 347–351; in Asia, 351; in Australia, 351–352; in EU, 341–342; in Middle East, 343–347; in Russia, 342–343. *See also* United States—queer politics in

queer/queerness: bilingual identity and, 166–167; as choice, 250; defined, 453; doubleness of, 175; "enfreakment" of, 386; Hinduism and, 300–302; identification as, 2; Islam and, 296–299; linguistic history of, 13–18, 25, 27, 316; parallel terms for, 2; racial/ethnic identity and, 148; religion and, 310–311; the sublime and, 360–361; use of term, 4–5, 7–9, 18–19, 153, 175, 247, 347; whiteness and, 123–124. *See also* queer identity; queer people; *specific topic*

queer rights, 377

queer sexuality: Buddhism and, 303; disability and, 276–280; monogamy and, 397

Queers for Economic Justice, 331

*Queers in American Popular Culture* (ed. Elledge), 437

queer sociality, 220–221

queer spaces, 115, 208, 226

queer spectatorship, 358–359

*Queer Spirits* (Roscoe), 441

queer sports teams/leagues, 274–275

queer studies, 15, 70, 87, 163, 210, 244, 294, 413

queer sublime, 360–361

queer theology, 292–296, 304

queer theory: binaries and, 311; body in, 87; defined, 5–6; emergence of, 15, 22, 95, 211; founders/pioneers of, 4–5, 72; homonormativity in, 53; language of, 16; queer theology and, 294

"Queer Theory: According to My Grandmother" (poem; Blanco), 175, 421–423

queer uncanny, 362–364

*Queer Uncanny, The* (Palmer), 362–363

queer youth, 254, 258–260, 269

Quesada, Uriel, 171

questioning, 26–27, 454

Quran, 298–299, 347

rabbis, gay, 288

race: feminism and, 159–160; hate crimes based on, 337; intersectionality and, 148; Issues for Investigation, 189–190; scholars of, 220–221; whiteness and, 148

race studies, 196

racial formation, 157, 454

"Racial Naturalization" (Carbado), 317–318

racial prejudice, 123

racial segregation, 135–136, 157–158

racism: African Americans and, 155–156, 330; AIDS epidemic and, 270; Asian Americans and, 181, 182, 184, 187; black lesbians and, 160; down low myth and, 161–162, 445; in gay ghettoes, 157–159; homonationalism and, 323; Latinx people and, 168, 174

Radical Faeries, 305–307, 395, 403, 454

*Radical Love* (Cheng), 294–295

Rainbow Project (Namibia), 350

Rainey, Ma, 156

Ramakrishnan, Jayati, 375

Ramer, Andrew, 403

Ramirez-Valles, Jesus, 234, 241–242

rape, 346, 348, 350

Rapoport, Paul, 262

Rauch, Jonathan, 329

Ravi, Dharun, 213

Reading (PA), 391

Reagan, Ronald, 14–15, 260, 264, 394

recess activities, 203

first experiences of, 208; lower-class, 141; medicalization of, 245–246; monogamous, 229–231; nonheteronormative, 13, 246, 362–363; performances of, 87; polysexual relationships, 231; "queer" linguistic history and, 16–17; reproductive philosophies of, 410; same-sex, 341, 342–343; schooling of, 194–195, 203, 252; as uncanny, 363–364

sexually transmitted diseases (STDs), 76, 208

sexual orientation, 214–215; as changeable, 246, 281; as choice, 201; citizenship vs. naturalization and, 318; gender identity vs., 337–338; of intersex people, 109–110; as uncanny, 363–364

sexual pleasure (*jouissance*), 410

sexual reassignment, 25, 112–115

sex work, 228, 259–260, 350

Shaer, Matthew, 336

Shaffer, L. S., 438

Shakespeare, William, 210

shamanism, 150, 305, 435

Shams (Sufi mystic), 298

Shelley, Mary, 359, 363

Shelley, Percy Bysshe, 359

Shepard, Matthew, 338

Sherry, Michael S., 358

Sherwood, Bill, 397

Shi'ite Muslims, 297, 343

Shilts, Randy, 261, 454

Shiva (Hindu deity), 301

*Short History of a Prince, The* (Hamilton), 8, 74, 416–421

showers, 138

Shriver, Eunice Kennedy, 276

Shultz, Jackson Wright, 86, 100–101

Sicha, Choire, 229

Sidibe, Gabourney, 398

sin, 284

Singer, Peter, 87

*sinthome*, 410, 454

sissy, 95, 175, 203

Sisters of Perpetual Indulgence (SPI), 379

*Size Queen* ('zine), 257

skepticism, 310

*Skin: Talking about Sex, Class and Literature* (Allison), 144–146

Slagle, R. Tony, 4–5

slang, 32

*Slant* (magazine), 395

slavery, 153–155

*Slouching towards Gaytheism* (Harris), 310–311

Slovenia, 342

Smith, Patti, 44–45

smoking, 235, 254–255

Snider, Stefanie, 257

Socarides, Charles, 250

social class. *See* class

social contract, 317

sociality, 220–221; bar culture and, 253–254; family bonds, 221–225; Issues for Investigation, 242–243; marriage and, 232–234; queer aging and, 235–239; romantic bonds, 225–232

socialization, 197

social media, 205

social mobility, 133, 139–140, 166, 188

social movements, 323–324, 325, 338–339, 454

social studies education, 199–200, 216–217

society, integration into, 64–65

*Society and the Healthy Homosexual* (Weinberg), 244, 246

Socrates, 45–46

Sodom, 284–287, 298, 326

sodomite, 14, 155, 246, 284, 454

sodomy, 284, 343

sodomy laws, 326–329, 343, 346, 348, 349

*Someday* (Levithan), 373

Sontag, Susan, 378–379, 380, 384, 402

Sophocles, 378

Soules, Marshall, 318

*Sounds of HIV* (Pajek), 396

South Africa, 299, 347–348, 350

South America, 351

South Asia, 351

South Asian immigrants, 179, 182

Southeast Asia, 351

Southern Baptists, 291

crimes and, 337–338; invisibility of, 244; medicalization of, 345; in Middle East, 345; in the military, 336; queer theology and, 295; sexual orientation vs., 338; as socially accepted/"normalized," 99; "transgender" usage and, 92; as uncanny, 362–363, 365; in young adult fiction, 372–375

transgender language, 22

transgender men, 102, 136, 138, 306, 341

Transgender Nation, 15

transgender rights, 339

*Transgender Studies Quarterly* (*TSQ*; journal), 99

transgender/transgender people: African policies concerning, 347–349; aging, 239; artistic production among, 389; Asian American, 183; binaries and, 99; black, 156, 164; butch lesbians and, 169–170; challenges facing, 100–103, 259; children of, 235, 236; citizenship and, 345; class experiences of, 122; code-switching by, 34; of color, 123, 158, 164; coming-out experiences of, 69, 122, 127; denaturalization of, 318; disability and, 280; discrimination against, 233–234, 323; drag vs., 383–384; employment difficulties of, 164, 239; gender identity and, 259, 363; hate crimes against, 337–338; health challenges of, 239, 259–260; HIV infection among, 389; intersex people and, 110; Islam and, 299, 345; Judaism and, 289–290; late-life transitions of, 236; LGB people vs., 138, 323; linguistic history of, 22, 24–26; medical/surgical interventions for, 92–93, 96–97; in Middle East, 345; military ban on, 337; military service of, 336–337; as parents, 410; passability of, 339; political issues, 338–341; psychological interventions for, 97–98; public sphere and, 319–320; queer activist exclusion of, 325; queer bodies of, 86, 90–92; same-sex marriage and, 233–234; in school contexts, 201, 214–215; sex/gender distinction and, 93–95; social bonding of, 220, 230, 236; in sports, 274; terms associated with, 40; Two-Spirit people vs., 149; as uncanny, 363; use of term, 153, 348–349, 457; violence against, 138, 214; visibility of, 98–100, 195, 201, 214; working-class, 136, 138; in young adult fiction, 365, 370–376; as young adult fiction authors, 371. *See also* transgender identity; transgender men; transgender women; transphobia

transgender women: Asian American, 183; of color, 164; discrimination against, 102–103, 386; drag queens vs., 383–384; fear of, 339–340; femininity of, 176; film portrayals of, 389; HIV infection among, 234, 270, 389; military service of, 336–337; radical feminism and, 22; women-centered neo-paganism and, 307–308; working-class, 136

transnational movements, 341–342

transnormativity, 321

*Transparent* (TV series), 98

transphobia, 93; AIDS epidemic and, 270; at colleges/universities, 212; of gay men, 158; in nursing homes/assisted-living facilities, 240; pinkwashing and, 323; in school contexts, 200; Two-Spirit people and, 150; white supremacy and, 206; young adult fiction and, 375

*Trans/Portraits* (Shultz), 100–101

trans sensibility, 358

transsexual, 24–25, 92, 93, 99, 112–115, 153, 410, 458

transsexual rights, 114

transubstantiation, 293

transvestite, 24, 90–91, 458

Trask, Stephen, 47

Travolta, John, 380

Treat, John Whittier, 391

Treichler, Paula, 270

*Trembling before G_d* (documentary film; 2001), 289

triads, 231

Triangle Square (Hollywood, CA), 241

Trinity, 291, 294

*Triumph of the Moon, The* (Hutton), 438

Troiden, Richard, 74–75
Troyano, Alina, 381–382
Trump, Donald J., 165, 196, 337, 399
Truvada, 269
Turcot Yards (Montreal, Quebec), 360
Turner, Lana, 114
*Two Boys Kissing* (Levithan), 373–374
Two-Spirit people: devaluing of, 150–151; growth of, as identity, 151–153; Native American spirituality and, 403; as shamans, 150; use of term, 149–150, 456

UCLA, 247
Uganda, 348
uncanny, the, 361–364, 365
"Uncanny, The" (Freud), 361–362
uncanny valley, the, 362, 363
undocumented immigrants, 196
Unitarian Universalism, 290, 312
United Church of Christ (UCC), 163–164
United Kingdom, 253
United Methodist Church, 163
United Nations, 347
United States: AIDS cases in, 268; AIDS response of, 260, 264, 296; bar culture in, 225, 253; citizenship discourse in, 176; class in, 121–122, 141; "coming out" origins in, 69; deindustrialization in, 139–140; exceptionalism of, 121; gay imams in, 299; individual identity in, 60–61; labor movement and masculinity in, 137; Latinx people and culture of, 165; police shootings in, 317; self-image of, 352; social-mobility ideology in, 133, 139–140, 166, 188; sodomy laws in, 326–329; student unrest in (1968), 53; transgender history in, 100. *See also* United States—queer politics in
United States—queer politics in: ballot measures, 323, 324–325; hate crimes/speech, 337–338; LGBTQ+ politicians, 325–326; military issues, 333–337; social movements, 323–324, 325; sodomy laws, 326–329; trans/intersex politics, 338–341. *See also* same-sex marriages

United States Air Force, 334
United States Air Force Academy, 337
United States Congress, 151, 223, 325–326, 338
United States Constitution: First Amendment, 322; Fourteenth Amendment, 327, 328–329, 331, 332
United States Federal Drug Administration (FDA), 268, 269
United States Health and Human Services Department, 263
United States House of Representatives, 325–326, 336
United States Military Academy (West Point, NY), 337, 339
United States Senate, 336
United States Supreme Court: *Bowers v. Hardwick*, 327–328; citizenship vs. naturalization and, 318; *Lawrence v. Texas*, 328–329; *Obergefell v. Hodges*, 65, 215, 234, 332–333; transgender military ban upheld by, 337; *United States v. Windsor*, 331–332
*United States v. Windsor*, 331–332
Université de Paris, 54
University of Michigan, 176–177
University of Pennsylvania, 249
"unknowability," 298
upper class, 133
upper middle class, 133
*U.S. News and World Report*, 196
*Utopia in Performance* (Dolan), 412
utopias, imperfection of, 411–412

*Valentine Road* (documentary film), 207
Valerio, Max Wolf, 153
Valiente, Doreen, 308
vampires, 363
Vanderbilt, Gloria, 125
Vanita, Ruth, 301–302, 455
Van Zant, Charles, 196
*Velvet Goldmine* (film; 1998), 35, 40
Velvet Underground, 395
*Very Recent History* (Sicha), 229
"victim art," 402
Vidal, Gore, 392